American Literary Criticism from the Thirties to the Eighties

American Literary Criticism
from the Thirties to the Eighties

VINCENT B. LEITCH

Columbia University Press
NEW YORK

Library of Congress Cataloging-in-Publication Data

Leitch, Vincent B., 1944–
   American literary criticism from the thirties to
the eighties.

   Bibliographical references, pp. 413–38
   Includes index.
   1. Criticism—United States—History—20th century.
2. American literature—History and criticism—Theory,
etc. I. Title.
PS78.L4   1987   801'.95'0973   87-15133
ISBN 0-231-06426-8
ISBN 0-231-06427-6 (pbk.)

Columbia University Press
New York   Guildford, Surrey
Copyright © 1988 Columbia University Press
All rights reserved

Printed in the United States of America
C 10 9 8 7 6 5 4 3
P 10 9 8 7 6 5 4 3 2

Clothbound editions of Columbia University Press are Smyth-sewn
and printed on permanent and durable acid-free paper

For all seekers

CONTENTS

PREFACE

IN THE 1880s departments of literary study first began to appear in leading American universities. Within a generation multifaceted struggles were under way between advocates of an elitist, literary aesthetic and advocates of a somewhat populist viewpoint emphasizing the sociological foundations of poetic art. In the 1930s the antagonistic dialogue between conservative New Critics and Marxist literary theorists constituted an especially strong form of this struggle, which manifested itself in other vigorous forms into the 1980s, as, for example, in the conflict during this decade between Yale School deconstructors and leftist proponents of cultural studies. American literary criticism between the 1930s and 1980s exhibited continuous struggles between various "formalistic" schools of criticism devoted to linguistic, ontological, and epistemological habits of mind and certain "cultural" movements committed to sociological, psychological, and political modes of thinking. On one side of this divide stood New Criticism, the Chicago School, phenomenological criticism, hermeneutics, structuralism, and deconstruction. On the other side were Marxist criticism, the New York Intellectuals, myth criticism, existential criticism, reader-response criticism, feminist criticism, and the Black Aesthetic movement. At their worst these two contending wings of academic literary criticism fostered characteristic disorders of reading: one tended to discount the reader and aggrandize the text whereas the other tended to ennoble the reader and dominate the text. One conceived of the literary work as a miraculous, semi-autonomous aesthetic artifact and the other conceptualized literature as a valuable cultural production grounded in anthropological, economic, social, and political history. Characteristically, one veered toward liberal and conservative political views and the other toward leftist and left-liberal perspectives. In the final analysis, however, this large-scale dialectic or allegorical division tells us remarkably little about the detailed *history* of American literary criticism between the 1930s and 1980s.

Following the struggles of the 1930s, the New Criticism gained and maintained ascendancy for almost two decades over the academic discipline of English and American literary studies, flanked on one side by relatively isolated literary historians, biographers, and Myth Critics and on the other by increasingly marginalized literary journalists, linguists, textual bibliographers, and assorted radicals and mavericks. Significantly, the late 1950s and the 1960s witnessed a reversal: myth criticism matured and a wave of Continental philosophy swept the discipline, both weakening the hold of an already flagging formalist crticism. Among the imported schools and movements derived from European philosophical traditions were existentialism, phenomenology, hermeneutics, structuralism, semiotics, deconstruction, and Neo-Marxism. In addition, the rise of certain indigenous schools and movements, notably reader-response criticism, feminism, Black Aesthetics, and new left Marxism contributed to the decline of New Criticism. Little by little, contemporary commentators characterized this whole historical shift as the superseding of modernism by postmodernism, which, though provocative, offers inadequate explanation.

After the early 1930s numerous literary critics in America started to move "beyond humanism" in three different ways. First, the Marxists, New Critics, Chicago Critics, and the New York Intellectuals dismissed the New Humanism of Irving Babbitt, Norman Foerster, Paul Elmer More, and Stuart Sherman. Propounded during the teens and twenties, Neo-Humanist doctrine struck leftist cultural critics as a reactionary amalgamation of aristocratic, moralistic, and religious ideas. At the same time more conservative formalist critics rejected Neo-Humanism because it relied on ethical criteria for aesthetic evaluation, confounded religion and art, and dismissed modern and experimental literature. Second, leading academic literary critics after the twenties rarely displayed any deep-seated attachment to ancient Greek and Roman literature. This signaled a significant erosion of foundations in classical learning and the undermining of long-standing intellectual traditions stemming from Renaissance humanism. With few exceptions, leading American critics were primarily preoccupied with post-Renaissance vernacular literature. However ambiguously, the values associated with classical humanism were subjected to more or less continuous interrogation from the 1880s and afterwards. Third, literary critics in growing numbers between the 1930s and 1980s mounted assaults against humanism's transcendental stance toward existence and its patriarchal and Caucasian domination of culture. Indeed, the "death of man" widely proclaimed in the 1960s culminated in explicit antihumanistic thinking, characterizing the founding premises of structuralism, deconstruction, feminism, Black Aesthetics, and much contemporary leftist criticism. Construed as a religious, cultural, and political philosophy perpetuated for centuries by white European male aristocrats, "humanism" seemed a repugnant creed for increasing numbers of American literary critics. Depending on the emphasis, the move "beyond humanism" came to signify the progressive destruction of the centrality of European aristocratic values, of classical learning, of religious foundations, of patriarchal hegemony, of "logocentric" theories of literature, and of self-effacing devotional modes of interpretation. This historical struggle occasioned considerable losses and gains, which critical schools and movements demonstrated in complex and special ways, as this history documents in detail. But to thematize the complicated developments in modern American literary criticism as an epochal move "beyond humanism" is to engage in a considerable simplification of history.

While a number of historical accounts of contemporary American literary criticism exist, there is no history covering the six decades from the thirties to the eighties. Of the four recent texts in this area, Grant Webster's *The Republic of Letters* (1979) stops at the early 1960s and limits its inquiry to two major schools; Arnold Goldsmith's *American Literary Criticism 1905–1965* (1979) also ends at the early 1960s and leaves out the New York Intellectuals, the phenomenologists, and the existentialists; Frank Lentricchia's *After the New Criticism* (1980) confines its investigation to the period from 1957 to 1977; and René Wellek's *American Criticism, 1900–1950* (1986)—the sixth volume of his *A History of Modern Criticism* (1955–86)—offers summary treatments of the Marxists, Chicago Critics, and New York Intellectuals. While the period preceding the 1930s is fairly well covered, the subsequent six decades in American criticism lack comprehensive historical documentation. Particularly scanted in recent histories are important contributions from feminists, Black Aestheticians, and Leftist Critics of the Space Age.

This book provides accounts of thirteen American critical schools and movements of the period from the early 1930s to the mid-1980s. Each chapter presents a history of a specific school or movement, covering pertinent social and cultural backgrounds, main figures and texts, key philosophical and critical theories and practices, and significant relations with allied and antagonistic contemporaneous movements both here and abroad. For each school the text examines pedagogical programs, ideological commitments, and processes of institutional emergence, formation, and influence.

In writing the history of modern American academic literary criticism, I follow many of my predecessors by employing the "schools and movements" method of organization. On the one hand, the "schools and movements" approach lends coherence to the works of the seventy-five or so critics treated here, which otherwise is difficult to obtain. On the other hand, this pragmatic method has the added advantage of dividing chapters into discrete histories. Thus, historical differences are not homogenized by larger, overarching or monistic patterns of cultural evolution, teleology, continuity, unity, devolution, or cyclicality. One inevitable disadvantage, however, is that independent figures appear only in marginal roles. Displaced from this history are the individual careers of such critics as René Girard, Hugh Kenner, Harry Levin, Lewis Mumford, Morse Peckham, and Helen Vendler, and such important poet-critics as Donald Hall, Richard Howard, Randall Jarrell, Charles Olson, and Wallace Stevens. The insights provided by individual critics who do not ally themselves with theoretical shifts are invaluable and innumerable. But the history of practical criticism and individual theoretical insights is not my subject. One assimilates it in studying the literature of particular times and places; it does not lend itself to comprehensive consideration outside this context. I console myself with the knowledge that in most cases these literary intellectuals get careful consideration in essays and books on their works and that many will be treated in the forthcoming *Dictionary of Literary Biography: Modern American Critics,* edited by Gregory Jay for the Gale Research Company.

In past studies, one liability of the "schools and movements" approach has been the oversimplification of core beliefs, commitments, and practices. To mitigate this tendency, I initiate investigations of the historically marginal and contradictory forces and elements that structure each movement. For example, related European critics and groups, internal disputes and struggles, historical precursors, contributions from minor figures, inner transformations, and external challenges and conflicts are treated so as to preserve the rich heterogeneity present within the boundaries of specific schools and movements. More important, the conventional "schools and movements" method of organization is supplemented here with a mode of institutional analysis that retrieves the formative roles played by journals, conferences, university presses, granting agencies, research institutes, professional organizations, educational foundations, pedagogical programs,

and the creations of new fields and subdisciplines (for instance, Comparative Literature, American Studies, Semiotics, Narratology, Women's Studies, Ethnic Studies, "Theory," and Cultural Studies). This attention to
institutional matters broadens and complicates the concept of school and of
movement through more material modes of historical analysis.

Practiced in America for eight decades, psychological criticism constitutes a type of criticism rather than a school or movement. While this
study offers no chapter on psychological criticism, it in fact devotes more
discussion to its pervasive presence than to any one school or movement. In
particular, much of the text concerns itself with the controversial legacies of
Freud, Jung, and Lacan.

I shall conclude by listing areas for future detailed investigation. Worthy
of inquiry are the linkages between the history of literary criticism and the
histories of scholarship, of literary journalism, of the immigration of literary
intellectuals, of translations, of textual bibliography, of literary history, of
pedagogy, of libraries, of publishers, of book stores, and of the university. In
the case of the university, especially in the period after World War II, topics
deserving extended consideration directly relevant to the history of literary
criticism include the proliferation of graduate literature programs, the
emerging definitions of "literary research," the pressures upon critics of
"professionalism," the specifications of criteria and credentials for tenure
and for advancement, the formations of composition and creative writing as
subdisciplines, the creation of learning skills and writing centers, the effects
of departmental expansions and retrenchments on literary canons and on
course offerings, the prevailing organization of knowledge into departmental units, and the general decline of higher education and of literary studies
during the 1970s and 1980s. One final topic warranting special scrutiny is
the complex role of the federal and state governments in establishing and
administering endowment funds, research guidelines, affirmative action
goals, and support for libraries, institutes, publications, translations, new
programs, conferences, and foreign-language study. My premise here, as
throughout the text, is that the history of criticism is not separable from
economic, social, political, cultural, and institutional history.

March 1986   V.B.L.

ACKNOWLEDGMENTS

SOME MATERIAL in this book appeared in earlier versions in *College English,* 39 (October 1977), *Studies in the Literary Imagination,* 12 (Spring 1979), *Critical Inquiry,* 6 (Summer 1980), *New Orleans Review,* 10 (Spring 1983), and my book *Deconstructive Criticism* (New York: Columbia University Press, 1983). I am grateful to the editors and publishers for permission to reprint.

This book draws upon much of my training, teaching, and research over the last decade. I am especially thankful for time spent at the School of Criticism and Theory as a Fellow in 1978, at the University of Tampere (Finland) as a Fulbright-Hays Senior Lecturer in 1979, at the International Institute for Semiotic and Structural Studies as a Mellon Fellow in 1981, and at the intersection of many fruitful debates fostered by the Society for Critical Exchange as a member of the Board of Directors from 1978 to 1983. I am appreciative of research support from the National Endowment for the Humanities in 1980, from Mercer University in 1982, from the American Council of Learned Societies in 1985, and from Purdue University in 1986.

Among the people who kindly offered assistance with this project, Geoffrey Hartman, Murray Krieger, Wallace Martin, and Gregory Ulmer deserve grateful mention. For love I thank Kristin and Rory.

CHAPTER ONE

Marxist Criticism in the 1930s

FOR THE CONTEMPORARY historian of literary theory and criticism in America perhaps what most distinguishes the decade of the 1930s is the formation of four significant groups: the Marxists, the New Critics, the Chicago Critics, and the New York Intellectuals. Needless to say, the histories of these schools lead backward to earlier times and forward to later years; and, too, the development of each movement links up with wider social forces and analogous groups in other places. While the emergence of heterogeneous and competing schools of criticism clearly calls for differentiated historical analyses, the field of economic, political, and intellectual forces of the 1930s serves as a common, however fragmented and complex, ground of development. The "Great Depression" nicknames the numerous socioeconomic phenomena and cultural problems that marked American history in the 1930s.

THE GREAT DEPRESSION

During the frenetic month of the "Stock Market Crash" in October 1929 the value of stocks on the New York Exchange plummeted thirty-seven percent. For the next dozen years America remained in a severe economic depression. At a high of 452 in September 1929, the stock average of the *New York Times* bottomed at 52 in July 1932. The personal income of Americans declined by more than fifty percent between 1929 and 1932. Unemployment reached roughly twenty-five percent in 1932 with 13 million people out of work. Whereas wheat earned $2.16 a bushel in 1919, it sank to thirty-eight cents in 1932. For the same dates, cotton peaked at nearly forty-two cents and bottomed at about five cents per pound. Approximately one million farms were lost to mortgage holders between 1930 and 1934. Traditional agrarian modes of existence were in serious jeopardy throughout the Depression. When Franklin D. Roosevelt took office as president in March 1933, four-fifths of the nation's banks were closed: the monetary system was near ruin. In the recent assessment of one moderate historian: "The crash had revealed the fundamental business of the country to be unsound. Most harmful was the ability of business to maintain prices and take profits while holding down wages . . . with the result that about one-third of the personal income went to only 5 percent of the population."[1]

The accumulation of capital and its unbalanced distribution during the 1920s resulted from swollen profits, huge dividends, and massive tax savings to the wealthy. The consequent large money supply created an era of feverish speculation. At the same time excessive savings led to a decline in demand. What characterized the economy was, on the one hand, low wages, high prices, capital concentration and monopoly and, on the other hand, weak enforcement of antitrust regulations and widespread suspicion of collective bargaining by labor unions. In short, governmental mechanisms to balance economic inequalities were ineffective or nonexistent.

The "New Deal" of Franklin Roosevelt sought to remedy the failures of governmental policies, charting a course between the excesses of laissez-faire and socialist economics. In a sense, the New Deal of the 1930s installed a welfare state upon a capitalist foundation. In 1935, for example, Roosevelt fostered the now landmark Social Security Act, the National Labor Relations Act, the Works Progress Administration, and the Revenue Act. The latter Act, to cite some specifics, raised surtaxes on income over $50,000, imposed graduated taxes on incomes over five million dollars (up to a seventy-five percent maximum rate), created an excess profits tax on corporate earnings, and established estate and gift taxes. Despite such reforms, Roosevelt himself memorably admitted in his Second Inaugural Address (1937): "I see one-third of a nation ill-housed, ill-clad, ill-nourished." Throughout the 1930s and into World War II such conditions persisted.

SOCIALISM AND COMMUNISM IN AMERICA

Given the ruinous economic conditions of the Great Depression, it was not surprising that Marxist thought became a vital force during the 1930s in America. But we can go back half a century into the American past and find evidence of a growing socialist movement. In 1877 the Socialist Labor Party was formed, later came the Socialist Democratic Party in 1897, the Socialist Party of America in 1901, and the Industrial Workers of the World (the "Wobblies") in 1905. American voters had a socialist option in the presidential elections of 1900, 1904, 1908, 1912, and 1920. In the election of 1912, for example, Eugene V. Debs received 900,000 ballots—six percent of the popular vote. The same year thirty-three cities had socialist mayors. At the time of the 1932 election the socialist Norman Thomas gained 900,000 votes and the communist William Z. Foster got 103,000. With a million voters in the early part of the twentieth century, Marxist-inspired movements in America constituted an active, if marginal, political force.

Left wingers departed the Socialist Party in 1919 to establish the Communist and Communist Labor Parties, which were united in 1923. Until the mid-30s, many American communists regarded socialists as dupes and fascists. In these early days the Communist Party of the United States pretty much followed the lead of Moscow. At first a secret organization, the Party became legal in 1923. Until 1935 the Communist Party was a sectarian, ultraleft organization. But between 1935 and 1939, the period of the populist "People's Front," the Party softened its approach, seeking support from liberals of many persuasions, including New Dealers. This dramatic turnabout was inspired by the Communist International. With 7,000 members at the start of the 1930s, the party attained a membership of 75,000 by 1939 and its influence in some circles often exceeded these numbers.[2] Among other things, the Spanish Civil War—like the later Vietnam War of the 1960s and 70s—radicalized many Americans, as did the economic depression. While the United States remained neutral in this struggle, the Soviets supported the Spanish Republic against the fascists, earning the admiration of many people. Key intellectuals supported the efforts of the Communist Party during the 1930s—some as members and others as sympathizers ("fellow travelers").

In September 1932 fifty-three artists and scholars, including, among others, Newton Arvin, Malcolm Cowley, Granville Hicks, Sidney Hook, and Edmund Wilson, signed a letter in support of the revolutionary Communist Party and of the presidential candidacy of William Z. Foster. The League of American Writers—a Popular Front group set up in 1935—included such writers as Nelson Algren, Van Wyck Brooks, Erskine Caldwell, John Dos Passos, Theodore Dreiser, Clifton Fadiman, James T. Farrell, Waldo Frank, Lillian Hellman, Ernest Hemingway, Langston Hughes, Archibald MacLeish, Lewis Mumford, William Saroyan, John Steinbeck, Nathanael West, William Carlos Williams, and Richard Wright.[3] During the 1930s leftist periodicals ranged from the dogmatic *Daily Worker* to the doctrinaire *New Masses* and from the scholarly *Science & Society* to the literary *Partisan Review*. To be sure, a generation earlier important literary intellectuals had supported socialist programs and works: William Dean Howells, Edward Bellamy, Jack London, Upton Sinclair, and Theodore Dreiser, to name just five leading figures. And earlier journals welcomed socialist criticism: *Comrade* (started 1901), *The Masses* (1911), *New Republic* (1914), *The Liberator* (1918), *The Nation* (after liberalization in 1918), and *The Modern Quarterly* (1923). Despite all their internal differences, organized Marxist-inspired groups persisted in America from the late nineteenth century till the mid-twentieth century. Artists, scholars, and intellectuals frequently participated in the various Marxist activities of the day.

While different socialist and communist cadres and parties experienced internal disputes, "red scares" brought outside threats into existence. The first significant scare came during the last days of World War I. Following the passage of the Espionage Act of 1917 and Sedition Act of 1918, many socialists landed in jail: more than a hundred Wobblies were convicted in Chicago for opposing the war and Eugene V. Debs received a twenty-year sentence for statements tending to cause resistance to the draft. (Debs was later pardoned by President Harding.) In 1919 The General Intelligence Division of The Department of Justice started to collect files on radicals. The same year 249 radicals, including Emma Goldman, were deported to Russia without the benefit of court hearings. The next year the New York Legislature expelled five duly elected socialist members. Hysteria against socialists and communists provided the essential backdrop for the judicial sentences in the infamous Sacco-Vanzetti case decided in 1921.

The second significant "red scare" spanned the years from 1947 to 1954; it was the internal counterpart of the external Cold War. In March 1947 President Truman issued an Executive Order requiring all future federal employees to sign a loyalty oath. (Over a four-year period the order affected three million people.) The Taft-Hartley Act of 1947, which restricted labor unions, called for labor leaders to take oaths that they were not members of the Communist Party. In 1948 Alger Hiss, a prominent citizen, was convicted in a celebrated case over lying about espionage. A more extreme fate befell Julius and Ethel Rosenberg, who were executed a few years later for espionage. The McCarron Internal Security Act of 1950 required communist or communist-front organizations to register with the attorney general. Enforcement was put in the hands of the Subversive Activities Control Board. (The Supreme Court ruled in 1965 that this Act was in violation of the Fifth Amendment.) In view of the prevailing atmosphere, it was not particularly anomalous that Senator Joseph McCarthy in February 1950 should declare the State Department to be infested with communists. Though he continued to make similar charges until 1954, Senator McCarthy never uncovered any communist agents. As a result of President Eisenhower's Executive Order 10450, issued in April 1953, the category "security risk" was used to screen federal employees who could lose their jobs because of dubious associations or personal habits. In December of that year the Atomic Energy Commission removed the security clearance of J. Robert Oppenheimer, father of the atomic bomb, because he had associated with communists in the past and had expressed doubt in the late forties about the hydrogen bomb. The "red scares" after each world war were not temporary: a line of continuity exists between 1917 and 1954. The House of Representatives established in 1938 the notorious Committee on Un-American Activities, which sought to harass communists, as did the Smith Act of 1940.

While "red scares" gradually weakened popular support for Marxist movements, finally putting the Communist Party out of action in the middle 1950s, it was the Hitler-Stalin Non-Aggression Pact of 1939 that most dramatically damaged leftwing politics. The specter of a jingoistic deal between fascists and communists undermined the widespread support for and the prestige of leftist parties and policies. The infamous Stalinist treason trials of 1936–38 also severely diminished the promise and possibilities of Marxist politics. To summarize, a history of Marxist activity and organization spanning two generations came to a virtual halt in the postwar period, having reached a peak of intensity in the 1930s. Ironically, the New Left of the 1960s and 1970s cared little about this American history, sometimes turning for inspiration and guidance toward European Marxist theories and thinkers.[4] If there was an American lost generation, it was perhaps that group of Marxist literary intellectuals active during the period of the Great Depression and living on into the era of the Vietnam War.

MARXIST PHILOSOPHY AND AESTHETICS

The tenets of classical Marxist philosophy insist on (1) the indissoluble priority of matter over mind (materialism); (2) the economic foundations of social actions and institutions (economic determinism); (3) the continuous struggle of social groups as the motor force of history (theory of class struggle); (4) the production of social value through work (labor theory of value); (5) the capitalistic "commodification" of relations and resultant alienation (reification); (6) the inevitable seizure of power by the working class (theory of proletarian revolution); and (7) the ultimate establishment of a classless society (communist utopia). That the socioeconomic conditions of existence determine human consciousness, and not vice versa, is central to Marxist thought, as is the view that the economic relations of production (the economic base or infrastructure) determine the ideological formations of society (the cultural superstructure). In Marxist thinking, *ideology* designates the political, legal, religious, philosophical, and aesthetic forms that consciousness assumes at a given stage of economic/material development. Finally, the theory of the successive "historical modes of production" (the Asiatic, the ancient, the feudal, the bourgeois, and the socialist), however schematic, is fundamental to much Marxist philosophy.

Because the comments of Marx and Engels on specifically aesthetic matters are scant, fragmentary, and unorganized, a "Marxist aesthetics" must be (re)constructed.[5] While unified doctrine in aesthetics is not to be found in Marxist philosophy, certain traditional lines of thought give direction and coherence to this field of inquiry. In their occasional writings on art and literature, Marx and Engels provide three very different perspectives: (1) art depends on a particular social formation; (2) art is (and should be) an instrument of political action; and (3) art is relatively autonomous. The first major theoretician of the initial perspective is Plekhanov, who promulgates systematically the view that art reflects life. The second perspective is developed early and effectively by Lenin and institutionalized later by Zhadanov: art must seek to further the socialist revolution. From this program emerge such phenomena as Proletkult, Agit-Prop Theater, and Socialist Realism. The third perspective finds support in early Trotsky, who, despite much hedging in *Literature and Revolution* (1924), allows creative art to unfold in a sphere of its own.

In early twentieth-century Marxist aesthetics four modes of analysis predominate. The first type undertakes historical and theoretical inquiry into the general status of art and literature in human societies. This resembles traditional aesthetics. The second kind attempts to specify the role of art and literature in society, particularly its political function. This mode usually promotes activist revolutionary programs. The third analytic examines past artworks and literary texts, especially masterpieces, to disclose their ideological configurations—to uncover the relationships between cultural productions and socioeconomic foundations. Such "ideological analysis" of great works parallels mainline historical scholarship. The fourth type engages in demystification of contemporary works to make visible their ideological leanings in relation to existing conditions. This kind of work is basically partisan literary journalism.[6]

The leading American literary Marxists of the 1930s most often practiced historical scholarship and especially literary journalism. Their purely aesthetic theories and their revolutionary programs were borrowed almost wholesale from earlier Marxist sources. The object of much native Marxist scholarship was the American "social totality" (the historical configuration of base and superstructure in a given time), usually of the period stretching from the Civil War to the Great Depression. Critics like V. F. Calverton and Granville Hicks, in their major historical projects, examined primarily ideology—the ideas, values, and sentiments expressed by writers in their particular milieus. Understanding the material conditions and ideological formations of the American past provided such critics a certain comprehension of the present and a vision of the future. In other words, ideological analysis furthered programs for revolutionary activity—as we shall see.

In Marxist aesthetic theory, there exist several long-standing areas of debate. The exact relation between art and ideology is a case in point. Art is part of the superstructure, the ideological framework, of social existence. Yet art not only embodies but transforms ideology; it reflects and (re)produces ideology *and* it deflects and revalues ideology. This relation of intimacy and distance between art and ideology is, in Marxist terms, "dialectical." The pattern of reciprocal interaction here repeats itself in the vexing relation of aesthetic form and content: each shapes the other, both are ideological and transformative. Another significant Marxist area of dispute concerns the role of the artist in relation to his work. The notorious Soviet doctrine of Socialist Realism, developed by Lenin in 1905 and later promulgated by Zhadanov as dogma in 1934, insists that writers should be self-consciously progressive and partisan in their work. But the classical Marxist "principle of contradiction" allows that the political views of an artist may (and often do) run counter to what the artwork may objectively show. Accordingly, a work of art can serve progressive ends in spite of the artist's intentions. A final area of debate involves the Marxist law of "unequal development," which provides for different stages of maturation within the ideological sphere in relation to the socioeconomic base. This means that the artist may be more or less retrograde, diagnostic, or prophetic in any particular social formation.

What often happens in Marxist analysis to the dialectical flexibility promoted between base and superstructure is a severe mechanization and reduction to simple and rigid causation. An iron law comes into play: as in the base, so in the superstructure. Such "vulgar Marxism" was fairly common during the 1930s—a time when the extremes of scientific Leninism and "humanistic" Trotskyism vied with one another and when party critics and independent Marxists engaged in heated polemics and divisive debates.

A PIONEER AMERICAN MARXIST PROJECT

V. F. Calverton's lengthy *The Liberation of American Literature* (1932) was "our first full-length Marxist study of the history of American letters."[7] In the opening words of his Preface, the Marxist Calverton told the reader "this book is as much a study of American culture as it is of American literature, for its aim is to interpret American literature in terms of American culture. The American cultural pattern, shaped as it has been by the conflicting class interests in American society, has revealed a number of new and contradictory characteristics. . . ."[8] At the outset Calverton firmly rooted literature in the soil of society and its class system. Straightway, he focused on the historical role of social contradictions in literary creations. That social forces determined artistic productions was never doubted by Calverton. The relation of such sociological poetics to aesthetics was clear: "I believe that aesthetic criticism is fundamentally social in character, and can only be significant when derived from a sound social philosophy" (xii). Society was the ground of art: the arts constituted the superstructure and society the base of existence. Aesthetics depended on social philosophy. Given his commitments, Calverton found it tactically necessary to defer "pure aesthetic" studies: "I have intentionally avoided the problem of aesthetic analysis and evaluation. In short, as an expedient, I have taken the aesthetic element for granted, and in almost all cases have immediately proceeded to an analysis of the philosophy, or ideology if you will, that underlay the individual author's work" (xii). Ideological analysis, not aesthetic evaluation, constituted the method of *The Liberation of American Literature*.

Taking the literary canon of leading writers as established, Calverton examined the social contradictions in the great writers of American literature. He argued that most major writers after the Civil War and up to the Great Depression were born into middle-class culture but, unable to find meaning in bourgeois culture's proclaimed values, they eventually experienced alienation and pessimism. According to Calverton, the doctrine of self-reliant individualism, in particular, became a target—intentionally or otherwise—of American writers' criticism and scorn. "The faith of Emerson and Whitman belongs to the past and not to the future. Their belief in the common man was a belief in him as a petty bourgeois individualist; our belief must be in him as proletarian collectivist. In that belief lies the ultimate liberation of American literature—and American life" (480). Here the thrust of Calverton's pioneer project became fully evident; he wanted to move from the American literary past into the social future (without forgetting the past) and to make the future a time of liberation in American life and literature. Since the socioeconomic movement of history, in his view, was from the aristocracy to the middle class to the proletariat, Calverton recommended joining the proletariat. Collectivism would replace individualism. The historical mode of production was changing. This prophetic, utopian strand, characteristic of Marxist analysis, allowed Calverton to assign literature a constructive role in society—one way out of the debilitating contradictions that characterized American capitalist life and art.

"The literary artist is not, therefore, as many people think, a hopeless victim of his environment, but is a creative part of it, able to help shape and rebuild it. Although he derives his ideas and direction from the social environment, he in turn, by virtue of those same ideas and direction, is able to assist in the transformation of that environment" (468). The artist both reflected and remolded society. He or she was potentially a diagnostician and a revolutionary capable of assisting in the work of social revolution and reconstruction. Just as the socioeconomic base of society determined the ideological superstructure, so the forces of ideology could feed back to transform social foundations. Art had a role to play in social revolution. Again, Calverton sought for liberation of literature *and* life.

It would be a mistake to regard Calverton's *The Liberation of American Literature* as something completely new in American literary studies. Leftist sociological criticism had appeared earlier in, for example, John Macy's *The Spirit of American Literature* (1913), Van Wyck Brooks' *America's Coming-of-Age* (1915), and Vernon L. Parrington's three-volume *Main Currents in American Thought* (1927–1930). The latter monumental study employed a sociological method founded on belief in economic and social determinism and expressed through a progressive or populist point of view. Starting with the colonial times of Roger Williams, Parrington unearthed and reconstituted radical democratic traditions in America. In addition, specifically Marxist analysis of American literary culture shows up in memorable works, written between the start of World War I and the onset of the Depression, by

Max Eastman, Floyd Dell, Michael Gold, and Joseph Freeman, among others. What was new about Calverton's pioneering critical work was that it was a full-length, revolutionary Marxist treatment of the history of American literature: it not only argued a certain diagnosis of the past, but propounded a certain program for the future linked indissolubly with the proletariat.

In his *Writers on the Left,* Daniel Aaron observed, "Calverton's career is almost a one-man history of the American radical movement between 1920 and 1940."[9] A quick survey of Calverton's biography bears out Aaron's observation. Born George Goetz in 1900 and educated at John Hopkins University, Calverton was a full-fledged radical in 1923 when he founded *The Modern Quarterly*—a journal destined to publish the era's leading radicals, ranging from ultraleft communists to rightist moderate socialists. (Calverton early adopted his pen name so as not to jeopardize his job in the Baltimore public schools.) Eventually, his eclecticism and tolerance would earn the enmity of many more single-minded associates and comrades. Calverton would be recklessly labeled a "social fascist" and "Trotskyite" by doctrinaire party members in the late twenties and early thirties—a time when the Communist Party was rigidly doctrinaire. A militant socialist as a teenager, Calverton worked closely with the Communist Party in the mid-20s and shifted in the late twenties and thirties to anti-Stalinism. This prophetic stance was adopted by Max Eastman in the mid-20s and a decade later by the New York Intellectuals. Author and editor of seventeen books, including texts on sex, marriage, and women's liberation, Calverton pioneered Marxist literary theory and criticism in America with *The Newer Spirit* (1925), *The New Grounds of Criticism* (1930), and his major work, *The Liberation of American Literature.* Never forswearing his ecumenism, Calverton remained an independent Marxist until his early death in 1940, maintaining his dream of a united front of all radicals against capitalism and fascism.

AN EXEMPLARY MARXIST CAREER

The career of Granville Hicks in the Depression era offers a revealing overview of revolutionary Marxism in America during the 1930s. Situated at the crossroads of leftist literary activities, Hicks served as both a model and a target for other Marxists, drawing out the lines of force in this contested field. Granville Hicks graduated from Harvard in 1923, studied for two more years at Harvard Theological School, taught for three years at

Smith College, returned to Harvard to earn a Master's degree, spent the first half of the 1930s as a professor in the Department of English at Rensselaer Polytechnic Institute, became an editor of *New Masses* in 1934, joined the Communist Party in 1935, obtained a Guggenheim Fellowship in 1935, worked assiduously as a publisher's reader, secured a brief post at Harvard in 1938–39, and resigned dramatically from the Communist Party in Autumn 1939, spurred by the notorious Nazi-Soviet Pact. Author of numerous articles and four novels, Hicks early published *Eight Ways of Looking at Christianity* (1928), *The Great Tradition* (1933; revised edition 1935), *John Reed* (1936), *I Like America* (1938), and *Figures of Transition* (1939), as well as the later anticommunist memoir *Where We Came Out* (1954) and the autobiographical *Part of the Truth* (1965). A socialist in the 20s, Hicks became a communist by 1932, though not a member of the Party until 1935.

In James T. Farrell's view, Hicks was a hypocritical, sectarian Stalinist, given to mediocre didacticism. An independent Marxist, Farrell was considered by Party critics to be an arch dissenter and "Trotskyite." (Those opposed by the Party were invariably called "Trotskyites" whether or not they actually were.) With perhaps more objectivity, Daniel Aaron found Hicks to be a liberal, decent fellow.[10] In any case, Farrell's assessment displays some of the intense inner dynamics of American Marxist polemics in the 1930s. Specifically, Farrell judged Hicks to be the worst of the communist literary commissars and mechanical materialists. In *A Note on Literary Criticism* (1936), Farrell pilloried two types of American leftists. The "revolutionary sentimentalist," like Michael Gold, demanded simple, even banal, literature, preferring irrational poems of sweat and stench and books that idealized workers and writer workers. The "mechanical determinist," like Granville Hicks, presupposed that literature immediately and faithfully followed economics, omitting considerations of craft and aesthetics. What Farrell, like Max Eastman at this time, abhorred was the tendency of certain doctrinaire revolutionary communists to require of artists a commitment in their works to specified political ends. Hicks, in Farrell's mind, confused propaganda with literature.

As a highly visible editor of *New Masses,* a presiding officer at the initial American Writers' Conference in 1935, an editor of *Proletarian Literature in the United States: An Anthology* (1935), and author of *The Great Tradition,* Granville Hicks "was probably the foremost American liberal literary critic of the decade."[11] Hicks is best remembered today for his lengthy study, *The Great Tradition,* subtitled *An Interpretation of American Litera-*

ture Since the Civil War. In the tradition of Macy, Van Wyck Brooks, Parrington, and Calverton, Hicks undertook here a sociological analysis of American literary culture focusing on the role of economic, political, and class struggle in canonical literary productions. He traced the decline of agrarian, mercantile modes of life and the triumph of capitalistic, industrial society following the Civil War. What Hicks sought, in addition, was a literary criticism more attentive to aesthetic matters than earlier leftist work. In particular, he wished to avoid Calverton's separation of craftsmanship and content, believing the "important problems of form are absolutely bound up in the problems of content and attitude."[12] His first sustained piece of Marxist analysis, *The Great Tradition,* urged the necessity for commitment to political action and argued the thesis that revolutionary literature was the authentic outcome of the great tradition of American literature. Given sternly to the mystique of the proletariat, Hicks celebrated or criticized the value of any particular author to the degree that he exhibited a revolutionary attitude. It was his commitment to the proletarian class and to the coming revolution that distinguished Hicks' doctrinaire criticism from that of the many independent nonrevolutionary Marxists of the thirties.

According to Hicks' critical theory, as outlined briefly in "The Crisis in American Criticism," published in *New Masses* (February 1933), there existed three main criteria of literary value for Marxist criticism. First, a work of literature had to deal with themes related to the central issues of life. Second, literature had to possess intensity, provoking the participation of the reader in the life portrayed by the work. And third, an author's point of view had to be that of the proletariat. Using such criteria, Hicks was enabled to praise Proust's *Remembrance of Things Past* because it presented a clear, convincing, and fine picture of the decay of bourgeois civilization. More than any modern revolutionary Marxist work, Proust's novel offered "an enormously vivid sense of the corruption and unworthiness of the system under which we live; we see that that system is decaying and deserves to collapse" (5). Though Proust's text lacked a utopian dimension of revolutionary hope and determination, it nevertheless successfully met the tests of centrality and intensity required by Marxist criticism. As time passed, however, Hicks became more insistent about the criteria of commitment to the revolutionary proletariat.

In the Preface to the revised edition of *The Great Tradition,* Hicks justified his new edition, saying "because of the absence of achievement in the ranks of the non-revolutionary writers, I have devoted the new chapter entirely to the revolutionary movement in literature. When I wrote the book, I was writing a history of bourgeois literature. I wanted to show that certain problems had arisen that could not be solved within the framework of bourgeois thought and feeling."[13] What was missing from the first edition of *The Great Tradition* was a full demonstration of the substance and power of contemporary revolutionary writers. The early text was mainly a diagnosis of the impasse of middle-class literature. Hicks closed off his new Preface dramatically: "Believing that criticism is always a weapon, I see no reason to disguise, either from others or from myself, the nature of the conflict in which I am engaged or the side that I have chosen" (x). For Hicks, criticism was fundamentally political activity, whether or not particular critics admitted this truth. Neutrality was a political position just as much as activism was. Brandished or not, criticism was a weapon in social struggle. Hicks openly threw in with the struggle for revolutionary socialism. In his judgment, revolutionary writers were "participating in a battle that is for civilization itself" (330).

About three-quarters of the way through his inquiry, Hicks revealingly focused on the weaknesses of key critics of the era around World War I, including James G. Huneker, Joel Spingarn, H. L. Mencken, and Irving Babbitt. According to Hicks, the Impressionists (Huneker, Spingarn, and Mencken) committed two main errors. First, they "refused to admit that the artist expresses more or less completely the civilization of which he is a part, the civilization that has made him what he is"; second, they did "not see that art not only expresses something but also does something, has consequences as well as causes" (248–49). What was wrong with Impressionism was that it privatized literary experience, falsely cutting off the writer from his society (the socioeconomic base) and obscuring the transformative potential of the artwork (the cultural superstructure). Without roots or relations to the social ground, art became purely personal and subjective, isolated and impotent. To marginalize literature in this way was to further the decline of creativity under advanced industrial capitalism. Even as unrelenting and energetic a critic of reactionaries and moralists as Mencken had ultimately "nothing to offer the hosts of bewildered agnostics except a blind nihilism" (249). Neither solutions to problems nor positive programs could be found in the Impressionist School. As far as Hicks was concerned, the Humanists (Paul Elmer More and especially Irving Babbitt) also fled problems and responsibilities: they turned to the past and to religion, producing "a defence of private property, the existing order, and Puritan morality" (250). Salvaging old standards, they "consolidate the position of the privileged class" and potentially "stifle protest and prevent revolution" (250–51). The philosophy of such defensive "Humanism" was reactionary: it upheld the crumbling capitalist order in the name of an obsolete ethics. Hate for the present and fear of the future motivated this conservative mandarinism, which robbed art of its social power and revolutionary potential. Earlier branded by Calverton as "literary fascism" in *New Masses* (April 1930), Humanism served Marxists in the early thirties as a productive foil for their own programs.

In *The Great Tradition*, Hicks developed a theory of American literary tradition, and he projected a future for this literature. He argued that "the best of American writers have always affirmed values that were not being realized under capitalism. Today . . . these values cannot be realized so long as private ownership endures" (294). That the Marxist theory of world history pertained to the American experience was never seriously questioned. Capitalism was crumbling and socialism was coming. In the meantime, a revolutionary struggle was underway. American literature reflected this development. "This is the great tradition of American literature. Ours has been a critical literature, critical of greed, cowardice, and meanness. It has been a hopeful literature, touched again and again with passion for brotherhood, justice, and intellectual honesty. . . . It involves not merely criticism but destruction of capitalism and its whole way of life" (329). Until the thirties, the ruinous effects of capitalism, which had steadily been documented by American writers, had never been so clear. The Great Depression illustrated catastrophically the need to continue the anticapitalistic tradition of American literature by accepting the need for revolutionary activity. For Hicks, contemporary revolutionary writers insured the continuity of American literary development.

There was a logic in Hicks joining the Communist Party in 1935—the year the revised *The Great Tradition* was published. "The revolutionary writers have proceeded from a belief that capitalism is unsound to a belief that it must be destroyed. Most of them have gone further and recognized that only the working class can destroy capitalism. . . . A majority of these support the Communist Party" (295–96). To continue the great line of American literary tradition required furthering the coming social transformation. Since the working class would play the main role in this struggle, it was essential to work with this elect group through the Party. With confidence Hicks traced in *The Great Tradition* a course of events from the past into the future. The source of his certainty was clear: "the future of the movement rests on confidence in the Marxian analysis of history" (327). As he turned from the past, documented in detail in his book, Hicks envisioned the literary future—which was thoroughly tied up with the proletariat and with revolutionary communism:

Proletarian literature will not only grow before and during the revolution, but also and more especially in the period of the class dictatorship. Its growth before the revolution is limited by capitalist powers, and, if capitalism is allowed to follow its natural development into fascism, may be temporarily checked, but in the period in which the foundations of a new social order are laid, proletarian literature will have its opportunity. . . . [It will] ripen into something finer and nobler than itself, something finer than any literature the world has ever known, broad as all mankind and free to devote itself to men as men and not men as enemies. (328)

The mixture of naive utopianism and political prescience about fascism, of hope for the future and criticism of the capitalist past, of sureness about the new social order and uncertainty about the intervening time—all this embodied faithfully the overriding optimism and underlying wishfulness characteristic of much radical Marxism in the middle 1930s before knowledge of the Russian famines, the Stalinist Purge Trials, and the Nazi-Soviet Pact had turned things around.

That Hicks never managed to integrate examination of content with analysis of craftsmanship in *The Great Tradition* was evident throughout the text. Like Calverton, Hicks both admitted the importance of aesthetic matters and postponed inquiry into this realm for more urgent tasks. In his concluding chapter, he reasoned,

no one imagines that mere adherence to a set of political principles, or even the complete mastery of a world philosophy, is any guarantee of literary talent. In the preceding chapters we have taken for granted a certain minimum qualification, so to speak, and have been principally concerned with what each writer did with the capabilities he had. This is not to say, however, that a discerning eye and a quick ear, the power of penetrating below the surface and the willingness to work for perfect expression, are unimportant. (298)

Politics was one thing and aesthetics another. Hicks limited aesthetics to each writer's "literary talent" and personal "capabilities" in achieving "perfect expression." The discernment and power, perceptiveness and diligence essential to aesthetic achievement were "taken for granted."

Like Farrell before him, the Marxist critic Bernard Smith, in his *Forces in American Criticism: A Study in the History of American Literary Thought* (1939), castigated Marxist critics for slighting aesthetics and separating form from content. At the same time Smith found little to admire in the aristocratic formalist criticism associated with Edgar Allan Poe, Henry James, and T. S. Eliot: artistry and taste divorced from social purpose and political commitment were no substitute for substance. In Smith's view, the reactionary individualism, philosophical idealism, principled restrictions, and limiting rules concomitant with traditional aesthetics were unacceptable to all Marxists.[14] In any case, Hicks, like Calverton, left himself open to criticism not just from intellectuals on the right, but from fellow travelers like Farrell, Smith, and especially the leftist group supporting *Partisan Review*.

As editor of *New Masses* (the main organ of Communist Party intellectuals), Hicks found himself in increasing conflict with the revitalized *Partisan Review* (1934–1936; 1937–present), edited by the independent left-wingers Philip Rahv and William Phillips. From its rebirth in 1937, following a year of suspension, *Partisan Review*, a literary periodical, tried to integrate aesthetics and politics, specifically modernist experiments à la Joyce and Eliot and sophisticated Marxist literary criticism. Publisher of many leading members of the literati, this journal was critical of Stalinism and somewhat sympathetic to Trotskyism. By the late thirties Rahv and Phillips, like Farrell, deplored both sentimental proletarianism and mechanical materialism. The result of such developments was a growing tension between the doctrinaire and propagandistic politics of Hicks' *New Masses* and the liberal Marxist aesthetics and literary modernism of Rahv's and Phillips' *Partisan Review*. By 1937, when it resumed publication after its suspension for financial reasons, *Partisan Review* was openly opposed to the Communist Party. Supported by such leading anti-Stalinist figures as Edmund Wilson, Lionel Trilling, John Dos Passos, Harold Rosenberg, Clement Greenberg, Meyer Schapiro, and Sidney Hook, the newly established *Partisan Review* acknowledged for a brief time Trotsky's critique of the degeneration of the Russian Revolution and his call for support of the revolutionary international proletariat rather than the Soviet bureaucracy. The split within the America Marxist movement pitted key literary intellectuals against *New Masses* and Granville Hicks.[15] Although it constitutes part of the history of Marxist criticism in the 1930s, the independent Marxist line of the *Partisan Review* critics shall be examined in chapter 4 rather than here.

In 1935 Hicks paid a price for his communism. After returning from the American Writers' Conference in April, he was informed by the administration of Rensselaer Polytechnic Institute, where he had been teaching since 1929, that he would not be rehired because of retrenchment. Tenureless,

Hicks protested, getting the American Association of University Professors to investigate and concur reluctantly with him that politics, not finances, occasioned his dismissal.[16] (Other universities and agencies engaged in similar tactics to harass left-wing intellectuals.[17]) After 1935 Hicks had to scramble to survive, which he did by reviewing books, refereeing numerous manuscripts for Macmillan Publishing Company, and writing books. Also he farmed some of his thirty acres, raising crops and harvesting wood for fuel.

Like other former Marxists of the thirties, Hicks advocated "New Liberalism" during the forties—which he discussed, for example, in a symptomatic special issue on the future of socialism published in 1947 by *Partisan Review*. Here Hicks modulated his earlier beliefs in the inevitable end of capitalism, in the takeover of the social order by the proletariat, and in the emergence of a classless society. This representative disenchantment with Russian communism and Stalinist totalitarianism, experienced belatedly by Hicks, was memorably prefigured by the dismay with the Russian Revolution revealed by, among others, Floyd Dell in the closing chapter of *Intellectual Vagabondage* (1926), by V. F. Calverton's break with the Stalinism of the Communist Party in 1931, by Max Eastman's critique of Party discipline expressed in *Artists in Uniform* (1934) and *The End of Socialism* (1937), by the attacks on the rigidities of Stalinism mounted by James T. Farrell, Bernard Smith, and the *Partisan Review* critics during the late 1930s, and by the advocacy of evolutionary, rather than revolutionary, democratic socialism promoted by Newton Arvin in *Whitman* (1938) and elsewhere. In a retrospective assessment of Marxism in the 1930s, Malcolm Cowley, once a Stalinist, described three distinct successive moods of the period: (1) anger at capitalism, (2) millennial hope for communism, and (3) discouragement about all socialism.[18] Because Hicks experienced and voiced millennial hopes longer and more intensely than most American Marxists, he emerged as a key figure, a rallying point, and a scapegoat.

Like many former party members and fellow travelers, Granville Hicks became a devout anticommunist soon after his break in 1939. "For anyone who knows Communism at first hand," he stated in *Where We Came Out,* "neutrality is, at least in the long run, impossible: if you aren't for it, you have to be against it."[19] Such sentiments, common among intellectuals in post-Depression America, explained why Hicks and other one-time radicals helped the FBI and legislative committees, especially during the early days of the Cold War with the Soviet Union, to fight communism. According to Hicks, the American Communist Party was a complete servant of Russia; its members were agents for Russia; and it sometimes engaged in espionage on behalf of Russia.

Despite the anticommunism and anti-Sovietism among numerous American intellectuals from the late 1930s onward, many felt, like Hicks, unwilling "to scrap our heritage from the liberals, reformers, progressives, and radicals of the pre-Communist era. Much can be salvaged . . ." (205). After the Red Decade, liberalism became the home for many former Party people. As others did, Hicks continued to promote economic equality, fair distribution of wealth, freedom of speech, the right to dissent, the right of unions to organize, and the protection of civil liberties. He deplored the McCarthy hearings and dogmatic anticommunism. In the 1950s he criticized both ex-communist conservatives like Whittaker Chambers, John Dos Passos, and Max Eastman and ex-communist Fake Liberals, Retarded Liberals, and Ritualistic Liberals—all of whom were dogmatic and theoretical in economics and politics, lacking pragmatism and flexibility. An exponent of a homegrown "Critical Liberalism," Hicks in the postwar era championed New Deal reformism, which he came to regard "as the best available means for the salvaging of civilization" (179). Although Hicks detested doctrinaire communism, he concluded of Marxism: "the contact of critical thought with historical materialism was in many ways fruitful."[20]

THE FRANKFURT SCHOOL IN AMERICA DURING THE THIRTIES

Many of the intellectuals associated with the German Marxist "Institute of Social Research," founded in 1923 in Frankfurt, produced scholary studies of the economic base of society in the 1920s, shifting their emphasis in the 1930s to interdisciplinary speculations on and examinations of the cultural superstructure. Directed by Max Horkheimer after 1930, the Institute fostered important Marxist aesthetic studies undertaken by, among others, Theodor Adorno, Walter Benjamin, Erich Fromm, Leo Lowenthal, and Herbert Marcuse, whose works were published in books and in the School's periodical—*Zeitschrift für Sozialforschung (Journal of Social Research)*. With the Nazi assumption of power in early 1933, the Institute was forced to relocate briefly in Geneva and the next year in New York in affiliation with Columbia University. (Branches stayed open in Geneva, London, and Paris for a few years during the thirties.)

From the outset in the early twenties most of the members of the Frankfurt School rejected both the moderate socialism of the Weimar

Republic and the doctrinaire Moscow-led communism of the German Communist Party. Like many leading American intellectuals of the thirties, they functioned as independent Marxists. (In this regard, the committed Party politics of major European Marxists like Georg Lukács and Antonio Gramsci offered a marked contrast.) What was of significance in this non-partisan leftist institution in New York was its unrelenting series of sophisticated critiques of vulgar Marxism both of the mechanical positivistic sort and of the dogmatic Stalinist sort. The Frankfurt School dedicated its energies to reexaminations of the foundations of Marxist thought; rather than systematize Marxist philosophy into dogma or a political party, the School revised and enriched Marxism for present and future uses. It pioneered, for example, the linkage of Marxism and Freudianism; it stressed the radical importance of women's liberation and of rational treatment of ecological issues. As we now know, the Neo-Marxism of the Frankfurt School—not the homegrown Marxism of Americans—provided important source material for leading members of the American left in the 1960s and thereafter. Among several others, Herbert Marcuse, a German Marxist who joined the Frankfurt School in 1933, served as a key figure in this transmission.

Why the Frankfurt School had no impact on the development of American Marxism in the 1930s is made clear in the following explanation: "Horkheimer's desire to keep the Institute self-consciously German [including the Zeitschrift] was rooted also in a serious appreciation of the need to maintain a link with Germany's humanist past, a link that might help in the future reconstruction of a post-Nazi German culture. To this end, the Institute's members remained impervious to the entreaties of their new colleagues at Columbia to integrate their work into the American social-scientific mainstream."[21] An opportunity to connect the reflective Hegelianism of the Frankfurth theorists with the often less philosophical Marxism of Americans had to wait a full generation. Indeed, much Western European Marxism of the interwar years arrived in America only with the reemergence of the left during the 1960s and later.

After 1940 the Institute of Social Research started to publish its journal and its books in English; key staff members took out naturalization papers; research topics shifted to analyses of American life and culture; methods mixed American empiricism with German philosophical theory. But this transformation of the Frankfurt School's enterprise came after the heyday of American Marxism. At the time the Institute returned to Frankfurt in 1951, its leading members were more pessimistic than ever—not merely about capitalistic culture but about the chances for positive Marxist transformations of society. Similar sentiments were felt by American radicals who survived the 1930s.

In the realm of aesthetics, the Frankfurt School insisted on the political nature of all art (including classical and bourgeois work) because it preserves human yearnings for utopian ways of life. Art not only reflects existing social realities (as all Marxists affirm) but also embodies radical impulses. The Kantian and Arnoldian notion that art is "disinterested" is erroneous: art protests domination. This dialectical view counters the vulgar Marxist notion that bourgeois art manifests (only) false consciousness. In Frankfurt School theory, the idea that the socioeconomic base determines the cultural superstructure of society is enriched: cultural works are not simply secondary, derivative phenomena reflecting class interests, they express both the contradictions and the utopian aspirations of the social totality. The presence of counterideological elements in artworks confers value on all aesthetic productions—elitist as well as proletarian ones. The masterpiece is as potentially useful as the proletarian text for revolutionary activity. This enriched poetics was not developed in America until the 1970s, when it fostered a rapprochement of aesthetic formalism with Marxism.

At about the same time that the American Communist Party's "Popular Front" was broadening its base of support and reaching out to progressive intellectuals and citizens, the Frankfurt School was working toward a wider conception of revolutionary activity. All this occurred during the time of the Stalinist purges. "Unlike more orthodox Marxists, the Frankfurt School never felt that the personal interaction of workers and intellectuals would be beneficial to either. As early as 'Traditional and Critical Theory' in 1937 [published in Zeitschrift, vol. 6], Horkheimer had denied the necessary connection between radical theory and the proletariat, arguing instead for an alliance with all 'progressive' forces willing 'to tell the truth'."[22] The scrapping of belief in the ideal union of the proletariat and the intelligentsia—an early tenet of doctrinaire American communists—had the effect of legitimating the traditional focus of scholars and critics on "high culture." (This apparent mandarinism, however, never relinquished the view that art reflects and mediates social existence.) Significantly, the insistence of Stalinist dogmatists in the 1930s on proletarian art and on Socialist Realism in literature was undermined by this conception. Had hard-line American Marxists adopted a similar notion, the harsh disagreements between literary liberals and radicals might have been softened. James T. Farrell and the

Partisan Review group might not have had to square off against V. F. Calverton and Granville Hicks. Still, to simplify, the political and aesthetic theories of Trotsky's line and those of Stalin's were fated to divide the Marxist movement: theoretical poetics and critical praxis were inextricably caught up in internal political struggle.

CULTURAL POLITICS: "NEW CRITICISM" VERSUS MARXISM

Although American "New Criticism" was nominally an apolitical, literary movement interested in the intrinsic qualities of literature, its cultural politics—usually implied yet occasionally expressed—were conservative and sometimes reactionary. A rightist point of view was most evident in the early texts of the Southern New Critics, especially John Crowe Ransom and Allen Tate. Associated with *The Fugitive* in the early 1920s and with the manifesto *I'll Take My Stand* (1930), the Southern Agrarians championed a traditional stable, religious, and rural social order in which family, kinship, and custom constituted the grounds of community. The Southern New Critics were in self-conscious reaction against both contemporary industrial commercialism and older forms of agrarian sentimentalism. Like Marxists, they propounded a strong critique of American industrial capitalism during its decline in the 1930s. At the same time the emerging New Critics deplored Marxist philosophy. Early on they considered naming *I'll Take My Stand* as "A Front Against Communism." In the Preface to his unabashedly titled *Reactionary Essays on Poetry and Ideas* (1936), Allen Tate condemned any connection between politics and poetry, stating "a political poetry, or a poetical politics, of whatever denomination is a society of two members living on each other's washing. They devour each other in the end. It is the heresy of a spiritual cannibalism."[23] Such "religious" condemnation of links between politics and poetics characterized New Criticism early and late.

Two important American harbingers of the New Critical School, Ezra Pound and T. S. Eliot, both pursued conservative cultural politics from the 1920s through the 1940s. Rightist politics, whether stated or submerged, permeated American formalist criticism.[24] In the case of Ezra Pound, the search for a new social order led to outright support of Italian Fascism. With Eliot the quest led to defense of the virtues of a Christian monarchical society. The politics of New Critical formalism, like that of Marxism, deplored the disorder and dislocation, the human alienation and loss of community, and the "commodification" of work and leisure that typified capitalist life during the interwar period. While literary Marxists tried to bring politics consciously to bear on poetry, New Critics sought to ban politics from poetics and to provide an aesthetic purity for literature and criticism.

In his *Modern Poetry and the Tradition* (1939), Cleanth Brooks castigated Marxists for committing the "didactic heresy." Marxists, according to Brooks—arguably the "purist" of the New Critics—fostered "propaganda art" designed primarily to "instruct and convert."[25] Such adulteration of art degraded authentic aesthetic values: "the truth of the doctrine enunciated in a poem cannot in itself make the poem good" (49). Additionally, the revolutionary Marxist need for literature to proclaim proletarian truths and messages risked producing "a poetry of exclusion," which omitted unfavorable aspects of experience and thus oversimplified life. "However revolutionary their economics," concluded Brooks of the Marxists, "the aesthetic theory of such critics is not revolutionary at all. It represents little advance over the Victorians with their 'message-hunting' and their Browning societies" (51). Despite the ridicule and name-calling, Brooks had a point, which the Marxist Farrell and the *Partisan Review* critics, not to mention both Calverton and Hicks themselves, had repeatedly registered. In 1932, Hicks, for example, insisted, "the correctness of a person's social theories is no guarantee of literary achievement, which depends on the power of perception rather than ideological soundness."[26] The problem of *literary* value, however, continued to haunt Marxist aestheticians.

R. P. Blackmur, in "A Critic's Job of Work" (1935), expressed strong dislike for "extrinsic" forms of literary criticism, including not only the moral philosophy of George Santayana and the sociology and psychology of Van Wyck Brooks, but particularly the "economism" of Granville Hicks. As far as the New Critic Blackmur was concerned, the beginning and end of criticism was the literary work itself—not philosophy, sociology, economics, or other nonliterary concerns. This stance represented the classical New Critical position on all *"extrinsic* criticism." Because Hicks' *The Great Tradition* examined and evaluated literature in relation to economic factors, class struggle, and Marxist ideas, Blackmur concluded that Hicks "is not writing criticism at all; he is writing a fanatic's history and a casuist's polemic. . . ."[27] Criticism should focus on literary form, not on social science and its theories and not on the separable content of works. Tate, Brooks, and Blackmur, leading New Critics of the 1930s, all concurred with "religious" fervor on these points.

Just as New Critics were scornful of Marxist politics and aesthetics, so

Marxists were hostile to the New Critics' formalist poetics and apolitical criticism. Early in the 1930s, for example, Granville Hicks observed of the Agrarians in his *The Great Tradition:*

The proclamation of Messrs. Davidson, Ransom, Tate, and the others who have taken their stand for agriculture as opposed to industry and for southern ideals as opposed to northern, may deserve whatever admiration one can accord to a quixotic gesture; but it is peculiarly futile. The young confederates ignore the economic forces that are spreading industrialism; they ignore the political forces they would have to contend with in order to bring about the kind of agrarian section they believe in. (282)

In Hicks' view, to ignore economics and politics was to engage in futile, quixotic gestures. Such forces could not be overlooked, repressed, forgotten. Quietism was no solution to the problems at hand; activism was essential. On such points New Critics and Marxists disagreed, even though they shared many insights about the evils of industrial capitalism made evident by the Great Depression.

For his part, Bernard Smith deemed the prevailing aestheticism of the New Critics unacceptable and dangerous. What bothered him, as he pointed out in *Forces in American Criticism,* was an aristocratic "strain of aloofness from the common life, of indifference to the fate of the community, of a sense of superiority to the passions and ideals of the mass of men" (359). While he admitted that Marxist critics "consistently slighted esthetic appreciation" and "failed to analyze the interaction of idea and form" (379), he judged the New Critics' emphasis on literary value to be part and parcel of a broader reactionary world view. Of Eliot, Ransom, Tate, and other New Critics, he observed, "They were esthetic critics; their inclinations were toward individualism and aristocracy; they are now religious and political reactionaries" (385). According to Smith's analysis, formalism was inherently aristocratic, conservative, and religious; moreover, nonliterary traditionalist corollaries always undergirded such perniciously "pure" literary criticism. Smith closed off *Forces in American Criticism* by pitting Marxism against New Criticism:

The literary criticism of this school [New Criticism] tends to create a literature that will express the sensibilities and experiences of a few fortunate men. The criticism of the opposing school tends to create a literature that will express the ideals and sympathies of those who look forward to the conquest of poverty, ignorance and inequality—to the material and intellectual elevation of the mass of mankind. To whom does the future belong?

CHAPTER TWO

The "New Criticism"

THE EMERGENCE AND GROWTH OF THE NEW CRITICAL SCHOOL

MOST OBSERVERS of the American literary scene agree that the major development in the history of criticism following the onset of the Great Depression was the overwhelming success of the "New Critics" in pioneering and institutionalizing formalist concepts and methods. The first stage of this development occurred during the 1920s when T. S. Eliot, I. A. Richards, and William Empson in England and the Fugitives and Agrarians (especially John Crowe Ransom and Allen Tate) in America began to express ideas and work out practices that would form the fundamentals of the New Critical School a decade later. Throughout the 1930s and 1940s—the second stage of development—the number of critics sympathetic to this emerging formalism increased, and the New Critics spread their beliefs effectively into literary quarterlies, university literature departments, and college textbooks and curricula. The major critics associated with New Criticism by the late 1940s were Eliot, Richards, Empson, Ransom, Tate, R. P. Blackmur, Cleanth Brooks, René Wellek, W. K. Wimsatt and, to some extent, Kenneth Burke, F. R. Leavis, and Yvor Winters. Numerous others could be named but these constituted the leading early New Critics. Journals sympathetic to New Criticism included, among others, Eliot's *The Criterion* (1922–39) and Leavis' *Scrutiny* (1932–53) in England, and in America the *Southern Review,* edited by Brooks and Robert Penn Warren from 1935 to 1942, the *Kenyon Review,* headed by Ransom from 1938 to 1959, and the *Sewanee Review,* run by Tate from 1944 to 1945 and thereafter by other sympathizers into the 1980s. Another stage of development, the third, happened over the decade from the late 1940s to the late 1950s when, as the movement lost a "revolutionary" aura and

occupied the mainstream, its followers produced intricate canonical statements of its theories. We can cite in this regard particularly René Wellek's
and Austin Warren's *Theory of Literature* (1949), W. K. Wimsatt's *The
Verbal Icon* (1954), Murray Krieger's *The New Apologists for Poetry* (1956),
and Brooks' and Wimsatt's *Literary Criticism: A Short History* (1957).

Just when some of the leading New Critics were turning away from strict
formalist practices to broader cultural concerns, their doctrines began to
spread to second- and third-generation followers who sometimes insured
the purity of New Criticism at considerable cost, reducing the movement to
a carefully refined dogmatic method. Among those first to move beyond
New Criticism was T. S. Eliot, who throughout the thirties and forties
wrote much social criticism. The interests of Richards after the late thirties
and Blackmur after the late forties went beyond "normal" New Criticism.
Others were associated with the School only for a short time as, for example,
Leavis, who early preferred cultural analysis; Yvor Winters, who practiced
moral criticism; and Kenneth Burke, who pioneered interdisciplinary theoretical systems. While these critics maintained certain New Critical habits of
mind and procedures of investigation, they supplemented formalism in a
rich variety of ways. The result of such departures is that the list of first-
generation, life-long American "true believers" is small: Ransom, Tate, and
Brooks. In this reduced version of the School, Wimsatt, Krieger, and
Wellek, while fervent longtime New Critics, appear latecomers who arrived
on the scene after the opening stages of development in the twenties and
thirties.

Of Ransom, Tate, and Brooks, the most influential populizer was arguably Brooks. Unlike Ranson and Tate, who considered themselves poets first
and critics second, Brooks, an academic critic, early initiated the refinement,
systematization, and dissemination of New Criticism throughout America's
colleges and universities. Neither an innovator like Eliot, nor a profound
interpreter like Blackmur, nor a fierce polemicist like Tate, Brooks proved to
be a rigorous and insightful analyst as well as an effective and enduring
representative of the School. Well into the 1980s he was frequently invited
to American university campuses to present his New Critical views.

That the New Criticism was over by the late 1950s as an innovative and
original School was clear to both adherents and opponents. Nevertheless,
after that time, the New Criticism served for growing numbers of academic
critics and scholars as "normal criticism" or simply as "criticism." This
transformation of a particular school into a cultural status quo distinguished
New Criticism from all other competing schools, marking a special—a

fourth—stage of development. Often critics practicing New Criticism during this phase were unaware that they were doing so: the ideas and methods of the School had become so deeply embedded and broadly generalized among critics as to form the very essence of "criticism." To delineate the fourth stage of development, we can cite the lucid observations of William Cain, a critical historian writing in the eighties:

> The New Criticism appears powerless, lacking in supporters, declining, dead or on the verge of being so. No one speaks on behalf of the New Criticism as such today. . . . But the truth is that the New Criticism survives and is prospering, and it seems to be powerless only because its power is so pervasive that we are ordinarily not even aware of it. So deeply ingrained in English studies are New Critical attitudes, values, and emphases that we do not even perceive them as the legacy of a particular movement. On the contrary: we feel them to be the natural and definitive conditions for criticism in general.[1]

The "death" of New Criticism in the 1950s signaled a kind of normalized "immortality"—a strange feat which no other critical school in this era was able to accomplish. What were the fundamental ideas, values, and beliefs that fostered so long a life?

THE FUNDAMENTALS OF A FORMALIST POETICS

In the *Princeton Encyclopedia of Poetry and Poetics* (enlarged ed., 1974), Cleanth Brooks offers a 1200-word condensation of New Criticism. Here he singles out a handful of distinguishing characteristics of this formalist School. First, New Criticism separates *literary* criticism from the study of sources, social backgrounds, history of ideas, politics, and social effects, seeking both to purify poetic criticism from such "extrinsic" concerns and to focus attention squarely on the "literary object" itself. Second, New Criticism explores the structure of a work, not the minds of authors or the reactions of readers. Third, New Criticism champions an "organic" theory of literature rather than a dualistic conception of form and matter; it focuses on the words of the text in relation to the full context of the work: each word contributes to a unique context and derives its precise meaning from its place in the poetic context. Fourth, New Criticism practices close reading of individual works, attending scrupulously to nuances of words, rhetorical figures, and shades of meaning as it attempts to specify the contextual unity and meaning of the work in hand. Fifth, New Criticism distinguishes literature from both religion and morality mainly because many of its adherents have definite religious views and seek no substitutes for religion, morality, or literature.[2] Though Brooks' summary list of traits needs refinement and supplementation, it can serve as a rough charter of New Critical formalist ideas and methods. For some members of the School, this cluster of concepts constituted an organized critical system, while for others it amounted to a temporary set of attitudes about literature and criticism.

To understand what New Critics stood for, it is useful to summon from the past what they stood against. In a retrospective assessment published in the late 1970s, Wellek recalled that New Critics reacted strongly against certain trends prevalent in American criticism and society during the early twentieth century. Specifically, they disliked the evocative mode of Impressionist criticism, the moralism of Neo-Humanism, the antimodernist cultural criticism of Mencken and Van Wyck Brooks, and the sociologizing of Marxist criticism. In addition, they protested against academic criticism, specifically philology, textual bibliography, historical scholarship, and literary history, which dominated university instruction, publication, and promotion. What they most uniformly deplored about academic criticism was its view of the literary canon: for example, no room was allotted for modern literature, and too little space was assigned the metaphysical poets. Finally, most American New Critics detested science, particularly Ransom and Tate, for whom science, according to Wellek, "is the villian of history which had destroyed the community of man, broken up the old organic way of life, paved the way to industrialism, and made man the alienated, rootless, godless creature he has become in this century. Science encourages Utopian thinking, the false idea of the perfectibility of man, the whole illusion of endless progress."[3] Taken together with their shared beliefs, the many dislikes of the New Critics served to unify this disparate group of literary men.

The leading first-generation New Critics practiced judicial criticism as part of their overall formalist program. Because they worked at revising the canon of great works, they were given regularly to judging the worth of literary texts. Standards of poetic value quickly emerged, as we shall see. The judicial practice fundamental to early New Criticism was not limited to literature; it glided into and emerged out of religious and social criticism. The first example of this comes from T. S. Eliot, who, as early as *The Sacred Wood* (1920), offered an influential account and critique of Western culture's decadent development. Once there was an ordered world, which disintegrated at the hands of skepticism and science, leading to a "dissociation of sensibility" and the alienation of man from himself and his world; the ongoing decay of Western societies through secularism and industrialism, however, could be resisted and wholeness sought; "unified sensibility," a complex (re)joining of intellect and feeling, was possible through rejection of modern fallen civilization and return to myth, religion, and homogeneous (Christian, rather than agrarian) culture. Like the Southern Agrarian's view of modern degenerate society, Eliot's account of social disintegration led to a set of combined moral-literary values: unified sensibility, complexity of thought, wholeness of being, and religious and mythical order were positive goods. Such values could be found, for instance, preeminently in the poets Dante and Donne—two of Eliot's and Tate's most esteemed masters. What we find is that New Critical formalist criticism was invariably linked with a conservative social, moral, religious, and political assessment of the past, present, and possible future. This axiology undergirded the judicial and specifically literary criticism practiced by the inner circle of early New Critics. In addition, it conditioned their conceptualization of poetry itself. Though they endeavored to purify criticism, the practice and theory of these American formalists was typically tied to a traditional conservative—a Tory—ideology and value system. Eliot was explicit when, near the end of his career, he declared that "it is impossible to fence off *literary* criticism from criticism on other grounds, and that moral, religious and social judgments cannot be wholly excluded."[4]

FORMALIST PROTOCOLS AND "CLOSE READING"

The New Criticism was distinguished from other schools of literary criticism by its rigorous "close reading" of relatively short texts, most often poems. That a strong and relentless form of *explication de texte* characterized the best practical New Criticism from the mid-30s onward is undeniable. Significantly, the presuppositions surrounding such reading determined a distinctive mode of formalist hermeneutics. Thus, it is not enough to say that New Critics practiced "close reading"; rather, it is essential to delineate the panoply of protocols which directed and delimited the formalists' interpretative activity.

"Genetic" and "receptionist" critical approaches were deemed anathema. Whatever went into the genesis of a text was considered merely preparatory and largely irrelevant (however interesting) for interpretive work. Consequently, source and background studies, whether historical, psychological, or sociological, played the smallest possible role in interpretation. In this way, poetry was distanced and depersonalized—objectified. Similarly, the personal response of the individual reader assumed little importance in the conscious criticism of poetic texts. It did not matter whether the response was that of a reader of the present day or that of a reconstructed historical reader of a previous era. The reader's reception of a text was ruled out beforehand as distracting to properly critical analysis. These constituted two main elements of the system of protocols delimiting and determining the carefully controlled activity of formalist interpretation as practiced by New Critics.

The formalist arguments against genetic and receptionist criticism were forcefully codified by W. K. Wimsatt, along with Monroe C. Beardsley, in the celebrated essays "The Intentional Fallacy" (1946) and "The Affective Fallacy" (1949)—both published first in *Sewanee Review* and later in *The Verbal Icon*. As is often the case in theoretical presentation, the argument for or against one concept requires the supporting presence of other concepts. The infrastructure of ideas constituting the New Criticism's formalist doctrine, later capsulized in Brooks' encyclopedia piece, found its way into these two canonical essays of the School. The whole formulation of formalist reading was conditioned by a network of dependent axioms. For instance, we can glimpse a certain cluster of essential concepts in this passage from "The Intentional Fallacy":

> Judging a poem is like judging a pudding or a machine. One demands that it works. It is only because an artifact works that we infer an intention of an artificer. "A poem should not mean but be." A poem can *be* only through its *meaning*—since its medium is words—yet it *is*, simply *is*—in the sense that we have no excuse for inquiring what part is intended or meant. Poetry is a feat of style by which a complex of meaning is handled all at once. Poetry succeeds because all or most of what is said or implied is relevant; what is irrelevant has been excluded, like lumps from pudding and "bugs" from machinery. In this respect poetry differs from practical messages, which are successful if and only if we correctly infer the intention.[5]

The odd images of the ideal poem as a pudding, a machine, and an artifact sought to objectify and spatialize literature—to establish an invariable ontological status in which literature was separated from its producers and consumers. It stood alone—timeless. Simply stated, literature exists; it *is*. What its artificers intended was "neither available nor desirable as a standard for judging the success of a work" (3). The job of the critic was to judge the text, as one judges an object or machine, to determine whether or not it worked efficiently. All parts had to work together; no part could be irrelevant. The poem—a verbal icon—was a spatial complex of meaning where all words and implications became relevant. The medium of poetry differed from practical language both ontologically and stylistically. The "all-at-onceness" of "meaning," its spatial configuration, meant interpretation came about following multiple retrospective analyses, which conferred a certain feeling of objectivity and omniscience upon New Critical close readings.

When a New Critic came to examine and to evaluate a text, he assumed at the outset that it was a spatial complex of intricately interrelated words. The poem as a well-wrought urn or efficient machine had from the start been constructed as an impersonal and ahistorical artifact. Although its poetic language was separated from ordinary discourse, it did proffer meaning—of a highly complex and special sort. Nevertheless, that the poem existed (as an autonomous object) was more important than the fact that it signified something: being preceded meaning. The New Critics valued the independence of the text over the meaning of it—without, however, giving up the idea of meaning. "In a manner of speaking," declared Allen Tate, "the poem is its own knower, neither poet nor reader knowing anything that the poem says apart from the words of the poem."[6] The effect of this pattern of concepts was to focus critical description and judgment fully and continuously on the text, excluding all else as much as possible. What was highly esteemed were complex, free-standing poems filled with intricate semantic interrelations. Given these values, it is not surprising that the works of John Donne and other metaphysical poets and those of T. S. Eliot and other high modernists were widely celebrated while those of Walt Whitman and other "loose" Romantics were condemned when not ignored. Ultimately, the New Critics' special way of reading engendered a widescale scholarly reevaluation of the entire canon of great poetic works. Put simply, reading for the New Critics involved technical rhetorical explication and literary evaluation based on a distinctive set of preexisting protocols—with poetic complexity assuming a primary place in the hierarchy of both literary and exegetical values.

The notion of *meaning* in New Critical theory and practice deserves further scrutiny because the slippery concept is lodged at an intense intersection of numerous fundamental ideas of this formalist School. It plays a key role in shaping the protocols of reading.

In "The Heresy of Paraphrase," the last chapter of his *The Well Wrought Urn* (1947), Cleanth Brooks, having examined ten superior works from *Macbeth* to the present, concluded "the common goodness which the poems share will have to be stated, not in terms of 'content' or 'subject matter' in the usual sense in which we use these terms, but rather in terms of structure."[7] The value of a poem for a New Critic depended not on its content but on its *structure*. To extract content from a poem, to summarize or paraphrase a text was heretical because it reduced "meaning" to proposition or statement, putting literature in competition with philosophy, science, and politics while divorcing form from content. Conceived as paraphrase, "meaning" was debased: "paraphrase is not the real core of meaning which constitutes the essence of the poem" (180). What was "meaning" then? An aspect of structure. "The structure meant is a structure of [textual] meanings, evaluations, and interpretations; and the principle of unity which informs it seems to be one of balancing and harmonizing connotations, attitudes, and meanings" (178). The task of reading was to examine and evaluate *structure*, which consisted of a *unified* complex of textual elements—linguistic, rhetorical, semantic, philosophical, and psychological. Structure—unified structure—became a master critical concept. Meaning for New Critics was both a subordinate category and an inseparable element of structure. As a hermeneuticist, Brooks proposed that critics understand—explicate—unified literary structure free not only from genetic and receptionist concerns, but from reductions to paraphrasable elements and extractable propositions. At most, statements of meaning served as scaffolds.

Typically, the formalist readings of New Criticism reached completion when structural unity, balance, or harmony had been demonstrated. Numerous forces of tension, conflict, and divergence were processed to attain this moment of structuration. "The attempt to deal with a structure such as this," according to Brooks, "may account for the frequent occurrences in the preceding chapters of such terms as 'ambiguity,' 'paradox,' 'complex of attitudes,' and—most frequent of all, and perhaps most annoying to the readers—'irony' " (179). Indeed, these key operators of New Critical exegesis functioned as mediators of disruptive tensions and conflicts, leading to "discovery" (or creation) of unified structure. "Irony," in particular, Brooks' own favorite hermeneutical instrument, worked to subdue into a unity the incongruities that pervaded texts. What New Critics ended with, then, was a theory and practice of reading which presupposed that unified structure of numerous tensions and divergences constituted the goal of analysis as well as the true nature of literature. The more harmonized the incongruities, the better the text and its exegesis.

Texts of all kinds were conceived as dramas filled with intricate conflicts: "the structure of a poem," proclaimed Brooks, "resembles that of a play," which "builds conflict into its very being" (186–87). According to the poetics of New Criticism, "The conclusion of the poem is the working out of the various tensions—set up by whatever means—by propositions, metaphors, symbols. This unity is achieved by a dramatic process, not a logical; it represents an equilibrium of forces . . ." (189). What a formalist reading in the New Critical manner invariably demonstrated—and set out to demonstrate—was a unified dramatic structure of numerous rhetorical, semantic, psychological, and symbolic forces in equilibrium. The model of drama, applied to all genres, enabled exegesis to center on tensions and forces in final balance. It also allowed critics to talk about "personae" and unnamed "speakers" rather than actual authors of works, facilitating both the stricture against genetic criticism and the belief in literary autonomy.

The hermeneutic of the New Criticism was ultimately conditioned by a certain contradiction or "dialectic" in its poetics. A cluster of concepts linked with Kantian "art for art's sake" theory contended with a pattern of ideas associated with older, classical philosophy. On the one hand, poetry was separated from morality, religion, science, psychology, sociology, and history while being unified internally by complex aesthetic and dramatic equilibriums and harmonies; on the other hand, poetry was "a simulacrum of reality," an "imitation," based on "experience" (*WWU*, 194), which offered "knowledge of a whole object" and "the full body of the experience" (*EFD*, 105). This peculiar mixture of textual, mimetic, and cognitive theories of literature allowed interpretations to be oriented in one or more directions. A New Critical reading of a text could stress aesthetic complexity and wholeness, or richness of life and reality, or realizations of experience and conflict, or—more likely—some combination of these values. The interpretative emphasis could be mainly aesthetic or moral, psychological or philosophical, linguistic or religious, rhetorical or judicial.

(The long-standing conventional and misleading image of New Critical "close reading" as the purely aesthetic and rhetorical interpretation of texts was the product of several forces: the tendency of the growing movement to narrow and codify its prevalent characteristics, the habit of its opponents in reducing its diverse practices, the success of its simplified textbooks and manifestos, and the dilution of its early diversity by latter-day imitators.)

What the New Critics owed to Kant and Coleridge was an aesthetic rooted in a theory of the imagination that privileged, above all, poetic unity, inclusiveness, and harmony. In addition, the New Critics followed both philosophical forebears in deploring utilitarian and sectarian theories of literature and criticism, which set interest and will above the disinterest and purposelessness characteristic of authentic beauty. Properly speaking, the true object of attention for aesthetic critics was the purposive and magical "internal form" typical of singular poetic works.

One recurrent concept in the development of New Critical poetics and hermeneutics was a "theological" notion of *metaphor*, which served as an essential protocol of close reading. In *Literary Criticism: A Short History*, Wimsatt and Brooks propounded this view succinctly:

> We can have our universals in the full conceptualized discourse of science and philosophy. We can have specific detail lavishly in the newspapers and in records of trials. . . . But it is only in metaphor, and hence it is *par excellence* in poetry, that we encounter the most radically and relevantly fused union of the detail and the universal idea.[8]

The linkage of the concrete and historical with the abstract and universal, of the newspaper and court record with philosophy and science—this union purportedly happened through metaphor, which is poetry. In other words, the mimetic and cognitive dimensions of literature were fused in a more fundamental textual, figurative domain. What made poetry different from both ordinary discourse and scientific discourse was metaphor. Poetry is metaphor. Metaphor is poetry. When he analyzed the ontology of poetry in 1934, Ransom concluded that "there is a miraculism or supernaturalism in a metaphorical assertion."[9] This theory of metaphor—developed by Ransom, Brooks, Wimsatt, and Krieger—underpinned an incarnational, Symbolist poetics indebted to Coleridge. By virtue of metaphor, poetry was the queen of human discourse. Whereas the classical purpose of metaphor was to decorate and illustrate, the New Critical function of metaphor was "to discover truth." It was a "means to insight." In poetry, metaphor was "structural" rather than simply "ornamental."[10] Characteristically, New Critics described *metaphor* in religious or sacred terms. The tendency of this spiritualizing of metaphor was to refocus exegesis on metaphor before and above all. Attention to metrics and genre, for example, was usually minimal, if not missing altogether. Given the central role and "theological" value assigned to all metaphorical language, we should not be surprised at a certain congruence between fundamentalist Protestant exegesis and New Critical "close reading."[11] Unlike the "higher criticism" of modern biblical scholarship with its attention to historical matters and textual flaws, the fundamentalist hermeneutic conferred divine status on the work and then proceeded worshipfully to unravel the text. New Critical formalism built on this tradition.

In its method of reading, the New Criticism required of a reader that he focus on the poem rather than on his responses and that he avoid extrinsic concerns and use objective, technical criteria. This assumed an ideal reader. As Brooks put it in "The Formalist Critics," published in *Kenyon Review* in 1951, "the formalist critic assumes an ideal reader: that is, instead of focusing on the varying spectrum of possible readings, he attempts to find a central point of reference from which he can focus upon the structure of the poem or novel."[12] Once again, the reader's goal was *structure*—in the special New Critical sense of the word. To get at structure, the ideal formalist reader had to inhabit a "central point of reference." But nowhere was the reader informed how to occupy this hermeneutic space. No matter, Brooks confessed a sentence later: "There is no ideal reader, of course, and I suppose the practicing critic can never be too often reminded of the gap between his reading and the 'true' reading of the poem" (75). In this extreme formulation, the New Critical reader was imagined to be seeking the one, true textual reading—which he knew to be a fiction. What he had to avoid, above all, was a "varying spectrum of possible readings." The specter of a relativistic hermeneutics haunted New Criticism.

Like the concept of an "ideal reader," the fundamental belief in "unity" was an enabling fiction. Tate reminded us: "we must heed Mr. Ransom's warning that perfect unity or integration in a work of art is a critical delusion" (*EFD,* 273). It was unusual for a New Critic to undermine in this way trust in his critical protocols. He preferred absolutism to relativism. Still, we can locate other such subversive moments. At one point, for example, Tate declared about his deepseated notion of unified or "organic society" (the old Agrarian ideal): the "point at issue is not whether unity of being in an organic society ever existed, or whether it could exist; we must affirm its necessity, if only to explain the disunity of being which is the primary fact of the human condition" (*EFD,* 378). The strategy here—modeled after Wallace Stevens' celebrated "necessary fictions"—occurred occasionally in the texts of other New Critics, most notably in Murray Krieger's later works, as we shall see. The effect is to moderate our understanding of the New Critics' dedication to extreme ideals—in this case the literary and cultural ideal of "unity."

The same tempering occurs when we catch Tate, in a discussion of Robert Frost's "The Witch of Coös," admitting: "Like every first-rate work of art—poem, picture, sculpture, film—it invites endlessly varied interpretations, and all of them may be 'right.' "[13] Out of the mass of materials written by the New Critics, an historian can create a narrow unified ideology or, attending to differences and subversive moments, he can construct a more disparate, heterogeneous School. The effect of Tate's statement is to broaden the understanding of this formalist hermeneutics, conferring on its distinctive protocols and practices of close reading a certain compulsive, exaggerated, and fictional quality.

We can effectively summarize the panoply of formalist protocols that conditioned and directed New Critical "close reading," keeping in mind the usual provisos which accompany such reductive idealizations. In performing a close reading, a New Critic would generally:

(1) Select a short text, often a metaphysical or modern poem;
(2) rule out "genetic" critical approaches;
(3) avoid "receptionist" inquiry;
(4) assume the text to be an autonomous, ahistorical, spatial object;
(5) presuppose the text to be *both* intricate and complex *and* efficient and unified;
(6) carry out multiple retrospective readings;
(7) conceive each text as a drama of conflicting forces;
(8) focus continually on the text and its manifold semantic and rhetorical interrelations;
(9) insist on the fundamentally metaphorical and therefore miraculous powers of literary language;
(10) eschew paraphrase and summary or make clear that such statements are not equivalent to poetic meaning;
(11) seek an overall balanced or unified comprehensive structure of harmonized textual elements;
(12) subordinate incongruities and conflicts;
(13) see paradox, ambiguity, and irony as subduing divergences and insuring unifying structure;
(14) treat (intrinsic) meaning as just one element of structure;
(15) note in passing cognitive, experiential dimensions of the text; and
(16) try to be the ideal reader and create the one, true reading, which subsumes multiple readings.

This system of protocols distinguished New Critical formalist "close reading" from the exegetical practices of other schools. American Marxist critics of the 1930s, for example, could have subscribed to few, if any, of these New Critical stipulations and procedures. Significantly, these protocols not only guided the activity of analysis but embodied criteria for critical judgment. For New Critics, "reading" required evaluation as well as explication. Some poems were unquestionably better than others.

PEDAGOGICAL MISSIONS

The New Criticism passed on its basic concepts and methods, notably its practice of "close reading," to thousands upon thousands of students and scholars. Behind this institutionalization of such formalist ideas and procedures lies a certain history, involving chiefly the early Fugitives, the Cambridge critics I. A. Richards and William Empson, and later Cleanth Brooks, René Wellek, and various collaborators. The details of the pedagogical missions of New Criticism merit serious consideration.

The Fugitives met weekly at Vanderbilt University from 1919 to 1925 to examine and to assess one another's poetry. This informal university study group, which evolved rigorous technical standards, sought to instruct itself about proper craftsmanship and reading methods. The practices of the group would later condition the mode of analysis characteristic of New Criticism. When Laura Riding, who had published in *The Fugitive* and who knew about Fugitive critical practice, moved to England in 1926 and collaborated with Robert Graves on *A Survey of Modernist Poetry* (1927), she may have introduced to England the method of analysis propounded by early American New Criticism. In writing his *Seven Types of Ambiguity* (1930)—a key text in establishing essential formalist procedures—William Empson admitted to relying heavily on Graves' and Ridings' intricate manner of exegesis.[14] After 1930 many New Critics pointed to Empson's text as a model.

When Empson published *Seven Types of Ambiguity*, he was a 24-year-old student of I. A. Richards at Cambridge. The influence of Richards on New Criticism in general (and on Empson in particular) was considerable and needs delineation here. Richards' long and productive career divided roughly into two parts. From the late teens to the late thirties he worked mainly in Cambridge on aesthetics, semantics, and literary theory and criticism; from the late thirties till the middle seventies he was associated with Harvard University, where he focused on education, basic English, and world literacy projects. It was the early work of Richards that influenced New Criticism. To be precise, certain strands of Richards' early thinking impacted significantly on American New Critical formalism. While his empirical and rationalist commitments and his devotion to science and psychology were overlooked, criticized, or deplored by New Critics, his theories of poetic language and of criticism were taken seriously, as were his studies of classroom pedagogy and teaching difficulties.

The most important of I. A. Richards' many books for American New

Critics were arguably *Principles of Literary Criticism* (1924) and *Practical Criticism* (1929). From the first book came such now familiar terms as "tension" and "balance," "emotive" and "referential" language, and "irony" and "pseudo-statement." What characterized aesthetic experience for Richards was an intricate balance or equilibrium of opposites in extreme tension: "This balanced poise, stable through its power of inclusion, not through the force of its exclusions, is . . . a general characteristic of all the most valuable experiences of the arts."[15] The highest poetry, moreover, depended on irony, which "consists in bringing in of the opposite, the complementary impulses" (250). A decade later Cleanth Brooks and others would make much use of such concepts in developing theories of poetry and protocols for reading. However, the psychological grounds of Richards' ideas were replaced by linguistic and rhetorical foundations. When Richards, near the end of *Principles of Literary Criticism,* came to discuss language, he distinguished between the referential or naming function of language used in science and the emotive function of language typical of poetry. While poetry often referred to verifiable things in the world, it had other purposes. Thus the sole test of correspondence between words and things was inappropriate to poetic language. In place of the criterion of correspondence, one could employ that of effect or that of coherence—which involved the ordering of attitudes and the "balanced poise" native to aesthetic experience. The language of literature consisted of pseudo-statements. With care Richards differentiated the language of poetry from that of science and philosophy—a project that predated and paralleled similar goals pursued by the New Critics.

Five years later Richards' *Practical Criticism* analyzed the written responses of several hundred Cambridge University students to a selection of short poems. Scrutinizing their work closely, Richards compiled a list of ten difficulties in reading poetry. The ten main problems of understanding were (1) trouble in making out plain sense, (2) misapprehension of meter and rhythm, (3) misinterpretation of figurative language, (4) application of irrelevant personal associations, (5) reliance on stock responses, (6) sentimental overreaction, (7) inhibited response or hardness of heart, (8) restricting religious doctrines, (9) disabling technical presuppositions, and (10) narrow critical preconceptions. "I believe," declared Richards, "that most of the principal obstacles and causes of failure in the reading and judgment of poetry may without much straining be brought under these ten heads."[16] Thus *Practical Criticism* pioneered pedagogical techniques, both in theory and in practice, for poetic interpretation and evaluation. In this work Richards accorded a central role to figurative language—a reading protocol that his student Empson and later the New Critics would further to great effect. Significantly, the overall goal of *Practical Criticism* was to analyze and ultimately improve the *teaching* of literary studies. It provided a highly articulated model to use in university classrooms. When Cleanth Brooks and Robert Penn Warren put together their influential textbook *Understanding Poetry* (1938), they built on the earlier work of Richards. Two final strands in Richards' work are worth noting. Implicitly, he criticized modern society as degenerate, documenting its shortcomings and defending high standards. In addition, he rarely displayed any historicist proclivities or antiquarian habits of mind. Both of these characteristics enabled further compatibility with New Criticism.

If the detailed examinations of texts offered by Richards suggested a rigorous mode as well as rich possibilities for classroom explication, the verbal analyses of Empson once and for all demonstrated sustained high standards of close reading. Empson's interpretations were positively "niggling," as he himself admitted. They easily rivaled in intricacy and intelligence competing contemporary historical scholarship and textual bibliography. Ironically, it was not his typology of ambiguity that took hold, but rather his rhetorical method of close reading. In adition, his scorn for simple "appreciative criticism" and his celebration of relentless "analytical criticism"—offered in the closing pages of *Seven Types of Ambiguity*—paralleled the emerging views of all those associated with American formalist criticism. Here indeed was a student who could read.

The values, prejudices, and methods of American New Criticism were broadly disseminated by Brooks' and Warren's *Understanding Poetry* (1938), their *Understanding Fiction* (1943), and Brooks' and Robert Heilman's *Understanding Drama* (1946). In René Wellek's retrospective judgment, *Understanding Poetry* alone did "more than any other single book to make the techniques of the New Criticism available in the classrooms of American colleges and universities and to present the techniques of analysis as something to be learned and imitated."[17] A. Walton Litz agrees with Wellek, adding, "For all its pedagogical virtues, *Understanding Poetry* accelerated the movement toward rigidity and dogmatism that would be one source of the New Criticism's undoing."[18] This pioneering anthology—complete with exemplary commentaries and discussions of key concepts—preferred metaphysical and modern poetry to Romantic and Victorian verse; it excluded biographical, historical, and social criticism in favor of formalist analysis of unified structure; and it unintentionally implied that uninformed yet sincere exegesis was worthy literary criticism.

Part of the pedagogical imperative that *Understanding Poetry* came to fulfill was first outlined by John Crowe Ransom in "Criticism, Inc." (1937):

[I]t is from the professors of literature, in this country the professors of English for the most part, that I should hope eventually for the erection of intelligent standards of criticism. It is their business.

Criticism must become more scientific, or precise and systematic, and this means that it must be developed by the collective and sustained effort of learned persons—which means that its proper seat is in the universities.

Ransom went on to propose:

Rather than occasional criticism by amateurs, I should think the whole enterprise might be seriously taken in hand by professionals. Perhaps I use a distasteful figure, but I have the idea that what we need is Criticism, Inc., or Criticism, Ltd. (*WB*, 328–29)

The net effect of Ransom's proposal, if effected, would be to locate literary criticism in universities, to make a profession of criticism, to bring about its systematization through collaborative effort, and to shift critical activity away from book reviewers and periodical essayists to professional academics. That something very like this happened is quite clear: in our era the gentleman-critic and poet-critic have been replaced by the professional university critic. Eliot excepted, all of the New Critics pursued lengthy careers teaching in colleges and universities. Many of their works were published by university-funded quarterlies and presses. As a collaborative anthology and a formalist primer, *Understanding Poetry* not only systematized New Critical principles by synthesizing the works of Richards, Empson, the Fugitives, and others, but also furthered the establishment of Criticism, Inc. by hastening the emerging institutionalization of the New Critics' formalist criticism. Ransom's proposal marked a turning point in the development of American New Criticism—the turn toward the universities and pedagogy. *Understanding Poetry* fulfilled this pedagogical imperative.

When the second edition of *Understanding Poetry* was published in 1950, the situation of the New Critics was considerably enhanced. Brooks, Wellek, and Wimsatt were professors at Yale, Blackmur was at Princeton, Burke was at Bennington, Eliot had just received the Nobel Prize, Krieger and Ransom were at Kenyon, where Ransom headed the influential Kenyon School of English (supported by the Rockefeller Foundation), Richards was at Harvard, Tate was at Minnesota, and Winters had just become a full professor at Stanford. Located at prestigious schools, the New Critics were in positions of authority that allowed them to spread their ideas through their publications and their day-to-day pedagogy. At about this time the full range of theoretical principles of the New Criticism were codified in what proved to be an influential textbook, René Wellek's and Austin Warrens' *Theory of Literature* (1949), which was aimed at graduate students and professors, unlike *Understanding Poetry*, designed for undergraduates. The establishment of "Criticism, Inc." was a reality by the late 1940s—built upon the pedagogical missions of the Fugitives, the Cambridge Critics, the Yale Critics, and others sympathetic to such formalist work.

INSIDE AND OUTSIDE NEW CRITICISM: AN EXEMPLARY CASE

During the later stages of its development, the New Criticism tended to become rigid and dogmatic, partly as a result of its intensive systematizations and codifications and partly as a consequence of its extensive and successful pedagogical missions. The progressive "purification" of the theory and practice occurred at the same time that leading "New Critics" were branching out in many other directions. By the late 1940s Eliot, Richards, Leavis, Blackmur, Winters, and Burke had all expanded their projects to include historical, sociological, and ethical matters, though they all retained certain formalist beliefs and practices. Of the group of major critics, no one broadened his enterprise more dramatically and self-consciously than Kenneth Burke. In doing so, he revealed some of the limitations of New Criticism—which makes his enterprise an exemplary case for inquiry.

Like most Anglo-American New Critics, Kenneth Burke throughout his career remained a strong critic of capitalist industrial society, preferring the mode of existence to be found in a cooperative agrarian community. He distrusted modern science and felt that its peculiar striving for perfection would lead to devastating technological wars. Evidently not a *practicing* Christian, he held Christian theology, nevertheless, to be the most complete "world vision" and ethical paradigm. In the manner of the New Critics, Burke continuously stressed the value of close reading, and he regularly undertook "scholastic" explications. He carefully distinguished literature from morality and religion and separated formalist criticism from sociological and cultural analysis. He not only shared but vastly expanded the New Critical beliefs that literature is knowledge, that metaphorical language is inherently "religious," and that drama is *the* model of poetry.

The differences between Burke's enterprise and that of purified American New Criticism were many and striking. It was these differences which increasingly pointed up important limitations and shortcomings of New Criticism. Burke's hermeneutic project fell *roughly* into three phases. In the twenties and thirties he explored literature as symbolic action; in the forties and fifties he analyzed literature as dramatic action; in the sixties and seventies he investigated literature as "logological" action. Significantly, the later undertakings not only expanded but included the earlier ones so that the project of logology encompassed the previous efforts of dramatism and symbolic action. What distinguished Burke's endeavors, early and late, was an overriding interest in human relations broadly understood. Because for Burke the finest source of information about and the best model for human relations were linguistic and literary forms, he could always be regarded as just one more literary critic devoted to rigorous formalist analysis. Yet as time passed Burke's broader concerns became more and more obvious to others; progressively, his interests widened to include biography, psychology, sociology, philosophy, politics, aesthetics, ethics, religion, and anthropology. Out of these materials he gradually fashioned a complex machine for textual analysis. Not surprisingly, dedicated New Critics deplored his importation of extrinsic concerns into literary study, accusing him of foregoing *literary* criticism. Meanwhile, Burke produced intricate and ingenious readings of poetic works as if to taunt his accusers. By the mid-1940s Burke had articulated a highly complex model of interpretation, which required for understanding the kind of attention one gives to systematic philosophy. As a result, he was charged with practicing obfuscation, with employing eccentric terms, and with seeking to convert rather than inform his readers. This most inclusive of critics seemed to be willfully inverting New Critical taboos into truths, turning forbidden procedures into positive practices.

At the heart of Burke's project was a formalist exegetical method supplemented by various other hermeneutical approaches. Since literary analysis did not exhaust the study of human relations and symbolic actions, Burke came to link Poetics with Grammar, with Rhetoric, and with Ethics. In Burke's system, Grammar focused on content—on literature as information and knowledge. Rhetoric attended to response—to literature as power. Poetics centered on beautiful objects—on literature as aesthetic form. And Ethics dealt with moral values—with literature as personal and social portraiture. In this mature scheme, poetics treated only one of the dimensions of symbolic action. To the formalist explication fundamental to poetics, Burke added psychological analysis of the poet's preoccupations and the audience's reception, sociological inquiry into embedded cultural mores and hierarchies, and epistemological investigation into stated and implied beliefs and definitions.

Burke maintained a critic could legitimately limit himself to formalist work or he could pursue other dimensions of study. Either way, he demanded methodological rigor. "[W]ith regard to Poetics in particular," insisted Burke in 1966, "I would propose to make rules in that dimension as strict as possible. Absolutely no biographical reference would be admissible. History itself would be admissible only in the sense that the meaning (and allusiveness) of a term will change through the centuries. . . ." Formalist analysis in the realm of poetics had to be limited and focused. For example, other poems by a poet, biographical details, and general historical information had no place in this method of inquiry. "[W]hen considering the work as an instance of sheer poetic action in and for itself, one should leave such matters out of account. Here the material must stand or fall by reason of its role in the story [or poem], regardless of whether it arose in the course of the writing, or was lifted from a notebook, or was even stolen or borrowed from someone else."[19] While Burke defined rigorously the domain of poetics and the methods of formalism, he saw no reason to limit all inquiry to this realm and these procedures. "At its best," close reading, as he experienced it, "sustains the intense contemplation of an object to the point where one begins to see not only more deeply into the object but beyond it, in the direction of generalizations about the kinds of art and artistic excellence, and even the principles of human thought and experience universally."[20] Here Burke revealed the quintessential movement of his mind—from textual analysis to human experience. As far as Burke was concerned, "The greater the range and depth of considerations about which a critic can be explicit, the more he is fulfilling his task as a critic" ("KC," 272). We may say that, characteristically, Burke worked through the text and *beyond* it. He gave himself more fully to the pursuit of textual implications than any of his New Critical contemporaries.

In one of his most celebrated early works, the monograph entitled "The Philosophy of Literary Form" (1941), Burke defined "imaginative works" at the outset as "answers to questions posed by the situation in which they arose. They are not merely answers, they are *strategic* answers, *stylized* answers."[21] Implied in this opening definition was a project for extrinsic as well as intrinsic criticism. "Situation" was interrelated with "style" and "solution." The "situation," which conditions the creation of a work, typically included cultural and historical backgrounds as well as biographical and purely literary matters: "situation" constituted the functional ground of a work. This variable ground licensed a plurality of critical approaches. For Burke literature was stylized self-expression that responded to a situation and sought to offer persuasive solutions. It was "equipment for living." As revelation, literature required biographical analysis; as ritualization (or stylization), it called for formalist criticism; as cultural response, it demanded sociological inquiry. Manifested forcefully in "The Philosophy of Literary Form," this pluralistic system of poetics and hermeneutics had been worked out gradually by Burke throughout the 1930s. In *Counter-Statement* (1931), for example, he declared: "The artist begins with his emotion, he translates this emotion into a mechanism for arousing emotion in others, and thus his interest in his own emotion transcends into his interest in the treatment."[22] Burke's thinking here moved swiftly from self-expression to persuasion to style, including them all in one synthetic view of the nature of imaginative works. What was missing in this very early formulation was a sociological dimension.

The role of sociology in Burke's theories of literature and criticism became evident in the early 1930s, when he added a Marxist perspective to his initial aestheticist premises. Of the leading early American New Critics, Burke was the only one to adopt a socialist line of thinking. He did not join the Communist Party, but remained an independent Marxist. In an essay published in the Marxist journal *Science & Society,* later collected in *The Philosophy of Literary Form,* Burke contended "that the analysis of aesthetic phenomena can be extended or projected into the analysis of social and political phenomena in general" (309). Burke would later come to call such analysis "socioanagogic criticism," which aimed to examine the forces and tensions produced by specific sociopolitical hierarchies as embodied in imaginative works. It was in "Literature as Equipment for Living," published in the thirties, that Burke proposed a large-scale project of sociological criticism, seeking "to take literature out of its separate bin and give it a place in a general 'sociological' picture" (296). Specifically, such a sociological project "would seek to codify the various strategies which artists have developed with relation to the naming of situations" (301). Like proverbs, works of literature provided exhortations, admonitions, forecasts, consolations, and instructions that bore directly upon human welfare. Like medicine, literature was equipment for surviving specific sociopolitical situations. Criticism could and should take account of such powerful motives in literature.

Burke insisted in "The Philosophy of Literary Form" that the primary "focus of critical analysis must be upon the structure of the given work itself," yet he added that "observation about structure is more relevant when you approach the work as the *functioning* of a structure" (74). Among the functions of literature, he included a sociological purpose: literature possessed therapeutic and cathartic powers applicable to the whole social body. The purgation and redemption wrought by literature applied to poets as well as readers. This "functionalist axiomatic" stood behind Burke's general theory of literature as *action*. Literature does things—for poets, readers, societies. The form and content of literature must be understood in this light. Accordingly, anthropology and psychology, sociology and biography, politics and ethics, religion and aesthetics all offered routes to depth, range, and fullness of understanding. "The main ideal of criticism," proclaimed Burke, "is to use all that is there to use" (23).

Burke pioneered not only coordinated interdisciplinary approaches to literature, but refined methods of formalist analysis. He employed a six-fold "formalist" hermeneutic, composed of structural analysis, cluster analysis, dramatic analysis, pun analysis, archetypal analysis, and symbolic analysis. To these he later added "indexing." Rather than rehearse all these modes of inquiry—which Burke's critics have carefully catalogued—let us sample the dimensions of "structural analysis" alone, as summarized by one of Burke's scholars:

Every kind of progression is covered under structural analysis. The most important of these are plot (sequence of external events); action ("spiritual movement," or sequence of internal reactions); pattern of experience (the simple and complex patterns of psychic and physical experience resulting from conflicts within an agent and the interaction between agent, other agents, scene, and the like); spatial movement (up, down, in, out, north, south, east, west); tonal progression; chronological progression (seasonal progression, biological growth, historical change); scenic progression; and qualitative progression (from dark, to gray, to light imagery; from rot, to purgation, to redemption imagery; from innocence to corruption to depravity). The first step in the analysis of a poem as symbolic action requires an exhaustive descriptive and analytic study of its structure in order to determine what follows what, and why.[23]

This is the first of six analytical procedures in Burke's formalist mode. The other procedures, depending on the particular text, can be equally intricate and thorough. Burke practiced "close reading" with a vengeance. What distinguished his exegeses from New Critical interpretations was a complex set of coordinated protocols linked firmly to the social sciences. Burke named this coordination of literary criticism with other disciplines "planned incongruity."

The wide-ranging speculations, sidetrackings, and "incongruities" of Burke's theory and criticism, combined with his peculiar thoroughness and interdisciplinarity, led New Critics to criticize while admiring him. R. P. Blackmur set the pattern in his influential "A Critic's Job of Work" (1935), where he surveyed Burke's strengths and many weaknesses. Two decades later in his codification of New Criticism, Murray Krieger allotted Burke some space in one footnote. About Burke, Krieger's *The New Apologists for Poetry* said dismissively:

Kenneth Burke has very different assumptions from which to attempt the definition of poetry. Although he is popularly referred to as a new critic and his is an unusual attempt, one which has not been without its influence, he is not being treated in this essay by very reason of his different assumptions. . . . In the work which is to satisfy the psychology of the poet and the psychology of the audience, there is insufficient provision made for the dislocations of stereotyped expressions. . . . This framework leads to Burke's "dramatistic" theory, which ends by denying any barrier between art and life. . . . While Richards differs from most of our critics in a similar way, his theories lent themselves to adaptation and transformation by those critics who are my central concern. Burke, on the other hand, simply represents an extremely divergent approach. . . .[24]

Here Krieger drummed Burke out of the New Critical School. Among his faults were his interests in the psychology of the poet and the reader, in the close connections of art and life, and in the symbolic value of *ordinary* language. Although very much like I. A. Richards in his interests, Burke lacked true influence on other New Critics, so he was dismissed, while Richards was allowed inside. Given Krieger's main goal of providing a purified systematic aesthetic for New Criticism, we can understand his tactical excommunication of Burke. Burke belonged on the outside.

NEW CRITICAL FORMALISM DEFENDED IN LATTER DAYS

At the time Murray Krieger's *The New Apologists for Poetry* came out, New Criticism was beset by hostile attacks from many sides. The Chicago Critics and New York Intellectuals, the Myth Critics and philosophical critics, various psychological and sociological critics all were challenging to some degree the enterprise of this formalist movement. Many of the leading New Critics had themselves branched out. As time went on, other theorists and scholars mounted more critiques of New Criticism, including Reader-Response Critics, structuralists, deconstructors, feminists, ethnic critics, and leftist cultural critics. From its earliest days, of course, New Criticism was contested by Marxists, Freudians, literary historians, and others. Still, the attacks on the School were so numerous, widespread, and intemperate by the early 1970s that its role became one of scapegoat. When caricatured, the New Criticism often emerged, in careless retrospect, as an unrecognizable monolith. Since many of the early New Critics were dead by the seventies, and others had long since left the ranks or become inactive, the only authoritative spokesmen left were Cleanth Brooks, René Wellek, and Murray Krieger. About twenty years younger than his colleagues, Krieger was in mid-career and at the height of his power during this most intense period of challenge. The youngest and apparently the last of the major New Critical theorists, Murray Krieger went on the defensive, seeking both to protect and extend New Critical formalism. It was Krieger's defense during the seventies that produced a sophisticated, supple, and rarefied latter-day version of New Critical formalism.

At a certain point in the 1970s Krieger felt positively caught between two somber alternatives. A choice had to be made. As far as Krieger could determine, the historical grounds of this decisive moment dated back to the days of Matthew Arnold and his crisis of faith. What especially exacerbated the grim situation now was the present threat to all humanists posed by deconstructive criticism. For Krieger the "Arnoldian choice," a century old, still involved questions of faith; his own latter-day position hinged on faith. He declared himself a believer.

If we share Arnold's loss of faith, we can go either of two ways: we can view poetry as a human triumph made out of darkness, as the creation of verbal meaning in a blank universe to serve as a visionary substitute for a defunct religion; or we can—in our negation—extend our faithlessness, the blankness of our universe, to our poetry. If we choose the latter alternative then we tend . . . to reject the first, affirmative humanistic claim about poetry's unique power, seeing it as a mystification arising from our nostaligia and our metaphysical deprivation.

Stubbornly humanistic as I am, I must choose that first alternative: I want to remain responsive to the promise of the filled and centered word, a signifier replete with an inseparable signified which it has created within itself. But I am aware also that my demythologizing habit, as modern man, must make me wary of the grounds on which I dare claim verbal presence and fullness.[25]

As a modern believer, Krieger insisted that poetry was a "human triumph," a "creation of verbal meaning," a "visionary substitute for a defunct religion," a "unique power," a "filled and centered word," a "signifier replete with an inseparable signified," a "verbal presence and fullness."

This theory of literature, in Krieger's assessment, was "stubbornly humanistic" and "affirmative." It came into play for him against a somber cultural background where the universe was blank, religion was defunct, metaphysics was insubstantial, and every belief underwent demythologization. In such a world, any affirmation required wariness and daring. Thus Krieger's declaration, "I want to remain responsive to the promise," self-consciously exhibited poised care mixed with faith, while his statement, "I must choose," accepted the necessity of boldness as it asserted his belief in poetry's visionary power and meaning—poetry's "verbal presence and fullness."

In Krieger's extreme formulation, the alternative to his choice was to extend faithlessness and blankness, to negate poetry and regard it as mystification and nostalgia. This second way separated the linguistic signifier from its signified, renounced faith in poetry as triumph, unique power, and vision, decentered the filled and centered word, and demystified meaning and presence. This other road was the heretical way of deconstruction, which we shall examine in detail in chapter 10. Throughout the seventies Krieger staged his formalist project in opposition to deconstruction, seeking to fashion an alternative to the negation and blankness of the deconstructive program and trying to halt the erosion of Western humanism. The challenge of deconstruction forced Krieger into becoming the main spokesman and defender of the New Critical tradition during the 1970s.

Krieger labeled himself a *humanist,* self-consciously conceiving his work as an extension and preservation of the Western cultural tradition. He also called himself an *existentialist*—a philosophic position that showed up in his awareness of and anxiety about the death of God, in his perception of the nothingness and blankness of existence, and in his consciousness of human death as an indisputable fact (*PPI,* 208). And Krieger presented himself as a *formalist*—an heir and revisionist of New Criticism, a believer in the unique and superior power of poetic language and in the separate and special status of the autonomous literary artifact. Against the dark backdrop of grim reality, the great works of Western literature came forth for him as luminous and visionary creations of verbal meaning, as miraculous and centered signs, offering the fullness and presence of the word.

To keep his latter-day formalism viable, Krieger had constantly to refine his theory of literature. In particular, he regularly confronted deconstruction, working to introject and modify its findings for his own project. In this regard, Krieger represented an important phenomenon, for he was the only

leading New Critical formalist to confront and absorb massively and impla-
cably the deconstructive threat. This confrontation aimed not at understanding deconstructive criticism, however, but at preserving a formalist
criticism.

Responding to an essay that championed American deconstruction,
Krieger asserted about the embattled status of poetry:

> If belief in the poet's power to find embodiment in the word is a myth, it has
> been, for the critical tradition in the West from its beginnings, the necessary
> fiction that has permitted more than two millennia of our greatest poems to
> speak to us. Few critical schools in our history have done more than the New
> Critics did to give them voice. Thanks in large part to these critics—but
> before them as well—the poems have been *there*, speaking as they do, as if
> there is a presence in them. They make their own case for presence, and it is
> out of no mere nostalgia that we continue to value it in them. For presence is
> present tense, and while we live we must not allow ourselves to be reasoned
> out of it. (*PPI*, 112)

Here Krieger praised the New Critics and linked them with the broader
Western critical tradition. Formalist and humanist, he insisted on the need
to preserve our greatest poems and to continue our ancient traditions. In
duress, he urged us "while we live" to oppose the end of humanism and the
desacralization of great literature. The odd phrase "while we live" imported
death into the argument, reminding us of Krieger's pressing existential
anxiety. When warned "we must not allow ourselves to be reasoned out of
it," it was clear that faith as much as reason motivated Krieger's position.

Throughout the seventies and into the eighties Murray Krieger affirmed
continuously that the poet possessed the power to discover "embodiment in
the word," that great poems "speak to us," that formalist criticism allowed
poems to have such "voice," that poems are "*there*," that they "speak" and
have "presence in them." Krieger's conception of literature clearly depended
on the linkage of voice and presence. The "verbal presence and fullness" of
poetry opposed head-on the absence and emptiness of *écriture*—the isolated, nonreferential, written signifiers celebrated in deconstructive poetics.

Krieger's subtle formulations about *poetic presence* were central to his
endeavor, serving as the ground of his poetics. He accepted that the
traditional belief in presence could be a "myth." He conceded that "verbal
presence" held the status of "as if." He tagged his latter-day incarnational
poetic a "necessary fiction"—a system of belief that "*permits*" poetry to
"speak." Noticeably, Krieger relied on "if" (as in the two citations above).
Still, he insisted that poems "make their own case for presence"—that the

poetic signifier was "replete with an inseparable signified which it has created *within itself.*" The phrases "own case" and "within itself" were peculiar figures of speech; these rhetorical devices, nevertheless, were native to formalist thinking about poetry as autonomous artifact. At all costs Krieger sought to reserve for poetry the sacred power to create full presence. Poetry, unlike ordinary discourse, was special. This New Critical notion, as Krieger now realized, was an illusion. Poetic presence was an illusion, a necessary fiction, a useful eucharistic myth for an era of demystification.

Having got this far with Krieger, we cannot fail to notice how different was his discourse of the 1970s from that of the first New Critical formalists of the 1930s and 1940s. The essays of Brooks and Wellek written during these latter days did not reflect the changes of terminology so obvious in Krieger. It was Krieger, alone among the major New Critics, who met the challenges of opponents by adopting their terminology for his own ends. Perhaps this was a tactical error, perhaps not. In any case, it was Krieger's distinctive way of fostering formalist values in a hostile environment. When he cofounded the influential School of Criticism and Theory in 1976, Krieger invited major spokesmen from most of the leading critical schools of the time. Incorporation, not exclusion, was Krieger's general strategy. Consequently, he produced a peculiar lexicon in his defense of New Criticism.

Through certain key tropes and figures, employed consciously and systematically, Krieger was able to maintain his beliefs and justify his faith. About one essential device of language he was direct and informative: "So there are several major paradoxes which I find our literary experiences to suggest—paradoxes in which I can see neither side yielding" (*PPI,* 204). For example, the poem for Krieger was through *paradox* both an aesthetic object *and* a reader's experience; both a discontinuous, separate metaphorical language *and* a continuous part of all discourse; both a closed, autonomous realm *and* an open network of linguistic elements; both, as Krieger put it,

the verbal miracle of metaphorical identity *and* the awareness that the miracle depends on our sense of its impossibility, leading to our knowledge that it's only our *illusion.* . . . We both learn to see *and* distrust our seeing, as we view poetic language both as breaking itself off from the normal flow of discourse to become a privileged object, worthy of idolatry, *and* as language self-deconstructed and leveled, joining the march of common *écriture.* (*PPI,* 204–05)

The formalist side of this system of paradoxes cast literature as object, vision, miracle, identity, and metaphor—all meriting idolatry. The "deconstructive" side staged literature as an impossible miracle, self-created illusion, untrustworthy vision, leveled language, and common writing. Krieger managed it both ways, though he preferred and continued to champion the sacred poetics of formalism, reserving for the "deconstructive" formulation strategic incorporation. He aimed to press the two sides of these tangled "impossible" paradoxes together, but his faith insisted on better and worse alternatives. He preferred the miraculous over the heretical in keeping with the tradition of New Criticism, which characteristically castigated heresies and kept the faith. *Poetry was metaphor* (and illusion).

In the 1970s Krieger found himself in something like the position of a theologian trying to explain and justify to heretics the mystery of the Incarnation. For Krieger poetic content was an aspect of form—the signified was in the signifier—just as God was in the man Christ. Miraculous and material realms met in the figure (metaphor). Krieger relied heavily on various paradoxes to explain this fundamental premise. Unlike some other American New Critics, Krieger championed paradox not just in individual poems, but in his overall theory of poetry. Paradox was Krieger's master trope, used to great effect in both his critical essays and poetic theories. "Paradox may well be less acceptable in critical discourse than it is in poetry," apologized Krieger, "but in my defense I can say only that I can do no better and can do no less if I am to do justice to what I find our literature requiring of its critic" (*PPI,* 203). Krieger allowed paradox to migrate from poetic to critical discourse. An account of literature demanded such literary treatment. Literary paradox produced critical paradox; one textual realm touched another. This blurring of the essential distinction between poetic language and critical language was not "acceptable" for a formalist. To defend this procedure, Krieger invoked "justice." He was "required," in being true to literature, to borrow the resources of literature. However he explained it, paradox was Krieger's main speculative instrument; it determined his literary theory. Poetry was both metaphor and illusion, both autonomous and open-ended, both special language and common language, both an aesthetic object and a reader's experience. Here a general structure of paradoxes—of systematic contradiction—undergirded a whole project of formalist poetics and hermeneutics.

However warily, Krieger did insist on verbal presence and fullness for poetry. What he also did was to temper such claims by declaring them to be illusions and fictions. He proclaimed the strategic necessity and value of all such paradoxes. Poetry was opened and closed discourse. A poem was an experience and an object. These paradoxes—fictions—were designed and marshaled to save both poetry and formalist criticism.

Heir to the Arnoldian legacy and faced with the challenge of contemporary deconstruction, Krieger, as humanist, constructed an intricate defense of literature and formalist criticism, using the rich materials of the Western tradition. Few New Critical formalists were as widely learned and eclectic as Krieger in building a complex and "coherent" system. However, no American theorist had ever deliberately based an entire aesthetic theory on a foundation of contradictions turned into a system.

For Krieger, the poem remained the origin and center of critical activity. Though traditionally a secondary art, criticism in the Space Age sometimes threatened to substitute its own text for the central poetic work. In Krieger's view, such centrifugal "play," such "criticism," should not replace the poem.[26] The language of literature, superior to critical discourse, should moderate the presumption and arrogance of any hermeneutic will-to-power over poems. In the role of moralist, Krieger pleaded with critics to remain faithful servants of the poetic text.

Like other New Critics, Krieger believed that a literary work shaped and ordered experience. The work was an artifact or special object possessing potent forms of aesthetic and of cognitive closure. These distinctive features elevated poetry, giving it a place different from and above other types of discourse. With its fundamental and characteristic drive toward closure, the work exhibited an internal purposiveness and coherence, separating it in kind from ordinary language and justifying its status as sacred object. Despite its connections with an author, a group of readers, a cultural tradition, and a historical language, the poem maintained its essential integrity, refusing to dissolve or erode under any such extrinsic and fragmenting force or entity. Throughout the 1970s Krieger affirmed these essentials of formalist doctrine, especially in his lectures of 1979 titled *Arts on the Level.*

The mounting assaults on New Critical articles of faith by Reader-Response Critics, semioticians, Marxists, and especially deconstructors threatened, but did not ruin, the inherent integrity of the sacred literary artifact so prized by Krieger. The idolatry of art, a long-standing feature of all formalisms, lived on for Krieger, who, in spite of and by virtue of his concessions and paradoxes, remained steadfastly committed to the old faith. In the end, such faith had little to do with "truth"; he conferred on it the status of "necessary fiction." This modernist strategy, adopted from Wallace Stevens, aimed to counter the undoings and deconstructions of the somber postmodern era.

Implicit in Krieger's system was a pattern of cultural and social ideas which occasionally came to the surface. The poem for him was an "elite object." The role of the critic was to read, explain, and evaluate such works for the culture. The brotherhood of critics, sharing a similar high regard for the stability and integrity of each text, settled disputes by reference to the work and by means of close reading. In this way, the great tradition underwent constant sifting and preservation in the present for the future. Only through restraint could the tradition persist and high culture continue. Sensing that this economy was disintegrating, Krieger became during the seventies increasingly zealous and urgent in his defense of both the great tradition and his formalist articles of belief.

With Krieger the close reading of literary texts was a controlled practice dependent on a set of articles of faith. When Krieger read, he "found" internal purposiveness and cohesion—closure and form. As artifact, the poem appeared unique and miraculous, a human triumph. The fullness of the poetic word, its presence, elevated it to a special and sacred place. The reader became a worshipper. In the modern godless age, the text served as a kind of religious experience. Poetic language embodied the richness and promise of man's most noble and holy self. The centered word spoke to us. This whole system—with its set of formalist protocols—continued the New Critical manner of reading and interpretation. Because critics sometimes misread poems on account of their self-interest or their inherent will-to-power over texts, Krieger urged restraint and moderation, deploring self-indulgence. Krieger emerged in the latter days of New Criticism as a stoical man of faith, an embattled conservative, the last of the leading New Critics.

EAST EUROPEAN AND AMERICAN NEW CRITICAL FORMALISM

At about the same time after World War I that New Criticism was being formed in England and America, a parallel movement was developing in Eastern Europe. An examination of these different Schools, focusing on significant similarities and differences, will provide an opportunity to clarify the distinctive traits and practices of American New Critical formalism. Such an examination deals with historical confluence, not direct influence, since the East European formalists and the New Critics were virtually unaware of each other's projects until the late forties and early fifties—a time when New Criticism was fully formed and Eastern European formalism had gone out of business.

The Russian formalist movement consisted of two groups: the Moscow Linguistic Circle, active from 1915 to 1920, and the Petersburg Society for the Study of Poetic Language (the so-called *Opoyaz* group), at work from 1916 to 1930. The leading members of the Moscow group were Roman Jakobson, Osip Brik, and Boris Tomashevsky; the main figures in the Petersburg Society were Victor Shklovsky, Boris Eichenbaum, Leo Jakubinsky, and Yury Tynjanov. The Moscow group dissolved after Jakobson went to Prague in 1920, where he remained for two decades, playing a leading role in the important Prague Linguistic Circle, which furthered the initial work of Russian formalism from the late twenties onwards and included, among others, the theorists Jan Mukařovský, N. S. Trubetzkoy, and René Wellek. The Petersburg Society stopped functioning by 1930, as did the Prague Circle about two decades later, on account of pressures from doctrinaire Soviet Marxists.

The work of the Slavic groups was first made widely known in America by Wellek and Warren's *Theory of Literature* (chaps. 13 and 16), published in 1949, and by Victor Erlich's definitive *Russian Formalism: History-Doctrine,* brought out by Yale University Press in 1955. Exemplary texts of the Slavic formalists, however, were not available in translation until the sixties and seventies. Between the world wars when New Criticism and East European formalism were developing, these Schools apparently knew little, if anything, about one another.

What the Russian formalists and American New Critics had in common was a language-oriented criticism, centered on the close scrutiny of autonomous verbal constructs, conceived as highly structured and unified patterns of miraculous poetic language. Both groups attacked academic literary studies, particularly biographical criticism, historical scholarship, and impressionistic evaluation. In effect, they ruled out extrinsic approaches to literature in favor of immanent modes of analysis. Both Schools engaged, formally and informally, in reevaluating the canons of great works, using *literary* standards to sift through past culture and tradition. To a large extent, both New Critical and Russian formalists derived their major premises from Kantian idealism as embodied in the *Critique of Judgment* (1790)—which made them early targets of Marxist critics committed to materialist and historicist philosophical presuppositions.

The Russian formalists and New Critics differed from one another in significant ways. In contrast to the Tory conservatism and theological ethos of the American group, the Russian School displayed an aestheticism unanchored by any uniform religious vision. In Russian formalism, there was nothing like the New Critics' philosophy of history rooted in a tragic view of man's loss of organic society and dissociation of sensibility. Early on most of the Moscow and Petersburg critics devoted themselves to a neo-positivist program of descriptive poetics based on faith in scientific methodology and in a science of literature. Conversely, the American critics generally disliked science and pushed beyond description to interpretation and evaluation. The result was that New Critical formalists typically engaged in practical and judicial criticism of individual works while their Russian counterparts undertook relatively large-scale projects in theoretical poetics, often avoiding interpretation and explicit evaluation altogether. In this regard, the New Critics continued the Western tradition of "aesthetic humanism" while the Russian formalists pioneered scientific structuralism—which the Prague Circle later brought to fruition. Essentially, the Americans were increasingly more absorbed, and the Russians progressively less so, with the cognitive dimension of literature—with the notion that art conveys a special nonparaphrasable, nonscientific knowledge. New Critics never fully renounced "meaning" for criticism; Russian formalists frequently practiced "interpretation-free" inquiry. Much Russian attention was devoted in the early years to analysis of poetic instrumentation—to rhythm, rhyme, and sound effects—using linguistic methods to uncover the phonetic laws of music in poetry. Later, attention was paid to genre studies, particularly to prose forms. By comparison, New Critical interest in poetic instrumentation, in genre, and in prose form was scant and non-systematic. Whereas the New Critics studied the convergence of elements in a textual structure, the Russian formalists examined the deviation of elements against the ground of literary norms. New Critical formalists were committed to unified structure and unified sensibility as standards of poetic perfection. Such values and judicial criticism played little role for the Russian formalists.[27]

As a school the New Criticism was much less cohesive than the Eastern European groups. The fact that the Russians and Czechs were compelled to disband meant that they did not get the opportunity to develop—which may partially account for their comparative cohesiveness. Ironically, the premature end of the Slavic formalists helped make them seem especially exotic pioneers when they first became widely known and read in France,

Germany, England, and America in the 1960s. While they were having a profound impact on structuralism and semiotics during this time, the New Critics were being attacked on all sides for numerous limitations and faults.

Shortly after World War I, I. A. Richards in England and Roman Jakobson in Russia began to distinguish systematically and scientifically the different functions of language. Soon New Critics and Slavic formalists alike came to make much of the difference between practical and poetic language. For Richards the language of poetry tended toward nonreferential pseudostatement; thus it was distanced from any mechanical one-to-one correspondence with reality. For Jakobson the discipline of literary studies needed to devote itself not to literature per se, but to the formal linguistic properties that distinguished literature from other types of discourse: the main topic of inquiry was to become "literariness"—conceived as a special function, not an essence, of language. The effect of the dichotomy between ordinary and poetic language was to focus formalist inquiry on matters intrinsic to literary works and to eschew examination of extrinsic factors. Textual structure replaced mimetic correspondence as the ground of literary analysis.

The first notable attack on formalism came in chapter 5 of Leon Trotsky's *Literature and Revolution* (1924). The Marxist Trotsky complained of the "superficial" and "reactionary," the "childish" and "superstitious," the "narrow" and "religious," the "defective" and "megalomaniacal" methods and theories of Russian formalism. At the same time Trotsky affirmed that formalist inquiry was "necessary," "useful," and "essential," though "partial" and "insufficient." While Trotsky accepted the relative autonomy of art, he insisted on its materialistic nature: "It is not a disembodied element feeding on itself, but a function of social man indissolubly tied to his life and environment."[28] The separation of the poetic from the practical, of literature from social life, of art from history, of the poem from the reader, of words from deeds, of the "superstructure" from the "base"—all these faults of formalism were discussed by Trotsky—devitalized and disembodied the material grounds of imaginative work, denying its utilitarian function and value and enthroning (pure) "art" as useless and mummified. However unreal and fantastic artistic creation may be—however much "a deflection, a changing and a transformation of reality" (175)—its material always derived from social reality and its class structure. Ultimately, Trotsky accused the Russian formalists of philosophical idealism: "The Formalist School represents an abortive idealism applied to the questions of art. The Formalists show a fast ripening religiousness. They are followers of St.

John. They believe that 'In the beginning was the Word.' But we believe that in the beginning was the deed. The word followed . . ." (183).

Just as the New Critics drew fire early on from the leading American Marxists of the day, so the Russian formalists experienced the barbs and critiques of Soviet Marxist theorists, starting with Trotsky in the early twenties and continuing with the Bakhtin School in the late twenties. Located near Leningrad, the inner circle of this competing School included Mikhail Bakhtin, Pavlev Medvedev, and Valentin Vološinov. In Medvedev's and Bakhtin's *The Formal Method in Literary Scholarship: A Critical Introduction to Sociological Poetics* (1928), the Marxist critique, initiated by Trotsky, continued but with more rigor and insight. Following Trotsky, Medvedev and Bakhtin complain that the formalists in their conception and their treatment of the literary work not only divorce literature from the subjectivity of the reader and the poet, but "estrange it from the whole ideological environment and from objective social intercourse. The work is cut off from both real social realization and from the entire ideological world."[29] The separation of the artwork from the socioeconomic base was compounded by its isolation from the cultural superstructure (the ideological world)— from politics, law, philosophy, religion, science, and ethics. Doubly divested of meaning, the formalists' poem became an empty shell in an ideological vacuum. "Their fear of meaning in art led the formalists to reduce the poetic construction to the peripheral, outer surface of the work. The work lost its depth, three-dimensionality, and fullness" (118).

What ultimately distinguished this critique of Russian formalism by the Bakhtin School was its own language-centered analysis. These Marxists objected to the nonreferential, hermetic function assigned to literary language by formalists. Unlike objects or physical processes, utterances—even if only one word—were social acts. In this Marxist thinking, "Every concrete utterance is a social act. At the same time that it is an individual material complex, a phonetic, articulatory, visual complex, the utterance is also a part of social reality" (120). Human language was inherently communicative, dialogical. Enmeshed in a sociohistorical environment, the act or performance of language always occurred in given circumstances under certain conditions. Language was both linguistic and sociological—involved with both abstract phonetics and social reality. The context of every utterance, poetic or otherwise, was social intercourse. As a function of discourse, meaning was inescapable. "It is impossible to understand the concrete utterance without accustoming oneself to its values, without understanding the orientation of its evaluation in the ideological environment" (121). Utterances produced meanings, which could only be deciphered in relation to *cultural* context. Given its theory of language, including poetic language, as dialogical, the Bakhtin School was able to mount a critique of Russian formalism not only on the grounds of bad language theory, but also on the bases of defective hermeneutics. The scientific analysis of instrumentation was insufficient; "meaning" remained to be deciphered in its full sociohistorical and ideological, rather than simple dictionary, sense.

The tendency of Russian and New Critical formalist theory to conceive of the literary text as an autonomous artwork constructed of poetic language led to "oddities" in the treatment of meaning. With the Russian formalists the value of "meaning" was often ignored or denied. With the New Critics, "meaning" was made ineffable (an unparaphrasable experience or actualization): "meaning" consisted of a cluster of unresolvable paradoxes or indeterminate balanced tensions. If a work did not display such qualities, the New Critics judged it defective. When threatened by the death of meaning promoted by deconstruction, Krieger, following the line of New Critical tradition and the path of humanism, rushed to save meaning—even if only in a special, self-subverting, paradoxical form. Unlike the Russian formalists, the New Critics always strained to maintain a theory of "meaning" and to resist any positivist projects for a purely descriptive poetics.

Ironically, the New Critics shared with the Russian Marxists a view of language as spoken discourse directed at a reader, though they were coy in saying so and in admitting their idealization of the reader. Even more ironically, the Russian formalists, who studied sound devices more thoroughly than any previous school, did not treat language as spoken to an audience; their poetics was more graphic than oral. Given different notions of language and of meaning, Russian formalists, American New Critics, and Bakhtinian Marxists produced different conceptualizations of poetics and hermeneutics. It was the early Russian Marxists, in trying to incorporate formalism, who revealed most forcefully the foundational role played by theory of language in the development of literary studies. With this understanding, we can clarify further the distinctive nature of New Critical formalism.

In an interview in 1975 Cleanth Brooks stated: "Nobody in his right mind, of course, is really interested in empty formality. Words open out into the whole world of emotions, ideas, actions. So that the 'arrangement of words' . . . is a kind of special reflection of manifold humanity itself. Words are not mere phonetic improvisations; they are meaningful." And a moment later he added that "language is the product of society and, like society, has its own history. The words of a literary work constantly point back to the human being who chose and patterned them. . . . The 'verbal artifact' can't be purged of human meanings."[30] There was a double motion in this statement. On the one hand, Brooks maintained a classic New Critical stance: the patterned words of poetry constituted a *special* reflection of life; the verbal artifact partook of language—which has its *own* history. In short, poetic language, however rooted in social reality, remained yet separate and special. On the other hand, Brooks assumed a "reflectionist" or mimetic position: the words of poetry were not empty and were not simply phonetic; poetic language was a product of the social world and opened itself to humanity; it possessed meaning. This position would have satisfied neither Jakobson nor Bakhtin; it represented something of a middle way between the extremes of "pure" formalism and Marxist sociopoetics.

When he came to discuss "meaning," Brooks insisted that literature offered *special* knowledge which was neither historical nor scientific but rather experiential. "Concrete," "dramatic," "revelatory," this knowledge was "civilizing," though incommunicable and unparaphrasable (46–58).

If we looked to Kenneth Burke or Yvor Winters, rather than to Brooks and Krieger, we would see a departure from the middle course of mainstream American New Criticism toward a cultural poetics. Here language retained practical rhetorical powers, meaning was specifiable, extrinsic criticism was encouraged, readers were "real" rather than "ideal." Winters' *In Defense of Reason* (1947) declared:

I believe that the work of literature . . . approximates a real apprehension and communication of a particular kind of objective truth. . . . The poem is a statement in words about a human experience. . . . The poem is good in so far as it makes a defensible rational statement . . . and at the same time communicates the emotion which ought to be motivated by that rational understanding of the experience.[31]

And about rhythm and form, Winters observed, "These aspects of the poem will be efficient in so far as the poet subordinates them to the total aim of the poem" (12). The stress on the communicative function of poetic language and the deemphasis of literary devices led Winters away from a mystical formalistic notion of meaning toward a rationalist concept of meaning as objective truth about human experience. As a result, Winters' hermeneutics, like Burke's, allowed a social usefulness for literature: literature potentially appealed to a wide audience rather than an aesthetic elite.

In *Criticism in the Wilderness* (1980), Geoffrey Hartman complained about the theory of meaning fostered by New Criticism. For New Critics meaning was *not* political, *not* scientific, *not* historical, *not* philosophical, *not* biographical, *not* sociological; it was *nothing*. "That 'nothing' has plagued us ever since. It acted as an unacknowledged theological restraint. The end of literary studies was not knowledge but rather a state of grace." All of this led "to an emptying out of the literary-critical enterprise."[32] In Hartman's perspective, New Criticism appeared as a severe and monkish asceticism, offering a negative knowledge equivalent to grace. Characteristic of it were restraint, denial, emptiness. The theological dimensions of New Criticism, centered in its hermeneutics of grace and its poetics of incarnation, distinguished it from Slavic formalism's project for a purely scientific poetics and a structuralist analytics. With the rise of structuralism and semiotics in the 1960s, East European formalism entered a heyday of influence. Meanwhile, New Critical formalism became a scapegoat for having impoverished literary studies. Because it could contribute little to either a scientific, a sociological, or a properly hermeneutical criticism, New Criticism lost influence with the advance guard of literary theorists in the 1960s and thereafter.

CHAPTER THREE

The Chicago School

PEDAGOGICAL FOUNDATIONS AND THE RISE OF THEORY

*C*ritics and Criticism: Ancient and Modern (1952) was the main text, the "manifesto," of the Chicago School. A lengthy scholarly book, it consisted of twenty articles by six members of the School—five pieces by Richard McKeon, five by Elder Olson, four by R. S. Crane, and two each by W. R. Keast, Norman Maclean, and Bernard Weinberg. Divided into three groups, the essays focused on, first, the limitations of contemporary criticism, primarily New Criticism; second, the pluralistic nature and continuing influence of past literary and critical theory, ranging from Aristotle to Samuel Johnson; and, third, the philosophical (or aesthetic) and methodological principles necessary for an adequate present-day criticism and poetics. Because the collection opened with pointed critiques of I. A. Richards, William Empson, Cleanth Brooks, and other New Critics and because it then promoted a revised and expanded formalism, the Chicago School at its outset was presented as a reaction to New Criticism and as an alternative formalism. Beyond the University of Chicago, the School exerted comparatively little influence during the fifties or thereafter. New Critical formalism gained sway across the nation.

As editor of *Critics and Criticism*, R. S. Crane provided a programmatic introduction to the School. From then on he was identified as the main spokesman for the Chicago Critics. Delivered as a course of lectures at the University of Toronto in the same year as the publication of the joint volume, Crane's own *The Languages of Criticism and the Structure of Poetry*, published in 1953, developed in detail the basic concepts outlined in the introduction to the collective text. We learn from Crane that this group of critics had been working together at Chicago for two decades, having first come into contact during the mid-thirties to consider curriculum matters and educational reforms. A half century later the details of the early pedagogical projects of the School were sketched and corroborated by Richard McKeon in his brief memoir "Criticism and the Liberal Arts: The Chicago School of Criticism" (1982). Significantly, the collected essays of the School and Crane's own book, though published in the early fifties, represented work initiated in the thirties and forties (roughly contemporary with American New Criticism) and work undertaken in a context of pedagogical reform.

During the thirties the humanistic disciplines were fast losing influence to the sciences and social sciences. Something had to be done. At the University of Chicago, as elsewhere, programs of renewal were being considered. What was undertaken initially was extensive reexamination of the assumptions and procedures of humanistic studies. In a state of disarray and inclined to imitate the sciences, the humanities increasingly lacked effectiveness and prestige. Ultimately, humanistic studies at Chicago were coordinated and a comprehensive curriculum was devised for undergraduate students. Under a new plan, four cooperating areas of humanistic education were conceived, including (1) Linguistics (very broadly construed); (2) Analysis of Ideas and Methods; (3) Comparative Examination of Art and Literature; and (4) Study of the History of Culture. Scholars from thirteen departments designed and staffed these interdisciplinary concentrations. Among the intellectuals recasting the curriculum and teaching in the various areas were the six Chicago Critics represented in *Critics and Criticism.* Richard McKeon, for example, originally a member of the Department of Greek and later a member of the Department of Philosophy, worked in the Program on Ideas and Methods as well as in the Program on History of Culture. Crane and McKeon collaborated for several years in teaching a course on the history of literary criticism. Numerous such linkages existed among the other members of this group. Thus the context for the formation of the Chicago School was a crisis in the status and function of the humanistic disciplines and a set of programs to reform and revitalize humanistic education. "The 'Chicago School of criticism,'" observed McKeon decades later, "began and developed in the context of such changes in the programs of the college and the division of humanities."[1]

While the Chicago Critics affirmed "the equal importance of linguistics, philology, the philosophic analysis of ideas, and history," they focused in their group collection not on "the place of criticism among the other humanistic arts but its present internal state," as Crane admitted in his introduction to *Critics and Criticism*.[2] Such an interest was long-standing, dating back to Crane's famous essay, "Literary Scholarship and Contemporary Criticism," published by the National Council of Teachers of English in the *English Journal* (College Edition) during 1934. In this early position paper, Crane debated the question of whether university departments of English should serve as centers for the study of the history *or* of the criticism of literature. According to Crane, the outcome of this decision would effect departmental courses, examinations, dissertations, appointments, and research. He portrayed the internal situation of the discipline of literary studies as in crisis. When later cast in institutional and pedagogical terms, his early conclusions would become significant for the future project of the Chicago School:

> Literary history, I should insist, is a good thing, and it is surely one of our functions to see that its values are safeguarded in the academic world of the future. As a handmaiden to criticism its importance is much less than has sometimes been thought, but one can easily go too far in contemning the real services, humble as they may be and in many respects chiefly negative, which it is capable of offering the interpreter of literary works.[3]

Amidst the battle intensifying throughout the thirties and forties between the older historians of literature and the younger critics of literature, Crane took his stand against the historians and with the critics. Before this time he was associated with "history of ideas" scholarship. Now literary history was a humble handmaiden whose importance was exaggerated and whose contributions were mainly negative. Students and scholars should chiefly study literature itself—not read *about* literature. Crane called for the reform of literary studies and departments of English. Literary criticism, rather than literary history, needed to become the new core of the discipline.

The two major interests of American university literature departments in the 1930s were literary history and literary criticism. Criticism was secondary to history in courses and lectures, in examinations and dissertations, in appointments and promotions, and in research and publication. Generally speaking, literary historians focused on the particulars of biography, the genesis of "types," the social backgrounds of literary periods, the establishment of texts, the details of bibliography and lexicography, and the proper methods of historical inquiry. They paid much attention to historical documents and comparatively little attention to poetic texts. Literary critics for their part were concerned with reasoned discourse about literary works themselves and with scrupulous exegeses of texts as aesthetic productions. At the close of his landmark position paper, Crane proposed two reforms for literary studies aimed at all levels of university education:

The first of these would comprise systematic work in the theory, generally of all the fine arts, and specifically of the art of literature; it would be of great advantage if this work could be organized and conducted, not by particular departments of literature separately, but by the division of humanities as a whole. In order to give it substance . . . it might be desirable to base it definitely on a reading and critical discussion of the principal classics of esthetic theory . . . from the Greeks to our own contemporaries. . . . But the end of theory, for criticism, is application; and so the second of our two groups of studies would consist of exercises in the reading and literary *explication* of literary texts. (23)

Criticism should become the core of literary studies. The two components of the new core consisted of, first, *theory* conceived as the history of aesthetics and poetics and, second, *practice* presented as close reading of individual texts. As reasoned discourse, criticism was theoretical; as analysis, it was exegetical or practical. Linguistics, philology, and literary history were to serve as aids to both critical theory and practice.

When John Crowe Ransom, in his influential "Criticism Inc." (1937), proposed to institutionalize a similar program of reform, he acknowledged the priority and leadership of R. S. Crane. In the event that criticism ultimately supplanted history as the center of literary studies, said Ransom, "the credit would probably belong to Professor Ronald S. Crane, of the University of Chicago, more than to any other man. He is the first of the great professors to have advocated it as a major policy for departments of English."[4] Chicago Critics and New Critics undertook to reform literary studies during the 1930s and 1940s: both groups sought to dislodge history and install criticism at the center. Where their formalist pedagogical missions differed was on the role of *theory*. Generally speaking, New Critics wanted explication to form the core of the discipline, while Chicago Critics placed (the history of) theory before exegetical practice. In his 1934 proposal, Crane insisted "much will be gained, especially in the way of securing a common ground of agreement within the limits of our philosophical approach, if the principles with which we operate are given explicit statement and subjected to rational examination before being used in the criticism of individual works" (13).

In the Preface to an abridged edition of *Critics and Criticism,* newly subtitled *Essays in Method* and published in 1957, Crane registered two complaints against New Criticism. It had routinized a narrow practical criticism and it had impoverished literary theory. Starting with I. A. Richards, theory proceeded "as if none of the essential problems of literature had ever been discussed before or any important light thrown on them in the more than a score of centuries during which literature had been an object of critical attention."[5] As a reformer, Crane wanted an enlargement rather than a restriction of the *theoretical* resources of criticism; he called for emphasis on the *history* of literary theory. Ironically, this call came the same year that Cleanth Brooks and W. K. Wimsatt published their monumental *Literary Criticism: A Short History*. And by then René Wellek had brought out two volumes of his seven-volume *A History of Modern Criticism* (1955– 86). Still, the Chicago Critics differed noticeably from New Critics in their early and continuous commitments to the history of literary theory and to the development of systematic and logical criteria for critical method. Moreover, they emphasized theory much more than practice in their publications. Only two of the twenty essays in their collective volume involved sustained textual exegeses.

NEO-ARISTOTELIAN POETICS

If anything united the six early members of the Chicago School in their fundamental devotion to the history of literary and critical theory, it was their fondness for Aristotle. Not that they ignored other historical figures and other periods, but they borrowed from Aristotle's *Poetics* both a systematic methodology and a set of perennial problems for inquiry. Aristotelianism conditioned both their critical approaches and topics of investigation. What was perhaps most characteristic of the Chicago Critics as Neo-Aristotelians was a certain continuing interest in "formalist" poetics and in genre theory, which they learned from Aristotle's *Poetics* but extended to a wide range of later literary issues and kinds.

According to the "general poetics" of the Chicago School, the poet or craftsman constructed from language and experience aesthetic wholes of various kinds composed of constituent elements. The job of the critic as theorist and practitioner, therefore, was to inquire, as Crane formulated it in his introduction to *Critics and Criticism,* into "the necessary constituent elements, of possible kinds of poetic wholes, leading to an appreciation, in individual works, of how well their writers have accomplished the particular sorts of poetic tasks which the nature of the wholes they have attempted to construct imposed on them" (13). Worthy of special notice here are the conception of literature as a collection of *individual* texts, the insistence on the "constructive" modality of all texts, the emphasis on works as constellations of "elements" and "wholes," the absence of references to language and to rhetorical figures, the notion of different kinds or genres of aesthetic wholes, and the commitment to evaluating the effectiveness of literary compositions. Significantly, literary productions "impose" upon writers certain tasks. Here we see a shifting of "intention" from the writer to the work. Each work manifests an internal intentionality which results from the constraints of genre and which can be determined inductively. "It is the merit of Aristotle," declared Crane, "uniquely among systematic critics, that he grasped the distinctive nature of poetic works as *synola,* or concrete artistic wholes, and made available, though only in outline sketch, hypotheses and analytical devices for defining literally and inductively, and with a maximum degree of differentiation, the multiple causes operative in the construction of poetic wholes of various kinds and the criteria of excellence appropriate to each" (17). The fundamental "formative principle" or "cause" of a work was conceived in generic terms; to interpret a work required differentiating inductively its driving generic "intention" or "cause." In effect, the Aristotelian interpreter must seek to occupy two positions: that of the poet as maker and that of the critic as evaluator. The Chicago formalists were interested primarily in aesthetic principles of construction rather than in verbal meaning.

What was literature for the Chicago School? A collection of individual and unique constructions of different kinds composed of elements wrought into wholes, each possessing a distinctive shaping principle.

Since literature consisted of "kinds," poetics as a field of inquiry and theory tended for Chicago Critics to be "special"—not general. Rather than "poetics," they wanted "poetics of"—of tragedy, of comedy, of epic, of lyric, of the novel, and so on. The "poetic" matters typically investigated by Chicago Critics included the particular elements of a work, the method(s) of artistic organization and presentation, and the principles and causes informing composition. As a discipline, poetics examined unique formal structures of dynamic wholes and parts. Form and content were inextricably linked. Avoiding the perennial form-content problematic, they divided works into four basic components: plot, character, thought, and language. The precise deployment of these constituent elements varied from genre to genre and from work to work.

Unlike the New Critics, the Chicago Critics privileged plot, character, and thought over language, integrating thereby traditional mimetic, affective, and didactic poetics with more modern textual poetics. Life entered art; morality played a role for readers of literature. As Crane put it, "The form or 'power' of a poem is determined primarily by the poet's representation of humanly significant or moving actions, characters or thoughts, to the end of achieving a particular over-all effect, mimetic or didactic . . ." (*CC,* 21).

According to Elder Olson in several key essays on general poetics, the two major branches of literature were mimetic and didactic. The formative principle or fundamental "intention" of a text was *either* to present a human activity in a system of probable, necessary, or effective incidents *or* to propound a doctrine (or attitude toward a doctrine) and provide proof of it (*CC*, 65–68, 588–92). If, for example, we were to read the *Iliad* as didactic or the *Divine Comedy* as mimetic, we would seriously misjudge them and find them wanting; we would have misinterpreted their "primary intention"—their generic "cause." In Olson's view, the aesthetic goal of mimetic literature was to proffer pleasurable beauty and that of didactic literature to produce pleasurable instruction.

As a heuristic device or point of departure for analysis, the simple generic division of all literature into two kinds had some limited uses. But it never caught on, and it amounted to a weak part of Neo-Aristotelian poetics. In one of his discussions, Olson considered supplementing this dyad with a third literary kind: "entertainment" aimed not at beauty or instruction but at raw pleasure. Yet such literature was frivolous and unreal so Olson excluded this "swill" from "high art" (588–89). This moment of crisis in the scheme of classification pointed up a certain lack in the system—which was never quite satisfactory. Perhaps the main trouble with this simplistic discovery was that it threatened to turn into an *a priori* model of all literature, closing off inductive inquiry and maximum differentiation—two cherished goals of Aristotelian methodology.

More useful and significant for Chicago poetics was Richard McKeon's subtler theory of literature based on Aristotle's three domains of language usage: logic, rhetoric, and poetic. In each domain, thought and subject matter received different treatments. Poetics (literature) was distinguished from logic (science) and rhetoric (politics and ethics).

> A poem, thus, may be considered in terms of its own unity, its effect on audiences, or its imitation of actual things. To consider a poem in itself, however, is to consider what Aristotle calls its "proper pleasure," that is, its effect on an audience so constituted and informed that its reactions may be traced to causes proper to the work of art. . . . To consider a poem in itself is likewise to consider it as an organization of incidents, a development of characters, and an expression of thoughts, and all of these are effective as imitations of nature and life; but they are effective not as a literal report of what actually occurs but as an artistic representation which has a life of its own and a probability which does not depend on historical accuracy. (*CC*, 214–15)

According to McKeon, a work could be treated (a) poetically by attending to its unity, (b) rhetorically by considering its reception, and (c) logically (or scientifically) by examining its mimetic accuracy. Properly conceived, however, a work belonged in the domain of poetics—not rhetoric or logic. From the perspective of poetics, the mimetic dimension of literature had to do not with literal, scientific, or historical accuracy, but with autonomous aesthetic probability. Its reception involved less the actual sentiments of an audience than an audience's reflection of intrinsic aesthetic causes. The whole effect of McKeon's theorizing was to formulate a broad formalist poetics, centered on such dominant aesthetic categories as unity, autonomy, organization, and (nonliteral) representation. Though he maintained mimetic and affective powers for literature, McKeon, like other Chicago Critics, emphasized a formalistic poetics of aesthetic wholes and parts distanced from actual readers and from reality.

Ultimately, the poetics of the Chicago School allowed for literature to have connections with life. The material of literature was human existence and literature re-presented this material. All literature instructed, moved, informed, or improved us. In Olson's account, literature influenced personal, social, and political action; it taught us to be wary of blind self-interest and it inculcated moral attributes. "The ethical function of art, therefore, is never in opposition to the purely artistic end; on the contrary, it is best achieved when the artistic end has been best accomplished, for it is only a further consequence of the powers of art" (566). All superior art possessed moral power, as Crane judged it (*CC,* 621–22). While the Neo-Aristotelian poetics of the Chicago School was formalistic in the main, it retained for literature subordinate mimetic, affective, and didactic powers. Moreover, it reserved for all art a generalized ethical force and function—which, strictly speaking, had to do with rhetoric, not poetics.

CRITICAL METHOD

In his program for the reform of literary studies proposed in the mid-thirties, R. S. Crane defined criticism as "reasoned discourse concerning works of imaginative literature the statements in which are primarily statements about the works themselves and appropriate to their character as productions of art" (*IH2,* 11). Two strands of thought emerged here that would later be influential in the formation of the critical project of the Chicago School. First, criticism required examining works formalistically as aesthetic constructions. Extrinsic concerns were ruled out. Second, criticism was a realm of discourse separate from literature and subject to standards and frameworks of formal logic. Criticism was two-sided: practice and theory—exegesis and reasoned discourse.

As a pioneering formalist reformer, Crane excluded from practical criticism all extrinsic approaches.

> The essential thing about the understanding to which the literary critic aspires is that it is understanding of literary works in their character as works of art. It is not criticism but psychology when we treat poems or novels as case books and attempt to discover in them not the art but the personality of their authors. It is not criticism but history or sociology when we read imaginative writings for what they may tell us about the manner or thought or "spirit" of the age which produced them. It is not criticism but ethical culture when we use them primarily as means of enlarging and enriching our experience of life or of inculcating moral ideas. It is not criticism but autobiography when we content ourselves with stating our personal preferences with regard to them. . . . Criticism . . . is simply the disciplined consideration, at once analytical and evaluative, of literary works as works of art. (*IH2*, 12)

The modes of approach dismissed here included biographical, historical, sociological, moral, and impressionistic criticism. Crane had no personal sympathy for Marxism, "Humanism," Impressionism, or Historicism. As a practitioner, he wanted only formalist criticism devoted to immanent analysis and aesthetic evaluation of individual texts. He was interested primarily in the poem itself—not the poet, not the reader's sentiments or enrichment, and not the sociohistorical contexts of the work.

According to Crane, there were two kinds of understanding: historical and critical. He preferred critical understanding, that is, formalist criticism, which attempted to get at the *what* and *how* rather than the *why* of imaginative works. Critical understanding deciphered the denotations, connotations, allusions, figures, ideas, and especially the formative elements and shaping principles of texts. Historical understanding explained the personal, social, political, literary, and cultural circumstances that conditioned the creation and reception of works. As far as Crane was concerned, historicist hermeneutics had so dominated literary studies that change was needed. While the thrust of his early program for reform was to jettison historical criticism in favor of formalist criticism, he yet reserved a subordinate place for historical understanding. In addition, he made a special plea for the usefulness of studying the history of literary theory.

Two decades later Crane took a broader view of critical practice. About the Chicago approach, he said, "The principles of the method, it is true, are the internal causes of poems, viewed as artistic products, in analytical separation from the activities which produced them; but it requires only a relatively easy shift in causal perspective to combine 'poetic' propositions about particular poems with philological, biographical, or historical propositions about their materials and the conditions and circumstances of their making" (*CC,* 22). Extrinsic critical approaches, though still secondary, were acceptable and useful modes of understanding. Such practices were no longer conceived as rivals but as ancillary supplements to formalist criticism.

Five decades after the formation of the Chicago School, Richard McKeon remembered this early formalist group adopting a crucial critical strategy, which had the effect of incorporating other key approaches. "We had agreed to talk about the art object as an independent entity and unity and to examine art objects in their particularity." But along with this founding formalist instant came another more inclusive moment. "We argued that although rhetorical criticism considered the poem in the context of the poet and the poet's audience, dialectical criticism in the context of ideas and the cosmos, and grammatical criticism in the context of elements and things, what the three types of criticism said could be restated in terms of the characteristics of art objects" ("CLA," 17). By using a "strategy of restatement," a formalist critic was able to talk about the poet, the audience, the cosmos, and so on. In other words, "extrinsic concerns" were reconceived and resituated: the text underwent expansion to become an inclusive microworld. This explains how the Chicago Critics could be formalist critics given to discussion not only of purely textual matters, but of mimetic, didactic, and affective dimensions of imaginative works.

As practical critics, the Chicago exegetes distinguished between, in Crane's terms, "interpretation" and "criticism." Programmatically, they were committed to criticism, not interpretation. Interpretation analyzed the diction, grammar, and syntax of any discourse (literary and otherwise) to isolate meanings and implications created by a writer's expressive intentions. Such hermeneutical investigation employed extrinsic methods of inquiry like psychology and history. Unlike interpretation, criticism sought to determine the formative principles or shaping causes of individual poetic wholes. Whereas interpretation analyzed the sentences and senses of discourse, criticism attended to the forms and structures of literary works.[6] In the realm of criticism, "meaning" occupied a space subordinate to "structure." The objective of the Chicago School in practical criticism was to determine the intrinsic rationale of a work's construction. In the end, criticism aimed to apprehend and explain the arrangements, proportions, and interconnections of the parts of a text in order to realize its overall formal structure.

To the Chicago Critics the semantic analyses characteristic of New Criticism, fixated on language—on paradox, irony, ambiguity—seemed a limited grammatical and "rhetorical" mode of interpretation. In the fourth of his lectures in *The Languages of Criticism and the Structure of Poetry*, R. S. Crane parodied New Critical close reading, demonstrating that such interpretation was both reductive and allegorical. Similar attacks on the New Criticism's manner of analysis were mounted in the opening five essays of *Critics and Criticism*. Since the Chicago School dealt with plot, character, and thought as well as language—always in the context of "forming intention"—its criticism examined not simply poetically crafted images, symbols, and figures but artistically-shaped human activities, personalities, and ideas. The Chicago Critics prided themselves on the broadness of their formalist criticism.

As an instrument of analysis and as "reasoned discourse," criticism was subject to certain standards. It needed to be both useful and adequate to its object and many-sided, economical, and comprehensive. To accomplish its tasks, criticism had to be inductive and differential. Anathema to the Chicago Neo-Aristotelians was any deductive—"Platonic"—mode of reasoning, which started with general concepts and then forced facts to fit concepts. Characteristic of the Chicago School was a pragmatic insistence on data and evidence for conclusions. This explains why, for example, the Chicago Critics had no patience for Marxism, Freudianism, Jungianism, or any other "transcendental system." To serve privileged hypotheses was to take an "a priori road." "The marks of a good scholar are many," observed Crane, "but surely one of the most important is what I would call a habitual distrust of the a priori . . ." (*IH2*, 29). What the Chicago Critics desired was to avoid altogether, or at least to reduce to a minimum, the a priori or deductive element in criticism. That is why they fostered "special" rather than "general" poetics and why they treated elements of genre as hypotheses to be tested rather than invariant structures simply to be observed.

Reminiscent of much twentieth-century philosophy with its interest in the formal logic of conceptual systems, the Chicago School undertook analysis or criticism of criticism along similar "scientific lines." This overriding theoretical interest in the logic of methodology (or in the grounds of criticism) distinguished the Chicago criticism from other contemporaneous critical movements. Part of the reform of humanistic study at the University of Chicago involved a separate program in Analysis of Ideas and Methods. And Crane's program for reform of literary studies required a dominant role for *theory* over practice. According to the manifesto of the Chicago School, all literary criticism possessed an underlying conceptual or theoretical framework that delimited its practice:

[C]riticism, as distinct from mere aesthetic perception or appreciation, is reasoned discourse, that is to say, an organization of terms, propositions, and arguments the peculiar character of which, in any instance, depends as much upon factors operative in the construction of the discourse itself as upon the nature of the objects it envisages or the mind and circumstances of its author. The reference of any critic's statement, general or particular, to the things he professes to be talking about is mediated, in the first place, by the special framework of concepts and distinctions which, out of all the others that might be, or have been, thought relevant to the things in question, he has chosen for one reason or another to employ. There can be no intelligible discourse about literature . . . that does not rest upon such a conceptual scheme; and, once chosen, it delimits what the critic can say about any of the questions with which he may be concerned. . . . (*CC*, 6–7)

Critics create the objects of their attention. Critical principles and approaches, whether or not consciously chosen, predetermine subject matter and frame findings. The combination of conceptual scheme and mode of reasoning constituted critical method. Invariably, practical criticism was a consequence of theoretical (methodological) commitments.

Since practical critics could not analyze everything at once, they had to select topics for inquiry. All criticism was thus truncated. This did not mean that what was omitted from study was nonexistent. Given such a state of affairs, it was not surprising that the Chicago Critics concluded, "We must have many critical methods, therefore, besides the 'Aristotelian' . . ." (*CC*, 19). "Pluralism" became the catchword of the Chicago theorists.

THE PLURALIST LINE

One of the salient characteristics of the Chicago Critics was their interest, as critical theorists, in examining the logical bases of variation among critical positions. Many of the studies undertaken by the members of the School investigated the different principles and methods adopted throughout the history of literary theory. The modes of reasoning and the theories of literature adopted by critics accounted, in large part, for the numerous variations in critical principles and methods. The results of inquiries into the grounds of methodology led the Chicago Critics to conclude that "there are and have been many valid critical approaches to literature."[7] As Elder Olson saw it, "pluralism, taking both doctrine and method into account, holds the possibility of a plurality of formulations of truth and of philosophic procedures—in short, of a plurality of valid philosophies" (*CC*, 547). "Pluralism" emerged as *the* philosophical banner of the Chicago School.

As pluralists, the Chicago Critics castigated critical dogmatists, skeptics, and syncretists. Dogmatists believed that the nature of poetry was discoverable and that their critical modes alone accounted for it. All other theorists and critics were wrong. Skeptics held that devotion to any system was vain since critics have never agreed on the essentials of poetry or criticism. All literary theories and analytical instruments were false. Syncretists, confronted with contending theories, insisted on the partial truth and falsity of conflicting theoretical positions, resolving such dilemmas by combining elements from different systems into newly integrated schemes. The pluralist stance advocated granting critics free choice in matters of literary theory and critical approach. However, all conceptual schemes and modes of analysis of whatever types were ultimately subject to judgment based on the possible testable and pragmatic solutions fashioned for problems undertaken by them. The capacities of different systems to conceptualize, understand, and evaluate literature became key indicators for assessing their effectiveness. Thus, "There is a great difference between 'pluralism' and 'relativism,' and also between 'pluralism' and a merely amiable tolerance of half-truths, bad reasonings, and preposterous interpretations" (CC2, v). Because the Chicago pluralists were dedicated to analyzing the limitations and partial views of different systems, they could not be accused of "amiable tolerance" or of "relativism." Put simply, they could and often did judge some theories and methods to be more comprehensive, coherent, and effective—better—than others. Nor were they reluctant to condemn faulty ideas and practices.

Concerning the Aristotelian critical approach specifically, the Chicago pluralists confirmed, "it can hardly be used effectively, as an instrument of practical criticism and literary history, except in conjunction with other methods—linguistic, historical, philosophical, for instance. . . . It would make no sense to think of it as an all-embracing system of critical philosophy . . ." (CC2, iv). Ideally, Neo-Aristotelian formalism was an aid to, not an enemy of, other systems. Here we can detect the broadening force of the fourfold scheme of humanistic studies developed at Chicago during the 1930s. All of the Chicago Critics were engaged for several decades in a joint project of teaching linguistics, theories of methodology, comparative aesthetics, and history of culture. It is unlikely that they would have insisted dogmatically on the truth of Aristotelian formalism to the exclusion of all other poetic and critical systems.

Of the three leading Chicago Critics, McKeon more than Crane or Olson served as the leading exemplar and demonstrator of critical pluralism. We have seen how Crane in the early thirties tended to dogmatism in his program for reform of literary studies. McKeon's most memorable illustration of pluralism at work occurred in his monograph-length "The Philosophic Bases of Art and Criticism," first published in *Modern Philology* (1943–44) and later in both versions of *Critics and Criticism*. Among other things, he laid out "the" six modes of aesthetic analysis developed in Western culture, showing in detail their strengths and weaknesses and their possible interrelations and productive combinations (*CC*, 530–44). While even-handed and learned in his elucidation of the underlying principles involved in methodological oppositions, McKeon yet quietly advocated a supple version of Aristotelian formalism.

In the closing words of his 1952 series of lectures, Crane made a strong plea for pluralism. He insisted that there could be no monopoly on truth and that there should be as many methods as there were critical problems. Of the Aristotelian approach, he observed, "It is a method that necessarily abstracts from history and hence requires to be supplemented . . ." (*LCSP*, 192). While he continued to criticize a whole array of dogmatisms, orthodoxies, and routinizations of all kinds, Crane came to celebrate the multiplicity of critical languages and systems. For him every method possessed, to some degree, both useful conceptual and logical means *and* limiting weaknesses and incapacities. "The best hope for criticism in the future, indeed, lies in the perpetuation of this multiplicity; nothing could be more damaging than the practical success of any effort to define authoritatively the frontiers and problems of our subject or to assign to each of its variant languages a determinate place in a single hierarchy of critical modes. Better far than that the chaos of schools and splinter parties we have with us now!" (*LCSP*, 193).

The pluralism of the Chicago School, influenced perhaps by William James' *A Pluralistic Universe* (1909), evidently resulted from studying the history of literary theory. In "An Outline of Poetic Theory," Elder Olson argued that recognition of methodological differences throughout history "establishes the fact that twenty-five centuries of inquiry have not been spent in vain. On the contrary, the partial systems of criticism correct and supplement one another . . . to form a vast body of poetic knowledge . . ." (*CC*, 552). Contemporary critics were urged to extend knowledge, which was possible by recourse to examining past accomplishments. The Chicago project for the history of theory went hand in hand with the philosophy of critical pluralism. In this regard, Crane was especially critical of René Wellek, the preeminent historian of theory, because he dogmatically assumed the possibility of only one adequate analytical method (*CC*, 6).

The culmination of the doctrines and methods of the Chicago School occurred arguably during the 1960s and 1970s in the works of Wayne C. Booth, who was a graduate student of Crane's in the late 1940s and who returned to Chicago to teach in the early 1960s. The pluralist philosophical line, in particular, came to fruition in Booth's *Critical Understanding: The Powers and Limits of Pluralism* (1979), which was initially developed as four lectures in 1974 for the Christian Gauss Seminars at Princeton University. Among other things, Booth examined the exemplary pluralist projects of Ronald Crane, Kenneth Burke, and M. H. Abrams on his way to designing his own commodious "pluralism of pluralisms."

Booth situated his Chicago-style project in several ways. To begin with, he restricted himself mainly to "metacriticism"—to critcism of criticism. In Chicago terms, he worked chiefly in the realm of "theory," though less in its historical aspects than in its methodological dimensions. (Throughout the 1970s Booth served as Chairman of the Program on Ideas and Methods.) Also, he initiated his enterprise against the backdrop of the situation of literary criticism in the 1970s—portrayed by him as a field of controversy, confusion, debate, rivalry, warfare, and chaos, exacerbated by contending formalisms, reader-response theories, and especially deconstruction. Perhaps inevitably, Booth emerged as something of a peacemaker in *Critical Understanding,* which promoted the values of collegiality and respect for others and called for a community of inquiry and a just commonwealth of critics.

The methodological pluralism Booth sought, unlike freer kinds, refused to renounce belief in critical understanding, in determinable textual meaning, and in the possibility of error. A mode of criticism of whatever type had to adhere to standards of comprehensiveness, coherence, and correspondence. Critical understanding, in Booth's formulation, required one critic to enter the mind of, or to incorporate the thinking of, another critic. The ability to reconstruct accurately and fairly the information, intention, and values imparted by a critic constituted the ground of understanding. "Wherever understanding is maimed, our life is threatened; wherever it is achieved, our life is enhanced."[8] By its very nature, critical understanding, as defined by Booth, fostered justice and vitality within the community of inquirers. Indeed, the quality of an act of understanding could be assessed, in part, in terms of its justice and vitality. What Booth's pluralism ultimately hoped for were ways of living with rather than subduing variety and means of reducing rather than increasing the amount of meaningless critical conflict.

Like the first-generation Chicago Critics, Booth excoriated monists, skeptics, and eclecticists. He too believed his heuristic pluralism to be ultimately more pragmatic than idealistic. In addition, he insisted on formalistic practical criticism while allowing all manner of "extrinsic criticism." The primary obligation of a literary critic or practitioner was to "understand the text," that is, to be able to reconstruct its ideas, motives, and values. The quality of such formalist recovery of a work depended on its own adequacy, accuracy, and validity vis-à-vis the work. For Booth the key to literary understanding was, as with earlier Chicago Critics, "shaping intention" or "formative cause." "It is only when texts are torn free of intentions that they become uninterpretable" (265).

Booth went further than previous Chicago Critics in linking intention to (implied) authors and thereby opening up potential biographical dimensions for critical understanding. In his homemade "law of disparate giftedness," he hypothesized that authors were inherently superior to and more gifted than readers (272–75). As a pragmatic principle guiding exegesis, this law permitted practical criticism to serve effectively its traditional role of handmaiden to great texts and to keep alive the ancient idea of authors as geniuses.

According to Booth, the second obligation of a practicing literary critic, after understanding, was "overstanding" a text. Works "by many authors will enslave us if we succumb to their wishes" (272). Criticism, therefore, needed not only to recover the richness of a work but to repudiate it on occasion. Yet such harsh judgments or "violations" were always supplementary. "Understanding is a first step toward whatever overstanding is to be added to our joint exchange" (256). In several comments, Booth warned us not to overemphasize either activity and not to engage in premature overstanding. Overstanding depended on accurate, adequate, and coherent understanding. After reading a literary text and having "experienced the unique form, I may want to move to some kind of overstanding, judging it by political, moral, psychoanalytical, or metaphysical standards. Pursuing such differences is as essential to the life of criticism as discovering the core of agreements on which they depend . . ." (284).

As a latter-day Chicago pluralist aware of deconstruction and reader-response theory, Booth expanded his formulation of critical reading to include both the broad program of early Chicago formalism (understanding) and a newer, more extreme project of extrinsic criticism (overstanding). Still, amidst political, ethical, psychoanalytic, and philosophical overstandings, he yet maintained the priority of literature's unique form and fundamental core of meaning. In this regard his project of the 1970s shared similarities with that of Murray Krieger's contemporary defense of New Critical formalism examined in chapter 2. Both critics tried vigorously to incorporate deconstruction into their formalist systems.

As a Chicago theoretician and pluralist, Booth affirmed "that every inquirer is inherently limited by his language, that we can see only what our equipment allows us to see" (33). Precisely the constraints of methodological and discursive frameworks created the need for critical understanding and methodological pluralism. The alternatives imagined by Booth included dogmatism, relativism, skepticism, and merciless controversy—all leading to dissolution of shared goals and critical community. The job of the pluralist metacritic was to analyze methodologies by understanding their conceptual systems and lines of approach and by assessing their strengths and weaknesses. To be effective, the latter task might require strong overstanding. The working assumption of the metacritical activity was that methodologies with more or less awareness defined their subjects and principles, pursued specified goals and questions, and employed self-contained modes of reasoning and critical approaches. One way Booth put all this was to affirm at the outset that formulations about literature and about criticism were "essentially contested concepts" and that supreme attempts to set up unified systems or master discourses were antithetical to the very nature of criticism. Pluralism, not monism, could best serve the survival and vitality of critical inquiry. Given an extreme choice, multiplicity and chaos were preferable to monopolistic monism and deadening harmony. Where Booth differed from his Chicago forbears was in his essentially Christian commitment to pluralism. The philosophical stance on pluralism was with Booth a transformation of the theology of the golden rule rather than an outcome of merely secular commitment to the formal logic of conceptual systems.

ON THE MARKS AND INFLUENCE OF THE CHICAGO SCHOOL

When he came in 1982 to write the story of Chicago criticism, Wayne Booth singled out six marks of the School. First, it made special use of history to serve philosophical or methodological purposes. Second, it advocated an inductive, differential mode of reasoning and demanded care with data and conclusions. Third, it conceptualized textual meaning as "shaping intention," seeking to recover this fundamental motive in sympathetic acts of reconstructive understanding. Fourth, it rejected deductive reasoning and transcendental thinking, deploring Plato, Hegel, Marx, and other "dialectical" monists. Fifth, it lodged all propositions in a theory of pluralism. And sixth, it proposed a Neo-Aristotelian formalist poetics.[9] About this last trait Booth was dismissive.

But there were many other distinguishing traits of Chicago criticism. We shall amplify Booth's short list with ten further marks of the Chicago School. Seventh, it conceived critical schools and movements as self-contained systems or languages. Eighth, it repudiated and regularly criticized critical relativism, dogmatism, and skepticism. Ninth, it situated at the center of literary studies criticism rather than literary history. Tenth, it promoted the systematic study of the history of theory as part of criticism in general. Eleventh, it propounded broad-based humanistic study and inquiry despite its own preferences for limited projects. Twelfth, it revived interest in genre theory while renouncing "general poetics." Thirteenth, it insisted on evaluative criticism based on articulated standards. Fourteenth, it usually examined traditional canonical texts and left aside modern and "frivolous" works. Fifteenth, it allowed space for mimetic, didactic, and affective poetics. And sixteenth, it demonstrated the limitations and weaknesses of the dominant formalism of the era—New Criticism.

One complicated part of the story of the Chicago School involved New Criticism. On the one hand, the School's *Critics and Criticism* attacked New Criticism; Crane's *The Languages of Criticism and the Structure of Poetry* parodied New Critical close reading; and Booth continued the critique of this monism in *Critical Understanding*. Indeed, an extensive bill of indictment of the many faults of New Critics, as formulated by the Chicago group, could be produced. On the other hand, the Chicago School was criticized by New Critics, including John Crowe Ransom, Kenneth Burke, W. K. Wimsatt, Yvor Winters, René Wellek, Murray Krieger, and others. Thus a detailed sketch of the errors of Chicago criticism, as unearthed by New Critics, could be drawn. Let us simply sample the representative charges made by Wimsatt against the Chicago School, resisting the temptation to settle or adjudicate this tangled dispute between these divided groups of formalists.

In "The Chicago Critics: The Fallacy of the Neoclassic Species" (1953), published in *The Verbal Icon*, W. K. Wimsatt began by recalling R. S. Crane's early essay seeking reform of literary studies. Wimsatt pointed out that Crane's program was belated and unoriginal, having been preceded by the earlier work on pedagogy of I. A. Richards and by the 1933 presidential address of John Livingston Lowes delivered to the Modern Language Association. Wimsatt then called to mind the attacks on New Criticism by the Chicago Critics—which first appeared in the Kansas City *University Review* during Winter 1942 and in the pages of *Modern Philology* (edited by Crane during the 1940s). The polemical point of this history was that the work of the Chicago School by the 1950s was repetitive. After belittling the Chicago Critics' marginality and repetitiveness, Wimsatt went on to document the "shiftiness of their tactics."[10] He singled out and marked for critique their vacillating position between pluralism and Neo-Aristotelian dogmatism, their alienated view of critical systems as self-contained, incommensurable frameworks, their reductive scheme of literature as either mimetic or didactic, their muddled a priori theories of genre, their bias in favor of dramatic and narrative rather than lyric forms, their latent intentionalism and affectivism, and their stylistic opacity. What especially disturbed and irritated Wimsatt was the poetics of the Chicago School. Specifically, he challenged the theory of literature as *nonverbal* artifact and the associated reductive theories of language, metaphor, and symbol. Against the Chicago group, Wimsatt insisted on a general poetics and a parallel generalized understanding of poetic language. In Wimsatt's view, no one could effectively differentiate poetic language along genre lines, isolating different modes of tragic, comic, satiric, and lyric language. Within the American formalist realm of holistic and organistic poetics, it was the New Critics rather than the Chicago theorists—argued Wimsatt—who were genuine pioneers.

Despite Wimsatt's angry suggestion that the Chicago group had exhausted its enterprise by the early 1950s, the original members and their students produced Chicago-style works well into the 1980s. The marks of the School, declared Booth, persisted for a half century. In his study of the movement, Booth listed as exemplary Chicago Critics not only the six founding fathers, but also ten productive second-generation scholars and eight third-generation intellectuals. Some of the second-generation critics founded the journal *Critical Inquiry* in 1974 at the University of Chicago; this quickly became the most catholic (pluralistic) of the leading journals in the vital area of theory. In its first decade, the journal regularly published the major spokesmen from all the most active contending schools, and it presented special issues on important topics of the day like feminist criticism and theory, the politics of interpretation, theories of metaphor, and so on. Chicago criticism lived on longer than Wimsatt and the other New Critics could have imagined.

Attempting to account not for the Chicago School's longevity, but its lack of wide influence, Grant Webster offered a handful of likely explanations. To begin with, the group produced almost no practical criticism of note—a serious failing in most American critical circles. Also, it was an old man's movement. Crane was born in 1886, McKeon in 1900, and Olson in 1909. Moreover, the Chicago "ethos" was centered in critical history, not literary modernity. Another failing was the prose style of the three leaders—which was uniformly turgid and opaque. When he assessed their contributions, Webster singled out the many fine scholarly works in the history and theory of criticism. Nevertheless, he added on this score another reason for the lack of influence: "the theoretical issues raised by the Aristotelians [had] become obsolete before the death of their defenders."[11] Finally, the project of Neo-Aristotelianism, intricate to the point of scholasticism, had the effect of burying Aristotle for contempory criticism. Similar conclusions were earlier reached by Walter Sutton in his *Modern American Criticism* (1963). He judged that the Chicago Critics' theories of imitation and of genre were inadequate, that their methods were inflexible and unwieldy, and that their formulations on metaphor and language were misguided.[12]

Notwithstanding Webster's and Sutton's assessments, the lack of broad influence of the Chicago School had mainly to do with the effective institutionalization of formalism in American universities around the time of World War II. Writing in 1957, Crane expressed surprise at how successful and rapid was the revolutionary shift from history to criticism within the literary academy. On this occasion he regretted the radicalism of his 1934 program for reform and recommended the partial restitution of history and philological scholarship (*IH2*, 25–44). Between the mid-30s and mid-50s, a widespread and profound change of orientation occurred—along lines first sketched by Crane and Ransom in the thirties. The shift affected university courses, examinations, dissertations, appointments, and publications. As chairman of the Department of English at Chicago from 1935 to 1947 and as editor of *Modern Philology* from 1930 to 1952, Crane played a key role in the "formalist revolution." Despite numerous differences, the formalists—New Critical, Chicago style, and others—formulated fresh objects of inquiry, new objects for exclusion, and innovative activities. In retrospect, the special activity of the close reading or immanent analysis of autonomous artifacts separated from cultural contexts was central to all American formalisms.

While the leading Chicago Critics promoted the general formalist project in their theoretical work, they themselves undertook little close reading. In addition, they did not create anthologies and textbooks to further the formalist program.[13] On these two counts, the New Critics overwhelmingly outperformed the Chicago Critics. As a group, the New Critics produced more practical criticism, more textbooks, and more handbooks of principles. And they did all of this before the Chicago School was able to present its case in its 1952 manifesto. That the New Critics were located in numerous colleges and universities rather than one furthered the spread and dominance of their program for formalism. They influenced more colleagues and students, controlled more journals, had wider access to presses, and produced immensely more publications. Because from the outset the Chicago Critics were committed to theory and to its history, their formalism seemed less forceful, pure, or effective than that of the New Critics. Moreover, the Chicago School's commitment to pluralism—an apparent objectivity instead of zealous advocacy—served to dilute its radicalism and to moderate the movement toward reform. That the discourse and style of the leading Chicago Critics was less crisp and literary or, to turn this around, more scholarly and ponderous than that of New Critics, diminished their allure and linked them to the old ways. Finally, the Chicagoans' devotion to the traditional canon—when compared with the New Critical fervor for modern literature and for reform of the tradition—lessened the relative radicality and attractiveness of their program for renewal.

To reiterate, leading Chicago Critics had little influence, in contrast to the New Critics, because they assembled no widely read textbooks, anthologies, and handbooks; they wrote very little practical criticism and published comparatively little of anything in the competitive thirties and forties; they moderated their appeal and radicalism by commitments to history, theory, pluralism, and scholarly style; they remained at one university and had only one journal and one press as outlets; they preserved with too great respect the traditional canon and traditional Aristotelian poetics; and they missed by a decade or so the timing of their manifesto. Though they contributed to the formalist revolution, their contribution was too minimal and moderate to gain them much impact. Even when interests in theory and in history revived several decades after the heyday of the Chicago School, these critics still exerted little influence: the new history was chiefly cultural, not literary; the new theory was mainly linguistic, psychological, and/or sociological, not historical and logical. In brief, the story of the Chicago School's influence is a matter of "too little, too late" and, perhaps, "too staid, too sensible."

CHAPTER FOUR

The New York Intellectuals

THE FORMATION OF THE SCHOOL

THE LEADING LITERARY critics among the first-generation New York Intellectuals were born around World War I, came into association mainly through the *Partisan Review* in the late 1930s, and maintained a distinctive critical project into the early 1970s. The heyday of the School lasted from the late thirties up to roughly the mid-fifties. The most important figures included (arguably) Richard Chase, Irving Howe, Alfred Kazin, Philip Rahv, and Lionel Trilling. Edmund Wilson, older by more than a decade, served as a model for the School. Other noteworthy writers associated with the Intellectuals were Lionel Abel, William Barrett, F. W. Dupee, the early Leslie Fiedler, Paul Goodman, Clement Greenberg, Elizabeth Hardwick, Sidney Hook, Dwight Macdonald, Mary McCarthy, Steven Marcus, William Phillips, Norman Podhoretz, Richard Poirier, Harold Rosenberg, Isaac Rosenfeld, Meyer Schapiro, Delmore Schwartz, Susan Sontag, Diana Trilling (wife of Lionel Trilling), William Troy, and Robert Warshow. Because many of the New York Intellectuals were Jewish (usually secularized), the group was sometimes characterized by outsiders and insiders alike as a Jewish clique. A large percentage of these critics started out as radical literary journalists—who wrote early on for *Partisan Review, The New Republic,* and *The Nation,* and later for *Commentary, Dissent,* and *The New York Review of Books*—and ended up as respected university professors who continued practicing literary journalism rather than academic scholarship. Their favorite genres were the critical review and the essay; their books typically consisted of collected short pieces. Many of them took to writing memoirs in later years. Early and late, the New York Intellectuals maintained a critical, often distrustful view of both the academy and bourgeois culture.

In his incisive history of these critics, entitled "The New York Intellectuals" (1968), Irving Howe assessed three decades of achievement, isolating for attention a dozen or so distinguishing traits of these writers. They felt a sense of apartness from society; they were radicals and democratic (not revolutionary) socialists opposed to Stalinism and Soviet totalitarian communism; they enjoyed polemics and sought self-consciously to be brilliant; they focused on post-Enlightenment European culture and on post-Romantic American culture; they came late but enthusiastically to avant-garde literary modernism as well as to Marxist theory; in literature they prized complexity, coherence, irony, rationality, ambiguity, seriousness, intelligence, and liberal values; they self-consciously, often programmatically, united cosmopolitan culture and radical politics; they wrote criticism with a strong social-moral emphasis; they took Edmund Wilson's work of the twenties and thirties as a model; they disliked parochial academic scholarship; they assaulted mass culture (following the Frankfurt School); they were Jews by birth or osmosis and often promoted Jewish literature; they aspired to lead the nation but were, in fact, a regional group; they became, in the early postwar or "Cold War" period, liberals, sometimes renouncing socialism; and they strongly opposed postmodernism and the new left.[1]

The New York Intellectuals were, in Howe's assessment, the first "intelligentsia" in American literary history. Unlike the gathering of Transcendentalists around Emerson in Concord, the New York Critics constituted "a circle of writers who think of themselves as deeply cut off from the society in which they live while nevertheless tied to it by bonds of criticism, a circle of writers, drawn from or desiring to attach itself to plebeian segments of society and thereby tending to see culture and politics as all but inseparable."[2] What was revealing in this depiction was the sociological dialectic underlying the intellectual vocation of the New York School. On one hand, these writers came from or aspired to the middle class; on the other hand, they felt separate from and critical of the world of the bourgeoisie. This explains how the New York Intellectuals could affirm democratic socialism, yet condemn mass culture. Not surprisingly, the leading Marxists of this middle-class intelligentsia denounced the mystique of the proletariat promoted by hardline members of the American Communist Party.

As a common project, the New York Intellectuals early sought to further both a socialist order and an elitist modernism. This program was announced in the "Editorial Statement" of the first issue of the revitalized *Partisan Review* in 1937. When he recalled the New York Intellectuals of the 1930s in his *New York Jew* (1978), Alfred Kazin concluded: "The aim was unlimited freedom of speculation, the union of a free radicalism with modernism."[3] The connections between politics and aesthetics, specifically between democratic socialism and literary modernism, formed the essential dialectic of the New York intelligentsia or "family," to use Normon Podhoretz's metaphor from his personal history of the School in *Making It* (1967). The family was deeply involved at once with bourgeois society and with the modernist avant-garde, with a realistic-social-liberal tradition and with an imaginative-literary-conservative tradition, with twentieth-century material culture and with modern poetic imagination.[4] Additionally, these critics, according to Podhoretz's account, were strongly united in their opposition to commercialism, mass culture, *kitsch,* middlebrowism, academicism, populism, American boosterism, and Stalinism.[5]

MARXIST POLITICS AND BEYOND

For many of the New York literary intellectuals, Edmund Wilson served as *the* model from the previous generation of critics and Philip Rahv evidently functioned, in the early years, as *the* embodiment of the values and beliefs of the group.[6] Both Wilson and Rahv expressed commitments to Marxist politics at the opening of the 1930s. Wilson wrote to Allen Tate in May 1930, "I am going further and further to the left all the time."[7] In his "An Appeal to Progressives," published in *The New Republic* of January 14, 1931, Wilson renounced faith in liberalism and progressivism while indicting the "monstrosities" and "meaningless life" of the "antiquated economic system" of American capitalism. He condemned American politicians as ineffective "racketeers" and celebrated the successes of the Soviet Union's "great Communist project." Ultimately, he urged American radicals to work for an American socialism in line with native traditions.[8] In a similar, though more militant, vein, Rahv expressed solidarity with the proletariat and with the project of communism in his "The Literary Class War," published in *New Masses* in August 1932. In this early piece, Rahv deplored the bourgeoisie, liberalism, moderate socialism, and criticism of Soviet Russia, recommending that intellectuals, specifically fellow travelers, "master Marxian theory" and "integrate themselves into the proletariat."[9] Two years later when Rahv and other associates established *Partisan Review,* the goals, as articulated in the initial editorial, were to fight against fascism and war, to defend the Soviet Union, and to advocate proletarian literature. For the New York Intellectuals there was never much doubt in the early days about the necessary and inescapable linkage of literary criticism and leftist politics.

By 1937 both Wilson and Rahv had become critical of Stalinism, of

Soviet communism, of the proletarian program for literature, and of the American Communist Party, including its Popular Front line. But neither man rejected out of hand socialism as such. In "American Critics, Left and Right" (January–February 1937), Wilson complained that "one of the worst drawbacks of being a Stalinist . . . is that you have to defend so many falsehoods" (*SL,* 643). Specifically, he despised the "falsification of history," the "suppression of opinion," the "terror," and the "unscrupulousness" characteristic of Stalinism, concluding, "I cannot see that the United Front is making a bit of difference" (644). Wilson advocated an independent, homegrown socialism free from the horrors of Stalinism and the sectarian struggles of Trotskyism. When the *Partisan Review* resumed publication in 1937, following a year of suspension, it publicly disassociated itself from the factionalism of the Communist Party, from the totalitarian communism of Stalin, and from the proletariat in favor of the intelligentsia. Here in 1937 emerged the roots of the Intellectuals' leftist anti-Stalinism, anti-Sovietism, and anti-communism—which in the later "Cold War" period would mesh with similar liberal and conservative sentiments. This political line, first evident in the Menshevism of *The New Leader* throughout the twenties and thirties, would subsequently show itself not only in the *Partisan Review* circle of the New York Intellectuals, but also in the neoconservatism, neoliberalism, and democratic socialism of numerous postwar critics and groups.

When leftist New York Intellectuals broke away from the communist movement in the mid-thirties and thereafter, they renounced Stalin, the Communist Party, the Soviet Russian model, and totalitarianism, but not Marxism and not the connection of criticism with politics. What was needed in the Soviet Union was reform—reform of the political superstructure rather than renewal of the socialist socioeconomic base. Party monopoly, bureaucracy, and state terror were the problems. Freedom of thought and expression, in their fullness, were essential to democratic socialism. The all too common faulty and narrow identifications in America of the Party with the proletariat, of Stalinism with Marxism, and of Russia with socialism constituted three fundamental errors in early leftist thinking. Accordingly, it was not surprising that an independent Marxism respectful of liberal values and committed to democratic socialist programs emerged from the crisis of the 1930s. In his 1940 essay "Marxism at the End of the Thirties," published as a summary to *To the Finland Station* (1940), Edmund Wilson asked himself "What remains of Marxism?" He answered: "When all this is said, however, something more important remains that is common to all the great Marxists: the desire to get rid of class privilege based on birth and on difference of income; the will to establish a society in which superior development of some is not paid for by the exploitation, that is, by the deliberate degradation of others—a society which will be homogeneous and cooperative as our commercial society is not . . ." (*SL*, 742–43). Wilson, like other Intellectuals, stayed committed to Marxist ideas and values long past the thirties. To cite two other examples, from 1953 up to the present, Irving Howe's magazine *Dissent* continued the tradition of independent socialist thinking initiated in the late 1930s; and Rahv maintained an independent Marxist line in *Partisan Review* until his departure in 1969 and then in his own journal *Modern Occasions* (started in 1970) until his death in 1973.

During the 1940s and afterwards, the New York Intellectuals often disagreed with one another on political matters. Some remained Marxists like Rahv, some became anarchists like Dwight Macdonald, some adopted liberalism like Lionel Trilling, and some later turned to conservatism like Norman Podhoretz. What united these critics politically was anti-Stalinism, anticommunism, and anti-Sovietism—all buttressed by faith in liberal democratic values, particularly freedom of thought and expression. In addition, they all conceived literary criticism within the broad context of politics. Lionel Trilling became representative of this latter-day position.

When he published *The Liberal Imagination* in 1950, a collection of sixteen essays written in the forties (six of which appeared originally in *Partisan Review*), Trilling offered a Preface on the subject of liberalism. Typical of his balanced dualistic approach to things, Trilling both promoted and criticized liberalism, which for him represented the dominant intellectual tendency of our cultural era. A formation of the Enlightenment, liberalism advocated a distinctive, rational set of moral, intellectual, and political beliefs and values: faith in human potential, respect for life, tolerance of differences, importance of individual rights and liberties, necessity for religious and intellectual freedom, limitations on governmental authority, and value of open-mindedness and moderation. Because this cluster of concepts presupposed social existence and political organization, it quietly opposed anarchy and thorough-going individualism as well as state authoritarianism and totalitarianism. In Trilling's view, liberalism in our time needed not only to foster "variousness" and "possibility," but also to respect "complexity" and "difficulty."[10] The weaknesses, mistakes, simplifications, and complacencies of the modern liberal imagination required constant examination and criticism. What vexed Trilling was the dual tendency of liberal ideals to become doctrinaire when codified and narrow when implemented.

Since politics and literature both dealt with sentiments and ideas, there existed for Trilling a natural connection between them. This link formed the basis for a political criticism. What was politics? According to Trilling, politics was "the organization of human life toward some end or other, toward the modification of sentiments, which is to say the quality of human life" (ix). Politics, liberal or otherwise, envisaged life and shaped sentiments. The same tasks were engaged by literature. Given such similarities, Trilling affirmed, as did the other New York Intellectuals, an "inevitable intimate, if not always obvious, connection between literature and politics" (ix).

THE ENTERPRISE OF CULTURAL CRITICISM

For the New York Intellectuals a work of literature was a cultural phenomenon open to analysis from many points of view. Their critical theory advocated numerous approaches to literary texts because culture was multifaceted and dynamic, involving economic and social organization, ethical and moral codes, religious beliefs and critical practices, political structures and systems of valuation, and intellectual interests and artistic traditions. Since the assumptions and conventions maintained by a culture were frequently unconscious and antagonistic, critical inquiry often needed to be not only sociological and aesthetic, but psychoanalytical and dialectical. The cultural criticism characteristic of the New York School was typically labeled by them "social criticism" because the concepts "society" and "culture" were used more or less interchangeably.

When he edited *Literary Criticism: An Introductory Reader* (1970), Lionel Trilling provided a succinct conspectus on cultural criticism. He allowed room in his model of criticism for many critical approaches: formalist aesthetic analysis, genre study, biography, sociology, psychoanalysis, history, moral criticism, stylistics, evaluative criticism, and phenomenology. Culture, in Trilling's definition, denoted "all of society's activities, from the most necessary to the most gratuitous, as these are conceived in their observed, or assumed, integrality."[11] As a manifestation of culture, a literary work could and should be examined from many perspectives.

The tendency of New York Intellectuals to link literature intimately with culture—to fuse them—enabled these critics to practice numerous forms of inquiry, ranging from intellectual biography to "history of ideas," from broad-based genre study to psychoanalysis, without renouncing either careful textual exegesis, evaluative criticism, or sociological analysis. We can adduce as significant examples of such variousness Trilling's *Matthew Arnold* (1939), Chase's *The American Novel and Its Tradition* (1957), Howe's *Politics and the Novel* (1957), and Wilson's *The Wound and the Bow* (1941). This abbreviated list does not take account of the Intellectuals' many journalistic essays, reviews, autobiographies, anthologies, editions, creative works, and memoirs. The range of forms here reflects the broad conception held by the New York writers of criticism as cultural analysis.

In a lengthy introduction to *Modern Literary Criticism: An Anthology* (1958), which contained pieces by thirty-one modern critics of whom eight were New York Intellectuals, Irving Howe argued against all doctrinaire modes of criticism, whether Marxist, Freudian, formalist, or otherwise, urging an eclectic panoply of approaches in the interest of such liberal critical values as "freedom, variety, and spontaneity upon which the literary life depends."[12] What Howe recommended was a criticism open to social and historical dimensions and sensitive to literature's fundamental relationships with human culture. A similar, yet more strenuous argument was pressed by Alfred Kazin in the last of his six dozen pieces in *Contemporaries* (1962)—which he titled "The Function of Criticism Today." Kazin believed that in our time "literature can exercise its classic functions of providing ideas central to social policy and moral behavior."[13] Evident in Kazin and Howe was a tendency, common to all the New York Intellectuals, to extend their social criticism beyond its hermeneutic function to its activist potential. In Kazin's view, the great tradition of criticism was "part of the general criticism of established values which must go on in every age. Its greatest single attribute is its force, its passionate declaration of the true nature of man and what his proper destiny must be" (496). Regardless of ideological persuasion, genuine criticism focused on the future as well as the past, thereby assuming a broad cultural and political significance and potential. Howe and Kazin wished to tap this potential.

The same year as the publication of *The Liberal Imagination*, Richard Chase published his credo, "Art, Nature, Politics," in which he adopted a stance representative of the New York Intellectuals not only in its anti-Stalinism, its secularism, its moral tone, and its polemical flashes, but also in its insistence on promoting a large-scale project of cultural criticism. Chase regarded such criticism as inherently political. As he formulated matters, "the literary critic will find himself inescapably a policical writer. For literature deals with moral action, with sentiment, with manners, with myth. . . . We may even say, speaking very generally, that the subject of literature is the establishment, the disintegration, and the regrouping of a society."[14] While the engagement of literary criticism with society and politics was inescapable, it could be handled more or less effectively. Some of the bad criticism of literature written in the thirties provided Chase a case in point. What was wrong with much of this work was that it had too narrow and doctrinaire a conception of politics and of criticism. With such failures in mind, many literary critics by mid-century had turned away altogether from political criticism. Chase wanted to reverse this escapist tendency: "our task now is to open up the category of political discussion once again. To do this we must shrug off the burden of our religiosity, our escapism, our archaism, our transcendentalizing, and our apathy" (593). All these stood in the way of an effective activist and secular critical practice.

Like Trilling, Chase was an advocate of liberalism. He wanted American politics "to provide a loose but efficient order within the state, to protect the civil rights of every part of the state from every other part, and from the whole, and to ensure the establishment and perpetuation of diversity in institutional life, in custom, and in thought" (589). Realizing that many great writers, particularly modernist ones, were political conservatives rather than liberals or revolutionaries, Chase all the same criticized conservatism for fostering both class privilege and anarchy—which led in extreme situations to totalitarian political formations. Not denying innate human depravity (the basis of conservatism), Chase yet held high expectations for broad liberal freedoms. Like Trilling, his colleague at Columbia University, Chase promoted cultural criticism with a distinctively liberal political slant.

Whether liberal or Marxist, the social criticism of the New York Intellectuals differed sharply from the formalism of the New Critics and the Chicago Critics, whose critical practice deliberately avoided sociopolitical themes and methods. Against such schools, Chase defended the New York writers' social criticism: "There are many other ways of literary criticism, but I do not know of any which so firmly insists that the critic should find his way fully into the real texture of the imagination on the one hand and of man's practical life on the other" (592). The joining of literary imagination and social existence provided by cultural criticism served as the keystone for the critical enterprise of the New York Intellectuals, distinguishing them from competing contemporary schools.

For the New York writers the intimate connection of criticism with culture was possible and essential because literature mirrored social experience and thus bore upon the social totality. This configuration meant too that criticism involved not only sociological, historical, and moral perspectives, but also literary and aesthetic ones. Thus the trouble with proletarian literature, as conceived in the 1930s by Stalinists like Granville Hicks, was precisely that it lacked an "aesthetic principle" and envisaged no frontiers between politics and art (Rahv, *ELP*, 295). That the literary works of the conservatives W. B. Yeats and T. S. Eliot were better than those of the leftists Jack Conroy and Michael Gold was clear to the New York Intellectuals. That is to say, these critics conceived criticism as a form of commentary and of evaluation. So politics, in the narrow sense, occupied ultimately a limited position in the practice of cultural criticism. As the editors of the *Partisan Review* declared in summer 1943: "We could never agree to 'subordinate' art and literature to political interests." Aesthetic criticism had an essential, though also restricted, role to play. Taken together, the uses of sociology, history, ethics, politics, and aesthetics made of the praxis of the New York Intellectuals a distinctive American mode of criticism during the early postwar era. Its nearest contemporary equivalent was the cultural criticism developed by the Frankfurt School and that practiced by the Harvard don F. O. Matthiessen.

The independent Christian socialist F. O. Matthiessen developed a form of cultural criticism—notably in *The Achievement of T. S. Eliot* (1935), *American Renaissance* (1941), and *Henry James: The Major Phase* (1944)— that combined commitments to socialist and religious values, that focused memorably on the history of American ideas, and that practiced close reading in a New Critical manner. What distinguished Matthiessen's project from that of the New York Intellectuals were his formalist mode of analysis, his religious (essentially tragic) perspective, and his continuing political faith in both the Russian Revolution and Soviet socialism. This politics, expressed most clearly in the travel book *From the Heart of Europe* (1948), led to Matthiessen being branded a "Stalinist." Matthiessen's stress on aesthetic criticism, more insistent than that of the New York Critics, surfaced in both his critical works and his theoretical credo "The Responsibilities of the Critic" (1949). Unaffiliated with any school, Matthiessen's impressive work ultimately influenced the development of American Studies more than the direction of literary and critical theory.

When in 1949 the Bollingen Award was given to Ezra Pound for his *Pisan Cantos*, some New York Intellectuals bitterly criticized the decision. Significantly, they did not debate the considerable aesthetic merits of Pound's poetry—which they admitted. Rather, they argued against awarding a prize to a fascist anti-Semite who furthered the causes of Mussolini and Hitler during the war. This incident pitted "pure" formalist aesthetics against the leftist political and liberal moral values informing the cultural criticism of the New York writers. In other words, the Pound affair forced the Intellectuals to decide on the relative "weights" of aesthetics and politics in practical cultural criticism. Three decades later in *A Margin of Hope,* Irving Howe explained the New York Critics' position, relying on the School's stance as articulated at the time by William Barrett, an editor at *Partisan Review:* "We had to agree, uneasily, with William Barrett that 'the category of the esthetic is not the primary one for human life, and that the attitude which holds esthetic considerations to be primary is far from primary itself, but produced by very many historical, social, and moral conditions.' And we had to cultivate, increasingly, a wariness regarding the claims of the formalist aesthetic . . ." (155). With manifest uneasiness, the New York Intellectuals assessed aesthetic claims: such claims were secondary to the primary conditions of history, society, and morality. As a category, culture subsumed aesthetics. Aesthetic analysis was fundamental and necessary, yet ultimately not sufficient, for an enterprise of cultural criticism.

In his "The Historical Interpretation of Literature" (1940), published in the revised edition of *The Triple Thinkers* (1938; rev. ed. 1948), Edmund Wilson offered a suggestive model of cultural criticism. In the opening sentence, Wilson defined what, in fact, he meant by "historical criticism": "the interpretation of literature in its social, economic and political aspects."[15] Derived from Vico, Herder, Hegel, and Taine, specifically *social analysis* conceived society and literary objects as works of man within the context of his geographical, national, and historical conditions—all of which ought to be studied by critics. The legacy of Marx and Engels, *economic analysis* took into account methods of production and influences of social class in the creation of cultural forms and artifacts. As cultural criticism developed from Vico to Marx, observed Wilson, it became "instead of simpler and easier, more difficult and more complex" (248). Primarily a Russian phenomenon, *political analysis* from the time of the czars up to Stalin required of artistic works that they pass certain ideological tests. American critics, stated Wilson, "can very well do without this aspect of the historical criticism of literature" (250). In addition to social and economic inquiry, Wilson's cultural criticism included psychoanalysis and aesthetics. Psychoanalytical investigation studied the attitudes, compulsions, and emotional patterns that recurred in the work of a writer within the context of his community and historical moment. Since neither social, economic, nor psychoanalytical study could assess artistic value, aesthetic analysis was necessary: "We must be able to tell good from bad, the first-rate from the second-rate" (252).

A part of his enterprise of cultural criticism, aesthetic analysis for Wilson grew out of emotional response and reasoned intuition. Emotional reaction was the "critic's divining rod" (253). With a first-rate work "we experienced a deep satisfaction: we have been cured of some ache of disorder, relieved of some oppressive burden of uncomprehended events. This relief that brings the sense of power, and, with the sense of power, joy, is the positive emotion which tells us that we have encountered a first-rate piece of literature" (255). The terms that characterized for Wilson aesthetic emotion fit into two domains: (1) affective terms included joy, satisfaction, relief, resolution, power and (2) cognitive terms combined order, discipline, harmony, symmetry, and comprehension. Wilson did not believe that establishing a set of fixed aesthetic criteria—like unity, universality, originality, suggestiveness, morality, or socialist realism, for example (252)—would insure either high artistic quality or sound critical judgment. A work could meet any or all of these standards and still not be good. "If you identify the essence of good literature with any of these elements or with any combination of them, you simply shift the emotional reaction to the recognition of the element or elements" (252–53). According to Wilson, such "objectivity" offered no escape from the inherent subjectivity involved in the realms of aesthetic creation, analysis, and evaluation.

The early program for cultural analysis propounded by Wilson insisted on the centrality and usefulness of social, economic, psychoanalytical, and aesthetic analyses. Writing in 1940, he had doubts about political analysis insofar as it tended to be prescriptive. (The same can be supposed of moral criticism.) As a democratic socialist, Wilson employed a liberal approach to specifically political analysis. In practice, he mixed reading of texts with biographical and historical examination, often using the complete works of a writer to illuminate his aesthetic evaluations. In the next section of this chapter, we shall examine an especially fine example of Wilson's critical approach when we discuss his reading of the Philoctetes legend published in *The Wound and the Bow.* What Wilson pioneered for the New York Intellectuals was a multifaceted conception of literary criticism based on a commitment to culture as the ground for achieving maximum understanding and appreciation.

Because the New York Critics believed preeminently in the social foundations of life and art, they characteristically assigned to specialized critical approaches like aesthetics, stylistics, and psychoanalysis a limited domain of inquiry within the broad enterprise of cultural criticism. We shall discuss in the next section how they circumscribed the practice of psychoanalytical criticism. In addition, we shall explain the crucial limitations set on the growing power and hegemony of culture over the modern self—a phenomenon most feared by Lionel Trilling, who wished to preserve a sense of man's ultimate separateness and freedom from the awesome reach of cultural forces. It was this element of independence from culture that allowed men to withstand, to assess, and to change society.

PSYCHOANALYTICAL SUPPLEMENT

Most of the leading New York Intellectuals supplemented their cultural criticism with psychoanalysis. Wilson, Rahv, Trilling, Kazin, Chase, and Leslie Fiedler all proclaimed a deep respect for the theories of Freud. In this regard, they differed from doctrinaire Marxists, New Critics, and Chicago Critics. Of course, the New York writers were not the first critics in America to make use of psychoanalysis. As early as 1915 Max Eastman published exegeses of Freudian theories in *Everybody's Magazine*. In 1920 Van Wyck Brooks brought out *The Ordeal of Mark Twain* and in 1926 Joseph Wood Krutch published *Edgar Allan Poe: A Study in Genius*—both works were biographical studies based on psychoanalytical concepts. Ludwig Lewisohn's *Expression in America* (1932) offered a large-scale history of American literature profoundly informed by Freudian learning. The project of Kenneth Burke was indebted to psychoanalysis, as noted in chapter 2.[16] In 1939 Hans Sachs reestablished as the *American Imago* the journal of psychoanalysis that he and Otto Rank had published in Germany. A bit later Frederick J. Hoffman in *Freudianism and the Literary Mind* (1945; rev. ed. 1957) and Simon O. Lesser in *Fiction and the Unconscious* (1957) made important contributions to American psychoanalytical criticism. In short, psychoanalytical criticism was practiced in America more or less continuously from the Jazz Age onward.

In his Introduction to *Modern Literary Criticism: An Anthology*, Irving Howe catalogued a lengthy list of the limitations of psychoanalytical criticism. Admitting its impressive potentials, Howe yet sought to restrict psychoanalytical inquiry to a limited area of literary criticism. This strategy roughly characterized the approach of other New York Intellectuals. In a negative review of Fiedler's *Love and Death in the American Novel* (1960), Howe again toted up the main limits of psychoanalytical criticism: it divorced literature from history; it did not credit socioeconomic factors; it evaded moral problems; and it often subordinated texts to reductive psychological categories.[17]

Writing a positive assessment titled "Freud and the Literary Mind"

(1949), Philip Rahv carefully articulated some essential constraints on psychoanalytical criticism while emphasizing its values and strengths. Ultimately, Rahv cast psychoanalysis as a useful adjunct to understanding certain texts. What he criticized was the tendency to overextend this instrument into a monopolistic method. In Rahv's representative judgment, "the best and most reputable literary criticism contains all sorts of observations drawn from diverse spheres of human interest. Manifestly, the value of psychoanalysis to criticism is simply a matter of its relevance to the particular text under examination. . . . When the Freudian approach is used in isolation from other methods and other approaches it tends to become an end in itself and to displace the art-object. . . ."[18] For Rahv the kind of text relevant to psychoanalytical scrutiny would not be the realistic, rational, or impersonal type rooted in the norms and ideals of society, but rather the kind that is "strongly individualistic and marked by the range and depth of its unconscious reference and meaning" (165–66). Like Howe, Rahv aimed to set limits on psychoanalytical criticism, judging it a useful supplement to a broader project of cultural criticism.

One of the most memorable early works of psychoanalytical criticism in America was Edmund Wilson's *The Wound and the Bow* (1941)—the bulk of which was published previously as separate essays. After discussing the works of Dickens, Kipling, Casanova, Wharton, Hemingway, and Joyce, Wilson turned in his last chapter to the myth of Philoctetes in order to develop a psychoanalytical theory of literary creativity according to which "genius and disease, like strength and mutilation, may be inextricably bound up together."[19] The symbol of the bow and that of the wound represented, respectively, the strength of genius and the mutilation of disease. These interconnected images suggested to Wilson "the conception of superior strength as inseparable from disability" (287).

What was noteworthy about Wilson's study of Philoctetes was its general critical mode. Nowhere did he use psychoanalytical terminology. While he offered a psychological interpretation of the legend, he buttressed his essay with lucid scholarly discussions of relevant details about Greek literary and political history, about later European literary history, about the biography of Sophocles, about the textual bibliography of Sophocles' work, about the sources of myth, about the nature of genre, about the beauty of some of the poet's lines, and about the moral implications of the Philoctetean legend. Along the way, Wilson also presented a reading of Sophocles' oeuvre, aligning Oedipus, Antigone, Electra, and other Sophoclean characters with Philoctetes so as to illustrate in Sophocles the "cool observation of the behavior of psychological disagreements" (290). In comparison with the philosophical Aeschylus and the romantic Euripides, Sophocles was "clinical"; he had "special insight into morbid psychology" (289). At the close of his economical, twenty-five-page study, Wilson offered a lucid social-moral reading: "The victim of a malodorous disease which renders him abhorent to society and periodically degrades him and makes him helpless is also the master of a superhuman art which everybody has to respect and which the normal man finds he needs" (294). The artist as Philocetean figure was here set in society and given an essential community function; his fate implicated the social order: "he shall be cured when he shall have been able to forget his grievance and to devote his divine gifts to the service of his own people" (294). Characteristic of the New York Intellectuals, Wilson employed various critical modes of analysis, including the psychoanalytical, on his way to enacting a broad-based cultural criticism.

Of the leading New York writers, Trilling was the most committed to *Freudian* psychoanalysis. Near the end of his life he observed, "upon my work in criticism, upon my intellectual life in general, the systems of Marx and Freud had, I have never doubted, a decisive influence."[20] But while he was a Marxist for a short period, he remained engaged with psychoanalysis until the end. What Trilling learned from Freud and Marx was, first, to unmask the "settled, institutionalized conception of reality" and, second, to acknowledge "the actuality and intimacy of history, of society, of culture" (236–37). Given such lessons, it was not surprising that Trilling should occupy himself as a critic "not with aesthetic questions, except secondarily, but rather with moral questions, with the questions raised by the experience of quotidian life and by the experience of culture and history" (228). As with Howe, Rahv, and Wilson, Trilling placed psychoanalysis in the context of cultural criticism. He too was mindful of the limitations of Freudianism.

The Liberal Imagination contained two landmark essays on psychoanalysis: "Freud and Literature" (1940; rev. 1947) and "Art and Neurosis" (1945; rev. 1947). The first essay sought a balanced historical assessment of Freud's strengths and weaknesses. Among many qualities, Trilling singled out for praise Freud's realistic, philosophical view of man as "an inextricable tangle of culture and biology," of man as "not simply good," and of compromise as man's "best way of getting through the world" (54). To these values he added Freud's rationalism and appreciation for complexity as well as his understanding of both the modulations of human motive and the crucial role of past experience in human existence. Quite obviously, Trilling found and sympathized with certain *liberal* philosophical qualities in Freud. He criticized, among other things, Freud's narrow epistemology, his identification of art with illusion and pleasurable escape (instead of reality), his view of the artist as neurotic, his conception of reality (as simply given instead of produced), and his idea of artistic meaning (unacceptably forgetful of audience effect). Lastly, Trilling argued, against the simple Freudian view, that "between the unconscious mind and the finished poem there supervene the social intention and the formal control of the conscious mind" (50). Taken together, Trilling's criticisms of Freud revealed his commitment to a theory of literature in which the formally crafted work of art embodies and reflects human experience and social reality to the end of sanely affecting man and his culture.

In "Art and Neurosis," Trilling summoned a battery of arguments against Freud's idea of the artist as neurotic and against Wilson's analogous theory of the wound and the bow. Of interest in this essay were some of Trilling's "incidental" formulations. For example, Trilling laid the blame for the erroneous neurotic theory of art not only on pyschoanalysts and poets, but on the "industrial rationalization and bourgeois philistinism of the nineteenth century" (157). Also, he concluded, extending Freud, that we are all ill and that "most of society is indeed involved in neurosis" (168)—which meant that the artist was not unique in this regard. Special to the artist was not his neurosis but his "successful objectification" of it by virtue of his "shaping it and making it available to others" (174). Here the perception and creativity of the artist, not his illness, received emphasis: the poet "shapes his fantasies, he gives them social form and reference" (169). Throughout these arguments, Trilling stressed again and again the social foundations of neurosis as well as the social functions of art. "A neurotic conflict cannot ever be either meaningless or merely personal; it must be understood as exemplifying cultural forces . . . and no doubt the writer who makes a claim upon our interest is a man who by reason of the energy and significance of the forces in struggle within him provides us with the largest representation of the culture . . ." (173–74). For Trilling, as for the other New York Intellectuals, the fundamental ground of human psychology was social existence. Significantly, however, Trilling "saved" art from the charge of illness by bringing in not only sociology but aesthetics. The ability of the artist to shape material, rather than his purported neurosis, formed the basis of his genius.

Not surprisingly, the role of society or culture risked becoming deterministic in the critical work of the New York Intellectuals. Trilling worried about the possibility of this vulgar causation, particularly in his essay,

"Freud: Within and Beyond Culture" (1955). Starting with the premise that man was a product of culture, Trilling proceeded to problematize and undermine this notion, using Freud as his source. In Trilling's account, Freud was ambivalent about culture: Freud saw man as both formed by culture and set against it; he believed "it was possible to stand beyond the reach of culture."[21] Specifically, the biologism of Freud and his theory of the death instinct—celebrated by Trilling—worked effectively to set limits on cultural omnipotence. Man could withstand or renovate culture: some part of him was apart from culture. For Trilling this was a liberating idea, preserving for the human self a stubborn core "that culture cannot reach and that reserves the right . . . to judge the culture and resist and revise it" (115).

In his Preface to *Beyond Culture* (1965), Trilling insisted on the adversarial force of modern literature, as he had done earlier in the Preface to *The Opposing Self* (1955). Against the growing hegemony of culture, he posed art, observing that a "primary function of art and thought is to liberate the individual from the tyranny of his culture" (xiii). What bothered Trilling in the 1960s about this liberating adversarial role of modern art was its growing institutionalization in the university and the formation around it of a new class estranged from the bourgeoisie. The self-aggrandizement and programmatic preconceptions of this class threatened to erode the liberating power of art and to smother the special independence of the self from culture.

More than the other leading New York Critics, Trilling made of Freud a model to both enrich and refine his cultural criticism. While man and his literature were formed by culture, there yet remained an autonomous element free from the absolutism of culture. Trilling wished to preserve this element against all threats. That he identified it variously with irreducible human physicality, biology, and mortality—with a stubborn, Freudian somatic core of existence—illustrated a certain liberal universalist faith in human life and its inherent corporeal drive for freedom.

Titled "Freud and his Consequences," the seventh chapter of Alfred Kazin's *Contemporaries* criticized vehemently the legacy of Freudianism. While Kazin deeply admired Freud's own heroic search for truth, his originality, his independence, and his literary skill, he detested the latter-day psychoanalytical works of Adler, Fromm, Jung, Rank, and Reich. His thesis was that "apart from Freud, Freudianism loses its general interest and often becomes merely an excuse for wild-goose chases" (*C,* 384). Kazin particularly disliked the degradation of psychoanalysis as found in its contemporary uses for perfecting techniques of market research, for encouraging adaptation to society, for enabling a mechanical psychoanalytical criticism, for licensing solipsistic searches for identity, and for disconnecting consciousness from external reality. Of Freudians, Kazin observed "the world—the surrounding and not always friendly reality of nature, history, society—had disappeared for these writers, and has taken with it everything which has given measure and definition to man's struggles in the world . . ." (369). What Kazin generally deplored was any and all contemporary nihilism and solipsism—the flaccid refusal to engage nature and culture in struggle—which psychoanalysis had aided and abetted.

Of Carl Jung, Kazin was especially critical. Whereas Freud was devoted to reality and truth, Jung was interested in needs and possibilities. Jung was a mere mystic; Freud a scientist. Jung turned psychoanalysis into a substitute religion for a godless age. The Jungian philosophy of life, derived from primordial impulses and attitudes, was useless for orientation in our alien, external world. Of the leading New York Intellectuals, Kazin was most severe in his criticisms of psychoanalysis, particularly of the Jungian variety.

None of the New York writers relied more on psychoanalysis in his cultural criticism than Leslie Fiedler. In the 1959 Preface to his *Love and Death in the American Novel* (the title adapted Freud's Eros and Thanatos), Fiedler stressed the usefulness of many critical approaches and the importance of not sacrificing the "sociological, psychological, historical, anthropological, or generic" critical modes.[22] Specifically, he acknowledged a contempt for formalist criticism, a high regard for Marxist analysis of the *Partisan Review* kind, and a deep indebtedness to Freudian and Jungian psychoanalysis. "Readers familiar with orthodox Freudianism and Jungian revisionism will recognize the sources of much of my basic vocabulary; I cannot imagine myself beginning the kind of investigation I have undertaken without the concepts of the conscious and unconscious, the Oedipus complex, the archetypes, etc. Only my awareness of how syncretically I have yoked together and how cavalierly I have transformed my borrowings prevents my making more specific acknowledgments" (14). Given the intensity and breadth of his commitment to psychoanalysis, it was easy to regard Fiedler as mainly a psychological critic, as most readers did. Add to this his general thesis about the American novel between the 1780s and 1950s and readers got a particularly firm impression of his major interests as chiefly psychoanalytical.

In Fiedler's account, American fiction writers failed to come to terms with adult heterosexual love and became obsessed with death, incest, and homosexuality. Broached initially in the infamous essay "Come Back to the Raft Ag'in, Huck Honey!," first published by *Partisan Review* in 1948 and collected later in *An End to Innocence: Essays on Culture and Politics* (1955), Fiedler's grandiose thesis appalled other New York Intellectuals, especially Kazin and Howe, who judged such archetypal or "myth" criticism to be reductive, ahistorical, and anti-aesthetic.

To preserve the rich realism and poetic quality of literary work, Richard Chase proposed the special study of myth as a substitute for psychoanalysis in his *Quest for Myth* (1949) and *The Democratic Vista* (1958) where he took to task typical contemporary "myth criticism" for avoiding experience, history, and literariness. According to Chase, myth was story—literature— not religion, psychology, philosophy, or magic. However much he accepted unconscious themes and forms, Chase wanted to save the conscious, imaginative elements of literature as well as the social and historical specificities of it. At the close of his *The American Novel and Its Tradition* (1957), he condemned the rigidity and abstractness of much myth criticism, which ignored "the whole reality of time and place and the whole illuminating cultural context."[23] Similar charges were registered earlier by Rahv in his landmark essay, "The Myth and The Powerhouse" (1953).

As a group, the New York Intellectuals expressed disdain for monolithic Freudian, Jungian, and myth criticism. To counter such criticism, they insisted on the important roles of politics, sociology, history, morality, and aesthetics in the job of understanding and evaluating literature. Those New York Critics who did value psychoanalysis allotted it a subordinate place, seeking both to limit its applicability and to escape its errors. While they respected greatly the work of Freud, they reacted very negatively to Jung. Leslie Fiedler's turn to and immersion in Jungianism marked for them his departure from the family.

THE FOCUS ON MODERN LITERATURE

Several months after Philip Rahv's death, Mary McCarthy published on the front page of *The New York Times Book Review* a brief memoir that commenced "for him, literature began with Dostoevsky and stopped with Joyce, Proust and Eliot," then quickly added "he despised most contemporary writing" (*ELP*, vii). Speaking generally, the leading first-generation New York Critics focused on post-Enlightenment literature of Europe and on post-Romantic American literature. In addition, they gravitated toward fiction rather than poetry or drama, and they chiefly admired fiction produced in the great tradition of realism. Opposed to mass culture and advocates of elitist modernism, the New York Intellectuals frequently expressed dismay when the culture of modernism began to be quickly and widely institutionalized in universities from the 1950s onwards. In a listing of two dozen of their favorite authors, there appear only four poets and eight Americans; the rest are European prose writers once considered avant-gardist and now part of the tradition: Bellow, Cummings, Dos Passos, Dostoevsky, Eliot, Faulkner, Freud, Gide, Henry James, Joyce, Kafka, Lawrence, Malamud, Malraux, Thomas Mann, Marx, Nietzsche, Orwell, Proust, Silone, Stendhal, Stevens, Tolstoy, and Yeats. The literature preferred by the New York Intellectuals tended to be not only realistic and modern, but highly complex and serious, mature and difficult.

In their enthusiasm for modernist literature, the New York Critics were about a decade behind Edmund Wilson and R. P. Blackmur, who in the twenties were publishing critical estimates of Eliot, Lawrence, Stevens, Yeats, and others. The American study most memorably and fully scrutinizing modernism during those early days was Wilson's *Axel's Castle* (1931)— a lengthy text that defined the Symbolism of the period 1870–1930 and that examined specifically the works of Yeats, Valéry, Eliot, Proust, Joyce, and Gertrude Stein. Wilson's first critical book, *Axel's Castle* established him as a lucid stylist and an expert exegete of the avant-garde, a learned man and a leader with foresight.

The dedication page of *Axel's Castle* defined ideal literary criticism as "a history of man's ideas and imaginings in the setting of the conditions which have shaped them." This formula depicted with precision Wilson's project in his study of Symbolism. When he reached his closing chapter, "Axel and Rimbaud," Wilson placed the ideas and visions of his writers in the context of the cultural situation obtaining in the Western world leading up to and following World War I. For all his deep admiration of the modernists, Wilson ultimately criticized them for taking the futile paths of "Axel" or of "Rimbaud." The way of Axel, hero of Villiers de l'Isle-Adam's "Axel" (1890), meant turning away from the real world and nourishing inner visions. The way of Rimbaud led to fleeing modern Western society and returning to primitive locales and exotic modes of life. Hopeless and escapist, neurotic and antisocial, the Symbolists, concluded Wilson, could "no longer serve us as guides."[24] As an antidote to the despair of Western society and literature, Wilson in his closing presented "Russia, a country

where a central social-political idealism has been able to use and to inspire
the artist as well as the engineer. The question begins to press us again as to
whether it is possible to make a practical success of human society, and
whether, if we continue to fail, a few masterpieces, however profound or
noble, will be able to make life worth living . . ." (293).

As a cultural critic, Wilson set the phenomenon of aesthetic modernism
within its economic, social, and political contexts, paying particular attention to the industrial revolution, the rise of the bourgeoisie, and the
calamity of World War I. All of these occurrences forced poets to occupy
marginal and maladjusted social positions, especially the War. "But when
the prodigious concerted efforts of the War had ended only in impoverishment and exhaustion for all European peoples concerned, and in a general
feeling of hopelessness about politics, about all attempts to organize men
into social units . . . in the service of some cultural ideal, for the accomplishment of some particular purpose, the Western mind became peculiarly
hospitable to a literature indifferent to action and unconcerned with the
group" (286). Modernism was the production of a demoralized culture.
Thus its indifference and alienation, its aimlessness and despair reflected not
simply the neurasthenic perceptions of a few isolated poets, but the actual
conditions of a culture in crisis.

In Wilson's view, the best hope for literature in the future was if "Naturalism and Symbolism combine to provide us with a vision of human life and
its universe, richer, more subtle, more complex, and more complete than
any man has yet known—indeed, they have already so combined, Symbolism has already rejoined Naturalism, in one great work of literature, 'Ulysses'" (294). Ideal literature would be rich, subtle, complex, and complete in
its imaginative rendering of life and the universe. Joyce's *Ulysses* would serve
as a model for this literature. The linkage of Naturalism and Symbolism—
the two great, though separated, modes of late nineteenth-century and early
twentieth-century literature—constituted Wilson's literary ideal. In his
assessment of Symbolism in *Axel's Castle,* he faulted the movement for its
lack of Naturalism. *Ulysses*—a complex, comprehensive, and subtle novel
tied to reality—served not just Wilson but most of the New York Intellectuals after him as *the* type of great modern literature.

Throughout the 1960s Irving Howe published one retrospective essay
after another concerned with modernism. As revealed in *A World More
Attractive: A View of Modern Literature and Politics* (1963) and *Decline of the
New* (1970), Howe, like Wilson, was ambivalent about modernist literature. He admired its formal perfection and imaginative richness, but de-

spaired especially of its solipsism and nihilism—its "loss of connection with the sources of life" (*DN*, 31). In Howe's account, nihilism, cast as a social disorder, "lies at the center of all that we mean by modernist literature, both as subject and symptom" (33). Joyce emerged for Howe as the greatest of the modernists precisely because he at once confronted the nihilistic nausea and disgust of existence, yet energetically affirmed life; he plumbed the solipsistic depths yet emerged "into the commonplace streets of the city and its ongoing commonplace life" (24). Not only did Joyce overcome solipsism and nihilism (the way of Axel), but he personally resisted the turn to primitivism and authoritarianism (the way of Rimbaud), which attracted so many of the major modernists. Although these ways admittedly sometimes served as the bases for great literary works, they were for Howe ultimately "unacceptable" on moral and political grounds. It "would have been much better for both literature and society if the modernist writers had kept themselves aloof from politics" (17). Whether this politics was of the right as with Pound, Yeats, and Lawrence or of the left as with Gide, Malraux, and Brecht, it took on an unfortunate authoritarian cast. Howe did not, however, finally recommend as an effective solution the monastic retreat of some modernists who renounced faith in the common reader, formed special bohemian cults, gave up ideas of responsibility, and sought salvation in art alone.

Of all the tendencies of modernism, Howe was most critical of Symbolism—the central movement of the modernist revolution.

> Stretched to its theoretic limit, Symbolism proposes to disintegrate the traditional duality between the world and its representation. It finds intolerable the connection between art and the flaws of experience; it finds intolerable the commonly accepted distance between subject and act of representation; it wishes to destroy the very program of representation, either as objective mimesis or subjective outcry. . . . Symbolism proposes to make the poem not merely autonomous but hermetic, and not merely hermetic but sometimes impenetrable. (19)

The Symbolists' breakdown of mimetic and expressive conceptions of literature, not to mention traditional didactic notions, spelled disaster for Howe. Textual poetics in the manner of Mallarmé and other Symbolists was anathema. For Howe the death of representation—of mirroring outer reality and of lightening inner life—was, though madly heroic, finally inadequate, reductive, and beyond sustaining. Pure Symbolism was impossible: "soon the world contaminates the poem and the poem slides back into the world" (20). Howe, like Wilson and the New York Intellectuals generally, demanded "realism" in art. Hermetic and autonomous literature, closed off from the world and from life, was unacceptable.

As the widespread praise of *Ulysses* implied, the literature actually valued by the New York Intellectuals contained both symbolist and realist tendencies, exhibited both solipsism and worldly commitment, explored both nihilistic and life-affirming depths, embodied both profoundly negative and positive elements. The complex dialectical interplay of Symbolism and Naturalism (to use Wilson's terms) formed the basis of the New York Critics' theory of literature. If a work favored heavily one aspect of this polarity—as did "hermetic Symbolism" and proletarian literature—it was subject to severe criticism. Rahv's condemnation of doctrinaire proletarian writings matched in severity Howe's critique of impenetrable Symbolist works (Rahv, *ELP,* 293–304).

In an expansive program for an ideal "realism," Trilling attempted to include not only realism in the ordinary, objective sense of whatever is external and perceptible in the present, but also realism in a subjective, moral sense of whatever could be internally conceived or fantasized in the past and in the future. This latter, inner realm of passions and feelings—of human motives—offered realism supplemental subtleties and depths. For example, so simple a motive as generosity often turned into cruelty. For Trilling, the complex, paradoxical nature of motives required the scrutiny of a realistic moral imagination whose creative exercise promised great "practical, political, and social use" as well as literary value (*LI,* 215). But because fine and righteous moral passions and conceptions could be "even more willful and impervious and impatient than the self-seeking passions" (214), the project for "moral realism" demanded especially refined scrutiny of human motives in order to unmask whatever may be truly engendering even our "best" impulses. What was "moral realism" for Trilling? The "perception of the dangers of the moral life itself" (213). "Perhaps at no other time has the enterprise of moral realism ever been so much needed, for at no other time have so many people committed themselves to moral righteousness. We have books that point out the bad conditions, that praise us for taking progressive attitudes. We have no books that raise questions in our minds not only about conditions but about ourselves, that lead us to define our motives and ask what might be behind our good impulses" (213). When he came to contemplate realism, Trilling desired more than accurate depictions of communal conditions; he wanted subtle accounts of social intentions. This formed the basis of moral realism—a Jamesian theory of literature that never really caught on.

The speculative theory of literature proposed by Trilling added to the mimetic and expressive functions of imaginative works an overt didactic purpose. Literature should teach—for the good of society. Though neither Wilson nor Howe nor Rahv were openly moralistic, they too presumed the cultural importance of literature's didactic powers. Of course, this didactic element was tied in with the broader sociopolitical project of the New York Intellectuals.

In his genre study *Politics and the Novel,* Howe asserted, "The criteria for evaluating a political novel must finally be the same as those for any other novel: how much of our life does it illuminate? How ample a moral vision does it suggest?"[25] The criteria for evaluating all fiction were the traditional mimetic and didactic tests broadly conceived.

(Parenthetically, Howe's model of political fiction more or less repeated the Naturalism-Symbolism dialectic characteristic of the New York Intellectuals. The structure of the political novel set in juxtaposition a dual world of real social conditions and human motives against an ideal world of political goals and ideologies. In a representative political narrative, ideological abstraction "is confronted with the richness and diversity of motive, the purity of ideal with the contamination of action" (23). The underlying dialectic of political fiction, according to Howe, consisted of ideological abstractions, programs, and ideals interacting and conflicting with the flux of experience, the diversity of motives, and the contamination of actions.)

The ideal literature propounded by Wilson, Trilling, and Howe constituted an aesthetic, moral, and sociological formulation. The linkage of mimetic, expressive, and didactic functions of art, in self-conscious opposition to autonomous textual poetics, insured the ethical interaction of literature with life and society. In Kazin's succinct phrasing, literature should "exercise its classic functions of providing ideas central to social policy and moral behavior" (*C,* 505). This ideal possessed importance for aesthetics: texts underwent evaluation in relation to their adherence to the ideal. Necessarily, judgment of a work was at once aesthetic, moral, and social. The ambivalence of the New York Intellectuals toward high modernist literature, especially Symbolism, reflected their negative assessments of its moral and social weaknesses, as the case of Ezra Pound and the Bollingen Award so dramatically demonstrated. Aesthetic perfection was necessary, but not sufficient, for first-rate literary creation.

THEORIES OF AMERICAN LITERATURE

All of the major first-generation New York Intellectuals wrote critical texts on American literature and a number of them made memorable contributions to "American Studies"—a field that emerged from the forties to the sixties. Several of Rahv's essays, Kazin's *On Native Grounds* (1942), and Chase's *The American Novel and Its Tradition* (1957) were especially noteworthy in this regard, as we shall see in a moment. A thorough study of the theories of American literature produced by the New York Critics would have to scrutinize the numerous essays of Wilson, Kazin, Howe, Fiedler, Schwartz, and others, and it would, in particular, have to examine Wilson's *Patriotic Gore* (1962), Kazin's *Contemporaries* (1962) and *Bright Book of Life* (1973), Fiedler's *Love and Death in the American Novel* (1960), and Howe's biography, *Sherwood Anderson* (1951), and his introductory *William Faulkner* (1952). Many more works could be added to this list.

Rahv's oeuvre of forty or so essays focused with roughly equal attention upon politics and culture, Russian and European fiction (especially that of Dostoevsky), and American literature. In his concern with American writing, Rahv also edited five books: *The Great Short Novels of Henry James* (1944), *The Bostonians* (1945), *Discovery of Europe: The Story of American Experience in the Old World* (1947), *Literature in America: An Anthology of Literary Criticism* (1957), and *Eight Great American Short Novels* (1963). Not only did Rahv contribute to the James revival and help to bring aesthetic modernism into American literary Marxism, but he also propounded a particularly well-known theory of American literature in his famous essay "Paleface and Redskin."

According to Rahv, there existed a distinctively American sociohistorical polarity affecting the literary tradition. He characterized this cultural dissociation of sensibility as a separation into two antipodal positions occupied by "palefaces" and "redskins." Palefaces, like James, Melville, Hawthorne, Dickinson, and Eliot, were patrician intellectuals given to solitude and a tragic sense of life derived from puritan religion and characterized by estrangement from reality, deep respect for highbrow traditions, and attraction to disciplined modes of life and allegorical symbolic forms of literature. Paleface culture, associated with the idealism of New England, dominated American intellectual life in the nineteenth century. The last of the palefaces in Rahv's own time were the Neo-Humanists of the 1920s. Redskins, like Whitman, Twain, Dreiser, Steinbeck, and Hemingway, were energetic and boisterous, plebeian mystics, often hostile to ideas and greedy for experience, materialistic and hedonistic, in tune with the environment and the rabble of the frontier and the city, and given to lowbrow forms of literary realism. Redskin culture, scornful of new developments and passive in the face of the *Zeitgeist,* dominated the twentieth century. After documenting the strengths and weaknesses of these antagonistic strands of American tradition, Rahv called for their balance, wholeness, and unification by means of "effort and understanding" (*ELP*, 7).

While Rahv's theory can be considered a variation on and amplification of Van Wyck Brooks' earlier "highbrow-lowbrow" distinction, Eliot's idea of the "dissociation of sensibility," and Wilson's concept of the "Symbolism-Naturalism" dialectic of modernism, it had the virtue of working out in unforgettable detail the theory for specifically American culture of the period between the American Renaissance and the Red Decade. Published in 1939, Rahv's essay pointedly recommended to reigning redskins careful attention to older paleface strengths. Interestingly, Wilson's *Axel's Castle*, published in the early thirties, took an opposite tact, advising modern Symbolists to adopt Naturalism. But both Wilson and Rahv hoped for the ultimate unification of the bifurcated strands of tradition: imagination and reality, consciousness and experience, patrician and plebeian should come together.

The fundamental category of Rahv's literary theory was "experience." In "The Cult of Experience in American Writing" (1940) and in "The Native Bias" (1957), he argued that Whitman and James—the initiates of modernism in American literature—both adopted positive approaches to experience, though they held different views of its content and significance. The widespread "surge toward and immersion in experience," enacted since the Civil War against the backdrop of morbid spirituality, jocose escapism, and abnormal conceptions of dignity, positively transformed and liberated American literature from its enervating subservience to European traditions.[26] The intense relation to experience and the break with Old World traditions, both begun in earnest during the later nineteenth century, served in Rahv's view as the founding instances of authentically modern American literature.

When he published his monumental *On Native Grounds: An Interpretation of Modern American Prose Literature*, Alfred Kazin became the leading Americanist among the New York Intellectuals, which he, along with Richard Chase, remained long past the heyday of the School. His thesis about major American fictionists between the 1880s and 1930s was that they responded primarily to the deformities of industrial capitalism and of science, committed themselves to realistic examination of social life, and experienced profound alienation in their disappointment with the failed hopes for America's early ideals. Significantly, Kazin framed his narrative history with two cultural crises. First, America in the 1880s stood "between one society and another, one moral order and another. . . . It was rooted in the drift to the new world of factories and cities, with their dissolution of old standards and faiths. . . ."[27] Second, "it is clear to me," declared Kazin in the waning years of the Great Depression at the start of World War II, "that we have reached a definite climax in [our] literature, as in so much of our modern liberal culture, and that with a whole civilization in the balance, we may attempt some comprehensive judgment . . ." (x). By setting his history between the "triumph" of Western industrial capitalism and its terrible decline, Kazin was enabled to approach his subject from a thoroughgoing social-moral perspective. American literature was "at bottom only the expression of our modern life," and "it was rooted in nothing less than the transformation of our society . . . rooted in that moving and perhaps inexpressible moral transformation of American life, thought and manners under the impact of industrial capitalism and science . . ." (viii). Like Rahv and Wilson, Kazin situated the history of literature within the broad confines of cultural history chiefly in its economic, sociological, aesthetic, and moral dimensions. Characteristic of the New York Intellectuals, he was deeply concerned with the crises of capitalism and of liberalism. Finally, he too believed that American literature was immersed in reality: "above all it was rooted in the need to learn what the reality of life was in the modern era" (ix).

For Kazin part of the general history of culture was the history of literature and part of literary history was critical history. Conditions in literary and critical domains paralleled those in economic and social realms. Criticism was not autonomous; it was one element of culture. Not surprisingly, Kazin devoted roughly a quarter of his narrative to the history of native criticism as one part of the story of American literature. His theory of American critical history went as follows:

From Emerson and Thoreau to Mencken and Brooks, criticism had been the great American lay philosophy, the intellectual conscience and intellectual carryall. It had been a study of literature inherently concerned with ideals of citizenship, and often less a study of literary texts than a search for some new and imperative moral order within which American writing could live and grow. Never more than incidentally concerned, save for men like Poe and James, with problems of craftsmanship and style, it had always been more a form of moral propaganda than a study in esthetic problems. It had even been the secret intermediary—read and practiced though it was by so few— between literature and society in America. (400–1)

Against the backdrop of this tradition, Kazin deplored the battle waged in the thirties between the Marxists and the formalists. These extremists of the left and right, in promoting doctrinaire sociological criticism and textual aesthetics, forced criticism to become totalitarian in an age of totalitarianism. For Kazin American criticism should be neither political weapon nor scholastic technique, neither propaganda nor anemic academicism. Sociology without aesthetics and aesthetics without sociology courted fanaticism and authoritarianism. The drift of formalists like Pound to fascism and of leftists like Hicks to Stalinism typified the worst dangers of critical extremism. Ultimately, the crisis in criticism during the 1930s was part of a wider crisis in the whole moral order of western civilization: "criticism had become a philosophical front where the great central forces seeking to rebuild the world were locked together in battle" (406).

What Kazin disliked about the warring camps of American critics in the thirties was the intellectual and moral retreat institutionalized in their enterprises. The only hope he saw rested with the New York Intellectuals: "In these writers criticism lived as securely as it had ever lived in America . . ." (447). Edmund Wilson became for him the only modern American critic to merit ungrudging praise. Not ensnared by the fatal either/or of social criticism or aesthetic criticism, Wilson "continued to write criticism as a great human discipline, a study of literature in its relation to civilization that sacrificed nothing to closeness of observation, yet kept its sights trained on the whole human situation" (447). In Kazin's view, the tradition of American criticism remained most alive and dynamic with the New York Intellectuals—not the doctrinaire Marxists or New Critics. It was the dual commitment to reality and to literary craft that distinguished our best critics and our best writers. Also characteristic of them was alienation from capitalist society and commitment to democratic values.

Widely recognized as an important leading Americanist, Richard Chase published six books and edited one casebook all dealing with American literature: *Herman Melville* (1949), *Emily Dickinson* (1951), *Walt Whitman Reconsidered* (1955), *The American Novel and Its Tradition* (1957), *The Democratic Vista* (1958), *Walt Whitman* (1961), and *Melville: A Collection of Critical Essays* (1962). Best known for *The American Novel and Its Tradition,* Chase offered here a theory of American literature similar at certain significant points to Rahv's and Kazin's, yet different in distinctive ways. Studying the American novel from Charles Brockden Brown and James Fenimore Cooper to F. Scott Fitzgerald and William Faulkner, he sought to distinguish American from English fiction by characterizing the great English works as realistic novels and the great American ones as romance-novels.

In Chase's theory, romance as practiced in America was a nineteenth- and twentieth-century adaptation and modification of traditional realism.

Among the many distinguishing traits of romance were its relative freedom from verisimilitude and actuality, its tendency toward melodrama or pastoral idyll, its privileging symbolic action over character development, its concern with universal moral problems rather than with the truth, its marked preference for alienation, contradiction, and disorder instead of harmony, reconciliation, and catharsis, and its treatment of experience as disconnected and uncontrolled, asocial and individual.

Romance is, as we see, a kind of "border" fiction, whether the field of action is in the neutral territory between civilization and the wilderness, as in the adventures of Cooper and Simms, or whether, as in Hawthorne and later romancers, the field of action is conceived not so much as a place as a state of mind—the borderland of the human mind where the actual and imaginary intermingle. Romance does not plant itself, like the novel, solidly in the midst of the actual. Nor when it is memorable, does it escape into the purely imaginary. (19)

In relation to realistic fiction, the romance-novel tended to turn away from reality and social existence toward the mind and the imagination. More abstract than concrete, it occupied a border position. Psychologically, it moved away from consciousness toward the subconscious, expressing "dark and complex truths unavailable to realism" (xi). Formally, it often preferred legend, symbol, or allegory over documentation of lived experience. It was content to explore new territories and anomalies of life rather than to appropriate and civilize such strange places and experiences. In contrast, English realism was "a kind of imperial enterprise, an appropriation of reality with the high purpose of bringing order to disorder" (4).

According to Chase's account, romance emerged out of a culture of contradictions engendered by (1) the geographical and political solitariness of early national American experience; (2) the powerful puritan manichaean melodrama of good and evil; and (3) the dual allegiance of Americans to the intellectual ways of the Old World and the New. Like Rahv and Kazin, Chase cast literature into the broader realm of national culture, which he too found to be bifurcated. Chase's realism and romance paralleled to some extent Rahv's redskin and paleface and Kazin's sociology and aesthetics as well as Wilson's earlier Naturalism and Symbolism. These analogous categories reproduced in distinctive ways the founding polarities of the enterprise of the New York Intellectuals: Marxist politics and modernist aesthetics. The project to combine and balance the two domains repeated itself in unique ways in the theories of American literature proffered by each of the New York Intellectuals.

Because the theory of romance seemed to place the American novel in a purely aesthetic realm, Chase added an appendix to his book where he used the ahistoricism and transcendentalism (the aesthetics) of myth criticism as a foil to emphasize his own commitment to cultural criticism and realistic literature. Of the Myth Critics, he declared, "They ignore the whole reality of time and place and the whole illuminating cultural context. . . . I have been mindful of this in saying that realism is the fundamental distinguishing quality of the novel and in going on to speak of romance as something that in the novel arises from and modifies realism . . ." (245–46). The strategy here aimed to keep romance within the realm of realism, avoiding its hypostatization into a paleface, symbolist aesthetic mode free from culture and historical reality. As a "border" phenomenon, romance was lodged, however unstably, between reality, experience, and society, on one side, and the mind, imagination, and autonomous aesthetic form, on the other. Here we uncover one version of the fundamental dialectic of the New York Intellectuals, which appeared in the theories of American literature propounded by Rahv, Kazin, Chase, and others.

ON THE INSTITUTIONALIZATION OF CRITICISM AND LITERATURE

Starting in the early 1950s, the New York Intellectuals began to express despair at the institutionalization of criticism and literature, a phenomenon linked in their view with the broad formation of mass society in the postwar period. The cooption of the avant-garde in literature, in criticism, and in politics threatened intellectual independence and begat conformism. "By mass society we mean," explained Howe, "a relatively comfortable, half-welfare and half-garrison society in which the population grows passive, indifferent, atomized; . . . in which coherent publics based on definite interests and opinions gradually fall apart; and in which man becomes a consumer, himself mass-produced like the products, diversions, and values that he absorbs" (*DN,* 196). The flattening out and passification of differences, of eccentricities, and of special interests created a cultural situation in which "disagreement, controversy, polemics are felt to be in bad taste" and "direct and first-hand experience seems to evade human beings" (197). Cut off from immediate experience and encouraged not to dissent, mass man was provided comfort, entertainment, education, and welfare in exchange for his independence and power of criticism.

In "American Intellectuals in the Postwar Situation" (1952), Rahv characterized intellectuals as no longer committed to dissidence and revolt, no longer feeling alienated and disinherited. "As their mood has gradually shifted from opposition to acceptance, they have grown unreceptive to extreme ideas, less exacting and 'pure' in ideological commitment, more open to the persuasions of actuality" (*ELP*, 329). The factors that had brought about this change included the exposure of the myths of Stalinist utopia, the comforting accumulation of national masterpieces during the modernist period, the intellectual enervation of Western Europe in the postwar era, the absorption of intellectuals into university and government service, and the increase of material wealth generated by a war-geared economy. In Rahv's judgment, the nation was witnessing the "*embourgeoise-ment* of the American intelligentsia" (330). Accompanying the mood of acceptance of America and of criticism of communism was a "neophilistine tendency," unchecked by the critical spirit, aimed at submerging traditions of dissent. To counteract "the ruthless expansion of mass-culture, the least we can do is to keep apart and refuse it favors" (334). The one option for intellectuals, in Rahv's mind, was the revitalization of an avant-garde to develop its own norms and standards and to resist the incentives to accom-modation.

The most memorable critique of mass culture and its institutionalization of criticism and literature was Howe's "This Age of Conformity" (1954). Decrying the accommodation of intellectuals, Howe formulated a provoca-tive equation: "the relation of the institutional world to the intellectuals is as the relation of middlebrow culture to serious culture, the one battens on the other, absorbs and raids it with increasing frequency and skill, subsidizes and encourages it enough to make further raids possible."[28] As popular culture fed off high culture, so institutions absorbed intellectuals. What was lost was the traditional humanist idea and vocation of critical indepen-dence—the willingness to be "committed yet dispassionate, ready to stand alone, curious, eager, skeptical" (33). Like Rahv, Howe believed that only a reconstituted, activist avant-garde could reverse the dreadful trend toward conformism. This vanguard had to accept alienation, which, after all, was the source of the best literature, criticism, and speculative thought pro-duced in the modern period. Also it had to beware of liberalism, which "contributes heavily to our intellectual conformity" (17).

Howe was especially concerned about the conformism fostered by the success of New Criticism. In addition, he criticized the Ph.D. system and all literary education. "What we have today in the literary world is a gradual bureaucratization of opinion and taste . . ." (26–27). In this age of confor-mity, "Literature itself becomes a raw material which critics work up into schemes of structures and symbol; to suppose that it is concerned with anything so *gauche* as human experience or obsolete as human beings . . . is to commit heresies" (27). As an industry more interested in poetic structure than human experience, criticism had become a mechanics complete with tools, trade secrets, and methods.

According to Delmore Schwartz's reading of events, mass culture, education, and New Criticism were all part of the same general massification of society. The "New Criticism naturally tends to attach literature to the university, so only a critical nonconformist intelligentsia, inside and outside the university, can right the balance. . . ."[29] Agreeing with Rahv and Howe, Schwartz called for a revitalized intellectual vanguard—with the added possibility that some of its members might reside inside the university.

In the revised edition of *Contemporaries* (1982), Alfred Kazin saw fit to add an introductory reflection on criticism since the Depression: he recalled that in the late 1930s "Criticism was still a matter of individual knowledge and taste, not a way of introducing students to literature. . . ."[30] Regretting the triumph of mechanical New Criticism, Kazin particularly resented its faulty professional identification of criticism with pedagogy. That the university had coopted criticism, monopolized literary study, and diminished independent literary journalism was both evident and depressing to the New York Intellectuals by the early 1950s. To be sure, the antiacademic ethos and the dislike of professional scholarship (in favor of independent journalism) dated back to the founding days of the School. In 1939 Edmund Wilson wrote from the University of Chicago to Allen Tate, "I'm a little dismayed—though perhaps unnecessarily—at seeing how many of the literati are taking to teaching as what *Partisan Review* calls a 'crutch'" (*Letters*, 321). While most of the Intellectuals would come in the 1950s to depend heavily on this crutch—with notable exceptions like Wilson—they continued to distinguish the functions of criticism and pedagogy and to prefer high journalism to academic scholarship. "Criticism should never be so professional," insisted Kazin in 1962, "that only professionals can read it. . . . I have been staggered lately by the absolutely worthless essays in so many recent academic journals devoted to modern literature and criticism" (*C*, 502). Throughout the whole tradition of modern letters, Kazin noted, the most powerful criticism originated in weekly reviews and magazines. His own *On Native Grounds* was written in a journalistic mode without footnotes or bibliography. The same nonprofessional style of criticism was favored by almost all of the New York Intellectuals. Increasingly, this meant that they exerted little influence among university critics.

The institutionalization of specifically modernist literature was a special source of deep ambivalence for the New York Critics. That the rebels of the interwar years—Eliot, Joyce, Pound, and so on—had become a cult in the universities particularly disturbed Lionel Trilling. For him this phenomenon was part of the larger institutionalization of adversary, vanguard culture, which was sadly formed into a distinctive class lodged mainly in the university world. As Trilling stated explicitly in the addendum to his Preface to the 1968 version of *Beyond Culture*, "I regard with misgivings the growing affinity between the university and the arts. Further, my uneasiness over the situation arises from my concern for the integrity and right influence of the arts" (xviii–xix). That the university speeded up the process of turning radical and subversive works into "classics" and that this legitimation or socialization of the subversive seemed almost effortless created a situation in which the difficult personal encounter with a work characteristic of earlier culture was disappearing in a peculiar process of massification. In "On the Teaching of Modern Literature," first published with a different title in *Partisan Review* in 1961, Trilling mused ironically: "We have to ask ourselves whether in our day too much does not come within the purview of the academy. More and more, as the universities liberalize themselves, and turn their beneficent imperialistic gaze upon what is called Life Itself, the feeling grows among our educated classes that little can be experienced unless it is validated by some established academic discipline, with the result that experience loses much of its personal immediacy for us and becomes part of an accredited societal activity" (*BC*, 10). The pedagogization of experience, of Life Itself, appeared limitless; it disciplined more and more of reality, making all things public with an "imperialistic gaze" that left little, if anything, uninspected. The realm of the personal and the private was shrinking, perhaps disappearing. Vanguardism and nonconformity, like everything else, were institutionalized almost in an instant. For Trilling these were the bad fruits of "beneficent" liberalism, which he had warned against in the 1940s and which fed in the 1960s a growing dismay and conservative mood among the New York Critics. In his memoir, *The Intellectual Follies* (1984), Lionel Abel surprisingly lamented that "the universities have abandoned a good deal of the life which used to lie outside them, and this, I believe, to the disadvantage of life and of learning too."[31]

Whereas the New Critics and Chicago Critics earlier had given themselves more or less enthusiastically to designing effective pedagogical instruments, the New York Intellectuals were less enthusiastic on several counts. To begin with, they regarded the life of the independent literary journalist as a model for the critic. That is to say, they were suspicious, if not scornful, of the academy and the professional scholar. Also they resisted the reduction of criticism to explication and classroom exegesis. Because criticism was a cultural activity aimed at a broad audience, it could not, and should not, be limited to university lecture halls and professional journals. Moreover, the New York Critics disdained mass culture and processes of massification: the pedagogical imperative partook uncritically of such dreadful "realities." (Disdain notwithstanding, many of the Intellectuals served as anthologists and editors of books designed for university and "mass" markets.) Finally, they distrusted pedagogy precisely because it served to socialize—to discipline—the vanguard culture they loved. Trilling stated their feelings succinctly when he said "pedagogy is a depressing subject to all persons of sensibility" (*BC*, 3).

Given the postwar massification of education, the socialization of adversary modernist art, the widespread reduction of criticism to professionalized pedagogical explication, and the cooption of vanguard intellectuals by the university, it was not surprising to hear Trilling and other New York writers expressing dismay at the growing trivialization of art and private experience. Nor was it surprising that they felt grim about any usefulness or efficacy of literary education. Because contemporary criticism and teaching taught intelligent passivity before the most aggressive modern texts, they failed to develop and refine critical intelligence and independence; in fact, they fostered conformity, professionalism, and passivity, not independent critical thinking. For the New York Intellectuals the usefulness of literary education in the postwar period was increasingly in doubt and its value was more and more uncertain.

While roughly half of the leading New York Critics had been associated with universities from the outset of their careers, they and most of the others came to occupy positions of academic prominence during the period from the early 1950s to the early 1960s. When in 1963 the *Partisan Review* left New York to set up at Rutgers University (where William Phillips accepted a professorship) and when six years earlier Philip Rahv had journeyed to New England to take a professorship at Brandeis University (where Howe had moved in 1953), the School can be said to have experienced the *embourgeoisement* and cooption that it had earlier decried. "The New York literary life had crumbled into success," said Howe of this period (*A Margin of Hope*, 289). Perhaps the New York Intellectuals constituted at this point a noncomformist intelligentsia within the university, which Delmore Schwartz had called for in the early 1950s. A less charitable view of these events would have it that the New York Critics "sold out." What this transformation of the School signified was, among other things, both the end of independent literary journalism as a powerful force in American criticism and the beginning of a new age in which the university became *the* home of literary criticism as well as creative writing. Despite the institutionalization of the New York Critics and the deaths by the early 1970s of Wilson, Rahv, Trilling, Chase, and Schwartz, nevertheless Kazin, Howe, and others managed to keep alive into the 1980s the ideas and interests, the methods and perspectives—the distinctive style—of the New York Intellectuals. In addition, many younger followers carried on the New York critical tradition in the pages of the remaining "literary" magazines.

Among the weaknesses and failures of the New York Critics were a comparatively narrow conceptualization of language, a limited appreciation of poetry, and a serious disregard for the intricacies of literary style. In these matters, the cultural criticism of Erich Auerbach and F. O. Matthiessen, also published in the forties and fifties, was considerably more sophisticated. That the New York Intellectuals could not appreciate postmodern literature—especially detested were the works of Norman Mailer and the Beats—pointed up the rather constricted range of their literary sympathies. Similarly, their contempt for the new left cut them off from the new generation of radicals and socialists, severely restricting their influence. Although they were among the earliest American literary intellectuals to be sensitive to European existentialism, they made little of this new philosophy, leaving it to other critics like the phenomenologists, existentialists, and hermeneuticists to further the fruitful lines of investigation opened by contemporary Continental thought. Among the New York Intellectuals were some superior women critics—Elizabeth Hardwick, Mary McCarthy, Diana Trilling, and later Susan Sontag—making this School the first "integrated" one in the contemporary era. Still, these women did not make sustained contributions to specifically feminist criticism, missing the opportunity to pioneer a new mode of inquiry. Ironically, the broad scope of the enterprise of cultural criticism meant that the project of the New York Intellectuals successfully resisted the effective codification essential for institutionalization. It was left, therefore, to the New Critics to triumph, however dubiously, in the universities and thereby to assure their long-term influence and survival. The alienation and bohemianism of the New York School—the source of its strength—ultimately became the weakness that kept it from spreading its ideas beyond a narrow circle. Successfully resisting institutionalization, the New York Intellectuals offered themselves to younger generations as a disparate fringe group of cranks and antiquated radicals.

CHAPTER FIVE

Myth Criticism

PERSPECTIVES ON MYTH IN THE MODERN ERA

ALTHOUGH MYTH criticism was undertaken in America from the 1930s through the 1980s, the heyday of the movement lasted from the late 1940s to the middle 1960s. During this pioneering period of activity the main figures included Richard Chase, Francis Fergusson, Leslie Fiedler, Daniel Hoffman, Stanley Edgar Hyman, Constance Rourke, and Philip Wheelwright. Among numerous others associated with the rise of myth criticism were Kenneth Burke, Joseph Campbell, and William Troy as well as the British critic Maud Bodkin and the Canadian scholar Northrop Frye—the latter being the leading Anglo-Saxon literary personage in the movement. Like the major Marxists, New Critics, Chicago Critics, and New York Intellectuals, most of the prominent Myth Critics were born during the first two decades of the century or earlier. (The critics to be discussed in subsequent chapters are from later generations.) Because the Myth Critics as a group did not share key journals or magazines, extensive networks of long-standing friendships, or specific institutional or geographical locations, they constituted less a school than a "movement." (Burke, Fergusson, Hyman, and Troy, however, were associated with Bennington College.) What united these literary critics was a certain way of thinking about literature and criticism more or less dependent on theories of myth often derived from European anthropology, philosophy, sociology, and/or folklore studies.

The success and popularity during the immediate postwar period in America of myth criticism can be attributed partially to the narrowness of the reigning formalism and historical scholarship, the impressive growth and attractiveness of early twentieth-century anthropology and psychology, and the dreadful spiritual state of modern man and civilization portrayed so memorably by contemporaneous existential philosophy and literature. More or less self-consciously, Myth Critics reacted against the aridities of formalism and antiquarianism and against the emptiness and absurdities of a godless scientific world; they responded favorably to the newly uncovered anthropological truths concerning the fullness and wonder of man's universal communal creation of sacred rituals, folktales, and myths. Characteristic of the Myth Critics were a distrust of technology, a yearning for spiritual significance, an implicit commitment to the idea of community, and an abiding interest in primordial human consciousness.

The memorable indictment of modern life provided by Friedrich Nietzsche in *The Birth of Tragedy* (1872) can serve as a representative tableau for understanding the deracinated world to which myth criticism was a positive response. According to Nietzsche, society had lost its essential foundations in myth with devastating consequences:

Let us consider abstract man stripped of myth, abstract education, abstract mores, abstract law, abstract government; the random vagaries of the artistic imagination unchanneled by any native myth; a culture without fixed and consecrated place of origin, condemned to exhaust all possibilities and feed miserably and parasitically on every culture under the sun. Here we have our present age. . . . Man today, stripped of myth, stands famished among all his pasts and must dig frantically for roots. . . .[1]

Without myth man had become abstract—homeless, godless, frantic. Giambattista Vico had foreseen this situation in the early eighteenth century. All of culture from art to law to government to education experienced terrible deracination. Significantly, it was science that "destroyed myth and, by the same token, displaced poetry from its native soil and rendered it homeless" (105). The grim condition of modern culture—its sickness— seemed to call for a rebirth of myth: "every culture that has lost myth has lost, by the same token, its natural, healthy creativity" (136).

When, a half century after Nietzsche, T. S. Eliot and James Joyce came to grips with the immense futility of the modern world, they relied heavily on myth: *The Waste Land* and *Ulysses* employed mythical methods deeply indebted to anthropology. Yeats pioneered this strategy. Many modernists used it. The turn to primitive or mythic consciousness—to "blood consciousness" as opposed to abstract "mental consciousness" in D. H. Lawrence's terms—characterized the course of much of the finest of the arts and social sciences from the late nineteenth century onward, forming an essential background for the rise of myth criticism. Such interest in primitivism had its roots in Romanticism. Upon Sir James Frazer and other anthropologists, upon Ernst Cassirer and other philosophers, and upon Carl Jung and other psychoanalysts, the Myth Critics depended most heavily for their knowledge and understanding of myth. Numerous social scientific studies of myth—produced in the earlier part of the century—laid behind the essential perspectives on myth later employed by literary scholars in America and elsewhere.

In the work of the Cambridge anthropologists—particularly in Frazer's *The Golden Bough* (1890; enlarged eds. 1900, 1911–15)—readers learned that ritual actions, gestures, and dances were the sources of primitive myth. The origin of rituals was magic: ancient peoples performed rituals to harness various powers for pragmatic social purposes. Through magic, ritual, and myth, early man established vital connections with transrational and numinous spiritual forces. Communal by nature, these primordial forms, accompanied by awe and wonder, made use of dramatic modes for social ends—which over time lost contact with their origins. "As the ancient rites die out in literal practice," according to Stanley Edgar Hyman who followed the Cambridge line, "their misunderstood and transformed record passes into myth and symbol, and that is the form in which they survive and color history, without being themselves the events of history."[2] Originally neither records of historical events nor persons, but more explanations of actual phenomena, myths were stories that sanctioned rites. Later they came to be misread sometimes as historical and sometimes as protoscientific documents.

Depending on the individual literary critic, myth was, alternately or in some combination, perceived as primarily magical, ritualistic, historical, narrative, cognitive, or functional. Critics following the Cambridge line (like Hyman) favored a ritualistic perspective on myth. The narrative view was promoted most insistently by Richard Chase, who believed man's poetry-making abilities produced myths (rather than the reverse) and who especially deplored any cognitive conception of myth. To his narrative formulation, Chase added a magical dimension: myths suffused "the natural with preternatural force toward certain ends, by capturing the impersonal forces of the world and directing them toward the fulfillment of certain emotional needs."[3] By expanding on Cassirer's findings, Philip Wheelwright fostered a perspective on myth that combined ritual, narration, and cognition while ruling out magic by dissociating it from ritual. The idea of the fundamental cognitive dimension of myth, derived from Cassirer's work of the 1920s, postulated that myth was a way of apprehending and envisioning the world. As a symbolic form like language and art, myth was an independent mode of conceptualizing reality.[4]

The connection between myth and consciousness was most usefully formulated for literary critics not by anthropologists or philosophers, but by psychoanalysts, particularly Carl Jung, whose influence upon Myth Critics was profound and pervasive from the 1930s onwards. Positing a collective unconscious below the threshold of a personal unconscious, Jung offered for consideration studies of universal collective images, themes, symbols, characters, and plots, which could be found in the most ancient and the most modern human works, ranging from carvings and sacred rites to dreams and fantasies, from paintings and dances to myths and poems. Such timeless materials from the depths of the psyche, recurrent in all human cultures and aesthetic forms, were stored in man's collective unconscious—the rich repository of ancient imaginings and wisdom. The Jungian psychological perspective on myth was essentially an ahistorical formulation that conceived myths to be, like daydreams, perennial messages from the unconscious revealing perdurable human needs, desires, and problems within the broad context of phases of psychic growth and maturation. Jungian psychoanalysis provided for cognitive, narrative, and cathartic functions of myth while allowing for spiritual interpretations of mythic creations.

From the days of Johann Gottfried von Herder onwards the study of "folk" focused on aspects of culture transmitted orally, which often involved customs, beliefs, rituals, crafts, costumes, foods, and verbal expressions such as riddles, proverbs, miracles, sagas, fairy tales, and legends. In the influential modern sociological perspective on folk narratives developed during the 1920s by Bronislaw Malinowski in his field-based studies of the Trobriand Islanders, three kinds of oral story were distinguishable among the Islanders: legends, folktales, and sacred myths. Legends were stories of the past in no prescribed format believed to be true and thought to possess historical (rather than spiritual) value; folktales had no relation to truth, being told dramatically by a specific person or group for entertainment; sacred myths embodied ancient social, moral, and spiritual values sanctioning current beliefs and actions.[5] What Malinowski's sociological perspective demonstrated for Myth Critics was a functional view of myth requiring differentiation not only of teller from tale and tale from audience, but also of the specific social functions of narrative from universal aesthetic effects.

American Myth Critics never came to any consensus on the relation of folk literature to myth: some believed folk forms preceded myths and others thought they followed them in the processes of formation and transmission. Nevertheless, several critics did employ folklore studies to good effect, especially Constance Rourke and Daniel Hoffman. Using native folk materials in his investigations of American literature, Hoffman was enabled to resist the marked tendency of myth criticism to universalize; he self-consciously aimed to limit his analyses to specifically native culture. What concerned him was *American* ritual, folktale, and myth. If a "universal" myth entered American culture, it underwent processes of revision at the behest of powerful preexisting folk traditions. In general, the perspective on myth provided by folklore studies emphasized the cultural and historical specificity as well as the primary indigenous and popular, communal character of all mythic materials. Accordingly, advocates of the folkloristic perspective typically detested and argued against the apparent leveling conceptions of ritual and myth promoted by Cambridge anthropology and Jungian psychoanalysis, favoring the views offered by contemporary sociologists and social anthropologists.

No matter what perspective on myth a particular modern intellectual adopted, a certain dialectic uniformly operated in the whole field of myth studies. On one hand, myth was opposed to ordinary knowledge and fact, to simple empiricism and positivism, and to reason, logic, and consciousness; on the other hand, it was closely linked with mystery and otherness, with magic and dreams, with the imagination and the unconscious, with the primitive mind and the folk, and with the intuitive and the pre- or translogical. The whole world of values, ideas, and beliefs attached to *mythos* was in open conflict with those connected to *logos*. The opposition of myths and science, prophetically dramatized by Nietzsche in *The Birth of Tragedy*, repeated itself in later myth criticism, structuring its domain of inquiry and its panoply of perspectives. Against the abstract, deracinated knowledge and reality produced by modern science, myth criticism offered higher truths and communal forms of life, ancient wisdom and meaningful sources for man in an indifferent, if not hostile, world.

In 1966 John B. Vickery compiled a casebook of three dozen previously published essays by the leading theorists of myth criticism. He prefaced this consolidation of the movement with a belated charter for myth criticism:

But to state briefly and precisely what myth criticism has to say is difficult, for it has more than its share of antagonistic sub-groups, internecine rivalries, and just plain mavericks. Nevertheless, most myth critics would probably subscribe to the following as general principles. First, the creating of myths . . . is inherent in the thinking process and answers a basic human need. Second, myth forms the matrix out of which literature emerges both historically and psychologically. As a result, literary plots, characters, themes, and images are basically complications and displacements of similar elements in myths and folktales. . . . Third, not only can myth stimulate the creative artist, but it also provides concepts and patterns which the critic can use to interpret specific works of literature. . . . Fourth and last, the ability of literature to move us profoundly is due to its mythic quality, to its possession of *mana*, the *numinous*. . . . The real function of literature in human affairs is to continue myth's ancient and basic endeavor to create a meaningful place for man in a world oblivious to his presence.[6]

This justification and codification of myth criticism sketched not only a philosophy of criticism committed to investigating enduring human needs and responses, but a model of literature derived from myths and folktales as well as a theory of literary hermeneutics based on prior interpretations of aspects of myth. Although Vickery hedged a bit by noting the internal struggles and disagreements within the domain of myth criticism, he envisaged a unified movement despite contending anthropological, philosophical, psychoanalytical, sociological, and folkloristic perspectives.

VARIETIES OF MYTHOPOETICS

The grounds for fashioning a theory of literature based on the nature of magic, ritual, folktale, and myth ultimately depended on a set of perceived relations between such "myths" and literature. Formally, myth and literature shared features of plot, character, theme, and image. Psychologically, literature derived from ritual and myth—man's original modes of responding to reality. Thematically, literature, like myth, concerned itself with certain perennial topics: the genesis of the world and people, the foundations of society and law, and the nature of the gods and demons. Historically, myth frequently served as a source, influence, or model for literature. Culturally, myth and literature functioned as essential narratives imparting knowledge and wisdom while reinforcing social and spiritual beliefs (*IL*, 67–73). With some or all of these connections in mind, an individual critic constructed a theory of literature dependent primarily on myth. Let us sample some representative "mythopoetics," paying particular attention to the significant formulations of Carl Jung, Maud Bodkin, Leslie Fiedler, and Philip Wheelwright.

Because Carl Jung influenced all Myth Critics, it will be useful to survey at the outset his key ideas about literature, which are expressed dramatically in his early essay, "On the Relation of Analytical Psychology to Poetry" (1922). Following Schiller, Jung distinguished between an inferior mode of literature, characterized by the author's successful assertion of his conscious intentions and aims against the unconscious demands of his work, and a superior mode characterized by the poet's subordination to the requirements of his art object. That the strength of the creative impulse arising from the unconscious in a superior work of literature dominated the poet was axiomatic for Jung. It was primarily the potent artwork out of the collective unconscious that interested Jung. "I am assuming that the work we propose to analyze . . . has its source not in the *personal unconscious* of the poet, but in a sphere of unconscious mythology whose primordial images are the common heritage of mankind. I have called this sphere the *collective unconscious*. . . ."[7] Here Jung located the impersonal, universal source of superior literature in the collective psyche, which he depicted as a sphere of mythology. The primordial images from this mythological realm—the *archetypes*—emerged in the materials of art, lending it mysterious thaumaturgic power: "when an archetypal situation occurs we suddenly feel an extraordinary sense of release, as though transported, or caught up by an overwhelming power. At such moments we are no longer individuals, but the race; the voice of all mankind resounds in us" (82). The remarkable affective power of literature—its ability to carry us away—resulted from its activation of mythological materials, which swept away individual consciousness, will, and intention for readers as well as poets.

What distinguished Jung's theory of literature was not only its foundations in ancient mythology and the collective unconscious and its celebrations of rapturous effect for poet and reader, but also its emphases on both the didactic value and the autonomy of literature. By activating archetypes, the literary creation assumed broad social significance: "it is constantly at work educating the spirit of the age, conjuring up the forms in which the age is most lacking" (82). The cultural education proffered by literature compensated the inadequacies of the present, serving broadly to balance and improve the spirit of man. However valuable the work of literature was for the society, it possessed for Jung a fundamental aesthetic independence like that theorized by formalist critics. According to Jung, "the meaning and individual quality of a work of art inhere within it and not in its extrinsic determinants. One might almost describe it as a living being that uses man only as a nutrient medium, employing his capacities according to its own laws and shaping itself to the fulfillment of its own creative purpose" (72). Within the realm of aesthetics, the literary object appeared an impersonal, autonomous, organic form. "Perhaps art has no 'meaning'. . . . Perhaps it is like nature, which simply *is* and 'means' nothing beyond that" (77).

The Kantian or formalist thrust of Jungian mythopoetics more than its anthropological, psychological, and ethical dimensions made it especially attractive to Anglo-Saxon Myth Critics who had to contend with the rise of New Criticism. This is evident in the works of such quasiformalist Myth Critics as Maud Bodkin, Francis Fergusson, and Northrop Frye, among others. Along with Jung's textual theory went a strong prejudice against traditional expressive poetics. At its best, poetry expressed not the individual will, intention, or personal unconscious of the poet, but the universal archetypes from the collective unconscious. The flaw in the Freudian view of art was precisely its reduction of artworks to the individual artist's neurotic psyche and to the personal sexual problems developed during infancy. Superior works of art "positively force themselves upon the author. . . . The work brings with it its own form; anything he wants to add is rejected, and what he himself would like to reject is thrust back at him. While his conscious mind stands amazed and empty before this phenomenon, he is overwhelmed by a flood of thoughts and images which he never intended to create and which his will could never have brought into being" (73). The work's own form took full precedence for Jung over the poet's personal will, consciousness, and intention. Poems expressed not the mind of the individual artist but the soul and genius of the race. Here Jung actually expanded the expressive theory of literature, shifting its foundations from the personal to the collective unconscious.

In her pioneering *Archetypal Patterns in Poetry* (1934), Maud Bodkin eclectically combined Jungian theories, especially those of the archetypes and the collective unconscious, with concepts from Freudian psychoanalysis and British anthropology, not to mention her use of various philosophers, theologians, sociologists, and literary critics. Specifically, she studied in detail the rebirth archetype, the paradise-hades archetype, the betrayed-betrayer woman archetype, and the archetypes of devil, hero, and god. Among other texts, she scrutinized "The Ancient Mariner" and *The Waste Land,* offering early exemplary instances of myth criticism in English. Though given to glorifications of irrationality, mysticism, and racial memory, Bodkin resisted the Jungian temptation to universalize; she credited the impact of historical conditions on the formations of particular versions of archetypes: "The images studied of man, woman, god, devil, in any particular instance of their occurrence in poetry can be considered either as related to the sensibility of a certain poet, and a certain age and country, or as a mode of expressing something potentially realizable in human experience of any time or place."[8] The roles of the personal unconscious and of social history received some emphasis in Bodkin's theory of literature.

Fundamentally, poetry for Bodkin communicated communal knowledge of archetypal characters, plots, and themes in so intensely emotional a manner that she wanted to develop a receptionist criticism based on an affective conception of art. In her Preface, Bodkin called for large-scale research in the future on the nature of response to poetry, which would require "intensive work on the experience of individuals" (vi). This project found fulfillment a generation later in the Freudian reader-response criticism of Norman Holland. It had been initiated in I. A. Richards' investigation during the 1920s of student response. Typical of Myth Critics, Bodkin reserved a privileged place for affective theory in her conceptualization of literature.

While Bodkin's conception of literature generously allowed for textual, didactic, expressive, and affective dimensions of imaginative works, it assigned a vague place to the mimetic powers of poetry. Distinguishing between scientific and poetic uses of language, Bodkin differentiated the literal truth of reference found in the discourse of science from the suggestive, visionary truth of reference produced in the discourse of poetry. (Her semantic theory derived doubtlessly from I. A. Richards.) They key to Bodkin's attenuated mimetic poetics was ritual dance, which operated as a model of complete communication in the arts. "In the dance, communication is achieved through a sequence of bodily attitudes so related that each, within the total rhythm, enhances the experience of the rest; this vivid sensuous experience becoming the vehicle of a shared imaginative vision of reality" (324). For Bodkin, mimesis involved an alluring *embodiment* of numinous reality rather than an accurate mirrorlike reflection of it. The role of mimetic poetics was usually discounted by Myth Critics, as we shall see in a moment.

Like Maud Bodkin, Leslie Fiedler relied heavily on Jungian psychoanalysis in developing his own distinctive system of mythopoetics. He too found it necessary to reserve a place for the personal unconscious while maintaining the role of the collective unconscious. What was involved here was the need to insure a space for history as well as biography. Early on, Jung attacked Freud for situating poetry in the infantile psychobiography of the individual poet; instead he stressed the universal, impersonal, and collective origins of art. This escape from biography entailed a flight from history, which later Jungians had to amend. As a Marxist, Fiedler was especially concerned to provide for sociological and historical factors shaping writers and their works during any given period of time.

In his "Archetype and Signature" (1952), Fiedler self-consciously chose the terms "Archetype" and "Signature" rather than "myth" to explain his poetics. "Archetype" for him designated "any of the immemorial patterns of response to the human situation in its most permanent aspects."[9] The Archetype belonged to the realm of the metapersonal, the unconscious, the id, and the community at preconscious levels. "Signature" meant "the sum total of individuating factors in a work" (537); it belonged to the domain of the ego and superego—the personality and the social collectivity—at conscious levels (539). "Literature, properly speaking, can be said to come into existence at the moment a Signature is imposed upon the Archetype" (537). Unlike myth and folktale (pure archetypes), literature exhibited individuating traits not only of genre, diction, meter, and imagery, but also of social rules and historical conventions which changed from place to place, time to time, and author to author. What Fiedler's formulation provided was a role for biography, history, and aesthetics as well as ritual, folktale, and myth. In other words, he fashioned a way of uniting literature and nonliterature without sacrificing literature's all-important magical power—its special ability—to transport us, to be agressively sublime, to put us in touch with the "marvelous." The "ecstatics" of literature, prized by Jung, Bodkin, Fiedler, and most other Myth Critics, distinguished them sharply from competing critics; their theory of literature set less value on instruction, craft, or (mere) delight than on "ecstasy" and "wonder."

With his special interest in the "ordinary reader" and his concept of "Signature," Fiedler set about studying the popular literature of America. Having redefined the Jungian "archetype" as a socially determined rather than simple eternal formation—as a combination Signature-Archetype— he was enabled to investigate relatively recent homegrown "myths" instead of strictly ancient ones or primitive folk works. In much of his finest criticism, he uncovered "American Archetypes." Best known in this regard was the archetypal American story explained in "Come Back to the Raft Ag'in, Huck Honey" (1948) and in Love and Death in the American Novel (1960). In the most celebrated of American popular classics, according to Fiedler, we encountered a society officially characterized by conscious fear of homosexual love and by open violence between whites and nonwhites, yet we repeatedly discovered idyllic literary scenes of fervent, though chaste, male bonding of whites and dark-skinned refugees from civilization. This native "archetype" revealed a dimension of American psychological fantasy life different from the official version of society. As far as Fiedler was concerned, whatever a society repressed returned in its literature (WWL, 41–42). This special dialectical concept of repression-compensation in the realm of archetypal theory derived from Jung, who used it as the foundation for erecting his didactic conception of art. For his part, Fiedler regarded such a cultural mechanism as a moral force and cause for hope.

About the mimetic potentials of art Fiedler was dismissive. He did not want to limit poetry to the domain of the probable, the verisimilar, the rational, the realistic. In his view, the popular audience is "as indifferent to the verisimilitude of plot and character as it is to the beauty of structure and style. Intuitively aware that the mode of the books they prefer is fantastic rather than mimetic or analytic, ordinary readers do not demand that their protagonists be psychologically credible. . . ."[10] Ultimately, Fiedler downgraded textual, didactic, expressive, and especially mimetic poetics in favor of the ecstatic, affective powers of art. It was less a question here of denial than of strong preference.

The dismissal of mimetic poetics from myth criticism was unflinchingly carried out by Northrop Frye in his essay, "The Archetypes of Literature" (1951), collected later in Fables of Identity (1963). "Art deals not with the real but with the conceivable; and criticism . . . can never be justified in trying to develop, much less assume, any theory of actuality."[11] The conceivable versus the real, the fantastic versus the verisimilar, numinous "reality" versus actuality—in these oppositions Myth Critics unswervingly preferred the conceivable, the fantastic, and the numinous over the real, the verisimilar, and the actual. "The criticism of literature," declared Frye, "is much more hampered by the representational fallacy than even the criticism of painting" (14).

An assault on simple concepts of representation and realism was memorably mounted by the philosopher and semanticist Philip Wheelwright in The Burning Fountain (1954). Championing a view of language propounded for myth criticism against that widely promulgated by logical positivism, Wheelwright criticized the literal, logical discourse of science—"stenolanguage": it was dogmatically limited to the public domain of law and necessity, of technical and conventional "truth," and of denotation and monosignation. Unlike steno-language, the translogical, expressive discourses of myth, religion, and poetry opened a private realm of possibility and freedom, of deep and integral truth, and of connotation and plurisignation. Wheelwright defended the suggestive, paradoxical discourse of myth against the declarative, univocal language of logic and science.[12] Like Nietzsche, he associated mimesis and realism with rigid scientific literalism; and like other Myth Critics, he opposed the possible to the real, the paradoxical to the known, and the mysterious to the actual.

In a secular age of science, Wheelwright sought to keep alive the spiritual "sense of a beyond." He deplored triumphant positivism, materialism, and naturalism, being offended by dogmas of plain sense and declarations against religious consciousness. Like Bodkin, he wanted to move modern aesthetics toward mysticism. All of these feelings and aims entered into Wheelwright's poetics. Just as he attempted to consolidate the emotive and the referential functions of discourse in the sphere of literary semantics, so he tried to link the narrative and the cognitive dimensions of myth in the field of poetics: poetry, like myth, was a narrative mode of apprehending reality. Both myth and poetry shared with ritual not a thirst for power, as the positivist Frazer believed, but a drive for communal participation in "the something beyond." Not surprisingly, Wheelwright condemned self-conscious didacticism and allegory in poetry because they tended toward the literal and abstract rather than the translogical and concrete. The wisdom of literature, communicated through archetypes, was embodied in paradoxical and plurisignative language. It was "closer to man's natural human vision than are the products of brain ingenuity" (92). Any separation of idea from image debased art. The deep wisdom and truths of mythic literature were depicted by Wheelwright as "transcending the limits of what can be said via ordinary literal speech" (159).

Perhaps most distinctive about Wheelwright's theorizing on myth and literature was his strong view of affective poetics. Unlike other leading Myth Critics, he criticized the notion that literature provided sublime pleasure or promoted healthy psychic balance. The problem with such simple hedonistic and therapeutic theories was that they separated the emotional from the intellectual response to imaginative works. Response to literature depended on apprehending its deep truths and wisdom in a spirit of awe and wonder.

In *King Lear,* for example, the language and imagery and character developments and story are inseparable aspects of the total poem and legitimate factors in its appeal. But *King Lear*'s principle claim to greatness transcends these components: it is great because in and through such poetic devices it reveals depth-meaning—it adumbrates truths and quasi-truths of high importance about such matters as human nature, old age, false reasoning, and self-confrontation through suffering. The depth-meaning of *Lear*—the "poetic truth" to be discovered in the play—is what mainly accounts for and justifies the Fit Reader's full response, an inseparable blending of emotive and intellectual. (46)

While Wheelwright credited in this passage a textual poetics concerned with language, imagery, character, and plot, he ascribed first priority to a combined didactic-affective theory focused on the inseparable wisdom and sublimity conveyed, however mysteriously, to the perceptive reader. Given such a poetics, we can understand why mimesis, in particular, was downplayed: accuracy in depicting the external world had little to do with the enigmatic higher truths of ritual, myth, religion, and poetry. At its finest, poetry expressed sublime ancestral wisdom in a discourse unto itself. Drained of emotion and sacred truth, poetic archetypes became stereotypes and myth degraded into mythology. Against such a demythified world Wheelwright, like all Myth Critics, waged earnest battle.

A certain unspoken philosophy of history permeated most varieties of mythopoetics. Whatever was primordial or ancient took precedence over whatever was modern or contemporary. The power of archetypes derived from the unspecified but massive accumulations of time. Things attached specifically to modernity, like science, technology, steno-language, and literary naturalism, paled in significance and received scorn in comparison with things connected with primitive times. In *"illo tempore,"* to use Mircea Eliade's phrase, men were nearer to sacred truths, to the gods, to genuine creativity, to authentic emotions, to psychic health, to communal well being—to ritual, folktale, and myth. Modern abstract man, rootless, materialistic, godless, and positivistic, was no match in imagination or in wisdom for his heroic ancestor. Giants were in the earth then. At its worst this philosophy of history was sentimental, nostalgic, conservative, fictitious. Its politics veered decidedly to the right. Turned toward the distant past, it disliked the present and ignored or dreaded the future. Unlike revolutionary Marxists who deplored the despotic past and looked forward to the communitarian future, the more reactionary Myth Critics, like some of the New Critics, sought communal harmony in a mythical, agrarian past. The course of time was degenerative. Civilized literature constituted a falling off and a derivative of ancient ritual, folktale, and myth. Wisdom and wonder was in that ancestral work.

OF DIVINATION, DESECRATION, AND WONDER

In *The New Science* (1725; 3d ed., 1744), Giambattista Vico insisted "the first science to be learned should be mythology or the interpretation of fables; for, as we shall see, all the histories of the gentiles have their beginnings in fables, which were the first histories of the gentile nations. By such a method the beginnings of the sciences as well as of the nations are to be discovered. . . ."[13] For Vico, myth had its sources in history: the best method to divine ancient wisdom and knowledge was to interpret the myths of a culture. Such interpretation must not be allegorical, as with the Platonists, but historical or, in Vico's terminology, "genealogical." The aim of Vico's new science was to examine the history of ancient customs, deeds, and ideas through interpretation of fables so as to derive the principles of human nature and history. About allegorical interpretation Vico declared impatiently, "all the mystic meanings of lofty philosophy attributed by the learned to the Greek fables and the Egyptian hieroglyphics are as impertinent as the historical meanings they both must have had are natural" (120). The allegorical interpretation of myths and scriptures, dating from classical Greek culture and from early Judeo-Christian times up to the present, focused not merely on literal and historical sense, but on spiritual significance—the latter often involving discreet typological, tropological, and mystical levels of meaning. The famous "four senses of interpretation," developed in the tradition of biblical hermeneutics by Philo, Origen, Augustine, and Aquinas, among others, presupposed that ancient texts were polysemous and that certain textual meanings were hidden from view. Such scriptural interpretations tended, in practice, to bypass genealogical inquiry in favor of philological and spiritual analysis. When historical interpretation did enter biblical hermeneutics in the nineteenth century, it brought about a significant transformation—the revolution of the so-called "higher criticism." The disagreement between the allegorists and the genealogists, depicted by Vico, has continued in one guise or another into the present time and into the ranks of the Myth Critics, as our broad profile here of their critical concerns and approaches will show.

Because modern myth criticism frequently dealt ahistorically with hidden significance, with ancient "types," and with moral and spiritual meanings, it was associated by friends and foes alike with allegorical interpretation. Wheelwright's theory of language, we recall, pitted the secretive, paradoxical, plurisignative discourse of myth, religion, and poetry against the declarative, denotative, monosignative steno-language of logic and science. Wheelwright asserted "literal meaning is only one aspect of the full poetic meaning" (*BF*, 69). The search beyond the literal for the spiritual significance of texts characterized all myth criticism, making it heir to the tradition of pagan and Judeo-Christian allegorical interpretation.

What concerned and dismayed many Myth Critics about all interpretation was its ever-present tendency toward destruction. The will-to-knowledge motivating interpretation set *logos* against *mythos*. Myth Critics found themselves demythifying beloved texts. Divination entailed the desecration of the wonder of sacred works. In his early essay on analytical psychology and poetry, Jung exhibited the deep ambivalence usually accompanying the hermeneutic project of myth criticism. On the one hand, "we ought not to understand, for nothing is more injurious to immediate experience than cognition" (78); on the other hand, "We must interpret, we must find meanings in things, otherwise we would be quite unable to think about them. We have to break down life and events . . . well knowing that in doing so we are getting further away from the living mystery" (78). By its very nature interpretation engendered separation and destruction as well as understanding and cognition. Like the sciences of anthropology and psychology, literary criticism rationalized the irrational, turning magic into explicated illusion, Id into Ego, the unconscious into consciousness, darkness into light. It questioned the very truthfulness along with the meaning of myth and poetry; it risked transforming living archetypes into moribund stereotypes.

Aware of the desacralizing powers of understanding, Maud Bodkin expressed a wish and a goal for criticism. "Yet thought need not be of the hard destructive type. Thought may be subtle, pliant, yielding itself to serve and follow the living imaginative activity" (*APP,* 320–21). Such programmatic reverence in the special presence of the sacred and irrational typified much myth criticism, distinguishing it from other modes of inquiry and often rendering it suspect to opponents.

Like Jung, Wheelwright, and Bodkin, Leslie Fiedler had grave doubts about both scientific understanding and literary criticism—*logos.* He proposed as a model for criticism not science but myth itself. In a confessional mood, Fiedler admitted, "I helped turn living myth to dying mythology, if not archetype to stereotype. Nevertheless, I remain convinced that there is a chance of raising such material to the level of full consciousness without utterly falsifying it, as long as the critic who does so remembers that he is himself writing literature about literature, fiction about fictions, myth about myth" (*WWL,* 131). It was this fundamental commitment, antiscientific in impulse, that thereafter rendered odious to Fiedler most "dis-enchanting" forms of modern criticism. If, following Fiedler, we could present or recreate in our criticism the *ekstasis* of myth and literature, we would "find ourselves speaking less of theme and purport, structure and texture, signified and signifier, metaphor and metonymy, and more of myth, fable, archetype, fantasy, magic and wonder" (*WWL,* 140). In the end, Fiedler argued against all methodology—formalist, structuralist, deconstructive, or whatever—advocating instead an eclectic, populist, *amateur* criticism.

The eclectic criticism promoted by the Myth Critics—early advocates of interdisciplinary study—was pioneered by Kenneth Burke, as we saw in chapter 2.[14] As prototype of the American Myth Critics, Burke was deeply concerned about the destructive power of criticism; specifically, he worried about the dangerous hubris of pure speculation and scientific curiosity. "Curiosity becomes malign when the kind of benefit sought, or the kind of assertion made, is too restricted from the standpoint of social necessities. Or it becomes malign when the incentive of *power* outweighs the incentive of *betterment*. . . ."[15] Like later Myth Critics, Burke opposed deracinated science and pure speculation insofar as they harbored destructive, antisocial potentials. Intellectual activity should serve to better community or to cure society.

A number of his ideas and theories linked Kenneth Burke with the Myth Critics. But like Fiedler, he too was essentially a maverick. Let us note, in passing, some of Burke's "anthropological" formulations. Burke argued that ritual drama constituted the structural "Ur-form" of all human action. He believed that language was inherently "magical" because the act of naming decreed that something be singled out. He insisted that poetry was "homeopathic medicine," proffering immunizations or antidotes aimed at the healthful purgation of the communal body. He gave a key role to the ritual "scapegoat" in the work of poetic purgation. His overall theory of "symbolic action," which theorized that poetry did something positive for poet and for community alike, assigned two opposing spiritual motives to literature—"pious awe" or "impious rebellion." However, Burke differed from many Myth Critics in his reliance on intricate rhetorical and biographical inquiries. Like Fiedler and Chase, Burke was enough of an eclectic and independent intellectual to make his critical allegiances far-ranging, yet tenuous. Among other things, the commitment of these three critics to overt politics and leftist theory distinguished them from mainline Myth Critics.

The critical approach employed by any given Myth Critic might be primarily receptionist as with Bodkin, or sociological as with Hoffman, or religious as with Campbell, or "formalist" as with Fergusson, or historical as with Frye. Biographical criticism was more or less relinquished to Freudian psychoanalysts and evaluative aesthetic criticism was left pretty much to New Critics and other committed formalists. Since almost all of myth criticism of whatever specific approach was focused on retrieving buried archetypes, it carried out its project in the tradition of allegorical interpretation. In other words, to the extent that its reading progressed from literal to spiritual—or from manifest text to latent psycho-social-anthropological (re)coding of text—it engaged in the allegorical interpretation long ago practiced by platonic exegetes and scriptural hermeneuts. As early as the closing years of the Great Depression, William Troy in his manifesto "A Note on Myth" prefigured an American project of myth criticism dependent on allegorical interpretation.

The sociological mode of myth criticism proved a great boon to the developing field of American Studies, particularly during the early postwar period. Numerous texts made significant additions to knowledge by unearthing distinctively American archetypes. Especially noteworthy in this regard were Constance Rourke's *American Humor* (1931), Henry Nash Smith's *Virgin Land* (1950), R. W. B. Lewis' *The American Adam* (1955), Richard Chase's *The American Novel and Its Tradition* (1957), Leslie Fiedler's *Love and Death in the American Novel* (1960), and Daniel Hoffman's *Form and Fable in American Fiction* (1961). These and other books produced detailed studies of archetypal American characters, themes, plots, images, genres, and settings. This harnessing of myth criticism for purposes of literary nationalism, while not in keeping with a certain universalizing drift of the movement, constituted a major contribution rather than an aberration. That American soil was a fertile ground of folktale, myth, and archetype became by the middle 1960s an undisputed, if unexpected, fact of scholarship. In this regard, American myth criticism succeeded in elevating the history of native literature in a grand manner that no other school or movement following the Great Depression ever approached. As carried out by Hoffman, Fiedler, Chase, and others, this special interpretative enterprise employed a sociological perspective and a genealogical method that tempered somewhat the tendency of myth criticism to spiritualize or allegorize literary texts.

In *Form and Fable in American Fiction,* Hoffman examined ten exemplary romances—key texts of Irving, Hawthorne, Melville, and Twain—by drawing on native materials dating from the seventeenth century and later as well as on universal materials from world culture originating in precivilized times. Hoffman's exegeses particularized the texts under scrutiny, rendering his readings and theorizings more subtle and less generalized than those of Chase and Fiedler—which were discussed in chapter 4. Among Hoffman's contributions were ten superior interpretations, a rich theory of romance (which extended Chase's work), and a subtle portrait of the archetypal American hero. It was in his understanding of romance that Hoffman revealed most fully his methodological manner.

According to Hoffman, American romance was a nonrealistic, poetic prose genre typically featuring a journey of self-discovery—a quest for (national) identity—cut off from the traditions of the Old World and seeking fresh myths for a new land. However discarded, the old mythic materials formed the background for the American romance. In part, national destiny rested on denial. In affirming independence, the American romance exploited native folk traditions of character, theme, action, and language. For example, oral tradition and nonbelletristic writings provided handy national character types like the self-reliant, naive Frontiersman and the Yankee. Characteristically, indigenous folk materials were in conflict with mythic themes from world culture: to become American required rebellion against ancestral fathers, kings, societies, and traditions. The political ideology of romance favored democratic egalitarianism. Unlike the novel of manners, the romance avoided the solidities of society and its conventions, preferring the unfettered world of nature and instinct. Seemingly primoridial, this condition did not simply encourage the reemergence of cosmic archetypes. Although there were in American romances dead gods and resurrections, scapegoats and demons, initiatory rites and rebirths, "the contexts of their presence in the works that embody them are scarcely twice alike, nor are their functions, and these are often determined by themes from folklore either analogous to or contradictory of these myths" (14). For Hoffman the relations between American folklore and world myth were multifaceted: a native tradition might corroborate, cancel, complicate, or contradict an ancient archetype. In any case, the emergence of either folk or mythic materials in a romance was specific to that work: Hoffman resisted the leveling tendencies of myth criticism.

When discussing the influence of Gothic fiction upon American romance, Hoffman was especially revealing of his sociological approach. It was a question for him less of the impact of eighteenth-century British Gothic literature than of the native folkloristic tradition standing behind the American Gothic imagination: the lore of witchcraft, fairies, and ghosts came with American settlers in the earliest days and did not need later British literary traditions to give it currency. So-called "Gothic" materials were both *folkloristic* and literary. American social history more than British literary tradition provided "Gothic" materials for native authors.

Depicting the archetypal American hero, Hoffman worked assiduously against the earlier universalist theories of the hero developed by Otto Rank, Lord Raglan, and particularly Joseph Campbell. "The American folk hero is startlingly different from most of the great heroes of myths or Märchen.

Unlike them, the American has no parents. He has no past, no patrimony, no siblings, no family, and no life cycle, because he never marries or has children. He seldom dies" (78). That is to say, the American hero was thoroughly different from the European hero as described by leading Myth Critics. He was the creation of an independent, indigenous folk whose cultural vision and social life were peculiar to itself.

The religious approach of myth criticism, employed dramatically by Joseph Campbell in *The Hero with a Thousand Faces* (1949), sought to uncover timeless human patterns in myth and literature. It worked on the level of the planet rather than the particular society. Methodologically, it preferred allegory to genealogy. Its point of view was deeply religious and unitarian in the manner of certain Eastern religions. As such, it constituted a polar opposite to the sociological approach of Hoffman, Chase, and Fiedler, being closer to the work of Jung, Bodkin, and Wheelwright. Whereas the Americanists were concerned with the impact of "Signature" upon "Archetype"—to employ Fiedler's terms—Campbell and other religious critics were devoted primarily to pure "Archetype" free from "Signature." Accordingly, biography, social history, and individual aesthetic form received scant emphasis. For Campbell, mythic forms were everywhere the same beneath regional variations. All heroes were one hero and all myths were one myth. According to Campbell, "The differentiations of sex, age, and occupation are not essential to our character, but mere costumes. . . . We think of ourselves as Americans, children of the twentieth century, Occidentals, civilized Christians. We are virtuous or sinful. Yet such designations do not tell what it is to be a man, they denote only the accidents of geography, birth-date, and income."[16] Time, place, religious affiliation, moral state, economic condition—those constituted the accidents, not the essentials, of human life. "The community today is the planet, not the bounded nation . . ." (388). Nationalism was inimical to Campbell.

The same year that Joseph Campbell published his work on the monomyth of the hero, Francis Fergusson brought out *The Idea of a Theater* (1949), which studied the details of ten plays within the context of a general theory of drama informed by myth criticism. Fergusson's scrupulous attention to individual works signaled a certain "formalist" aesthetic approach. Influenced by British anthropology, Fergusson in his broad theory as well as in his particular exegeses relied heavily on notions of ritual and myth. For example, Oedipus in Sophocles' play functioned for him as a dismembered king and scapegoat while Thebes constituted a wasteland complete with infertile crops, herds, and women. Beyond such mythic archetypes, *Oedipus*

Rex, like all drama, possessed a fundamental histrionic dimension, a primitive performative substratum, linked with ancient ritual, that took priority for Fergusson over its civilized literary or textual aspects. As public performance, the play unfolded "at the center of the life and awareness of the community."[17] Theater at its best, as in Periclean Greece or Elizabethan England, was ritualistic, popular, communal; it offered society a healthy mode of understanding as well as a living reflection of social life antecedent to philosophy, science, and the arts. Oedipus enacted a dramatic rite not simply of his own growth and development, but "of the precarious life of the human City" (41). Literary plot, characterization, and dialogue were built upon collective psychic phenomena—*mythos* preceded *logos.*

What Fergusson shared with American formalists, particularly early New Critics, was a meticulous care for the specificities of individual works and a religious view of culture rooted in Eliot's conception of the dissociation of sensibility. According to Fergusson, rationalism and philosophical idealism took over in the mid-seventeenth century, divorcing feeling and intuition from intellect and thought. The triumph of the scientific mind spelled the end of ritual, myth, and organic community. In our epoch, myth was reduced to ornament or lie. The task of criticism was to recover our traditional ritual sensibility—mythic consciousness—which operated before all rational predication: "the histrionic sensibility is a basic, or primary, or primitive virtue of the human mind" (252). Prior to our epoch of rationalism, man "had a free use of the reason without having lost the habits of feeling, and the modes of awareness, associated with the ancient tribal religion" (245). Like the New Critics, Fergusson deplored modern man's bifurcated sensibility, his loss of religion, and his abdication to science and rationalism.

Significantly, the immediate experience of a dramatic performance was for Fergusson precritical. The authentic work of drama put us in touch with "the deepest level of experience, where the mysterious world is yet felt as real and prior to our inventions, demands, criticisms" (47). Criticism followed the mystery of experience: it was secondary, belated, inferior. *Logos* supervened upon *mythos.* Thus "critics must assume that works of art, even those of the remote past and of foreign cultures, are in some sense directly understandable; and that what we learn about them may modify or deepen, but can never replace, our immediate acquaintance with them" (23). Like ritual, drama was self-evident, however mysterious. While the secondary work of criticism could supply learning and enrich knowledge, it could never substitute for wondrous immediate experience. In its present form, drama was "an art which eventuates in words, but which in its own essence is at once more primitive, more subtle, and more direct than either word or concept . . ." (22). Fergusson's model for drama was prediscursive and prerational primitive ritual—pure action—immediately accessible to the community. The obligation of criticism was to work back reverently through concepts and words to action and mystery lodged at the center of communal life. Ideally, the trajectory of criticism progressed from *logos* to *mythos*. In this endpoint we see how different was the myth criticism of Fergusson from the formalism of the New Critics, who ruled out extrinsic concerns, worshipped the isolated autonomous text, refused to separate content and form, and condemned all genetic modes of inquiry.

Among other contributions, Fergusson offered a superior reading of *Hamlet,* becoming part of a significant tradition of myth criticism centered on Shakespeare. Other fine works in this line included those of Gilbert Murray in 1914, Colin Still in 1921, G. Wilson Knight in 1930, J. I. M. Stewart in 1949, C. L. Barber in 1959, John Holloway in 1961, and Northrop Frye in 1965 and 1967. Numerous other critics could be listed. The point being made here—that myth criticism positively affected Shake-spearean studies—could easily be generalized to include Medieval, Renais-sance, and especially Romantic studies, not to mention other period studies. Significantly, myth criticism worked equally well as a critical instrument with poetry, drama, or fiction and with seemingly any period of literature. The same cannot be said, for example, of Marxism and New Criticism, which favored certain genres and periods.

Given the broad applicability of myth criticism, it was not surprising that it emerged during the late 1950s as the strongest rival of New Criticism and its likeliest replacement. The publication of Northrop Frye's monumental *Anatomy of Criticsm* in 1957 signaled for many critics and scholars both the fruition of myth criticism and the end of the uncontested dominance of New Criticism. Neither the Chicago Critics nor the New York Intellectuals nor the leading historical scholars of the time could match in range, ver-satility, or appeal the growing quantity of myth criticism. That myth criticism was, furthermore, highly compatible with the emerging fields of American Studies and Comparative Literature—which began to expand in the 1940s—meant that it could serve both pioneering and traditionalist literary critics. It could accommodate allegorical as well as genealogical modes of inquiry; it allowed for receptionist, sociological, religious, historical, and "formalist" critical approaches. However much it worried about desecration, it proffered an ambitious and multifaceted program for divination.

SYSTEMATICS OF MYTH CRITICISM

A certain grand culmination of myth criticism came with the publication of Northrop Frye's *Anatomy of Criticism: Four Essays* (1957). This masterwork of modern critical theory demonstrated impressively the wide scope of myth criticism, influenced a broad group of younger literary critics, effected single-handedly a significant challenge to all competing contemporary schools, and summed up the movement by providing a far-reaching systematics for its project. Produced during four active decades, Frye's other works, consisting of reviews, essays, radio talks, cassette tapes, educational television shows, and roughly twenty books, served to initiate, elaborate, and refine—without quite surpassing—his ambitious enterprise detailed in the *Anatomy*. Although myth criticism was more or less successfully challenged from the middle 1960s onwards by philosophical, reader-response, structuralist, deconstructive, feminist, ethnic, and leftist criticism, the *Anatomy* maintained a seemingly impervious position as influential masterpiece in a class with such earlier critical works as Eliot's *The Sacred Wood* (1920), Richards' *Principles of Literary Criticism* (1924), Wilson's *Axel's Castle* (1931), Brooks' and Warren's *Understanding Poetry* (1938), Wellek's and Warren's *Theory of Literature* (1949), and Trilling's *The Liberal Imagination* (1950).

What made Frye's endeavor so memorable was his working premise that literature as a whole constituted a coherent and closed system and that criticism, accordingly, needed to articulate all the elements of the system. In a manner of speaking, Frye aimed to complete the scientific task initiated by Aristotle in his unfinished *Poetics*—to systematize all literature. In the judgment of his more enthusiastic admirers, Frye's encyclopedic effort succeeded admirably, giving criticism an epistemological underpinning and intellectual status equal to contemporary sciences and social sciences.

In his first essay in the *Anatomy*, Frye depicted a historical pattern of five literary modes found in classical literature and postclassical literature: the five modes were myth, romance, high mimetic, low mimetic, and irony. In each of the five modes, literary works could be sophisticated or naive and tragic or comic. Thus, there were numerous possible combinations: sophisticated comic romance, naive low mimetic tragedy, and so on. In this theory of modes, Frye argued that, while a work always contained an underlying dominant mode, it might partake of any or of all the other modes. Finally, embedded in the epochal "linear" progression of modes was the theory that romantic, high mimetic, and low mimetic modes formed a series of displaced myths and that irony effected a cyclical return or movement back toward myth. This cyclical theory set myth as the *arche* and the *telos* of literature.

Myth opposed mimesis in Frye's system of poetics.

Our survey of fictional modes has also shown us that the mimetic tendency itself, the tendency to verisimilitude and accuracy of description, is one of two poles of literature. At the other pole is something that seems to be connected both with Aristotle's word *mythos* and with the usual meaning of myth. That is, it is a tendency to tell a story which is in origin a story about characters who can do anything, and only gradually becomes attracted towards a tendency to tell a plausible or credible story.[18]

As literature moved from the mythic to the ironic model, it tended toward the plausible, credible, and verisimilar (which should not be confused with truth or reality) and then back toward the mythic, as was evident in the ironic myths of Joyce, Eliot, and other modernists. Frye surrounded mimesis with myth.

Significantly, a certain pattern of oppositions structured Frye's system, as it did all Myth Critics. In polar tension with one another were myth and mimesis, oral culture and written culture, religion and science, revelation and truth of correspondence, poetry and prose, metaphor and simile, community and the individual, the language of hope and belief and the language of concept and proposition, conservative political forms and liberal political forms, *mythos* and *logos*. As a systematic critic in the tradition of Aristotle, Frye valued writing, science, individualism, prose, the language of concepts, and liberal thinking. As an independent private reader, however, he favored myth and romance to realism and irony, poetry to prose, metaphor to simile, comedy to tragedy, revelation and ritual to empiricism and demonstration.

Like some other Myth Critics, Frye believed that a dissociation of sensibility occurred in Western culture, creating two domains, which he labeled the "mythological universe" and the "scientific universe." Copernicus symbolized the point of separation, which the modern intellectual, in Frye's view, must seek to reconcile. In the Preface to *Spiritus Mundi: Essays on Literature, Myth, and Society* (1976), Frye summed up his view of the mythological universe, declaring "that all literature is written within what I call a 'mythological universe' . . . ; that this mythological universe is not really a protoscientific one . . . ; and that literature is written within this universe because literature continues the mythological habit of mind. The latter, being an imaginative habit, is quite as subtle, profound, and in touch with 'reality' among Australian aborigines as among twentieth-century poets."[19] This linkage of the human imagination with myth, irrespective of time, place, and culture, cast science as a derivation and displacement of mythological consciousness. The universe of myth lay at the "origin" of human consciousness and culture.

In his second essay in the *Anatomy,* Frye developed a five-phase semantic theory of literary symbols and fashioned a stratified hermeneutics to go with it. In its "descriptive" phase, literary language was referential; in its "literal" phase, it was nonreferential; in its "formal" phase, it offered autonomous, exemplary images; in its "mythical" phase, it communicated archetypes; and in its "anagogic" phase, it presented symbols of the whole of existence unconstrained by references, examples, or the known. (Of the five types of criticism aligned with the five phases of literary language, Frye was most interested in archetypal criticism, to which he devoted his third essay.) The basis of Frye's theory of language and of criticism was a division between ordinary discourse (instrumental communicative language) and poetic discourse (autonomous language and imagination).

In literature, questions of fact or truth are subordinated to the primary literary aim of producing a structure of words for its own sake, and the sign-values of symbols are subordinated to their importance as a structure of interconnected motifs. Wherever we have an autonomous verbal structure of this kind, we have literature. Wherever this autonomous structure is lacking, we have language, words used instrumentally to help human consciousness do or understand something else. Literature is a specialized form of language. . . ." (74)

This semantics, reminiscent of I. A. Richards' and Philip Wheelwright's theories of language, lent Frye's whole systematics a "formalist" direction that was supplemented by his denial of intention in literature, his dislike of paraphrase and didacticism, his tendency toward a totalizing spatial hermeneutics, and his condemnations of various types of "extrinsic criticism." Still, Frye did not deny that literary language had a relation to reality; rather he presented the relation as potential and variable, as subordinate, rather than simply direct, negative, nonexistent, or dominant.

The inward-turning tendency of literary language favored the pleasure-principle over the reality-principle, delight over instruction, emotion over truth, wonder over understanding. That is to say, Frye advocated an affective rather than didactic poetics without renouncing the latter. Here, as elsewhere, we glimpse the key strategy of Frye. He admitted almost everything, denied almost nothing, and included, while hierarchizing, everything. In hermeneutic matters, he preferred archetypal to rhetorical, judicial, or other types of criticism. In poetic matters, he preferred myth to mimesis (realism), wonder to instruction, the autonomous artifact to the self-expressive document. In addition, he preferred the communal to the individual, the oracular to the discursive, poetry to science, and myth criticism to New Criticism or Marxism. Hypothetically, Frye should never have had to express any preferences: his synoptic vision sought to affirm all and deny nothing. That he priviliged myth in the cycle of modes and archetypal interpretation in the phases of criticism meant that he emerged as a Myth Critic—a stance which, ironically, restricted his broad scope and his "ideal" potential.

Here and there Frye distinguished between an ordinary, amateur, or public "reader" and a professional, scientific, or scholary "critic." The former he associated with Longinus and the latter with Aristotle. The Longinian reader focused on the immediate process of reception and the temporal dimensions of reading—on ekstasis. The Aristotelian critic studied the finished literary product in its unified spatial fullness. Though a devoted Aristotelian, Frye emerged from time to time as an enthusiastic Longinian, celebrating the mysterious power, beautiful exuberance, and wondrous apprehension of art. Such admittedly "pre-critical" responses were rare with Frye. He did not want to credit the direct experience of literature over the critical understanding of it. In this matter, Francis Fergusson took the opposite path.

The main problem with New Criticism, according to Frye, was that it separated a work of literature from the system of literature, isolating the text from its "full" context. The communal or archetypal ground of the literary system was repressed. The formalist critical method functioned best with lyrical literature in an ironic mode; it did less well with the other genres and modes. "What is called myth criticism," on the other hand, "is not the study of a certain kind or aspect of literature, much less a patented critical methodology, but the study of the structural principles of literature itself, more particularly its conventions, its genres, and its archetypes or recurring images."[20] With its broad scheme of five literary modes and five critical phases, Frye's myth criticism suggested how narrow were the projects of other schools (especially New Criticism), which limited themselves to certain modes, genres, and phases.

In his third essay in the *Anatomy,* Frye indicated at length and in detail what was involved in the work of archetypal or myth criticism. Concerned with the system of literary archetypes and conventions, myth criticism stressed the social or communal aspect of literature. The ground of a literary work was the literary system. One text emerged against the backdrop of a network of other texts, all leading back to myth, "the most abstract and conventional of all literary modes" (134). The job of the third essay was to provide taxonomies of literary images, plots, and characters—all modulated to account for the full richness and variety of existing literature. The immense amount of data to be systematized forced Frye into a terminological buccaneering rivaled only by Kenneth Burke and later by Harold Bloom.

According to Frye, there were four pregeneric literary categories or *mythoi*—romance, tragedy, irony, and comedy—each having six cyclical phases, allowing for twenty-four forms. The four *mythoi* constituted aspects or episodes of a central unifying quest-myth. In other words, all literary genres derived from the quest-myth. Such derivation was more logical or theoretical than historical. What Frye did here was to elevate romance and its quest to the status of superior or controlling "archetype." The total work of literature told of the passage from struggle through confusion, catastrophe, and ritual death to recognition and rebirth. This movement from *mythoi* to monomyth enacted a shift from properly archetypal to anagogic criticism.

Like the third essay, the fourth essay of the *Anatomy* covered so much data and offered so many taxonomies as to be at once grandiose and muddled. This final essay examined literary conventions of diction, rhythm, and visual presentation—rhetorical aspects of literature—in the four main genres: *epos*, fiction, drama, and lyric. At points in this examination Frye connected the four genres under scrutiny with his earlier historical modes, symbolic phases, and literary *mythoi*. It took Frye's most thorough critic, Robert Denham in *Northrop Frye and Critical Method* (1978), twenty-four diagrams and 250 pages to disentangle and elucidate Frye's total systematics. We shall not attempt a new summary.

Among important ancillary issues discussed in the fourth essay were a theory of "literary initiative" and a theory of "source myth." Like New Critics, Chicago Critics, and some Jungian Myth Critics, Frye deplored the tendency of critics to limit the understanding of a work to the conscious or subconscious "intention" of the poet. In other words, Frye discounted expressive poetics and biographical criticism (which was unusual for a critic devoted to Romantic literature as Frye was). What motivated a text was not personal "intention" but impersonal "literary initiative"—a controlling and coordinating aesthetic power that assimilated everything to itself and became the containing form. The "initiative" might be a meter, a mood, a genre, a pattern of imagery, theme, or some combination of these or other literary elements. Significantly, the theory of "initiative" displaced "intention" from the realm of personal psychology to the realm of impersonal literary system, linking it with convention rather than individual character. This meant that "controlling or shaping motive" was a fit subject for archetypal criticism.

The Bible was for Frye the primary source for undisplaced myth in the postclassical Western tradition. As such, it held a singularly privileged place in his system. He considered it the central encyclopedic work in the mythical mode. As Frye noted, many of our images, symbols, character types, plots, tropes, genres—archetypes—derived from biblical materials. In a revealing move, Frye dismissed the genealogical "higher criticism" of the Bible, which focused on textual corruptions, redactions, insertions, and conflations. Instead he advocated a critical "synthetizing process which would start with the assumption that the Bible is a definitive myth, a single archetypal structure extending from creation to apocalypse. Its heuristic principle would be St. Augustine's axiom that the Old Testament is revealed in the New and the New concealed in the Old. . . . We cannot trace the Bible back, even historically, to a time when its materials were not being shaped into a typological unity . . ." (315). Rather than regarding the Bible as a mishmash of texts joined together through a millenium-long process of editing, Frye envisaged it as a single unified and coherent myth organized around the heroic quest of the central figure called Messiah. Materials in the Bible were there because they were mythically significant, not because they were historically "true." Setting aside textual and historical criticism, Frye's archetypal criticism, here tied in with Patristic typological hermeneutics, conferred upon both biblical testaments pristine originality and priority, literary and structural perfection. The culmination of this special treatment of the Bible occurred in Frye's *The Great Code: The Bible and Literature* (1982).

In theory, Frye's systematics accorded space to textual, formalist, historical, biographical, and receptionist criticism; in practice, archetypal criticism tended to subsume all other critical modes. Such archetypal criticism was formalistic insofar as it actively resisted extrinsic criticisms. The problem with such criticism as Marxism, Freudianism, and phenomenology was that they attached criticism to outside frameworks instead of finding a conceptual framework within literature. "Critical principles cannot be taken over ready-made from theology, philosophy, politics, science, or any combination of these. To subordinate criticism to an externally derived critical attitude is to exaggerate the values in literature that can be related to the external source, whatever it is" (7).

Although criticism was an autonomous discipline and body of knowledge, distinct from other disciplines and from the experience of literature itself, it did enter into relations with other areas while maintaining its independence. For example, "the moment we go from the individual work of art to the sense of the total form of the art, the art becomes no longer an object of aesthetic contemplation but an ethical instrument, participating in the work of civilization" (349). On one side, archetypal criticism was flanked by ethics and, on the other, by history. The totality of literature was an historical phenomenon, which Frye's cyclical theory of five literary modes made clear. Ethical criticism had to do with the internal social context of literature—not with canons of morality and not with criteria of aesthetic value. The "debauchery of judiciousness" characteristic of evaluative criticism disgusted Frye, who insisted "criticism has no business to react against things, but should show a steady advance toward undiscriminating catholicity" (25). What Frye did was to shift the work of civilization to the inside of literature. This idealistic or anagogic strategy meant that such "extrinsic" concerns as history, sociology, and religion became part of the mythological universe to be worked on by archetypal criticism.

Among the kinds of criticism incorporated into the work of archetypal criticism was allegorical interpretation. The problem with unaffiliated or pure allegorical reading, however brilliant and ingenious, was that it generated a potentially "infinite amount of commentary," depressing critics and fostering a sense of "futility." "The only cure for this situation is the supplementing of allegorical with archetypal criticism. Things become more hopeful as soon as there is a feeling, however dim, that criticism has an end in the structure of literature as a total form, as well as a beginning in the text studied" (342). Properly speaking, the relation envisioned here between archetypal and allegorical criticism was one of incorporation rather than supplementation. To accept the enabling premise of literature as total form or complete system was to accord a limited hermeneutic potential to the isolated text. Ironically, the one possible exception here would be the primary source myth or bible of a culture—the very text that spawned allegorical interpretation in the first place. Evidently, Frye regarded the migration of allegorical reading from sacred source myths to secular literary genres as troublesome and unfortunate.

In his later work, Frye sought to revise some of the extreme positions staked out in the *Anatomy*. In *The Critical Path* (1971), for example, he backed away from the anagogical ingestion of culture that marked his conception of the internal structure of literature. "Criticism will always have two aspects, one turned toward the structure of literature and one turned toward the other cultural phenomena that form the social environment of literature. Together, they balance each other. . . ."[21] This view of critical activity did not renounce the autonomy of literature, nor did it compromise the independence of criticism from extrinsic nonliterary disciplines of thought; it did, however, allow commerce between various separate realms of human existence. Here Frye's project came around to the cultural criticism earlier advocated by, for example, Chase, Fiedler, and Burke.

Although feared by other Myth Critics, the desecration brought by critical divination seemed not to bother Frye. In adopting the role of scientific theorist in the tradition of Aristotle, he banished the private reader—the Longinian enthusiast—to the peculiar domain of "precriticism." In a few later essays, however, he "rehabilitated" the private reader without renouncing his larger scientific project. Frye's "Criticism, Visible and Invisible" (1964) argued that "scientific criticism" was flanked on one side by "triumphant criticism" and on the other by "militant criticism." At its best, criticism triumphant sought the inner, invisible, subjective possession of literature as intense imaginative force and power. At its best, militant criticism aimed to visibly judge works of literature as good or bad for the public interest and in defense of freedom of thought and expression. In its worst form, however, militant criticism became destructive: it exploited aesthetic and moral criteria in order to distance, damn, and censor literary works. What was destructive in criticism for Frye was the permanent objectification of literature, the censorships of it, and the restrictions on its power to move us. The triumphant end of criticism, according to Frye, was "not an aesthetic but an ethical and participating end: for it, ultimately, works of literature are not things to be contemplated but powers to be absorbed."[22] Triumphant criticism was private and positive; scientific criticism was impersonal and informative; militant criticism was public and usually negative. In its worst manifestations, militant criticism desecrated literature. Projecting moral, aesthetic, social, or religious anxieties, such criticism exhibited the "debauchery of judiciousness" excoriated by Frye in the opening pages of *Anatomy of Criticism*. By maintaining triumphant criticism as private and precritical, Frye was enabled belatedly to protect the power and wonder of literature from the public ravages of all criticism whether scientific or militant.

MYTH CRITICISM AND THE INSTITUTION OF LITERARY STUDIES

During the 1960s in America, myth criticism was rapidly accepted into the institution of academic literary studies. On a growing scale major university presses published works in this mode, as they had done previously with the books of the early leaders of the movement. Published in 1965, the definitive *Princeton Encyclopedia of Poetry and Poetics* offered an entry on myth criticism longer than those on New Criticism and the Chicago School. Walter Sutton's and Richard Foster's textbook anthology *Modern Criticism: Theory and Practice* (1963) contained representative selections from eight Myth Critics, including Barber, Bodkin, Chase, Fergusson, Fiedler, Frye, and Lewis. The Modern Language Association's widely read conspectus on contemporary scholarship, *Relations of Literary Study* (1967), provided a guide to myth criticism and a lengthy, detailed bibliography—both by Frye. John B. Vickery's casebook, *Myth and Literature* (1966), was reprinted four times in the closing years of the decade. Thus by the early seventies David Lodge could, in his textbook, *20th Century Literary Criticism: A Reader* (1972), unself-consciously situate samples of myth criticism amidst a comprehensive framework of six types of modern criticism: formalist, historical, sociological, *archetypal,* psychoanalytical, and prescriptive. Two years later William Handy and Max Westbrook divided their classroom anthology, *Twentieth Century Criticism: The Major Statements* (1974), into five types of criticism: formalist, genre, *archetypal,* historical, and interdisciplinary. Unlike the Marxists of the 1930s, the Chicago Critics, or the New York Intellectuals, Myth Critics almost immediately enjoyed, and continue to enjoy, a highly visible and widely acknowledged place in the academic critical establishment.

Among the obvious reasons for the quick acceptance of myth criticism was its flexibility: it worked as a critical instrument on any genre from any period and place. Also it apparently posed no singular or radical threat to the established canon of great works. In the fields of American Studies and Shakespeare studies particularly, it had the immediate effect of enriching understanding of already acknowledged masterworks. At the same time it furthered the contemporaneous projects of revaluing Romantic literature, of institutionalizing Comparative Literature, and of accrediting popular literature as a worthy university subject. Because it could function as a supple formalist methodology, myth criticism was much more easily adapted to existing dominant patterns of inquiry than the cultural criticism propounded by Marxists and New York Intellectuals. In addition, the highly touted flamboyant work of Fiedler, the unparalleled achievement of Frye, the unforgettable contribution of Joseph Campbell, and related enterprises imparted an aura of success and promise unrivaled by other schools in the late fifties and early sixties. That myth criticism could so easily serve pedagogical imperatives insured all the more rapid institutionalization.

Myth criticism drew its share of hostile critiques. Among the New Critics, for instance, Brooks and Wimsatt in their *Literary Criticism: A Short History* (1957) registered serious complaints, as did the Marxist and New York Intellectual Philip Rahv in his well-known essay, "The Myth and the Powerhouse" (1953). Of the Chicago Critics, it was mainly R. S. Crane who, in his *The Languages of Criticism and the Structure of Poetry* (1953), catalogued some major weaknesses in a parodic manner. Later attacks on myth criticism are simply too numerous to list, though the vigorous critiques of Frye by the young Marxists John Fekete in *The Critical Twilight* (1977) and Frank Lentricchia in *After The New Criticism* (1980) deserve mention because they illustrate the longevity and ongoing influence of Frye and of myth criticism. Like New Criticism, myth criticism lived on and thrived well into the 1980s in American academic circles.

Perhaps the most acrimonious complaints against myth criticism had to do with its overt and covert politics. While it bothered formalists that Myth Critics eschewed stylistic texture, shunned scrupulous close reading, and borrowed abstruse terminology from the social sciences, it positively antagonized Marxists that myth criticism avoided the realities of social history, sought ecstatic moments of transcendence, and fostered certain "unreal" social-political attitudes. At the close of *The Hero with a Thousand Faces,* for example, Campbell declared "a transmutation of the whole social order is necessary, so that through every detail and act of secular life the vitalizing image of the universal god-man who is actually immanent and effective in all of us may be somehow made known to consciousness. And this is not the work that consciousness itself can achieve" (389). Further, "It is not society that is to guide and save the creative hero, but precisely the reverse. And so every one of us shares the supreme ordeal—carries the cross of the redeemer—not in the bright moments of his tribe's great victories, but in the silences of his personal despair" (391). The future revolution imagined here by Campbell—a religious transformation—pictured each individual as a potential hero seeking self-transformation amidst the background of a despairing collectivity. Nevertheless, chance more than conscious activity would precipitate the revolution. The denigration of "society" and of "consciousness," the celebration of the redeeming "god-man" and the "hero," the enforced isolation of the crucified "individual" and his alienation from "tribe"—all these were propounded almost as if to taunt Marxists. Interestingly, the philosophical idealism behind this anti-collectivistic and alienated understanding of history were singled out not only by hostile Marxists, but by "sympathetic" Myth Critics like Burke, Chase, Fiedler, Hoffman, and Hyman. What this makes clear is that the politics of myth criticism could, in fact, range all the way from traditional Christian conservatism and liberalism, as with Fergusson and Frye, to secular socialism as apparently with, say, Burke and Fiedler. Invariably, such politics—whether of the right, center, or left—professed moments of transcendental vision. Here, then, is another set of reasons why myth criticism was so quickly incorporated into the institution of American literary studies: it could tolerate almost any politics, any religion, and any critical approach. All this was possible while imbuing its practitioners with a sense of community, of optimism, of work to be done, and of transcendence. Seemingly, neither deracinated science nor technology could match myth criticism in its range and comprehensiveness, in its power to adopt multiple perspectives, in its ability to explain all human artifacts and imagination, and in its programs to pacify desacralizing *logos* through numinous *mythos*.

One highly significant, distinguishing feature of American literary theory and criticism from the 1950s and afterwards was its increasing enclosure within the academic world of colleges and universities. We have already noted the turn to the academy of the New Critics and the New York Intellectuals during the 1940s and thereafter. The depression-era Marxists were by this time mostly out of business and the Chicago Critics were from the start located in the university. With the advent of the Space Age in the late 1950s, innovative literary criticism in America was largely confined to the academy. That Edmund Wilson, T. S. Eliot, and Granville Hicks survived into this time served to highlight the end of the era of the influential "independent" man of letters, who earlier had made a living by writing reviews and books, reading publishers' manuscripts, giving occasional lectures, penning prefaces, and undertaking other "odd jobs." The leading postwar Myth Critics in America were all associated with colleges and universities. In the Space Age, to reiterate, innovation in literary theory and criticism took place in association with academia. Almost all independent criticis and magazines had either passed from existence or been absorbed into the university world. Like subsequent critical movements, myth criticism was predominantly an academic affair. Of the leading Myth Critics, it was mainly Leslie Fiedler, a long-time academic, who kept self-consciously and stubbornly alive the old ideal of the independent critic by scorning scholarly style and apparatus, seeking "popular" outlets and commercial publishers, and playing into old age the *enfant terrible* and the man of letters. In this project, however, he showed himself heir to the avowed tradition of the New York Intellectuals rather than that of the professional Myth Critic.

CHAPTER SIX

Phenomenological and Existential Criticism

FROM THE ATOMIC TO THE SPACE AGE

IN OCTOBER 1957 the Soviet Union launched *sputnik*, the first manmade satellite, which it followed a few weeks later with another satellite carrying an animal wired for monitoring on earth. Hastily, America responded in 1958 with the launching of Explorer I in January, the creation of the National Aeronautics and Space Agency in July, and the establishment of the National Defense Education Act for improved training in the sciences and mathematics in September. The fear of a "missile gap" between America and the rival Soviet Union prompted the placement by America of Jupiter and Thor missiles in Britain, Italy, and Turkey during 1958. The globalization of the Cold War, begun in the immediate postwar years, quickened its pace in the 1950s and thereafter as science and technology were increasingly harnessed by governments for purposes of "defense." In his farewell address of 1960, President Dwight Eisenhower, an Army general and war hero, warned Americans: "In the councils of governments we must guard against the acquisition of unwarranted influence, whether sought or unsought, by the military-industrial complex." Eisenhower hoped to avert the control of policy by "a scientific-technological elite." From the dawning of the Atomic Age, technology and science were increasingly felt to be potentially life-threatening as well as awe-inspiring.

The triumph of science in the postwar period was symbolized positively by the discoveries of DNA, polio vaccine, and antibiotics. The success of technology manifested itself most dramatically in the computer machinery that enabled space flight. Worldwide systems of communication as well as nationwide telecasting testified also to the achievements of science and technology, though on less fearful terms than the new atomic weaponry and rocketry. In the domain of theoretical science, astrophysics in particular brought to dramatic realization the post-Einsteinian universe with disclosures of startling new concepts and phenomena: big bang, expanding universe, curvature of space, black holes, supernovas, pulsars, quasars, antimatter, quarks. Closer to earth, American homes and offices reaped the benefits of technology and science in the form of numerous gadgets and innovations, ranging from televisions to air conditioners, from dishwashers to push-button phones, from automatic car transmissions to electric typewriters.

By the late 1960s American society was three-fourths urban and one-fourth rural in population. A century earlier the figures were the exact opposite. Ninty-seven percent of the population increase from the 1940s to the 1960s was an urban phenomenon. Disguised by such highly publicized figures was the reality of growing suburbanization, which especially characterized American social life during the expansive years of the Atomic and Space Ages. From 1950 on, the Census Bureau included suburban figures in urban statistics. Not only did rural society experience loss during the postwar period, but so, in fact, did strictly "urban" centers. By the late sixties 76 million Americans dwelled in suburbs and 64 million lived in cities. Suburban sprawl brought freeways, shopping malls, and isolated pockets of inner-city poverty.

While the Gross National Product went from $58 billion in 1932 to $504 billion by 1960, the expanding national wealth did not filter evenly through society. In 1960, for example, the top 5 percent of the population received approximately 13 percent of the wealth whereas the bottom 20 percent received 6 percent. More than 20 million people lived below the government poverty line during the 1960s. The postwar image of an "affluent society," composed of suburban, well-heeled, comfortable consumers, left out the reality of widespread poverty, devastated cities, and decaying rural communities.

The increasing massification of postwar society, epitomized by growing "Levittowns" and "Daly Cities," with their homogenized houses and lifestyles, was manifested not only by the suburbanization of the expanding population, but also by the spread of systems of mass transporation, mass communications, and mass marketing. Despite the apparent mobility, comfort, and wealth of American life, many intellectuals saw in contemporary mass society as well as postwar technological science much decadence and danger, much alienation and absurdity, much repression and sickness.

Numerous influential sociological studies offered grim portraits of American society, including David Riesman's *The Lonely Crowd* (1950), C. Wright Mills' *White Collar* (1951) and *The Power Elite* (1956), Herbert Marcuse's *Eros and Civilization* (1955), William Whyte's *The Organization Man* (1956), Vance Packard's *The Hidden Persuaders* (1957), John Kenneth Galbraith's *The Affluent Society* (1958), Norman O. Brown's *Life Against Death* (1959), and Paul Goodman's *Growing Up Absurd* (1960). What emerged from such analyses, among other things, was an urgent historical narrative about the dispossession of rugged individualists in favor of outer-directed conformists who were manipulated by government bureaucracies and corporations and stripped of political and psychological potency. Mass man was puny, weak, dependent, repressed, controlled, and absurd. The subduers of man were corporate capitalism, big government, mass advertising, rampant technology, rigid social conventions, coopted science, and total administration—all of which tamed forms of opposition and fostered docile conformity.

During the immediate postwar years the upsurge in university enrollments and the consequent expansion of the teaching corps led to the massification of higher education. The GI Bill contributed to this phenomenon, as did the Korean War. Starting in the late forties, veterans flocked to the universities. Students could and did avoid military service in Korea by enrolling in colleges. Between 1946 and 1957 enrollments nationwide rose from 1,677,000 to 3,138,000 students. The number of university faculty members increased in the same years from roughly 136,000 to 344,000. Not incidentally, the simplified classroom procedures of the New Criticism were well suited to these conditions, unlike the more complicated pedagogies of sociological and historical criticism, which generally required considerable amounts of background education. Veterans, in particular, tended to be indifferent to social and political issues, wanting to get on with their own interrupted lives rather than to change society. By the late fifties, however, the conformity and quietism characteristic of the first postwar decade began to be challenged on numerous fronts.

Not surprisingly, many programs appeared urging liberation and revolt, ranging from the fostering of small independent communes to beginning artistic countercultures, from dropping out of society to turning on to mind-expanding drugs, from creating special political interest groups to seeking erotic freedoms. Flourishing particularly in the late 1950s and the 1960s, such programs, often cast as "pastoral" alternatives, invariably envisioned the enemy as the technological-bureaucratic mindset aided by scientific, social, and educational methods of control. Some of America's finest young literary intellectuals turned to Continental philosophy, particularly phenomenology and existentialism—formed abroad before mid-century— as means for developing vital new modes of literary criticism in the 1950s and the 1960s.

CONTINENTAL PHILOSOPHY IN AMERICA

In twentieth-century Europe the dominant traditions in philosophy were the analytical/positivist and the phenomenological/existential lines of thinking. The latter mode of thought had an important impact on American literary criticism during the postwar period, beginning roughly in the mid-50s. Before examining American Phenomenological and Existential Critics, we shall briefly survey some essential philosophical backgrounds relevant to phenomenology and existentialism.

Of the many European philosophical phenomenologists, the most important was Edmund Husserl, the founder of the movement at the turn of the century. While other phenomenological thinkers made significant contributions, they exerted a less profound influence in the 1950s and 1960s on American literary criticism. In this category fall—arguably—Roman Ingarden, Maurice Merleau-Ponty, Gaston Bachelard, Emil Staiger, and Mikel Dufrenne. In American literary studies, Husserlian phenomenology was largely mediated and transformed through the Geneva criticism of Georges Poulet (whom we shall discuss in the next section of this chapter).

In his *Logical Investigations* (2 vols., 1900–1901; 2d rev. ed., 1913) and *Ideas* (1913), Husserl aimed to establish the foundations of knowledge and the criteria of scientific truth by going beyond empiricism and philosophical idealism. Whereas Lockean empiricism pictured the mind as a blank sheet that received and associated sensory data, Kantian idealism presented consciousness as active rather than passive in constituting knowledge through universal mental categories. To avoid *both* the associationist psychologism and the "objectivism" of empiricism *and* the categorizing and subjectivism of idealism, Husserl urged a return to objects as experienced by subjects. The basis of phenomenology was contemplative description of experience—of a perceptual arena where subject and object worked in tandem. While objects came to a subject through direct intuition, the subject constituted the objects in acts of bestowing meaning. Because subject and object were mutually implicated, consciousness for Husserl was never blank or empty: a pure "I think" was impossible. Consciousness always had content and was conscious *of*—something. The fundamental linkage of subject and object in experience, the essential fact of mind as being "consciousness of," was labeled by Husserl *intentionality*. The inherent intentionality of consciousness meant that phenomena did not exist independent of subjects; subjects constituted phenomena while bestowing meaning; phenomena for human consciousness were "intentional."

To enable a "return to things themselves," Husserl developed the *epoche*— a method of "bracketing" or "suspending" extraneous presuppositions, inferences, judgments, and emotional projections, which distort experience. In this manner Husserl jettisoned the Kantian categories that made "things in themselves" unknowable, just as he subverted empiricism through intentionality, all of which left consciousness content-dominated rather than empirically empty or blank. To carry out a full phenomenological project, a Husserlian phenomenologist first described, in adherence with the *epoche*, objects of consciousness in all their many perspectives, then intuited through a "transcendental reduction" what was revealed in the stream of consciousness, and finally grasped by means of "eidetic reduction" what emerged as essential in the experience of the overall field of objects. Ultimately, phenomenological method aimed to secure for knowledge neither a random flux of phenomena nor an eccentric or merely personal testimony, but an unchanging and universal essence (*eidos*).

Among the chief contributions of Husserlian phenomenology were its insistence on the epistemological co-implication of subject and object and on the primacy of the world of experience (*Lebenswelt*). In addition, it called into question the "natural attitude" or "commonsense" view that objects existed in the outside world independent of observers. Phenomenology subverted not only empiricism and idealism, but Cartesian dualism and modern scientific method. It worked to heal the rift between self and world, experience and knowledge, and consciousness and the creation. With its transcendental and eidetic methods of analysis, it (re)dignified human beings in the wake of Darwin and Freud.

Of the numerous European existentialist thinkers, the most influential for American critics were Martin Heidegger and Jean-Paul Sartre. The latter came to prominence in the immediate postwar years and passed on to Americans what was originally from Heidegger, whose popularity came considerably later. One of the peculiar features of existentialism, which appeared in a self-conscious form in Heidegger's *Being and Time* (1927), was its ability to incorporate in its project all manner of thinkers, including earlier writers like Kierkegaard, Dostoevsky, and Nietzsche as well as many later modernists like Kafka, Eliot, and Gide. In a 1945 lecture on the topic, published in 1947 in a popular English translation titled *Existentialism,* Sartre outlined a handful of traits characteristic of the philosophy. According to his early conspectus, existentialists insisted that existence preceded essence; that human subjectivity was the proper starting point of philosophy; that human beings had no essence and were thus obliged continuously to define existence; that the making of choices inescapably produced anguish; that God did not exist and man was forlorn as a result; that man was "condemned" to freedom in the absence of all determinisms; that ethics had constantly to be invented in the context of specific world situations; that reality resided in actions and involvements undertaken in the presence of others; that man could want but one thing—freedom; and that man, in constantly reaching outside himself, in passing beyond, favored transcendence. Developed more fully in Sartre's early masterwork *Being and Nothingness* (1943), these core themes and premises were helpfully amplified for Americans by William Barrett's widely read monograph-length introduction to existentialism published in 1947 in *Partisan Review* and later supplemented in his *What is Existentialism?* (1964).

While Heidegger and Sartre were both phenomenologists, they focused their labors on the question of being rather than the question of knowledge. Existentialism was ontological philosophy whereas Husserlian phenomenology was epistemological philosophy. The former tended to examine traditional humanistic matters, the latter veered toward perennial scientific concerns. Existentialism brought with it a cluster of distinctive thematic preoccupations and key concepts: absurdity, abyss, anguish, authenticity, bad faith, being, caring, commitment, contingency, crowd, death of God, finitude, forlorness, freedom, historicality, lostness, nausea, nothingness, otherness, ontology, responsibility, situation, temporality, world. Very few of these primary existential topics appeared in Husserlian phenomenology.

Perhaps because it developed in the context of the French Resistance to German Occupation during World War II, early Sartrean existentialism attended to the philosophical practicalities and problems of everyday living; it possessed a distinct moral tone and praised ethical engagements. It was a humanism, as Sartre acknowledged. Heideggerian existentialism was neither an ethics, nor an activism, nor a humanism, which Heidegger pointed out in his "Letter on Humanism" (1947). Both versions of existentialism found almost immediate applications in fields other than philosophy. In the discipline of psychoanalysis, Ludwig Binswanger appropriated Heideggerian concepts for a full-fledged existential psychoanalysis; Sartre himself developed an existential psychoanalysis in *Being and Nothingness*. Almost at the outset both Heidegger and Sartre themselves turned to literary criticism, producing readings of major writers. As a novelist and dramatist, Sartre fashioned an immensely influential existential literature. Fields of inquiry affected by existentialism included religious studies, sociology, and fine arts as well as psychology, literary criticism, philosophy, and literature.

The general effect of contemporary philosophical criticism, whether of the phenomenological or existential variety, was to affirm the value of human subjectivity, to deny conventional scientific objectivity, to celebrate the individual as opposed to the crowd, to credit intersubjective intimacy, to resist mechanical or technological leveling and framing, to foster personal engagement rather than detachment or disinterest, to complicate and enrich American critical methodology, and to offer alternatives to other modes of criticism, particularly New Criticism and myth criticism. In effect, philosophical criticism worked to counter the dubious triumphs of social massification, technological science, and formalist criticism, which seemed all of a piece to American philosophical critics. In the following sections, we shall examine the philosophical criticism produced in America from roughly the mid-1950s to the early 1970s, focusing on representative and/or influential Phenomenological and Existential Critics, including especially J. Hillis Miller, Paul Brodtkorb, Geoffrey Hartman, Susan Sontag, William Spanos, and Ihab Hassan, all of whom belong to a generation of critics born between 1925 and 1934. Later modes of philosophical criticism developed from the late 1960s to the mid-1980s—particularly hermeneutics and deconstruction—are discussed at the close of this chapter and in separate chapters.

PHENOMENOLOGICAL CRITICISM
GENEVA STYLE

While a relatively small number of American literary intellectuals were interested in and undertook philosophical criticism during the 1950s and 1960s, an even smaller number of them practiced phenomenology that excluded existential themes and commitments. Of such Phenomenological Critics, the most influential and significant were J. Hillis Miller and Geoffrey Hartman. The main line of American criticism in a strict phenomenological mode loosely followed the lead of the Geneva School, particularly the work of the Belgian critic Georges Poulet, who taught in America from 1952 to 1957 and whose books gained considerable domestic readership during the 1960s. While discussing in this section the critical work of J. Hillis Miller, we shall interweave an account of the Geneva School and of Georges Poulet. In the next section, we shall consider Paul Brodtkorb's phenomenological study of Melville, which offered some enrichments of the Geneval approach, and we shall scrutinize Geoffrey Hartman's work— ultimately the least aligned and most modulated of American phenomeno- logical undertakings during the 1950s and 1960s.

Phenomenological criticism in the Geneva manner was best known to Americans through the influential works of J. Hillis Miller, including his *Charles Dickens: The World of His Novels* (1959), *The Disappearance of God: Five Nineteenth-Century Writers* (1963), *Poets of Reality: Six Twentieth-Century Writers* (1965), *The Form of Victorian Fiction* (1968), and *Thomas Hardy: Distance and Desire* (1970). In studying each of his many authors, Miller dedicated himself to drawing a detailed portrait of the *consciousness* of each writer. The details of portraiture were gathered consistently from each artist's oeuvre. Miller's unit of analysis was self-consciously not the individ- ual artwork of formalist criticism but the canon of the author, including letters, notes, diaries, and so on. In other words, Miller focused solely on the consciousness of the writer and eschewed valuing (beforehand) a poem, play, story, or novel over a letter, diary entry, literary fragment, or lecture. Any piece of writing, whether it was a masterwork or a minor fragment, could, in Miller's view, reveal the mind of its author. As he went about constituting the total consciousness of a writer, Miller alternately assumed a calculated relationship to the writer as that of fellow traveler, of brother meditator, or of cocelebrant. Such methodological intimacy or intersubjec- tivity distinguished Miller from other (nonphenomenological) American critics. Significantly, both the method and the goal of Miller's Geneva criticism contrasted sharply with the various means and ends characteristic of Marxist criticism, New Criticism, Chicago criticism, New York criticism, and Myth criticism.

Miller described his method incisively in an essay titled "The Geneva School" (1966). Here he offered an introductory section, two sections of general theory, six sections on six leading European members of the School, and a brief concluding section. Not surprisingly, he revealed much about his critical ways in those parts discussing his cobelievers as well as in the theoretical parts. "The Geneva Critics," according to Miller's opening remarks, "consider literary criticism to be itself a form of literature. It is a form which takes as its theme not that experience of natural objects, other people, or supernatural realities about which the poet and novelist write, but those entities after they have been assimilated into the work of some author. Literary criticism is literature at a second degree."[1] To (re-)constitute in criticism the themes and visions of a writer meant to enter his or her world—to relive and share such reality from within. There was no pretense in this procedure to scientific objectivity or neutral exposition; the co-implication of critic and author formed the foundation of critical engagement. As Miller put it, "the literary critic, like the novelist or poet, is pursuing, however covertly or indirectly, his own spiritual adventure. He pursues it not by way of his own experience, but by the mediation of the experience of others. His work is far from disinterested or detached" (306; see also Preface to *Thomas Hardy*). By nature the critic's work was inescapably personal, if not openly intimate. Miller replaced the traditional goal of "aesthetic distance" with a provocative suggestion about Geneva criticsm: "it might be best to define it not in terms of its relation to other kinds of literary criticism, but as a special form of that literature of meditation, reverie, or spiritual quest which is historically associated with Switzerland and most often with Geneva" (306). Geneva criticism was meditation, dream, or mystical journey, and the Geneva Critic was meditator, dreamer, or spiritual quester. The basic method, as Miller conceived it, was ultimately to experience, extend, and complete the visionary consciousness of the writers from the inside: the Geneva Critic was an explorer into the interior spaces of human consciousness whose method was to reincarnate in writing his unique experience of an author.

Revealingly, Miller started his manifesto with the italicized fragment, "*Consciousness of consciousness, literature about literature.*" He meant to signify by this two key aspects of Geneva criticism. What he did with the first tag, "consciousness of consciousness," was to identify cryptically the goal of the Geneva phenomenologists. The second tag suggested the method of the School. Essentially, these critics conceived of literature strictly as a form of consciousness (see the Preface to *The Disappearance of God*). This conception denied that literature was manifestation of social reality, or objective structure, or revelation of the collective or personal unconscious, or mere orchestration of sign codes. "For Geneva Critics, then, criticism is primordially consciousness of the consciousness of another, the transportation of the mental universe of an author into the interior space of the critic's mind. Therefore these critics are relatively without interest in the external form of individual works of literature" (307). Accordingly, Geneva Critics mostly ignored the supposed autonomy of particular artworks, since they sought to behold the living center of the artist's mind revealed in the complete works.

There was genuine significance in the fact that citations by a Geneva Critic referred to page numbers in the collected works instead of using the title of the work along with page numbers. The individual work was desubstantiated; the author's consciousness was hypostatized. "Often the subject of one of their essays is the total work of an author, including his notes, his diaries, his unfinished works, his fragmentary drafts. Such incomplete writings may allow better access to the intimate tone or quality of a mind than a perfected masterpiece" (307). To sum up, the goal of Geneva criticism was to reveal through the consciousness of the critic the structure of the writer's consciousness as embodied in his or her complete works[2]— which explains why this literary phenomenology was nicknamed "criticism of identification."

The leading European members of the Geneva School were Marcel Raymond, Albert Béguin, Georges Poulet, Jean Rousset, Jean-Pierre Richard, and Jean Starobinski. These critics were linked through friendships as well as shared ideas. Miller himself came to know Poulet and Starobinski when he was a young professor in the early and mid-1950s at the Johns Hopkins University. In several later essays Miller discussed in detail the criticism of his mentor—Poulet. Here Miller took great pains to elucidate Poulet's similarities with and differences from other Geneva Critics. About Poulet's general approach, Miller observed: "As long as some specific quality of inner experience is successfully expressed in the work of a writer, Poulet will find it worthwhile to relive that quality from within. The aim of each of his critical essays is to re-create as precisely as possible the exact tone which persists in a given writer throughout the variety of his work" (313). After this observation, Miller went on to demonstrate that, strictly speaking, Poulet's concept of consciousness was not phenomenological, but Cartesian, since Poulet believed in "pure consciousness" as opposed to the phenomenological belief in "consciousness of" something. This was an important point, leading Miller to conclude: "Poulet's criticism, then, may more exclusively be defined as 'consciousness of consciousness' than either the religiously oriented criticism of Raymond and Béguin or the thematic criticism of Bachelard and Richard" (315). In short, Poulet's was the most Genevan of Geneva criticism insofar as his criticism was more exclusively a consciousness of "pure" consciousness. Here Geneva criticism, however, ignored the whole thrust of Husserlian phenomenology, seeking to transcend the contents of consciousness so as to arrive at pure mind—an idealistic end-point later condemned by some historians of criticism.[3]

Significantly, Miller's personal debt to Poulet was openly declared in his introduction to his first book—the study of Dickens—where he initially described the Geneva phenomenological method. A dozen years later he characterized Poulet's approach and summed up his own values and goals in an essay titled "Georges Poulet's 'Criticism of Identification'": "Poulet's criticism is first of all mimesis, and the duplication of an author's mind in a critic's mind is accomplished when the critic can, as it were, speak for the author, alternately in the author's language and in the critic's language, for the two languages have become the same."[4] Indeed, it was Miller's uncanny protean identification with his author's ideas, feelings, and words that distinguished his work from the dominant formalism and myth criticism of the 1950s and 1960s.

In 1970 Miller dropped Geneva phenomenology in favor of deconstructive criticism—a telling event signaling a new wave of philosophical criticism. We shall discuss deconstruction in chapter 10.

The first full-length account of Geneva criticism—Sarah Lawall's *Critics of Consciousness* (1968)—provided American intellectuals an informative, scholarly introduction to the School, devoting a chapter to each of the eight leading critics. Lawall's approach was to discuss chronologically the major works of each critic; using this method, she covered Miller's first three books in detail. On the opening page Lawall characterized the work of the Geneva Critics: "They look upon literature as an act, not an object. They refuse to make distinctions between genres; they look for a single voice in a series of works by the same author; they will not consider each work as an autonomous whole. What is more, they seek latent patterns of themes and impulses inside literature, and do not discuss the symmetries and ambiguities of the formal text."[5] Put negatively, for Geneva phenomenologists a literary work was not an object; genre was an unproductive extrinsic concept; an individual work in isolation from the oeuvre did not offer coherence of vision; the individual work, in effect, was not self-enclosed; and objective patterns of images and themes in individual works did not often or necessarily reveal the significant meanings of works. Furthermore, Geneva Critics conceived literary criticism as itself a creative form of writing in which the critic sympathetically relived and recreated through his own personal consciousness and literary prose the unique consciousness of an author as it was contained in his complete works.

Among the noteworthy aspects of Geneva criticism, as practiced by Miller during the 1950s and 1960s, were the vital role accorded the reader, the importance assigned to critical *writing*, the implied critique of other modes of criticism (particularly formalism), the emphasis on immanent criticism, the conception of language as transparent, the disregard of social and historical determinants (in line with the transcendental reduction), the concept of "work" as oeuvre (in harmony with the eidetic reduction), and the treatment of the concept of "intention." With regard to "intention," Geneva criticism exhibited no interest in an author's purpose—in the psychology of an author preceding his writing. Rather, "intention" was construed phenomenologically as that which resulted from the encounter of author and world as embodied in the text and experienced by the critic.[6] Geneva criticism was, therefore, uninterested in ordinary biographical criticism. Finally, worthy of note in Miller's phenomenological inquiries was a certain religious or mystical tone and vocabulary, a result of his marked preference for epiphanic moments regularly sought in the authors he examined. What such intensities demonstrated was a disregard of the law of the *epoche*—of the necessity of bracketing presuppositions and prejudices. Since similar religious preoccupations appeared in many of the Geneva Critics, it constituted a distinguishing characteristic of the School.

PHENOMENOLOGICAL CRITICISM PLURALIZED

For most philosophically minded American literary critics and theorists during the opening years of the Space Age, the dominant mode of phenomenological criticism remained the Geneva approach of Georges Poulet and J. Hillis Miller. Nevertheless, other enriched and pluralized versions of critical phenomenology emerged in works by, among others, Paul Brodtkorb, David Halliburton, Geoffrey Hartman, LeRoi Jones, Joseph Riddel, and Edward Said. This diversity can be sampled by examining the book by Brodtkorb on Melville published in the middle sixties and the essays and books by Hartman published between the mid-1950s and early 1970s. Like Miller, Brodtkorb and Hartman resisted the growing tendency to subsume their work under the aegis of existentialism. This does not mean that either one ignored Sartre, Heidegger, or other Continental philosophers, but that each kept faith with basic phenomenological insights and concerns.

At the outset of his *Ishmael's White World: A Phenomenological Reading of MOBY DICK* (1965), Paul Brodtkorb lucidly staked out his phenomenological project: he would read *Moby Dick* by focusing exclusively on the narrator's consciousness through description of the dimensions of its fictive world. According to Brodtkorb's Husserlian theory of consciousness, "consciousness is always consciousness *of* something: to be aware of anything at all is to 'intend' it in a certain, often characterizable, way. Mind and matter are thus inseparable; subject alters, colors, and shapes what is present to it, so that 'subject' and 'object' spring together."[7] The contents or matter of *Moby Dick* could be characterized through a description of the "intentional consciousness" or mind of the narrator Ishmael. To depict with precision the topography of Ishmael's life-world (*Lebenswelt*), Brodtkorb employed a Heideggerian schematic as articulated by the Dutch psychologist J. H. Van den Berg in his *The Phenomenological Approach to Psychiatry* (1955). "Ishmael's existence as an intentional consciousness may be divided into his apprehension of (1) his world, excluding other people; (2) his body, and his consciousness of the bodies of others; (3) other people, including himself as a character; (4) time" (10). Accordingly, Brodtkorb devoted a separate chapter to each aspect of the narrator's *Lebenswelt*, using, in passing, insights from Bachelard, Blanchot, Kierkegaard, Poulet, Sartre, and other Continental thinkers. Not surprisingly, Brodtkorb examined existential themes— boredom, death, despair, dread, nonbeing, nothingness, others, situation, void—but he did so within the broad framework of a Husserlian theory of consciousness.

Brodtkorb's phenomenological approach differed in several significant ways from that of Geneva criticism. To begin with, it displayed little interest in the author, adhering strictly to analysis of character. And it scrutinized one work only and avoided cross references to other works in the author's oeuvre. Lastly, it foregrounded the text by relying on continuous bulky citation, erasing the presence of the reader almost altogether: thus it courted critical "objectivity" rather than intimacy. What all this pointed to was clear—Brodtkorb accommodated phenomenology to the dominant formalism of the time. He dwelled upon a self-enclosed individual work; he eschewed both the "intentional fallacy" (the presence of the author) and, to a lesser extent, the "affective fallacy" (the shaping role of the reader); and he investigated carefully the text per se in a mannered version of close reading. From the outset Brodtkorb committed himself to exegesis of "symbolic structure" aimed at demonstrating "coherence" and "unity" (10): like a formalist, he sought structural unity, though in this case the critic worked through language to get at unified *consciousness*. Finally, he bracketed social and historical concerns in the manner of a New Critic (a formalist "strategy" shared with Geneva phenomenologists).

Whereas Brodtkorb dedicated himself to discipleship at the start of his project, Geoffrey Hartman avoided such commitments throughout his more than three decades of critical work. As a phenomenologist and later as a deconstructor, he worked to remain independent. It's almost as if Hartman were playing gingerbread man, daring anyone "catch me if you can." Evidently, Hartman did not care to be catechized or enrolled in any school.

Hartman's evasiveness manifested itself, for instance, in the peculiar attitude he displayed toward his phenomenology in the "Retrospect 1971," added to the new printing of his *Wordsworth's Poetry: 1787–1814* (1964): "What I did, basically, was to describe Wordsworth's 'consciousness of consciousness.' Everything else—psychology, epistemology, religious ideas, politics—was subordinated. If that is phenomenological procedure, so be it."[8] Indeed, it was phenomenological procedure. In this book Hartman scrupulously reconstituted the development of Wordsworth's consciousness over the period of a quarter century. As he announced in the Preface to the original edition of the text, he aimed to track Wordsworth's "emerging phenomenology of mind" and to describe sympathetically the "drama of consciousness and maturation."[9] He characterized his study as "a new and comprehensive view of Wordsworth's 'consciousness about consciousness,' " and he argued phenomenologically that the "fundamental relation, as between subject and object, posited by Wordsworth, is not something intrinsic and inalienable, but part of a deeply operative principle of generosity . . . the imagination goes out to nature, becomes fertile, and produces a 'creation' . . ." (391). The meeting of mind and world in Wordsworth's poetry, according to Hartman, constituted a deliberate phenomenological act of love and generosity. What Hartman illustrated in Wordsworth was a phenomenological dialectic: the extreme poles of the poet's consciousness included, on one hand, ideal union of self with nature and, on the other hand, solipsistic withdrawal of self from world.

Hartman's interest in phenomenological matters can be glimpsed in his first book, *The Unmediated Vision* (1954). Although he was clearly not a card-carrying Phenomenological Critic at this point, Hartman's interests ran instinctively to concerns central in phenomenology: the relation of self and world, the nature of consciousness, the "intentional" character of knowledge, and the epistemological priority of "experience" in literature. In his introductory "Short Discourse on Method," he insisted that great poetry "is written by men who have chosen to stay bound by experience" and that "the poem should be taken as a whole, and the poet's work as a whole."[10] Within a phenomenological context of literature as embodiment of human experience, Hartman sought to respect the aesthetic integrity of the individual work in relation to the oeuvre. In the end, however, he formulated a *general* thesis about modern poetry: "The modern poet has committed himself to the task of understanding experience in its immediacy" (164). The category "experience," conceived phenomenologically, formed the ground of Hartman's work: he found modern poets to be frantic bracketers in their quest for direct or unmediated experience.

Craving the most intense and pure representation of self and reality, modern poets practiced radical forms of bracketing. Often they suspended history, perception, and language itself in their search for direct knowledge or experience of nature, body, and consciousness. The extremist desire for or creative possibility of unmediated knowledge—a legacy of Cartesian philosophy—drove modern poets to radical forms of withdrawal from and denial of mediations. Some poets cherished silence; some dreamed of purified voice or language; some imagined pure perception or pure consciousness.

As poets, Wordsworth, Hopkins, Rilke, and Valéry are at one in their quest for a pure representation. But as *modern* poets they are related by their effort to gain pure representation through the direct sensuous intuition of reality. Each has a greater or lesser trust in unmediated vision. . . . The eye and the senses are made to supply not merely the ornaments but the very plot of truth. Consciousness becomes, in its contact with the physical world, the source and often the end of cognition. (156)

What Hartman demonstrated was that the post-Cartesian split of philosophical understanding into idealism and empiricism repeated itself in the major European poets from the Romantics to the Moderns and that these poets intermittently fashioned phenomenological solutions to this split. Some poets tended toward idealism and some toward empiricism—some desired a domain of pure intellect and some a realm of pure perception. Ultimately, however, the co-implication of self and world, the fact of experience, solved their dilemmas: "Consciousness becomes, in its contact with the physical world, the source and often the end of cognition."

In his critical works from the mid-fifties through the early seventies, Hartman exhibited a continuous dedication to three integrated modes of inquiry. He practiced textual exegesis in the context of literary history. The epistemological and thematic foundation of this aesthetic or philological criticism was essentially phenomenology: Hartman's analyses typically progressed from form to consciousness. Along with philology and phenomenology, Hartman engaged in religious or, better yet, anagogical criticism. This latter mode of questioning manifested itself in various ways—concern about scripture, about mysticism, about myth, about spirituality, about "ghostly" or uncanny dimensions of literature. In *The Unmediated Vision*, for example, Hartman saved for his closing words a certain lament about the death of God in modern poetry: "The four artists here considered, chosen from among the greater modern poets, have in varying degrees and even when most Christian, lost the full understanding of revealed religion, accepted the individual quest for truth and forced by this same quest to seek mediation, sought it neither in Christ nor in tradition but in the very things that caused them to seek: personal experience and sense experience" (172). Given the spiritual dilemma of modern poets, as depicted by Hartman, it was not surprising that he characterized post-Enlightenment poets as "Self-Tormentors." A final example of Hartman's early spiritual interests should suffice. Throughout *Wordsworth's Poetry*, Hartman documented apocalyptic and eschatological themes in his poet's work. Of the poet, he declared: "While Wordsworth generally limits himself to the growth of the individual mind . . . his poetry does suggest, however mildly, the possibility of a providential (ecological?) change in human consciousness" (407). That the uncertain revolution in question may have been ecological rather than providential was a secondary, not primary, possibility. Spirit came to mind first. Like Poulet, Miller, and other Phenomenological Critics, Hartman displayed a marked penchant for religious thematics.

When Hartman talked about "consciousness of consciousness," he had in mind poets' awareness and thematization of personal mental activity. This interest in literary self-consciousness, an epochal inward turn of mind, differed from the Geneva Critics' dedication to interpretative intimacy or identification. For Geneva phenomenologists "consciousness of consciousness" designated the critic's intuition of the poet's interior universe: the critic was implicated in the act of literature. Hartman did not extend phenomenological intentionality to the critical act. As a philologist and literary historian, he kept some distance between himself and his poets. It was this distance, bred of a certain formalism and historicism, that distinguished Hartman from the Geneva Critics. Concern for spiritual matters, however, he shared with many Geneva phenomenologists, though in Hartman's case spirituality had less to do with immanent textual epiphanies than with historical reflections on the state of religious consciousness in his authors.

From the late 1960s onwards Hartman conceptualized the general situation of American criticism as a field of struggle between the dominant Anglo-American formalism (the tradition of empiricism) and the emergent Continental philosophy (the tradition of idealism). He despised pure formalism and feared undistilled philosophical criticism. What he promoted was a merging of the two modes. In the context of American criticism, this meant that Hartman emerged as an advocate of philosophical criticism. Such a commitment became increasingly more evident from *Beyond Formalism: Literary Essays 1958–1970* (1970) to *Saving the Text: Literature/Derrida/Philosophy* (1981). Throughout this later period Hartman fought against the domestication of literature by Anglo-American formalists and for the defamiliarization of it by Continental philosophers and critics. Increasingly, Hartman presented literature as strange, mysterious, magical, unfamiliar, ghostly. This "anagogical" dimension of his criticism linked up with a growing historical curiosity about sacred and secular hermeneutics as practiced by ancient rabbis and church fathers as well as more modern German Hermeneutical Critics. Part of Hartman's latter-day project involved a transformation of the plain-style prose of Anglo-American criticism into the literary or creative prose associated with European critical practice. Here Hartman's effort made contact with the Geneva phenomenologists' critical program earlier nicknamed "literature about literature." As we shall see in the penultimate section, Ihab Hassan proposed a similar turn to "creative criticism."

In *Beyond Formalism,* Hartman attempted to bring "literary criticism closer to philosophy" without renouncing formalism. "Despite an allegiance to the Continental style of criticism, I feel strongly what James called 'the coercive charm of form.'"[11] Nevertheless, the devotion to form in America "proved to be dangerously narrowing" (xii). In Hartman's assessment, New Critical exegesis impoverished the work of literary criticism. This was the situation in 1970: "We witness today the pedagogical triumph of the auxiliary science of exegesis: of the repetitive, compulsive analysis of works of art in terms of theme and formal relations. Great exegetes, however, have always, at some point, swerved from the literal sense of the text. This text, like the world, was a prison for Rabbinic, Patristic, or Neoplatonic interpreters, yet by their hermeneutic act the prison opened into a palace and the extremes of man's dependence and of his capacity for vision came simultaneously into view" (xii). Taking his lead from ancient scriptural interpreters, Hartman wanted to move criticism from text and theme to life-world and vision—from philology to philosophy and hermeneutics, from formalist exegesis to phenomenological and anagogical criticism. Given such a goal, we can understand Hartman's harangue against formalism voiced in his celebrated essay "Beyond Formalism" (1966):

The dominion of Exegesis is great: she is our Whore of Babylon, sitting robed in Academic black on the great dragon of Criticism, and dispensing a repetitive and soporific balm from her pedantic cup. If our neoscriptural activity of explication were as daring and conscious as it used to be when Bible texts had to be harmonized with strange or contrary experience, i.e., with history, no one could level this charge of puerility. . . . To redeem the word from the superstition of the word is to humanize it, to make it participate once more in a living concert of voices, and to raise exegesis to its former state by confronting art with experience as searchingly as if art were scripture. (56–57)

The proper end of criticism was to reach through text to human experience. Experience here was variously characterized as "strange" and "contrary," as "history," as a "living concert of voices." The model for criticism was ancient biblical hermeneutics. Contemporary formalism was heresy, idol, superstition; it tamed and weakened American critics.

The same year that Hartman lambasted formalism, he attacked myth criticism in a dissection of Northrop Frye. Once again, he insisted on experience as the foundation of literature and criticism. As in his attack on formalism, he identified experience with "history" and with the "human voice." "This surely is what the great work of fiction (or criticism) achieves: it recalls the origin of civilization in dialogic acts of naming, cursing, blessing, consoling, laughing, lamenting, and beseeching. These speak to us more openly than myth or archetype because they are the first-born children of the human voice" (39). To put flesh on the dead word, image, or archetype, the critic must recover a primordial sense of voice, of dialogue, of human community, of experience. Oral poetics, used by Hartman as a defense against formalist devaluation and mythic appropriation of art, instituted "dialogue" as a founding category of literature. About texts, Hartman pronounced, "if they do not reveal 'the voice of the shuttle' as well as 'the figure in the carpet,' they are expendable" (xiii). The theory of dialogue—of interaction of poet's text and critic's word—installed a phenomenological ground for literature and criticism, which accounted for the *Lebenswelt* of author as well as reader and for the intentionality of the literary artifact.

The multifaceted criticism of Hartman retained a phenomenological core while it relied on philology and resuscitated ancient hermeneutical insights. It sought to preserve for criticism formalist practice, historical sensitivity, and spiritual significance. Needless to say, this independent pluralized form of phenomenological criticism recruited no followers: it was a unique blend seemingly designed to resist imitation and categorization. What it lacked was the distinctive intimacy of the affective critical approach of the Geneva Critics. It compensated the weaknessess of the Geneva mode, however, by adding to its special expressive poetics a programmatic concern for literary form and for literary history. Like Geneva phenomenology, it displayed little interest in matters related to judicial criticism. Finally, Hartman's project self-consciously highlighted with increasing drama the conflicts between philosophical criticism and native formalist modes. Myth criticism was a desiccated inkhorn child of bookcraft and erudition (40) and New Criticism was a whore of Babylon (56). Continental philosophy promised vitalization through estrangement: "Literature is today so easily assimilated or coopted that the function of criticism must often be to defamiliarize it."[12]

FROM EXISTENTIAL PHENOMENOLOGY TO CHRISTIAN EXISTENTIALISM

During the late forties and early fifties when it first aroused interest, existentialism in America seemed to be predominantly a French affair. Only a few early existentialist literary critics took Heidegger or other German philosophers to heart. Sartre and Camus more or less dominated the field of initial native interest. Perhaps because both men were superb novelists and dramatists as well as critics and philosophers, their influence spread to American poets, playwrights, and fiction makers as well as literary critics. Thus by the 1960s W. S. Merwin, Edward Albee, and Norman Mailer, for example, were as much existentialists in American literary estimates as any contemporary literary critics. All this is to say that the growing popularity of existentialism tended to broaden its historical, philosophical, and thematic reach with each new anthology, casebook, introduction, and symposium. After a relatively short time, existentialism became neither simply a French affair nor merely a critical movement.

In his *Casebook on Existentialism* (1966), William Spanos included as representatives of existentialism the philosophers Pascal, Kierkegaard, Nietzsche, Heidegger, Jaspers, Berdyaev, Sartre, Tillich, Camus, and the writers Dostoevsky, Kafka, Unamuno, Hemingway, Dürrenmatt, Ionesco, Sartre, Camus, and Auden. He argued in his Preface that "existentialism is more than a philosophical movement. It has become *the* perspective from which the sensitive and concerned modern man looks at his world."[13] In his introductory essay, he observed, "The roots of existentialism extend deeply into Western history, even beyond St. Augustine to the pre-Socratic philosophers and the author of the Book of Job" (1). Put another way, existentialism during the later stages of its development became a generalized perspective concerned with unaccommodated man and his experience of nothingness, with meaningless social life and the fact of alienation, with death and its absurdity, with authentic existence and the burden of freedom, with spiritual dread and personal rebellion. Given such a broad scope, it was not surprising that existentialism gained a varied following in America. Numerous texts elucidated and popularized its premises, preoccupations, and major figures, as did—to cite only six examples—the inaugural number on "Existentialism" of *Yale French Studies* (Spring–Summer 1948), H. J. Blackham's *Six Existentialist Thinkers* (1952), William Hubben's *Four Prophets of Our Destiny* (1952), Arturo B. Fallico's *Art & Existentialism* (1962), Eugene F. Kaelin's *An Existentialist Aesthetic* (1962), and Davis Dunbar McElroy's *Existentialism and Modern Literature* (1963). Among the most interesting existential literary critics were Susan Sontag and William Spanos, whose works we shall scrutinize here. In the next section, we shall examine the utopian existentialism of Ihab Hassan.

A graduate of the famous humanities program at the University of Chicago, a trained philosopher, a filmmaker, novelist, critic, and perhaps the most provocative of the younger New York Intellectuals, Susan Sontag burst on the literary scene in the early 1960s with a remarkable spate of essays later collected in *Against Interpretation* (1967) and *Styles of Radical Will* (1969). A cultural critic steeped in contemporary French philosophy and literature, Sontag practiced an unencumbered, suave form of existential criticism in the self-conscious manner of a New York essayist and literary reviewer rather than a university scholar or professional philosopher. She combined a phenomenological sensibility with existential thematics—which renders her a useful transition figure for our study of philosophical criticism in its existential form.

In "The Aesthetics of Silence" (1967), Sontag described "the" two stages of post-Romantic literary consciousness. According to Sontag, art moved in our epoch from being a noble expression of human consciousness to being a tragic, self-estranged antidote to consciousness. As it progressed from confession to deliverance, art became a form of "purgation" of both human self and creative form. Ultimately, art sought silence, yet not the preparatory silence of ripening depicted by Valéry, but the terminal silence of renunciation dramatized by Rimbaud, Duchamp, and Wittgenstein. Such apparently debilitating renunciation disguised "the wish to attain the unfettered, unselective, total consciousness of 'God.'"[14] When it did not

abandon art altogether, such an aesthetics of silence promoted either immediate, sensuous experience of life or confrontations with the conceptual
boundaries of art. What it wanted to counter or cancel, above all, was the
burden of historical consciousness, which produced an enervating sense of
belatedness and alienation and which befouled present perception, language, and consciousness. "Behind the appeals for silence lies the wish for a
perceptual and cultural clean slate. And, in its most hortatory and ambitious
version, the advocacy of silence expresses a mythic project of total liberation. What's envisioned is nothing less than the liberation of the artist from
himself, of art from the particular artwork, of art from history, of spirit from
matter, of the mind from its perceptual and intellectual limitations" (192).

The existential ordeal of modern consciousness, the basis of the literary
aesthetics of silence, centered invariably on the inauthenticity of ordinary
language. Various projects of creative renovation and destruction were
conceived by post-Romantic writers. Some, like Tristan Tzara, recommended the abandonment of the written word and the revival of oral
poetics. Others, like Samuel Beckett, fostered an interminable "ontological
stammer" in the face of the "void" (199). Still others, like Rilke and Ponge,
sought to cleanse language by cutting back its scope to the simple art of
naming. Related attempts to return to things themselves, to purify perception, to reestablish communal culture, to behold uncontaminated consciousness, to become mute—all of these were part of the modern aesthetics
of silence, and they testified to man's extreme existential alienation and
emptiness. While other American philosophical critics had earlier examined
aspects of this grim cultural situation, among them Geoffrey Hartman and
George Steiner, Susan Sontag gave the ordeal of modern literary consciousness and its concomitant aesthetics of silence a nearly definitive formulation.
She did not privilege "experience," as did Hartman, nor did she blame the
desiccation of language and art on "technological mass-society" and contemporary "political inhumanity," as did Steiner,[15] rather she credited a
wide array of forces—all of which were entangled with the burdens of
historical consciousness and its curtailments of free creativity. In this she
followed her master, Friedrich Nietzsche.

Sontag's most celebrated essay of the 1960s was "Against Interpretation"
(1964)—a manifesto written in an aphoristic style that argued a phenomenological thesis based on an existential view of modern existence. "All the
conditions of modern life—its material plenitude, its sheer crowdedness—
conjoin to dull our sensory faculties. . . . What is important now is to
recover our senses. We must learn to *see* more, to *hear* more, to *feel* more"

(104). In place of utilitarian interpretations that darken and encumber artworks, we needed an erotic and transparent, descriptive criticism. "To interpret is to impoverish"; "interpretation is largely reactionary"; "a great deal of today's art may be understood or motivated by a flight from interpretation" (99, 98, 101)—such aphorisms energized Sontag's call for an end to scholastic interpretation. Ironically, this call came at a time when hermeneutics was on the threshold of a considerable expansion in America, as suggested by the publication of E. D. Hirsch's *Validity in Interpretation* (1967) and Richard Palmer's *Hermeneutics* (1969). Sontag's revulsion against interpretation, her rebellion in search of genuine perception, her demand for critical freedom, her disgust with the crowd in society and in critical work constituted an existential stance against the modern condition. Rebellion rather than silence seemed to her the most authentic option. Self-consciously, she worked against the grain.

At the opening of his introductory text *Existentialism* (1945), Jean-Paul Sartre admitted a certain difficulty in defining existentialism. "What complicates matters is that there are two kinds of existentialist; first, those who are Christian . . .; and on the other hand the atheistic existentialists, among whom I class Heidegger, and then the French existentialists and myself."[16] From the 1950s onward a number of important Christian existential studies of literature were written by American theologians and literary critics, among whom were Stanley Romaine Hopper, William F. Lynch, Nathan A. Scott, Jr., Amos Wilder, and William V. Spanos. The latter literary critic edited a popular anthology of existentialism, mentioned above, which assigned considerable space to theological "existentialists" from Augustine to Tillich. In his lengthy study, *The Christian Tradition in Modern British Verse Drama* (1967), subtitled *The Poetics of Sacramental Time,* Spanos cast modern life, the "modern predicament," as a "boundary situation" in which "man, stripped of protective philosophical or theological systems, naked, unaccommodated, and alone, stands face to face with Nothingness."[17] This essentially religious encounter constituted the fundamental fact of modernity, serving as the foundation of Christian existentialism.

Like most Christian writers of our era, the British verse dramatists— associated with the Festivals at Canterbury Cathedral from the late 1920s to the late 1960s (interrupted only during the war years)—faced the modern "boundary situation" in trying to create a vital religious literature. Chief among these writers were Gordon Bottomley, T. S. Eliot, Christopher Fry,

John Masefield, Dorothy Sayers, and Charles Williams—all of whom were studied by Spanos in an effort to develop an existential "sacramental aesthetic," which opposed the secular "aesthetics of silence."

As did many modern literary people, Spanos believed a dissociation of sensibility set in during the seventeenth century, producing a positivistic "naturalistic imagination" and an idealistic "angelic imagination." The task of the modern Christian intellectual was to heal this split on religious grounds. "What was necessary—and most difficult—here within the boundary situation was a genuinely existential ontology that could potentially integrate the whole range of human experience . . ." (12). The Christian verse dramatists found a solution in the "sacramental realism" of the medieval miracle play based on the "doctrine of the Incarnation, the Word made Flesh, which reconciles time and eternity and salvages the past from the refuse heap of history" (13). Similar incarnational solutions were fashioned in the "crisis theology" propounded by Continental Christian existentialists such as Barth, Berdyaev, Bonhoeffer, Bultmann, Marcel, and Tillich. For poets the incarnational or sacramental aesthetic, respecting the divinity of the Word and the humanity of the flesh, allowed literature "to employ the objects of nature to express transcendent significance without sacrificing their identity, their particular reality" (27). History, instead of being a dreadful burden, emerged in the sacramental aesthetic as endowed temporality in which "time and eternity, the many and the one, motion and stillness, perpetually inform each other. Every moment in history, every human action, is infused by a discoverable universal and permanent significance without loss of its unique actuality, its historicity" (29).

Unlike myth criticism, which suffused modernity with timeless archetypal value yet diminished contemporary reality, the Christian existential aesthetic provided ontological rather than merely psychological value to present and past existence. Where myth criticism repeated the stance of philosophical idealism, the sacramental aesthetic recuperated on an ontological plane the phenomenological solution. "Sacramental vision reconciles the concrete reality and value that the empirical world view dichotomizes; and, in so doing, it rescues value from naturalistic and reality from idealistic art. By means of it, all objects in space (nature) and all events in time (history) are placed according to a universal scheme and given transcendent significance" (50). What this meant for drama was that human actions, whether they occurred in the past or the present, possessed contemporary as well as transcendent value. Time became the authentic vehicle of the spiritual life. "Torn between the claims of time and eternity, body and soul, evil and good, the Christian hero . . . discovers in his anguish that the way of salvation necessitates an existential immersion in time . . ." (335). Return to myth—escape from time—violated the sacramental aesthetic. By virtue of the Christian existential aesthetic, the dramatic hero was enabled to embrace the chaos and pain of temporality. Whether a Christian chose the *via positiva* and accepted affirmatively the gifts and burdens of nature and time, or whether she decided on the *via negativa* and rejected ascetically the fallen self's abuse of the gifts and burdens of nature and time, she confirmed all the same both the incarnational redemption of time and the necessity of existential immersion in it.

The sacramental aesthetics developed by Christian existentialism amounted to an ontological solution to the painful epistemological dilemmas embodied in the secular aesthetics of silence. The role of time and history was crucially different in each aesthetics. For the atheist, time was burdened with the oppressive and immense bric-a-brac of history; it imported the future fact of death into the present; yet it left the future opened and undefined. Time was fallen, but proffered freedom. For the Christian, time was sedimented with past deeds redeemed by the Incarnation; it rendered the painful present as spiritually significant as the past; and it offered a transcendent material future. Both atheistic and religious existentialism acknowledged the predicament of the present, the boundary situation—"existence precedes essence" in Sartre's words—in which man, alone, confronting Nothingness and death, had both responsibility and freedom to define his existence through acts undertaken in anguish and uncertainty. It was the view of the past, of history, that distinguished religious from atheistic existentialists. For the latter, the solutions to the burden of historical consciousness ranged from destruction to willed forgetfulness, from parody to silence. For the former, history gave a vast reservoir of significant analogues to the present. The Christian view engendered a conservatism; the atheistic understanding generated various radicalisms. The Christian project of verse drama, unlike the extremist enterprises of, say, Valéry and Rimbaud or Beckett and Duchamp, harkened back to the golden days—the era of Elizabethan and medieval theater. The past became boon, not burden.

In the 1970s William Spanos turned away from Christian existentialism to Heideggerian "destructive hermeneutics," renouncing the religious solution of sacramental aesthetics and confronting the dilemmas of the aesthetics of silence. Like many phenomenologists and existentialists, he continued the efforts both to overcome the separation of idealism and empiricism—to merge transcendentalism and naturalism—and to maintain for contemporary man creative possibilities and freedom.

UTOPIAN EXISTENTIAL CRITICISM

Among the most suggestive and productive of the American Existential Critics was Ihab Hassan, who published numerous essays and several widely praised books in this philosophical mode, especially *Radical Innocence: Studies in the Contemporary American Novel* (1961), *The Literature of Silence: Henry Miller and Samuel Beckett* (1967), and *The Dismemberment of Orpheus: Toward a Postmodern Literature* (1971). Later works by Hassan remained existential in spirit, but added to this foundation an increasingly dominant cultural utopianism and fragmented style exceeding a strictly existentialist project. This change occurred about 1970 and was first fully manifested in the collection *Paracriticisms: Seven Speculations of the Times* (1975). Born and raised in Egypt, Hassan came in 1946 to American where he pursued graduate study and an academic career. He became a naturalized citizen of the United States in 1956.

A contribution to the growing field of American Studies, Hassan's *Radical Innocence* ostensibly offered a literary historical and sociological survey of a dozen or so major novelists writing in the postwar era. (A considerable amount of Hassan's material here was published in the fifties as journal articles.) Among the writers examined were Bellow, Capote, Cheever, Donleavy, Ellison, Mailer, Malamud, McCullers, Salinger, and Styron. Expanding on Northrop Frye, Hassan argued that there were three distinctive forms of ironic fiction in contemporary American literature: the ironic-tragic with victim or scapegoat as hero; the ironic-comic with impostor, rebel, or outsider as hero; and the ironic-romance with self-deprecating man as hero. The foundation of Hassan's historical, sociological, and formalist critical modes was existentialism.

Regarding genre, Hassan insisted, "form is the way the mind acknowledges experience," involving a "concrete and existential encounter" of the "self with world" or of the "hero with experience."[18] That contemporary American fiction conformed to the shape and spirit of irony testified to the nature of human experience in this time and place. In other words, technique followed life, not vice versa. This view of genre allowed Hassan to resituate Frye's "formalism" on existential grounds. It amounted to an existentialist attack on myth criticism as well as a critique of the romance theory of the American novel: "if the contemporary hero seems mythic in the sacrificial quality of his passion, his actions have the concrete self-definition of an existential encounter" (114). As far as Hassan was concerned, "the pattern of experience in contemporary fiction is largely existential," not fundamentally mythic or generic. The postwar novel did not conform to the traditional genres of comic or tragic fiction; its unique existential pattern had its roots in the tradition of irony and the stuff of life. For Hassan the virtue of such a conception of fiction was that it allowed the critic "to view the peculiar tensions of American culture and the formal bias of contemporary fiction in a single perspective" (122).

The existential sensibility behind Hassan's social criticism was evident throughout *Radical Innocence,* in which he depicted the modern self in various extreme relations to society.

The alienation of the self, its response in martyrdom or rebellion or both to the modern experience, has been briefly observed in history, in the body politic, in man's psyche, and in his existence. (20)

The central fact about fiction in a mass society may be this: that as the modes of behavior congeal into a hard, uniform crust, the hero attempts to discover alternate modes of life on levels beneath the frozen surface. (107)

The dominant political trend of the age fortifies the collective and technical organization of society. (20)

But technology has not only reduced individual freedom, it is taking over the State itself. (15)

This is the . . . paradox of mass culture: that enforced uniformity not only produces, in depth, levels of dissent beneath the surface; it also breeds pockets of heresy in the lateral direction. (108)

The contemporary self recoils, *from* the world, *against* itself. It has discovered absurdity. (5)

The contemporary world presents a continued affront to man. . . . (5)

The picture of modern social life presented in these and similar passages was broadly representative of the prevailing existentialist indictment of mass society. In the context of the uniformities imposed by technological social organization, man was alienated and resentful, victimized and rebellious, self-destructive and heretical. He sought, above all, freedom.

Hassan's was a cultural criticism that shuttled adroitly between contemporary fiction and social life, resolutely refusing to respect the aesthetic autonomy posited by formalist criticism and suspicious of the leveling ahistoricism or universalism of myth criticism. The ontology and historicity of literature preceded its aesthetic and archetypal forms. Patterns of experience determined the nature of artistic form. Hassan's politics, implied between the lines, was unrelentingly antinomian and ultimately anarchist. For him literature bore a relation to life. Writers showed people "how they may actually live in the lion's mouth" (335). Accordingly, "This is not a time for professors of literature to ignore the judgment of human passions" (326). Like many existentialists, Hassan regarded history as a burden. "Revulsion has indeed become a modern attitude toward history. . . . It is a confession that man finds no redemption in history. Eden is far behind, the millennium not appreciably nearer. The prevalent sense is one of cataclysm or else of transience" (13). However much a nightmare history was, the future remained open. Existentially, we were free to act and shape our existence. It was characteristic of Hassan to stress this utopian element of the openness of time. Acts of rebellion and resistance signified for him man's positive unwillingness to be a victim of his future. But the future contained death, which had to be accepted. To deny death was to refuse time and history—to be radically innocent.

At about mid-point in *Radical Innocence,* Hassan catalogued five general traits of contemporary fiction—all of which were decidedly existential. First, "Chance and absurdity rule human actions." Second, "There are no accepted norms of feeling or conduct . . ."; courage alone conferred dignity in the face of such meaninglessness. Third, the hero "remains an alien to society, a misfit," and for him time "serves to eventuate only in defeat." Fourth, "Human motives are forever mixed; irony and contradiction prevail." And fifth, the perception of any situation "remains both limited and relative" (116–18). Despite such a grim portrait, Hassan emphasized everywhere the positive potentials for transcendence that existential philosophy and literature contained: it displayed courage, commitment, freedom, responsibility—affirmations of world and life.

In his works after *Radical Innocence,* the utopian direction of Hassan's cultural criticism became more insistent and evident, though he continued to examine the unspeakable depths of existential experience. In *The Dismemberment of Orpheus,* for example, he studied the despairing works of Sade, Hemingway, Kafka, Genet, and Beckett. Admittedly, these authors "exemplify, in some hieratic order of despair, the sovereignty of the void."[19] But to counterpoint such a movement, Hassan strategically inserted two Interludes and a Postlude designed to show that "the destructive energy of the avant-garde seems finally redemptive" (x). The possibility of a redemptive transformation of human consciousness thrust Hassan from avant-garde literature toward present life. "Yet we must also move onward, to a personal fate closed finally by mortality, and a collective destiny unknown to children of the old earth or new moon. Literature does not suffice" (ix). This imperative to move beyond literature surfaced on the very first page of *The Dismemberment of Orpheus*.

What the literature of the silent void disclosed were fundamental questions of being and nothingness, of consciousness and death. These were vital issues not just for avant-gardists, but for all intellectuals in the modern world. It was essential to Hassan that this literature not pass rapidly from fashion to history without pressing its powers on us. "The face of silence that drives through literature from its modern to postmodern phase will merely flash as personal intuition or fade as critical abstraction unless we allow it the resistance of example. In choosing these examples, we deliver ourselves of a judgment which is not wholly literary, and draw the experience of the authors into our own constructions. Thus critics finally attest to the energies they exchange with art" (22–23). As an existential cultural critic, Hassan wanted modern and postmodern literature to exceed both the abstract coldness and distance of mere history and the personal warmth and intimacy of simple fashionable criticism; he advocated instead a crucial intermediate task of making this literature an energetic interpersonal and communal experience—a tough example. The literature of the void intimating a transformation of human consciousness must energize criticism to help effectuate change. The didactic potentials of literature depended on the sympathetic and activist responses of the critic, whose job it was to offer testimony and to further change. Hassan deemphasized slightly the traditional mimetic, expressive, and textual or formal dimensions of literature in the interests of its affective and didactic powers, understood in existential terms to involve consciousness of being and nothingness and in utopian terms to involve new forms of existence. As an existential cultural critic in a utopian mode, Hassan valued history, biography, and sociology as means to extend the project of existentialism to remake and reconceive not only criticism but consciousness.

Hassan ended the brief foreword to *Dismemberment*—dated Fall 1970— admitting "It is all too likely that some uneasiness in this work may betray a manner that I consider no longer my own" (x). Indeed, a transformation had occurred. No longer would Hassan operate within the traditional modes of literary scholarship. His texts soon became fragmented, aphoristic, personal. While the sentence and paragraph as units of composition remained firm, larger structures gave way. Exuberant and innovative forms of dismemberment disrupted his critical texts. The "aesthetic of silence" invaded his prose compositions. The line between literature and criticism was crossed. Criticism became creative. In his own way, Hassan fulfilled the admonition of Geneva criticism to make critical writing "literature about literature." But none of the Geneva Critics went nearly as far as Hassan. A similar transformation occurred during the early 1970s in the style of other philosophical critics like Geoffrey Hartman and Harold Bloom. In this as in other things, Susan Sontag was a precursor, though she never went so far in her analyses of postmodern themes and her assaults on scholarly style as did Hassan and others. With the project of *paracriticism*, Ihab Hassan accepted also the lure of utopianism. "At the center of my concerns is an awkward vision of change, a pressing query about the destiny of our race. What role will expanding human consciousness play in the universe?"[20] From the "Personal Preface" (dated 1974) of *Paracriticisms*, this statement and query described the direction of Hassan's work during the 1970s. At heart an existentialist, he became a full-fledged utopian and orphist interested in gnostic forms of consciousness. In 1970 Hassan urged: "Let criticism, then, become a design for life. Let it envision a new man. Let it also praise, and thus foster mutability."[21] A dozen years later, in a new edition of *Dismemberment*, Hassan posed a telling rhetorical question, asking "is some decisive historical mutation—involving art and science, high and low culture, the male and female principles, parts and wholes, involving the One and the Many as pre-Socratics used to say—active in our midst?"[22] Evidently, he believed so. It was no time for literary intellectuals to ignore the positive possibilities of the coming future.

CONTINENTAL PHILOSOPHY IN AMERICA— THE FIRST AND SECOND WAVES

Phenomenological and existential literary criticism emerged and matured in America between the mid-1950s and the early 1970s. Rooted in the Continental philosophy of early Husserl and Sartre, among many other sources, such philosophical criticism in America found itself in deep opposition to native formalism and myth criticism, which were the dominant critical modes of the 1950s and 1960s. (The "marginal" work of the early Marxists and New York Intellectuals posed no apparent threat.) While the older formalists and Myth Critics paid comparatively little attention to the post-war wave of Continental philosophy—with some notable exceptions, including Murray Krieger and Leslie Fiedler—philosophical critics remained deeply conscious of their older native rivals. All of the American philosophical critics examined in this chapter were born in the decade between 1925 and 1934; they were of a different generation from the New Critics, Chicago Critics, and Myth Critics as well as the depression-era Marxists and the leading New York Intellectuals. They came to the universities at the dawn of the Atomic Age and began their professional careers on the eve of the Space Age. Many of them were in contact with Continental intellectuals. Most were deeply sympathetic to, if not trained in, the discipline of Comparative Literature. As young intellectuals, they witnessed the formation of a growing and impressive critique, propounded by sociologists, theologians, and psychologists, of mass society and technological reason. Similar critiques had been developed earlier by New Critics, Marxists, New York Intellectuals, and Myth Critics. Their chosen European mentors were similarly critical of social massification and technological reason. Steeped in phenomenology, all of the American philosophical critics deplored, in particular, positivist scientific epistemology with its impersonal objectifications of physical and cultural phenomena and its dissociations of subject and object, existence and essence, reader and text. Many of these critics were distressed by the scholarly and cold conversational style of American criticism. The transformations they sought involved not only revising impersonal epistemology and critical style, but also revaluing the literary canon. Unlike the formalists and Myth Critics, none of these critics displayed much interest in literature before Wordsworth or Blake. And few were dedicated in the long run to American Studies. Interestingly, none of the American Phenomenological and Existential Critics expressed any overt political beliefs: they were adherents of neither the right nor the left. And regarding religion, most of them exhibited interest in spirituality, but of a nonsectarian, mystical sort.

In the area of poetics, most of the early philosophical critics in America were more or less in agreement about the valuable affective and didactic potentials of literature. While they credited the importance of textual exegesis, none of them were content to hypostatize the literary text as sacred autonomous artifact. Although they were evenly split on the pertinence or usefulness of expressive poetics, they shared a consensus on the mimetic dimensions of literature, though none—except Hassan—was genuinely interested in literature as social record or revelation. On the possibilities of psychopoetics, few of the philosophical critics expended much energy, though Hartman, Brodtkorb, and Hassan made some use of Freudian (not Jungian) insights. In general, the preoccupation of the Phenomenological and Existential Critics with consciousness did not extend very often to the unconscious. Presumably, that realm was left to the Myth Critics.

When it came to the area of critical approach, these literary intellectuals uniformly avoided judicial criticism, evidently leaving such business to the formalists. They were all more or less deeply interested in the reader's response to literature, as befits their roots in phenomenology, which insisted on the co-implication of subject (reader) and object (text). Where they differed here was in how far they promoted the divinatory intimacy of reader with work. Although a few of the philosophical critics showed an interest in writers' biographies, none of them allotted much weight to actual biographical criticism. Careful scrutiny of the formal text characterized all of these critics—testimony, no doubt, to the powerful influence of the New Criticism and of the Anglo-Saxon empirical tradition. The one exception was Susan Sontag, who worked in the waning tradition of New York literary journalists rather than the university scholar. The attention to textual detail characteristic of the group distinguished them from their Continental models, who were considerably more relaxed in this regard. While all of the American philosophical critics displayed some degree of commitment to historical criticism, they often disagreed on what this work entailed and on how history itself was to be construed. In this matter, they showed a remarkable heterogeneity that was the direct antithesis to the relative homogeneity of the historical criticism practiced by the Depression-era Marxists. Several of the philosophical critics, namely Sontag and Hassan, engaged in cultural criticism that extended beyond the confines of strict literary history.

By the early 1970s the most productive of this generation of critics had attained considerable stature in the academic world. While philosophical criticism was still a relatively marginal endeavor, these critics evidently had little trouble in publishing their books and articles with leading journals and presses. The institution of literary studies accommodated Phenomenological and Existential Critics effortlessly and early. Perhaps because all of them, except Sontag, were perceived early on as scholarly "practical critics" rather than nonliterary or philosophical "theorists," they were received with relatively little trouble or suspicion. Unlike New Criticism, philosophical criticism had no appreciable impact, nor did it seek to, on pedagogical methods. It was left to later Reader-Response Critics to advocate programs of classroom reform along lines sympathetic to basic phenomenological insights. If philosophical critics had any significant impact on the teaching of literature in America, it was in facilitating the spread of existentialism, which started to appear widely in university course content during the 1950s. The credit for this change doubtlessly belonged to social conditions and the combined work of psychologists, sociologists, theologians, and philosophers rather than to the efforts of a relatively few committed literary critics.

In the late 1960s and early 1970s a second wave of Continental philosophy, more multifaceted and diffuse than the first, made its way into the domain of literary studies in America. What characterized this influx was, first, its division into four distinguishable projects—hermeneutics, structuralism, deconstruction, and Marxism—and, second, its complicated relations with phenomenological, existential, and psychoanalytical modes of inquiry.

Following the tradition of German hermeneutics, the American Hermeneutical critics, including, among others, E. D. Hirsch, Richard Palmer, and William Spanos, derived their projects from the works of Martin Heidegger and Hans-Georg Gadamer, although in the case of Hirsch such derivation was plainly antithetical, leading him to resuscitate the older German tradition of philological rather than phenomenological hermeneutics, as embodied in the texts of F. D. E. Schleiermacher and Wilhelm Dilthey. The main literary structuralists, including Jonathan Culler, Seymour Chatman, Claudio Guillén, Gerald Prince, Michael Riffaterre, and Robert Scholes, had intellectual roots in various national traditions of linguistic and stylistic analysis, though the contemporary French tradition was dominant. They came from two distinct generations—those born during the twenties and those born during the forties. In the work of the increasingly influential contemporary philosopher Jacques Derrida, deconstruction derived from, while being critical of, Husserlian and Heideggerian phenomenology, Saussurian and Lévi-Straussian structuralism, and Freudian and Lacanian psychoanalysis. In addition, deconstruction was ambiguously steeped in the texts of Nietzsche. Among the first American intellectuals in the late sixties and early seventies to adapt deconstruction for literary criticism were Harold Bloom, Paul de Man, Geoffrey Hartman, J. Hillis Miller, and Joseph Riddel, all of whom, like the rival Hermeneutical Critics, were members of the generation born between the mid-twenties and mid-thirties.

Significantly, a "Marxist" element of the second wave of Continental philosophy developed in the 1970s and 1980s, involving, among others, Fredric Jameson, Frank Lentricchia, Michael Ryan, Edward Said, and Gayatri Spivak. These critics were mostly born after the mid-thirties, coming from a later generation than the first American hermeneuts and deconstructors. The cultural criticism of these younger leftist intellectuals had roots in later Sartrean existential phenomenology, in Foucaultian structuralism, sometimes in Freudian and Lacanian psychoanalysis, in Derridean deconstruction, and in twentieth-century Neo-Marxist thought as embodied in the projects of the Frankfurt scholars, Georg Lukács, and numerous others. Unlike the earliest American deconstructors, who were established critics when they turned to Derridean philosophy, these younger Leftist Critics were near the beginnings of their careers when they adopted the Continental philosophy of the second wave and its various supplements.

The hermeneutical criticism initiated in America in the late 1960s underwent some significant expansions in response to the rapid spread of deconstruction in the first half of the 1970s. An important new European source was added to this tradition: the work of the contemporary French hermeneutical phenomenologist Paul Ricoeur—a dozen of his books appeared in translation between 1965 and 1977—became quickly influential because it confronted in detail and with care structuralism, psychoanalysis, and deconstruction without renouncing hermeneutics. From the mid-sixties into the eighties, Ricoeur taught part of the time in America. Moreover, a new ally was recruited in the early 1970s to the hermeneutical project when William Spanos turned from Christian existentialism to Heideggerian "destructive hermeneutics," which moved toward deconstruction without abjuring the phenomenological tradition as did, for example, Miller and Riddel. Finally, renewed relevance and urgency was conferred upon hermeneutics because it offered a sophisticated alternative to, as well as a critique of, the growing deconstructive movement. Just as deconstruction reinvigorated Murray Krieger's formalism during the seventies (as we saw in chapter 2), so it energized the enterprises of Hermeneutical Critics like Spanos and Hirsch, the latter of whom gained added notoriety by attacking deconstructors as upstart skeptics and "cognitive atheists."

From the late 1960s to the mid-1980s interest in European hermeneutics, structuralism, deconstruction, Marxism, and psychoanalysis (especially of the Lacanian variety) was increasingly widespread. The second wave managed to gain a much broader audience and larger following than the first. This turn to Continental sources, widely characterized by literary intellectuals as a move to "theory," had numerous impacts and manifestations: many journals in this new interdisciplinary field of inquiry were started; presses published a growing number of "theory-oriented" books; scores of conferences and symposia were convened; translations poured off the presses; careers were made; new authorities were established; institutes and schools were formed; and new questions and terms broadly infiltrated American criticism and scholarship. The discipline of literary studies seemed transformed from within. The manners and conventions of the profession underwent reexamination. In the works of Hartman, Hassan, and Bloom, as we noted, the style of critical discourse itself gave way to new freedoms and excesses. In all of this change, existentialism faded into the background and phenomenology became a scapegoat while hermeneutics, structuralism, deconstruction, and Marxism expanded their scope and influence.

The second wave of Continental philosophy rendered prominent the works of Marx, Nietzsche, Saussure, Freud, Heidegger, Gadamer, Lacan, Derrida, and Foucault. What these thinkers had in common, as Ricoeur suggested in *De l'interprétation* (1965), was more or less distrust in the surface of things and in manifest "reality." Aiming to demystify surfaces and illusions, these European "destroyers" developed and advocated a "hermeneutics of suspicion." All of the philosophical lines of the second wave in America reflected this tendency. In addition, they continued and expanded the intense doubts, fears, and criticism, initiated during the early days of the New Critics and elaborated during the period of the first wave of Continental philosophy, of technological science and mass society.

In conjunction with reader-response, feminist, and Black Aesthetic criticism, hermeneutics, structuralism, deconstruction, and leftist cultural criticism made the field of literary studies in America during the Space Age seem a carnivalesque site; it appeared less a loosened hierarchy than, say, a series of interlocking sideshows. At work in the early 1970s were New Critics, Chicago Critics, New York Intellectuals, Myth Critics, phenomenologists, existentialists, Hermeneutical Critics, Reader-Response Critics, structuralists, deconstructors, feminists, Black Aestheticians, and leftists as well as textual scholars, linguists, literary historians, biographers, literary journalists, bibliographers, and numerous poets, playwrights, and novelists writing criticism as a sideline. In future chapters we shall have more to say about this diversification of literary studies and proliferation of theoretical orientations in American literary criticism during the Space Age.

CHAPTER SEVEN

Hermeneutics

THE VIETNAM ERA

B Y T H E E A R LY part of 1965 there were 125,000 American combat troops in South Vietnam and massive aerial bombings of North
Vietnam were getting underway. A large-scale antiwar March on Washington, involving roughly 25,000 students, took place later the same year.
The presence of so many troops in Vietnam and the mass protests against
them would persist for almost a decade—until the last U.S. soldiers departed Vietnamese soil in 1973 and Saigon had "fallen" in 1975. How did
America get involved in Vietnam—the first war it admittedly lost? And
what happened during the Vietnam era?

In the early fifties America sent aid and arms to Vietnam in order to assist
the French in their effort to regain their former empire in Indochina. By
1954 America was paying approximately eighty percent of the French war
expenses, which involved annually hundreds of millions of dollars. At the
same time China and Russia sent assistance so that Vietnam constituted, in
fact, a contested site in the international "Cold" War waged by the U.S.
against communism and its potential spread. Among other unstable sites in
this period were Korea and various countries in Central Europe. After the
cataclysmic defeat of the French at Dien Bien Phu in 1954, Vietnam was
divided into North and South at the seventeenth parallel. As part of the
1954 Geneva agreements, Vietnam was supposed to hold elections, which
Ngo Dinh Diem (the leader in the South) refused to allow in 1956, with
President Dwight Eisenhower acquiesing in this violation. Soon afterwards
the Vietcong emerged in the South in active and armed opposition to Diem,
who, nevertheless, received continued support from the U.S.

When President John Kennedy took office in 1961, America had had an
extensive, decade-long involvement in Vietnam. He furthered this part of

the war against communism in several ways: by ordering the Department of Defense to make plans to save Vietnam (which he approved in May 1961), by committing 7,000 troops for base security in November 1961, and by secretly authorizing a coup against Diem in November 1963. Other flash points in the international struggle against communism at this time included the Berlin Wall Crisis of 1961, the Cuban Missile Crisis of 1962 (preceded by the invasion of the Bay of Pigs in 1961), and the "Space Race" with the Soviet Union. (Uri Gagarin was the first man in space in 1961, followed by John Glenn in 1962.) Behind the political decisions of the early Vietnam era was the postwar liberals' commitment to internationalism and to anticommunism, which the Kennedy presidency symbolized.

Shortly after President Lyndon Johnson assumed office, the North Vietnamese evidently attacked some American ships in the Gulf of Tonkin during August 1964. Passed by Congress, the "Gulf of Tonkin Resolution" authorized the President to protect U.S. troops. Within a year, more than a hundred thousand American troops were fighting in Vietnam and bombing of the North was undertaken on a large scale.

As the war escalated from the mid-1960s onward, opposition increased at home and abroad. In 1965 came the March on Washington and in 1966 Martin Luther King, winner of the Nobel Peace Prize in 1964, spoke out against the war. Over the course of the decade, opposition expanded, manifesting itself in especially dramatic ways at the March on the Pentagon in 1967 (memorialized by Norman Mailer in *The Armies of the Night* [1968]), at the disruptive convention of the Democratic Party in 1968, and at the siege of Kent State University by the National Guard in 1970. Marches, sit-ins, draft-card burnings, desertions to Sweden, exile in Canada, and other forms of protest were common and well-publicized in this period. Meanwhile, the "monolith" of international communism showed signs of breakage. In 1960 came the Sino-Soviet split; in 1968 the invasion of Czechoslovakia by Soviet troops; in 1969 armed clashes along the border between Russia and China; and in 1970 a workers' strike in Poland. The effect of such incidents was to call into question the fundamental concept of the Cold War—the threat of coordinated worldwide communist aggression and the resultant "domino theory"—which motivated and "justified" American involvement in Vietnam.

Among the most influential of antiwar intellectuals was the linguist Noam Chomsky, who in 1967 published in *The New York Review of Books* a series of challenging essays, especially "The Responsibility of Intellectuals" and "On Resistance." Several years later Chomsky collected these and other antiwar essays in *American Power and the New Mandarins* (1969), which was dedicated "to the brave young men who refuse to serve in a criminal war." In Chomsky's assessment, the Vietnam War was a criminal act of immorality, an obscene example of American imperialism, an expression of an agressive, depraved will to power—all of which scholar-experts in and out of government had a responsibility for fostering.

Citizens of the Vietnam era witnessed not only growing radicalization of the intellectual community (especially university students) but increasing calls for civil rights and justice by blacks, women, American Indians, homosexuals, and other disenfranchised groups. In 1963 a mass demonstration for civil rights by blacks took place in Washington, D.C., during which Martin Luther King delivered his now famous speech "I Have A Dream." The next year King received the Nobel Prize and Congress passed the Civil Rights Act. In 1965 violent riots broke out in the Watts ghetto in Los Angeles; in 1966 the radical Black Panther Party was founded; in 1968 several American black athletes made a black power salute upon receiving medals at the Olympic Games in Mexico City. The women's movement, initiated symbolically by the publication of Betty Friedan's challenging *The Feminine Mystique* (1963), came to preliminary fruition in the 1966 founding of the National Organization of Women, which issued a Bill of Rights for Women in 1967. The agitation of women led to liberalization of abortion laws in three states by 1970 and the opening of Senate hearings on an Equal Rights Amendment during the same year. This was also the year that Kate Millett published her influential *Sexual Politics*. The protests of women, blacks, and other groups, the highly visible criticism of the war, and the general disenchantment with all forms of repression, authority, and domination were manifested not only in mass marches, riots, and rallies, but in movies, popular songs, books, and "political" movements. Among the latter were the unisex, civil rights, antiwar, "human potential," gay rights, commune, beat, hippie, and psychedelic movements.

What the various movements and protest groups across the country revealed were dramatic changes taking place in attitudes and awareness, in morals and manners, and in sensitivity and sensibility. The grounds of consciousness and ethical behavior seemed to be shifting. Heterodoxies proliferated, making the whole era appear a gaudy carnival. This cultural change approximated less conventional struggle than guerrilla warfare, having many fronts and numerous invisible troops. The whole idea of a university, for example, was called everywhere into question—especially in California at Berkeley, in New York at Columbia and Cornell Universities, and in Ohio at Kent State University. In fact, in all sectors of the country campus upheavals occurred. Simultaneously, movements toward liberalization or liberation happened in numerous places around the globe: in America, France, Germany, Czechoslovakia, Poland, and Vietnam, to be sure, and in Algeria, Ghana, Cuba, the Congo, Bolivia, Ireland, Quebec, Puerto Rico, Cambodia, Chile, Portugal, Angola, Mozambique, and South Africa. Many "Third World countries," in an impoverished condition analogous to the Third Estate in prerevolutionary France, sought to escape the economic control and cultural hegemony exerted by "First World countries" via multinational corporations and political-economic alliances. America was frequently portrayed, in such countries, as the worst of the "new imperialists." When added up, the demands for liberation both at home and abroad constituted something of a widespread, broad-based consensus, casting the nation into a period of fecund, however threatening, instability and soul-searching. The conscience of the nation demanded careful examination and national presuppositions needed reconsideration—two tasks engendered by the many heterogeneous and multifaceted protests lodged against the country and sustained throughout the Vietnam era.

American intellectuals participated in protest movements, seeking variously to liberate oppressed groups, to realign fundamental values, to promote an examination of conscience, to liberalize restrictive laws and cultural practices, and to get us out of Vietnam. Within China, in contrast, intellectuals experienced purges during the "Cultural Revolution," starting in 1966 and lasting till 1969. Under the direction of Mao Tse-Tung, Chiang Ching, and other leaders, and with the approval of the Communist Party, the young Red Guards dismantled the cultural superstructure of the nation: schools were shut down, libraries destroyed, dance companies and symphonies closed, books burned, foreign influences stamped out, artists dismissed from posts, and teachers publicly humiliated. Estimates suggest that as many as 400,000 people died at the hands of the Red Guard.[1]

In the domain of literary theory and criticism, America witnessed an amazing growth of new schools and movements during the Vietnam era. The most prominent were hermeneutics, reader-response theory, structuralism and semiotics, deconstruction, feminist criticism, Black Aesthetics, and leftist criticism. More or less antinomian, all of these movements sought to counter prevailing and dominant modes of critical theory and practice. Within these schools, critics were more or less radical in their efforts to forge new instruments of inquiry and new grounds for analysis. Above all, the new schools had one project in common: to dismantle or discredit New Critical formalism, which proved to be a highly productive whetstone. Paradoxically, the attacks on New Criticism gave renewed life to this waning formalism, insuring its longevity all through the sixties and seventies. Caricatured, pilloried, subverted, American formalism lived on, seemingly as much because of the relentless attacks on it as because of its continuing attractiveness and viability. What characterized the field of American literary studies during the Vietnam era was a proliferation of new schools of criticism, an increase in the financial resources of literature departments, universities, and foundations, a tremendous numerical expansion of academic posts, journals, conferences, and book publications, a relentless drift toward further institutionalization and professionalization of literary study, and a diversification of academic power and prestige. Given the antinomian spirit and the instability of the era, the various calls and programs for liberation, and the expansion of this field of inquiry, it was not surprising that literary criticism flourished in a way suggestive of a renaissance, though some intellectuals regarded the times as chaotic and degenerative—as an end rather than a new beginning.

The forces at work in literary studies during the Vietnam era included not only a seemingly anarchic and destructive assessment of past endeavors and achievements, but also an ecumenical openness to and tolerance of diversity, dispersal, and indeterminacy. A vast will to deconstruct coexisted with a will to affirm all human effort. In many critical circles, nevertheless, partisanship typically prevailed over pluralism. Laments about the loss of coherence and the end of tradition persisted throughout the sixties and seventies. Here is how William Phillips, editor of *Partisan Review* for over five decades, characterized the literary scene during the 1960s and 1970s: "there is no central idea in our culture, no leading tradition, no main direction, only divergent themes and visions, expressing the chaos of modern life."[2] Behind this representative complaint was despair about both the kaleidoscopic quality of the present and the loss of the supposed unity of the past. Those who weren't complaining were evidently busy chipping away at past monuments. Unlike Phillips, Morris Dickstein, a fourth-generation New York Intellectual and an editor at *Partisan Review*, deemed the time a renaissance comparable in energy and cultural significance to the peak moment of High Modernism during the 1920s. Though not uncritical, Dickstein, in *Gates of Eden: American Culture in the Sixties* (1977), celebrated certain key values and modes of thinking of the era: its skepticism about conventions, its criticism of old habits of belief, its new ethic of participation, its constructivist poetics, its renunciation of disinterested and impersonal (objective and value-free) inquiry, its critique of all formalisms, its politicization of life, literature, and critical inquiry, and its openness to excluded groups and new cultural possibilities. What most distressed Dickstein as well as others was the unstable and self-consuming nature of the art, popular culture, and politics of the time.

The flowering between the late 1960s and the mid-1980s of hermeneutics within critical circles reflected some of the key preoccupations of the Vietnam era. Among these important and pressing concerns were the desires to eschew false commitments to disinterested criticism, to promote practices of interpretative participation, to credit forces of history and culture in the formation of understanding, and to scrap the stifling conventions and habits of mind fostered by critical formalism. It was a certain strand in the work of Martin Heidegger that served as the starting point for the new project of hermeneutics—a project which in the mid-seventies entered a second phase of development in its confrontation with deconstruction.

HEIDEGGER'S HERMENEUTICAL "REVOLUTION"

Of the Continental contributors to modern hermeneutics, none was more significant than Martin Heidegger, who in *Being and Time* (1927) laid the grounds for a full-scale transformation of this special area of German philosophy. Later European hermeneutical philosophers, including Emilio Betti, Hans-Georg Gadamer, Paul Ricoeur, and Peter Szondi, worked in the wake of the Heideggerian "revolution." Present-day historians of hermeneutics now refer to the pioneering works of F. D. E. Schleiermacher and Wilhelm Dilthey, produced in the nineteenth century, as the "old hermeneutics" and the efforts of Heidegger, Gadamer, and their disciples, developed in the twentieth century, as the "new hermeneutics." During the late 1960s and thereafter certain American literary critics, philosophers, and theologians took up the project of hermeneutics as a way to manage, in a contemporary manner, textual understanding and interpretation.

What Heidegger accomplished in hermeneutics was, first, to install phenomenological ontology as the grounds of understanding. The descriptive project of phenomenology ultimately required interpretative labor. To depict *being* meant to interpret it. Being didn't simply manifest itself, it had to be uncovered. Second, Heidegger developed a sophisticated account of the circular process of hermeneutical activity, building on the insights of

Schleiermacher. To simplify *Being and Time* (sections 32–33), hermeneutical labor progressed in a process involving prereflective intimacy of text and reader, which Heidegger called "fore-having" and "understanding." The descriptive articulation of such understanding included complex acts of "fore-sight" in which the reader's concerns and point of view found (or produced) relevant textual elements—all of this work Heidegger labeled "interpretation." At a certain point the interpretation was conceptualized through a process of "fore-conception" into objective, propositional thoughts, which Heidegger named "assertion." In the three strata of hermeneutical effort—understanding, interpretation, assertion—circularity occurred because various presuppositions (fore-having, foresight, fore-conception) were inescapable and essential to the activity. Significantly, the interaction here of reader and text (subject and object) did not require bracketing of context, neutralization or reduction of personal concerns, or respectful sympathy for the author. For these and other reasons, Heidegger's hermeneutical phenomenology differed from the old "objective hermeneutics" of Schleiermacher and Dilthey and from the transcendental phenomenology of Husserl.

Heidegger's third area of achievement in hermeneutics occurred with his later eccentric readings of the poetry of Trakl, George, and Hölderlin and with his attendant reflections on language. These exegetical and linguistic ventures, however, like hermeneutics in general, found relatively few followers in America during the 1960s in comparison with the enormous popularity and influence of existentialism. It was mainly in the 1970s and 1980s that Heideggerian hermeneutics flourished in some American literary circles—a period in which the made-up or constructed nature of meaning or significance and the participation of the critic in such construction demanded full-scale consideration and explanation.

HERMENEUTICS NEW AND OLD

The "new hermeneutics" of Heidegger and Gadamer found interested followers among American philosophers, theologians, and literary critics, primarily from the late 1960s to the mid-1980s. One of the earliest substantial American works in this tradition was Richard Palmer's *Hermeneutics: Interpretation Theory in Schleiermacher, Dilthey, Heidegger, and Gadamer* (1969)—the work of a literary critic intended as an introduction and manifesto. The "old hermeneutics" of Schleiermacher and Dilthey (mediated through Emilio Betti) found a powerful advocate in E. D. Hirsch, whose *Validity in Interpretation* (1967) presented an aggressive and lucid case on behalf of a rigorous philological interpretation.

Palmer's *Hermeneutics* was significant for two reasons: first, it offered the first full-length exposition in English of hermeneutics as an historical discipline and, second, it strenuously advocated the "new hermeneutics" against both the dominant formalism of American criticism and the philological interpretation of Hirsch. It is as manifesto that we shall discuss Palmer's book. Although Palmer labeled the third and final part of his work "A Hermeneutical Manifesto to America Literary Interpretation," the whole text foregrounded both the merits of phenomenological over the older philological hermeneutics and the strengths of the new hermeneutics over reigning Anglo-American formalism. Palmer admitted his commitments in his "Introduction," where he initiated his philosophical attacks against his various opponents.

What was wrong with the dominant New Criticism and myth criticism was their mutual basis in "philosophical realism," which posited the fundamental separation of subject and object (reader and text), rendering the literary work separate from its historical context as well as its reader. Such "realism" made tragically irrelevant to interpretation reader's response and historical milieu. In Palmer's assessment, these exclusions showed Anglo-American criticism to be technological and violent, imitating the approach of the impersonal scientist. "We have forgotten that the literary work is not a manipulable object completely at our disposal; it is a human voice out of the past, a voice which somehow must be brought to life. Dialogue, not dissection, opens up the world of the literary work. Disinterested objectivity is not appropriate to the understanding of a literary work. . . . One must risk his personal 'world' if he is to enter the life-world of a great lyric poem, novel, or drama."[3] As "work" rather than "object," the literary text solicited an historical encounter that called forth personal experience of being in the world. Against philosophical realism Palmer set existential phenomenology: subject and object were co-implicated; human concern, not disinterest, was the proper critical attitude; dialogue instead of dissection constituted authentic critical activity; and understanding—with its personal risks—rather than impersonal knowledge, was the genuine goal of criticism. Because literature was closer to event and proclamation than to mere information, it possessed a fundamental historical dimension slighted by scientific rationality.

Palmer privileged the speaking voice over the dead letter, hearing over reading. Written language was weak; it alienated the word from its living,

primordial powers. Criticism must "make up for the weakness and helpless-
ness of the written word" (17). At its finest, literature was oral happening in
time—not spatial or visual, autonomous artifact. "The saying done by a
literary work is a disclosure of being . . ." (248). It brought a world into
presence. "Oral poetics" characterized the new hermeneutics from Heidegger to Gadamer, from Palmer to Spanos. (We shall examine William Spanos'
"hermeneutics" in the next section.) A similar project involving comparative historical analysis of preliterate oral cultures and later literate societies
was initiated in the 1960s in a series of well-received books published by
Walter Ong. In *The Presence of the Word* (1967), for example, Ong contrasted the two kinds of cultures, observing: "The old more or less auditory
syntheses had presented the universe as being, which was here and now
acting, filled with events. For the new, more visual synthesis, the universe
was simply there, a mass of things, quite uneventful. The shift from a
universe where activity welled up from within to a universe of objects
relatively devoid of internal resources can of course be detected in many
developments within intellectual history."[4] The theory of orality, in Ong
and in Palmer, linked together speech, dialogue, saying, hearing, eventful-
ness, being, and primordiality, opposing them to visuality associated with
print, impersonality, writing, reading, stillness, objectivity, and modernity.
Oral poetics, as such, served as a philosophical foundation for the new
hermeneutics, drawing together many of its key doctrines and themes.

In *Hermeneutics,* Palmer distinguished interpretation proper from observation, explanation, analysis, reflection, and methodology. Implicated necessarily in the act of interpretation were the ontological, historical, and
linguistic worlds of the work and the reader. To observe, explain, analyze, or
reflect upon a text rationally was to distance the reader instead of enabling
"the language event to seize and overpower and transform the interpreter
himself" (226). Furthermore, to methodize the activity of interpretation
was to structure in advance the reader's encounter with a work. All such
predeterminations made of interpretation dogmatic testing or cross-exam-
ination rather than experiential exploration. The tendency to bracket the
horizon of the reader and to focus on the horizon of the text produced
antiquarian criticism. To reconstruct or restore an artifact—to seek to
understand an art object in terms of itself and its time (even if possible)—
was to exclude the world of the interpreter and her present interests.

Interpretation for Palmer had to "relate to the present or die" (251). This
explained why Palmer included in his general hermeneutics Rudolf
Bultmann's practice of "demythologizing," an interpretative process of

sifting the meaning possible for modern man from ancient, more or less alien texts. It also explained why Palmer argued for a special concept of "significance": "Significance is a relationship to the listener's own projects and intentions . . ." (24). The "significance" of a work was a function of the relationship between it and the reader. No relationship, no significance. Finally, it explained why he refused to begin interpretation with considerations of form: the separation of form from theme was a reflexive act, having no basis in one's experiential encounter with a work.

Since the world of the work and that of the reader were historical, interpretation was necessarily historical activity. No work stood outside history; no interpreter existed independent of time. A reader's modes of conceiving, hearing, and understanding were bequeathed from the past. Nonhistorical interpretation was impossible. (Husserl and Heidegger disagreed on the inescapability of the historicality of consciousness, understanding, and world.) The popular concept of critical "objectivity," based on the notion of nonpositionality in time, was a dangerous delusion of Anglo-American criticism in Palmer's view.

On the perennial questions of author's intention and of literary value, Palmer was largely silent. The new hermeneutics did not concern itself with judicial criticism, nor was it interested in biographical inquiry. The author dissolved into the world of the work. Here was a point on which the new hermeneuticists and New Critics agreed. On almost all else they were in conflict.

Phenomenological hermeneutics, unlike New Criticism, credited history and celebrated the reader. (However, reader-response criticism from the late 1960s and throughout the 1970s was considerably more rigorous in its treatment of the reader, as we shall see in the next chapter.) The history dealt with by hermeneutics was decidedly not socioeconomic, as in Marxist criticism, but linguistic and "epistemological": problems in history involved differences primarily in language and world views. The ability of literary works to transform the world of the reader made reading a risky personal venture, conferring on literature very special power. To maximize this power, literature had to be spoken and heard. The important move from textual to oral poetics had the effect of deemphasizing the formal features of literature and activating its affective potentials. Both of these consequences undermined formalist criticism. Though at the time that Palmer attacked New Criticism and myth criticism the first-round creative energies of both schools were spent, they were both then undergoing more or less refined processes of institutionalization and entrenchment. American hermeneutics, like phenomenology and existentialism, took as part of its earliest mission a strong critique of all formalisms. Consequently, one derived an especially sharp sense from all such philosophical criticism during the 1960s that irreconcilable differences and permanent divisions fragmented the field of literary studies (which, in fact, was a site of numerous contending forces at least since World War I). Of the multiple differences and divergences among and within separate schools during the Vietnam era, none seemed more profound than the split of American philosophical and formalist critics, which helped set the tone of critical struggle for several decades to come.

Within the ranks of hermeneuticists there existed very deep differences. The "old hermeneutics" of E. D. Hirsch bore little resemblance to Palmer's project for the "new hermeneutics" in America. It was evident that philology and phenomenology could not be reconciled. The divergences between the two modes of hermeneutics widened throughout the 1970s as Hirsch published further essays collected in *The Aims of Interpretation* (1976) and as other "new hermeneutical" phenomenologists like William Spanos and Robert Magliola picked up where Palmer left off.

The philological tradition in Germany, associated with nineteenth-century figures like Schleiermacher, Humboldt, Boeckh, and Dilthey, sought for all textual interpretation a correct method of obtaining objective truth through genuine re-cognition of an author's meaning. This tradition, though attenuated, survived in America in the well-known works of the German expatriates Erich Auerbach and Leo Spitzer, who were Romance scholars practicing well into the 1950s historical and stylistic philology. The early twentieth-century hermeneutic projects of Heidegger and Bultmann, culminating in Gadamer's monumental *Truth and Method* (1960), constituted massive assaults against the philological tradition.

Aided by the contemporary philological hermeneutics developed from the mid-1950s to the mid-1960s by the Italian jurist Emilio Betti, E. D. Hirsch set about constructing for American criticism a general hermeneutics in the mode of Schleiermacher, Dilthey, Betti, and the nineteenth-century philologists. Hirsch's basic strategy was to attack the conventions and presuppositions of the reigning criticism, offering philological hermeneutics as a powerful solution to current problems. This way of proceeding immediately lodged Hirsch at the center of controversy that lasted, especially in American hermeneutical circles, for more than two decades. Argumentative, tough-minded, and unrelenting, Hirsch did for hermeneutics, though on a smaller scale, what Brooks did for New Criticism: he defined the basic issues and made popular the central doctrines. *Validity in Interpretation* was reprinted a dozen times in the fifteen years following its publication.

The foundations for Hirsch's project were first laid in a lengthy essay, "Objective Interpretation," published in 1960 in *PMLA* and incorporated in *Validity*. Seeking to make literary studies "a corporate enterprise and a progressive discipline" and wanting to avoid the destructive errors of "subjectivism" and "relativism," Hirsch proposed to establish a set of authoritative and consistent principles capable of generating correct interpretations and of adjudicating disputes.[5] Committed to protecting the stable determinacy of meaning, Hirsch deplored critical individualism and solipsism, which undermined the possibility of humanistic knowledge and the basis for a unified discipline.

Among the key concepts of Hirsch's philological hermeneutics, none were more important than "meaning" and "significance," which he derived from Boeckh, Frege, and Husserl. For Hirsch, "meaning" (*Sinn*) designated author's meaning—an unchanging, self-identical, and reproducible object. Meaning was both determinate and determinable. In the case of an ambiguous text, the specification of the precise ambiguities was possible and essential: interpretation could determine ambiguous meaning. Because the meaning of a work was fundamentally auctorial, Hirsch criticized the formalists' "text-centered" concept of meaning and the Myth Critics' archetypal, impersonal notion of meaning. Significantly, Hirsch distinguished between the "public stance" and "private attitude" of an author—between what an author actually, verifiably said and what he might possibly or unconsciously have intended. In ruling out the nontextual "private attitudes" of authors, Hirsch found himself in sympathy with the New Critics about the dangers of the "intentional fallacy" and the foolishness of "biographical meaning." With the distinction between the public and private views of an author, Hirsch was enabled to handle anonymous texts. The interpreter of such texts simply posited a particular verifiable "public" author.

"Significance" (*Bedeutung*) for Hirsch involved building onto determinate auctorial meaning supplementary interests, associations, and contexts as, for example, the present concerns of the critic, or certain standards of value, or questions of contemporary relevance. "Significance" exceeded "meaning" in its own terms and for its own sake. The meaning of a text might over the course of time come to have a different significance. Such a mutation, however, depended on stable meaning. To relate meaning to larger realms required distinguishing meaning from significance. In theory, the significance of a text was unlimited since the number of contexts, associations, and interests arising in the course of time was indefinitely large. Hirsch credited the importance and value of significance: texts should speak to us. For this to happen, however, they first had to have determinate meaning.

Based on the fundamental difference between meaning and significance, Hirsch distinguished between "interpretation" and "criticism." (In this he followed Boeckh.) The goal of "interpretation" was meaning; the aim of "criticism" was significance. Criticism, in Hirsch's logic, was a secondary discipline to interpretation. In his project he was interested in interpretation, not criticism. He wanted to base all humanistic studies on hermeneutics—the science of interpretation. This meant that questions of fact and interpretation took precedence over questions of relevance and value. Thus, receptionist and judicial criticism were deferred, if not summarily banished. Biographical and historical criticism were sometimes recruited as aids to the main enterprise of textual interpretation. Anchored in a certain respect for history and biography and respectful of oeuvre as well as individual works, Hirsch's theory of textual interpretation constituted something of a peculiar "formalism" different in important ways from New Criticism and Chicago criticism. All the same, *Validity in Interpretation* was dedicated to W. K. Wimsatt and R. S. Crane, suggesting its nearness to the American formalist tradition.

As a theoretical project in general hermeneutics, *Validity in Interpretation* aimed to establish normative principles of valid interpretation. Hirsch opposed, therefore, "historicism," "psychologism," and "autonomism"— all of which denied the possibility of normative validity. What disturbed Hirsh in such skepticisms was the interpretative and disciplinary disorder, solipsism, and anarchy fostered by them. "The wider implications of such hermeneutical skepticism are usually overlooked by its adherents. At stake ultimately is the right of *any* humanistic discipline to claim genuine knowledge. Since all humane studies, as Dilthey observed, are founded upon interpretation of texts, valid interpretation is critical to the validity of all subsequent inferences in those studies" (viii). Cast in the dual role of conscience and law-giver of the discipline, Hirsch's work adopted a Mosaic tone and high moral stance; his self-assurance and impatience seemed to irritate almost everyone. The immediate secondary criticism on *Validity* was enormous and is still growing. When in the opening pages of the nine essays collected in *The Aims of Interpretation* Hirsch declared "these essays do not, in any respect that I am aware of, represent substantive revisions of the earlier argument,"6 he presented himself as unscathed by his numerous dedicated antagonists. More secondary criticism ensued. In *Aims,* Hirsch clarified, elaborated, and extended his project while attacking newly formed skepticisms, notably the "cognitive atheism" of deconstruction. For over a quarter of a century Hirsch worked to resituate the field of literary studies on the solid ground of philological hermeneutics.

Hirsch distinguished two phases in the act of interpretation: one was an intuitive phase of divination and the other was an intellectual phase of interpretation proper. "To understand a poem by Keats a reader must imaginatively reenact the doubts, glories, and mysteries which inform Keats' sense of life, but afterwards the reader can subject his imaginative construction to a severe discipline . . ." (*VI,* x). Interestingly, Hirsch's first phase depicted something akin to the Geneva and Heideggerian modes of phenomenological criticism. Opposed to this prereflective, personal, and emotional reenactment of the text was reflective, impersonal, and intellectual reconstruction. The severe discipline required of such philological reconstruction admittedly depended on empathic response subjected to retroactive tests of verification and standards of probability. Ultimately, author's intended meaning, not reader's response to text, was the proper object of interpretation. In this regime, history played a crucial role, but it was the history situating the author and text rather than the history determining the reader's understanding, or the combined history conditioning auctorial work and critical reception. In all such distinctions, Hirsch exhibited a tendency to "philosophical realism" despite his citations of Husserl: divination/interpretation, reenactment/reconstruction, personal/impersonal, reader/author, value/fact, subjectivity/objectivity—all permutations of significance/meaning.

In 1984 Hirsch published "Meaning and Significance Reinterpreted," an article designed to expand and strengthen his original theory without undermining the project of philological hermeneutics. Partially incorporating Gadamer's divinatory and historicist notion of "application" into his interpretative theory of reconstruction, Hirsch was enabled to add to auctorial meaning the possibility that an author's historical intent might have been originally future-oriented, as in Shakespeare's sonnet 55 addressed to posterity. In any case, since language was inherently "provisional" (directed at futurity), it was possible for "meaning" per se to be more than simply historical or permanently dated. What these new distinctions meant for Hirsch's hermeneutics was that "interpreters can adjust old concepts to new beliefs, so long as the adjustment is in the spirit of the historical speech-intention and is not greatly distant in character."[7] In other words, Hirsch allowed the force of relevance to slip a bit from the domain of significance to the realm of meaning—subject, of course, to severe constraints, requiring tests of probability, verification, and author's "public" intent.

Though Hirsch gave a little here to the new hermeneutics, he wanted above all to hold to his original theory of history—which constituted a main point of difference between the old and the new hermeneutics. The belief of the latter school was that meanings must change over time since history changes and, as it does so, human understanding changes. The former school held that an historical event did unquestionably determine forever permanent features of its meaning. In other words, meanings were historically stable over time. The new modification made by Hirsch was that an historical event "can determine forever the permanent, unchanging features of meaning" (216). In going from "did" to "can," Hirsch allowed the possibility of change in historical meaning—again subject to tests of validity. Nevertheless, he continued to oppose the "must" of the new hermeneutics, which insisted that meanings necessarily changed over time.

In 1964 Hirsch was well on his way to completing *Validity in Interpretation*, which was essentially a grand elaboration of his 1960 essay, "Objective Interpretation." Palmer in 1964 was working on his *Hermeneutics* at the University of Heidelberg and at the University of Zurich's Institut für Hermeneutik. Hirsch was in contact with Betti while Palmer studied with Gadamer and conversed with Heidegger. Links with the Continental tradition of hermeneutics were personally and philosophically strong in 1964— the year Susan Sontag published "Against Interpretation." In 1964 Sontag opposed the general critical mode of both the old and the new hermeneutics. What she advocated was something akin to the intuitive and transparent, creative divination practiced by the Geneva Critics. This kind of supple criticism flourished during the early 1960s in the work of J. Hillis Miller, congealed in the accommodations of Paul Brodtkorb, and solidified in the accomplishments of Geoffrey Hartman. By the early 1970s the type of criticism called for by Sontag existed hardly anywhere, the phenomenologists having turned to the rigors of deconstruction and the Hermeneutical Critics having gained a modest, though growing, following for their intricate projects. Only in existentialism could one still find a certain intuitive and transparent criticism, although it was firmly anchored in a cultural thematics that, however lightened by creative style, weighed it down more and more with the complexities of despair and nothingness. When Ihab Hassan turned to utopian cultural criticism, he lightened his style but complicated all the more his existential mode of vision. The same increase in analytical scope and density occurred when Sontag herself moved from phenomenology to existentialism—from "Against Interpretation" to "The Aesthetics of Silence" (1967)—and when William Spanos turned from Christian existentialism to destructive hermeneutics. Thus American philosophical literary criticism became increasingly more rigorous and speculative as time passed, and it became, above all, less devotional and more suspicious. This was an important development and a distinctive feature of the era of the Vietman War. By the early 1970s Hirsch had emerged as a major figure. Heidegger was coming to be known by all but the drowsiest of critics. Hermeneutics really came into its own in the 1970s and 1980s.

DESTRUCTIVE HERMENEUTICS

Many modern philosophers, critics, and poets attempted to counter or cancel the increasingly crushing burdens of history and tradition, both of which engendered a debilitating sense of belatedness and distorted present consciousness, language, and understanding. The pervasive desire (or drive) for a perceptual, linguistic, and cultural clean slate manifested itself in a variety of drastic projects: it sought refuge in silence, it celebrated psychedelic liberation of consciousness from the limits of perception, it promoted abandonment of the written word and revival of oral poetics, it advocated cleansing language by defamiliarizing normal discourse, it attempted to return to things themselves, it dreamed of pure perception, it argued against interpretation, it recommended creative destruction of history and tradition. In the realm of modern philosophy, one such project was Martin Heidegger's plan for "Destroying the History of Ontology" outlined in the Introduction to *Being and Time* (sec. 6). Here Heidegger called for *destruction (Destruktion)*, not destruction (*Zerstörung*): his project ultimately entailed a violent creative preserving of history.

For Heidegger the destruction of the history of ontology opened anew the fundamental "question of Being," allowing it to attain its proper primordial dimension, its particularity, its vitality. History and tradition concealed truth.

> If the question of Being is to have its own history made transparent, then this hardened tradition must be loosened up, and the concealments which it has brought about must be dissolved. We understand this task as one in which

by taking *the question of Being as our clue,* we are to *destroy* the traditional content of ancient ontology until we arrive at those primordial experiences in which we achieved our first ways of determining the nature of Being. . . .[8]

But this destruction is just as far from having the *negative* sense of shaking off the ontological tradition. We must, on the contrary, stake out the positive possibilities of that tradition. . . . On its negative side, this destruction does not relate itself towards the past; its criticism is aimed at 'today'. . . . (44)

Tradition, while transmitting more and more knowledge, concealed truth; repository of self-evident, disembodied "truths," tradition, in the role of authority and master, blocked access to the genuine sources and primordial experiences in which truth originated. Since the well-springs were well hidden and forgotten, the work of return had to seem at first unnecessary and incomprehensible. Once the return did appear essential, the work of destruction could begin in earnest to reclaim those elements of tradition which remained useful for today. The project of destruction, therefore, emerged as both negative and positive activity. Negatively, it rummaged resolutely through tradition in a disruptive search for authentic materials of use to contemporary projects; it burned and blew away in a black wind of impatient criticism much that was conventionally regarded as sacred; it left in disrepute vast amounts of treasure, abjuring the antiquarian efforts at and pious respect for preservation and museum archeology. Positively, destruction renewed tradition by conserving selected materials of value; it revivified present thinking through concernful and genuine, yet critical, care of the past; and it payed homage to history by repeating the self-same founding operations of tradition. The project of destruction assumed that tradition was two-faced. In one aspect tradition concealed truth by preserving only deadened "truths" (which appeared insidiously as self-evident to us), thereby blocking off in forgetfulness all primordial and authentic origins. Yet, in another respect, tradition offered a way back to the founding and inaugurating moments of Being and truth. However it was viewed, man could not escape history. His mode of being-in-the-world kept him within time and his heritage.

Whereas Richard Palmer followed the "new hermeneutics" of Heidegger and his disciples through the work primarily of Hans-Georg Gadamer, William Spanos adopted his "new hermeneutical" project directly from Heidegger. Moreover, it was the early Heidegger of *Being and Time* and of the *destruction* that directed Spanos' phenomenological hermeneutics. A few years after he cofounded the important journal *Boundary 2: A Journal of Postmodern Literature* in 1972, Spanos turned from Christian existentialism to "destructive hermeneutics." Over the next decade Spanos published a series of lengthy essays dedicated to developing the theory of destructive hermeneutics and to applying it to major modern and postmodern authors. This enterprise, difficult and dense, extended the new hermeneutics, casting it as a self-conscious rival of deconstruction, which had gained growing numbers of followers from the early 1970s onwards. In its confrontation with deconstruction, hermeneutics in America entered a second, more complex, phase of development.

Following Heidegger, Spanos regarded the dominant "ontotheological tradition," which spanned from Plato to Husserl, from Greek tragedy to High Modernism, as pernicious in its covering over and forgetting of being and time. He devoted much energy to "destroying" this tradition, particularly its systematic mishandling of temporality. In Spanos' view, the tradition transformed, in two parallel ways, the temporality of being-in-the-world into an overall insidious "world picture":

(1) a flattened out, static, and homogeneous Euclidean space—a totalized and ontologically depthless system of referents (a map)—if the objectifying consciousness is positivistic or realistic; or (2) a self-bounded or sealed off and inclusive image (icon or myth), if the objectifying consciousness is idealistic or symbolistic. In either case, this transformation allows *Dasein* [human being] to *see* existence from the beginning, i.e., all at once. In so doing it dis-stances him, i.e., disengages his Care, makes him an objective, a disinterested or careless, *observer* of the ultimately familiar or autonomous picture in which temporality—its threat and its possibilities—has been annulled.[9]

The "map" and "icon" paradigms of existence, which sprang, respectively, from the world views of the positivistic-scientific and the idealistic-symbolist mindsets, situated human consciousness above the tumult of life, affording man a measure of objectivity and distance from things as they were. As observer, man was enabled to look over the whole of life and to grasp its order, to make sense of its origins and ends. In constructing a view of the world and of existence, ontotheological man assumed a stance of disinterest and impersonality; he distinguished through observation the permanent from the changing; he withheld his care and interest. Thus man was able to place before or to present to himself in presence and in certainty objects for analysis, manipulation, and calculation; he exercised will and power over the world. In all of this, metaphysical man expressed a profoundly spatial view of existence.

Spanos aimed to "destroy" the traditional spatial model or world view in favor of a temporal systematics. What did such destruction entail? "By 'destruction' I do not, of course, mean 'annihilation'; I mean, rather, a hermeneutic project grounded in an understanding of truth . . . as *a-le-theia*—bringing into the open from hiddenness or oblivion [*BT,* 57]—and assuming the form of a destruction—a dis-assembling of a spatial figure— such as that which Heidegger undertakes in his dialogue with . . . the systematic philosophy of what he has called the Western 'onto-theo-logical' tradition."[10] In a Heideggerian manner, Spanos conceived destruction as an interpretive enterprise oriented toward overturning the systematic philosophy of tradition, especially its spatial paradigm, in order to reveal hidden and forgotten possibilities through careful de-structuring of the now dominant metaphysical formations of truth.

Destructive inquiry, as it opened a text and progressed through time, disarticulated the spatial point of view, bringing into the open the indefinite or vague insights into being that lie hidden in tradition. It discovered being as *be-ing* in the actual temporal process itself, and disclosed that interpretation was a ceaseless experience of concealing and unconcealing the truth of being. As an historical being-in-the-world, the destructive interpreter proceeded with interest and care to move independently yet intimately into the being of the text to re-enact for himself and his time the truth of being in an activity of retrieval or repetition (*Wiederholen*). As *repetition,* interpretation repeated and recaptured primordial historical existence, transforming it into a new beginning. Here the beginning was not reduced to the past (or to a form of detemporalized *recollection*), but was begun again with all the dangers and insecurities of authentic beginning. This process of destructive interpretation "makes time man's element and ceaseless exploration in the openness of time his (saving) activity."[11] Thus man was thrown into an endless interpretative existence. There was never closure.

Revealingly, Spanos took out after formalism, myth criticism, Geneva criticism, structuralism, and other forms cf "metaphysical" thinking. Each of these modes of criticism purportedly initiated inquiry with a predetermined sense of the "whole picture" or with an opening commitment to "overall form." The end was in sight before the reading began. Sure expectations of one sort or another coerced the temporal medium of literature into an inclusive message or immobile object—a closed circle, a detemporalized presence. That meaning, like form, was infinitely open eluded these "metaphysical" interpretive systems. In their demands for and expectations of totality, in their will-to-power over texts, in their repressed anxiety in the face of continuous uncertainty, these spatial methods turned disorder into Order, differences into Identities, and words into the Word. Unable to let texts be in openness, traditionalist criticisms sealed off the unfolding disclosures of truth. Spatializing the temporal processes of be-ing, all metaphysical criticism practiced a particularly invidious strategy: *"It is, in other words, a strategy that is subject to a vicious circularity that closes off the phenomenological/existential understanding of the temporal being of existence, and, analogously, of the temporal being—the sequence of words—of the literary text."*[12]

What was fundamental for Spanos' poetics was his opening of the text to the individual creative activities and discoveries—the being—of the reader. In effect, Spanos withdrew both the critic's and the author's authority over and spatial perspective on the text. No longer could the critic or poet hover above the text in Olympian contemplation and complete understanding. To come to life, the poem had to be unfolded care-fully and intimately in a continuous dialogue between reader and text. The "form" of the text was a belated and recollective construction; it did not exist. Readers did not experience form. The flow of words, the temporal being of the text, required from the reader active involvement and interested exploration. Thus the text was an event—an event occurring within the reader's temporal horizon, an event experienced necessarily as interpretation, an event discovering the temporality of being in and for the present ("BC," 445). As action and event, the poem produced Form through process, Meaning through interpretation, Being through be-ing; these were not entities or substances inserted into or extractable from texts. They were retrospective constructions. Engaging the reader in open-ended actualizing, the literary work deferred closure, demanding an ongoing interrogative mood and projective stance while refusing totalizing interpretation. The text set going an activity of continuous participation and revision. When it was stopped, reduction and reification ensued as pernicious *recollection*.

Significantly, Spanos assigned parallel and equiprimordial status to Existence, Understanding, and Discourse. (In this he adhered closely to Heidegger's teaching in *Being and Time*.) Like being and thinking, discourse emerged primordially in (as) the founding moment of existence ("HK," 138). Nevertheless, words too often appeared to us as images, that is, they became static pictures for us to oversee and to contemplate, not to hear. Such spatializing required destruction. To Spanos' mind, "the essential existential structure of human life is language as human speech" ("HK," 138).[13] Holding this view of language as primordial speech, Spanos worked within the tradition of the "new hermeneutics" and against the drift of much contemporary literary criticism and theory.

Ultimately, the scope of Spanos' project reached beyond fashioning a new hermeneutics for reading literary texts. What he envisioned was a new literary history. *"This temporal, as opposed to spatial, orientation is the key not only to reading a literary text but to the discovery of a new literary history"* ("HK," 116). In Spanos' view, destructive hermeneutics "opens up the possibility of a perpetually new—a postModern or an authentically modern—literary history, a history that, in focusing on dis-closure, both validates the inexhaustibility of literary texts (i.e., literary history as misreading) and commits literature to the difficult larger task of 'overcoming metaphysics'—a history, in other words, that puts literature at the service of being rather than being at the service of literature" ("BC," 446). Using this new hermeneutics, the destructive critic discovered that texts were inexhaustible. To read a text was necessarily to "misread" it. All readings were misreadings. Texts were perpetual. Therefore, literary history was by definition permanently open and continuously new. Such a hermeneutics was destructive precisely in that it revealed, accepted, and extended the inexhaustibility of texts and of literary history. In his view of a new literary history, Spanos extended Heidegger's distinctive performative mode of phenomenology toward a theory of history and tradition as ceaseless happenings and inexhaustible performances. At the same time he appropriated insights from deconstruction for his phenomenological hermeneutics.

What Spanos did for the new hermeneutics was bring it firmly into literary theory and criticism, for he was not dedicated, as was Palmer, to a general hermeneutics. Though narrowing the ambitions of phenomenological hermeneutics, he extended its reach into the various recesses of literary studies. Nowhere was this more evident than in his suggestions about developing a new literary history. While this endeavor was undertaken in piecemeal fashion, it dramatized the implications of the new hermeneutics for the field of literary criticism. The obsessions with temporality and historicity exhibited by Spanos pertained, not to the past of the text or the author, but to the present of the text and the reader. The stress on "oral poetics" aimed to actualize the affective and didactic powers of literature in the here and now. The whole goal of destructive hermeneutics was to bring the past alive today, not to enshrine former monuments in the manner of antiquarian philology. To overleap the deadening respect for the past of historicism and the old hermeneutics—that was the point. If a text didn't live today, it was dead. Unlike Palmer, Spanos showed little interest in the historicality of earlier world views and linguistic forms, which posed problems for a reader of older texts. Focused on modern literature, Spanos was enabled to give full reign to his preoccupation with temporality in the here and now. His dislike of spatial formations embodied the traditional phenomenological animus against philosophical realism and idealism. In giving up during the 1970s the "sacramental aesthetics" of Christian existentialism for the destructive hermeneutics of Heideggerian phenomenology, Spanos altered his philosophy of history: past works could no longer live in the present—unless they underwent destruction at the hands of the reader. Yet at bottom such violence was devotional: it preserved the past with contemporary vigor and vitality.

Whereas the writing style of American Phenomenological and Existential Critics tended toward "creative" or literary modes, as in the works of J. Hillis Miller, Geoffrey Hartman, Susan Sontag, and Ihab Hassan, the style of Hermeneutical Critics remained resolutely and uniformly "philosophical," as was evident in the texts of Palmer, Hirsch, and Spanos. This feature, among others, distinguished hermeneutics (old and new) from phenomenological and existential criticism. Of all the philosophical critics in America, none had a more dense style than Spanos—a trait more marked in his hermeneutical than in his existential criticism.

In the early 1980s Spanso expanded his project by adding a new dimension to his destructive analytic. In addition to the Heideggerian dis-assembling adopted in the mid-1970s, he advocated and practiced Foucaultian genealogy, which he adapted from Edward Said and various Marxists as well as Michel Foucault. Other younger members of the group associated with *Boundary 2* moved in a similar direction, including Jonathan Arac, Paul Bové, and Daniel O'Hara, among others. The later version of destructive hermeneutics involved not only unconcealing spatial rigidities and ontotheological formations, but also uncovering cultural or archival grounds and constraints engendering widespread hegemonic control and disciplinary power. This new "worldly criticism" led Spanos to negative assessments of bourgeois culture, capitalist economics, and Calvinist Christianity. What had occurred to Spanos was clear: to ask the question of being was also to ask questions of consciousness, language, nature, history, epistemology, law, gender, politics, economics, ecology, literature, criticism, and culture. As an equiprimordial site on a "continuum of being," each of these domains, however unevenly formed at any historical moment, implicated all the others. To initiate inquiry into one area was, to some degree, to open all others to question. The concept of the "continuum of being," fundamental to Spanos' later hermeneutic, led almost inevitably to genealogical cultural criticism in a leftist mode. Among American Hermeneutical Critics, Spanos was special in trying to join the traditions of Heidegger and Marx—in seeking to incorporate ideological analysis into a project of phenomenological hermeneutics.

HERMENEUTICS AFTER DECONSTRUCTION

The historical development of the hermeneutical movement in American literary studies involved two phases. A turning point came in the mid-seventies—the moment when deconstruction sprang to the attention of most hermeneutical theorists. Before the advent of deconstruction, hermeneutics, whether phenomenological or philological, derived from the German tradition running from Schleiermacher to Gadamer. After deconstruction, it began to take into account and often to accommodate French poststructuralist thought without renouncing the commitment to a project of hermeneutics. This is the moment when the work of Ricoeur became prominent and the enterprise of Spanos was initiated—both labored at incorporating "deconstructionist thinking." Coinciding with the close of the Vietnam era, the second phase of hermeneutics witnessed the publication of a number of books coping with the implications of deconstruction for hermeneutics. Among the dozen or so varied texts representative of this later phase of development were David Couzens Hoy's *The Critical Circle: Literature, History, and Philosophical Hermeneutics* (1978), Paul A. Bové's *Destructive Poetics: Heidegger and Modern American Poetry* (1980), Gerald L. Bruns' *Inventions: Writing, Textuality, and Understanding in Literary History* (1982), Susan A. Handelman's *The Slayers of Moses: The Emergence of Rabbinic Interpretation in Modern Literary Theory* (1982), and—taken together—Robert R. Magliola's *Phenomenology and Literature* (1977) and his *Derrida on the Mend* (1984), as well as T. K. Seung's *Structuralism and Hermeneutics* (1982) and his follow-up, *Semiotics and Thematics in Hermeneutics* (1982).

Under the influence of French poststructuralism, hermeneutics in Germany itself moved into a period of "post-hermeneutics" in the work of Manfred Frank, Friedrich Kittler, and others. Interestingly, Frank in *Das Sagbare und das Unsagbare: Studien zur neuesten französischen Hermeneutik und Texttheorie* (1980) accepted the linguistic foundations of Being while working to preserve integral subjectivity against the onslaughts of Jacques Lacan and especially Jacques Derrida. Returning to Schleiermacher and Sartre, Frank sought to modulate contemporary deconstructive linguistic determinism by developing a nonontological—a language-based—theory of the self. Whether successful or not, this representative effort demonstrated the intrusion into German hermeneutics of philosophical problematics formulated by French deconstruction.

During the second phase, the confrontation of Hermeneutical Critics with deconstruction took various forms. In *Inventions*, for example, Gerald Bruns portrayed deconstructive philosophy as an elaborate epistemology committed to thinking in terms of ahistorical, self-enclosed systems and their logical structures. According to Bruns, "Derrida is our most intimate and fabulous connoisseur of systems, a fearsome and abandoned Leibniz."[14] For Bruns the fundamental ground of language and of its understanding was history conceived as an inescapable movement of events and situations that produced social practices. Understood not as formal mental acts but as time-bound social practices, textual interpretations simply appeared in history—always subject to relativistic norms of rationality and rooted in specific forms of life. Therefore, to understand interpretation was to understand its history, not to possess some universalist or structuralist idea of it. This historicist critique of deconstructive systematics served other Hermeneutical Critics as an essential line of defense against Derrida and his followers. Developed first by Gadamer, Heidegger's student, the historicist line emerged in the work not only of Bruns, but also of Hoy and Seung— the first of whom genially incorporated deconstruction while the second excoriated it from the project of hermeneutics.

What made Spanos' confrontation with deconstruction unusual in hermeneutic circles was his particular strategy. He neither deplored Derridean philosophy like Seung, nor politely disarmed and incorporated it as did Hoy, nor overemphasized its structuralist dimensions in the manner of Bruns. Rather, he fell back on the untapped resources of Heidegger's *destruction* articulated in *Being and Time*. Developed between 1975 and 1980, Spanos' first approach toward *"destructive* hermeneutics" was ontological; his second approach, worked out from 1980 onwards, was genealogical (or ideological) as well as ontological. In essence, Spanos sought neither to dismiss nor to devour deconstruction, but rather to counter it by means of alternative procedures and explanations derived from Heidegger and Foucault, not from Gadamer or Ricoeur—the usual sources of support for beleaguered latter-day American hermeneuts.

The confrontations with deconstruction enacted in the works of Magliola and Handelman were at once fascinating and eccentric. By the time he published *Derrida on the Mend*, Magliola was no longer simply a Heideggerian, as he had appeared at the close of his *Phenomenology and Literature*.

As a Carmelite Christian, Magliola attempted to concoct a "differential mysticism" out of strands of Heideggerian phenomenology, Derridean deconstruction, Nagarjunist Buddhism, and Trinitarian Christianity. Without judging the success of his theological project, we can observe that Magliola, taken solely as a critical theorist, remained in the orbit of phenomenological hermeneutics.[15] For her part, Handelman in *The Slayers of Moses* argued that German hermeneutics from Schleiermacher to Gadamer had roots in Patristic modes of textual understanding while "deconstructivist hermeneutics" from Freud to Derrida to Bloom had foundations in Rabbinic modes of interpretation. The thrust of Handelman's enterprise was to remove deconstruction from its uncomfortable "place" in the history of European hermeneutics, setting it in its "proper" Jewish tradition—a long history of "heretic hermeneutics." Without assessing Handelman's theology, we can state that she worked as a hermeneutical critic not in a phenomenological but in a midrashic tradition linked to Jewish aggadah.

During the second phase, an important and influential account of hermeneutics appeared in Richard Rorty's *Philosophy and the Mirror of Nature* (1979). As a leading American philosopher steeped in the modern traditions of analytic philosophy and pragmatism, but not of Continental phenomenology, Rorty found himself jettisoning the post-Renaissance "analytical" projects of epistemology, philosophy of mind, and theory of language—the philosophies of Descartes, Locke, Kant, Husserl, and Russell—in the interest of a nonsystematic philosophical hermeneutics indebted to Heidegger, Wittgenstein, Dewey, Sartre, and Gadamer. In Rorty's historical assessment, foundational epistemology had come to a dead end and hermeneutics had to take over. The homemade hermeneutical philosophy Rorty had in mind was definitely not derived from the "old hermeneutics" of Schleiermacher, Dilthey, Betti, and Hirsch—which was part of the dead-end tradition of epistemology committed to objective frameworks for inquiry and scientific standards of verification. Rorty's hermeneutics was historicist and relativist. The aim of the hermeneutical project, in Rorty's own words, was "to undermine the reader's confidence in 'the mind' as something about which one should have a 'philosophical' view, in 'knowledge' as something about which there ought to be a 'theory' and which has 'foundations,' and in 'philosophy' as it has been conceived since Kant."[16] What distressed Rorty about the Cartesian-Kantian tradition of philosophy was its "attempt to escape from history—an attempt to find nonhistorical conditions of any possible historical development" (9). Like other new hermeneutical theorists, Rorty rejected "disinterested," "objective," "impartial," and "rational" inquiry because it turned men into knowable, ahistorical, empirical phenomena or objects rather than mysterious and free moral agents.

For Rorty, as for Gadamer, hermeneutics was *attitude,* not method. It involved a "willingness to view inquiry as muddling through, rather than conforming to canons of rationality—coping with people and things rather than corresponding to reality by discovering essences."[17] His model for the activity of hermeneutics was conversation or open-ended dialogue. Such pragmatic conversation or dialogue presupposed no epistemological matrix or common ground; it proceeded simply in the hope of agreement or fruitful disagreement. Significantly, his model for the hermeneutical philosopher was not the scientist but "the informed dilettante, the polypragmatic, Socratic intermediary between various discourses" (*PMN,* 317).

Following his hermeneutical work in the 1970s, Rorty in the 1980s sought to subordinate hermeneutics to a revised and expanded pragmatism in the tradition of William James and Friedrich Nietzsche. In this latter project, tutelary figures included not only Heidegger and Gadamer, but Foucault and Derrida. The textualist enterprise of French poststructuralism conformed to and aided the new pragmatism: "we shall best understand the role of textualism within our culture," declared Rorty, "if we see it as an attempt to think through a thoroughgoing pragmatism. . . ."[18] What was significant here was Rorty's merging of hermeneutics and deconstructionism for other, broader philosophical and critical purposes. Instead of a confrontation of hermeneutics and deconstruction, Rorty attempted a synthesis of them in his opposition to Anglo-American analytical philosophy and scientific method.

In the second phase, Hermeneutical Critics sometimes extirpated deconstruction, as did Bruns, Seung, and Hirsch; sometimes they incorporated it into hermeneutics, as did Hoy; sometimes they merged it with broader "eccentric" projects, as did Magliola, Handelman, and Rorty; and sometimes they both greeted and challenged it, as did Spanos, Bové, and other *Boundary 2* critics. The intellectual stance or politics here ranged from conservative reactionism to libertarian tolerance to liberal annexation to progressivist diplomacy. That is to say, the institutional political tactics of Hermeneutical Critics in the second phase spanned a spectrum from intolerant conservatism to wily progressivism. In surprising ways, then, deconstruction galvanized the hermeneutical movement, exposing its ideological heterogeneity and bringing out its various possibilities.

In the Vietnam era and the decade following it, literary hermeneutics remained a relatively small movement. Other than *Boundary 2,* no journal regulary published hermeneutical criticism. Ironically, only Hirsch emerged as a major figure in contemporary American criticism. The irony lay in the fact that most Hermeneutical Critics worked in the tradition of Heidegger and Gadamer, not that of Schleiermacher and Dilthey. The impact of hermeneutics on pedagogical practice and textbook publication, like that on practical criticism and institutional politics, was negligible. Among the growing number of avant-garde critical theorists, however, hermeneutics, like all other forms of philosophical criticism indebted to modern Continental thinking, typically received serious consideration, forming part of the discourse and citation system of this influential subdiscipline within literary studies. That hermeneutical criticism rarely offered sustained readings of texts—rarely engaged in pure practical criticism—partially explained its lack of wide influence in the domain of American literary criticism. Also much of the message and novelty of hermeneutical philosophy had been prefigured by phenomenological and existential criticism, which earlier pioneered an antinomian critique of disinterested inquiry, propounded an ethics of participation, and promoted an impatience with formalism. What hermeneutics added to this effort—for example, the interests in temporality, in history, in oral poetics, and in interpretative circularity—was apparently not momentous enough to propel its project into the forefront of critical activity or concern.

Some of what hermeneutics might have contributed to "normal" literary interpretation was contributed by reader-response criticism, which, in literary circles, commanded a greater amount of attention during the Vietnam era and its immediate aftermath. Like hermeneuticists, reader-response theorists conceived literature as an event and disclosure of temporal being, involving exploration and risk for the reader and requiring dialogical transactions for the construction of meaning. What this rival criticism lacked were philosophical foundations in ontology, fundamental engagement in historicism, commitment to oral poetics, and strong roots in theology, philosophy, and the human sciences—all of which bestowed on hermeneutics a distinctiveness and breadth that sustained it in its later stages of development among comparatively small groups of theologians, philosophers, and social scientists as well as literary critics.

Literary hermeneutics was part of a broader "general hermeneutics." On this linkage Palmer and Hirsch agreed at the outset in the late sixties. A decade or so later, Spanos would come to consent, as would Magliola, Hartman, Hoy, Rorty, Handelman, Seung, Bruns, and others. Unlike reader-response criticism, hermeneutics was not limited to literary criticism; it was aligned with wider interdisciplinary endeavors. Its energies were scattered across a spectrum of disciplines, which at once diluted its impact while increasing its allure and promise. "Hermeneutics," declared Richard Palmer a year after the end of the Vietnam War, "is not an 'ism.' It is not the property of Heidegger and Gadamer, although I find that they are very helpful. . . . Hermeneutics is the discipline of bridging gaps and of theorizing about what is involved in this process."[19] Among the dozen exemplary gaps fit for hermeneutical inquiry, according to Palmer, were God and man, past and present language, extraordinary and ordinary reality, unusual and everyday experiences, Eastern and Western minds, women and men, blacks and whites, and native and immigrant Americans (first-, second-, or twelfth-generation). Over time the focus of hermeneutics expanded to include not simply traditional religious, historical, and philosophical matters but also contemporary sexual, social, and political issues. French Space Age philosophy helped incite this expansion.

The connection of hermeneutics to social criticism was early demonstrated by Fredric Jameson in his *Marxism and Form: Twentieth-Century Dialectical Theories of Literature* (1971) and his *The Political Unconscious: Narrative as a Socially Symbolic Act* (1981). In both texts he developed an eclectic Marxist hermeneutics indebted fundamentally to Paul Ricoeur's *De l'interprétation*. From Ricoeur came the crucial distinction, essential to Jameson's project, between negative, destructive hermeneutics and positive, restorative hermeneutics. The former aimed to demystify illusions in the manner of Marx, Nietzsche, Freud, and Derrida; it was at one with the Marxist critique of ideology and false consciousness. The latter sought to provide access to some essential sources of life in a move reminiscent of sacred hermeneutics, of Ernst Bloch's ideal of hope, of Mikhail Bakhtin's liberating concepts of the dialogical and the carnivalesque, and of the Frankfurt School's notion of promises of happiness inscribed in aesthetic works: positive hermeneutics was in keeping with the long-standing Marxist commitment to utopian thinking. According to Jameson, "a Marxist negative hermeneutic, a Marxist practice of ideological analysis proper, must in the practical work of reading and interpretation be exercised *simultaneously* with a Marxist positive hermeneutic, or a decipherment of the Utopian impulses of these same still ideological cultural texts."[20]

Just as Spanos and Palmer expanded their early positive phenomenological hermeneutics that initially sought access to being to include a later negative cultural analysis that aimed to diagnose social divisions and repressions, so Jameson added to his primary demystifying ideological criticism a restorative utopian hermeneutic, inspired by Ricoeur, by ancient anagogical interpretation, and by revolutionary Marxism. As we shall see in chapter 13, Jameson's Marxism, like Rorty's Pragmatism, incorporated hermeneutics and poststructuralism into a broad affirmative project, attesting thereby to the importance and usefulness, during the days following the Vietnam War, of hermeneutics as well as deconstruction for a new cultural criticism. However given to ahistoricism, deconstruction contributed, in Jameson's views, to the critiques of ideology and of illusory consciousness. Like other textualist theories, deconstruction forcefully "liberates us from the empirical object—whether institution, event, or individual work—by displaying our attention to its *constitution* as an object and its *relationship* to the other objects thus constituted" (297). In other words, deconstruction complemented Marxist negative hermeneutics by similarly revealing the made-up quality, the time-bound nature, and the interrelatedness of all so-called "empirical" phenomena. Poststructuralism, in general, opened to view the grounds of social formations for hermeneutical inquiry.

CHAPTER EIGHT

Reader-Response Criticism

THE ERA OF THE READER

FROM THE Great Depression to the onset of the Space Age, American critics tended primarily to focus either on literary texts, or on the historical and cultural contexts of literature, or on both. During the early years of the Space Age, the focus of concern for many leading critics and theorists shifted to the activities of reading and readers. The rise of reader-oriented criticism manifested itself more or less forcefully in numerous and varied critical projects, including those carried out by literary phenomenology, hermeneutics, structuralism, deconstruction, and feminism. While an interest in text reception appeared before World War II in the works of I. A. Richards, Maud Bodkin, D. W. Harding, Kenneth Burke, and Louise Rosenblatt, it was not until the late 1950s and shortly afterwards that a veritable landslide of studies started to concentrate self-consciously on readers and reading, initiating a broad-based movement opposed to earlier text-dominated and context-dominated criticism. Among the many critics in America contributing to the development of a reader-centered criticism were David Bleich, Stephen Booth, Wayne Booth, Jonathan Culler, Paul de Man, Judith Fetterley, Stanley Fish, Norman Holland, Simon Lesser, J. Hillis Miller, Richard Palmer, Mary Louise Pratt, Gerald Prince, Alan Purves, Michael Riffaterre, Walter Slatoff, and William Spanos. Significantly, half of these critics associated themselves with specific schools rather than this broad movement: Wayne Booth with Chicago formalism; de Man and Miller with phenomenology, then with deconstruction; Palmer and Spanos with hermeneutics; Prince and Riffaterre with structuralism; Culler with structuralism, then with deconstruction; Fetterley with feminism; and Pratt with speech-act theory, then with Marxism. As a result, the roster of leading American Reader-Response Critics, established by the peak of the movement's vitality in the late 1970s, was limited arguably to Fish, Holland, and Bleich—listed here in order of their chronological entry into the field and treatment in this chapter.

Whether or not the membership of the movement is construed narrowly or broadly, certain tenets characterized reader-response criticism during its heyday from the late 1960s to the early 1980s. It argued against the text-centered criticism of formalism, advocating instead a reader-oriented approach. It often stressed the temporality of reading, resisting tendencies toward spatial hermeneutics and toward organicist poetics. It pioneered accounts of textual discontinuity over doctrines propounding literary unity. It investigated the epistemological, linguistic, psychological, and sociological constraints on the activity of reading and the labor of readers. It often ignored explicit questions concerning aesthetic value and the role of history. It did not tamper with the canons of scholarly style, and it pushed critical inquiry toward pedagogy, typically locating the text and reader in the classroom. Not surprisingly, it fostered various didactic poetics. It tended toward a politics of liberal pluralism, which advocated the rights of readers against the prescriptions and dogmas of doctrinaire methodologies. Focused tightly on the reader, it developed a rich panoply of types of readers—informed readers, ideal readers, implied readers, actual readers, virtual readers, superreaders, and "literents." Like other schools and movements during the Space Age, it cast New Criticism as a scapegoat responsible for many of the ills and errors of contemporary literary criticism. Unlike some other groups, Reader-Response Critics did not constitute a tightly knit cadre or circle of colleagues with access to certain journals, presses, institutes, and universities. Instead, the movement had an increasingly broad geographical and intellectual base—more so than all other schools of American criticism from the thirties to the eighties except feminism and leftist criticism during the Space Age.

Given the wide scope of the movement, reader-response criticism was characterized by numerous differences and disagreements. As the movement expanded, many explanatory articles and essays appeared, increasing exponentially the bibliography in this field of inquiry. Whereas reader-oriented criticism did not dramatically alter literary canons or textbooks nor engender specialized dictionaries or handbooks, it did generate a large number of special sessions at conferences and special issues of journals. The proliferation of helpful published materials reached a high point in 1980 with the publication of two exemplary anthologies of reader-response criticism, complete with useful introductions and lengthy bibliographies:

(1) *The Reader in the Text: Essays on Audience and Interpretation,* edited by Susan Suleiman and Inge Crosman, published by Princeton University Press, containing sixteen original articles; and (2) *Reader-Response Criticism: From Formalism to Post-Structuralism,* edited by Jane Tompkins, published by the Johns Hopkins University Press, reprinting eleven key texts of the movement. Sponsored by major university presses and frequently reprinted, these anthologies signaled a certain culmination of the shift from text-centered to reader-oriented criticism within the field of literary studies in American universities.

In her extensive introduction, "Varieties of Audience-Oriented Criticism," Susan Suleiman surveyed six approaches to receptionist criticism, including rhetorical, structuralist-semiotic, phenomenological, psychoanalytical, sociological-historical, and hermeneutical modes. She argued that "audience-oriented criticism is not one field but many, not a single widely trodden path but a multiplicity of crisscrossing, often divergent tracks that cover a vast area of the critical landscape. . . ."[1] Unlike Jane Tompkins in "An Introduction to Reader-Response Criticism," Suleiman allotted considerable space to European critics who played a significant role in the "revolution" set off by reader-oriented theory. Her canon of important American critics included Bleich, Booth, Fish, Holland, Prince, Riffaterre, and certain Yale deconstructors, namely de Man, Hartman, and Miller. While Tompkins too presented reader-response criticism as heterogeneous, observing it was "not a conceptually unified critical position,"[2] she nevertheless argued that the movement exhibited a "coherent progression" over its two decades of growth and displayed a "main line of theoretical development" (ix, xxvi). According to this account, two stages characterized the internal history of the movement as it progressed from formalism through structuralism and phenomenology to psychoanalysis and post-structuralism. First, reader-response criticism envisaged the reader's activity as instrumental to the understanding of the literary text without denying that the ultimate object of critical attention was the text. Second, it conceived the reader's activity as identical with the text so that this activity became the source of concern and value. This "revolutionary shift" from text to reading, from product to process, opened new areas of inquiry, resituated theories of meaning and interpretation, and reconnected criticism with ethics and eventually with politics. The key American critics in this development, in Tompkins' view, were Prince, Riffaterre, Fish, Culler, Holland, and Bleich. Unlike Suleiman, Tompkins left out of account the works of European sociological and historical Reader-Response Critics and of Continental and native Hermeneutical Critics. Both editors omitted consideration of feminist reader-oriented critics. Perhaps this was so because feminist criticism did not reach its peak until the mid-1980s, evidently some years after the reader-response anthologies were first planned. As with other historians of reader-response criticism, Suleiman and Tompkins disagreed about the actual scope of the heterogeneity and disunity within the movement. That it constituted a more or less fragmented site of inquiry was never in question. Usually presented as a cultural paradigm shift, the new focus on the reader seemed to preoccupy an era rather than one school or another.

READING: FROM PHENOMENOLOGY
TO POSTSTRUCTURALISM

During the sixties the most well-known and popular work of reader-response criticism was Stanley Fish's *Surprised by Sin: The Reader in Paradise Lost* (1967). Here and in his *Self-Consuming Artifacts: The Experience of Seventeenth-Century Literature* (1972), Fish focused single-mindedly on the reader's experience of literature. In contrast to the long-standing formalist idea that a literary text was an autonomous object like a well-wrought urn, Fish insisted that a work of literature entered reality for the critic through the act of reading—the process of reception. Because reading occurred through time, the experience of literature involved a continuous readjustment of perceptions, ideas, and evaluations. The meaning of a work, therefore, was to be encountered in the experience of it, not in the detritus left after the experience. Literature was process, not product. Criticism required the microprocessing of phrases and sentences in a slow sequence of decisions, revisions, anticipations, reversals, and recoveries. Here the phenomenology of reading replaced both the traditional formalist project of spatial unity and the old hermeneutical project of recollective interpretation.

Fish described the basis of his phenomenological theory in the 1971 Preface to the paperback edition of *Surprised by Sin:* "Meaning is an *event*, something that happens, not on the page, where we are accustomed to look for it, but in the interaction between the flow of print (or sound) and the actively mediating consciousness of a reader-hearer. *Surprised by Sin*, although it nowhere contains any reference to such a theory of meaning, is nevertheless the product of it."[3] True to this description, the focus throughout Fish's book was on Milton's reader in *Paradise Lost*, particularly on the reader's participation, humiliation, and education during the course of the poem. As Fish conceived it, Milton's procedure was to render in the reader's mind the action of the Fall of Man, thereby causing the reader himself to fall just as Adam did. The meaning (or content) of the poem was embodied in the experience of the reader, not in the poem. Such experience was intellectually and morally uplifting.

Fish's concept of meaning entailed an unorthodox conception of literary form. He was unabashed about this matter, arguing that "if the meaning of the poem is to be located in the reader's experience of it, the form of the poem is the form of that experience; and the outer or physical form, so obtrusive, and, in one sense, so undeniably there, is, in another sense, incidental and even irrelevant" (341). Fish dismissed the traditional dualistic notion of the artwork as constructed object composed of form and content, replacing it with a monism (reader's experience = meaning = form), which earlier the New Critics had labeled a fallacy—the so-called "affective fallacy." Fish staked out a clear position on this presumed liability:

I am courting the "affective fallacy." Indeed I am embracing it and going beyond it. . . . That is, making the work disappear into the reader's experience of it is precisely what should happen in our criticism, because it is what happens when we read. The lines of plot and argument, the beginnings, middles, and ends, the clusters of imagery, all the formal features that are observable when we step back from the reading experience, are, during that experience, components of a response; and the . . . structure of response. (ix–x)

Methodically, Fish asserted a temporal basis for literary form as well as meaning. Spatial forms—poetic patterns objectified retrospectively—were illusory. Meaning and form were coextensive with the reader's experience; they were not produced after the reading activity. The phenomenology of time determined both the meaning and the form of a work.

Like the phenomenological criticism practiced earlier by J. Hillis Miller, Fish's reader-oriented criticism abolished the text as the sole object of attention and advocated a primary role for the reader's consciousness. The interaction of reader and text, the co-implication of subject and object, effected a strong antiformalist emphasis on the experiential features of the engaged critical mind rather than on the formal features of the text (imagery, plot, genre). Fish, like Miller, more or less bracketed extrinsic social realities and historical issues, substituting for such broad matters an all-consuming sense of engagement experienced by the reader-critic working with the text. Despite their shared antiformalism and their tendency to ahistoricism, these two critics had different views of the text, of the text-reader relationship, and of meaning. Whereas Miller regarded the oeuvre as the unit text, Fish considered the individual work as text. For Miller, the "text" embodied the consciousness of the author which was shared mystically with the sensitive reader: the reader served as acolyte or cocelebrant of the holy "text." For Fish, however, the text functioned as a rigorous, authoritative controller of the reader's developing responses. According to Miller's formulation, the meaning of a "text" emerged from the persistent themes, motifs, and tones that recurred throughout the works of an author, revealing an essential selfhood or center of consciousness. To re-create the quintessential spiritual adventure of the author was to render the meaning of his work. According to Fish, however, meaning was created in the reader by the author as the text developed in the reading process: meaning was the reader's sequential experience of the work unfolding. To constitute meaning required describing in detail the moment-by-moment experience of reading.

Several years after *Surprised by Sin*, Fish articulated at some length and for the first time the basis of his reader-response theory in "Literature in the Reader: Affective Stylistics" (1970), which he later appended to *Self-Consuming Artifacts* as an essential theoretical credo. In addition to depicting his theories of meaning, of form, and of the text, he offered in this manifesto a profile of his "informed reader." In moving from the text to the reading process to the reader, Fish opened for consideration a new array of problems, which would dominate his criticism throughout the seventies and eighties. The informed reader, in Fish's account, was "neither an abstraction nor an actual living reader, but a hybrid—a real reader (me) who does everything within his power to make himself informed."[4] The informed reader possessed both linguistic and literary competence—language experience and knowledge of literary conventions. Such minimal competency formed the necessary precondition for all potential reader responses. Not until the late 1970s would Fish begin to work out the implications of his theories about competence and convention. In the meantime, he attracted much harsh criticism, serving as *the* point man for the reader-response movement in America.

During the early seventies, Paul de Man criticized Fish for his theory of meaning and his view of the author. According to de Man, Fish substituted "a regressive notion of unmediated 'experience' for meaning,"[5] which had the effect of covering over the inherent duplicity of language. The materiality and complexity of language were dissolved by Fish. In addition, Fish posited an intentional auctorial consciousness that controlled the complications of meanings through manipulation of linguistic and poetic conventions. This dubious formulation cast the reader in an eternal catch-up role with the author and actually minimized the reader's labor and creativity. What especially bothered de Man was a retrograde concept of intention surviving in Fish's reader-response criticism. According to de Man's assessment, Fish unwittingly projected the author as the ideal reader of the text.

Jonathan Culler criticized Fish in the mid-seventies for his refusal to take seriously the concepts of linguistic competence and literary convention, which formed the foundation of his theory of the informed reader. Given the logic of his position, Fish ought to have carried out "an investigation of reading as a rule-governed, productive process."[6] Instead, he retreated to individualistic thematic interpretation in a phenomenological mode. By simply assuming that the informed reader had internalized essential knowledge and ability, Fish closed off a whole area for inquiry—"to make explicit the procedures and conventions of reading, to offer a comprehensive theory of the ways in which we go about making sense of various kinds of texts" (125). This project, the goal of structuralist literary theory carefully outlined in Culler's *Structuralist Poetics* (1975), required a shift of focus from the individual to the communal reader.

In 1976, Fish recast his early view of the informed reader with the productive concept of "interpretive communities," first introduced in the important essay, "Interpreting the *Variorum.*" This new turn initiated a shift from phenomenological to poststructuralist modes of thinking. Fish sought to account for the variety as well as the stability of reader responses to a text. He did so by theorizing that "interpretive communities are made up of those who share interpretive strategies not for reading (in the conventional sense) but for writing texts, for constituting their properties and assigning their intentions. In other words, these strategies exist prior to the act of reading and therefore determine the shape of what is read rather than, as is usually assumed, the other way around."[7] Each community of interpreters deciphered texts in the manner demanded by its interpretive strategies. Thus numerological and psychoanalytical strategies, for instance, each reproduced one text. Moreover, any one reader could respond in different ways at different times because he or she could change to or belong to other communities. In any event, a reader always employed a set of interpretive strategies in spite of the desire for or impression of objectivity. Traditionally, meanings were thought to be embedded in a work prior to, and independent of, any individual interpretation. According to Fish, all meanings were created through particular reading acts and interpretive strategies during the reader's moment-to-moment experience of the text. As such, Fish proposed not just an informed reader, but an informed reader as a member of one community of interpreters or another, that is, a communal reader predisposed to create particular meanings.

When he moved from the informed reader to the interpretive community, Fish altered the nature of his enterprise. He left behind former notions about authors, about texts, and about individually cultivated readers, adopting new concepts about institutional readers, about interpretive strategies and (re)writing protocols, and about the sociology and professional politics of interpretation. He concerned himself not with the events of reading but with the systems of constraints controlling interpretive activity and with the communally based rationality engendering predictable interpretations. He denied the possibility of disinterested inquiry and "objective" facts. Communal interests, beliefs, and values shaped knowledge, formed facts, and directed inquiry and interpretation. The understanding of a text—its (re)writing—emerged out of the preexisting interests and beliefs of the particular reading community. "One can only read what one has already read."[8]

From the mid-1970s through the mid-1980s, Fish promoted a pragmatist view of linguistic competence, literary convention, and interpretive strategy, opposing the universalism of traditional Baconian science and rationalism, the abstract mathematical structuralism of Chomskian linguistics, and the general hermeneutics of Hirschian criticism. He preferred the special differential historicism of Foucault, the "ordinary language" ideas of Wittgenstein and Grice, and the antifoundationalist philosophies of Rorty and Derrida. About language competence, for example, he insisted: "Linguistic knowledge is contextual rather than abstract, local rather than general, dynamic rather than invariant; every rule is a rule of thumb; every competence grammar is a performance grammar in disguise. This then is why [universalist or foundational] theory will never succeed: it cannot help but borrow its terms and its content from that which it claims to transcend, the mutable world of practice, belief, assumptions, point of view, and so forth."[9] All interpreters were situated. No point of transcendence—free from situation, context, and values—existed. Literary criticism could not bracket communally established and historically determined interests and beliefs. As a result, Fish was led to initiate inquiries into the sociology of knowledge and the nature of literary professionalism.

While Fish changed his approach over the course of two decades from a phenomenological to a poststructuralist mode of inquiry, he was in the 1980s subject to mounting criticism from numerous theorists, particularly those of the leftist cultural studies movement. According to Edward Said, for instance, "If, as we have recently been told by Stanley Fish, every act of interpretation is made possible and given force by an interpretive community, then we must go a great deal further in showing what situation, what historical and social configuration, what political interests are concretely entailed by the very existence of interpretive communities."[10] In other words, Fish needed to move much further in the direction of sociology, history, and politics. Frank Lentricchia concurred, complaining that "Fish's reader is purely literary: his membership in a community of literary critics somehow cancels out the forces that shape his political, social, or ethnic status. . . . A literary community walled off from larger enclosures of social structure and historical process is a repetition of aestheticist isolationism."[11] Similar criticisms appeared in William Cain's *The Crisis in Criticism* (1984), Terry Eagleton's *Literary Theory* (1983), and other works published in the opening years of the 1980s. Having moved from the text to the informed reader to the interpretive community, Fish jumped beyond formalism to phenomenology and poststructuralism, stopping short of the ideological analysis characteristic of cultural studies as practiced in America during the seventies and eighties.

PSYCHOANALYSIS OF READERS

Over the course of two decades, Norman Holland developed a detailed account of literary transactions in a series of articles and books, particularly *The Dynamics of Literary Response* (1968), *Poems in Persons* (1973), *5 Readers Reading* (1975), *Laughing: A Psychology of Humor* (1982), and *The I* (1985). These works emanated from an abiding interest in the psychoanalytic nature of response. While the traditional insights and methods of Psychoanalytical Critics in the past elucidated the activities of authors and of literary characters, Holland's studies focused primarily on the transactions between readers and texts, using the findings of "ego psychology" as a means of understanding the nature of text reception. By analyzing transcripts of actual readings performed by experimental subjects, Holland was enabled to conceptualize the dynamics of response in a refined psychoanalytical formulation. Essentially, he propounded a model in which the identity (or personality) of the reader constructed from the text a unified interpretation of the text: he offered a psychological account of the way personality affected the perception and interpretation of literature. Holland argued that belief in uniformity of response was erroneous because individual personality determined response in all cases.

Whereas in *The Dynamics of Literary Response* Holland used his own personal responses to extrapolate a schematic view of the reader-text transaction, he later employed the responses of others to formulate an empirically derived transactive model, especially in *Poems in Persons* and *5 Readers Reading*. In a key essay written just after these three books, he distilled the essentials of his model and, in so doing, put his project in its most succinct form. At the outset of "UNITY IDENTITY TEXT SELF" (1975), published in *PMLA* and reprinted in Tompkins' anthology, Holland briefly defined the four terms of his title (since they underpinned his basic formulation). By "text" he meant the words on the page; by "self" he designated the whole person of an individual—mind and body. Using standard notions, Holland conceived literary "unity" in a traditional way as a union of parts or a structural whole resembling a living organism. And he conceptualized "identity" as a unified configuration of subordinate themes and patterns in a life—an unchanging and invariant essence typically called "character" or "personality." Correlating these four concepts, Holland outlined various sets of mathematical relationships among them: "*Unity* is to *text*," to cite only the most important ratio, "as *identity* is to *self*."[12] That is to say, the unity of a text is like the identity of a self.

The point of all this preliminary labor was quickly made clear: "The ratio, unity to text, equals the ratio, identity to self, but the terms on the right side of the equation cannot be eliminated from the left side. The unity we find in literary texts is impregnated with the identity that finds that unity" (816). To put it another way, the literary transaction between reader and text ended with a sense of the unity of the text because of the shaping and unifying presence of the identity of the reader. As Holland summed it up, "*interpretation is a function of identity*" (816). Elaborating on this basic model of the reader-text transaction, Holland explained: "The overarching principle is: identity re-creates itself, or, to put it another way, style—in the sense of personal style—creates itself. That is, all of us, as we read, use the literary work to symbolize and finally to replicate ourselves. We work out through the text our own characteristic patterns of desire and adaptation. We interact with the work, making it part of our own psychic economy and making ourselves part of the literary work—as we interpret it" (816).

To account for the sequence of specific operations in the reader-text transaction, Holland depicted three psychological phases of response discovered in his research. The first phase of the process brought into play the reader's desire for pleasure and fear of pain. That is, the operation of the pain-pleasure mechanism and its attendant defense system constituted the initial set of events in the response process. Essentially, the reader shaped the work or found in the material what he or she both wished and feared, defending in a habitual way against what was feared and adapting through characteristic strategies what was desired. If the process did not take place, the reader shut out the experience. (Holland presented an exemplary case study of blockage in *Poems in Persons*.) The second phase of the response process brought to bear the reader's pleasure in fantasy. The reader re-created from the text a personal fantasy and thereby realized deep gratification. The third phase of the process brought into action anxiety and guilt over raw fantasy and the fantasy's consequent transformation into a coherent and significant experience of moral, intellectual, social, or aesthetic unity and wholeness. In the end, therefore, a synthesis of the reader's responses typically occurred in which defenses, gratifications, and anxieties were balanced so as to maintain mental and emotional stability.

Holland succinctly summarized and generalized this operational process of response transaction in "The New Paradigm: Subjective or Transactive?" (1976):

> Very briefly, the literent (or the perceiver of another person or any other reality) comes to that other reality [a text, for instance] with a set of characteristic expectations, typically a balance of related desires and fears. The perceiver adapts the "other" to gratify those wishes and minimize those fears—that is, the perceiver re-creates his characteristic modes of adaptation and defense (aspects of his identity theme) from the materials literature or reality offers. He or she projects characteristic fantasies into them (and these fantasies can also be understood as aspects of identity). Finally, the individual may transform these fantasies into themes—meanings—of characteristic concern. . . .[13]

Because the phases of response involved *d*efenses, *e*xpectations, *f*antasies, and *t*ransformations, Holland employed the acronym DEFT to designate his model of literary transaction.

DEFT, the process of identity re-creation, was derived from the reading practices of experimental subjects (undergraduate students) recorded in great detail in *5 Readers Reading*. However, as Holland's generalized description implied, this model accounted for the manner in which identity or style shaped all interpretations of experience and all human transactions, including the interactions of institutions, cultures, and nations—not just interpretations of literary experience.[14]

Significantly, Holland extended the application of identity re-creation theory by analyzing the thematic preoccupations and techniques of writers, specifically of Hilda Doolittle in *Poems in Persons* and of Robert Frost in "UNITY IDENTITY TEXT SELF." In addition, he subjected his own critical interests and methods to DEFT analysis in *Poems in Persons*. Thus, by the mid-seventies, the point at which Fish had turned from the informed reader to interpretive communities, Holland had applied the model of identity re-creation with its phasic components to texts, authors, readers, and himself, suggesting that it could be extended to institutions and societies.

The main features of Holland's mature reader-response criticism resembled traits characteristic of Miller's Geneva criticism and Fish's early phenomenology. To be sure, there were differences also. It exhibited little commitment to historical inquiry, formalist explication, or ideological analysis. It attended to the reader-text transaction, allotting a primary role to the reader in shaping and determining the text. Whereas Miller's and Fish's work examined the role of temporality and consciousness in the creation of meaning, Holland's project scrutinized the drive of the unconscious toward producing organic unity. The reader had little freedom in interpreting the text; identity determined response. The reliance of Holland's enterprise on science, mathematics, and ego psychology distinguished it from other kinds of reader-oriented criticism. Where Miller spoke of mystical insights and moments of transcendence and Fish wrote about readers' continuous readjustments and consequent cognitive improvements, Holland talked of psychosexual fixations, defense strategies, and fantasy wishes.

Holland's psychological criticism represented a break with the main line of psychological criticism in American literary studies. The important books by Holland published in the 1970s revealed no indebtedness to Van Wyck Brooks, Kenneth Burke, Leslie Fiedler, Frederick Hoffman, J. W. Krutch, Ludwig Lewisohn, Lionel Trilling, or Edmund Wilson. Moreover, Holland downplayed contemporary existential, Jungian, Lacanian, Frankfurt School, and third-force psychology (which was made clear in "Guide to Further Reading" in *Poems in Persons*, and in the Appendix on "Other Psychoanalyses" in *The I*). He relied most heavily on ego psychology as developed in certain key works by Erik Erikson, Anna Freud, Ernst Kris, Heinz Lichtenstein, Roy Schafer, Robert Waelder, and D. W. Winnicott.

In *Out of My System* (1975) Frederick Crews, a fellow Psychoanalytic Critic, roundly criticized Holland for relying on the theory of identity derived from ego psychology, which he characterized as impoverished and reductive. As far as Crews was concerned, Holland was "forgetting the entire raison d'être of critical activity" and was "conducting a highly unusual going-out-of-business sale."[15]

Critics of Holland's psychoanalysis of readers registered numerous complaints. Among such criticisms were: he imprudently shifted the concept of unity from the text to the self; he renounced literary criticism for case studies; he rendered all reading self-interested; he undermined standards of interpretative validity, professional authority, and classroom procedure; he reductively modeled criticism on the Freudian theory of transference; he characterized reading as a neurotic process of filtering and subtracting; he unwisely presented all criteria of aesthetic value as matters of individual psychology; he portrayed readers as fixated and static egos; he fostered an apolitical pluralism denuded of communal and social values; his own readings were solipsistic and merely confessional; his type of criticism made the literary text a victim; his depictions of "ego style" remained caught in an interpretive circle; and his "transactive paradigm" retained vestiges of a commitment to the obsolescent goal of objectivity. Because Holland's work attracted a great deal of attention, often of a negative sort, it served as a site of intense focus within the American reader-response movement. Holland, like Fish, was a point man in the movement for over a decade.

THE SUBJECT OF PEDAGOGY

When Stanley Fish collected in book form his many credos and essays of the seventies, he titled the work *Is There a Text in This Class?*. When Norman Holland shifted in the early seventies from an objective to a transactive paradigm, he grounded his research in analyses of student responses as his magnum opus of the decade, *5 Readers Reading*, memorably demonstrated. When David Bleich wrote *Readings and Feelings* (1975) and *Subjective Criticism* (1978), he committed both books unequivocally to effecting "changes in existing pedagogical institutions" and to outlining new teaching methods based on "actual classroom experiences."[16] Characteristically, the leaders of the American reader-response movement closely linked literary criticism and theory with classroom pedagogy and academic practices. Such a linkage, however, seemed neither inevitable nor desirable to other groups of critics ranging from the early Marxists and New York Intellectuals to the later existentialists and deconstructors. Lionel Trilling put the issue pointedly in the opening pages of *Beyond Culture* when he observed that "pedagogy is a depressing subject to all persons of sensibility." No doubt, the characteristic preoccupation with pedagogy reflected the growing absorption of most criticism into the university and the widespread student demands for "relevance" typical of the sixties. Starting in the mid-sixties and continuing to the mid-eighties, Geoffrey Hartman, like several other influential philosophically minded critics, was prompted to warn against the increasing reduction of criticism to pedagogy.

No Reader-Response Critic was more insistent than David Bleich in promoting the gains for pedagogy of adopting an antiformalist and nonobjectivist paradigm for literary studies. His project, as first detailed in *Readings and Feelings: An Introduction to Subjective Criticism* (published by the National Council of Teachers of English), advocated the virtues of tutorial modes of teaching based on small classes and personal interactions of teachers and students. Holland's enterprise similarly advised small seminar formats where student-teacher interactions engendered intimacy and trust, conditions essential to reader-response pedagogy. "In large classes," insisted Bleich, "this method is impossible. . . ."[17] Located at mega-universities regularly offering large literature classes, reader-response teachers like Bleich, Holland, and others positioned themselves as critics of the widespread practice during the Space Age of presenting literature in huge lecture halls. The concern with pedagogy became the ground of criticism.

In Bleich's view, *interpretation* of literature entailed the belated re-creation and presentation of primary emotional response, consisting of personal (1) perceptions, (2) affects, and (3) associations. The fourth phase of a complex psychological process, interpretation involved objectification and potential falsification of individual subjective experience. "The true scope of feeling—or perhaps the true limitations of feeling—is essentially denied by intellectual reformulations" (69). What Bleich stressed and sought to demonstrate was the subjective ground of all objective formulations. He distrusted "objectivity." Epistemologically, feeling and passion preceded and directed thinking and knowledge. "Ultimately, the separation of conscious judgment from its subjective roots is false and artificial" (49). As a classroom teacher, Bleich was mainly interested in what a student felt rather than what she thought; he cared most about affect, not interpretation.

Because reading depended on personal psychology, it necessarily engendered "distortions"—exaggerations, omissions, associations, insertions, errors. No response to a text could meet the unreal orthodox criteria of objectivity and completeness. As an inherent element of response, "distortion" for Bleich was both revealing and valuable: it displayed features of perceptual style and testified to authentic engagement with a text. Valuing subjectivity required crediting personal peculiarities. Objectivity sought to eradicate just such essential and predetermining personal idiosyncrasies. Bleich deplored the critical taboo on private feelings and subjective values.

For Bleich, response was one thing and interpretation was another: one was private; the other was communal. To make an interpretation was to go public with a private experience: "experience of peremptory feelings and images precedes the onset of deliberate thought" (5). Thus, "dealing with subjective experiences in a community should be preceded by the student's working things out on an individual basis . . ." (79). Unlike Fish, Bleich pictured the community as a late arrival in the formulation of a response rather than as the determining factor in the formation of an interpretation. Like Holland, Bleich worked as a psychological rather than a sociological critic. Without question, the community helped shape interpretation, but it did so late in the process and it involved risks of falsification. In particular, the conventional social format for interpretation—the proposition-proof argument—directed primary reader response, especially personal affect and association, away from actual experience. Although he didn't say so in *Readings and Feelings,* Bleich evidently would have liked to scrap altogether the genre of the critical essay as inimical to reader-oriented pedagogy.

Like Fish, Bleich regarded literature as an experience, not as an autonomous object. Unlike Fish, he showed no interest in the temporality of reading. From his students he expected multiple readings of a text as a prerequisite of response as well as interpretation. A reader's "initial" response to a whole text might hinge completely on a work's last word. Bleich was no phenomenologist. As with other Reader-Response Critics, Bleich joined a didactic to an affective poetics: the emotional experience of literature "can produce new understanding of oneself—not just a moral here and a message there, but a genuinely new conception of one's values and tastes as well as one's prejudices and learning difficulties" (3–4). The strong emphasis on subjectivity in Bleich's work made him the least attached of all the leading Reader-Response Critics to a textual poetics. The power of the text to direct reading and survive distortion was inconsiderable. In literary study, ontological priority belonged to written response statements, not poetic texts. Criticism was not an operation of textual decoding but an experience of developing important personal feelings and associations.

Readings and Feelings was based on six years of experience teaching in reader-response classrooms and analyzing the actual responses of numerous undergraduate students. Thirty such responses were examined in Bleich's book. Where other contemporary literary intellectuals like Myth Critics and hermeneuticists prized erudition, philological rigor, and scholarly mastery, Reader-Response Critics working in the empirical mode of Holland and Bleich valued depth of personal engagement, individual frankness and authenticity, and freedom from institutional authority. They made public their own private responses as well as the responses of their students. As Susan Suleiman noted, such "criticism takes us as far as we can go in the investigation of reading as private experience—an experience in which the determining factor is the individual 'life history,' not the history of groups and nations" (31–32). Privileging the idiosyncratic over the norm and the singular over the collective, Bleich's subjective criticism left the text completely behind as a regulator of response. In this he differed from Holland, whose transactive criticism credited textual constraints.[18] Both critics, however, promoted efforts to renew literary pedagogy and to value individual student readers. Such a project prompted even sympathetic critics to doubts, as was clear in Steven Mailloux's *Interpretive Conventions* (1982) and William Ray's *Literary Meaning* (1984), both of which stressed the absence of adequate sociological and institutional analyses inherent in contemporary reader-response psychological criticism.

READING AS RESISTANCE: FEMINISM AND MARXISM

During the heyday of the reader-response movement, none of the leaders explicitly addressed the matter of gender—an issue that Feminist Critics began to raise in the 1970s. Do women read differently from men? Does sexual identity influence understanding? What role does gender play in literature? In criticism? Here Fish, Holland, and Bleich had nothing to say. Neither Suleiman and Crosman nor Tompkins considered such questions in their anthologies. In fact, the issue of gender remained unexplored by leading Phenomenological, Existential, Hermeneutical, Structuralist, and Deconstructive Critics during the early Space Age. Yet important work was done in the field of feminine reader response.

Among the most influential of feminist works of the 1970s in the area of reader-response theory was Judith Fetterley's *The Resisting Reader* (1978), which argued that classic American fiction from Irving and Hawthorne to Hemingway and Mailer was not "universal" but masculine and that women readers of this literature were constrained to identify against themselves. What Fetterley aimed to do was offer a "survival manual for the woman reader lost in 'the masculine wilderness of the American novel.' "[19] She took her inspiration from Kate Millett's *Sexual Politics* (1970)—a pioneering book that first examined texts in light of their male assumptions.

Fetterley argued that to be an American woman reading the nation's classic fiction was to find oneself excluded: one's experience was neither expressed nor legitimized in art. Reading such literature required identifying with it as a male. Under such conditions women were powerless. "Not only does powerlessness characterize woman's experience of reading, it also describes the content of what is read" (xiii). Ultimately, Fetterley criticized both male-dominated literature and the sexist academic institutions of criticism grown up around it. "As readers and teachers and scholars, women are taught to think as men, to identify with a male point of view, and to accept as normal and legitimate a male system of values . . ." (xx). Committing herself to feminist criticism, Fetterley aimed to remedy the anomalous situation of being sexually female and intellectually male. Accordingly, "the first act of the feminist critic must be to become a resisting rather than an assenting reader and, by this refusal to assent, to begin the process of exorcizing the male mind that has been implanted in us" (xxii). This project entailed not only psychological and sociological analysis but political criticism. Feminist resistance had to do with one's identity, one's class, and one's power relations. Fetterley never doubted "the power of men as a class over women as a class" (xvii), nor the present-day oppressive "function of literary sexual politics" (xx).

Following in the wake of other Feminist Critics, especially Carolyn Heilbrun, Kate Millett, Adrienne Rich, and Lillian Robinson, Fetterley indicted the patriarchal exclusions and sexist practices endemic to American institutions of literature. What characterized such male-dominated culture was sex-class hostility and oppression. The task at hand was clear:

> To expose and question that complex of ideas and mythologies about women and men which exist in our society and are confirmed in our literature is to make the system of power embodied in the literature open not only to discussion but even to change. Such a questioning and exposure can, of course, be carried on only by a consciousness radically different from the one that informs the literature. . . . Feminist criticism provides that point of view and embodies that consciousness. (xx)

By foregrounding female consciousness, feminist reader-response criticism could uncover, expose, and question the ideas, myths, and power relations

encoded in culture as a way to foster change. This program depended on a
new and radically different *female* consciousness. The goal was clear. "To
create a new understanding of our literature is to make possible a new effect
of that literature on us. And to make possible a new effect is in turn to
provide the conditions for changing the culture that the literature reflects"
(xix–xx). The job of feminist criticism was to produce new interpretations
as a means to alter consciousness and change society.

In Fetterley's feminist project, poetics encompassed affective, didactic,
and mimetic frameworks. To begin with, "what we read affects us" (viii).
We can be moved by literature. Moreover, we can be instructed and shaped
by it. For example, we can construe ourselves as powerless, schizophrenic,
or unworthy, as Fetterley personally testified. Finally, literature both embodies and reflects the reigning culture. American society and art, in Fetterley's account, were patriarchal and sexist. So too was academic criticism.
What most obviously distinguished the literary theory and criticism of
Fetterley from that of Fish, Holland, and Bleich was its recuperation of
mimetic poetics and its dedication to a political program. These two were of
a piece.

Since literature and its criticism moved, shaped, and mirrored our minds
and worlds, both possessed the power to effect positive change. "At its best,
feminist criticism is a political act whose aim is not simply to interpret the
world but to change it by changing the consciousness of those who
read . . ." (viii). Like other reader-response theorists, Fetterley linked reading with identity formation; however, she credited literary texts with much
more power over readers. As a result, she envisaged feminist critical activity
as an operation of resistance to power. For Fetterley, as for Fish, the reader
was not isolated and idiosyncratic, which Holland and Bleich believed, but a
member of an interpretive community. The readers represented in Fetterley's work belonged to a particular class with a specific experience of
history, set of goals, and program of protocols. About the sociology and
politics of the community, Fetterley was much more deeply concerned than
Fish. In this regard, the enterprise of Fetterley had a great deal in common
with the cultural studies movement initiated in the 1970s and less in
common with contemporary phenomenology, hermeneutics, structuralism, deconstruction, or male reader-response criticism.

As is typical of most reader-response criticism, Fetterley's work had close
connections with pedagogy. Her text's opening words were: "This book
began in the classroom." She then related her eight years of experience
teaching women's literature, revealing that her book started as a classroom

journal kept during a course and shared with students. "I have continued to develop, refine, and change my ideas through interaction and exchange with my students. It is my sincere wish that this book will extend that dialogue even further and that it will be itself a form of teaching" (vii). Here, as elsewhere in the reader-response movement, the beginning and the end of criticism was pedagogy, which was in keeping with its affective-didactic poetics and its student-oriented critical methods. What Fetterley added to this common nexus was a mimetic-political dimension, which lodged her work in an objective paradigm.

That some female practitioners and theoreticians of reader-response criticism were committed to both sociological and political analysis was evident not only in the book of Judith Fetterley, but in the later works, for instance, of Jane Tompkins and of Mary Louise Pratt. At the conclusion of her anthology Tompkins, for example, surprisingly offered a strong critique of the reader-response movement, singling out six weaknesses. First, it did not undermine New Criticism but "merely transposed formalist principles into a new key" (201). Second, it limited critical activity to specifying "meaning." Third, it continued to restrict analysis to individual texts. Fourth, it maintained the long-standing pernicious separation of literature from the forces of political and social life, exacerbating its puerile privatiza-tion and loss of moral effectiveness. Fifth, it accepted the removal of literature from history and the tendency to monumentalize or universalize art. And, sixth, it regarded literary language as special or as aesthetic rather than as a form or instrument of power.

In her important essay, "Interpretive Strategies/Strategic Interpreta-tions: On Anglo-American Reader-Response Criticism" (1982), Mary Louise Pratt employed the ideological analysis typical of the cultural studies movement to criticize American reader-oriented theory and criticism. Using insights from the Marxist intellectuals Louis Althusser, Raymond Williams, and Terry Eagleton, Pratt condemned reader-response criticism as a new formalist practice tied closely to "bourgeois esthetics, notably to a kind of consumerist view of art which calls for dehistoricizing the art object, detaching it from its context of production and making it available for privatized leisure use."[20] Like Fetterley and Tompkins, Pratt deplored the avoidance of history, sociology, and politics. What Pratt recommended for reader-response criticism was an expanded program that would undertake "exploring the specifics of reception as a socially and ideologically deter-mined process and coming to grips with the question of artistic *produc-tion*. . . . Obviously it is not in the slightest degree necessary for reader-response criticism to exclude questions of production from the domain of literary studies" (205). Reader-response criticism needed to extend its notion that reception was psychologically and communally determined to the idea that artistic production itself was similarly determined. Actually, argued Pratt, the movement could profitably apply the model of production also to the act of reception: response to literature was itself a form or process of production.

Though Fish's work came closest to meeting Pratt's goals for reader-oriented criticism, it provoked her dismay on several grounds. While Fish's theory of interpretive communities propounded the useful axioms of the socially constituted subject and of the social constitution of literature, it did so at considerable cost: it overlooked or ignored the reality of disagreements, uncertainty, and change within interpretive groups (ideological circles). It thus denied the possibility of power struggles. In Pratt's assessment, Fish portrayed "interpretive communities as spontaneously forming, egalitarian entities which couldn't be coercive" (225). In this way "the question of power relations is ruthlessly avoided" (226). The harmony within such communities was established by Fish's utopian concept of consensus—a happy endpoint always insured because the self-selected members of each community perfectly shared beliefs and reading conventions. Instead of politicizing the labors of interpretive communities, Fish depicted the variability and relativity of their critical efforts as signs of the healthy equality and fraternity within groups and the vital freedoms and energies between groups. Where Bleich celebrated the individual liberty of readers, Fish championed the communal agreements of like-minded critics. In both cases, these critics suppressed the fundamental fact of power relations and struggles.

In her earlier work, *Toward a Speech Act Theory of Literary Discourse* (1977), Pratt had attacked formalist and structuralist poetics because they distanced literary language from ordinary language, divorcing literature and criticism from the broad realm of social existence. She looked with hope toward new developments in reader-response theory as well as speech-act theory since both promised to reintegrate literary studies into material social life. In her later essay, she continued to hope for a renewal of criticism by its adoption of an account of discursive production indebted now to Marxist and feminist critical ideas and theories. She singled out Fetterley's work as a model for her enterprise. In Pratt's vision, the intersection of reader-response criticism with the Marxist concept of production and the feminist practice of sociopolitical analysis stood to broaden and improve the movement. In the early 1980s mainline American reader-response criticism lacked adequate treatment of sociological and political realities, as feminist and Marxists in increasing numbers documented. While the shift from a text-centered to a reader-oriented criticism was widely heralded as a positive transformation of literary studies by both feminists and Marxists, matters needed to go further so as to make contact with the facts of gender, class, power, and resistance.

GERMAN RECEPTION THEORY IN AMERICA

Independent of the American reader-response movement, a school of reception theory developed during the sixties and seventies in West Germany, primarily at the University of Constance. The leaders of this tight-knit group were Hans Robert Jauss and Wolfgang Iser, whose works frequently appeared in the biannual series *Poetik und Hermeneutik: Arbeitsergebnisse einer Forschungsgruppe (Poetics and Hermeneutics: Findings of a Research Group)*, which presented material from important colloquia regularly held at Constance. From the mid-seventies and lasting for a decade, the phenomenological project of Iser drew a great deal of attention in America whereas the historicist work of Jauss did not receive much consideration until the early eighties when his *Aesthetic Experience and Literary Hermeneutics* (1977) and his collected essays, *Toward an Aesthetic of Reception* (1982), obtained a sympathetic hearing. Iser's major books, *The Implied Reader* (1972) and the *Act of Reading* (1976), were translated by 1974 and 1978, respectively, and were widely and promptly reviewed in American journals. Throughout the seventies both Jauss and Iser lectured at American universities, which included several long sojourns at various major institutions. Significantly, however, the American anthologies of reader-oriented criticism, published by Suleiman and Crosman and by Tompkins in 1980, contained contributions only from Iser, not from Jauss. When a selection of the Constance material from *Poetik und Hermeneutik* was translated and published in 1979 as *New Perspectives in German Literary Criticism*, edited by Richard Amacher and Victor Lange, it offered two essays by Jauss and two by Iser—a more balanced presentation than other English-language collections of reader-oriented materials. Even though Jauss and Iser appeared in translation equally often during the seventies in the influential journal *New Literary History*, it was Iser who most often represented German reception theory for American intellectuals. There were two major reasons why Wolfgang Iser was hospitably received by American literary critics: first, he specialized in classic English fiction, unlike Jauss, whose main interest was in early romance-language literature; and, second, he practiced close reading in a phenomenological mode, whereas Jauss engaged in wide-ranging historicist speculations.

Just as American reader-response criticism provoked attacks for its apparent indifference to sociological and political issues, so West German reception theory incited parallel, though earlier, assaults from East German Marxists. By the opening years of the 1970s the East Germans, particularly Manfred Naumann and Robert Weimann, had lodged a series of critiques, published mainly in the pages of *Weimarer Beiträge*, the leading journal of literary theory during the post-Stalinist era in the German Democratic Republic. The Marxists had three major complaints. First, they condemned Constance reception theory for focusing exclusively on the consumption of literature, leaving out all consideration of its production. Second, they complained about the tendency of West German reader-oriented critics to subjectivize human cultural history. And third, they deplored Western receptionists' proclivity to privatize the reading process—which was a bourgeois idealization that circumvented all analysis of the social origins and determinants of individual response. Neither Jauss nor Iser escaped these charges similar to ones later made against Fish, Holland, and Bleich.

Americans interested in Iser were most attentive to his accounts of the "implied reader," the reading process, and the role of "textual gaps." Positing an implied reader prestructured by a text and actualized by a critic, Iser was able to focus reception theory on a transcendental or transhistorical reader, thereby bracketing actual, empirical readers and predetermined informed readers. In other words, Iser avoided entanglement with the history of reception in favor of involvement with potential response. This strategy comported well with long-standing formalist doctrines. As depicted by Iser, the reading process entailed a continuous readjustment of expectations and evaluations in a dynamic event dedicated to consistency-building. Unlike the holistic unity pictured as the endpoint in Holland's model of identity re-creation, the sequential consistency portrayed in Iser's account respected the unfolding temporality of the reading experience. The copartnership of reader and text emphasized the aesthetic and didactic dimensions of reading rather than the psychological, sociological, or historical aspects. Patterning the elements or schemata of the text, the reader actively engaged in a self-correcting operation that heightened self-awareness and reinforced humane openness. Because texts contained gaps, blanks, vacancies—indeterminacies—readers were constrained in the process of concretizing works and producing consistency to attend carefully and creatively to textual cues. Iser's reception theory thus respected the text, reminiscent of "objective" modes of criticism; it refused to transform or dissolve the text into the reader's subjectivity or the interpretive community's codes and conventions. At the same time it depended on and promoted the creativity of the reader in the work of surmounting indeterminacies.

In 1981 a debate broke out between Stanley Fish and Wolfgang Iser in the pages of the poststructuralist journal *Diacritics*. The main issue turned out to be epistemological. Fish insisted that "perception" was inherently interpretive, that "facts" were predetermined by values, that "knowledge" was always interested, that the "given" was in fact supplied, and that the "text" was constituted by the reader. Not only was perception thus mediated, but it was conventional. That is to say, perception was prestructured by public and communal rather than individual and unique categories. Consequently, the textual gaps or indeterminacies activating the labors of reading in Iser's model were not built into the text but resulted from the interpretive strategies or perceptual proclivities of the communal reader. Iser replied: "Interpretation is always informed by a set of assumptions or conventions, but these are also acted upon by what they intend to tackle. Hence the 'something' which is to be mediated exists prior to interpretation, acts as a constraint on interpretation, has repercussions on the anticipations operative in interpretation, and thus contributes to a hermeneutical process. . . ."[21] By insisting that the text preexisted and constrained interpretation, Iser unabashedly made clear the "objectivist" or textual poetics that distinguished his overall interactive or phenomenological model of interpretation from the various models proposed by Fish, Miller, Holland, Bleich, Fetterley, and others.

In his introductory book on German reader-oriented criticism titled *Reception Theory* (1984), Robert Holub separated American reader-response criticism from German reception theory. None of the American critics campaigned under the banner "reader-response criticism"; instead this designation was applied after the fact to a number of theorists having little contact with or influence upon one another. "If reader-response criticism has become a critical force," argued Holub, "it is by virtue of the ingenuity of labeling rather than any commonality of effort."[22] In contrast, German reception theory was a cohesive, self-conscious, collective enterprise responding to similar circumstances and predecessors. Forerunners included Slavic formalists and structuralists, European phenomenologists and hermeneuticists, and various sociologists and speech-act theorists. Significantly, psychoanalysis and feminism were conspicuously absent. As far as Holub was concerned, "the similarities in general critical perspective between reader-response criticism and reception theory are ultimately too superficial and too abstract for a merging here" (xiii–xiv). Yet Holub's subsequent account of the numerous internal disagreements and differences within the German enterprise illustrated a lack of cohesiveness easily a match for American diversity. This important similarity—diversity and struggle—highlighted the operation within all reader-oriented work of differing philosophical commitments (formalism, phenomenology, hermeneutics, Marxism) characteristic of German and of American reader-oriented criticism. Whether part of a tight-knit group or a loose movement, reader-centered critics in Germany and in America typically operated at the intense intersection of numerous contending philosophical forces. Iser was as different from Jauss as Miller was from Fish. What significantly separated the leading Americans from the main Germans were preoccupations with pedagogy and with psychology. Later the concern with feminism would further differentiate the American movement from the German School of Constance.

OF LIMITS AND CHANGES

Except for feminist and leftist criticism, no critical group or school appeared as "pluralistic" or heterogeneous during the 1970s in America as the reader-response movement. In Jane Tompkins' account, this movement encompassed various formalist, phenomenological, structuralist, poststructuralist, and psychoanalytical modes of approach. In the view of Susan Suleiman, it included a half dozen discreet methodologies, ranging from rhetorical, semiotic, and phenomenological to psychoanalytical, hermeneutical, and sociological-historical modes of analysis. (The latter category admittedly applied mainly to European reception theory.) The limits of the movement could have been expanded even further by including in such accounts the receptionist work undertaken by new hermeneuticists like Spanos and by feminists like Fetterley—both of whom promised to reinvigorate reader-oriented practice during its first period of stagnation in the late seventies. It was the force of the ideological analysis promoted by these latter two representative critics—and by certain of the emerging cultural studies theorists—that signaled change for the reader-centered enterprise.

Despite its broadness, the evident pluralism of American reader-response criticism could not accommodate the text-dominated methodology of certain formalists, structuralists, deconstructors, and hermeneuts. In addition, it could not comfortably accommodate the programmatic, theme-centered criticism common to most Myth Critics, existentialists, and Black Aestheticians.

In a certain sense, reader-response criticism was the least pluralistic of contemporary schools and movements. Generally, pluralists seek to avoid two main dangers: they resist any theory that insists there is (only) one correct interpretation of a work; and they deny any theory that promotes as many acceptable readings as there are readers. Pluralists encourage yet constrain hermeneutic liberty; they characteristically celebrate limited diversity and condemn outright arbitrariness. Because reader-response critics like Bleich, Holland, and Fish located meaning in individual readers, they exceeded, quite forcefully, the limits essential to pluralism. The reader-response movement assaulted traditional American pluralism not only by giving the critical franchise to individual readers, but paradoxically by insisting that for each reader there was really only one "valid" interpretation. Just as the conventions of an interpretive community directed reading along certain preestablished paths, so the personal psychology or identities of readers predetermined the outcomes of their reading experiences. Reader-response criticism undermined the two main limits of traditional pluralism.

Various telling changes characterized American higher education during the formative years of the reader-response movement. Among these were widespread expansions in the sizes of universities and classrooms, successful cries for students' rights, effective demands for relevance in subject matter, fulfilled requests for individualized majors, utopian attempts at deschooling society, scattered triumphant efforts to dismantle traditional grading policies, and heeded calls for formal teacher evaluations. What occurred was a broad shift of emphasis in education from the teacher to the student, from erudition to experience, from disinterested scholarship to personal self-development. The new reference source appeared to be the diary, not the encyclopedia. The source of authority became the self rather than the scholar. Confession seemed a productive activity. The small seminar was preferable to the huge lecture hall. The response statement replaced the critical essay. In such an environment, it was not surprising that text-centered literary studies faced a challenge from reader-response criticism. Nor was it surprising that charges against reader-oriented analysis included accusations of narcissism, of anti-intellectualism, of capitulation to vulgar consumerism, and of making classroom pedagogy *the* measure of effective theory and practice. In this context, the receptionists' early strategy of attacking New Criticism became symbolic of much broader changes taking place in American education during the Space Age.

In its later stages reader-response criticism often broke through its earlier limiting personalism and narcissism, catching glimpses of the impersonal sociological and cultural forces that conditioned the self and its activities. The result was that the magnified self of early formulations soon became a minimal self in later theories. The work of Fish and Fetterley best illustrated this significant change. By the time Holland published *The I,* he had added a new dimension to his theory of identity re-creation so as to account for the essential role of culture: "culture enables and limits the individual" or, put in terms of identity theory, "identities are social and political as well as individual" (149). Similarly, Bleich's *Subjective Criticism* marked an expansion of his earlier project precisely because it added a detailed account of how interpretations were negotiated collectively. According to Bleich, all knowledge "finds itself, at least in part, under the authority of communal and societal motives" (265). What distinguished such latter-day sociological theories formulated by leading receptionists was the degree to which they credited for the first time the determining powers of social practices and communal conventions.

While most of the leading critics associated with the reader-response movement sought to change traditional pedagogical practice and theory, they did not attempt to alter the canon of established great works. Consequently, they limited the scope of their entreprise. What was, in part, at issue here was the applicability of the techniques of personalized reading promoted by receptionists. Because reader-response methods applied to any literature from any period and genre, there was no drive to invent or privilege a special canon the way the New Critics did. However, Reader-Response Critics, particularly of the phenomenological and hermeneutical variety, slowed the pace of "normal" reading (as did certain Deconstructive Critics). This change entailed an attack on theories of spatial form in favor of new concepts of serial, or sequential, or temporal "form." Unlike the New Critics, who preferred short, poetic kinds of literature, Reader-Response Critics were as comfortable with long as with short kinds and as content with prose as with poetry. Consequently, long-standing limits on the canon were loosened somewhat. Although a more generous and inclusive view of the canon evolved, a countervailing need to assess and judge works aesthetically did not emerge. Like historical criticism, judicial criticism remained out of favor. In the absence of these two discredited practices, reformation of the canon was unlikely to occur in reader-response criticism. Not surprisingly, feminists, Black Aestheticians, and other ethnic critics had reason to complain about the status of the canon in the hands of leading Reader-Response Critics. Even in later years, when they turned toward sociological theory, Reader-Response Critics focused primarily on small communities of students and professors, avoiding analysis of society and culture at large. Starting in the late seventies, feminist receptionists set out to change this narrow focus and to revise the limited canon—a project in line with the new turn to historical, political, and ideological analysis.

To arrive at a fuller understanding of the various branches of American reader-response criticism, we shall have to consider the contributions of certain Structuralist Critics to theories of reading and the reader. In the fourth section of the next chapter, we shall examine the accounts of textual reception proffered by Michael Riffaterre, Gerald Prince, Jonathan Culler, and Robert Scholes.

CHAPTER NINE

Literary Structuralism and Semiotics

PROGENITORS AND PROGENIES

THE HEYDAY of structuralism and semiotics among American academic literary intellectuals lasted from the early 1970s to the early 1980s. The leading critics included Seymour Chatman, Jonathan Culler, Claudio Guillén, Roman Jakobson, Gerald Prince, Robert Scholes, and Michael Riffaterre, all of whom, except Jakobson, were deeply indebted to the French tradition of structuralist analysis, stemming from Ferdinand de Saussure and culminating with Claude Lévi-Strauss and Roland Barthes. It was the triumph of structuralism in France during the 1960s that most immediately prompted the rise of literary structuralism and semiotics in America. The first signs of the crucial French impact on American criticism occurred in 1966 with the publication of a speciall issue on "Structuralism" of *Yale French Studies* and the convening of an important conference focused on the "Structuralist Controversy" at the Johns Hopkins University. Several years later the special issue and the conference proceedings were published in book form. Both *Structuralism* (1970), edited by Jacques Ehrmann, and *The Structuralist Controversy* (1970; new ed. 1972), edited by Richard Macksey and Eugenio Donato, became at once key documents for American structuralist and semiotic critics. Put together by professors of French, these texts signaled the emergence of American interest in literary structuralism within the context of contemporary Gallic accomplishments.

By the time structuralism arrived in America, however, it had already developed a rich and complex tradition linked not simply with early Saussurean linguistics, but with Slavic formalist and structuralist poetics, with British and French structural anthropology, with American descriptive linguistics, and with more recent French structuralist psychoanalysis, political theory, historiography, cinema studies, and literary theory. To this mixture some Americans later added the native semiotics of Charles Sanders Peirce and Charles Morris, the generative grammar of Noam Chomsky, and the myth criticism of Northrop Frye. Because structuralism in the sixties and seventies gained some worthy adherents not only in America, but also in several East European countries, Germany, Holland, Israel, and Italy, it became common by the late seventies for American critics to refer to contemporary works emanating from these places. Two cases in point were the increasing currency in the United States of the books of the Italian semiotician Umberto Eco and the Russian semiotician Yuri Lotman. The coming of structuralism and semiotics to America in the seventies represented the arrival of a multifaceted international movement with considerable potential to affect nascent modes of interdisciplinary inquiry. During the seventies, various American art historians, historiographers, musicologists, philosophers, theologians, and other specialists had begun to explore the possible applications of the family of structuralist and semiotic methods and models for their fields. Thus, the structuralist movement both in the United States and elsewhere was not limited to literary theory and criticism; it had roots and applications in many fields as well as in numerous national settings.

Common to most varieties of structuralism and semiotics was a set of interlocking formulations and key concepts derived in the first instance from Saussure and formed in opposition to historicist and hermeneutical modes of investigation. To avoid various problems typical of nineteenth-century historical linguistics and philology, Saussure at the turn of the century proposed to focus analysis on the underlying rules and conventions of a language rather than on the surface configurations of speech acts. In other words, Saussure pioneered the analysis of the social or collective dimension of language rather than the individual events produced by speakers. He fostered inquiry into rules rather than expressions, grammar rather than usage, models rather than data, competence rather than performance, systems rather than realizations, *langue* (language) rather than *parole* (speech). To reconstruct a language system as a whole required arresting its historical evolution and attending to its elements at a given time. Unlike historical research, structural analysis tended to examine the synchronic instead of the diachronic dimensions of systems. For example, when N. S. Trubetzkoy, a leading member of the Prague Linguistic Circle, came in the thirties to scrutinize sounds in language, he distinguished between the study of actual speech sounds (phonetics) and the study of the limited pattern of phonemes essential to the functioning of a language (phonology). Like Saussure, Trubetzkoy was interested in the unconscious, synchronic infrastructures of phenomena. Following both Saussure and Trubetzkoy, Claude Lévi-Strauss during the forties first directed the anthropological study of primitive myth toward analysis of the rule-bound regularities of collective cultural texts, regarding all historical variants as parts of an underlying timeless synchronic system of myth.

In the early seventies, the programs for structuralism promulgated by America literary critics reflected principles stemming from the Saussurean legacy. In *Structuralism in Literature: An Introduction* (1974), Robert Scholes claimed special status for structuralism in literary studies "because it seeks to establish a model of the system of literature itself. . . . By moving from the study of language to the study of literature, and seeking to define the principles of structuration that operate not only through individual works but through the relationships among works over the whole field of literature, structuralism has tried—and is trying—to establish for literary studies a basis that is as scientific as possible."[1] Typical of most structuralists, Scholes conceived of his object of analysis as the totality of phenomena in his domain (not as autonomous, atomistic entities), conceptualizing the goal of analysis as the establishment of *a* model for *the* system of literature. In his *Structuralist Poetics: Structuralism, Linguistics and the Study of Literature* (1975), Jonathan Culler championed structuralism in opposition to reigning interpretive forms of criticism: "The type of literary study which structuralism helps one to envisage would not be primarily interpretive; it would not offer a method which, when applied to literary texts, produced new and hitherto unexpected meanings. . . . The study of literature, as opposed to the perusal and discussion of individual works, would become an attempt to understand the conventions which make literature possible."[2] Structuralist critics, in Culler's view, needed to uncover and comprehend the systems of conventions enabling literature and its interpretation. Such criticism was not dedicated to interpretation per se; nor was it restricted to individual works. While Scholes and Culler tended to conceive literature synchronically as well as systematically, the literary historian Claudio Guillén in *Literature as System* (1971) argued that "the history of literature—as distinct from language and society—is characterized not so much by the operation of full systems as by a tendency toward system and structuration."[3] This tempered view of literary systems was further modified because such "systems" were "not metatemporal or metahistorical" (389). Essentially, Guillén warned critics against the pursuit of universal categories, wanting them to reserve a place for literary history within structuralist criticism.

Because Saussure valued deep structures over surface phenomena, his work paralleled, in part, the projects of Marx and Freud. Marx's interest in underlying causes and Freud's concern for unconscious motivations dramatically diminished the traditional status of individual human consciousness, shifting attention to transpersonal forces in a manner similar to Saussure's. The "disappearance of the subject" engendered by structuralism, not to mention Marxism and Freudianism, pictured the self as a construct and consequence of impersonal social systems. The individual neither originated nor controlled the codes and conventions of his psychic life, his social existence, or his linguistic experience. Not surprisingly, structuralism was compatible with Marxism and psychoanalysis, as was evident, for example, in the influential work of Julia Kristeva, a Bulgarian theorist who worked in France from the mid-sixties and part time in America from the late seventies.

Saussure foresaw the possibility of a new discipline, a general science of signs and sign systems, which he tentatively labeled "semiology." He believed that his kind of structural linguistics could play a key methodological role in the new field. C. S. Peirce, Saussure's contemporary, envisaged a similar science which he called "semiotic" and which he tried to the methods of logic rather than linguistics. When Claude Lévi-Strauss delivered his inaugural lecture in 1961 at the Collège de France, he situated his structural anthropology within the broad domain of "semiology." In this increasingly common usage, the word "semiology," like its non-French relative "semiotics," designated a field of study dedicated to analyzing sign systems, codes, and conventions of all kinds, ranging from natural to animal languages, from traffic signals to sign languages, from the language of fashion to the systematic lexicon of food, from the rules of folk narratives to those of phonological systems, from the codes of diagnostic medicine to the conventions of primitive myth and civilized literature. Though it often depended on linguistic methods, semiotics (or semiology), in this broad sense, extended way beyond the confines of linguistic and literary research. The tendency during the sixties and seventies was for the word "structuralism" to be replaced by "semiotics" or "semiology." This terminological shift, which occurred in America in the late seventies, signaled a broadening of the horizons of Saussure's various progenies. Literary structuralism or semiotics was part of a bigger enterprise. Saussure's vision proved prophetic.

What characterized the numerous branches of worldwide semiotics after the mid-sixties, whether it involved zoosemiotics or narratology, kinesics or text linguistics, was a marked inventiveness in terminology undergirded by a tendency to methodological conservatism. The two basic operations common to semiotic analysis involved (1) constituting a synchronic domain or field of data (a *langue*) and (2) subjecting it to segmentation, classification of the segments, and specification of their underlying rules of combination. Semioticians typically determined for their various systems the smallest constituent units and the formal rules of relationship of these units. The classic model was Trubetzkoy's phonology with its limited number of phonemes patterned into binary oppositions amenable to ternary mediations. To study myth, Lévi-Strauss similarily constituted and examined "mythemes" (or miniscule narrative units) in their relations of opposition and mediation. When he came to examine primitive codes of cooking, he investigated systematic patterns of "gustemes." To organize their data, semioticians characteristically had recourse to mathematical formulations, indicating an essential linkage to and respect for classical science.

It was the connection to traditional science, among other ties, that generated within semiotic circles skepticism and criticism, leading in France, for example, to a schism that ended in "deconstruction," "sem-analysis," "critical semiology," "schizoanalysis," and other antithetical projects. The publication of Barthes' *S/Z* (1970) came to symbolize this crisis in the discipline. So too did the publications commencing in the late sixties by Jacques Derrida, Michel Foucault, Julia Kristeva, and others associated with the journal *Tel Quel*. Thus, the dream of a truly contemporary Space Age science that would generate new knowledge in a coherent fashion was soon called into question, as we shall see in the next chapter. Despite such skepticism about and attacks on the structuralist-semiotic enterprise, it produced much important work during its heyday and it promises to continue to do so.

LINGUISTICS AND SEMIOTICS
OF POETIC DISCOURSE

During the three decades following the start of the Space Age, the majority of literary structuralists and semioticians worldwide focused on narrative prose literature. Although poetry received comparatively little attention, some interesting and important works were published concerning poetic discourse. In the 1960s the most significant "structuralist" works on poetry employed the rigorous linguistic methods of stylistics, as was evidenced by Samuel Levin's *Linguistic Structures in Poetry* (1962), Michael Riffaterre's *Essais de stylistique structurale* (1971; a collection of articles from the sixties), and Roman Jakobson's many essays from this decade. In the 1970s the new science of semiotics was effectively applied to poetic discourse by, for example, Paul Zumthor in *Essai de poétique médiévale* (1972), Yuri Lotman in *Analysis of the Poetic Text* (1972; trans. 1976), and Michael Riffaterre in *Semiotics of Poetry* (1978). The two critics of poetry contributing most influentially to the development of literary structuralism and semiotics in America were Roman Jakobson and Michael Riffaterre, both of whom worked in the United States for more than three decades.

Significantly, Jakobson served between 1915 and 1920 as chairman of the Moscow Linguistic Circle and between 1927 and 1938 as vice-president of the Prague Linguistic Circle. He taught in the forties at Columbia University, in the fifties and sixties simultaneously at Harvard University and at the Massachusetts Institute of Technology, and in the seventies at numerous American institutions, including Brown, Brandeis, Yale, and New York Universities. Not only did Jakobson have intimate familiarity with Russian formalism and Prague structuralism, but with the structural anthropology of Claude Lévi-Strauss, with whom he worked during the early forties in America. In fact, it was Jakobson who first introduced the young Lévi-Strauss to structural linguistics. More than perhaps any single person, Roman Jakobson embodied the history of structuralism in the twentieth century.

Among Jakobson's contributions to the study of poetry were his exemplary analyses of poetic texts and his general theories about poetic function. Published in Thomas Sebeok's *Style in Language* (1960; proceedings from a conference), his manifesto "Linguistics and Poetics" (1958) set the terms for much future debate and development in structuralist-semiotic research. Coauthored with Lévi-Strauss, his essay, "Charles Baudelaire's 'Les Chats'" (1962), quickly became an influential demonstration piece in the struggle to establish a viable structuralist approach to poetry.

In "Linguistics and Poetics," Jakobson argued there were six factors involved in verbal communication and six corresponding linguistic functions (see figures 1 and 2).

	Context	
	Message	
Addresser	——————————————	Addressee
(Encoder)	Contact	(Decoder)
	Code	

FIGURE 1. Six Factors of Verbal Communication

Referential
Poetic

Emotive ————————————————————————————— Conative

Phatic
Metalingual

FIGURE 2. Six Functions of Verbal Communication

While Jakobson isolated six separate functions of communication, he insisted that verbal messages rarely ever fulfilled only one function. Instead of monopoly, there was diversity of function. What determined the verbal structure of a message, therefore, was the predominance of one function in a hierarchy of others. For poetic analysis the main effect of Jakobson's model was to break down the conventional conception of "poetry" as metrical language set in standard generic forms. The poetic function manifested itself not only in poetry but also in political jingles, commercial advertisements, and many other forms of discourse. Whether predominant or not, the poetic function appeared widely and frequently in verbal messages. As a result, the scientific study of "poetry" could not be limited by linguists and poeticians to traditional genres.

When he did study conventional poetic genres, Jakobson characterized them by differentiating hierarchical patterns of verbal functions. For example, epic poetry, typically oriented toward third-person discourse, involved the referential function as well as the poetic function. Lyric, linked with the first person, activated the emotive or expressive function along with the poetic. The poetic function per se was distinguished by three features: (1) an intense focus on the verbal message for its own sake; (2) a marked tendency to obscure the referential function; and (3) a potent drive toward parallelism on all linguistic levels (phonological, morphological, syntactical, and lexical). "This function, by promoting the palpability of signs, deepens the fundamental dichotomy of signs and objects."[4] Because the poetic function manifested itself in paintings, movies, ballets, and musical pieces as well as in verbal messages including literary works, it could profitably be studied within the context of general semiotics rather than simply linguistics or poetics. "Any attempt to reduce the sphere of poetic function to poetry or to confine poetry to poetic function would be a delusive oversimplification" (93). Although Jakobson envisaged a place for poetry within semiotics, he personally continued to study it within the framework of linguistics.

Perhaps the most influential of Jakobson's many linguistic analyses of poetry was his article, coauthored with Lévi-Strauss, examining Baudelaire's sonnet, "Les Chats." The piece came to symbolize "microstructuralism"—a scrupulous kind of close analysis attentive to mathematical patterns of contrast, correspondence, connection, and parallelism in the realms of grammar, syntax, semantics, rhetoric, thematics, tone, stanzaic structure, and especially phonic texture. In regard to phonic texture, Jakobsonian structural inquiry focused almost obsessively on the intricate modulations and chimings of vowels, consonants, rhymes, and metrical units, which had the effect of hypostatizing the poetic function of the individual text in a manner reminiscent of Slavic formalism. When coordinated, the numerous elements of a work like "Les Chats" endowed the poem "with the value of an absolute object."[5] As Lévi-Strauss put it, "each poetic work, considered in isolation, contains in itself its variants which can be represented on a vertical axis, since it is formed of superimposed levels . . ." (124). Indeed, the synchronic study carried out by Jakobson and Lévi-Strauss disregarded biography, literary and cultural history, and reader response, leaving the work separated from the context of production and reception.

The microanalysis of the poem characteristic of Jakobson's linguistic structuralism provoked criticism from various American sympathizers, including especially Michael Riffaterre. In a celebrated essay "Describing Poetic Structures: Two Approaches to Baudelaire's 'Les Chats'" (1966), first published in the special issue on "Structuralism" of *Yale French Studies,* Riffaterre initiated the American structuralist critique of Jakobson. He complained that many of the linguistic features examined by Jakobson and Lévi-Strauss were not literarily active and that structural linguistics without the support of literary stylistics could not differentiate pertinent from impertinent aesthetic elements. The trouble with Jakobsonian analysis was its evenhanded, indiscriminate processing of all aspects of a text and particularly its pursuit of irrelevant parallelisms to the point of blindness. While Riffaterre shared with other structuralists a distaste for biographical criticism, he insisted on the necessity for a criticism based on reader response. (Other American structuralists followed him in this regard, as we shall see in the fourth section of this chapter.) It was the refined reader, attentive to aesthetic value and literary significance, who kept descriptive criticism from theoretical sterility. "No segmentation can be pertinent that yields, indifferently, units which *are* part of the poetic structure, and neutral ones that are not."[6] To escape the misguided hands of the technicians, criticism had to depend on the informed reactions of sensitive readers. "The pertinent segmentation of the poem must therefore be based on these responses . . ." (203). What Riffaterre did was to activate the role of the *addressee* in the communicative process. In addition, he expanded the potential usefulness and pertinence of the *context* of communication by situating the work of the poet within the framework of the history of language and literature. References to nineteenth-century French lexicons and literary works permeated Riffaterre's reading of Baudelaire's sonnet. This restoration of the historical dimension of literature for a project of structuralist criticism was the main point of Claudio Guillén's essays of the same period. Critical of the isolation of the poem typical of Jakobsonian analysis, Riffaterre advocated a significant role for reader responses and historical contexts in structuralist criticism.

When he turned from stylistics to semiotics in the early 1970s, Riffaterre resolutely refused to renounce the practice of close analysis of autonomous texts derived from the formalist tradition. In *Semiotics of Poetry*, in *Text Production* (1979; trans. 1983), and in numerous essays of the seventies, he retained his commitment to literary history, to receptionist criticism, and to close reading of individual texts. What changed was a new dedication to a larger project of macrostructuralism: he sought to create a theoretical model of poetry applicable to Western literature in general. To account for difficult surface features or "ungrammaticalities" typically encountered when reading poetic discourses, Riffaterre propounded a theory of the deep structure or grammar of poetry. Through a series of more or less complex transformations, a poem derived from a simple word or sentence (a matrix). As it underwent expansions and/or conversions into the mimetic language of reference (the reigning sociolect), the deep-seated semiotic matrix (encoded in a literary idiolect) became distorted and produced obscurities. To read a poem referentially was to progress horizontally and superficially in an operation of harvesting content and meaning. To read a poem retroactively or "hermeneutically" was to move vertically up and down a system of equivalences to harness form and significance. What was ungrammatical on the mimetic level was grammatical on the semiotic level. For the reader the moment of maximum difficulty invariably signaled the crucial manifestation of the matrix. That the matrix was characteristically linked with or filtered through earlier texts (so called "hypograms") meant that reading depended on literary as well as linguistic competence. Riffaterre's reader was a careful student of literary history. In Riffaterre's generative-transformational semiotic model of poetry, the matrix was subject to transformations—to complicated hypogrammatizations, expansions, and conversions—which accounted for the production of the text and determined its proper reception.

What bothered some American structuralists and semioticians about both Jakobson and Riffaterre was their tendency to monumentalize poetry, cutting it off from society by drastically minimizing or dissolving the referential-mimetic function of language. Because Riffaterre went further than Jakobson in canceling mimesis and referentiality, he incurred more criticism. Culler, Scholes, and Guillén all complained about such formalist tendencies in the semiotics of poetry.[7] The structural linguistics of Jakobson and the semiotics of Riffaterre shared with formalism abiding interests in textual unity and spatial form, in literary over ordinary language, and in close reading of autonomous texts. To this combination, however, Riffaterre added concerns for the participation of the reader, the role of the historical intertext, and the underlying system of Western poetry—all of which ameliorated strict formalist commitments. Revealingly, Jakobson and Riffaterre differed from Soviet semioticians working during the sixties and seventies in their unwillingness to situate poetry within a typology of culture where modeling systems from all the arts were coordinated with a view to studying mutual influences, shared hierarchies, and similar sign systems. These two European-born American structuralists tended to isolate the poetic text reminiscent of New Critical forebears.

NARRATOLOGY: FROM SYNTAX TO RHETORIC TO DISCOURSE

From its inception in Europe during the sixties the discipline of narratology had for its corpus all existing and possible narratives, ranging from myths, legends, and fables to epics, novels, and short stories, from dialogues, news accounts, and movies to tragedies, comedies, and histories, and from certain relief sculptures, stained-glass windows, paintings to dances, pantomimes, and case studies. Narratology was self-consciously not limited to the history of the novel, the discovery of the meanings of narratives, or the assessment of the aesthetic values of canonized stories. The task of narratology was essentially the analysis of the features and functions of all narrative. In the modern Anglo-American tradition, important nonstructuralist, literary contributions to the understanding of narrative came from Percy Lubbock, Joseph Frank, Mark Schorer, Frank Kermode, Northrop Frye, Wayne Booth, William Labov, and numerous others. A significant line of Slavic theorists of narrative ran from Victor Shklovsky, Vladimir Propp, and Mikhail Bakhtin to Boris Uspensky, Yuri Lotman, and the Czech emigré Lubomír Doležel. Others could be named. The French tradition, just since the mid-sixties, included most prominently the structuralists Roland Barthes, Gérard Genette, Algirdas Greimas, Tzvetan Todorov, Julia Kristeva, and Claude Bremond. Some Dutch, German, Italian, and Israeli intellectuals contributed significant work to the new field of structuralist narratology. What characterized the study of narrative over the course of several generations were multifaceted methodologies and broad disciplinary boundaries. Important work in this area was done by literary Marxists, formalists, Myth Critics, structuralists, and semioticians as well as by folklorists, anthropologists, biblical scholars, historians, and psychoanalysts. Among American literary structuralists and semioticians in the seventies, the most innovative narratologist was arguably Gerald Prince. In addition, important projects in structuralist narratology were carried out by the historiographer Hayden White and the former stylistician Seymour Chatman.

Revising and systematizing his essays of the seventies and his *A Grammar of Stories* (1973), Gerald Prince in *Narratology: The Form and Functioning of Narrative* (1982) offered a lucid general introduction to the science of narratology, indebted to much previous research in the field. Unlike the literary studies of narrative carried out by Culler, Guillén, and Scholes, for example, Prince's project displayed a universalist ambition grounded in algebraic methods, which stemmed from Chomsky's *Syntactic Structures* (1957) and which sought to formalize and map in a macrostructuralist manner the finite set of grammatical rules of narrative. Like many contemporary students of narrative, Prince took account of semantics, reader responses, and conventional fictional functions (point of view, setting, character, etc.), but, unlike other American narrative theorists, he developed a generative-transformational grammar to account for the structural, logical, and narratorial elements and mechanisms of narrative.

Given a finite number of constituent features, according to Prince's model, an infinite number of narratives could be generated. Some of the possible narratives would inevitably be forms not yet realized by storytellers. Just as the grammar of a language allowed speakers to create fresh sentences, so the grammar of narrative empowered the raconteur to compose new stories. For Prince the fundamental or minimal unit of analysis was the event. To be a narrative, a text had to represent at least two events in a time sequence where neither event presupposed or entailed the other. Each bit of narrative was permitted one modification. Starting from such kernel narratives, Prince built up a set of ordered rewrite rules, depicting events conjoined by conjunctive elements or conjoined by strings of episodes. To deal with expanded narratives, where series of kernel narratives joined, alternated, or interrupted one another, Prince formulated a group of transformational rules. With his limited set of rewrite and transformational rules, he was able to account for all narrative structures. Additionally, to accommodate the formalization of content, narration, and translation (into natural languages), he sketched directions for future grammatical formulations. "As it stands, the grammar is clearly in need of much elaboration and its ultimate construction is not for the immediate future."[8] Despite limitations, Prince's grammar handled the rules of narrative *structure* quite well, which his twelve-page algebraic description of "Little Red Riding Hood" demonstrated by means of several dozen rules worked out in *A Grammar of Stories*.

Typical of a scientific structuralist, Prince believed that a finite set of rules could account for an infinite set of real and possible phenomena and that the most effective model for his purpose was the syntax of language (*langue*). His interest was not in the surface structure of individual texts but the deep structure of all narratives. Characteristic of a semiotician, his object of inquiry was all narrative, ranging from recipes to literary texts. Finally, he programmatically excluded considerations of history, aesthetics, and hermeneutics—a methodological maneuver fostered by the Saussurean legacy and featured as a necessity of scientific structuralist inquiry.

Throughout the 1970s the structuralist historiographer Hayden White appeared often at literary conferences and in the pages of literary journals. He was a frequent faculty appointee at the School of Criticism and Theory cofounded by Murray Krieger and Hazard Adams in the mid-seventies. Indebted heavily to Northrop Frye's theory of literary modes and Kenneth Burke's theory of rhetorical figures, his model of historical narrative reduced complex phenomena to a relatively few "rules." Along with Culler and Scholes, White became a favorite representative of structuralism on the nationwide academic lecture circuit. His *Metahistory* (1973) and *Tropics of Discourse* (1978) were widely read by literary theorists.

Focusing on the major historians and philosophers of history in nineteenth-century Western Europe (including Hegel, Michelet, Ranke, Tocqueville, Burckhardt, Marx, Nietzsche, and Croce), White in *Metahistory* observed that history, as narrative discourse, favored particular modes of emplotment: an historical text was predominantly either a romance, a tragedy, a comedy, or a satire. Other genres were subsumed under these dominant ones. Furthermore, each such controlling form exhibited an affinity for a particular mode of ideology. Correlated with the types of plot were, respectively, anarchist, radical, conservative, and liberal points of view. Variations, within limits, occurred. Homologous with the kinds of plot and ideology were specific forms of argument. Such broad explanations, hypotheses, or laws of history displayed certain preferred modes of deduction, including so-called formist, mechanistic, organicist, and contextualist methods. Taken together, the structural sets of emplotment, ideology, and argument generated the manifest aesthetic, ethical, and epistemological dimensions of historical works.

Ultimately, White grounded his model of historical narrative in a theory of language—a move typical of most structuralists. Before a historian could represent, value, or explain the data of an historical field, she had to prefigure or constitute the field as an object of thought. This generative act was linguistic in nature. "This preconceptual protocol will in turn be—by virtue of its essentially *prefigurative* nature—characterizable in terms of the dominant tropological mode in which it is cast."[9] Preceding her analysis of the field, the historian created her object and thereby predetermined her manner of presentation. The four tropological modes or master tropes, correlated with the modalities of emplotment, argument, and ideology, were metaphor, metonymy, synecdoche, and irony. As human thought made contact with the world of experience, relationships within and among phenomena occurred. The tropes described these relationships or, to put it more accurately, "thought remains the captive of the linguistic modes in which it seeks to grasp the outline of objects inhabiting its field of perception" (p. xi). Thus tropes undergirded and informed all preconceptual materials in the historical field: they constituted the latent level or deep structure of every historical text. As an historian prefigured an historical field linguistically, she committed herself implicitly to particular modes of emplotment, ideology, and explanation. Within this structural set, as defined by White, few permutations seemed possible.

With the establishment of a rhetorical base for historiography, White's literary model of historical narrative gained added significance. The aesthetic, moral, and cognitive levels of narrative emerged as projections of various founding tropes. Narration became the formalization of life's phenomena and experiences in line with preconscious linguistic determinations. Writing history entailed the working out of possible plots, ethical implications, and arguments contained in tropological formations.

White's fourfold structural model specified how historical narratives were produced and how they were linguistic and literary (tropological and generic). Tropological modes determined the paths of thinking and the generic patterns of narration. Authors were not free to alter such linguistic controls or deep structures. As in Prince's generative grammar of narrative,

White's model demonstrated how relatively few rules accounted for the production of numerous different narratives. Where White differed from Prince was in his overt concern with history, aesthetics (especially genre theory), politics, and hermeneutics. Indeed, White's range of concerns distinguished his project from that of all American literary structuralists, whether it was Jakobson or Riffaterre, Guillén or Scholes, Culler or Chatman. His commitment to a certain Marxist line of thinking explained his interests in history, politics, and hermeneutics, aligning him more nearly with French structuralists, many of whom were Marxists. Regarded as the production of an historical author, a narrative for White inescapably embodied a politics and a hermeneutics of social existence.

Seymour Chatman's *Story and Discourse: Narrative Structure in Fiction and Film* (1978), the most popular book of American structuralist narratology, attempted a lucid and judicious synthesis of Anglo-American and European theories of narrative. Booth was as much admired as Barthes; Lubbock received praise equal to Bakhtin. What distinguished Chatman's work was less its concern with the deep structure or grammar—the *story*—of narrative than its innovative attention to the formal articulation or transmission—the *discourse*—of story. Chatman had little use for the algebraic or rhetorical reductions characteristic of Prince and White. Where he was most original was in his revision and enrichment of point of view theory. Inspired by speech-act philosophy, Chatman scrapped as inadequate traditional categories: first-person narrator, third-person narrator, omniscient narrator, and so forth. "It is less important to categorize types of narrators than to identify the features that mark their degrees of audibility. A quantitative effect applies: the more identifying features, the stronger our sense of a narrator's presence."[10] Chatman constructed a spectrum of narrator-prominence, ranging from minimal to covert to overt narrators with about a dozen and a half different identifiable degrees of narrator audibility. Rather than renounce the conventional concept of narrator, he added substance and sophistication to it. Here, as elsewhere, an antireductionist tendency characterized Chatman's work.

Where European narratologists like Propp and Greimas offered economical typologies of character and conceptualized character as a function of plot, Chatman argued for characters as autonomous beings independently memorable and, in cases of certain great literary characters, inexhaustibly ponderable. In narrative, character was the ultimate residence of personality manifested in a name (a noun) endowed with abiding traits (adjectives).

Whereas narrative events occurred horizontally or syntagmatically along the temporal chain of the story, traits of character accumulated paradigmatically over the time spans generated by events. "The paradigmatic view of character sees the set of traits, metaphorically, as a vertical assemblage intersecting the syntagmatic chain of events that comprise the plot" (127). Drawing inspiration from the turn-of-the-century character analyses pioneered by the Shakespearean critic A. C. Bradley, Chatman called for an "open theory of character" more in line with humanistic scholarship than structuralist narratology.

Because he refined theories of narrators and characters and because he renounced reductionism of all sorts, Chatman, in fact, resisted the "death of the subject" concomitant with structuralism. Still, like most literary structuralists, he showed little interest in aesthetics, in hermeneutics, and in history, preferring to map the intricacies of discursive systems in a rationalist manner typical of the Saussurean legacy.

In a retrospective assessment of the progress and problems of narratology published in 1984, Jonathan Culler pointed out four contributions worthy of special note. He praised work done on the differences between deep structure and surface phenomena (story and discourse); he celebrated various sophisticated contributions to the theory of narration and point of view; he assigned high value to the study of narrative as a fundamental system of understanding and intelligibility (in the manner of Hayden White); and he proclaimed the importance of reflection on narrative audiences and reader response.[11] In structuralist circles, serious interest in reception was not limited to narratologists. The stylistic studies of poetry undertaken by Michael Riffaterre initiated in the sixties the interest in the reader later characteristic of American structuralist criticism. Ultimately, narratology at its best illustrated the power of structuralist methods to offer economical, simple, coherent, and testable formulations to account for the numerous and complicated features of narrative.

THE CONVENTIONS AND CODES OF READING

When they were published in 1980, the two leading anthologies of reader-oriented criticism, Jane Tompkins' *Reader-Response Criticism* and Susan Suleiman's and Inge Crosman's *The Reader in the Text*, contained essays by three American literary structuralists—Culler, Prince, and Riffaterre. Others could have been added. Often American Structuralist Critics made detailed observations about and contributions to theories of the reader and of reading. In his *A Glossary of Literary Terms* (1981), M. H. Abrams noted: "The focus of structuralist criticism is on the activity of reading which, by bringing into play the requisite conventions and codes, makes literary sense—that is, endows with form and significance the sequence of words, phrases, and sentences which constitute a piece of literary writing."[12] To give a straightforward example, Chatman formulated a working distinction between "reading" the surface level of a narrative and "reading out" its deep structures, which entailed laborious interlevel deciphering of conventions and codes. In general, the structuralist project could not have proceeded without amplifications and renovations of the ordinary understanding of reading, as we shall see in the works of Riffaterre, Prince, Culler, and Scholes.

In his essay, "Describing Poetic Structures," Riffaterre insisted that the segmentation and analysis of poetry depended on readers' perceptions of pertinent features of the text, which frequently were unpredictable obscurities unclear in content. To account for such relevant and crucial textual aspects, he posited the presence of a "superreader"—an imaginary composite reader who respected the unfolding temporality of the work and responded with hypersensitivity especially to its telling ungrammaticalities. This theoretical construct enabled Riffaterre to carry out formalistic microanalysis focused on significant moments of perceptible pecularity. In Riffaterre's view, the text determined response and response invariably required linguistic and literary knowledge. The superreader possessed an encyclopedic store of information as well as aesthetic hypersensitivity.

When the French translation of "Describing Poetic Structures" was published five years later in his *Essais de stylistique structurale,* Riffaterre added a new paragraph outlining three interlocking phases of reading. In the first phase, the reader faithfully followed the unfolding event of the text. In the second, he examined certain contradictory passages retroactively as a way to resolve dilemmas. In the third, he performed a global and memorial rereading. All three moments were essential to the dynamics of reading. When he turned from stylistics to semiotics, Riffaterre collapsed these three phases into two. First, "heuristic reading" attended to the linear, mimetic aspects of a work, confronting surface linguistic ungrammaticalities. Second, "hermeneutic reading" entailed a retroactive focus on the vertical, semiotic features of a text, particularly its deep structural hypograms and matrix. A set of oppositions characterized the two levels of reading: ideally, the process of reading progressed from *parole* to *langue,* sociolect to idiolect, meaning to significance, content to form, mimesis to semiosis, ungrammaticalities to grammaticalities, syntagm to paradigm, transformation to matrix, surface to depth. Such shifting of levels was labeled by Chatman "reading out." In Riffaterre's account, this process was highly stimulating, though disturbingly circular and unstable: "the reader is reconverted to proper reading when the structural equivalences become apparent all at once in a blaze of revelation. This revelation is always chancy, must always begin anew. . . ."[13] Semiotic "double reading" forced the reader into a productive and continuous shuttling between textual levels—a process construed by Riffaterre as a hallmark of literariness.

In his essay, "Introduction à l'étude du narrataire" (1973; trans. 1980), Prince added to the growing typology of readers by distinguishing the "narratee" from the real reader, the virtual reader, and the ideal reader. Like Riffaterre's superreader, the ideal reader understood the text fully. The virtual reader was the one the author believed himself to be addressing, whereas the real reader was the one actually reading the work. The narratee was the one or the ones to whom the text was directed as, for example, the Caliph in the *Thousand and One Nights* or the four companions of Marlow in *Heart of Darkness*. "All narration, whether it is oral or written, whether it recounts real or mythical events, whether it tells a story or relates a simple sequence of actions in time, presupposes not only (at least) one narrator but also (at least) one narratee, the narratee being someone whom the narrator addresses."[14] The narratee occupied a position like a character in a novel; he was immanent to the text. In Prince's model of reading, the line of communication flowed from the author to the narrator to the narratee to the virtual reader to the real reader to the ideal reader. To be able to characterize the narratee, Prince posited a hypothetical "zero-degree narratee" against whom he could measure the actual narratee. Unlike most overt or covert real narratees, the zero-degree narratee existed in a psychological, social, and ethical vacuum, possessing mainly minimal linguistic competence, a literal mind, and a good memory. With this fixed point of reference, Prince was able to sketch portraits of various textual narratees in a highly formalistic operation faithful to individual works. Among the functions served by narratees were establishing narrative frameworks, revealing the personalities of narrators, contributing to plot developments, relaying messages from narrators to·readers, and pointing to the morals of stories. According to Prince, to read a narrative adequately depended on taking into account the functions served by narratees.

Concerning the extratextual "real reader," Prince had something to say in *Narratology*. He distinguished between minimal and maximal reading. To understand and to paraphrase linguistic or denotational meaning was to read minimally. To grasp all the relevant and meaningful aspects of a text was to read maximally. Prince also distinguished between propounding a reading of a text and producing a response. In a reading, the critic selected, developed, and reordered materials gathered while reading. In a response, the reader allowed free associations and personal fantasies to condition his reception. Prince denigrated response on the grounds that it introduced irrelevancies and that it lost contact with the text by avoiding textual constraints. Just as Riffaterre insisted that "the literary text is first of all a grid of constraints upon and directions for a very special type of reading behavior,"[15] so Prince declared that "the text I read acts as a constraint on my reading" (112). Prince wanted a real reader to go beyond minimal reading in order to create a reading attentive to the constraints of the text in the process of extracting a maximum of meaning. For Prince, as for Riffaterre, meaning resided in the text and was extracted by the reader.

It was essential to Prince's real reader, as it was to Riffaterre's superreader and hermeneutic reader, to be familiar with linguistic and literary conventions and codes. According to Prince, "reading a narrative, understanding it, implies organizing it and interpreting it in terms of several codes" (125). Among requisite codes and conventions, he included knowledge of language, mastery of elementary logic, familiarity with interpretive conventions, and appreciation of traditional symbols, genres, and characters. Such information constituted a set of norms, limitations, and rules that rendered texts decipherable and understandable. Given textual constraints, linguistic conventions, and literary codes, reading emerged in Prince's account as an impersonal and restricted activity.

Generally speaking, the structuralist theorists of reading, especially Riffaterre, Prince, and Culler, differed from other reader-response theorists, like Bleich, early Fish, and Holland, in their depictions of reading as a highly determined operation of decoding directed by textual and cultural constraints rather than by psychological and emotional proclivities. When Fish in the mid-seventies introduced the concept of interpretive communities into his theory of reading, he adopted a structuralist perspective, that is, he acknowledged the limitations on reading enforced by conventions and codes. What the structuralist concept of convention (or code) introduced was the sense of an underlying social and historical system (or deep structure) of rules determining literature and its interpretation, as Claudio Guillén following Harry Levin memorably demonstrated (*Literature as System*, 59–68). No one did more to promote the study of conventions and codes in American literary circles than Jonathan Culler.

In *Structuralist Poetics* and elsewhere, Culler argued that readers of literature acquired mastery of codes and conventions, which allowed them to process sets of sentences as literary works endowed with shape and meaning. The task of structuralist criticism, therefore, was "to render as explicit as possible the conventions responsible for the production of attested effects" (31). Among interpretive conventions and codes shared by authors and readers, Culler singled out, for example, the following six. The "rule of significance" dictated that a literary work expressed a significant attitude about man and/or his world. The "convention of metaphorical coherence" affirmed that metaphorical tenors and vehicles were always coherent. The "code of poetic tradition" provided a stock of symbols and types with agreed upon meanings. The "convention of genre" offered stable sets of norms against which to measure texts. The "rule of totality" required works to be coherent on as many levels as possible. And the "convention of thematic unity" indicated that semantic and figurative oppositions fit into symmetrical binary patterns. In Culler's view, the whole system of such rules, codes, and conventions constituted literary competence and comprised the institution of literature.

Although reading conventions were often unconscious and sometimes changeable, they were social rather than subjective phenomena and thus capable of being analyzed the way grammar was examined in linguistics. What Culler advocated for literary studies, therefore, was a shift from scrutinizing separate works to investigating interpretive conventions. This turn from personal performance to social competence, from individual critics at work to the institution of literature, from surface phenomena to deep structure, recapitulated Saussure's move from *parole* to *langue*. Not surprisingly, Culler criticized the American preoccupation since the days of New Criticism with the close reading of individual texts. He discounted hermeneutics and championed semiotics for "granting precedence to the task of formulating a theory of literary competence and relegating critical interpretation to a secondary role" (128). Culler particularly deplored the tendency of contemporary critical interpretation toward premature foreclosure in the interests of unity and meaning, as was most clear in his *Flaubert: The Uses of Uncertainty* (1974)—a book that celebrated Flaubert's various strategies of undermining conventional modes of understanding. What the book on Flaubert illustrated was the crucial role not only of conventions but of convention-breaking for the institution of literary studies.

Throughout the seventies and early eighties, Culler incorporated more and more of deconstruction into his project of semiotics. While this effort was a minor affair in *Structuralist Poetics,* it became a major endeavor by the time of *The Pursuit of Signs* (1981) and *On Deconstruction* (1982). In the latter text, Culler almost seemed to have given up semiotics in favor of deconstruction while in the former he unequivocally aimed to appropriate deconstruction for semiotics. Such a change in his theoretical commitments altered his conception of the reading activity. In *On Deconstruction,* for example, he presented reading as itself a type of narration. Readings of texts were cast as stories of reading texts. By nature such stories were dualistic; they depended on "an interpreter and something to interpret, a subject and an object, an actor and something he acts upon or that acts on him."[16] To account for the linkages in the reading process, literary theorists had to construct various monisms in which the borders between texts and readers or between textual contents and interpretative inferences were, in Culler's view, ultimately undecidable. This paradoxical logic, typical of deconstruction, seemed to undermine Culler's earlier structuralist goal of mapping the system of conventions underlying the institution of literature. However, Culler portrayed structuralism and deconstruction as complementary projects: the one categorized the grammar of texts and the other charted textual ungrammaticalities. Each dealt with systems and their breakdowns but from different vantage points. In a way, *On Deconstruction* sought to systematize the new conventions and codes brought into being by various deconstructionist protocols of reading.

What the structuralist theories of reading and readers worked out by Riffaterre, Prince, and Culler had in common was a foundation in deep structures linked to society. Communal conventions or codes took the place typically occupied in other theories by the individual reader. Systems replaced subjectivity. Reading emerged as a rule-governed process subject to textual and interpretive constraints. The various readers posited by structuralists had this in common: they were impersonal, collective, theoretical constructs, not empirical or real readers. For structuralists, the main interest in the reader concerned, in Culler's words, "not what actual readers happen to do but what an ideal reader must know implicitly in order to read and interpret works" (*SP,* 123–24). The empathetic reading cherished by certain Phenomenological, Hermeneutical, Psychoanalytical, and Feminist Critics epitomized the approach most at odds with structuralist and semiotic criticism. To produce a maximal reading, the ideal reader had to decode the text in a manner consonant with superior competence in all matters of linguistic and literary convention. More or less ignored or downplayed in this process were the full resources of biographical, historical, and judicial modes of criticism.

Unlike other leading American literary semioticians, Robert Scholes became increasingly preoccupied with both classroom pedagogy and "ideological analysis," as attested especially in his *Textual Power: Literary Theory and the Teaching of English* (1985), the third in a sequence of books dealing with structuralism and semiotics. These twin interests emerged out of a concern with the conventions and codes of culture and its various institutions. In constructing a three-phase semiotic model of "reading," Scholes was heavily influenced by the "structuralism" of Michel Foucault, whose political and sociological works influenced significantly the cultural studies movement with which Scholes had increasingly more in common during the eighties.

The encounter with a text involved three interlocking and ascending stages labeled by Scholes as "reading," "interpretation," and "criticism." Reading entailed the submissive decipherment of a work dependent on largely unconscious knowledge of generic and cultural codes. Interpretation took place when difficulties occurred in reading, precipitating a conscious thematizing of oppositions and implications linked with shared cultural codes. Criticism entailed an antagonistic critique of the themes and/or codes in the name of certain specified group or class values. In Scholes' view, the encounter with a text ultimately required not passive consumption but active production, not reverential exegesis or close reading but judicious and skeptical questioning. Consequently, critics and teachers "must open the way between the literary or verbal text and the social text in which we live."[17] In his own readings and demonstrations, Scholes continually linked the literary text with the social text and engaged in ideological analysis indebted to psychoanalysis and feminism as well as structuralism and semiotics. He was committed to analysis and teaching of both interpretive codes and conventions and cultural codes and their values, rendering him the least formalistic of leading American literary semioticians. Scholes was not content with formulations like Prince's minimal/maximal reading or Riffaterre's heuristic/hermeneutic reading. He sought to add to such textual criticisms a judicial worldly criticism so as to empower the institution of criticism and render students as well as critics effective citizens. What Scholes did was to restore the referential and mimetic functions of discourse and dissolve the formalistic constraints erected by early structuralism. To Chatman's process of "reading out" texts, he added "reading against" texts, emerging in the eighties as one of a growing number of important and influential "resisting readers."

THE DISCIPLINE OF SEMIOTICS

All of the leading literary structuralists and semioticians in America operated primarily as theoretical rather than practical critics. Their main focus was on general literary issues, not individual texts. Riffaterre and Jakobson took Western poetry as their object; Prince and Chatman conceived all narrative as their proper domain; and Scholes, Guillén, and Culler cast the system and institution of literature as their primary topic. While these critics did examine individual works, such investigations were invariably undertaken in the interest of illustrating a broad point. Taken as purely practical critics, structuralists and semioticians favored formalistic scrutiny of texts and analysis of codes of textual reception, more or less ignoring biographical, judicial, and historical approaches. The concern with poeticity displayed by Jakobson and Riffaterre, for instance, had little to do with rendering aesthetic judgments on individual works and all to do with defining poetic or semiotic function in general. Similarly, the attention paid to history by Guillén and Culler, for example, was limited to literary history—the history of literary genres, conventions, and codes—not economic, social, or political history. The theory of literature propounded by critics working in the structuralist-semiotic tradition minimized its expressive, mimetic, affective, and sociological dimensions. Emphasis rarely fell on how or why poets produced texts, or how much or little poetry reflected reality, or how deeply it moved or stirred particular readers, or how fully it embodied elements of its sociohistorical contexts. By definition, the referential function of literature was at most a secondary matter, though Scholes in later years tried to restore it to prominence—which was one consequence of his turn to cultural studies. With regard to the affective aspects of literary discourse, structuralists and semioticians cared more about reading than about readers, more about general codes and conventions delimiting response than about personal reactions and associations. The institution, not the individual, was the site of inquiry. Depending on the critic, the text dissolved more or less completely into deep structure, generic grammar, matrix, founding trope, or literary convention. Thus, literary semiotics displayed a framework of distinctive features distinguishing it sharply from the approaches of competing contemporaneous critical schools and movements.

Much of the work produced by American Semiotic Critics was for the purpose of demonstrating the values, virtues, and powerful techniques available in the structuralist tradition. Because these critics were so often engaged in promoting structuralism and semiotics, they presented themselves as reformers, usually of a liberal sort. Culler and Scholes, in particular, quickly emerged as leading spokesmen since they regularly addressed issues of pedagogy, commenting on undergraduate teaching, graduate programs, the protocols of criticism, and the nature of literature departments—all within a context of a pressing need for change.

As a discipline, semiotics was not limited to literary studies. The pioneer programs at Brown, Vanderbilt, and Indiana Universities made this plain. Nowhere was the broad scope of semiotics made more evident than in the annual program of studies offered by the International Summer Institute for Semiotic and Structural Studies (*ISISSS*)—a four-week intensive institute starting in 1980 and offering numerous courses and seminars, colloquia and symposia, and workshops and special lectures. Started by the Toronto Semiotic Circle and the Structuralist Research Information Center of Vanderbilt University, the Institute attracted leading semioticians from around the globe to lecture and teach, and it received the endorsements of numerous national organizations of semioticians. Among major leading lecturers were Lubomír Doležel, Umberto Eco, Michel Foucault, Algirdas Greimas, M. A. K. Halliday, Benjamin Hrushovski, Daniel Patte, Michael Riffaterre, John Searle, Thomas Sebeok, and René Thom, representing such diverse fields as anthropology, history, linguistics, literary studies, mathematics, philosophy, and religious studies and also representing such varied traditions as those developed in Canada, England, France, Israel, Italy, the United States, and the Soviet Union. Many other lecturers and countries took part. Courses offered covered such areas as architectural semiotics, biological foundations of semiosis, issues in musical semiotics, nonverbal dimensions of human communication, semiotic analysis of performing arts, semiotics and archaeology, semiotics and art history, semiotics and feminism, semiotics of marketing, and symbolic process in nonhuman primates. Numerous courses in literary semiotics were presented, studying such topics as fictionality and semantics, Greimassian literary theory, Jakobsonian linguisitic analysis, methods of structural exegesis, narrative and lyric structures, polysystem theory, principles of literary semiotics, semiotics of didactic discourse, semiotics of fiction, and semiotics of poetry.

Despite its international and interdisciplinary diversity, semiotics emerged in the late sixties as an increasingly well-organized global discipline. Most adherents of the new field shared commitments to linguistic modeling and to sign theory; they were more or less steeped in ideas developed by Peirce, Saussure, Jakobson, Lévi-Strauss, Eco, and others; they published and read certain key journals, especially *Semiotica*, founded in 1969 by the International Association for Semiotic Studies; and they shared basic research methods and goals. No one represented more the formative organization of the emerging discipline than Thomas Sebeok, the Hungarian-born, American-educated impresario of the field, whose base from the forties to the eighties was Indiana University. To begin with, Sebeok, a linguist and anthropologist, served as editor for two decades of *Semiotica* and as executive director for a decade of the Semiotic Society of America, publisher of the *American Journal of Semiotics*. He edited several key book series, including "Current Trends in Linguistics" (started in 1963), "Approaches to Semiotics" (1969), "Studies in Semiotics" (1974), and "Advances in Semiotics" (1974). The latter series alone published important texts in English by Eco, Greimas, and Riffaterre; it also offered a history of semiotics by John Deely, an introductory anthology by Robert Innis, and introductions to various separate specialties like anthropological, architectural, cultural, gestural, and literary semiotics. Indiana University's Center for Language and Semiotic Studies, established in 1959 and chaired by Sebeok, hosted the *ISISSS* several times. Because Sebeok had little personally to do with literary semiotics—his own interests were in general semiotics and in zoosemiotics—he played no appreciable role in the development of structuralism and semiotics among members of the American literati, who were most indebted to French structuralism of the sixties and seventies. From a global point of view, American literary structuralists and semioticians were only loosely linked with worldwide networks of general semiotics research.

There were four phases in the development of literary structuralism and semiotics in America. In the sixties, linguistic and stylistic analysis of a formalist/protostructuralist kind predominated. In the early seventies, French structuralism of the sixties dominated native thinking, as was clear in the projects of Culler, Guillén, Prince, and Scholes. In the late seventies, "semiotics" replaced "structuralism" as the designation for the school, which signaled a loosening and broadening of boundaries. This was the point at which the works of Eco, Lotman, Peirce, and other non-French theorists began to have an impact. In the early eighties, the challenge from poststructuralism made itself visible, engendering a softening of scientific claims and an increase in methodological skepticism. While Prince and

Riffaterre sought to ignore or minimize poststructuralist thinking, Culler worked to incorporate it and Scholes and White tried to extirpate it. Chatman and Guillén were largely silent on this challenge. In the middle phases, the pedagogical imperative was strong. Even though the era of structuralist classroom anthologies had ended in the mid-seventies, it was at this point that the introductory overviews by single hands started to appear. So too did essays calling for pedagogical reforms and changes along structuralist lines. Still, canons did not alter nor did new literature textbooks appear. What did emerge throughout the seventies and eighties were new American journals and newsletters, including, among others, *American Journal of Semiotics, Diacritics, Enclitic, Semeia, Semiotext(e), Semiotic Scene, Structuralist Research Information,* and *Structuralist Review.* All of these were interested in literary structuralism and several championed poststructuralism. What impact, if any, semiotics had on American literary studies in the classroom was unclear. Insofar as it paralleled the general shift to "theory" promoted by literary hermeneuticists, reader-oriented critics, deconstructors, feminists, and others, the discipline of semiotics offered a sophisticated scientific option attractive to some of the best minds of the time.

As time passed, the field of literary semiotics was defined almost as much by its complex relations with other schools and movements as by its own distinctive methods and goals. The example of phenomenology was a case in point. Because early structuralism in France was conceived self-consciously as an antagonist and replacement for existential phenomenology, the relationship of American structuralists and phenomenologists was often one of rivalry. Several important differences separated these schools. Phenomenology cherished existential temporality whereas structuralism prized synchronicity; the one championed human consciousness and freedom, while the other credited the unconscious and social determination; the one modeled itself upon meditation, the other upon scientific analysis; the one favored semantic inquiry, the other preferred grammatical (or syntactical) investigations; the one believed the world came to stand in literature, the other considered the semiotic function of literary language dominant over the mimetic function. Not surprisingly, some analysts tried to heal the divisions between phenomenology and structuralism. The main tactic here was to cast the two schools as complementary—which is the stance that Paul Ricoeur pioneered in the sixties. Among Americans attempting this task were Vernon Gras in his introduction to *European Literary Theory and Practice: From Existential Phenomenology to Structuralism* (1973), Robert Magliola in *Phenomenology and Literature* (1977), Robert Detweiler in

Story, Sign, Self: Phenomenology and Structuralism as Literary Critical Methods (1978), and Wesley Morris in *Friday's Footprint: Structuralism and the Articulated Text* (1979).[18] Such projects were usually undertaken by phenomenologists and hermeneuticists. Structuralists seemed uninterested in reconciliation with the phenomenological tradition.

The discipline of semiotics had mixed relations with other major schools, which often involved simultaneous positive and negative alignments. On the one hand, for example, key semioticians shared with Reader-Response Critics a preoccupation with the crucial role of reading in the critical act. On the other hand, such semioticians decried the emphasis of leading Reader-Response Critics upon individual readers and subjective reactions. The proper object of receptionist criticism was the underlying codes and conventions determining the response of ideal or theoretical readers. Although semiotics shared with the formalist tradition a textual criticism largely uninterested in biographical and sociohistorical analysis, it criticized the formalist preoccupation with surface features of style and with individual texts, advocating instead study of deep structures and of literary systems.

The same pattern of mixed relations occurred with psychoanalysis and with deconstruction. Where semiotics and psychoanalysis, for instance, focused on underlying infrastructures of phenomena and on conventions of representation and interpretation, they disagreed on the importance and status of desire, personal identity, and language. When in the mid-fifties the French psychoanalyst Jacques Lacan conceived the unconscious as the whole structure of language, he linked psychoanalysis and structuralism, creating a structural psychoanalysis. Even though none of the leading American structuralists and semioticians followed Lacan, a number of important critics did, including, for example, Julia Kristeva in her numerous books (she lectured regularly at Columbia University) and Marc Eli Blanchard in *Description: Sign, Self, Desire* (an American work published in 1980 as part of Sebeok's series "Approaches to Semiotics"). Thus certain semioticians linked their work with psychoanalysis while most did not. The case of structuralism and deconstruction was quite complicated, as we shall see in the next chapter. For now it is enough to note that structuralism and deconstruction concurred on the determining roles of language, of textual systems, of the sign, and of reading conventions, while disagreeing on the precise nature and function of language, systems, signs, and reading. Culler tried to effect a rapprochement of semiotics and deconstruction whereas Scholes worked to exclude deconstructive concepts from latter-day literary semiotics. Other structuralists regarded deconstruction as an evolutionary replacement of structuralism, as was the case, for instance, with Jeffrey Mehlman and Eugenio Donato.[19]

In chapter 12 we shall examine the structuralist work undertaken by Houston A. Baker, Jr., who in the post-Vietnam era was a leading critic of Afro-American literature and became a convert to poststructuralism.

The relationship of structuralism and Marxism deserves special notice. Many French structuralists of the sixties were Marxists, notably Althusser, Barthes, and Lévi-Strauss. None of the leading American literary structuralists was a Marxist. White was sympathetic to Marxist thinking, as was Scholes in later years. Structuralism and Marxism had much in common. They excavated hidden structures, which invariably had social foundations. They assigned considerable powers of determination to deep-seated infrastructures, seeking to work through superstructures to infrastructures. However, Marxism credited historical determinism and philosophical materialism whereas structuralism discounted history and belonged to philosophical idealism. The one rested on economic foundations while the other operated on linguistic bases. The relationship of structuralism and Marxism in America was initially defined by Frederic Jameson in *The Prison-House of Language: A Critical Account of Structuralism and Russian Formalism* (1972)—a book which gave French structuralism of the sixties something of a bad name in American Marxist circles. Many subsequent Marxist commentators on structuralism followed Jameson's lead. Early on, Jameson registered some serious objections to structuralism. He deplored its antihistoricist commitment to synchronic analysis, which avoided the realities of time and history. He decried its formalistic bracketing of semantics, which denuded all phenomena of content and meaning. He denounced its empiricist habit of isolating autonomous objects for analysis and its idealist tendency to divorce consciousness from socioeconomic foundations. Finally, he despaired over its arbitrary and thoroughgoing allegiance to linguistic modeling, which engendered a reductive linguistic determinism.

The relationship of semiotics and myth criticism was limited largely to the work of Frye, especially *Anatomy of Criticism,* which most literary semioticians admired. Frye had stressed the value of theoretical over practical criticism and the importance of scientific method; at the same time he rejected biographical, judicial, and New Critical exegetical approaches to criticism—all of which harmonized with the work of American semiotics. It was Frye's devotion to the systematicity of literature that elicited the warmest response. Thus, for example, Scholes in *Structuralism in Literature* praised Frye's comprehensive theory of modes, going on to revise and enrich his theory of fictional forms. Culler, in his important essay "Beyond Interpretation" (1976), celebrated Frye's commitment to a coherent and all-encompassing poetics, complaining, however, about Frye's failure to attack head-on the preoccupation of Anglo-American criticism with textual interpretation. "Though it began as a plea for a systematic poetics," observed Culler, "Frye's work has done less to promote work in poetics than to stimulate a mode of interpretation which has come to be known as 'myth-criticism' or archetypal criticism."[20] To the extent that myth criticism engaged in textual exegesis, it was a disappointment to semioticians.

Pioneered by certain French theorists, the linkage of feminism with Lacanian language-based psychoanalysis and with semiotics opened new and promising directions in the late seventies and early eighties. In *The Subject of Semiotics* (1983), to take only one example, Kaja Silverman argued the necessity and the merit of a psychoanalytical semiotics from a feminist point of view. As a branch of semiotics, psychoanalysis presented human subjectivity as constructed within discourse and as constituted by discourse. The activity of signification—the proper object of semiotics—depended on both discourse and the subject as situated within one cultural order or another. The study of signifying phenomena entailed scrutiny of the subject and cultural codes. Significantly, sexual difference played a central role in the formations of subjectivity, discourse, and cultural codes. In the Western world the cultural order presented the subject with sexually differentiated and unequally represented discursive roles. Silverman's project was, in part, "to denaturalize the condition of woman and to isolate its cultural determinants," which would facilitate woman looking "beyond the nightmare of her history."[21] In Silverman's view, semiotics could be usefully harnessed for feminist resistance that attended to the contradictions within the discourse of culture and attempted to recast female subjectivity and the cultural order.

Looking back over the early development of the discipline of semiotics, Thomas Sebeok in "Semiotics: A Survey of the State of the Art" (1974) declared "the year 1969 may thus well turn out to have been a milestone in the history of semiotics."[22] This was so because in 1969 the International Association for Semiotic Studies, its journal *Semiotica,* and its important book series "Approaches to Semiotics" were founded. With the hindsight afforded by a decade and a half, we can confirm Sebeok's assessment. Semiotics flourished in the Space Age. *ISISSS* was a tangible sign of its growing vitality and increasing diversity. Its ability to form productive alliances with literary-critical schools and with other fields seemed to insure its future. At the same time as Sebeok, Eugenio Donato came to assess the past and future of the newly formed movement in specifically literary studies, concluding "structuralism as a critical concept has outlived its usefulness."[23] This was so because the work of poststructuralists, especially that of Jacques Derrida, undermined the foundations of structuralism and semiotics. Donato's words turned out to be prophetic for the field of literary studies, where the spread of poststructuralism throughout the seventies and eighties dramatically outpaced semiotics, which declined in influence as time passed. As a new transdisciplinary field or discipline, semiotics steadily expanded, but as a subspecialty of literary studies its impact increasingly diminished. Literary theorists had two ways of describing this phenomenon. Poststructuralism swept over semiotics, leaving behind very little; or poststructuralism swept up semiotics, raising it to new levels of sophistication and subtlety. Deconstructors generally took the first view, while many semioticians, including Culler, Kristeva, Silverman, and others, took the second. One consequence of the first view was that most American deconstructors pursued their own projects, taking into consideration little, if any, of the work of structuralists and semioticians. To be a poststructuralist in America meant to be beyond structuralism. There was no need to work carefully through the tradition of semiotic studies. This view served to subordinate semiotics more and more as poststructuralism's success spread. In hindsight, the year 1969 turned out to be very significant for literary semiotics in America: the first work of Derrida was published in English in 1969.

CHAPTER TEN

Deconstructive Criticism

THE EMERGENCE AND FORMATION OF
DECONSTRUCTIVE CRITICISM

W HEN DECONSTRUCTION first emerged in public during
the early 1970s among literary critics in America, it was limited to a
group of critics born during the interwar period, including—among others—Harold Bloom, Eugenio Donato, Paul de Man, Geoffrey Hartman,
J. Hillis Miller, and Joseph Riddel. By the mid- and late seventies a group of
younger critics, mostly born after 1940, had emerged as deconstructors.
Among the leaders of such deconstructive critics were Shoshana Felman,
Barbara Johnson, Jeffrey Mehlman, and Gayatri Chakravorty Spivak. Several dozen more young critics could be listed here. Almost all of the above
named deconstructors, young and old, were associated at one time or
another with either the Johns Hopkins University, or Yale University, or
both. When Miller and de Man in the early seventies left Hopkins, joining
Bloom and Hartman at Yale, the so-called "Yale School" came into being
and lasted till the mid-eighties. Younger colleagues and students of the four
main Yale critics included Felman and Johnson among others. Because
deconstruction spread quickly and widely in the late seventies and early
eighties, it was not limited for long to one or two universities nor to a small
group of a dozen or so critics.

The key figure in the establishment of American deconstruction was the
French philosopher Jacques Derrida, who taught in France and part-time in
the United States, mainly at Yale, Cornell, and the University of California
at Irvine from the early seventies through the eighties. At the 1966 conference on structuralism, convened at the Johns Hopkins University, Derrida delivered a decisive critique of structuralist thought. The next year he
published three books—*Of Grammatology* (trans. 1976), *Speech and Phe-*

nomena (trans. 1973), and *Writing and Difference* (trans. 1978). The first text extended the assault on structuralism; the second undertook a rigorous critique of Husserlian phenomenology; and the third offered eleven essays expanding the attacks on structuralism and phenomenology and presenting inquiries into psychoanalysis and literature. From the outset Derridean deconstruction was not only "post-structuralist" and "post-phenomenological," but positively oriented toward certain psychoanalytic and literary topics. Because the initial American reception of Derrida was limited to those adept at reading French, the wide spread of Derridean thought occurred only in the late seventies when numerous translations started to appear. The translation of *Of Grammatology* by Gayatri Spivak played a particularly important role in this transmission, since it offered a prefatory monograph explaining in detail the historical context, the interdisciplinary scope, and the philosophical and critical significance of Derrida's project.

A second wave of translations appearing several years later involved a half dozen books, especially Derrida's *Positions* (1972; trans. 1981), *Dissemination* (1972; trans. 1981), and *Margins of Philosophy* (1972; trans. 1982). (Many pieces of *Positions* and *Margins* had been translated and published during the seventies.) The first work offered lucid interviews in which Derrida explained his enterprise. The second contained exemplary deconstructive readings of texts by Plato, Mallarmé, and the novelist Sollers. Finally, the third presented additional essays on structuralism and phenomenology as well as on the important concept of *difference* and the status of rhetoric. Of the six books by Derrida mentioned, all were published in French by the early seventies. The extensive work of Derrida from 1974 onward played a relatively minor role in the formation of deconstructive criticism in the United States. Within the numerous ranks of American deconstructors in the eighties, disagreements occurred between true followers of Derrida and less faithful, more independent and pragmatic critics. Of the leading literary deconstructors, old and young, few were dogmatic Derrideans, so they were sometimes charged with diluting authentic deconstruction and/or with distorting the actual drift of Derrida's work. This was a common critique lodged against members of the Yale School. Oftentimes this debate centered around the relevance of Derrida's later (post-1973) texts, particularly *Glas* (1974; trans. 1986) and *Spurs* (1976; trans. 1976, 1979). Conversely, some critics disregarded Derrida's later texts— the works of his "American phase"—perhaps because of an emergent dadaistic style. The lament was that America had ruined Derrida. Although all deconstructors shared a certain legacy stemming from the critiques of structuralism and of phenomenology, they differed from one another in their degrees of faithfulness to Derridean philosophy, their views of the relevance of psychoanalysis, their judgments about the pertinence of Derrida's later work and style, and their assessments of the "political" import of deconstruction.

The first phase of the development of deconstruction in America, lasting from 1968 to 1972, entailed the formation of the doctrine. The second phase, from 1973 to 1977, involved passionate debates on and reviews of the early texts. The third phase, dating from 1978 to 1982, witnessed the dissemination and institutionalization of the school. It was during this phase that numerous translations appeared, including six of Derrida's books and many essays. Also several introductions were published, as, for example, Jonathan Culler's *On Deconstruction: Theory and Criticism after Structuralism* (1982), my own *Deconstructive Criticism: An Advanced Introduction* (1982), and Christopher Norris's *Deconstruction: Theory and Practice* (1982). The fourth phase, beginning in 1982, saw the extension of deconstruction to other areas, including, for instance, theology, literary pedagogy, and politics. Among theological books were *Deconstructing Theology* (1982) by Mark C. Taylor and *Deconstruction and Theology* (1982), edited by Thomas J. J. Altizer and others. In the domain of literary pedagogy appeared a special issue of *Yale French Studies* on "The Pedagogical Imperative" (1982), edited by Barbara Johnson; certain essays in the symposium on "Professing Literature," published by the *Times Literary Supplement* (December 1982); *Reading Deconstruction/Deconstructive Reading* (1983) by G. Douglas Atkins; *Applied Grammatology* (1985) by Gregory L. Ulmer; and *Writing and Reading Differently: Deconstruction and the Teaching of Composition and Literature* (1985), edited by G. Douglas Atkins and Michael L. Johnson. Finally, a number of books considered deconstruction within the context of politics, including Michael Ryan's *Marxism and Deconstruction* (1982), *The Yale Critics* (1983), edited by Jonathan Arac and others, Christopher Butler's *Interpretation, Deconstruction, and Ideology* (1984), Howard Felperin's *Beyond Deconstruction: The Uses and Abuses of Literary Power* (1985), Michael Fischer's *Does Deconstruction Make Any Difference?* (1985), and *Rhetoric and Form: Deconstruction at Yale* (1985), edited by Robert Con Davis and Ronald Schleifer. In the latter two phases, deconstruction spread far beyond its early adherents, galvanizing large numbers of intellectuals in a struggle over the meaning and significance of this School. Commencing in the late 1970s, the debate over deconstruction energized the field of literary theory, mobilizing numerous antagonists and generating a massive secondary literature.

It was not uncommon by the late seventies to find strands of deconstruc-

tive thinking interwoven into the projects of certain formalists, phenomenologists, hermeneuticists, Marxists, structuralists, feminists, Black Aestheticians, and cultural critics. We have already seen that deconstruction
affected the projects of such critics as Krieger, Booth, Magliola, Spanos,
Jameson, and Culler. We recall that Susan Suleiman cast deconstruction as
part of the hermeneutic branch of reader-response criticism. Its ability to
spur critics of all persuasions, ranging from the ultraconservative to the
radical, from the traditional humanist to the committed Marxist, from the
empiricist and pragmatist to the philosophical idealist and materialist, made
of deconstruction a phenomenon reminiscent of New Criticism, which a
generation earlier came to occupy the center stage of the field of literary
studies, making competing schools appear for a time marginal in comparison. Not surprisingly, deconstruction was dubbed the "New New
Criticism." This was so because it too came to occupy center stage, its
leaders also were located at Yale, and its preferred critical approach was
similarly text-centered.

THEORIES OF LANGUAGE
AFTER STRUCTURALISM

In *Of Grammatology* and in "Structure, Sign, and Play in the Discourse of
the Human Sciences" (the conference paper delivered in 1966 at Johns
Hopkins University), Jacques Derrida criticized the structuralism and semiology of Saussure and Lévi-Strauss, using the concepts of the sign and of
structure as wedges to create fissures in traditional thinking about language
and about textual interpretation. The conceptual mode of inquiry pioneered here by Derrida, like the rhetorical mode of investigation developed by the Harvard-educated Belgian émigré Paul de Man, served later
intellectuals as exemplary means of deconstructive analysis tied to close
scrutiny of language and its formations. In synthesizing the work of Derrida
and de Man and in championing the benefits of such deconstruction,
J. Hillis Miller emerged in the mid-seventies as the main spokeman and
representative of American deconstructive criticism. In fact, however, Miller advocated mainly the virtues of the work of the early Yale School
(Bloom, de Man, Derrida, Hartman, and himself), being less enthusiastically attentive to similar poststructuralist projects initiated by Roland
Barthes, Gilles Deleuze, Michel Foucault, and Jacque Lacan in France and
Eugenio Donato, Jeffrey Mehlman, Joseph Riddel, and Gayatri Spivak in
America. Miller's own deconstructive criticism focused on canonical texts of

literary masters and effectively excluded, in its earliest phase, overt involvements with philosophy, psychoanalysis, and French poststructuralism broadly conceived. This purified or narrow kind of deconstruction came under suspicion from more "eclectic" deconstructors.

In *Of Grammatology* Derrida framed Saussure's structuralism as a final gasp of Western philosophy, that is, of a metaphysical system spanning from Plato and Aristotle to Heidegger and Lévi-Strauss. By Derrida this system was called "logocentrism." The logocentric tradition, as portrayed by Derrida, always assigned the origin of truth to the *logos*—to the spoken word, to the voice of reason, or to the word of God. Moreover, the being of any entity was always determined as *presence:* the "object" of science and metaphysics was characteristically the "present entity." In these circumstances, the full presence of the voice was valued over the mute signs of writing. Writing, in fact, was conceived by the tradition as secondary speech, as a device to convey the voice, as an instrumental substitute for full presence. It was belated or secondary, representing a fall from speech. Insistently, logocentrism collapsed writing into speech, particularly in its preference for phonetic writing (writing as imitated speech). The dynamics of such "phonocentrism" had generated an entire historical and cultural matrix of axiological oppositions: voice/writing, sound/silence, being/nonbeing, consciousness/the unconscious, inside (interiority)/outside (exteriority), reality/image, thing/sign, essence/appearance, truth/lie, presence/absence, signified/signifier. The first term of each pair received privileged status in the logocentric tradition. Saussurean structuralism, according to Derrida, was situated squarely within this epistemological system or matrix (as was the work of Trubetzkoy, Jakobson, and other structuralists).

Against structuralism, Derrida argued that *writing* (*écriture*) was the origin of language; the orign was not the voice transporting the spoken word (*logos*). Derridean grammatology was self-consciously designed to replace Saussurean semiology. In Derrida's extended conceptualization, *writing* signified any practice of differentiation, articulation, and spacing. Understood in this new sense, *writing* included all forms of inscription, ranging from penning a legal code to recalling a dream to carving a path through a forest. Using this concept of *generalized writing* or *archi-écriture,* Derrida effected a reversal of traditional logocentric polarities: writing/voice, silence/sound, nonbeing/being, the unconscious/consciousness, signifier/signified, etcetera. Presented as traditional signifier-signified, to take one example, the sign resided firmly within the phonocentric-logocentric system, marking there the proximity of voice and truth, of voice and being, of voice and meaning. The silent and unconscious, differentiating operations of *writing* underwent repression and censorship during the logocentric epoch, keeping hidden the formative absences, differences, and spacings essential to the production of signs. Derrida's project entailed, in part, bringing these operative and disruptive forces into play. "Absence," "difference," and "spacing" became key words in Derrida's lexicon.

In "Structure, Sign, and Play," Derrida called into question the logocentric conceptualization of structure. Invariably, structure required and depended upon the concept of center whose function it was to stabilize the panoply of elements in a system whether it was metaphysical, linguistic, anthropological, scientific, psychological, economic, political, or theological. Taken together, all traditional centers fulfilled the same purpose, always determining "being" as "presence." This ontological ground, a stabilizing factor affording certitude, kept the center, the structural matrix, out of play. However vast and complicated a particular logocentric system, the center of its structure insured balance, coherence, and organization, all deployed around a controlled point. Derrida conceived of the historical series of stable elements as a sequence of metaphors and metonymies all playing a similar structural role. He depicted the center not as a locus, or a site, or an entity but as a systematic function whose purpose it was to orient structure and whose history consisted of a chain of concepts or sign substitutions. In the end, the historical set of these central signifieds (or transcendental signifieds) collapsed into a play of privileged names, which Derrida characterized simultaneously as structural necessities and floating signifiers.

In Derrida's view, Lévi-Strauss's exemplary structuralist interpretations of myth depended on the self-conscious imposition of centered structure to limit the play of elements. Play was ruled out. In fact, however, the possibility and operation of play allowed and preceded the very structurality of structure and the imposition of a center. Before the alternative of presence or absence and prior to the possibility of center or structure, play operated. It disrupted presence and undermined the solidifications of centered structure. Accordingly, Derrida outlined two historic modes of interpretation— one was logocentric and the other was deconstructive. Here was Derrida's formulation as pronounced at the Johns Hopkins University conference on structuralism in 1966:

> There are thus two interpretations of interpretation, of structure, of sign, of play. The one seeks to decipher, dreams of deciphering a truth or an origin which escapes play and the order of the sign, and which lives the necessity of interpretation as an exile. The other, which is no longer turned toward the

origin, affirms play and tries to pass beyond man and humanism, the name of
man being the name of that being who, throughout the history of metaphysics or of ontotheology—in other words, throughout his entire history—
has dreamed of full presence, the reassuring foundation, the origin and the
end of play.[1]

Under the proclaimed aegis of Nietzsche, Freud, and Heidegger (forerunners of deconstruction), Derrida opened to deconstructive attack the logocentrism of the structuralist project. Unlike traditional forebears, Derridean
deconstructive man affirmed the play of signs and the activity of interpretation, traced around the center the free play of signifiers and the tendentious
productions of structure, renounced the dream of illusory origins and
foundations, and wrote off ontotheological man and metaphysical humanism.

   Whereas Derrida wrote early and often about semiology and grammatology, about the sign and difference, about logocentrism and phonocentrism,
about writing and spacing, about structure, center, and play, and about
Freud, Saussure, and Lévi-Strauss, Paul de Man almost never mentioned
any of these topics, concepts, or people. The recurrent and dominant words
in his critical lexicon were "language" and "rhetoric." The one shared
forerunner was Nietzsche. De Man eschewed overt theorizing about theories of ontology, metaphysics, anthropology, psychoanalysis, or hermeneutics. He preferred to practice close textual exegesis, punctuated now and
then with theoretical generalizations. "My tentative generalizations," proclaimed de Man in the Foreword to his collected essays from the late 1960s
titled *Blindness and Insight* (1971), "are not aimed toward a theory of
criticism but toward literary language in general."[2] Later he confirmed his
preoccupation with language and rhetoric, which always frustrated and
undermined ontology and hermeneutics, in the concluding analysis of his
collected essays of the 1970s entitled *Allegories of Reading* (1979): "The
main point of the reading has been to show that the resulting predicament is
linguistic rather than ontological or hermeneutic," and the specific aim was
to demonstrate a profound "discontinuity between two rhetorical codes."[3]
However different Derrida and de Man were, they grounded their projects
in theories of language—of writing and rhetoric.

   De Man's most revealing expression of his notions about language and
rhetoric occurred in 1973 during a conference presentation on Nietzsche's
theory of rhetoric. Significantly, Nietzsche shifted the study of rhetoric
from methods of persuasion and eloquence to the prior theory of figures
and tropes. About Nietzsche's provocative formulation that "Tropes are not

something that can be added or subtracted from language at will; they are its truest nature," de Man generalized:

[T]he straightforward affirmation that the paradigmatic structure of language is rhetorical rather than representational or expressive of a referential, proper meaning . . . marks a full reversal of the established priorities which traditionally root the authority of language in its adequation to an extralinguistic referent or meaning, rather than in the intralinguistic resources of figures. (*AR*, 106)

Nietzsche, the decisive forerunner, presented a categorical rupture in the theory of language, starting a new historical epoch in which language was first consciously conceived of as always, at once and originarily, figural or rhetorical, rather than referential or representational. No primordial unrhetorical language existed. As the distinctive feature of language, *rhetoricity* necessarily undermined truth and opened up "vertiginous possibilities of referential aberration" (*AR*, 10). Thus the linguistic sign was the site of an ambivalent and troubling relation between referential and figural meaning.

The problematic of the sign brought into question thematic interpretation and encouraged rhetorical reading. For de Man the revisionary project of criticism, therefore, was to create a nonthematic figural criticism or a deconstructive rhetoric. Ultimately, de Man's theory of *rhetoricity* operated, like Derrida's concept of *écriture*, as a disruptive and decentering force, an instrument of deconstruction, in the work of "interpretation." One got the impression, almost genuine, that Derrida need not have existed at all for de Man to have fashioned his understanding of language.

J. Hillis Miller's deconstructive work derived from that of Derrida and de Man. In a 1970 essay he first sketched a deconstructive theory of language, which was dependent on Derrida's seminal essay, "La Différance" (1968). In a later essay he offered a succinct formulation: "Each leaf, wave, stone, flower, or bird is different from all others. Their similarity to one another arises against the ground of this basic dissimilarity. In a similar way, language is related to what it names across the gap of its incorrigible difference from its referent."[4] All similarities were produced out of differences so that *difference* per se was constitutive of resemblances, repetitions, and similarities. To say that two birds resembled one another was to affirm their initial difference. What was true for birds was true of words also. A bird was not a b-i-r-d; that is, the body and feathers were not the four black ink marks on white paper. Words and referents were incorrigibly different. Here Miller situated the linguistic sign amid the disruptive forces of *difference*.

Because *difference* produced or constituted the sign, the status of linguistic presence, being, and origin were called into question in a way indebted to Saussure and Derrida. What Miller's observations emphasized was that the relations between entities were not based on unity and continuity; rather, they were composed as differential and decentered formations.

For Miller all signs were rhetorical figures—all words were metaphors. Following de Man's theory of rhetoricity, Miller in a 1972 piece declared: "Rather than figures of speech being derived or 'translated' from proper uses of language, all language is figurative at the beginning. The notion of a literal or referential use of language is only an illusion born of the forgetting of the metaphorical 'roots' of language."[5] Situating the sign amidst the discontinuous and divisive forces of rhetoricity, Miller undermined referentiality and set the sign free to generate dizzying effects of semantic aberration.

Miller synthesized elements of Derrida's and de Man's theories of language, merging *difference* and *rhetoricity* and thereby forging an instrument for the work of deconstruction. Unlike the early Derrida but like de Man, Miller mainly practiced deconstructive rhetorical criticism, tracing the aberrations of figures and the destabilizing flights of reference in texts. Derrida focused upon concepts, reversing their terms and substituting new notions in place of old truths. Generalizing his rhetorical approach, Miller offered this program for future literary studies: "The study of literature should certainly cease to take the mimetic referentiality of literature for granted. Such a properly literary discipline would cease to be exclusively a repertoire of ideas, of themes, and of the varieties of human psychology. It would become once more philology, rhetoric, an investigation of the epistemology of tropes" ("NLM," 451). Next to historical, hermeneutical, and psychological criticism, Miller wanted rhetorical criticism. Such a move to deconstructive rhetoric was conceived, not as a happy escape from the simplicities of conventional criticism, but as a painful philological confrontation with the baffling epistemology of literary language. In essence, rhetoric provided a way to move beyond the fallacy of referentiality and a means to break through the logocentric enclosure.

The whole complex of propositions about language advanced by deconstructors came to be called *textuality,* which formed the cornerstone of deconstruction. Theories of language propounded by deconstructors had this in common: they installed fissures in traditional notions of reference, which had the effect of loosening language's ties to concepts and referents.

The resultant aberration or play of language called into question all stabilizing notions of unity, coherence, presence, voice, structure, and center.
Assigned a powerful foundational role, language determined man more
than he determined or directed it. In a sense, language constituted a
(prison) house of being. It engendered man and his reality. Nothing stood
behind: there were neither origins nor foundations outside language. Irre-
ducibly, the world was text. Extralinguistic reality was an illusion. "*There is
nothing outside of the text,*" proclaimed Derrida in *Of Grammatology* (158).

Examining French structuralist and poststructuralist theories of the linguistic sign developed during the sixties, Jeffrey Mehlman observed that at
this time "the most adventurous tendencies in French thought were beginning to converge in a reflection on textual dynamics which resembled
nothing so much as a radicalization of the inoffensive craft we had come to
know as 'literary criticism.' "⁶ Where deconstruction differed most from
structuralism was in its skepticism and subversion of linguistic stability, of
structuration per se, of philosophical binarism, of logical reading protocols,
of metalanguage, and of large scientific claims. In addition, the death of the
subject proclaimed earlier by structuralism was exacerbated by deconstruction, which declared the end of man and humanism. At this point some
American deconstructors, notably Bloom and Hartman, balked, wishing
somehow to preserve the human subject and the voice, testimony to earlier
commitments to psychoanalysis and phenomenology, as we shall see.

BEYOND PHENOMENOLOGY

Many of the leading American deconstructors born in the interwar period
had intellectual roots in phenomenology. This was true of Paul de Man,
Eugenio Donato, and Joseph Riddel as well as J. Hillis Miller and Geoffrey
Harman—the latter two have already been discussed as Phenomenological
Critics in chapter 6. Derrida was steeped in phenomenology: his first book
was a translation of Husserl's *Origin of Geometry* (1939; French trans.
1962); his second book, *Speech and Phenomena,* presented a critique of
Husserl's theory of language; and his other early works up to 1973 contained five important essays and numerous passing observations on Husserl,
Heidegger, and other phenomenologists. To arrive at deconstruction, Derrida had worked through both structuralism *and* phenomenology. Most of
his American allies, however, passed from phenomenology to deconstruction without confronting structuralism. This occurred because in the
United States both structuralism and deconstruction emerged as alterna-

tives for literary critics at about the same time. In the early 70s some critics, like Culler, Prince, Riffaterre, and Scholes, chose structuralism while others, like de Man, Donato, Riddel, and Miller, decided on deconstruction. Those who opted for deconstruction, unlike those who selected structuralism, were often former phenomenologists. However, most of the younger deconstructors, educated in the sixties and seventies, came to deconstruction as students, meaning that often they did not have to work through structuralism or phenomenology. What happened in America, therefore, was that various mature critics became poststructuralists without benefit of close contact with structuralism and other younger intellectuals became postphenomenological critics without having passed through phenomenology. Hence the complaint that American deconstruction was anomalous because American deconstructors were poorly grounded in essential philosophy. Despite the pertinence of such criticism, the route to deconstruction in America entailed for the leaders of the school a passage through and beyond phenomenology.

When dealing with Husserl and Heidegger, Derrida's strategy was to create counterreadings of their logocentric "metaphysics of presence" and "ontologies of being" by scrupulously locating and foregrounding in their works the unnoticed constituting forces of *difference* and *writing*. While Derrida appreciated the critiques of traditional metaphysics lodged by phenomenologists, he deplored their avowed projects to reawaken and restore metaphysics to its most authentic and original purpose: the determination of being as presence. Husserl, for example, founded his enterprise on the *lebendige Gegenwart* (living present), the universal and ultimate ground of all experience. Upon this ground the perception or intuition of self by self in presence functioned as a principle of principles. Husserl insisted that this primordial constitution of self-presence occurred without the agency of signs or the operation of signification. This pre-expressive experience of pure or ideal self-present identity took place in silence. Language was secondary. According to Derrida, Husserl's whole project "confirms the underlying limitation of language to a secondary stratum of experience and, in the consideration of this stratum, confirms the traditional phonologism of metaphysics. If writing brings the constitution of ideal objects to completion, it does so through phonetic writing: it proceeds to fix, inscribe, record, and incarnate an already prepared utterance."[7] For Husserl self-present being, pure being, preceded language. Language appeared, but as belated, instrumental, and phonetic. To disrupt and reverse this founding phenomenological formulation, Derrida demonstrated Husserl's suppression of primordial *difference:* "pure difference, which constitutes the self-presence of the living present, introduces into self-presence from the beginning all the impurity putatively excluded from it. The living present springs forth out of its nonidentity with itself and from the possibility of a retentional trace" (*SP*, 85). Where Husserl envisioned self-presence, Derrida sighted difference and written traces. Here textuality invaded ontology. For Derrida the living present was an effect of difference, of spacing, of writing.

The Derridean deconstructive critique of phenomenology pitted the constituting and uncanny forces of language explicitly against the metaphysical concepts of consciousness, being, presence, and voice and implicitly against the logocentric procedures of reduction, bracketing, and "description." From the outset deconstruction was critical of phenomenology's tendencies toward subjectivism, phonologism, and idealism. Because it focused upon the underlying system of concepts and the rhetorical matrices of traditional Western philosophy, Derridean deconstruction could cast phenomenology as the last gasp of logocentrism. The American deconstructive critiques of phenomenology, partially indebted to Derrida's pioneering work, lacked grandeur and sweep in comparison.

Paul de Man's connection with phenomenology was most apparent in his essays of the 1950s, while his self-conscious separation from phenomenology appeared in his articles of the late 1960s. In "The Dead-End of Formalist Criticism" (1956), for example, de Man criticized the faults of Marxist, Geneva, and Myth criticism as well as the errors of logical positivism and formalism. However, he singled out for praise the eccentric work of William Empson because it showed that "true poetic ambiguity proceeds from the deep division of Being itself, and poetry does no more than state and repeat this division." Here was de Man's broad characterization of Empson's exemplary progress: "Having started from the premises of the strictest aesthetical formalism, Empson winds up facing the ontological question."[8] What de Man did was to privilege ontology—rather than sociology, psychology, theology, or logic—as the essential discipline or domain of literature. In other words, the phenomenological "question of being" dominated his attention. Whereas in the early work de Man was preoccupied with the matter of being, in the later work he was absorbed by the problematic of language (rhetoricity). In "Criticism and Crisis" (1967), for instance, he surveyed the tumultuous state of Continental criticism in the Space Age, pointing out fundamental weaknesses in phenomenology and staking out the terrain of deconstruction. Asserting that "unmediated expression is a philosophical impossibility," de Man declared of literature "its separation from empirical reality, its divergence, as a sign, from a meaning that depends for its existence on the constitutive activity of this sign, characterizes the work of literature in its essence" (*BI,* 9, 17). In this deconstructive formulation, literature was mediated by language and language was inherently differential, problematical, nonidentical, aberrant. The shift from ontology to linguistics, from being to textuality, marked the move from phenomenological to deconstructive thinking.

J. Hillis Miller practiced phenomenological criticism of the Geneva kind during the fifties and sixties, as we discussed in chapter 6. He turned to deconstruction in the closing years of the sixties. The change was most dramatically revealed in print in a lengthy essay on Georges Poulet's criticism published in 1971. Here Miller offered a meticulous and fair-minded description of his mentor's phenomenological criticism, closing his text with an impersonal deconstructive critique and concluding, "the tradition represented by Derrida and that represented by Poulet must be set against one another as an irreconcilable either/or. A critic must choose either the tradition of presence or the tradition of 'difference,' for their assumptions about language, about literature, about history, and about the mind cannot be made compatible."[9] Having chosen Derrida and the "tradition of difference," Miller called into question Poulet's concepts of time, consciousness, language, and literary history. (A similar wide-ranging critique by Miller of a leading American literary historian M. H. Abrams was published in 1972, drawing up the first battle lines in America between deconstructors and orthodox literary historians.) The key point in the critique of Poulet concerned the proper relation of language and consciousness. "The concept or word 'consciousness,' or even consciousness itself . . . is generated as one element in a systematic interplay of linguistic elements which is the ground of the mind, rather than the other way around" (213). Like Derrida and de Man, Miller set language as the ground of consciousness, putting linguistics before ontology. The play of language produced the very possiblity of mind. Calling on Nietzsche, Freud, and Heidegger, Miller here subverted the foundations of phenomenology, aligning himself with certain French poststructuralists (Roland Barthes, Gilles Deleuze, Michel Foucault, and, preeminently, Jacques Derrida).

The deconstructive move beyond phenomenology involved a complex passage through the work of Martin Heidegger, by whom several leading deconstructors were heavily influenced. A telling debate broke out between J. Hillis Miller and Joseph Riddel bearing on the role of Heideggerian phenomenology. This same year—1975—William Spanos initiated in print his project for a "destructive hermeneutics," which was designed to counter deconstruction by foregrounding the "deconstructive" elements in Heidegger's philosophy, as we saw in chapter 7.

In his review of Riddel's *The Inverted Bell: Modernism and the Counterpoetics of William Carlos Williams* (1974)—the earliest large-scale work of American deconstructive criticism—Miller attacked Riddel's conceptualization of language.

Riddel's theory of language, like that of Heidegger, with his belief in "ein einziges, das einzige Wort," is in fact literal or mimetic. He tends to take the Heideggerian figures literally, as referring to extra-linguistic reality. . . . For Derrida, on the other hand, language is "originally" figurative. . . .[10]

According to Miller, Riddel held a mimetic theory of language and literature derived from Heidegger. What he needed as a deconstructor was a differential or, rather, a rhetorical theory modeled after Derrida. Revealing here was not only the stark confrontation of mimetic and rhetorical formulations of language, but the erroneous depictions of Heidegger and Derrida. Heidegger's notion of language was hardly literal or mimetic, nor was Derrida's account of language rhetorical. That was de Man's view. In his "corrective" discourse, Miller wanted deconstructors to relinquish Heidegger and take up Derrida.

Rather than offer a defense, Riddel constructed a critique of the whole Yale School in his reply. He accused the Yale Critics of taming Derrida by their privileging of both *literary* language and great works in a manner reminiscent of New Criticism. He correctly pointed out that Hartman and Bloom refused to adopt Derrida's theory of language and that Miller was just a "footnote" to de Man, who had erroneously limited Derrida's philosophy of language to literature. Thus, the first public division within the ranks of deconstructors and the first insider's criticism of the Yale School was occasioned by struggle over the work of Heidegger. To the charge of literalism, Riddel responded, "to say that I really believe in some originary, pre-linguistic event is ridiculous."[11] Riddel presented himself as more faithful to Derrida than any of the Yale Critics, opening for the first time the issue of "authentic Derrideanism," which would thereafter plague the growing community of deconstructors.

Despite some weaknesses in his argument, Miller was right to characterize *The Inverted Bell* as phenomenological. It was situated midway between Heidegger and Derrida, marking a point of transition in Riddel's turn to deconstruction. The next year Riddel brought out "From Heidegger to Derrida to Chance: Doubling and (Poetic) Language" (1976)—published in Spanos' *Boundary 2* and later in *Martin Heidegger and the Question of Literature* (1979)—which showed recognition of Heidegger's limits and acceptance of Derrida's "definitive" deconstruction of phenomenology. Here Riddel indicated he was "not Heideggerian." Characteristically merging Heidegger's and Derrida's distinctive lexicons, he affirmed that linguistic difference indeed "functions to upset the illusion that in literature there can be truth, or the 'appearance' of an unrepresented in the represented, the concealed which is unconcealed yet hidden, a unity of consciousness or the 'reality' of an imaginary 'world.' "[12] Thus, Riddel gave up phenomenological illusions about truth as *aletheia* (unconcealing), about consciousness as unified, and about literature as somehow real. Riddel, like Derrida himself, reserved an important place for Heideggerian phenomenology in the work of deconstruction. The only other American deconstructor to follow this line was Rodolphe Gasché, who argued the impossibility of fully comprehending Derrida without understanding Heidegger.

While Derrida, de Man, Miller, Riddel, and others turned away from phenomenology, William Spanos sought to fashion a "destructive" hermeneutics out of the early works of Heidegger as a way to meet the challenge of deconstruction. What Spanos wanted to protect was the relevance of literature for life against the antimimeticism and formalistic rhetoricity typical of deconstructive theorizing. He criticized deconstruction for its purported spatial rather than temporal hermeneutic and for its privileging of language over being. As far as Spanos was concerned, "writing" in the Western tradition insidiously preserved presence, stabilized being, and spatialized time. It was, in fact, "speech" as Heideggerian *Rede,* not as Derridean *parole,* that engendered authentic explorative language open to being and grounded in existential no-thingness (non-presence).

When he wrote the Preface to the Yale School manifesto *Deconstruction and Criticism* (1979), which contained essays by Bloom, de Man, Derrida, Hartman, and Miller, Geoffrey Hartman characterized de Man, Derrida, and Miller as "boa-deconstructors" and himself and Bloom as "barely deconstructionists."[13] This was an accurate depiction because Bloom and Hartman were reluctant to set language unequivocally before being, to accept the death of the human subject, or to replace voice with writing. This much of phenomenology remained in the "deconstructive" work of Hartman, whose engagement with phenomenological thought dated back to the fifties. Early and late, Hartman was committed to philological exegesis and hermeneutics in the context of literary history, to anagogical inquiry into uncanny and sacred themes of literature, and particularly to phenomenological recovery of consciousness and voice—the experiential grounds of literature. What worried Hartman about deconstruction, as it had earlier worried him about formalism, was its depersonalized view of language, which eliminated altogether voice and intention (or will), rendering literature nonreferential and ghostly. Here was how Hartman figured the relation of language and subjectivity in *Criticism in the Wilderness* (1980): "'In the beginning was the Word' means that there is no time of which it can be said, here time was and language was not. The subject or self is not denied but is the very locus that discloses that relation."[14] The site for the emergence of language and time was the self. Neither language nor history nor subjectivity could be disengaged from one another. Words both dispelled and produced presence and identity. Thus, when Hartman declared "Nothing can lift us out of language,"[15] he confirmed the deconstructive notion of the prisonhouse of language but not the attendant death of the subject.

The relation of deconstruction to phenomenology constituted an important part of the history of criticism in America because many of the leading Phenomenological Critics converted to deconstruction. This happened during the Vietnam era—a time when the derealization of consciousness and orthodox thought as well as resistance to such "deconstruction" were powerful forces in the land. There was an undeniable millenarian dimension to early deconstruction which envisaged itself at the dawn of a monstrous new epoch. In the role of seer, Derrida hailed the end of logocentrism. The prefatory "Exergue" to *Of Grammatology* declared: "The future can only be anticipated in the form of an absolute danger. It is that which breaks absolutely with constituted normality and can only be proclaimed, *presented,* as a sort of monstrosity."[16] Derrida rejected utopian consolation and recommended Nietzschean joyous affirmation—the one depended on impatient dreams and the other required patient deconstructive labor.

DOUBLE READING, MISREADING, MISPRISION

How does a deconstructor read? At the conclusion of "The Ends of Man," a conference presentation delivered in America during the fall of 1968, Jacques Derrida outlined various options for deconstructing the logocentric system. He observed that deconstructors had two potential strategies. First, a critic could attempt a reading without changing ground, repeating the original logocentric problematics and using the system against itself. (This approximated Heidegger's strategy of "destruction.") Second, a critic could change ground and abruptly step outside, affirming total discontinuity and difference. In the end, Derrida recommended that both forms of reading be employed. Between the two interpretations announced in "Structure, Sign, and Play," there existed no effective choice. Derrida urged double reading.

One of the most influential early readings undertaken by Derrida appeared in the second half of *Of Grammatology*, where Rousseau's *Essay on the Origin of Languages* was subjected to an exemplary double reading. This work was chosen because it organized an energetic defense of phonocentric and logocentric notions about writing. In isolating and tracking the specific operation of the mysterious *supplement* in Rousseau's text, Derrida initiated a mode of reading destined to distinguish the project of deconstruction. What was the *supplement?* Many writers and philosophers throughout the Western tradition posited or employed the opposition "nature/culture." According to the traditional logocentric account, archaic man, living in an innocent and blissful state of nature, came upon a danger or insufficiency of one sort or another, bringing about a need or desire for community. In the evolution of man from nature into society, the latter stage of existence was pictured as an addition to the original happy state of man. In other words, culture supplemented nature. Before too long, culture came to take the place of nature. Culture, then, functioned as a supplement in two ways: it added on and it substituted. At the same time it was potentially both detrimental and beneficial.

Significantly, the structure of the nature/culture opposition repeated itself in other traditional oppositions: for example, health/disease, purity/contamination, good/evil, object/representation, animality/humanity, and speech/writing. Temporal priority distinguished the first term in each pair; the second entity came as a *supplement* to the first. In the case of speech/writing, for instance, the conventional explanation related how writing came late in the history of man, arriving as a double-edged supplement that offered gains and losses to man. It protected yet menaced. Traditionally, the first term in each opposition constituted the privileged or better state or entity. Nature over culture.

Derrida pointed out, however, that nature untouched by the force of *supplementarity* possessed no truth-value; there was no original unsupplemented nature—only a desire for it or a myth creating it. Inverting the nature/culture opposition, and thus overturning this metaphysically pure idea, Derrida sighted the emergence of an "undecidable" concept (the *supplement*), tracing its pervasive operations throughout the text of Rousseau. The effect was to "deconstruct" nature and culture, demonstrating that culture did not supplement nature but that ~~nature~~ was *always already* a supplemented entity.

To indicate the double status of a concept, Derrida wrote it then crossed it out. This tactic of putting a concept "under erasure" ("sous rature") derived from Heidegger. In addition, Derrida often invoked the "always already" formula to interrogate notions of "natural origin" or "unsupplemented purity": the effect was to insert the *supplement* into any seemingly simple or pure metaphysical pair of binary opposites. These and other methods of "double writing" were required for deconstructive double reading.

The logic and economy of the *supplement* showed that the outside and the belated were really the inside and the primordial. In the state of "nature," the *supplement* had always already started its work. In a manner of speaking, man's departure from "nature" toward "culture" was instantaneous and interminable.

The most disturbing aspect of the mysterious *supplement* was its lack of substance and essentiality: it could not be touched, tasted, heard, smelled, seen, or intuited; it could not be thought—within the logocentric system. As such, it exhibited kinship with other Derridean *undecidables*, including *difference, writing,* and *spacing*. By the mid-eighties Derrida had isolated roughly three dozen *undecidables*, which were nonsynonymic "substitutions" of *difference* with textual specificities all their own. What was especially significant about the *supplement* was that Derrida marked its operation in the text of Rousseau. It was not an alien importation. Like all other textual *undecidables*, the *supplement* escaped appropriation into the binary oppositions and conceptual hierarchies of classical philosophy and literature, yet it dwelled amidst them, resisting and disorganizing them while refusing inclusion as a third or master term. Double reading entailed using the resources of the logocentric tradition to dramatize its closure and its breakdown. The formula for deconstructive double reading was "reverse and displace key terms in the text"—invert oppositions and mark undecidables. Given that "there is nothing outside of the text," deconstructive reading involved strict immanent analysis.

Paul de Man's deconstruction of rhetoric differed markedly from Jacques Derrida's deconstruction of philosophical conceptuality. In an early text de Man declared that "the determining characteristic of literary language is indeed figurality, in the somewhat wider sense of rhetoricity, but that, far from constituting an objective basis for literary study, rhetoric implies the persistent threat of misreading." More precisely, "the specificity of literary language resides in the possibility of misreading and misinterpretation."[17] In short, if a text ruled out or refused all misreading whatsoever, it could not be literary. A text was literary to the degree that it permitted and encouraged "misreading." As a consequence, any criticism or theory of reading that aimed to achieve "controlled" or "correct" interpretations was seriously deluded. What de Man's account of (mis)reading did, in essence, was to coordinate and invert the traditional pairs literal/figurative and reading/ misreading. Because literature was figurative, its reading inescapably entailed misreading. Paradoxically, de Man distinguished between valid and invalid misreadings and good and bad misreadings. A good misreading, for example, "produces another text which can itself be shown to be an interesting misreading, a text which engenders additional texts."[18]

The theory of misreading applied to authors as well as critics. Any reading by an author or by a critic was ultimately unable to control or delimit the text. In *Blindness and Insight*, de Man demonstrated how major critics (Lukács, Binswanger, Blanchot, Poulet, and Derrida) unwittingly manifested a discrepancy between their explicit theories of literature and their actual interpretations. Paradoxically, critics "seem to thrive on it and owe their best insights to the assumptions these insights disprove" (*BI*, ix). The *blindness/insight* pattern was "a constitutive characteristic of literary language in general" (*BI*, ix). In *Allegories of Reading*, de Man showed how major authors (particularly Rousseau and Nietzsche) revealed the inescapable operations of the misreading phenomenon. The fault rested with language, not with the reader.

In de Man's deconstructive project, the conception of the text as self-deconstructing ultimately subsumed the phenomenon of the critic as bold deconstructor or the author as wily self-deconstructor. "A literary text simultaneously asserts and denies the authority of its own rhetorical mode. . . . Poetic writing is the most advanced and refined mode of deconstruction . . ." (*AR*, 17). Literary texts deconstructed themselves; they were always already deconstructed whether the critic or author realized it or not. No one was free to hem in the play of figures and the aberrations of semantic references. Texts misread themselves.

What critical reading confronted was language that vacillated uncontrollably between the promise of referential meaning and the rhetorical subversion of that promise. De Man's term for such undecidability was *aporia* (semantic impasse). Truth was permanently threatened. De Man never renounced referentiality; he problematized it, undermined it, exploded it—yet preserved it, as did other deconstructors.

The disorienting events in reading could be recorded. Critical writing, in fact, narrated reading experience. As a narrative using figurative language, criticism was inherently *allegorical* (fictitious). Criticism could never simply describe, repeat, or represent a text. There was no unrhetorical or scientific metalanguage for critical writing. Even scrupulous paraphrase blurred textual discontinuities in the forced homogeneities of its own discourse. Since both literature and criticism partook of figurative language, the difference between them was "delusive" (*AR*, 19). Both writing and reading were duplicitous.

Following Paul de Man, J. Hillis Miller adhered to the theory of misreading, the practice of rhetorical deconstruction, the notion of the text as self-deconstructing, and the idea of critical writing as allegorical. Like Derrida, he occasionally sought to interrogate the logocentric system by foregrounding undecidable conceptual elements in texts.

All literary texts were unreadable—or undecidable—for Miller. To reduce a text to a correct or a single homogeneous reading was arbitrarily to restrain the free play of its elements. However, "this does not mean," emphasized Miller, "that the narrator or reader is free to give the narrative any meaning he wishes, but that the pattern is subject to 'free play,' is formally 'undecidable.' "[19] Consequently, there were "obviously strong and weak critical misreadings, more or less vital ones" ("DD," 24). But always *misreadings* because an interpretation could neither reach an illusory "original" meaning of a text, nor contain all potential readings. There could never be "objective" interpretation—only more or less vital misreadings.

One of Miller's tactics in reading a text—derived from Heidegger—was to trace the meaning of a key word back to its etymological "roots." In so doing, he shifted the apparent stability of the master term out of a closed system into an ongoing bifurcating labyrinth. The effect of such semantic *dissemination*—an undecidable concept formulated by Derrida—was to deracinate the text, revealing inexhaustible possibilities for interpretation and the futility of logical orderings or totalizations. After reading an exemplary poem, Miller characteristically concluded: "Such a poem is incapable of being encompassed in a single logical formulation. It calls forth potentially endless commentaries. . . ."[20] Significantly, a commentary could neither exhaust a text nor employ a language safe from figural errancy—free from rhetoricity and allegory. There was no metalanguage, despite the scientific claims of structuralists and semioticians.

Deconstructive critics championed immanent reading. Carefully tracing and repeating selected textual elements (figures, concepts, themes), the deconstructors unleashed the disruptive powers inherent in all repetition. Essentially, critical repetition set in motion the operations of *difference*, summoning up a disorienting chain of substitutions and displacements to destabilize textual systems. Miller demonstrated the critical force of such differential repetition in his book of readings of English novels aptly titled *Fiction and Repetition* (1982).

The deconstruction of a text entailed the broad subversion of the logocentric tradition. "The so-called 'deconstruction of metaphysics,'" argued Miller, "has always been a part of metaphysics, a shadow within its light . . ." (*LM*, 62). All texts contained both the traditional materials of metaphysics and the subversion of these materials. "This subversion is wrought into the conceptual words, the figures, and the myths of the Occident as the shadow in its light. . . ."[21] What this argued was that deconstructive reading involved immanent historical critique: there was no need and no possibility of stepping outside the age-old self-deconstructing logocentric system. Western literature, philosophy, and culture already contained the incompatibilities, duplicitous tropes, discontinuities, and undecidables essential to contemporary deconstruction. History and tradition were encrypted or inscribed in a massive and labyrinthine prisonhouse of texts, which were metaphysical and deconstructive at once.

"A literary text is not a thing in itself, 'organically unified,' but a relation to other texts which are relations in their turn. The study of literature is therefore a study of intertextuality. . . ."[22] For deconstructors *intertextuality* designated a text's dependence on and infiltration by prior concepts, figures, codes, unconscious practices, conventions, and texts. As a crucial critical instrument, *intertextuality* brought to the fore the labyrinthine grounds of texts, facilitated dissemination of meaning, and enforced contextual instability. Because intertextuality posited both an uncentered historical enclosure and an abysslike decentered ground for texts, it constituted a liberating determinism. Simplifying, Joseph Riddel stated, "a 'work' of art always originates in the historical field of predecessors" ("HD," 249).

With the exception of de Man, leading American deconstructors solicited more or less regularly the literary intertext in the labors of reading. None was more dedicated to this enterprise than Harold Bloom, especially in his tetralogy on "poetic misprision," which included *The Anxiety of Influence* (1973), *A Map of Misreading* (1975), *Kabbalah and Criticism* (1975), and *Poetry and Repression* (1976). According to Bloom, every literary text was necessarily an "intertext." The ground of any text was always another text. Poems did not exist—only "interpoems" did. Significantly, the relations between and among texts involved fundamental *misprisions* (misreadings, mistakes, misinterpretations). Misprision, both necessary and inescapable, occurred between one poet and another and between a critic and a text because, essentially, exact repetition or identification was impossible and because, quintessentially, identity was slavery and death; difference was freedom and vitality.

Bloom acknowledged three levels of misprision. The late-comer poet misread precursors; the critic misinterpreted texts; and the poet mistook his own works. "Poets' misinterpretations or poems are more drastic than critics' misinterpretations or criticism, but this is only a difference in degree and not at all in kind. There are no interpretations but only misinterpretations. . . ."[23] The theory of misprision insisted there was always only misreading. This formulation, derived from de Man, was delimited by Bloom: "I do not agree wholly with de Man that reading is impossible, but I acknowledge how very difficult it is. . . . The task of restituting meaning or of healing a wounded rhetoricity is a daunting one. Yet it can and must be attempted" (*D&C*, 16). Published in the Yale manifesto of 1979, this declaration revealed Bloom's conservatism. He wished to restore meaning and to deny the extremist textuality of de Man's concept of rhetoricity. On the safe side of the abyss of misreading, his theory of misprision deliberately and desperately set limits to the dissemination of literary meaning. It did so by charting in considerable detail the complex phases of aberration evident in the language of poetry. In Bloom's work, meaning was ultimately restored in disruptive and tattered intertextual forms. Unlike de Man, Bloom and the other leading deconstructors situated the intertext as the ground of the text. The language of a text was always intertextual. What made Bloom's enterprise special was its almost exclusive focus on poets' misprisions of precursor poets rather than on critics' misreadings of texts. Bloom was a literary historian first and foremost.

Whereas Reader-Response Critics examined the literary reader from psychological, phenomenological, sociological, cultural, or political vantage points, Deconstructive Critics investigated the text and its reading rather than the reader. Of his change from phenomenology to deconstruction, Miller observed: "The shift back from 'consciousness' to 'language' as the category to be investigated allows in principle a closer look at what is actually there on the page. . . . I think more is to be gained by talking about the words of the work, its rhetorical texture, than by talking about the reader as such and his responses."[24] Whether it involved double reading, misreading, or misprision, the accounts of reading propounded by deconstructors tended away from the reader most obviously because the concepts of the "self" and of "identity" had been questioned and undermined. The "self" was a linguistic construct, as was the text: the "death of the subject" was an axiom of deconstruction. Bloom and Hartman resisted this proposition, as we shall find in the next section. According to Hartman, "Writing is a labyrinth, a topological puzzle and textual crossword; the reader, for his part, must lose himself for a while in a hermeneutic 'infinitizing' that makes all rules of closure appear arbitrary" (*CW*, 244). What was retrograde about this formulation from a deconstructive point of view was the phrase "for a while." The "infinitizing" characteristic of deconstructive reading was not temporary, nor was the text momentarily a puzzle. "Misreading," explained Riddel, "is not an incorrect reading, but the errancy or deviation of every reading."[25] There was no escape from such errancy. To work through textual aberrations, contradictions, and discontinuities so as to arrive at and fix meaning was necessarily to exclude, repress, and violate essential segments of a text. Where Reader-Response Critics rationalized such distortion, Deconstructive Critics refused rationalization and dwelled on distortion. The undecidable and the aberrant directed reading.

PSYCHOANALYSIS, POSTSTRUCTURALISM, DECONSTRUCTION

Of deconstructive critics born during the interwar period, several were deeply interested in Freudian psychoanalytic theory, particularly Bloom, Derrida, and Hartman. Of deconstructors born after 1940, almost all were involved with psychoanalysis stemming not only from Sigmund Freud but from Jacques Lacan. A key figure here was Eugenio Donato (born 1937), who apparently first introduced Lacanian psychoanalysis in America during the mid-sixties while teaching at the Johns Hopkins University. The widening influence and role of psychoanalysis in deconstruction can be traced through the publication of certain special issues of journals, especially "French Freud: Structural Studies in Psychoanalysis," *Yale French Studies*, no. 48 (1972), edited by Jeffrey Mehlman; "Literature and Psychoanalysis—The Question of Reading: Otherwise," *Yale French Studies*, no. 55–56 (1977), edited by Shoshana Felman; "The Tropology of Freud," *Diacritics*, 9 (Spring 1979), edited by Richard Klein; and "Lacan and Narration: The Psychoanalytical Difference in Narrative Theory," *MLN*, 98 (December 1983), edited by Robert Con Davis. That some leading American deconstructors largely disregarded psychoanalysis, as in the notable cases of de Man and, in part, Miller, signaled a significant internal difference within the School.

There were many Lacanian Psychoanalytical Critics who were not, strictly speaking, deconstructors. Generally, such critics were labeled "poststructuralists." Here a problem in terminology arose. In some usages, "poststructuralism" and "deconstruction" were synonymous. In others, "deconstruction" was part of a larger movement named "poststructuralism," which derived not only from Derrida but also from Lacan and Foucault. Other influential French figures of the Space Age were often added to the list of leading poststructuralists, as, for example, Louis Althusser, Roland Barthes, Gilles Deleuze, Félix Guattari, Julia Kristeva, and Jean-François Lyotard. The broad boundaries of the poststructuralist movement were sketched by Josué Harari in his anthology, *Textual Strategies: Perspectives in Post-Structuralist Criticism* (1979), and by Robert Young in his anthology, *Untying the Text: A Post-Structuralist Reader* (1981). Young, coeditor of the important British poststructuralist journal, *Oxford Literary Review* (established 1976), depicted poststructuralism this way:

> Post-structuralism, then, involves a shift from meaning to staging, or from the signified to the signifier. It may be seen from this how the premises of post-structuralism disallow any denominative, unified, or "proper" definition of itself. Broadly, however, it involves a critique of metaphysics (of the concepts of causality, of identity, of the subject, and of truth), of the theory of the sign, and the acknowledgment and incorporation of psychoanalytical modes of thought. In brief, it may be said that post-structuralism fractures the serene unity of the stable sign and the unified subject. In this respect, the "theoretical" reference points of post-structuralism can best be mapped via the work of Foucault, Lacan and Derrida, who in different ways have pushed structuralism to its limits. . . .[26]

What most obviously distinguished the more inclusive domain of poststructuralism from that of deconstruction was the incorporation of the historical, sociological, and political researches of Foucault and the psychoanalytical formulations of Lacan. A sociological critic like Edward Said, a follower of Foucault and a critic of Derrida, was, properly speaking, more a poststructuralist than a deconstructor. A critic like Miller, faithful to Derrida and unmindful of Foucault and Lacan, was most accurately called a deconstructor and not a poststructuralist. A hermeneutical critic like William Spanos added insights first from Derrida then from Foucault to his original Heideggerian principles, making him a representative of "poststructuralist hermeneutics." But such terminology often engendered confusion, which suggested that new terms or ways of thinking needed to be fashioned. Some theorists, notably Jonathan Culler, wanted to scrap altogether the term "poststructuralism."

In the formation of deconstructive criticism, the role of psychoanalysis was so complex that it deserves a separate monograph. We can, however, sample this difficult domain by briefly examining (1) the celebrated critique of Lacan by Derrida, (2) the *Yale French Studies* issue of 1977 on "Literature and Psychoanalysis," edited by Shoshana Felman, (3) the musings of Hartman on Freud and Lacan, and (4) the Freudian psychopoetics of misprision developed by Bloom.

Derrida manifested a meticulous and growing concern with psychoanalysis from the sixties to the eighties. His essays on Freud and on Nicholas Abraham and Maria Torok, particularly "Freud and the Scene of Writing" (1966; trans. 1972) and "Fors" (1976; trans. 1977), constituted some of his most compelling texts. When he criticized Lacan in *Positions*, Derrida promised to substantiate his rough critique on a later occasion. He did so in "The Purveyor of Truth" (1975; trans. in part in 1975). In his first attack, Derrida lodged several complaints against Lacan: he worked within the logocentric system; he succumbed to phonocentrism; he relied on phenomenological concepts derived from Hegel, Husserl, and Heidegger; he simplified Freudian texts; he practiced an evasive and anachronistic, elliptical style; and he utilized Saussure's sign and thereby reduced *écriture*. Still, Derrida judged the Lacanian project to be historically important within the broad field of psychoanalysis.

In his second attack, Derrida criticized the "Seminar on 'The Purloined Letter'" (1957), the famous lead study of Lacan's monumental *Écrits* (1966). Despite his criticism, Derrida expressed earnest appreciation for Lacan's tempering of naive hermeneutic semanticism, for his sensitivity to the enigmatic nature and activity of the signifier, and for his refusal to valorize biographical constraints on the flights of textual meaning. Nevertheless, Lacan's seminar exhibited major faults.

In his analysis of Poe's tale, Lacan omitted the narrative frame and fixed on two triangular relationships. Having left out the scene of writing, Lacan's reading, according to Derrida, displayed "an analytical fascination with a content."[27] Even though the mysterious stolen letter functioned as a floating signifier in Poe's story, Lacan analyzed it as a stable signified. The omission of the narrator forced him to specify the truth of the letter and to ignore the full textual activity of this mobile signifier. Thus, writing turned into the written, the text into a message, process into product, signifier into signified. Lacan exhibited a "demand for the truth" (57); appearing as an orthodox analyst, he was a "purveyor of truth" (65).

The logocentrism of Lacan was most apparent to Derrida in his phonocentric orientation. In Lacanian analysis the truth (*logos*) shone forth as spoken or voiced: "he always resorts ultimately to a writing sublated by the voice" (82) and "the law of the signifier unfolds only in vocalizable letters" (83). With Lacan psychoanalysis remained "talking cure" founded on spoken truth.

According to Derrida, the Lacanian project positioned the phallus as a master signifier. Because the possibility persisted that every and any signifier could partake of this most peerless signifier, the phallus occupied a transcendental position in Lacanian psychoanalysis. The singular function of the phallus as sovereign signifier was to center and regulate systematically the process of interpretation, the unveilings of truth, the imports of the voice, and the flights of the signifier. Thus, Derrida criticized Lacan's phallocentrism as well as his phonocentrism, which were complicit with logocentrism. Derrida called this ideological complex "phallogocentrism."

Published as a book five years after it first appeared in *Yale French Studies* as a special issue, *Literature and Psychoanalysis—The Question of Reading: Otherwise* (1982) contained texts not only by important American and French poststructuralists, Marxists, and Lacan himself, but by three young deconstructors influenced by Lacan—Barbara Johnson, Gayatri Spivak, and Shoshana Felman. The epigraphs to the volume, taken from Lacan and de Man, suggested that reading for meaning entailed disabling mysteries, if not permanently subversive impasses. In "The Frame of Reference: Poe, Lacan, Derrida," Barbara Johnson deconstructed Derrida's reading of Lacan's seminar on Poe, presenting Lacan as a poststructuralist who resisted the lures of logocentrism. Gayatri Spivak's "The Letter as Cutting Edge" sketched the limits and uses of Lacanian psychoanalysis for philosophical and rhetorical deconstructive criticism. Among other things, she reserved a space within deconstruction for the theory of the subject and the intersubjective theory of transference. And Shoshana Felman's monograph, "Turning the Screw of Interpretation," examined the controversy surrounding Edmund Wilson's "The Ambiguity of Henry James" (1938; rev. 1948), a Freudian analysis of James' *The Turn of the Screw*, as a way to theorize in a manner indebted to de Man and Lacan the relations between textuality and sexuality and the connections between (mis)reading and transference. Taken together, these three texts dramatized the pertinence of Lacanian psychoanalysis to the work of deconstruction. Jeffrey Mehlman pioneered this line of thinking in the early seventies, and it was picked up later by Geoffrey Hartman—the only one of the older deconstructors hospitable to Lacan with the notable exception of Eugenio Donato.

In a characteristic deconstructive move, Shoshana Felman grounded sexuality in language. Like rhetoric, sexuality generated conflicting forces and complex contradictions, revealing a lack of unity and an essential ambiguity. Accordingly, "sexuality *is* rhetoric, since it essentially consists of ambiguity: it is the co-existence of dynamically antagonistic meanings."[28] The divisions, contradictions, and ambivalences inherent in language marked the disruptions of sexuality.

Given this sexual/texual theory, it was not surprising that Felman cast older, conventional American psychoanalytical criticism as a repressive and totalizing mode of reading dedicated blindly to mastering ambiguities and contradictions. Paradoxically, such efforts at mastery made disruptive textual and sexual forces reappear amidst the writings of the critics in an unnoticed process of transference. To read in this manner meant to appropriate knowledge from the Other (text or person) in a devouring act of love. In this act, the detective-doctor turned unwittingly into a criminal-patient. To behold the symptom was to be held by it. The flaws in such readings were linked by Felman to older American Freudian criticism: "A reading can be called 'Freudian' with respect to *what it reads* (the *meaning* or thematic *content* it derives from a text) or with respect to *how it reads* (its interpretative *procedures,* the techniques or *methods* of analysis it uses). While it is almost exclusively in the first of these two senses that the concept 'Freudian reading' is understood and used in the American cultural context, in France, it is on the contrary rather in the second sense that a new reading of Freud has been elaborated by Jacques Lacan" (117–18). What Felman advocated was a new psychoanalytical criticism derived from Lacan that renounced the old search for meaning and content in favor of inquiry into procedures and methods of reading meaning. For her, as for other deconstructors, meaning was never final, literal, fixed; it remained contradictory, unreadable, rhetorical.

In the Preface to *Psychoanalysis and the Question of the Text* (1978), a selection of papers from the annual English Institute of 1977 edited by Geoffrey Hartman, Hartman criticized the identity psychology of Norman Holland and others, holding up for praise both the older psychoanalytical criticism of Wilson, Burke, and Trilling and the new French Freudianism of Derrida and Lacan. In replacing the wounded artist with the eager-worded student and critic, identity theory reduced the strong dream interpretations and psychosomatic researches of early psychoanalysis to "a free speech movement, an evangelism of the Academy whose good tidings expel the old, repressive word in favor of the new."[29] In this context, Hartman preferred Lacan, who insisted "on the heroic Freud, on the stern or terrible father" (xvii) reminiscent of Wilson, Burke, and Trilling. Hartman opted for a conservative, strong Freud over a liberal, mild reduction of psychoanalysis. The repression hypothesis was more to his liking than the promise of liberation. He preferred psychoanalysis that attended to language—"its ambiguous origin and uncertain affect, its metaphorical energy however restrained or purified, its residual bodily or hieroglyphic aspect, its irreducible 'sounddance' (Joyce)" (ix).

In the closing chapters of *Saving the Text* (1981), Hartman offered "a counterstatement to Derrida" based on a psychoanalytical theory of "word-wounds" and "spectral names" derived from Lacan.[30] According to Hartman, language exposed us to continual psychic hurt: whether experienced or fantasized, certain word-wounds played a constitutive role in the mysterious formation of the self. It was the magical power of spoken as well as written words that interested Hartman. To the extent that Derridean deconstruction subverted the spoken word and undermined subjectivity, it threatened to undo the foundations of poetry as well as psychology. Hartman sought a restoration of rhetoric as oral performance in order to reclaim "the mimetic and affectional power of words, their interpersonal impact" (120). Ultimately, he insisted that the psyche was uncannily created, defined, and affected by direct speech. In all of this, Hartman's earlier commitments to phenomenological criticism and anagogical or spectral themes survived his encounter with deconstruction.

Like Hartman, Harold Bloom offered his own counterstatement to Derrida, particularly in regard to the concept of the self and the subject of psychoanalysis. Unlike Hartman, Bloom had no use for Lacan, preferring the work of Freud and several of his early followers. Since he self-consciously ignored the work of Derrida and Lacan as well as Foucault and other related French thinkers and since he relied on Nietzsche, Emerson, Freud, and certain Jewish Kabbalists, Bloom was, strictly speaking, neither a deconstructor nor a poststructuralist. Nevertheless, his work bore close resemblance to native deconstructive criticism, which was why Miller, Hartman, and others considered him a member of the Yale School. In the mid-seventies, Joseph Riddel argued that neither Bloom nor Hartman were deconstructors. The Yale manifesto presented both critics as "barely deconstructionists." The line of demarcation here concerned the concepts of the self and of language.

In his tetralogy of books published between 1973 and 1976, Bloom concerned himself with the post-Enlightenment poetry of major English and American poets; he conceived of the entire period between 1740 and the present as "Romantic." Opposing a "scene of instruction" to Derrida's "scene of writing" (*écriture*), Bloom elaborated a six-phase psychology of poetic origins and growth. According to this account, the young post-Enlightenment poet was seized by an older poet's power (*election*), whereupon ensued an agreement of poetic visions (*covenant*), followed by the choice of a counter-inspiration (*rivalry*), after which the apparently liberated ephebe offered himself as the true manifestation of the authentic poet (*incarnation*); eventually the later-comer comprehensively revalued the precursor (*interpretation*) and ultimately recreated him in a new way (*revision*).[31] Using Freudian notions as analogues, Bloom pictured this formation of the strong poetic *ego* as an unconscious and unavoidable process in which the precursor was lodged, not in the *superego*, but in the *id*. The relations between poets, similar to those in the Freudian "family romance," commenced with a "primal fixation of influence" in the emergent poetic psyche. Accompanying the initial fixation was a "primal repression" of the new strong poet's ravenous wish or desire for autonomy and for immortality. Without such an overpowering "will-to-divination," a newcomer could not succeed as a strong poet. The repression, more a continuously modified force than a stable state of being, brought into play various processes of revision designed to insure the survival, independence, and triumph of the belated strong poet against the precursor.

The site of the scene of instruction was the psyche. The self preceded poetic language. Resolutely, Bloom refused to "abandon the self to language."[32] He denied the scene of writing (*écriture*). "A poetic 'text,' as I interpret it, is not a gathering of signs on a page, but is a psychic battlefield upon which authentic forces struggle for the only victory worth winning, the divinating triumph over oblivion" (*PR*, 2). The indomitable will to overcome death and time, to survive belatedness and gain immortality—to be canonized—motivated the work of the strong poet. This will or intention, repressed from the moment of the primal fixation of influence, defended itself against extinction, deadening influence, and loss of poetic power through rhetorical troping. Rhetoric played a fundamental role in Bloom's literary theory. Rhetoric *served* the poetic will. Bloom denied the deterministic theories of language put forth by Derrida, Lacan, de Man, and Miller. He held onto the "subject."

Bloom admitted his logocentrism. His poet's will to poetic power, the dynamo that drove the psyche, functioned as a transcendental signifier that centered the significations of texts. In Bloom's account, the successful strong poet possessed a degree of autonomy and freedom—Emersonian self-reliance—out of keeping with the "death of the subject" proclaimed by structuralism, poststructuralism, and deconstruction. However "deconstructed" was the self of Bloom's poet by unconscious and mutilating fixations, repressions, and defenses, this self retained an aggressive posture and an identity.

Because Bloom added a rhetorical dimension to the psychoanalytical foundation of his psychopoetics, his literary theory bore important resemblance to the theory of rhetoricity developed by de Man and Miller. Bloom's poet had recourse to a panoply of unconscious "psychic defenses" that manifested themselves in poems as tropes. Bloom correlated six defenses with six tropes, creating a structural map which coordinated the six defenses and tropes with six patterns of images. Taken together, the homologous defenses, tropes, and images constituted six processes (or ratios) of revision. When he read a poem, Bloom analyzed images, tropes, and defenses as a way to assess poetic revisions. Ultimately, meaning emerged out of unstable, though chartable, relations between language and psyche or between writing and will, linking the Other and the self. Against deconstruction, Bloom aimed to save the psyche, will, and self from extinction by language, writing, and the Other. The revisions that he studied entailed the misreadings of canonized poets by competing new poets—a defensive psychological operation necessary for creativity. In Bloom's view, misreading occurred not because of inescapable linguistic slippage but because of necessary psychological defense. Since all defenses were embodied in tropes, Bloom shared with de Man and Miller the insight that tropes were the source of misreading. In the end, Bloom's psychopoetics promoted an expressive, not a textual, theory of poetry. When Bloom in 1982 declared, "I reject all Gallic modes of recent interpretation because they dehumanize poetry and criticism,"[33] he offered a revealing defense.

Despite the "death of metaphysical man" and the "end of humanism" proclaimed by poststructuralists and deconstructors, the subject remained a site of much speculation. The subject in question was anything but unified. The powers of language, simultaneously constituting and deconstituting the self, produced internal cleavages. Whether it involved the unconscious, the libido, the spectral name, primal fixations, repressions, or defenses, the destabilizing forces in the formation of subjectivity arrived in language—in the signifier, in the rhetorical figure, in the name, or in the trope. At the intersection of deconstruction and psychoanalysis, language undermined human identity and subjectivity. On either end of a spectrum ranging from Bloom's mutilated poetic subject to de Man's superseded hollow figure, humanistic man appeared at or near the end. On this point poststructuralists and deconstructors agreed.

DECONSTRUCTION AND FEMINISM

Just as the impact of the feminist movement was manifested on reader-oriented criticism and semiotics in the late seventies and early eighties, so its force was registered upon American deconstruction at about the same time. With the exception of Derrida, it was primarily female deconstructors who pursued the question of the feminine. In a special 1982 issue of *Diacritics* titled "Cherchez La Femme: Feminist Critique/Feminine Text," Derrida enigmatically observed: "What remains undecidable concerns not only but also the line of cleavage between the two sexes."[34] Like all other logocentric hierarchical polarities, the "male/female" pair stood in need of deconstruction. Not surprisingly, the biblical account of human genesis depicted the creation of woman from man's rib: woman was secondary, subordinate, supplementary. Even the Freudian and the Lacanian formulations presented the feminine psyche in terms of phallocentric "penis envy" and "phallic lack." Starting in the seventies, French, Anglo-American, and other feminists launched numerous critiques against such patriarchal and phallogocentric conceptualizations. The deconstructive reversal of the male/female opposition produced the undecidable concept of a generalized femininity consisting of male (clitoral) and female (vaginal/uterine) sexuality. Both male and female partook of fundamental bisexual femininity. Ideologically, therefore, feminists could emphasize the primacy of the feminine in an act of counter-mythmaking or the ambiguous doubleness of all sexuality in an act of subversive questioning. The danger of the tactic of reversal, in the absence of further critical displacement, was to install and solidify a feminist hysterocentrism in symmetrical and stable opposition to phallocentrism. Feminism would remain a form of logocentrism. In an interview published in 1985, Derrida stated: "So for me deconstruction is a certain thinking of women which does not however want to immobilize itself in feminism. I believe feminism is necessary. Feminism has been necessary and is still necessary in certain situations. But at a given moment, to close oneself in feminism is to reproduce the very thing one is struggling against."[35]

In "Gender Theory and the Yale School" (1985), Barbara Johnson discussed "patterns of female effacement already well established by the phenomenon of the Yale School—and indeed, with rare exceptions, by the phenomenon of the critical 'school' as such. Like others of its type, the Yale School has always been a Male School."³⁶ Johnson revealed that she, Shoshana Felman, Margaret Ferguson, and Gayatri Spivak had planned but unfortunately never carried off a feminist companion volume to the Yale manifesto published in 1979. What Johnson found in the work of the Yale Critics, including her own *The Critical Difference: Essays in the Contemporary Rhetoric of Reading* (1980), was both an official indifference to gender and an underlying logocentric system of sexual partitioning—all of which displayed occasional signs of self-deconstruction. This pattern of silence, discrimination, and flickering disruption characterized the general gender codes of contemporary criticism as well as literature. Woman was dramatized as silence, simulacrum, absence, decorative sign, difference on the verge of coming into presence, voice, language, and knowledge.

In "Rereading Femininity," published in a special issue in 1981 of *Yale French Studies* on "Feminist Readings: French Texts/American Contexts," Shoshana Felman read Balzac's text "The Girl with the Golden Eyes" as a means of illustrating the undecidability of "femininity." She used as a foil the evident logocentric patriarchalism of Freud as well as Balzac. From a conventional masculine point of view, "man alone has thus the privilege of proper meaning, of literal identity: femininity, as signifier, cannot signify *itself*; it is but a metaphor, a figurative substitute; it can but refer to man, to the phallus, as its proper meaning, as its signified. The rhetorical hierarchization of the very opposition between the sexes is then such that woman's *difference* is suppressed, being totally subsumed by the reference of the feminine to masculine identity."³⁷ This masculine misprision of femininity was undone in Balzac's tale by the dynamics of bisexuality and of rhetorical reversal. "Femininity" came to signal otherness, ambiguity, and difference, threatening to ruin stable definitions of sex roles and attendant principles of social hierarchy and order. The undecidability of femininity subverted the essentializing and reification characteristic of sexual differentiation: "femininity as real otherness, in Balzac's text, is uncanny in that it is not the opposite of masculinity, but *that which subverts the very opposition of masculinity and femininity*" (42).

Like other deconstructors working with feminism, Felman showed interest in the "social text" manifested in the literary text. Her analysis of Balzac attended not only to sexuality and rhetoricity, but also to economics and class differentiation. Just as the hierarchical order of the sexes came undone, so did the economical regime of the classes collapse in Balzac's work: a mobile "principle of universal economical *equivalence*" upset rigid principles of classification (39). An uncanny, coordinated free play of language, sexuality, and money disturbed fixed borders and overflowed established boundaries. Though Felman didn't mention it, this characterization of social existence in Balzac evidently reflected the forces at work in early nineteenth-century capitalist society.

It was Gayatri Spivak who linked deconstruction and feminism with ideological analysis stemming from Marx. While it was not uncommon for contemporary Marxists to use insights from deconstruction, it was unusual for deconstructors to even mention Marx. Though an independent socialist, Derrida himself rarely referred to Marx. To put this another way, very few deconstructors dealt with social or political history. Even coming to grips with literary history was a burden. What distinguished de Man and Miller from Bloom and Hartman was, among other things, the refusal of the former pair to engage in literary history as did the latter two.

To understand the force and direction of Spivak's Marxist deconstructive feminism, let us take a short detour to consider the question of history. The opening words of de Man's second book confessed: "*Allegories of Reading* started out as a historical study and ended up as a theory of reading. I began to read Rousseau seriously in preparation for a historical reflection on Romanticism and found myself unable to progress beyond local difficulties of interpretation. In trying to cope with this, I had to shift from historical definition to the problematics of reading" (*AR*, ix). Similarly, the Preface to de Man's *The Rhetoric of Romanticism* (1984) admitted the frustration of literary history by the breaks and interruptions that reading ceaselessly produced. So tangled up did de Man get in the epistemological abysses of figurative play that he never consciously arrived at history. The stark conclusion to his essay in the Yale manifesto "warns us that nothing, whether deed, word, thought or text, ever happens in relation, positive or negative, to anything that precedes, follows or exists elsewhere, but only as random event whose power, like the power of death, is due to the randomness of its occurrence" (*D&C*, 69). Such total discontinuity, randomness, and aberration, introduced through the operations of rhetoricity and reading, disrupted and disallowed any history. That we regularly recuperated and integrated things and events in aesthetic and historical systems did not deny the fallaciousness of all such fabricated continuities; it merely affirmed a linguistic necessity. The making of history brought randomness to order in monumental fictions wrought by language.

Following Derrida, Miller pictured the logocentric tradition, embodied in language, as an immense historical enclosure—a structural unconscious or intertext. Unlike Derrida, he envisaged no monstrous outside and no escape. Since the system carried within itself its nihilistic shadow, it provided internal openings for the work of deconstruction. Because the "beyond" was already "in place" inside, repetition and not revolution was the means of interrogating logocentric history. Such repetition introduced difference, opening fissures and proffering change. Like de Man, however, Miller did not believe that any history of literature was possible (*LM*, xxi).

Bloom and Hartman, unlike de Man and, in part, Miller, continually took account of history. This was what Bloom had to say about history: "that there is no literary history, but that while there is biography, and only biography, a truly literary biography is largely a history of the defensive misreadings of one poet by another poet."[38] This version of the great man theory of history turned "history" into psychoanalytical literary biography. Neither Bloom, nor Miller, nor de Man dealt with economic, political, or social history. While Bloom studied the history of literary influence and Miller sometimes scrutinized the history of privileged logocentric concepts and metaphors, de Man generally avoided such broad entanglements. He even suspected that the historicist notion of "logocentrism" was really a fiction created by Derrida as an effective mechanism for reading (*BI*, 137–39). Unlike the other members of the Yale School, Hartman resembled a traditional literary historian in his concern with the history of literature, criticism, hermeneutics, and cultural institutions. He acknowledged the cultural and political stakes of literature and criticism. "Some of us," urged Hartman in *Criticism in the Wilderness*, "must be willing to write a theory of criticism that is not simply a new version of pastoral: a theory of the relation of criticism to culture and of the act of writing itself as a will to discourse with political implications. . . . The situation of the discourse we name *criticism* is, therefore, no different from that of any other" (259). For Hartman critical writing entailed a will to discourse that had political and historical as well as intellectual and literary consequences. To hide from such realities was to lodge oneself in a pastoral retreat.

When young deconstructors turned to feminism, they put their textualist criticism into direct contact with questions of social history and politics. Whereas Johnson and Felman remained hesitant to depart from immanent analysis of specific phallocentric literary texts, Spivak as a Marxist displayed comparatively little hesitation in her essays of the late seventies and eighties. In this she resembled Derrida, who for a decade starting in 1974 became an activist, in collaboration with the Group for Research on Philosophic Teaching (GREPH), working against proposed government "reforms" of

French education. Here was Spivak's deconstructive view of history: "Even if all historical taxonomies are open to question, a minimal historical network must be assumed for interpretation, a network that suggests that the phallocentric discourse is the object of deconstruction because of its coextensivity with the history of Western metaphysics, a history inseparable from political economy and from the property of man as holder of property."[39] A Marxist feminist deconstructor had to carry on the critique of phallocentrism as part of a larger ideological analysis of logocentrism, which was a historically determined and determining system that assigned sexual, political, economic, and social roles to women. Phallocentrism was part of a larger historical network or text—the "social text" of Western logocentric society. Ultimately, Spivak aimed to transform society and not just literary criticism: "as women claim legitimation as agents in a society, a congruent movement to redistribute the forces of production and reproduction in that society must also be undertaken" (192n).

Among the various projects undertaken by feminists in general, Spivak was attentive and sympathetic to five in particular. She supported efforts to restore women's history and literature, to found a vanguard women's discourse, and to reread classic texts as incriminatingly phallocentric. All such projects, however, were part of a bigger collective enterprise—to rewrite the social text. In the absence of this project, feminist endeavors risked complicity with one or another part of the reigning phallocratic multinational capitalistic order. In addition, Spivak, a native of Bengal who pursued graduate education and a career in the United States, sought to integrate Third World with First World feminism. To exclude the "colonial woman" was to exclude the "other," exhibiting social, racial, and class biases.

As a feminist, Spivak had a special relation with deconstruction. "My attitude towards deconstruction can now be summarized: first, deconstruction is illuminating as a critique of phallocentrism; second, it is convincing as an argument against the founding of a hysterocentric to counter a phallocentric discourse; third, as a 'feminist' practice itself, it is caught on the other side of sexual difference" (184). Deconstruction, whether of the Derridean, Yale School, or other variety, was male-oriented. Despite Derrida's own pioneering forays into thinking the feminine, "even the strongest personal goodwill on Derrida's part cannot turn him quite free of the massive enclosure of the male appropriation of woman's voice" (190). Spivak wanted a special and specifically feminist deconstruction in coordination with Marxist ideological analysis.

What made Spivak's deconstruction noticeably different from that of

Johnson, Felman, and others was her concept of textuality. American deconstructors, especially followers of de Man, usually construed textuality as thorough. As Riddel put it, "Derrida does textualize the world, or sees it reduced everywhere to a text" ("RC," 242). In Spivak's view, it was "a mistake to think of such a thematic of textuality as a mere reduction of history to language."[40] Textuality did not, according to Spivak, close off access to socioeconomic, political, or historical realms, as many deconstructors evidently thought. In his work of the 1980s, Derrida had staked out a position consonant with Spivak's understanding: "when it is said about the deconstructive perspective that there is nothing outside the text, then I say to myself: If deconstruction *really* consisted in saying that everything happens in books, it wouldn't deserve *five* minutes of anybody's attention" ("DA," 15). With the exceptions of leftist and feminist deconstructors, leading American followers of Derrida and of de Man were studious in their avoidance of political criticism and engagements with social history. Non-Marxist feminist deconstructors hesitated to broach directly political economy.

INTERPELLATING DECONSTRUCTIVE CRITICISM

By the mid-eighties there were evidently more books, articles, reviews, and conference papers dedicated to explaining, assessing, applying, and/or criticizing deconstructive criticism than any school or movement had received in the period covered by this history of American literary criticism. After the mid-seventies complaints began to mount against deconstruction's apparent antimimetic and antiexpressive textuality, which cut off the literary work from the world and the author and inhibited valuable ethical and emotional responses from readers. Many critics were troubled by the evident antihumanism of deconstruction since it rendered inoperative not only ordinary biographical and receptionist approaches to criticism, but also traditional historical and judicial modes of analysis. Yet another area of concern was the denial of metalanguage promoted by deconstruction: the refusal to separate in principle critical from literary language collapsed the distance between the critic and the text, undermining the distinction between criticism and literature and fostering a "creative criticism" that usurped the power of art. Finally, the ambiguous political ideology embedded in deconstruction— which was compatible with certain anarchist, libertarian, and socialist views—provoked criticism for its undecidability.

Some of these charges were hasty and ill-founded. The complaint about antiexpressivism, for example, clearly did not pertain to the work of Bloom and Hartman, both of whom respected the creative psyche of the poet as well as the biographical dimensions of literature. Similarly, the accusation of antihistoricism did not reflect understanding of the projects undertaken by Bloom, Derrida, Hartman, and Spivak. Lastly, charges of antimimeticism were often crude and careless. The theory of language propounded by deconstructors was not, in fact, antireferential. De Man and Miller, for instance, continuously interrogated referentiality, as did Felman and Johnson, without, however, renouncing it. Since Bloom, Hartman, and Riddel attended often to the intertextual root systems of figures and images, they displayed little interest in the mimetic aspects of referentiality, but they did not give up the referent. Nor did Derrida: "never have I said that there is no referent" ("DA," 19). Eugenio Donato observed: "We do not have signs because of an existing or recoverable intimacy with things and each other, we live in the world of signs because such intimacy is forever forbidden to us."[41] Characteristically, there was no denial here that words and things were linked—that texts and reality were interconnected—only that linguistic linkages and connections with the world lacked closeness, proximity, intimacy. The space and time of *difference* inserted inescapable gaps into the process of signification, disturbing mimesis and making it problematic.

In several previous chapters we discussed the galvanizing effect of deconstruction, showing how certain critics dealt with it: some intellectuals tried to incorporate deconstruction; others sought to counter and challenge it; still others aimed to effect mergers; and finally, some wanted to extirpate it. Krieger attempted the strategy of introjection, Spanos that of countering, and Rorty that of synthesis. Numerous critics took bits and pieces from deconstruction to aid their own projects, as was the case with Booth, Culler, Jameson, and Said. Among those seeking to discredit or eradicate deconstruction were some of the most prominent humanists in America, including, for example, M. H. Abrams, W. Jackson Bate, Denis Donoghue, Gerald Graff, E. D. Hirsch, Robert Scholes, and John R. Searle. A monograph could be written about the antagonism to deconstruction displayed by prominent intellectuals between the late seventies and mid-eighties. We shall sample some of this material, focusing on several celebrated attacks.

In "Fear and Trembling at Yale" (1977), published in *American Scholar,* Gerald Graff treated the enterprise of the Yale Critics sarcastically, singling out for special criticism its histrionic self-absorption, its confessional agonies, its bankrupt antireferentiality, its defeatist renunciation of the self, its no-fault theories of (mis)reading, its boredom with truth and value, its disguised roots in New Criticism, and its bad style. Especially unhappy with the "clogged style" and "general opacity" of Hartman, Graff noted that such "elimination of logical connectives, like Bloom's dropping of the definite article, is reminiscent of the disjunctive technique of modern poetry. . . . Criticism should not mean but be."[42] In Graff's view, the concept of "undecidability" merely extended the New Critics' ideas of "ambiguity" and the "heresy of paraphrase," ultimately revealing the linkages of Yale deconstruction with the exhausted century-old Modernism that derived from nineteenth-century Symbolism—a dehumanized, antimimetic philosophy of art hostile to objectivity, realism, truth, politics, and industrial society. Graff speculated, "it is possible that the true source of the malaise of current criticism is not so much epistemological or ontological as institutional, that it is a reflection of the confusion of the literature department" (476). Living in an era of critical overproduction, the Yale Critics evidently came to resent conventional criticism which seemed increasingly uninspired, irrelevant, mechanical.

In his "How to do Things with Texts" (1979), M. H. Abrams assessed the losses to literature and criticism engendered by the radical projects of Derrida, Bloom, and Fish. As a self-conscious defender of traditional humanistic learning, Abrams had earlier criticized the work of Miller in a debate published in 1977 in *Critical Inquiry*. Five years before, Miller had written a thorough deconstructive critique of Abrams' *Natural Supernaturalism* for *Diacritics*, a journal published at Cornell University where Abrams was a long-time faculty member. In his engagements with deconstruction, Abrams praised certain novelties while pointing out major problems. He especially criticized the disregard of auctorial intention, the voiding of referentiality, and the renunciation of criteria of interpretative correctness. Believing that literature was by, for, and about human beings, Abrams deplored deconstruction's "textual universe whose reading is a mode of intertextuality whereby a subject-vortex engages with an object-abyss in infinite regressions of deferred signification."[43] The death of the self of the reader and the undecidability of the text produced the demise of meaning: in place of reader, text, and meaning were vortex, abyss, and infinite regress. Hence, Derrida was a "Zen master"; deconstruction was a "deliberate exercise in ultimate futility" (574); and its "unsouled reading-process" was "suicidal" (567, 568). Worst of all was Bloom's project, which exaggerated the literary motives of "self-assertiveness, lust for power and precedence, malice, envy, revenge" (586), denying artists all opportunity to sublimate such infantile Oedipal compulsions for higher goals and more mature human relations.

One of the most despairing attacks on deconstruction from a prominent literary figure appeared at the close of W. Jackson Bate's "The Crisis in English Studies" (1982), an article addressed to university administrators and the general learned public. Bate was a Harvard professor and holder of the National Book Award, three Gauss Awards, two Pulitzer Prizes, and the National Book Critics Award. Among his many works were the popular anthology, *Criticism: The Major Texts* (1952; rev. ed. 1970), which introduced students to the history of literary criticism from Plato and Aristotle to Sartre and Frye. Bate traced the decline in literary studies between the period 1880–1980, casting deconstruction as the suicidal endpoint of this degeneration. What Bate longed for was a return and rededication to the Renaissance ideal of *litterae humaniores,* which made the coordinated study of literature, history, and philosophy the center of liberal education and the formation of intelligence, knowledge, and moral character the goal of "humane letters." The enemies of this ideal were (1) arid formalism commencing with turn-of-the-century Symbolism; (2) modern academic specialism, including especially early textual bibliography, source studies, and philology; (3) contemporary studies in popular culture, particularly women's, ethnic, and gay studies; and (4) present-day critical theory, especially structuralism and deconstruction. All of these trends and movements fragmented and decentered literary studies, separating humane letters from common human experience, moral values, and cultural history. To characterize the widespread interest in theory of literature prevalent in the Space Age, Bate quoted Milton's "Lycidas": "The hungry sheep look up, and are not fed, / But swoln with wind, and the rank mist they draw, / Rot inwardly, and foul contagion spread." Bate urged the importance of classical mimetic and didactic poetics, the virtues of critical pluralism and commonsense, and the recognition of man's capacity for vision and his genesis in original sin. Deconstruction revealed not only a deplorable antimimeticism and anti-intentionalism, but a childish philosophical skepticism and nihilism. As a method, deconstruction was "gloriously free of any necessary relationship to history, to philosophy, or to human lives," declared Bate.[44] Like Abrams, Bate self-consciously represented the judicious views of traditional humanists and literary historians in his hostile interpellation of deconstructive criticism.

Whereas traditional critics linked with literary humanism judged deconstruction to be extremist, radical critics, often associated with the leftist critical movement, regarded it as conservative. According to this view, leading deconstructors privileged major canonized texts of English, American, and Continental literature: the canon remained undisturbed by Deconstructive Critics. Most deconstructors avoided all mention of politics. Many maintained connections with orthodox religions. Although it was a form of philosophical criticism, deconstruction favored formalistic analysis of literary masterpieces, staying steadfastly and narrowly entangled with rarified webs of regressive textuality. The only noteworthy differences between New Criticism and native deconstruction were the change from spatial to serial concepts of poetic structure, the shift from unity to heterogeneity as the dominant model of literary form, and the reluctance of the deconstructive School to produce textbooks, anthologies, and pedagogical guides—the latter testified to a purported elitism characteristic of deconstructors. Moreover, Deconstructive Critics held positions at major universities, published books and articles with leading presses and journals, maintained leadership roles in mainline professional organizations, and regularly won awards and fellowships from prestigious agencies and foundations, all of which illustrated further the complicity of Deconstructive Critics with the reigning intellectual establishment. Postwar academic professionalism solidified all the more with the triumph of deconstruction. Yet despite its alleged conservatism, deconstruction offered some radical critics significant assistance in the formation of a project of cultural criticism, as we shall see in subsequent chapters.

CHAPTER ELEVEN

Feminist Criticism

FEMINIST CRITICISM AND THE WOMEN'S MOVEMENT

THE INCEPTION and later success of American feminist literary criticism were neatly symbolized by the publications in 1970 of Kate Millett's *Sexual Politics* and in 1985 of Sandra Gilbert's and Susan Gubar's monumental *Norton Anthology of Literature by Women*. Over the course of fifteen years numerous women critics, mostly born between 1934 and 1944, took part in the development of feminist criticism, including notably Josephine Donovan, Judith Fetterley, Sandra Gilbert, Susan Gubar, Florence Howe, Alice Jardine, Annette Kolodny, Kate Millett, Ellen Moers, Lillian Robinson, Elaine Showalter, Patricia Meyer Spacks, Gayatri Chakravorty Spivak, and Catharine Stimpson, among numerous others. What unified the highly diversified methods and works of feminist literary critics was a threefold commitment: to expose patriarchal premises and prejudices; to promote the discovery and revaluation of literature by women; and to scrutinize the social and cultural contexts of literature and criticism. In general, the focus of American feminists fell more on gender than on sex— more on social than on purely biological factors. In its first phase feminist criticism attacked male sexism; in its second phase it investigated women's writing; and in its third phase it concentrated on literary, critical, psychosocial, and cultural theory.[1] Politically, it was situated at the outset amidst contending programs for liberal and socialist reform, radical separatism, and cultural revolution. Renunciation of all politics was rare, being antithetical to the critical movement. Political differences both energized and fragmented the feminist enterprise from the start.

Feminist literary criticism was part of the broader new women's movement initiated in the early 1960s, particularly by Betty Friedan's *The Femi-*

nine Mystique (1963), a book that anatomized and criticized the dominant cultural image of the successful and happy American woman as a housewife and mother. Promoted especially during the forties and fifties, this mystique made the housewife-mother the model for all women, portraying women's ideal reality as a narrow domestic round of cooking, cleaning, washing, and childbearing. To find fulfillment and achieve identity in this regime, women had to accept sexual passivity, male domination, and nurturing motherhood. Simultaneously, women were led to discount earlier feminists who fought for women's rights to higher education, careers, and the vote. According to Friedan, the post-Depression feminine mystique, "this image—created by women's magazines, by advertisements, television, movies, novels, columns and books by experts on marriage and the family, child psychology, sexual adjustment and by the popularizers of sociology and psychoanalysis—shapes womens's lives today and mirrors their dreams."[2] The task of the women's movement, therefore, was both to demystify the counterrevolutionary, ubiquitous feminine mystique and to renew the long struggle for women's emancipation.

Like the movements against racism, poverty, and war and for civil rights, economic justice, and peace during the sixties and early seventies, the women's movement against sex discrimination and for equal rights and the right to abortion manifested itself in the creation of new organizations, the issuing of manifestos, the introduction of new legislation, the staging of public protests and demonstrations, and the publication of widely read books and articles. Among important feminist organizations established were Friedan's own National Organization for Women (1966) and the National Black Feminist Organization (1973). Manifestos included NOW's "Bill of Rights for Women" (1967), the "Red Stocking Manifesto" (1969), the "Bitch Manifesto" (1969), and the "Fourth World Manifesto" (1971) by Detroit feminists and Indochinese women. Noteworthy legislation occurred not only with the Civil Rights Act (1964) and the reintroduction in Congress of the Equal Rights Amendment (1970), but also with the liberalization of abortion laws in Alaska, Hawaii, and New York (1970). Memorable protests included the Women's March on the Republican National Convention in 1968, the Speakout Against Rape of the New York Radical Feminists in 1971, and the release of the "Three Marias" in Portugal after an international feminist campaign in 1974. Among numerous significant books published were Friedan's *The Feminine Mystique*, Mary Ellmann's *Thinking about Women* (1968), Robin Morgan's edition of *Sisterhood is Powerful: An Anthology of Writings from the Women's Liberation Movement* (1970), and Kate Millett's *Sexual Politics*.

Millett's book was doubtlessly the most popular literary doctoral dissertation published in the early Space Age. Focused polemically on four male authors (D. H. Lawrence, Henry Miller, Norman Mailer, and Jean Genet) and on male supremacy and sexual violence, it opposed reigning critical formalism while modeling the social and cultural critique characteristic of much of later feminist criticism. Like Friedan, Millett depicted the period from the thirties to the sixties as counterrevolutionary, recommending a resurrection of earlier feminist radicalism. She too criticized contemporary popular culture and the social sciences, especially Freudian psychoanalysis, for sexist devaluation of women. Assessed as literary criticism, *Sexual Politics* pioneered both feminist cultural criticism and antiauthoritarian demystification of respected male authors. As a resisting reader, Millett made up in polemical power for what she lacked in sensitivity to thematic nuance and literary style. Politically more radical than the liberal Friedan, Kate Millett hoped for social revolution rather than reform. "As the largest alienated element in our society, and because of their numbers, passion, and length of oppression, its largest revolutionary base, women might come to play a leadership part in social revolution, quite unknown before in history."[3]

The women's movement initiated in the sixties constituted a second wave of American feminism, preceded by numerous feminist activities and projects that commenced in the pre-Civil War period and lasted until post-World War I times. Contemporary feminists retrieved this history. In the 1840s the Seneca Falls Convention marked the beginnings of the political movement for women's rights. It was during this decade that Margaret Fuller wrote *Woman in the Nineteenth Century* (1845) and worked as editor of *Dial* and the *New York Tribune,* serving as an inspiring model of assertive and independent womanhood. In 1869 Susan B. Anthony and Elizabeth Cady Stanton founded the National Woman Suffrage Association that promoted a suffrage amendment to the Constitution, which took until 1920 to pass as the Nineteenth Amendment, giving women the right to vote. Exemplary feminist political activity manifested itself both in the Settlement House Movement of the 1880s (particularly noteworthy was Jane Addams' Hull House in Chicago, which agitated on behalf of the oppressed) and in the founding of the National Women's Trade Union League in 1903, which worked for the economic benefit of women unionists. In 1923 the Woman's Party introduced in Congress an Equal Rights Amendment. The effect of reviving such history was to impart a sense of continuity and historical purpose to the new women's movement of the 1960s and 1970s. The later movement had some notable political successes: Title VII of the 1964 Civil Rights Act forbade sexual discrimination in the workplace; Title IX of the 1972 Educational Amendments Act required universities to establish programs of "Affirmative Action" to insure equal opportunity for women; and the 1972 *Roe versus Wade* decision of the Supreme Court struck down state laws forbidding abortion.

From the early seventies to the mid-eighties, feminist literary criticism displayed the political and methodological diversity characteristic of the broader women's movement. As the number of participants in the critical movement quickly proliferated, so too did the number of critical approaches increase. In *Feminist Literary Studies: An Introduction* (1984), K. K. Ruthven identified seven distinct types of feminist criticism:

There are sociofeminists whose interest in the roles assigned to women in our society prompt studies of the ways in which women are represented in literary texts ("images of women"); there are semiofeminists whose point of departure is semiotics, the science of signs, and who study the signifying practices by means of which females are coded and classified as women in order to be assigned their social roles; there are psychofeminists who forage in Freud and Lacan for a theory of feminine sexuality unconstrained by male norms and categories, and who examine literary texts for unconscious articulations of feminine desire or traces of where it has been repressed; there are marxist feminists more interested in oppression than repression, and who process literary texts in a recognisably marxist manner, infiltrating "woman" into their discourse at precisely those points where in a non-feminist marxist analysis you would expect to encounter "the working class"; and there are socio-semio-psycho-marxist feminists who do a little bit of everything as the occasion arises. There are lesbian feminists who promulgate a somatic theory of writing, exploring the connection between sexuality and textuality by looking to the labia as the source of a distinctively feminine writing (*écriture féminine*), thus countering that dominantly phallocentric myth of writing as an erectile and ejaculatory activity. And there are black feminists, who feel themselves to be doubly if not triply oppressed: as blacks in a white supremacist society, as women in a patriarchy, and as workers under capitalism. . . . [They indict] recent feminism for concentrating almost exclusively on the problems of middle-class white women in technologically advanced societies. . . . (19)

To this list could have been added feminists who practiced existential, reader-response, speech-act, and deconstructive criticism as well as Jungian myth criticism and Third World anticolonialist critique. Ruthven supplemented the list with poststructuralist antifeminist feminists who resisted patriarchal accommodations and treated the "feminine" as an excluded signifier rather than something connected with women. By the late seventies all of these fourteen types of feminist criticism had adherents in American critical circles. What this multiplicity illustrated was the most salient feature of feminist literary criticism in the eighties: it was a loose movement (not a tight-knit school) situated at the intersection of many Space-Age disciplines and at the various political crossroads of the post-Vietnam era.

THE FOCUS ON WOMEN'S LITERATURE

During the mid-seventies many Feminist Critics adopted a female-oriented perspective focusing on literature by women and forsaking earlier exclusive emphasis on exposing sexist distortions and patriarchal stereotypes. This shift from the negative analysis of male-centered works (androtexts) to the positive inquiry into women-centered works (gynotexts) was reflected notably in Patricia Meyer Spacks' *The Female Imagination: A Literary and Psychological Investigation of Women's Writing* (1975), Ellen Moers' *Literary Women* (1976), Elaine Showalter's *A Literature of Their Own: British Women Novelists from Brontë to Lessing* (1977), Nina Baym's *Women's Fiction: A Guide to Novels by and about Women in America, 1820–1870* (1978), Sandra Gilbert's and Susan Gubar's monumental *The Madwoman in the Attic: The Woman Writer and the Nineteenth-Century Literary Imagination* (1979) and their edition of the *Norton Anthology of Literature by Women* (1985), Elizabeth Janeway's "Women's Literature" in *The Harvard Guide to Contemporary American Writing* (1979), Margaret Homans' *Women Writers and Poetic Identity: Dorothy Wordsworth, Emily Brontë, and Emily Dickinson* (1980), Annis Pratt's and others' *Archetypal Patterns in Women's Fiction* (1981), and numerous other books and articles. Where the initial mode of feminist reading attacked masculinist stereotypes, distortions, and omissions, the later gynocentric criticism examined female creativity, styles, genres, themes, images, careers, and literary traditions. One important aspect of this project entailed the scholarly rediscovery of overlooked, forgotten, and neglected women authors and the concomitant (re)creation of a canon of significant women writers. The basic premise of the gynocritical enterprise was that all writing was marked by gender and that androcentric criticism missed this fundamental fact. By extension, the trouble with nonfeminist female critics like Susan Sontag and Helen Vendler was their refusal to credit the sexist psychosocial determinants detectable in the formation of gender identity and in the literary works of women writers.

The passage from Betty Friedan and Kate Millett to Ellen Moers and Elaine Showalter involved a shift from criticizing the influential works of males to celebrating the powerful literary production of females. The purpose of Moers' *Literary Women* was to offer a detailed appreciative narrative of the "Epic Age" of British, American, and French literature by examining the careers of "great literary women" from the 1780s to the 1930s. Moers attended to women's themes, images, traditions, and lives, fixing mainly on the novel—the women's genre par excellence. The fifty-page "Dictionary Catalogue of Literary Women," appended to the book, listed the best works by and about roughly 250 women writers from Sappho to Anna Akhmatova, indicating Moers' ultimate dream of one day treating all national literatures of all ages. Perhaps the most memorable effect of her book was Moers' enthusiasm for the works not only of such major figures as Jane Austen, Elizabeth Barrett, George Sand, and Harriet Beecher Stowe, but also of such undervalued writers as Willa Cather, Harriet Martineau, Mrs. Tonna, and Flora Tristan. Moers wrote infectiously about feminist factory and antislavery novels, about female landscape and bird imagery, and about women's financial successes and their utopian dreams. What she lacked in theoretical sophistication and concern for literary form, she compensated for by generous attention to biography and a general tone of affirmation. Her ultimate theme was the admirable "heroinism" of leading literary feminists. In the end, Moers resisted the temptation to homogenize women's literature. "There is no single female tradition in literature. . . ." "There is no such thing as *the* female genius, or *the* female sensibility." "There is no single female style in literature, though in every country and every period it has been wrongly believed that a female style exists."[4] Unlike Patricia Meyer Spacks and some other leading Feminist Critics in the seventies, Moers argued against an identifiable, homogeneous, "essential" female consciousness, literary tradition, or style.

In *A Literature of Their Own*, Elaine Showalter set out to rectify the flaws of traditional literary history that had reduced the ranks of British female novelists to a tiny group by privileging only great authors. "Having lost sight of the minor novelists, who were the link in the chain that bound one generation to the next, we have not had a very clear understanding of the continuities in women's writing. . . ."[5] To reconstitute the female tradition of British novelists from the 1840s to the 1970s, Showalter had to look beyond great writers in an operation of rescuing minor figures. Unlike Moers' "Dictionary Catalogue," Showalter's thirty-page "Biographical Appendix" listed dozens and dozens of virtually unknown women authors. Casting British women novelists as a literary *subculture* like other minority subcultures, she scrapped traditional periodization and sketched three phases of women's literary historical development. The initial "Feminine phase," from 1840 to 1880, involved imitation by women novelists of the dominant tradition and internalization of its literary and social standards. The second "Feminist phase," from 1880 to 1920, entailed protest against prevailing modes and advocacy of minority values and rights. The final "Female phase," from 1920 onward, evidenced a turning inward in search of identity and a relaxation of dependency on opposition. According to Showalter, "when we look at women writers collectively we can see an imaginative continuum, the recurrence of certain patterns, themes, problems, and images from generation to generation" (11). In other words, women had a literature of their own with a distinctive history and tradition. Showalter's project was to define in detail the long tradition of realistic British fiction from the Brontës to Doris Lessing, which required not merely rediscovering numerous texts but also reforming a reduced and rigidified canon. It also entailed demonstrating the limitations of a historiography focused only on great figures.

Unlike Ellen Moers, Elaine Showalter was self-conscious about her critical theory. She considered her project part of the emerging discipline of women's studies. She sought to practice a cultural criticism rooted in the understanding that society molded and constrained women's lives, including their language, consciousness, and literary education. At different times and in different places, such "shaping" took on unique political, economic, and social forms. The trouble with the reigning masculinist formalism and structuralism was that both evaded the facts of social-historical conditioning and of gender identity. Despite her commitment to gender as a founding category of critical inquiry, Showalter denounced attempts by writers and critics to hypostatize female consciousness or celebrate a female aesthetics. All such theories of a female sensibility or style risked repeating essentialist sexual stereotypes and enshrining universalist archetypes, thereby discounting the shifting material realities of women's experience. In this resistance, Showalter demonstrated more consistency and success than Moers.

In the opening of *The Madwoman in the Attic,* Sandra Gilbert and Susan Gubar affirmed "the recent demonstrations by Ellen Moers and Elaine Showalter that nineteenth-century literary women *did* have both a literature and a culture of their own."[6] This understanding came initially, as it had earlier for Spacks in *The Female Imagination,* through teaching: "This book began with a course in literature by women that we taught together at Indiana University in the fall of 1974. Reading the writing of women from Jane Austen and Charlotte Brontë to Emily Dickinson, Virginia Woolf, and Sylvia Plath, we were surprised by the coherence of theme and imagery that we encountered in the works of writers who were often geographically, historically, and psychologically distant from each other" (xi). Focusing on the female literary tradition of the nineteenth century, Gilbert and Gubar aimed to articulate an historical feminist poetics modeled on Harold Bloom's patriarchal poetics of the male tradition. Instead of an "anxiety of influence," female writers experienced an "anxiety of authorship" that required them to negotiate alienation and disease on the way to attaining literary autonomy and authority achieved by (re)establishing links with an archetypal Sibyl figure or female Ur-poet. In order to create, women authors had to destroy the inadequate and debilitating cultural roles of "angel" and "monster" assigned to them by Western patriarchal society. The precursor poet sought in this revisionary struggle emerged as a sister or mother whose pioneering example enabled the creativity and power of the latecomer against the confining and sickening backdrop of forbidding male literary authority. The way of the angel was tried by Jane Austen and Maria Edgeworth and that of the monster by the Brontës and Mary Shelley. George Eliot and Emily Dickinson opted for withdrawal. All dreamed of a utopian land of female wholeness and energy.

Some of the finest passages of *The Madwoman in the Attic* examined striking themes and images of illness characteristic of the female literary tradition. Gilbert and Gubar traced recurring instances of physical and psychological diseases, observing that "patriarchal socialization literally makes women sick, both physically and mentally" (53). Among illnesses memorably treated were agoraphobia, amnesia, anorexia, aphasia, bulimia, claustrophobia, hysteria, and madness in general. Investigating dramatic examples of the madwoman embodied in numerous fictional characters, they found this figure "is usually in some sense the *author's* double, an image of her own anxiety and rage" (78). Whereas Showalter's commitment to social history restrained broad generalizations, Gilbert's and Gubar's tendency toward archetypal psychological criticism licensed some far-reaching, almost universalist statements about women's images, themes, poetic practices, and angry sensibilities. The angel, monster, madwoman, and Sibyl figures inhabited a collective unconscious of women writers, surfacing dramatically in the realistic, though duplicitous, literature of nineteenth-century authors.

At the same time that a great deal of positive gynocritical work was done on post-Enlightenment women's literature, the task of rereading and exposing the negative forces of patriarchal sexist literature continued undaunted. Major writers like Shakespeare received widespread feminist scrutiny. The point is that gynocriticism and feminist critique complemented one another, opening for full consideration both the question of a women's aesthetic and the status of the standard male canon. A critic like Judith Fetterley could produce both *Provisions: A Reader from Nineteenth-Century American Women* (1985) and *The Resisting Reader: A Feminist Approach to American Fiction* (1978)—both an anthology of American women's writing and an attack on American men's sexist texts. As time passed, theoretical questions about critical methodology, poetics, and politics became increasingly more pressing, though they were present from the start. As Elaine Showalter put it, "there can be no practice without theory, even if theory is unformulated or incomplete."[7]

CRITICAL THEORY, POETICS, AND POLITICS

In earlier chapters of this history we encountered feminist reader-response criticism (chapter 8), psychoanalytical semiotic criticism (chapter 9), and psychoanalytical and Marxist deconstructive criticism (chapter 10) in discussions of the works of Judith Fetterley, Mary Louise Pratt, Jane Tompkins, Kaja Silverman, Shoshana Felman, Barbara Johnson, and Gayatri Spivak. Thus far in this chapter we have considered the social criticism of Betty Friedan, the "images of women" criticism of Kate Millett, the literary historical criticism of Ellen Moers, the cultural criticism of Elaine Showalter, and the psychological criticism of Sandra Gilbert and Susan Gubar. In the next section we shall glance at the poststructuralist "gynesic" criticism developed by influential French critics and in the next chapter we will explore issues in black feminist criticism. In retrospect, the list of fourteen distinctive types of feminist criticism given earlier was suggestive rather than definitive. Viewed positively, such diversity in critical approaches prompted Annette Kolodny, in a celebrated essay of 1980, to formulate a capacious theoretical stance for all feminist criticism: "our task is to initiate nothing less than a playful pluralism, responsive to the possibilities of multiple critical schools and methods."[8] The problem with pluralism, however, was that it fostered chaos rather than consistency and it favored liberal tolerance over radical commitment. Pluralistic or not, feminist critical theorists generally sought (1) to counter conscious and unconscious patriarchal presuppositions, (2) to explore women's literature, and (3) to examine the biological, linguistic, psychological, social, historical, and/or political shaping forces on life, literature, and criticism. Showalter labeled the first of these tasks "feminist critique," the second "gynocritics" after the

French coinage *la gynocritique,* and the third "cultural criticism."[9] These terms quickly became common in depicting the three main critical projects of literary feminists. Not surprisingly, many feminists regarded these three endeavors as dialectically interrelated, which Josephine Donovan early made clear in the Afterword to her collection of essays by diverse hands titled *Feminist Literary Criticism: Explorations in Theory* (1975).

Many leading American feminists practiced a coordinated mode of critical analysis involving receptionist, judicial, and sociohistorical approaches to literature. Traditionally discredited, women's subjective and intuitive responses to literary texts became a means to resist the exclusions produced by purported "objective criticism" while affirming the personal commitment and sense of awakening engendered by the women's movement. The analogue to such critical receptionism was the small consciousness-raising groups fostered by the movement during its earliest days. The judicial tendency of feminist criticism revived the whole issue of aesthetic value, which had been repressed or downplayed by almost all schools of postwar criticism.[10] What made a literary work superior? inferior? valuable? worthless? On what grounds were so many women writers excluded from the canon? omitted from textbooks? consigned to the dustbin of history? When women were belatedly added to the canon, was it because they were "representative" women or great writers? The general effect of such feminist inquiries was to suggest that conventional aesthetic standards needed overhauling. Finally, the sociohistorical approach, as manifested variously in the work of Friedan, Moers, Showalter, Gilbert, Gubar, and others, not only refused to separate writing from cultural contexts, but resisted the divorce of literature from life. What all this made plain was that American feminist critical theory called into question reigning formalist doctrines while revamping affective, didactic, mimetic, and expressive theories of literature.

Many American feminist poeticians asserted that literary texts reflected the personal, social, and political realities of writers and that readers were moved and shaped by works of literature. "We do not believe," declared Josephine Donovan, "that we can separate literature from life any more than we believe that a critic can separate her/himself from her/his social, cultural and personal identity."[11] When narrowly construed, this poetic theory sometimes led to prescriptive political criteria for literature. "To earn feminist approval," proclaimed Cheri Register, "literature must perform one or more of the following functions: (1) serve as a forum for women; (2) help to achieve cultural androgyny; (3) provide role-models; (4) promote sisterhood; and (5) augment consciousness-raising" (*FLC,* 18–19). Here critical questions of aesthetic value were forgotten in a rush toward a didactic and a political poetics. When broadly conceived, a multifaceted feminist poetic led to a revisionary cultural theory of literature like that promoted by Josephine Donovan, Annette Kolodny, and Elaine Showalter, all of whom believed that literature reflected the inner and outer realities experienced by writers and that literature moved and shaped readers.

Feminist characterizations of women's literature differed on the relative importance assigned in the formation of gender identity to biology, psychology, and linguistics. Did women's biological differences engender differences in their literature? Was there a distinctive primordial female psyche? If so, did it form a distinct feminine poetry? Was there a women's language—or a special style—that rendered female writing different? Some feminist poeticians believed and some didn't that there existed a separate women's biology, psychology, and/or language, making women's literature recognizably feminine. Key texts surrounding the debates on these issues were Annette Kolodny's "Some Notes on Defining a 'Feminist Literary Criticism'" (1975), which argued against biological determinism; the essays and poems of Adrienne Rich during the early 1970s, which entertained the likelihood and the significance of a psychic "female principle" and of an original matriarchal world order; and Robin Lakoff's *Language and Woman's Place* (1975) and the collection of twenty-one essays, *Women and Language in Literature and Society* (1980), edited by Sally McConnell-Ginet, Ruth Borker, and Nelly Furman, which both investigated the distinctiveness of women's language and style. Earlier we saw that Moers and Showalter argued against a female sensibility and for a distinctive women's literary tradition while Gilbert and Gubar propounded a special feminine psychology and poetic heritage.

Whatever their disagreements on poetics and on critical theory, most Feminist Critics remained steadfast in their commitment to an "ideology" based on gender and in their dedication to a political project aimed at social change. Fearing that the growing turn to literary and critical theory would diminish political activism, Showalter, for instance, argued against any feminist criticism "abandoning in the process the political priorities and the concerns for the personal that have made it so effective in the past" ("WT," 41). Abhorring the increasing separation of successful feminist scholarship and vigilant political activity, Kolodny denounced the loss of engagement implicit in all such academic isolationism: "to include segments on 'Women in the Labor Movement' in our American studies or women's studies courses, while remaining willfully ignorant of the department secretary fired for her efforts to organize a clerical workers' union; to glory in the delusions of 'merit,' 'privilege,' and 'status' which accompany campus life in order to insulate ourselves from the millions of women who labor in poverty—all this is not merely hypocritical; it destroys both the spirit and the meaning of what we are about" ("DM," 163). Despite the early studied apoliticism of Ellmann and Spacks, the majority of Feminist Critics stayed committed to an "ideology" of gender and a politics of social transformation.

In a controversial essay, "Archimedes and the Paradox of Feminist Criticism" (1981), Myra Jehlen criticized feminist ideology and politics for being overwhelmingly separatist and consequently ineffectual. What was needed was direct engagement of the dominant male intellectual system. The woman-centered works of such critics as Spacks, Moers, Showalter, Gilbert, and Gubar were misguided in fostering adversarial political or ideological criticism instead of appreciative aesthetic criticism. To deny female dependence on male culture was both foolhardy and historically inaccurate. And to forget that truly great works of literature sometimes contained bad and inhuman ideas was to be blind to *literary* value and success. "We should begin, therefore, by acknowledging the separate wholeness of the literary subject, its distinct vision that need not be ours—what the formalists have told us and told us about: its integrity. We need to acknowledge, also, that to respect that integrity by not asking questions of the text that it does not ask itself, to ask the text what questions to ask, will produce the fullest, richest reading."[12] In order to avoid the pitfall of feminist separatism, Jehlen advised reliance on the formalist doctrine of the autonomy of the literary text and its concomitant restraints on critical reading. The main task of *all* literary criticism was aesthetic appreciation and evaluation, not ideological inquiry and political assessment.

The literary and critical issues raised by Jehlen's controversial call to formalism had been argued in the earliest days of the formation of American feminist criticism. For example, in her "Dwelling in Decencies: Radical Criticism and the Feminist Perspective" (1970), published in a groundbreaking special issue of *College English* containing eight essays presented at the 1970 forum and workshops of the Commission on the Status of Women of the Modern Language Association, Lillian Robinson observed: "Criticism has progressed so far into formalism that we have forgotten not so much that art has content but that *content* has content."[13] As far as Robinson was concerned, neither literary form, nor style, nor history were independent of content, ideology, and politics. There were no objective aesthetic standards by which to judge literary texts. No separate domain of ideas existed. Such formalist notions served ruling-class interests. High culture systematically excluded women, nonwhites, and working-class people. Thus, Feminist Critics had to study literature within a broad social realm characterized by sex, race, and class oppression. "Feminist criticism, as its name implies, is criticism with a Cause, engaged criticism. But the critical model presented to us so far is merely engaged to be married. It is about to contract what can only be a *mésalliance* with bourgeois modes of thought and the critical categories they inform. To be effective, feminist criticism cannot become simply bourgeois criticism in drag. It must be ideological and moral criticism; it must be revolutionary" (3). Recalling that formalist criticism triumphed over Marxist criticism in the 1930s, Robinson self-consciously sought a reversal of that history; she cautioned Feminist Critics about reverting to nonideological, amoral, and apolitical textualist criticism whose biased values and spurious objectivity served sexist, racist, and class interests. In Robinson's view, feminist criticism was by definition moral, ideological, revolutionary—everything formalist criticism was not.

In her Marxist critique of formalist theory, Lillian Robinson referred at one point to "the greatest bourgeois theme of all, the myth of pluralism, with its consequent rejection of ideological commitment as 'too simple' to embrace the (necessarily complex) truth" (11). Whereas liberal feminists advocated theoretical pluralism, radical feminists championed a separatist ideological criticism while socialist feminists called for engaged political criticism attentive to race and class as well as sex. Conservatives wanted nothing to do with any ideological or political programs for feminist criticism. Some moderates, like Ellmann and Spacks, tried to avoid politics.

For all its diversity and contradictions on matters of critical theory, poetics, and politics, American feminist theory and practice from the outset in the early seventies displayed a characteristic toughness of spirit: it generally did without sentimentality, nostalgia, and deference, though it was sometimes defiantly personal. Feminist Critics were broadly discontent with patriarchal civilization and often worked angrily toward reform and occasionally toward revolution. They regarded formalism as an unworldly and unworthy sterile form of passivity devoid of moral and political force in the face of male cultural hegemony. Even though "the full conjoining of feminist literary criticism and politics has yet to be done," as Catharine Stimpson observed,[14] Feminist intellectuals persisted in such an effort from the start, as was clear in the early works of Millett, Robinson, and numerous others. While they eroded the classical rationales for producing lucid, economical, and elegant prose, Feminist Critics very rarely bothered with stylistic innovation, preferring revisionary work on the matter rather than the manner of patriarchal discourse. Feminist literary critics maintained a special solidarity with feminist academics in many other disciplines, with women's studies students of varying ages, and with sympathetic journalists, writers, and artists of different backgrounds. Finally, the women's movement engendered and sought to preserve a tangible *esprit de corps* characteristic of people sharing a special awakening and a similar calling.

FRENCH PSYCHOANALYTICAL THEORY: *L'ÉCRITURE FÉMININE*

Starting in the late 1970s, American Feminist Critics became increasingly interested in feminist theory produced in France after 1968. Special issues of journals testified to this interest: "Textual Politics: Feminist Criticism," *Diacritics* (Winter 1975); Elaine Marks' "Women and Literature in France" and Carolyn Greenstein Burke's "Report from Paris," *Signs* (Summer 1978); "Feminist Issue," *Enclitic* (Fall 1980); "Versions/Feminisms': A Stance of One's Own," *SubStance,* no. 32 (1981); "Feminist Readings: French Texts/American Contexts," *Yale French Studies,* no. 62 (1981); "French Feminist Theory," *Signs* (Autumn 1981); "Cherchez La Femme: Feminist Critique/Feminine Text," *Diacritics* (Summer 1982); "L'Écriture féminine," *Contemporary Literature* (Summer 1983); and "On Feminine Writing," *Boundary 2* (Winter 1984). A number of French-reading American critics served as key mediators in this process of transmission, including particularly Verena Andermatt Conley, Shoshana Felman, Jane Gallop, Alice Jardine, Peggy Kamuf, Elaine Marks, Nancy Miller, and Gayatri Chakravorty Spivak, not to mention dozens of translators. Several texts played an important role, especially *New French Feminisms: An Anthology* (1980), eds. Elaine Marks and Isabelle de Courtivron, and *The Future of Difference* (1980), eds. Hester Eisenstein and Alice Jardine. It was clear from all these sources that certain French feminists were of genuine interest to Americans, namely Hélène Cixous, Luce Irigaray, and Julia Kristeva, some of whose most important works were available in translation by the mid-eighties.

Whereas American Feminist Critics usually investigated women's experience and history, leading French feminist writers typically examined the construction of the "feminine" in language, philosophy, psychoanalysis, and other systems of discourse. Influenced by poststructuralism, especially by certain of Lacan's works, Cixous and others theorized an *écriture fémi-nine*—a utopian practice of avant-garde writing, pioneered by such writers as Mallarmé, Joyce, Artaud, and Duras—which subverted the linguistic and metaphysical conventions of Western discourse. Associated sometimes with the special powers of the feminine psyche, "feminine writing" disrupted the silences engendered by the repressive phallocentric system; it emerged as a radical form of *difference*. Not surprisingly, the style of some French femi-nists seemed "surrealistic" to many American intellectuals trained in the tradition of commonsense exegetical criticism. Characterizing the main difference between American empirical and French theoretical modes of feminism, Elaine Showalter in "Feminist Criticism in the Wilderness" observed: "French feminist criticism, essentially psychoanalytic, stresses repression; American feminist criticism, essentially textual, stresses expres-sion" (249).

According to Alice Jardine, there were three areas of significant difference between American feminist criticism and French "gynesis."[15] First, Ameri-can critics took into serious account the sex of authors; French gynesic critics, in the wake of the (post)structuralists' "death of the self," dismissed the empirical author as a locus of fruitful inquiry. Second, native critics regularly scrutinized images of women, gender stereotypes, and fictional characters—all elements of literary mimesis; French analysts abjured mime-sis, regarding images, types, and characters as mere tropes or effects of language. (It's worth noting that many American Feminist Critics centered inquiry on realistic literature.) Third, American critics sought the "truth" in or behind literary works; French intellectuals, seeing the relation between truth and fiction as undecidable, dismissed as illusory the humanistic search for truth. What subverted the "subject," "representation," and "truth" was precisely "woman," as the history of Western symbolic thought made clear. The "feminine," which historically signified otherness, alterity, the un-spoken, the unconscious, was identified by gynesic critics with disruptive *writing (écriture)* rather than with people of the female sex. Such French critics as Cixous and Kristeva were "antifeminist" because the basic prem-ises of feminism depended on humanistic distribution of clear and decidable sexual identities cast into binary opposition—male/female. Escaping this essentializing dialectic required demolishing its pernicious premises. "For these women, feminism is hopelessly anachronistic, grounded in a (male) metaphysical logic . . ." (64). Significantly, some gynesic critics tried to overcome sexual binarism by recourse to a third term—bisexuality or androgeny—which a number of American feminists sought to do also.

In *New French Feminisms,* Elaine Marks and Isabelle de Courtivron described American feminist criticism as "empirical, inductive, anti-speculative" and French gynesis as Marxist and psychoanalytical extensions of "the death of God, the death of man, the death of the privileged work of art."[16] In addition, they noted that French feminists more vigorously than Americans attacked male systems, values, and misogyny. Lastly, they pointed out the tendency of French intellectuals to form distinct ideological groups and salons, as in the cases of Kristeva and the "Tel Quel" group and Cixous and the "politique et psychanalyse" collective which established its own newspaper, publishing house, and bookstore. What they omitted mentioning was the acceptance by French critics, unlike the revision by Americans, of the traditional canons of male literature.

As Showalter observed, French feminist work was "essentially psychoanalytical." Cixous, Irigaray, and Kristeva were heavily indebted to Lacan's concept of the Imaginary, which served as a starting point for their own speculations about the position of the feminine in Western philosophical discourse.[17] In Lacanian psychoanalysis, the Imaginary referred to the pre-Oedipal period of child development when separations between the self and the mother and the self and the world had not yet occurred. In the Imaginary all was identity and presence. The Oedipal crisis marked the entry into the Symbolic Order when psychological differentiation of self and Other, language acquisition, and the unconscious first emerged. This moment of "primary repression" entailed not only loss of unity with the Mother and the world, but also association with the Law of the Father and the phallus. To stay in the Imaginary was to be psychotic. To enter the Symbolic Order was to open the self not simply to society, language, and the unconscious, but to loss, alienation, and desire. In *The Newly Born Woman* (1975; trans. 1986) and elsewhere, Cixous portrayed a utopian primeval realm of feminine creativity and imagination, free from difference, discord, and binary sexuality, linked ultimately with the voice of the Mother—the source of feminine writing. A similar feminist version of the Imaginary appeared in Luce Irigaray's *Speculum of the Other Woman* (1974; trans. 1985) in her chapter titled "La mystérique" (the "mystic/hysterical woman"), which examined female mysticism. Entailing the loss of subjectivity (a masculinized state), the ecstasy of the orgasmic mystic state returned abject women to a powerful imaginary realm from which they could speak a special discourse. This space of femininity offered escape from the impositions of patriarchy. Derived from Lacan's concepts of the Imaginary and the Symbolic Order, Kristeva's distinction between the "semiotic" and the "symbolic" portrayed the "semiotic" as a pre-Oedipal domain of primary drives and processes associated with a bisexual fantasmatic Mother and with literary "genotexts"—revolutionary and avant-garde writings.

The impact on American feminist criticism of such French theories was most apparent with Psychoanalytical Critics. For example, in the Preface to *The (M)other Tongue: Essays in Feminist Psychoanalytic Interpretation* (1985), the three American editors declared: "It makes a difference, we maintain, where one stands as reader as well as writer, and whether one constructs or responds to a mother-based or a father-based fiction. On the whole, Oedipally organized narrative (as well as interpretation) that is based on the determining role of the father and of patriarchal discourse tells a different story from pre-Oedipal narrative, which locates the source of movement and conflict in the figure of the mother."[18] Here a design for a distinctively feminine poetics and hermeneutics was initiated, using Lacanian feminist insights. But the possibility of a pre-Oedipal, mother-centered polysexual feminine writing, a utopian possibility promoted by gynesic critics, stirred American cultural critics, particularly sociologists, into opposition. Leading British feminists, many of whom were Marxists, were the first to raise objections, as was the case, for example, in Juliet Mitchell's widely read *Psychoanalysis and Feminism* (1974) and her later *Women: The Longest Revolution* (1984). "Any discourse phallicizes," declared the American Jane Gallop in *The Daughter's Seduction: Feminism and Psychoanalysis* (1982),[19] which suggested that to write was to enter inescapably the flawed phallocentric Symbolic Order. Writing from a realm like the Imaginary was impossible.

The view of pre-Oedipal sexuality held by many American feminists was formed by the psychoanalytical sociologist Nancy Chodorow in her influential *The Reproduction of Mothering: Psychoanalysis and the Sociology of Gender* (1978). In her (non-Lacanian) Freudian-Marxist account, the pre-Oedipal state of identification with the mother was experienced differently by male and female children. Whereas males in Western societies were encouraged early to seek differentiation and autonomy, females remained embedded in primary love and dependence with their mothers well into adulthood. As a result, sexual relations for adult heterosexual women entailed primary emotional attachment to mothers and secondary erotic relations with men: "women have different and more complex relational needs in which an exclusive relationship to a man is not enough."[20] Chodorow was ambivalent about all this. On the one hand, women had richer and more diverse psychic lives. On the other hand, the asymmetrical Oedipal experience of boys and girls created later frustrations in heterosexual relationships and families. As a Marxist, Chodorow wanted sexual equality, which ultimately led her to recommend equal parenting (mothering) by men and women as a way to redress the overdependence of their daughters and the inflexible independence of their sons—both of which traits furthered the patriarchal organization and division of labor necessary for industrial capitalist society. In short, while certain French theorists portrayed pre-Oedipal identification with the Mother as a utopian mode of radical polysexual femininity (a kind of lesbianism), Chodorow ultimately disallowed such a separatist fantasy on the grounds that it furthered regressive political and economic ends.

The gynesic criticism propounded by Cixous, Irigaray, and others did not go unquestioned in France. Written by the editorial collective, the lead article in the newly formed French feminist quarterly *Questions féministes* (established 1977), edited by Simone de Beauvoir, declared: "Under the pretext that we are 'women,' 'different,' we are prevented from fully leading the life of free and independent individuals. It is the patriarchal system which posits that we are 'different' in order to justify and conceal our exploitation. It is the patriarchal system which prescribes the idea of a feminine 'nature' and 'essence.'"[21] For all its sophistication, the utopian concept of a pre-Oedipal bisexual realm, linked with femininity and/or the Mother, partook of the patriarchal idea of essential "womanhood" and "feminine difference." The feminists associated with *Questions féministes* resisted opposing to the phallocentric psychosocial order a separate utopian hysterocentric realm. Similar resistance to the idea of a unique *écriture féminine* came from many Anglo-American feminists, including Gallop, Jones, Jehlen, Mitchell, Showalter, and Spivak. Carolyn Heilbrun generalized this resistance to feminist separation: "I suggest that we resolve not to limit ourselves to modes hitherto only female, whether these be semiotic, pre-Oedipal, cultural, maternal, or lesbian."[22]

THE INSTITUTION OF WOMEN'S STUDIES

Just as the black power movement brought about the establishment of black studies programs and the students' movement fostered the growth of free universities and experimental colleges, so the women's movement led to the creation of university courses and programs in women's studies. By 1975 there were 150 such programs; by 1980 another 150 had emerged; and by 1985 yet an additional 150 had appeared. These 450 programs were offering approximately 30,000 courses annually, of which roughly 3,000 were focused on literature. Of the seventy-odd divisions of the Modern Language Association set up in 1975 (1975 membership—30,000), the Division of Women's Studies in Language and Literature ranked in the top five in terms of size, with over 2,000 members. In September 1970, San Diego State College put in place a ten-course curriculum of women's studies, which was the first officially established integrated program in the nation. In December 1970, the newly formed Commission on the Status of Women of the MLA collected sixty-six course outlines and bibliographies on women's studies and published them in *Female Studies II*, edited by Florence Howe, the chairwoman of the Commission. Founded in 1977, the National Women's Studies Association signaled the culmination of early feminist efforts to institute across the nation this new domain of research and inquiry.[23] In their books, Fetterley, Gilbert and Gubar, Spacks, and others testified passionately to intimate connections between their research and their teaching of women's studies.

Although some *departments* of women's studies were established and some *graduate* curricula eventually created, the vast majority of women's studies programs were interdepartmental networks designed for undergraduate concentrations and majors. In this they resembled the American Studies programs set up in the immediate postwar period. The favorite methodology was interdisciplinary and historical; the preferred classroom pedagogy, when possible, involved small groups engaged in personal interactions modeled after feminist consciousness-raising collectives. The immediate goals included not only criticizing and compensating for patriarchal oppression, but also collecting materials and constructing traditions as a means of creating new conceptualizations of women. The long-range goal was to change the male bias of both university curricula and social practices. Not surprisingly, there were from the outset internal as well as external criticisms of women's studies programs.

In a 1973 essay, Catharine Stimpson isolated five different ideological groups within feminist scholarship. At odds with one another were "pioneers," "ideologues," "radicals," "latecomers," and "bandwagoneers." Stimpson hoped that a national organization would solidify the various contending communities of feminist scholars and teachers.[24] Perhaps the main external critique of women's studies was that such programs were political entities interested more in ideology and consciousness-raising than in scholarship and learning. The feminist response entailed both numerous critiques of self-interested patriarchal ideology and massive outpourings of academic scholarship. To retain existing curricula, argued feminists, was as "political" as seeking to change them.[25] To the extent that feminist scholarship examined questions of historical fact, interpretation, and value, its practitioners were engaged in traditional academic pursuits. The long-range goal to transform society (more than the short-range efforts to alter the structure of knowledge and the university) stirred overt criticism from opponents of women's studies. Two supplementary features provoked special antagonism: (1) the commitment of many programs to formal outreach work with women's counseling centers, rape crisis centers, and activist community groups, and (2) the growing feminist dedication to studying racism, homophobia, and class oppression as well as sexism. Neither community activism nor sympathetic interests in colonialism, lesbianism, and class struggle were considered proper academic pursuits by some opponents of women's studies.[26]

Within the MLA the presence of the women's movement manifested itself in various ways. In addition to the Commission on the Status of Women and the Division of Women's Studies in Language and Literature, the MLA formed within its Delegate Assembly a special interest group called Women in the Profession; it granted affiliate status to the Women's Caucus for the Modern Languages; and it published between 1975 and 1985 a dozen monographs and books on behalf of the Commission on the Status of Women. During the period from 1956 to 1970, one woman, Marjorie Nicolson, had served as president of the Association. But during the years from 1971 to 1985 seven women occupied this prestigious position—Florence Howe (1973), Germaine Brée (1975), Edith Kern (1977), Jean Perkins (1979), Helen Vendler (1980), Mary Ann Caws (1983), and Carolyn Heilbrun (1984). Half of these leaders were involved with women's studies. Of the twelve members of the Executive Council in 1985, five were women and three of these were feminists—Elaine Marks, Mary Louise Pratt, and Catharine Stimpson. The five members of the Executive Committee of the Division on Literary Criticism in 1985 were Sandra Gilbert, Barbara Johnson, Michael Riffaterre, Susan Suleiman, and Jane Tompkins. It was mainly MLA women who agitated successfully in the late seventies for a policy of "blind submission" to the Association's influential journal *PMLA*. This change followed upon a study showing a tendency of manuscript reviewers to rate more highly works and résumés assumed to be from men rather than women.

As the women's studies movement was spreading and the MLA was changing, new feminist journals, textbooks, and series were coming into being. Among leading American academic journals were *Women's Studies* (founded 1972), *Feminist Studies* (1972), *Women's Studies Newsletter* (1972) (it became the organ of the National Women's Studies Association in 1977 and changed its name in 1981 to *Women's Studies Quarterly*), *Signs: Journal of Women in Culture and Society* (1975), *Feminist Issues* (1980), and *Women's Review of Books* (1983). Early representative anthologies published in one year included *By a Woman Writ: Literature from Six Centuries by and about Women* (1973), ed. Joan Goulianos; *Images of Women in Literature* (1973), ed. Mary Anne Ferguson; *American Voices, American Women* (1973), eds. Lee R. Edwards and Arlyn Diamond; *No More Masks! An Anthology of Poems by Women* (1973), eds. Florence Howe and Ellen Bass; and *Fragments from a Lost Diary and Other Stories: Women of Asia, Africa, and Latin America* (1973), eds. Naomi Katz and Nancy Milton. Influential pedagogical texts were Jo Freeman's *Women: A Feminist Perspective* (1975), Esther Stineman's *Women's Studies: A Recommended Core Bibliography* (1979), and Gloria Bowles' and Renate Duelli Klein's *Theories of Women's Studies* (1980). Important series were early published by KNOW, Inc. (founded 1969) and the Feminist Press (1970), both of which shared responsibility for the ten pioneering volumes of *Female Studies* (1969–76), which offered exemplary syllabi, reading lists, and practitioners' reflections on the pedagogy of women's studies. Later, university and commercial presses undertook women's studies publications, including Chicago, Columbia, Cornell, Illinois, Indiana, Massachusetts, Michigan, and Rutgers, as well as Arno, Burt Franklin, and Garland presses.

The assault on the male-biased canon of standard literary texts mounted by feminist scholarship and criticism came from three main directions. To begin with, adherents of feminist critique uncovered pernicious images of women and sexist stereotypes, calling into question the stature, morality, and universality of major male authors. The work of Millett and Fetterley was representative of this endeavor. Secondly, gynocritics restored lost, neglected, and undervalued women's texts, showing the continuity and power of female literary traditions and redressing the age-old imbalance and overestimation of the masculinist canon. Exemplary critical texts here were those by Moers, Gilbert and Gubar, and Showalter. Numerous anthologies of women's literature paralleled such critical efforts. Finally, feminist critical and pedagogical theorists developed sophisticated instruments and practices to further the ideological criticism and classroom teaching essential to the research and development empowering the institution of women's studies programs. Influential in this regard were both the cultural criticism elaborated by such figures as Kolodny, Robinson, Showalter, and Spivak and the pedagogical work pioneered by such leaders as Howe, Rich, Showalter, and Stimpson.

In the realm of pedagogy, Rich and Showalter each produced during the early years a handful of widely read essays, as Marilyn Boxer documented in her account of the rise of women's studies in the seventies. More than Showalter's pragmatism, Rich's utopianism, particularly in her collection, *On Lies, Secrets, and Silence: Selected Prose 1966–1978* (1979), lambasted the oppressiveness of masculinist and compulsory heterosexual education, opening for consideration the future possibilities of transformed educational systems. Stimpson's contributions to the pedagogy and prominence of women's studies included (1) dozens of uncollected succinct articles and reviews, the latter often published in nonacademic outlets like *Ms., The Nation, The New Republic,* and *New York Times Book Review;* (2) the founding and editing for six years of *Signs: Journal of Women in Culture and Society* (published quarterly by the University of Chicago), the leading periodical in women's studies; (3) the successful solicitation of grants for *Signs* from major donors, including the Ford, Exxon, Lilly, and Rockefeller Foundations; and (4) active consulting and committee work with the MLA, the National Endowment for the Humanities, the U.S. Office of Education, the Educational Testing Service, the National Public Radio, and UNESCO. Moving out from her academic literary base, Stimpson was able successfully to link the emerging women's studies with influential nonacademic and/or nonliterary periodicals, foundations, and agencies. However difficult to assess, the effect of this kind of work made it easier for nonfeminist university intellectuals and administrators to support the institutionalization of women's studies.

Within academic literary circles the earliest prominent impresario of women's studies was Florence Howe. As first chair of the MLA Commission on the Status of Women, cofounder of Feminist Press, president of the MLA, author of important essays later collected in *Myths of Coeducation* (1984), consultant to numerous agencies and universities, editor of *Women's Studies Newsletter* (1972 to present), and early editor of pedagogical materials, Howe functioned as a pioneer in the field. At the 1970 MLA Convention, the Commission on the Status of Women distributed free of charge a list of 110 women's studies courses, edited by Howe and Carol Ahlum and published by KNOW, Inc., titled *A Guide to Women's Studies.* In October 1971, they edited *The New Guide to Current Female Studies,* published for the Commission by KNOW, Inc., listing 524 courses at 188 institutions. The next year they edited *The Guide to Current Female Studies II*, published by the Clearinghouse on Women's Studies of the Feminist Press, adding 344 new courses at 135 other institutions as well as naming forty-five programs in existence or formation. Howe's Feminist Press published *Female Studies*, numbers 6, 7, and 10 in 1972, 1973, and 1976, respectively, and *Who's Who and Where in Women Studies* (1974), edited by Tamar Berkowitz and others and funded by the Ford Foundation. All of this early material not only documented but facilitated the development and expansion of women's studies by distributing bibliographies and course outlines and by fostering new programs and scholarly networks. Several years later Howe engaged in reviewing the state of the new field first in her report to the National Advisory Council on Women's Educational Programs titled *Seven Years Later: Women's Studies Programs in 1976* (1977), funded by the federal government, and then in her and Paul Lauter's *The Impact of Women's Studies on the Campus and the Disciplines* (1980), undertaken for the National Institute of Education. Among feminist literary critics, Howe was one of the most active and visible in helping to enable, publicize, and assess women's studies programs.

Not until 1976 did the majority of women's studies curricula become structured in order to offer majors and minors to undergraduate students. Up until then, they were add-ons or supplements to other programs. This was the point at which the critical restorations of the female literary tradition, undertaken by gynocritics, started to appear in print. It was also the moment when plans were finalized for setting up the National Women's Studies Association. This turning point in the movement was marked in Howe's career by a shift from interest in establishing to reviewing programs of women's studies.

Guiding Howe's thinking and writing was an underlying cultural poetics common to many leading American Feminist Critics. Speaking in 1976, Howe declared, "the critic, the writer, and their audience—all are rooted in their biographies and historical circumstances. Art is neither anonymous nor universal; it springs from the particulars of gender as well as class, race, age, and cultural experience." Succinctly, she stated, "I do not think literature is, was, or ever can be pure, that is, disengaged from its place in history."[27] Not surprisingly, Howe urged feminist scholars and teachers to include in their research and their programs relevant materials about class and race as well as sex. She recommended in *Seven Years Later* that the government supply funds to help create teaching materials on Hispanic, Black, Asian-American, Appalachian, and Native-American women, particularly from the working class. Such material would help "to avoid replicating in women's studies the errors of white, middle-class, male-centered curricula."[28]

Looking back in 1979 over a decade of feminist scholarship, Howe observed:

In the past ten years, we have helped to build a body of knowledge about women and gender significant enough to suggest an epistemological shift qualitatively and quantitatively comparable to the nineteenth century's shift from theology to science. Like our nineteenth-century forefathers, we are also shifting the object of study, even as we are making the lenses of study a new issue.[29]

Institutionalized in hundreds of women's studies programs across the nation, revolutionary feminist work constituted a paradigm shift. What role could men play in this epochal shift away from androcentric oppression of women? "Can men come to this understanding? Of course. Though they may not be able to replicate female experience, men can understand and study its existence. Provided they are alert to the differences between their experiences and those of women, men can develop a feminist perspective."[30] Howe had reason to know because she had worked with Paul Lauter since the late sixties on many feminist projects, including cofounding the Feminist Press and writing several books together. If Lauter was the first American male feminist literary critic, others followed in his footsteps. During the early eighties quite a few men expressed sympathy for and sometimes commitment to feminism, including Wayne Booth, Jonathan Culler, Terry Eagleton, Lawrence Lipking, and Robert Scholes, to name only five prominent academic literary critics. The shift in epistemological paradigm was clearly relevant to all intellectuals.

In 1976 a controversy flared in the pages of *Critical Inquiry* between Annette Kolodny and William Morgan about the "problem" of "male feminism." Morgan, a "feminist," argued that the revolutionary implications of feminist literary study could not be limited to women scholars. He found unacceptable Kolodny's separatism in her 1975 essay, "Some Notes on Defining a 'Feminist Literary Criticism.'" Kolodny responded that "the presence of the male professor as intellectual authority figure and potential role model, especially in the Women's Studies or Women Writers classroom, could surely be detrimental. . . . As Virginia Woolf so well understood, women need a room of their own; in some instances, that may mean a classroom."[31] Unlike Howe, Kolodny erected posted signs around women's studies. A decade later, Alice Jardine, in a special issue of *Critical*

Exchange on "Men in Feminism," took a similar stance: "I think that you—our male allies—should issue a moratorium on talking about feminism/women/femininity/female sexuality/feminine identity/etc."[32] This gag order was confirmed by another contributor when she observed, "men are carriers of the patriarchal mode" (41). Here a radical feminist position, rooted in a separatist and essentializing ideology, cast the project of women's studies in an exclusionary mode—paradoxically the very mode that both explosively energized and inherently limited the reach and influence of women's studies.

Following upon the numerous liberal and radical activities and movements of the Vietnam era, a conservative backlash began to emerge and coalesce in the seventies. Symbolized in the eighties by the triumphs of Ronald Reagan at the polls and by the successes of the Christian fundamentalist Moral Majority in the courts, state houses, and media, the gradual rise to prominence and power of the political right posed threats to all the political wings of the women's movement—whether liberal, socialist, radical, or revolutionary.[33] Widely contested were the recently won legal rights of women to obtain abortions, to secure equal pay at work, and to receive affirmative action protection from the government. Numerous groups of rightist women increasingly protested the whole women's movement and all its various gains. Antifeminist women's works, like Midge Decter's *The New Chastity and Other Arguments against Women's Liberation* (1972), Arianna Stassinopoulas' *The Female Woman* (1973), and especially Betty Friedan's *The Second Stage* (1981), undermined the ideological grounds of women's studies, exacerbating the internal political differences within the women's movement while simultaneously suggesting the need for solidarity and continued political activism. Increasingly, feminists inside and outside the university found themselves on the defensive rather than the offensive. Despite the successes of women's studies, many programs never did secure adequate and stable institutional allocations of faculty, staff, library resources, research grants, office space, and essential equipment. In the eighties the future of programs in women's studies seemed precarious in view of the conservative backlash across the nation, the growing ranks of outspoken antifeminist women on the political right, and the uncertain financial and administrative support systems within universities. Nevertheless, feminist scholarship flourished and women's studies programs proliferated.

CHAPTER TWELVE

Black Aesthetics

THE BLACK LIBERATION MOVEMENT
IN THE SPACE AGE

DATING FROM colonial times, the history of black people in North America involved slavery, oppression, and struggle. When the United States broke with England during the revolutionary era, the quarter of the population that was black was not covered by the Declaration of Independence or the Constitution. From the early days of the founding of the Republic, growing numbers of black and white people agitated for the abolition of slavery. During pre-Civil War times some black leaders, like Martin R. Delany, advocated black nationalism while others, like Frederick Douglass, recommended social reform and integration. It was in this period that pioneering American blacks migrated to Haiti and others founded Liberia. Later, in the World War I era, Marcus Garvey promoted black independence in Africa while Booker T. Washington believed that full citizenship of blacks in America should be earned gradually by hard work, vocational education, and moral improvement. Taking issue with Washington's conciliatory program, W. E. B. Du Bois demanded redress from white America, militantly urging immediate political enfranchisement as a means to economic and educational progress. Like Garvey, Du Bois promoted Pan-Africanism; his last years were spent in Ghana. These different political programs—conciliation and integration, militant reform and redress, and nationalism and African freedom, all rooted in nineteenth-century black American history—surfaced forcefully during the black liberation movement spanning the years from the mid-1950s to the early 1970s.

There were two main phases of the postwar struggle for black liberation: (1) the civil rights movement dating from 1954 to 1964 and (2) the black power movement lasting from 1964 to 1973. The year after the landmark

Brown versus Board of Education decision was rendered in 1954 by the Supreme Court, making public school segregation illegal, Rosa Parks was arrested in Montgomery, Alabama, for illegally refusing to take a seat in the back of a city bus. A city-wide, year-long black boycott of the bus line and the contemporaneous creation of the Montgomery Improvement Association headed by Martin Luther King, Jr., initiated acts of nonviolent civil disobedience and political organizing, which would characterize the movement for a decade to come. Institutionalized in the Southern Christian Leadership Conference founded in 1957, King's Christian-inspired liberal integrationist philosophy would reach its peak of publicity and persuasiveness in 1963 in his famous "I Have a Dream" speech delivered during the massive March on Washington, and in 1964 in his obtaining the Nobel Peace Prize. At this point the historic Civil Rights Act of 1964 was enacted by Congress. A year later the Voting Rights Act was signed into law. In the meantime, several significant events had occurred. Early in 1960, four black college students staged a prolonged sit-in at a segregated Woolworth's store and were soon joined by other students. Over the next few months dozens and dozens of similar sit-in demonstrations were held throughout the South. By the end of the year the black student movement formed the Student Nonviolent Coordinating Committee—a group that during the next year agitated for integration by launching a Freedom Ride, ending in the arrest and imprisonment of several dozen peaceful protesters. The first such Freedom Ride, lasting two weeks and ending in violence, was undertaken in May 1961 by thirteen black and white people under the sponsorship of the Congress of Racial Equality. The idea was to challenge segregation laws at interstate bus terminals, which in September 1961 were finally desegregated by the Interstate Commerce Commission. What characterized the decade-long civil rights movement were widespread and growing resistance to segregation, the formation of activist nonviolent organizations, the philosophy of racial integrationism, and significant victories registered in the courts and in the mass media.

Having the right to eat in restaurants with and ride busses with white people did not measurably improve the economic or political situation of black people. Life in large urban ghettos as well as small rural towns remained miserable for large numbers of blacks. Despite gains in civil rights, urban riots broke out in many Northern cities. The Watts riot in Los Angeles during August 1965 came to symbolize black discontent and rage, which existing civil rights organizations and philosophies could not channel. During the years from 1966 to 1968, Martin Luther King launched

Poor People's Campaigns as a way to protest the economic plight of black people. However, his previous coalition of white liberals, black middle-class activists, and the black poor fell apart, signaling a new phase in the struggle for black liberation. It was during this period that the calls for black power made by Malcolm X, Adam Clayton Powell, Jr., Stokely Carmichael, and others fell on receptive ears. The earlier method of nonviolence and the previous goal of integration both seemed increasingly untenable. Inspired by anticolonial movements in the Carribbean, Latin America, Asia, and especially Africa, new leaders called for black nationalism and sometimes for revolution. Pride in negritude, marked visibly by the growing popularity of African names, dress, and hairstyles, manifested itself in an increasingly radical politics, symbolized memorably by the formation of the Black Panther Party in 1966 and by the black power salutes of two American athletes receiving Olympic medals in 1968. What distinguished the decade of the black power movement from the earlier decade of the civil rights movement were the dramatic turns to separatism and nationalism rather than integrationism as political goals, to riots, armed resistance, and revolution rather than nonviolence and passive resistance as methods, to the black lower class and poor people rather than the black and white middle classes as activist constituencies, and to racial pride, negritude, and Africanism rather than white Euro-American conventions and norms as standards of value.

During the period of the black liberation movement in America, a rebirth—a "New Renaissance"—occurred in black arts, including poetry, drama, fiction, and literary criticism.[1] It was especially during the days of the black power movement that black criticism took on a new urgency and vigor, as, for instance, in the work of the writer-critics Amiri Baraka and Larry Neal, the editor Hoyt Fuller, and the academic critics Addison Gayle, Jr., Stephen Henderson, and Darwin T. Turner. During the seventies and the eighties, two noteworthy phenomena occurred. First, a younger generation of black critics emerged, as was evident in the contributions of Houston A. Baker, Jr., and Henry Louis Gates, Jr. Second, a distinctive black feminism came to the fore, notably in the critical works of, among others, the writers Toni Cade Bambara, Mari Evans, Audre Lorde, and Alice Walker as well as the academic critics Barbara Christian, Gloria T. Hull, Barbara Smith, Erlene Stetson, and Mary Helen Washington. Finally, much energy was expended in scholarship and pedagogy centered around the institutionalization of black studies programs, which first began to appear in the late sixties and which preoccupied university intellectuals well into the eighties.

THE BLACK AESTHETIC

When, in June 1964, Malcolm X founded the Organization of Afro-American Unity (modeled after the Organization of African Unity established in May 1963 in Ethiopia), he drafted a "Statement of Basic Aims and Objectives" that declared: "We must launch a cultural revolution to unbrainwash an entire people. Our cultural revolution must be the means of bringing us closer to our African brothers and sisters. It must begin in the community and be based on community participation. Afro-Americans will be free to create only when they can depend on the Afro-American community for support and Afro-American artists must realize that they depend on the Afro-American for inspiration."[2] Perceiving a growing and debilitating political, economic, social, and cultural fragmentation among American black people, Malcolm X sought to unite blacks in a nonreligious and nonsectarian organization militantly devoted to freedom from oppression and to black solidarity. He opposed integration as a political goal, instead seeking cultural autonomy based on the brotherhood of all people of African descent. In his view, black artists emerged from and were responsible to the black community. The standards for all black arts were rooted in and derived from black communal life. White Euro-American aesthetics were not relevant to black people in this most influential and representative philosophy of black power.

Among those literary intellectuals promoting a distinctively Black Aesthetic from the mid-sixties to the early seventies was Hoyt W. Fuller, the highly respected editor of *Negro Digest* (renamed *Black World* in 1970) and the mentor of the Chicago-based Organization of Black American Culture, which convened weekly workshops of black artists among whom were such leaders as Gwendolyn Brooks and Don L. Lee. In his "Towards a Black Aesthetic" (1968), Fuller explicitly linked the project to found a Black Aesthetic with the black power movement, observing the "black revolt is as palpable in letters as it is in the streets."[3] As far as Fuller and others were concerned, the situation of the black populace in America amounted to internal colonialism. Between the races stood "high, thick dividing walls which hate and history have erected" (585). To achieve unity and strength within the black community, black people needed to recover and revere their distinctive cultural roots: "the road to solidarity and strength leads inevitably through reclamation and indoctrination of black art and culture" (587). What was needed was a "mystique of blackness" free from the influence of white racist cultural values. Fuller celebrated the distinctive styles, rhythms, and techniques of black music and black language, which reflected the special character and imperatives of black experience. Despite his tone of affirmation, he revealed doubts about the project of developing a Black Aesthetic. "The road to that place—if it exists at all—cannot, by definition, lead through the literary mainstreams" (582). What was essential in "this delicate and dangerous experiment is the emergence of new black critics who will be able to articulate and expound the new aesthetic and eventually set in motion the long overdue assault against the restrictive assumptions of the white critics" (587).

Like Fuller, the poet and editor Larry Neal linked the emerging black arts movement with the black power movement. In a widely read essay of the period, "The Black Arts Movement" (1968), Neal reviewed the nascent efforts of new black artists both to break away from the dominant (white) artistic modes and to pioneer African-based modes of creativity. He regarded the Afro-American community as part of the burgeoning colonial Third World in search of lost native traditions—not only in social, economic, and political organization, but also in mythology, history, culture, and ethos. Without a distinctive culture, a colonial people constituted a set of reactions to its oppressors. Derived from Frantz Fanon and Ron Karenga, this cultural theory called for jettisoning mainstream standards and developing anew previously denigrated ethnic artistic modes and traditions. In this light, the celebrated Harlem Renaissance of the early interwar period was a failure.

It did not address itself to the mythology and the life-styles of the Black community. It failed to take roots, to link itself concretely to the struggles of that community, to become its voice and spirit. Implicit in the Black Arts Movement is the idea that Black people, however dispersed, constitute a *nation* within the belly of white America. This is not a new idea. Garvey said it and the Honorable Elijah Muhammed says it now. And it is on this idea that the concept of Black Power is predicated.[4]

In the realm of aesthetics, the regressive philosophy of integration required adopting mainstream practices and relinquishing native ones whereas the progressive philosophy of nationalism—whether derived from Pan-African political programs, or Black Muslim religious ideas, or Third World revolutionary projects—recommended respecting indigenous ways of life and art while disregarding imposed, alien ones. Stokely Carmichael, chairman of the Student Nonviolent Coordinating Committee and coauthor of *Black Power* (1967), put it plainly: "what must be abolished is not the black community, but the dependent colonial status that has been inflicted upon it. The social and cultural personality of the black community must be preserved and the community must win its freedom while preserving its cultural integrity. This is the essential difference between integration as it is currently practiced and the concept of Black Power."[5] Politics and aesthetics—black power and black arts—went hand in hand.

Larry Neal personally attempted to anchor the emerging Black Aesthetic in a ritualistic theory of art reminiscent of the myth critic Francis Fergusson. In his Afterword to *Black Fire: An Anthology of Afro-American Writing* (1968), edited by LeRoi Jones and himself, he cast black music as the fundamental primordial form of black expression. He wanted black poetry to eschew textualism and to return to ritualistic oral performance: "Poets must learn to sing, dance and chant their works, tearing into the substance of their individual and collective experiences. We must make literature move people to a deeper understanding of what this thing is all about, be a kind of priest, a black magician, working juju with the word on the world" (655). As far as Neal was concerned, written literature was an elite Western form irrelevant to the mass of black folks. "The text could be destroyed and no one would be hurt in the least by it" (653). Since the springs of authentic black art were communal music and oral folktale, the new art had to return to these sources so as to become an integral part of contemporary black life. The broad context for the emerging Black Aesthetic was the decadent and antihuman Western world. "The white world—the West—is seen now as a dying creature, totally bereft of spirituality. This being the case, the only hope is some kind of psychic withdrawal from its values and assumptions" (648).

No black artist of the period did more to promote and publicize the project for a Black Aesthetic than LeRoi Jones, who changed his "slave name" in 1968 to the Muslim name Ameer Baraka (Blessed Prince) and then in 1970 to the Swahili, Amiri Baraka. Between 1958 and 1965 Baraka lived in Greenwich Village, associated with the avant-garde Beat Generation, and was married to Hettie Cohen, a white woman. In 1965 he left the Village for Harlem and then for his native Newark (a predominantly black city); in 1966 he married the black woman Sylvia Robinson, having divorced Hettie Cohen in 1965; and in 1966 he became a black nationalist under the influence of Malcolm X and later of Ron Karenga, founder and leader of the West Coast nationalist organization US. During the period from 1965 to 1973, Baraka was the key figure in the black arts movement. With much publicity, he promoted the Black Aesthetic, black nationalism, and black community involvement. His leadership roles in the short-lived

Black Arts Repertory Theater and School in Harlem, in the Spirit House in Newark, and in the 1970 Congress of African People held in Atlanta were highly visible signs of the widespread shift among black intellectuals from the philosophy of interracial integration linked with the civil rights movement to the philosophy of nationalism associated with the black power movement. Between 1965 and 1973, Baraka published roughly a dozen plays, four volumes of poetry, four books of essays, three edited anthologies, and one book of stories. He gave numerous lectures, set up various community organizations, wrote a screenplay, established a press, and cofounded a music journal. Much of this work was related to the development of the Black Aesthetic.[6] When Baraka shifted in 1974 from cultural nationalism to political internationalism, becoming a Marxist-Leninist, his leadership role in the waning black arts movement was symbolically ended.[7]

In *Home: Social Essays* (1966), Baraka collected twenty-six prose pieces from the transitional period 1960 to 1965, recording his shift from phenomenological poetics to black aesthetics and black nationalism. His early phenomenological theory of art insisted on the primacy of process over product, of function over form, of art-making over artifacts, of spirit over matter, of being (verb) over Being (noun). It constituted an assault on formalist poetics.

The academic Western mind is the best example of the substitution of artifact worship for the lightning awareness of the art process.[8]

Worship the verb, if you need something. (175)

Formal art, that is, artifacts made to cohere to preconceived forms, is almost devoid of this verb value. (174)

I speak of the verb process, the doing, the coming into being, the at-the-time-of. Which is why we think there is particular value in live music. . . . (174)

The imitator is the most pitiful phenomenon. . . . (176)

Baraka's antimimetic and antiformalist philosophy of art underwent revision when he articulated a Black Aesthetic. Because black art had to have social and political dimensions, the privatized expressionism of phenomenological poetics needed to be scrapped. In "State/Meant" (1965), Baraka declared: "The Black Artist's role in America is to aid in the destruction of America as he knows it. His role is to report and reflect so precisely the nature of society, and of himself in that society, that other men will be moved by the exactness of his rendering . . ." (251). The sociopolitical mission of black art required a combined didactic-affective poetics rooted in mimesis: the precise reportage of the artist would instruct and move the

black audience to correct political understanding and action. In the poem
"Black Art," published in *Black Magic: Collected Poetry 1961–1967*, Baraka
wrote:

We want "poems that kill."
Assassin poems, Poems that shoot
guns. Poems that wrestle cops into alleys
and take their weapons leaving them dead
with tongues pulled out. . . .

In a time of riots and violence, poetry had to promote revolutionary activity.
The poet, politician, preacher, and revolutionary were one.

A key essay in Baraka's *Home: Social Essays* was "The Legacy of Malcolm
X, and the Coming of the Black Nation" (1965), which outlined the
rudiments of a cultural poetics. According to Baraka, politics, social theory,
religion, and art all produced orderly patterns of images fostering cultural
consciousness and national autonomy. The task of contemporary black art,
therefore, was to assault mainstream (white) images and promote black
images as a means of fostering autonomous black consciousness, nationhood, and culture. "By the time this book appears," proclaimed Baraka, "I
will be even blacker" (10).

In 1968 Hoyt Fuller had called on black literary critics to articulate and
expound the new Black Aesthetic—a task undertaken preeminently by
Stephen Henderson and Addison Gayle, Jr., among other black academic
critics. In a monograph-length introduction titled "The Forms of Things
Unknown" to his anthology *Understanding the New Black Poetry* (1973),
Henderson offered a sophisticated scholarly treatment of the Black Aesthetic, using "poetry" as his primary material. To account for the specificity
of black experience, Henderson posited the "Soul-Field," which was an
historically formed, cohesive repository containing the social experiences,
moral and political values, linguistic forms, religious practices, and emerging aspirations of black people in America. A few years earlier, he had
labeled "Soul-Field" simply "Soul" and characterized it as the black "unconscious."9 Out of this domain emerged all forms of black expression, including revelations of self-hatred (the "nigger component"). The roots of
negritude, of black nationhood, and of the Black Aesthetic stemmed from
the communal Soul-Field, which more or less saturated the works of black
artists. Historically speaking, the black liberation movement, including its
cultural manifestation in the black arts movement, bore witness to the
eruptions of "Soul" in Space-Age America. As a literary critic, Henderson

sought to specify the distinctive structural and thematic features of black poetry. He did so by memorably outlining ten traits of black speech and ten traits of black music, covering special modes of folk and formal rhyme, allusion, diction, imagery, rhythm, tone, character, and genre, all of which shaped and characterized black poetic expression.

The cultural poetics articulated by Henderson served as the foundation for a critical practice:

> Art, of course, including literature, does not exist in a vacuum, and re-flects—and helps to shape—the lives of those who produce it. It is able to do these things, moreover, because of the special heightening and refining of experience that is characteristic of art. Literature, accordingly, is the verbal organization of experience into beautiful forms, but what is meant by "beauti-ful" and by "forms" is to a significant degree dependent upon a people's way of life, their needs, their aspirations, their history—in short, their culture.[10]

Henderson did not believe that *universal* forms of "the beautiful" existed; all aesthetic forms were culturally specific. What constituted beautiful form in Euro-American aesthetics and Afro-American aesthetics was neither neces-sarily nor factually the same. To describe as well as to evaluate the poetry of the black arts movement required, therefore, a specifically Black Aesthetic rooted in the Soul-Field of black experience and history. Only black literary critics could properly and effectively understand and assess the language, rhythm, imagery, tone, structure, meaning, and value of contemporary black poetry. "Who is best qualified to judge Black poetry? Black people obviously should judge, since the poetry—at least the contemporary po-etry—is directed to them" (10). In brief, "the ultimate criteria for critical evaluation must be found in the sources of the creation, that is, in the Black Community itself" (66). Although the closing words of Henderson's study allowed for nonblack readers to have their values altered positively and their sensibilities enlarged by black literature, he was not personally concerned about such matters.

No academic literary critic did more to solidify and popularize the emerging Black Aesthetic than Addison Gayle, Jr., who in 1971 edited a landmark anthology of thirty-three articles, excerpts, and manifestos, in-cluding contemporary works by Baraka, Fuller, Karenga, Lee, and Neal as well as by older figures like W. E. B. Du Bois, Langston Hughes, John Oliver Killens, Alain Locke, and Richard Wright. In the opening and closing texts to *The Black Aesthetic* (1971), Gayle articulated his own view of the Black Aesthetic, which he presented as a corrective political and artistic effort at de-Americanizing black consciousness and literature, a project having roots deep in Afro-American tradition. He railed against the "inept, sterile critiques of American academicians,"[11] particularly formalists and liberals. He urged all black artists not only to retrieve and rely on their special heritage and culture, but also to resist the temptations of assimilationism, which undermined the literary works of numerous earlier black writers like James Weldon Johnson, James Baldwin, and Ralph Ellison.

Gayle's *The Black Aesthetic* was one of a number of important anthologies published during the time of the black power movement, including LeRoi Jones' and Larry Neal's *Black Fire* (1968), Abraham Chapman's *New Black Voices* (1972), and Stephen Henderson's *Understanding the New Black Poetry*—all of which disseminated information about the growing black arts movement and the goal of articulating a Black Aesthetic. Earlier, Gayle's *Black Expression* (1969) had offered an extensive anthology of twentieth-century black literary criticism—the first of its kind in America.

In his Preface to *Black Expression* and elsewhere, Gayle called upon black critics to practice moral criticism and to promote moral art. This call was linked firmly with the black power movement.

In 1965, Stokely Carmichael cast himself against the tide of American history, removed himself from the back of the diseased tiger, and many of us followed him. When we did so we began to dream different dreams from those of our fathers. We dreamed not of integration but of nationalism, not of a melting pot but of a pluralistic theory, not of a great society but of a new one. More important, we dreamed of fashioning Canaan out of the debris of the American society, of erecting a nation predicated not upon the gun but upon morality, and if these dreams are hopeless, then so too is the future of mankind.[12]

Black literary criticism had to further the cause of justice; it was not enough to explicate intricate artistic craft or to explore exquisite metaphysical voids, as did Formalist and Existential Critics. Gayle wanted a moral criticism and a moral literature attentive to political, social, and historical dimensions of life. In his full-scale history of the black novel, *The Way of the New World* (1975), he insisted that "in order to cultivate an aesthetic sensibility, given an oppressive society, the first prerequisite is that the oppression must end . . . ; in more concrete terms, before beauty can be seen, felt, heard, and appreciated by a majority of the earth's people, a new world must be brought into being; the earth must be made habitable and free for all men. This is the core of the Black Aesthetic ideology and forms the major criterion for the evaluation of art. . . ."[13]

While black literary intellectuals like Fuller, Neal, Baraka, Henderson,

Gayle, and others committed themselves to the project of a Black Aesthetic, many did not. Such distinguished older black figures as Robert Hayden, J. Saunders Redding, Nathan A. Scott, Jr., and Melvin Tolson opposed the Black Aesthetic. To take only one example, Scott, in his history of postwar black literature, published in *The Harvard Guide to Contemporary American Writing* (1979), criticized the Black Aestheticians for recalcitrant partisanship, for philosophical incoherence, for intolerance particularly of white critics, for damning important black writers (especially Ralph Ellison), and for ethnic separatism. Scott and others wanted black art to meet the highest standards of universal art; any specifically national or racial aesthetic was unacceptable.

CRITICAL THEORY AND PRACTICE

In his autobiography, *Wayward Child: A Personal Odyssey* (1977), Addison Gayle lamented the sudden loss of collective commitment and the outbreak of internecine struggles which marked the community of black intellectuals in 1973. The next year Amiri Baraka turned to socialist internationalism, embracing the worldwide working class. In 1975 Hoyt Fuller's periodical, *Black World,* was discontinued. Coinciding with the close of the Vietnam War, the dissolution of the black power movement and the project for a Black Aesthetic signaled the apparent end of the New Renaissance of black letters, issuing in a time of theoretical diversification and individual effort, of the emergence of younger critics, and of the rise of black women writers and feminists. Historically speaking, the generation of Baraka, Fuller, Gayle, Henderson, King, Malcolm X, and Neal, born between the mid-twenties and mid-thirties, was superseded by a group of new intellectuals born between the onset of World War II and the Korean War.

During the heyday of the New Renaissance, a wide array of methods characterized black literary criticism, ranging from the early phenomenological theory of Baraka to the myth criticism of Neal, from the social criticism of Fuller to the historical aesthetic practice of Henderson, and from the moral criticism of Gayle to the later cultural criticism of Baraka. In the late sixties, these critics were united by their impatience with the isolations fostered by formalism and existentialism as well as by their firm commitments to black social history and to separatist politics, all of which rendered their criticism at once sociological, political, historical, and judicial. Parenthetically, Gayle published a biography of Paul Laurence Dunbar in 1971 and a critical study of Claude McKay in 1972. None of these critics displayed any serious interest in hermeneutics, reader-response criticism, structuralism, deconstruction, or feminism, which, of course, came to prominence at the end of their movement. Nor were they dedicated followers of Marx or Freud.

Like Baraka, some of the leading black feminists, such as Angela Davis and Barbara Smith, turned to Marxism. Perhaps the most interesting and influential of the older black socialist intellectuals, sympathetic to black nationalism and to the Black Aesthetic, was Harold Cruse, who published two widely read books in the sixties—*The Crisis of the Negro Intellectual* (1967) and *Rebellion or Revolution?* (1968). As a New York intellectual in the forties and a member of the Communist Party until the early fifties, Cruse was able to document in convincing ways the complex experience of the older generation of black literary people with organized Marxism. Ultimately, he found the strictures of Socialist Realism, of compulsory internationalism, and of Party racism and internal politics increasingly intolerable, leading him to independent socialism developed from the fifties onward. Not only was Cruse opposed to the Party, but to black integrationist organizations like the National Association for the Advancement of Colored People, the Urban League, the Congress of Racial Equality, the Southern Christian Leadership Conference, and the Student Nonviolent Coordinating Committee. His discontent with integrationism flared in 1960 in a debate with the prominent black academic literary critic J. Saunders Redding. Of this experience, Cruse concluded "that integrationists such as Redding present a greater liability in terms of an intellectual renaissance in black thought than the Marxist integrationists."[14] Significantly, Cruse collaborated with Baraka in the Harlem Black Arts Repertory Theater in the mid-sixties, and he championed the black nationalist movement, though not uncritically.

In Cruse's judgment, "the black situation has three important sides, a political side, an economic side and a cultural side. And each side calls for specific kinds of approaches."[15] While he encouraged interplay amongst the three fronts of the struggle for black liberation, Cruse argued for relative autonomy and independence on the cultural front. What he feared was the complete control of the cultural struggle by political ideologues. In the late sixties, he criticized Baraka's Black Arts Repertory Theater for confusing the artistic and the political sides of the black revolution. To change the content of drama required changing society and not vice versa. In addition, Baraka's Black Arts Theater was neither nationalistic nor separatist enough.[16] Repeatedly, Cruse called for the emergence of new and independent black cultural critics who could articulate distinctive black standards, ethics, politics, codes, and methods of criticism.

Included in Gayle's *The Black Aesthetic* was a brief history of black literary criticism from World War I to 1970. Written by Darwin T. Turner, this survey focused on six groups of black critics. First were black critics dedicated mainly to mainstream white literature, as, for example, William Stanley Braithwaite, Benjamin Brawley, and Nathan A. Scott. The second group consisted of cultural historians, like W. E. B. Du Bois, Alain Locke, and John Hope Franklin, who devoted fine, though partial, attention to black writers. Third came such social critics as Eldridge Cleaver and Harold Cruse, known mainly for their outrageous assessments of certain writers or movements. The fourth category was composed of numerous poet-critics, ranging in the interwar period from James Weldon Johnson and Countee Cullen to Wallace Thurman and Langston Hughes and in the postwar era from Arna Bontemps and Richard Wright to Ralph Ellison and James Baldwin. Fifth were prominent academic critics, including Benjamin Brawley, Sterling Brown, J. Saunders Redding, Nick Aaron Ford, Hugh Gloster, and Blyden Jackson. The sixth and final group was made up of the Black Aestheticians, among whom were academic critics like Addison Gayle, Jr., Stephen Henderson, and George Kent and writers like Amiri Baraka, Hoyt Fuller, and Larry Neal. Somewhat anxiously, Turner applauded the turn to theory effected by the Black Aestheticians. "It is important that these new critics are explaining theory rather than merely commenting on practice. Previously, as I have said, most Afro-American critics assumed that the desirable standards were necessarily those currently favored by the American literary establishment. This attitude inevitably restricted black writers to imitation rather than innovation. . . . Today, however, black critics are postulating theories about what literature is or should be for black people, according to a Black Aesthetic. . . ."[17] In Turner's assessment, the development of the Black Aesthetic in the Space Age signaled an important turn to theory in the history of black literary criticism. Since he was writing in 1970, Turner was unable to cover in his account the theoretical projects of younger critics (including the feminists), who began work in the seventies and eighties. These later critics extended the theoretical diversification characteristic of black literary criticism during the Space Age.

Among black male critics born after the onset of World War II, few, if any, were more prolific or promising than Houston A. Baker, Jr., and Henry Louis Gates, Jr. During the seventies, Baker edited *Black Literature in*

America, a full-scale anthology covering black literature from the early folklore to the Black Aestheticians; he published many articles and a few books of poetry; and he edited and wrote several critical books. Especially important were *Long Black Song: Essays in Black American Literature and Culture* (1972) and *The Journey Back: Issues in Black Literature and Criticism* (1980). Over the course of the decade Baker received prestigious fellowships from various mainstream foundations, and he was active in the leadership of the Modern Language Association. In succession, he taught at Yale University, the University of Virginia, and the University of Pennsylvania.

Baker was a literary historian interested in the persistence throughout the history of black literature of folk elements derived from tales, songs, oratory, sermons, blues, and jazz. These elements, among others, made black culture in America distinctive and separate. In his cultural criticism, Baker assumed the existence of a unique whole way of life common to black people. Influenced by the philosophy of black nationalism developed in the sixties, he regarded the black community as a colonized nation different from both white America and from emergent African countries. Black culture in America possessed a collectivistic rather than an individualistic ethos, a repudiative rather than an accommodative psychology, and an oral-musical rather than a textual tradition of communication.[18] As a cultural relativist, Baker saw no reason to privilege any one culture over any other culture. As far as he was concerned, values and standards were specific to individual cultures and not universal or somehow objective. "Black America can justifiably say that it possesses a true culture—a *whole* way of life that includes its own standards of moral and aesthetic achievement. . . . And only that same culture can evolve the standards by which its intellectual and imaginative work is to be judged" (6). Not surprisingly, Baker repudiated the exclusive architechtonic criteria of art propounded by Formalist and Structuralist Critics, stressing in the Preface and introductory Overview to *Black Literature in America* the important role played in literary judgment by sociohistorical factors. Following the Black Aestheticians, he rejected white American standards, seeking both to revive and reassess the separate tradition of black literature.

In *The Journey Back,* Baker altered his course, adopting a project inspired by structuralist research and theory. "There has been a great deal of muddled thinking about black literature during the recent past. An excessively nationalist prospect is probably not the most fruitful approach to the black literary text. And it is, no doubt, time to move on to a more descriptively accurate and theoretically sophisticated level."[19] However uncertainly, Baker dedicated himself to an "anthropology of art"—a scientific interdisciplinary method of studying (1) the status of art objects and performances within given cultures, (2) the relationships of specific aesthetic "works" to other entities and systems in a designated culture, and (3) the general nature and function of artistic production and reception therein. Consequently, Baker located works of black literature within *black* American culture. What he sought was a means of depoliticizing, deidealizing, and depersonalizing the powerful premises propounded by the Black Aestheticians. Relying on structuralist thought, he envisioned culture as linguistic discourse based on systematic rules, principles, and conventions, all of which regularized the social production of art. Black culture constituted a "discourse"—a holistic organization of social existence "in which rule-governed systems (e.g., religion, politics, language, economics, kinship, and so on) operate in strategically interrelated ways" (165). With this structuralist methodology, Baker was able to reassess, among other things, the contributions of the Black Aestheticians, who produced "conative utterances" designed to bring a utopian world into being by verbal fiat. Such exercises in will and desire, characteristic of much black literary criticism, were no substitute for critical reason and analysis (132–37). What the Black Aestheticians promoted in the sixties was the formation of self-conscious black artists and black audiences. Since this had been achieved, Baker felt he could leave behind their idealistic sociopolitical programs and calmly "study the expressive manifestations of black American culture in ways that allow one to interpret such works as structured creativity that derives its meanings from a rich cultural context" (138). Baker's turn to anthropological structuralism was designed to move black criticism from polemics to analysis. Because such a project depended on the intimate familiarity of the analyst with the semantic universe of black American culture, white critics unfamiliar with black discourse were at a serious disadvantage and risked ethnocentric distortion.[20]

In *Blues, Ideology, and Afro-American Literature: A Vernacular Theory* (1984), Baker once again altered his project, incorporating materials from various new sources, notably Marxism and poststructuralism. Without renouncing his anthropology of art, he extended his critical attention to economic subtexts of classic black works. Reminiscent of Henderson, Baker theorized that individual Afro-American texts emerged out of a long-standing vernacular matrix rooted in the collective historical realities of commercial deportation and the economics of slavery—a paradigmatic "discourse" symbolized for Baker by the "blues." To ignore this strand in critical analysis of black literature was to engage in formalistic blindness, which, according to Baker, characterized the work of some younger black critics dedicated to the careerist politics of professionalism rather than the politics of the black community. Significantly, Baker pictured the ideal contemporary black critic as a nomadic hobo prepared to employ a rich array of methods to further his journey. That this mythical jack-of-all-trades was an outcast black American hobo rather than a mainstream white European *bricoleur* was no accident: the historian Baker sought self-consciously to refigure the excluded margins as the cultural matrix of American culture.

Beginning his academic career in the late seventies, Henry Louis Gates, Jr., had by the mid-eighties edited an influential book and written a number of significant essays. In addition, he served as guest editor of an important special issue on " 'Race,' Writing, and Difference" of *Critical Inquiry* (Autumn 1985), which contained contributions from such figures as Jacques Derrida, Barbara Johnson, Mary Louise Pratt, Edward Said, and Gayatri Chakravorty Spivak. This issue was evidently the first one published on racial questions by a major American theoretical journal in the post-Vietnam era. Winner of the highly prestigious MacArthur Prize Fellowship in 1981 and a leading black poststructuralist in the eighties, Gates, like Baker, conceived the American black community as a colonialized people, having a special, indigenous culture. He wanted to harness the full resources of sophisticated mainstream critical theory in order to strengthen black criticism and literature. For Gates such a project of appropriation could not proceed uncritically, lest it substitute one colonial discourse for another: mainstream critical theory and practice in the eighties, despite their sophistication, remained racist in line with the general logocentric heritage stemming from the ancient Greco-Roman and Judeo-Christian traditions.[21]

In his introductory essay to *Black Literature and Literary Theory* (1984), a collection of thirteen theoretical and practical essays by diverse hands, Gates propounded a useful theory of text-milieu in order to describe the complex two-stranded heritage of black literature and to depict the situation of contemporary black literary critics. According to Gates, a black literature written in a Western language, whether English, French, Spanish, or Portugese, was heir to (1) a *standard* language, tradition, and canon derived from Greco-Roman, Judeo-Christian, and European cultures and (2) a *vernacular* language, tradition, and emerging canon descended from African, Caribbean, or Afro-American cultures. For present-day black critics, the white heritage of written discourse was part of an oppressive, ethno-centric colonial order, unlike the black heritage of native oral discourse. The task of the critic was both to draw upon and diverge from mainstream traditions and to delve into and derive principles and practices from the marginal traditions. Thus, Gates sought to negotiate the two heritages while maintaining their split. What he most deplored were the com-monplace anthropological, sociological, and linguistic fallacies that rele-gated vernacular black literature to the social sciences rather than to literary criticism. However, he excluded from condemnation the "anthropology of art" developed by Houston A. Baker, Jr., since it constituted a method of careful critical reading attentive to black literary language. Above all, Gates wanted black critics to practice *literary criticism*, by which he meant scrupu-lous analysis of the figurative language of black texts. His type of close reading or microanalysis was most indebted to the deconstructive rhetoric of Paul de Man, to whom he dedicated *Black Literature and Literary Theory*.

In Gates' view, the most distinctive feature of Afro-American literature was its figurality.

The Afro-American tradition has been figurative from its beginnings. How could it have survived otherwise? . . . Black people have always been masters of the figurative: saying one thing to mean something quite other has been basic to black survival in oppressive Western cultures. Misreading signs could be, and indeed often was, fatal. 'Reading,' in this sense, was not play; it was an essential aspect of the 'literacy' training of a child. This sort of metaphorical literacy, the learning to decipher complex codes, is just about the blackest aspect of the black tradition.[22]

Given the historical rhetoricity of American black literature, the analytical project of close reading appeared to Gates in the eighties a more pressing task for contemporary black literary critics than the older polemical enter-prise of valorizing sociopolitical separateness. "Because of this curious valorization of the social and polemical functions of black literature, the structure of the black text has been *repressed* and treated as if it were *transparent*. The black literary work of art stood at the center of a triangle of relations (M. H. Abrams' 'universe,' 'artist,' and 'audience'), but as the very thing *not* to be explained, as if it were invisible, or literal, or a one-dimensional document" (5–6). In place of older politicized and simplifying mimetic, expressive, didactic, and affective theories of black literature, Gates installed a textual theory rooted in a figural view of black language. The rhetorical nature of the black text, its multidimensionality and signify-ing density, required, above all, close reading. While such textual scrutiny could rely on a plurality of methods, Gates personally preferred the rhetorical reading developed by deconstructors at his alma mater, Yale University. In a key essay published in *Critical Inquiry* in 1983, Gates worked as a literary historian, building upon the poststructuralist concept of intertextuality to illustrate and analyze the complex interrelations characteristic of the "canonical" texts of Afro-American literature. Focused on Ishmael Reed's novel *Mumbo Jumbo* (1972), this major essay, reprinted in *Black Literature and Literary Theory*, articulated a model of Afro-American intertextuality as "signifyin(g)," which derived from a long-standing black American tradition with roots in African mythology. Among other things, "signifyin(g)" traditionally designated consummate verbal skill in troping, reversing, revising, or parodying another's speech or discourse. According to Gates, one type of "formal signifyin(g)" characteristic of Afro-American literature, was "tertiary revision" in which an author revised or signified upon at least two antecedent texts. Ishmael Reed, for example, parodied the naturalism of Richard Wright and the modernism of Ralph Ellison in his postmodern fiction. Of the "signifyin(g)" in *Mumbo Jumbo,* Gates declared:

It is indeterminacy, the sheer plurality of meaning, the very play of the signifier itself, which *Mumbo Jumbo* celebrates. *Mumbo Jumbo* addresses the *play* of the black literary tradition and, as a parody, is a *play* upon that same tradition.[23]

Reed's most subtle achievement in *Mumbo Jumbo* is to parody, to signify upon, the notions of closure implicit in key texts of the Afro-American canon. *Mumbo Jumbo,* in contrast to that canon, is a novel that figures and glorifies *indeterminacy.* In this sense, *Mumbo Jumbo* stands as a profound critique and elaboration upon the convention of closure, and its metaphysical implications, in the black novel. In its stead, Reed posits the notion of aesthetic *play:* the play of the tradition, the play on the tradition, the sheer play of indeterminacy itself. (304–5)

The concept of signifyin(g) enabled Gates to study the internal literary history of specifically Afro-American fiction while emphasizing mainstream poststructuralist themes like "indeterminacy," "play," and "intertextuality." In other words, Gates managed to coordinate the standard and the vernacular traditions, drawing upon while diverging from the former so as to elucidate and enrich the latter.

Like Baker, Gates sought self-consciously both to move beyond the polemical sociopolitical criticism of the Black Aestheticians and to appropriate poststructuralist insights for black criticism. Both critics devoted themselves to examining canonical texts in the history of black American literature; they were academic literary historians as well as emerging critical theorists. And both critics wished to practice rigorous critical reading of literary texts in line with certain Euro-American textualist modes of analysis.

In the eighties, the preoccupation of black critics with theory was motivated less by a search for critical independence than by an avowed commitment to critical sophistication and analytical rigor. This development did not mean that the old political goals of either assimilation or integration were again in vogue. Generally, black critics in the eighties presupposed the separate and distinctive status of black communal life and culture in America. Like earlier black critics, the new generation continued to write in standard English prose and to respect the exigencies of mainstream scholarship. Significantly, several noteworthy differences persisted between leading black and white American poststructuralists: black poststructuralists refused to divorce the social from the "literary" text and they refused to submerge the vernacular in the standard tradition. What poststructuralism provided black literary critics of the eighties was a sophisticated means of dealing with the legacies of deportation and slavery.

BLACK FEMINIST CRITICISM

Black feminists began to organize in the early seventies and black feminist literary critics started to appear in print in the mid- and late seventies. During an interview in 1970, the black philosopher and Marxist theoretician Angela Davis observed: "As Black women, we must liberate ourselves and provide the impetus for the liberation of Black men. . . ."[24] The sense of separation suggested here between the interests of black women and black men reached a decisive culmination in late 1973 when the National Black Feminist Organization was founded. Similar black feminist groups emerged at about the same time, as, for example, the Black Women's Organization for Action (San Francisco), the League of Black Women (Chicago), Black Women Concerned (Baltimore), National Black Women's Political Leadership Caucus (Detroit), and the Combahee River Collective (Boston), named in honor of Harriet Tubman, who had led a successful and inspiring guerrilla action during June 1863 in South Carolina that freed more than 750 slaves. Although many black women initially rejected as racist the feminist movement of the sixties, they increasingly perceived the ills of sexism as racial barriers began to weaken. The modest advances made during this time by blacks in jobs, in education, and in political elections were distributed unevenly to black men,[25] which suggested not simply that sexism persisted independently of racism, but that sexist practices were as fundamental a problem as racial prejudice and class oppression. Black women had to struggle, therefore, on various fronts—against white racism (including white feminist racism), against economic domination (including black exploitation), and against black and white sexism (including militant heterosexism). In their manifesto of April 1977, the black feminists of the Combahee River Collective declared: "we are actively committed to struggling against racial, sexual, heterosexual, and class oppression. . . . As Black women we see Black feminism as the logical political movement to combat the manifold and simultaneous oppressions that all women of color face."[26] With regard to black men specifically, these feminists stated: "We struggle together with Black men against racism, while we also struggle with Black men about sexism" (275).

Like white feminists, black feminists traced the roots of their movement to the nineteenth century. In the 1890s, in particular, several important black women's organizations were established, including the Congress of Colored Women of the United States and the National Association of Colored Women—the latter of which united the preexisting National Federation of Colored Women and the National League of Colored Women. Such groups built on earlier antebellum programs for abolition of slavery and for women's rights, as Angela Davis documented in her history, *Women, Race & Class* (1981). Among nineteenth-century black feminists were a number of important literary women like Frances E. W. Harper and Pauline Hopkins, whose novels contributed to the struggle for social change.[27]

Black feminists in the seventies felt themselves to be acutely isolated and marginalized in American society. In Michele Wallace's words, written in 1975, "we exist as women who are Black who are feminists, each stranded for the moment, working independently because there is not yet an environment in this society remotely congenial to our struggle. . . ."[28] When combined with moral outrage against oppression and longing for a voice in shaping the future, this sense of enforced isolation created the immediate conditions necessary for black feminist organizing, for retrieving a black women's tradition, and for forging feminist coalitions. Despite their anger and isolation, black feminists generally advocated remaining a part of the wider black liberation movement in fighting against race and class oppression. When black feminists' calls for separatism did surface, they were usually made in relation to white society and to white feminism.

Among American black literary women active in the seventies and eighties, some important contributors to feminist work were Toni Cade Bambara, Barbara Christian, Mari Evans, Gloria T. Hull, Audre Lorde, Barbara Smith, Erlene Stetson, Alice Walker, and Mary Helen Washington. All of these intellectuals were more or less seriously interested in the specific social situation of black women, the history of black women's literature, the usefulness of feminist solidarity, the evils of race and class oppression, the pressing ills of black and white patriarchalism, the plight of other Third World women, and the possibilities for future social change. As critics, they practiced both feminist critique of pernicious distortions and omissions regarding black women and gynocritical inquiry into black women's aesthetics and literary traditions. Most were committed to cultural criticism rooted in an abiding personal concern with the sociological and historical realities of black life, language, and sexual politics. While they had little use for formalism, psychoanalysis, or modern Continental philosophy (phenomenology, existentialism, hermeneutics, structuralism, deconstruction), they often exhibited interest in biographical research, receptionist modes of inquiry, and sociopolitical analysis. According to an emerging black feminist cultural poetics, literature by definition organized in rhythmical language and in form the personal feelings and observations of an author, reflecting communal realities and thereby moving readers toward understanding. Since the traditional criteria of Western aesthetic evaluation did not apply wholesale to Afro-American literature, black feminist critics usually avoided judicial criticism based on conventional standards of excellence. Finally, a great deal of sympathy among black feminists existed for black lesbian literature.

In her pioneering polemical essay, "Toward a Black Feminist Criticism" (1977), Barbara Smith opened for serious consideration several key issues. She angrily criticized black male intellectuals for sexism and misogyny and white female critics, particularly Ellen Moers, Elaine Showalter, and Patricia Meyer Spacks, for racism and heterosexism. Calling for the creation of an autonomous rather than separatist black feminist movement, Smith recommended strong links not only between black critics and artists, but among all Third World women. She sketched the rudiments of a program for cultural criticism. "A Black feminist approach to literature that embodies the realization that the politics of sex as well as the politics of race and class are crucially interlocking factors in the works of Black women writers is an absolute necessity."[29] Given the specificity of black women's literature, Smith advised against reliance on white male critical ideas and methods and argued for creating innovative and personal black feminist modes of analysis. She wanted literary criticism to align itself politically with the wider black feminist movement in order to work toward cultural revolution. As a lesbian, she engaged in special pleading on behalf of black women-identified literature. Finally, she theorized a special black women's aesthetic and literary tradition: "thematically, stylistically, aesthetically, and conceptually Black women writers manifest common approaches to the act of creating literature" (174). In short, "Black women writers constitute an identifiable literary tradition" (174).

In her anthology, *Black Sister: Poetry by Black American Women, 1746–1980* (1981), Erlene Stetson engaged in the gynocritical work advocated by Smith. She retrieved many forgotten black writers and provided the materials for a tradition. She offered a list of works for each of her five dozen poets, a list of fifty anthologies of black poetry (forty were published in the sixties and seventies), and a list of forty important critical books and articles on black literature. In her Preface and Introduction, Stetson called for revisions of both the canon and the history of American literature. Regarding black women's poetry as a coherent tradition, she isolated common traits of style, theme, imagery, and structure. Recurring images included flowers, masks, and houses and traditional themes were the quest for identity, the strategic use of subterfuge, and the subversive perception of reality. In black women's poetry, "the house," for example, "represents the historic quest by black women for homes of their own—apart from the house of slavery, the common house of bondage, the house of patriarchy. The house embodies women's search for place and belonging and for a whole and complete identity, as well as representing the historical house that was so difficult to get."[30] What Erlene Stetson did for poetry, Mary Helen Washington did for prose in her *Black-Eyed Susans: Classic Stories by and About Black Women* (1975) and her *Midnight Birds: Stories of Contemporary Black Women Writers* (1980). Stetson and Washington were not alone in the work of gynocritical restoration and discovery.

The tasks of anthology-making and of canon formation were complemented by the project of critical assessment aimed at revising literary history. In this area, Gloria T. Hull, for example, produced several informative articles assessing the historical importance of key women writers.[31] In one essay, published in Sandra Gilbert's and Susan Gubar's well-known critical anthology *Shakespeare's Sisters: Feminist Essays on Women Poets* (1979), Hull observed of standard black literary historiography that "the overall definition of the Harlem Renaissance automatically excludes or devalues the contribution of the women writers."³² In other words, black male sexist criticism created a faulty literary history. In her *Black Women Novelists: The Development of a Tradition, 1892–1976* (1980), Barbara Christian analyzed major black women fiction writers while situating them in a black women's tradition of the novel. Like Hull, Christian self-consciously worked to expand the scope and depth of traditional American and Afro-American literary history.

Reprinted in Showalter's influential *The New Feminist Criticism* (1985), Deborah McDowell's "New Directions for Black Feminist Criticism" (1980) ratified many of the positions first staked out by Barbara Smith in her 1977 ground-breaking essay while objecting to Smith's general lack of rigor and precision as well as her reliance on polemic. McDowell was critical of white feminist racism, singling out the works of Patricia Spacks and Mary Ellmann as examples. She deplored male sexism in books on black literature by Robert Bone, Donald B. Gibson, David Littlejohn, and Robert Stepto. She called for an end to the negative project of feminist critique and urged more positive work in gynocriticism and critical theory. However pluralistic such theory might ultimately become, it had to retain its feminist ideology and cultural orientation: "feminist criticism is a valid and necessary cultural and political enterprise"; it necessarily "exposes the conditions under which literature is produced, published, and reviewed."³³ What McDowell most wanted was a black feminist criticism rigorous in textual analysis. In this matter, she resembled Houston Baker and Henry Louis Gates. For McDowell a precise textualist criticism was essential for formulating the details of a specifically black women's aesthetic. Black women's language, images, themes, and fictional characters had to be clearly and convincingly differentiated from black men's literary modes. Writing in 1980, McDowell judged that such scrupulous work remained to be done by black feminist critics. While she employed and appreciated some insights from white feminists (especially Annette Kolodny and Lillian Robinson), McDowell sought to sidestep the issue of black feminist separatism. "Whether Black feminist criticism will or should remain a separatist enterprise is a debatable point. Black feminist critics ought to move from this issue to consider the specific language of Black women's literature, to describe the ways Black women writers employ literary devices in a distinct way. . . . If they focus on these and other pertinent issues, Black feminist critics will have laid the cornerstone for a sound, thorough articulation of the Black feminist aesthetic" (196–97).

The same year that Deborah McDowell called for both a halt to polemical criticism and a commitment to precise textual analysis, Barbara Christian published *Black Women Novelists,* which answered McDowell's call. Buttressed by some social history, Christian's book offered extended close readings of major novels, attending to the development of themes, characters, and structures in individual works. Although her overall goal was to document the negative images of black women in American life and literature, Christian's most memorable accomplishment was to provide detailed studies of landmark texts and thereby to produce a broadened conception of the Afro-American tradition of women's fiction.

Of seventeen essays written by Christian in the early eighties and collected in her *Black Feminist Criticism: Perspectives on Black Women Writers* (1985), almost all continued the project of careful analysis of black women's fiction, adding to her earlier critical mode a firmer sense of feminist politics, a clearer view of the extraordinary Renaissance of black women's literature initiated in the 1970s, and a budding interest in African culture. In a headnote to one of her essays, Christian reaffirmed her commitment to textual analysis, stressing her dedication to *literary* value:

In-depth critical analysis of Afro-American women writers is for me the very foundation of the body of criticism we are developing. Often outlets of publication are more interested in issues, problems, general themes, overviews than in this kind of concentrated analysis. Yet, without this approach, our writers will be reduced to illustrations of societal questions or dilemmas, in which people, for the moment, are interested, and will not be valued for their craft, their vision, their work as writers.[34]

Increasingly, leading black feminists identified with Third World women, often aligning themselves with all "women of color"—a broad group including Afro-American, Asian-American, Latin, and Native-American women as well as indigenous peoples of underdeveloped countries around the globe. In her Foreword to *This Bridge Called My Back: Writings by Radical Women of Color* (1981), edited by Cherríe Moraga and Gloria Anzaldúa, Toni Cade Bambara recommended coalitions of Third World women as effective means to counter masculinist "divide and conquer" tactics, to compete successfully in the political "numbers game," and to "create new powers in arenas where they never before existed."[35] In a conference presentation delivered in 1979 at New York University, Audre Lorde stated: "It is a particular academic arrogance to assume any discussion of feminist theory in this time and in this place without examining our many differences and without a significant input from poor women, black and third-world women, and lesbians."[36] Lorde went on to endorse the forging of coalitions and the making of common cause with all women of color. In the Introduction to *Home Girls: A Black Feminist Anthology* (1983), Barbara Smith observed "that there is a vital movement of women of color in this country . . . it is safe to say in 1982 that we have a movement of our own" (xxxi). As far as Smith was concerned, the emergence of Third World feminism was "the single most enlivening and hopeful development in the 1980s" (xlii). Black feminists dedicated to Third World feminism were generally uncommitted to as well as critical of white middle-class European and American women's movements. To differentiate such contending activists, Alice Walker advocated using the term "womanist" rather than "feminist."[37] One of the main targets of Third World womanists was ethnocentrism. As the radical black poet and Third World womanist Pat Parker angrily put it in 1980: "For too long I have watched the white middle class be represented as my leaders in the women's movement. I have often heard that the women's movement is a white middle class movement. I am a feminist. I am neither white nor middle class. . . . I, for one, am no longer willing to watch a group of self-serving reformist idiots continue to abort the demands of revolutionary thinking women."[38]

During the early eighties, the accomplishments of black women writers and critics attracted the attention of leading black male intellectuals. For example, Amiri Baraka wrote an admiring and sympathetic Introduction to *Confirmation: An Anthology of AfricanAmerican Women* (1983), edited by himself and Amina Baraka. According to Baraka, women's oppression was incontestably of a piece with money capitalism and white supremacy, so that only a wide-scale working-class revolution could create conditions favorable to the end of sexism, classism, and racism. Perhaps the most telling evidence of black male attention to the works of black women appeared in Mari Evans' edition of *Black Women Writers (1950–1980): A Critical Evaluation* (1984), which contained critical texts by twenty-four women and fifteen men, including Addison Gayle, Stephen Henderson, George Kent, Haki Madhubuti (Don L. Lee), and Darwin Turner. Significantly, Evans' epigraph read: "For Hoyt W. Fuller, Jr., who planned to be a part of this book; for Larry P. Neal, who did not have a chance to respond; and for George E. Kent, who provided a revision for his article two weeks prior to his death. Their names are here in figure and in fact; earned space. They were our clear voices, our 'long-distance runners.' They bless our efforts."[39] Unequivocally, Evans sought to link black women's criticism of the eighties with the work of the male Black Aestheticians of the sixties and seventies. Invoking Fuller and Neal and recruiting Gayle and Henderson amounted to ways of dispelling the discontinuity in the critical projects of feminist intellectuals and male Black Aestheticians. In his Introduction to this landmark critical compendium on fifteen leading women writers, Henderson assigned high value to the work of black women writers and acknowledged the emergence of a distinctive black women's aesthetic. For his part, Gayle implicitly praised radical black literary women for fostering political, moral, and cultural awareness of and love for racial identity in racist white America.

Like McDowell in 1980, Stephen Henderson in 1983 worried about the lack of interest among black feminist critics in new theoretical developments, particularly structuralism and poststructuralism. He complained that *Black Women Writers* did not contain contributions from Houston Baker, Henry Louis Gates, and others interested in vanguard critical theory, though he allowed that certain sociological matters might presently be more pressing for black feminists. In any event, the new frontier for academic black feminists after the mid-eighties seemed destined to be critical theory. In the Introduction to *Black Feminist Criticism*, Barbara Christian expressed skepticism and irritation as well as anxious concern about the growing prominence of theory:

What is a literary critic, a black woman critic, a black feminist literary critic, a black feminist social literary critic? The adjectives mount up, defining, qualifying, the activity. How does one distinguish them? The need to articulate a theory, to categorize the activities is a good part of the activity. . . . What do these categories tell anyone about my method? Do I do formalist criticism, operative or expressive criticism, mimetic or structuralist criticism . . . ? I'm irked, weighed down by Foucault's library as tiers of books written on epistemology, ontology, and technique peer down at me? (x–xi)

No doubt, the need to cultivate theoretical sophistication would weigh more heavily upon black feminist critics as time passed.

ETHNIC STUDIES IN THE UNIVERSITY

America has been from the seventeenth century a land of immigrants whose arrivals spanned from the early entries during the European Renaissance of Dutch, English, French, and Spanish settlers to the most recent comings during the Space Age of Cubans, Haitians, Indo-Chinese, Mexicans, and Puerto Ricans. Historically speaking, a growing number of ethnic groups has constituted the fabric of American society. For example, more than thirty-five million aliens came to the United States from the West between 1815 and 1914. Historians divide this great migration into three stages.

The Celtic migration from 1815 to 1860 brought five million people primarily from Ireland, Scotland, and Germany. The Teutonic migration from 1860 to 1890 involved ten million people mainly from Scandinavia, Germany, England, and Bohemia. And the Mediterranean-Slavic migration from 1890 to 1914 amounted to twenty million émigrés largely from Eastern Europe, Italy, Asia Minor, and the Balkans. This great migration was interrupted by World War I and ended by legislation during the twenties. Despite long periods of such open-door practices and despite the almost continuous expansion of America's multiethnic society, various virulent forms of discrimination and prejudice against ethnic groups persisted from the earliest days up to the present. Sociologists and other thinkers in the postwar period argued the case that assimilation of ethnic groups into the "melting pot" of America had not occurred as was earlier expected and hoped for by politicians and social visionaries. Observing that ethnic consciousness and identity endured through generations, intellectuals during this period initiated theories of ethnic pluralism, rather than assimilation, to begin to account adequately for the multiethnic fabric of American life. In 1980 the *Harvard Encyclopedia of American Ethnic Groups* found it necessary to provide histories of 106 different ethnic groups.

Summarized by Werner Sollors in his highly informative article "Theory of American Ethnicity" (1981), the scholarship and intellectual activity in this field during the Space Age was immense and growing.[40] Not until the seventies did the rich ethnic diversity of American *literature* elicit significant responses from literary intellectuals. The Modern Language Association (MLA) served as a barometer of the times, creating a special-interest group on Ethnic Studies for its Delegate Assembly, establishing a Commission on the Literatures and Languages of America, setting up formal Divisions of Ethnic Studies and of Black American Literature and Culture and formal Discussion Groups on American Indian Literature, Asian American Literature, Chicano Literature, and Jewish American Literature, and compiling an annual list of Ethnic Studies Programs in universities. In addition, the Association published five books: *Minority Language and Literature: Retrospective and Perspective* (1977), ed. Dexter Fisher; *Afro-American Literature: The Reconstruction of Instruction* (1979), eds. Dexter Fisher and Robert B. Stepto; *Three American Literatures: Essays in Chicano, Native American, and Asian-American Literature for Teachers of American Literature* (1982), ed. Houston A. Baker, Jr.; *Studies in American Indian Literature: Critical Essays and Course Designs* (1983), ed. Paula Gunn Allen; and *Ethnic Perspectives in American Literature: Selected Essays on the European Contribution* (1983), eds. Robert Di Pietro and Edward Ifkovic. Symptomatically, an increasing number of journals were devoted primarily to ethnicity, including *Ethnicity, Ethnic Groups, Ethnic and Racial Studies, Ethnic Studies, Immigration History Newsletter, International Migration Review, Journal of Ethnic Studies* (two by this name), *Migration Today, Novak Report, Polyphony,* and *Spectrum.* Especially important was *MELUS,* set up in 1975 by the Society for the Study of the Multi-Ethnic Literature of the United States, an organization that held annual meetings as an affiliate of the MLA. The phenomenon of ethnicity lay at the heart of increasing numbers of new books and journals, conferences and discussion groups, organizations and commissions, anthologies and pedagogical aides, grants and research projects, and university programs and centers all devoted to studying ethnic groups in America.

Generally speaking, immigrants to the United States were expected to assimilate into the "core" Anglo-Saxon society, which encouraged renouncing ancestral culture and adopting mainstream values and behaviors. But rather than accept incorporation, immigrants frequently resisted Anglo-conformity, maintaining links with their ancestral origins, national or tribal histories, inherited religions, traditional languages or dialects, and distinctive cultural forms and customs. In addition to such voluntary ties to ethnicity, immigrants often bore witness to their ethnic identities involuntarily by virtue of physical attributes like size, hair texture, skin color, and other distinguishing anatomical features. Significantly, certain ethnic groups differed markedly from others since they were *colonized* rather than immigrant groups: they were incorporated by force into America; they were subject to special repression and misrepresentation; and they were largely consigned to the lowest strata of the labor force. Among such "minorities" were African Americans, certain Asian Americans, Chicanos, Native American Indians, and Puerto Ricans. To study the history of these people was essentially to engage in a counterhegemonic cultural analysis of internal colonialism,[41] as was first made clear to many American intellectuals by radical black artists and scholars during the stormiest years of the black liberation movement in the late sixties and early seventies.

Started in the late sixties, the movement to establish programs and/or departments of black studies (or Afro-American Studies) reached a culmination in 1976 when the National Council for Black Studies (NCBS) was founded. Of all the disenfranchised ethnic groups, the blacks were the most active and successful in setting up ethnic studies in the university, serving as models for other groups. At the heart of the black studies movement were the needs to document and analyze the historical experiences of black people and to work for constructive social changes. Like W. E. B. Du Bois, Carter G. Woodson, and other earlier scholar-activists, black intellectuals in the Space Age emphasized race, class, nationality, and culture as salient distinctive features of Afro-American ethnicity. The historical foci of black studies were, chronologically, pre-diaspora Africa, the slave trade, slavery, emancipation, rural life, migration, urban life, and contemporary black liberation.[42] Since the history of American blacks was clearly so unlike that of other ethnic groups, some justification existed for special, separate treatment of this subject.

In the cultural domain, the articulation of the Black Aesthetic served to mark off the boundaries and specify the special contents of the black arts in America. This task meshed with the contemporaneous project to develop an *ethnopoetics* sensitive to the ritual origins of art, the performative oral dimensions of poetry and drama, the vernacular traditions and modes of marginalized people, and the communal contexts of colonized cultures. Assimilating ethnic literatures to "Euro-American" traditions invariably resulted in the denigration of such literatures. Instead of narrow monocultural standards, flexible multiethnic criteria were needed. "America is pluralistic, but traditional literary studies and the educational system have been based upon an [exclusive] ethnocentric and homogeneous set of values that reveal only one aspect of man and society, greatly limiting knowledge of cultures and literatures outside the dominant group."[43] What was essential, therefore, were not only a new aesthetic and a new criticism, but also a new canon and a new curriculum for American literature. Anglo-Saxon literature was only one among many ethnic literatures. Just as American society was an amalgamation of many ethnic groups, so was its culture and specifically its literature.[44] The project of ethnopoetics aimed to bring the hegemony and repression fostered by intellectual Anglo-conformity to an end. The work of the Black Aestheticians was arguably one of the most important and memorable outcomes of this endeavor.

The movement to establish black studies in the university was initiated mainly by black students at predominantly white institutions, as was evident in early documents like *Black Studies in the University: A Symposium* (1969), edited by Armstead Robinson and other students at Yale University; *New Perspectives on Black Studies* (1971), edited by John W. Blassingame; and *Black Studies: Threat or Challenge* (1973), by Nick Aaron Ford. Between 1968 and 1971 approximately 150 programs and departments were set up in American colleges and universities. This number rose and fell over the next decade, reaching roughly 225 in the early 1980s. By this time over a million university students, teachers, and administrators were involved with black studies. Of the twenty-six major professional journals in the new field, nine were inaugurated between 1967 and 1974 and ten between 1975 and 1983. Seven preexisted the sixties, dating from the time when venerable black institutions and organizations carried on research into American negro culture. In its first fifteen years, black studies went through several overlapping stages of development: innovation, experimentation, crisis, and institutionalization. The fourth stage was marked by the founding of the NCBS in 1976 and by its development in 1980 of a recommended nationwide core curriculum for black studies.[45] Characteristically, programs in black studies focused on undergraduate interdisciplinary education, emphasizing inquiry into black history, sociology, and culture and stressing scrutiny of disciplinary methods of mainstream and minority scholarship. Some programs maintained commitments to community outreach, most often through internships.[46]

Threats to the strength and survival of black studies came from both outside and inside the programs. Externally, sources of funding posed continuous problems; conservative colleagues and administrators remained suspicious; and new vocationally-oriented black students saw little value in black studies. Internally, faculty with superior interdisciplinary credentials were difficult to find and to keep. (No Ph.D.-granting program in black studies existed in the United States.) Sometimes departments of black studies engaged in extensive remedial education, draining time and energy away from advanced scholarship and instruction. And differences in ideology and politics posed serious challenges to departmental harmony. Strife arose among blacks from Africa, the Caribbean area, and the United States and among nationalists, Pan-Africanists, integrationists, and revolutionaries (Marxist and otherwise).[47] For example, Harold Cruse in a review of Ron Karenga's influential *Introduction to Black Studies* (1982) complained angrily about Pan-African and Third World orientations in black studies programs, arguing that "too much of the Black Studies movement's alleged interest in Africa comes across as a mental avenue for romantic political escapism from the hard realities of Afro-American political survival in the United States."[48] Cruse resented the professionalization, depoliticization, and Africanization of American black studies. He wanted black studies to engage in scholarship and activism on behalf of the American black community and its students. Despite internal and external problems, strong programs in black studies survived the retrenchment of the 1970s and solidified their institutional status in the 1980s.

Among academic literary critics associated with the black studies movement, Darwin Turner was one of the leading figures during the early stages of formation. He edited a popular classroom anthology, *Black American Literature* (1969), which appeared in separate volumes on poetry, fiction, and essays and then in 1970 in a combined volume that included drama. He compiled a comprehensive bibliography for students titled *Afro-American Writers* (1970). He wrote essays on pedagogy; worked actively with the MLA, the College Language Association, and the National Council of Teachers of English; and co-authored the useful *Theory and Practice in the Teaching of Literature by Afro-Americans* (1971)—a monograph aimed at literature teachers from elementary school through college. Starting in 1972, Turner served for over a decade as chairman of the Afro-American Studies program at the University of Iowa. In the seventies he was on the first board of directors of the NCBS; he functioned as an advisory editor to such journals as *American Literature, Bulletin of Black Books, CLA Journal,* and *Obsidian;* and he labored as a referee for such agencies as the American Council of Learned Societies, the National Endowment for the Humanities, the National Humanities Center, and the Rockefeller Foundation. During this period, he penned several dozen essays for book collections and many introductions to reprinted classics of black literature. Unlike many other black literary scholars and historians, Turner extended his work into the areas not only of classroom pedagogy and university administration, but also of mainstream professional organizations and major granting agencies. All of this activity helped gain visibility and legitimacy for the emerging field of black studies.

Like other black literary intellectuals born between the mid-twenties and mid-thirties, Turner affirmed the existence of a Black Aesthetic and articulated its general features. "The literature which I regard as distinctively Afro-American is that which reproduces characteristics derived from the oral tradition of the folktale, depends upon language usage common in or unique to the black community, derives from and recreates significant aspects of black culture, such as the sermon, utilizes rhythms characteristic of the music composed by blacks, and advances attitudes unique to the black community."[49] Unlike leading Black Aestheticians, however, Turner argued single-mindedly for the primacy of literary values over sociological, political, historical, psychological, or moral values. He insisted that "in a literature class the primary criteria for selecting works should be literary" (18). Because he wanted to integrate black literature into the canon of American literature and into classroom textbooks, Turner deemed it essential to promote black works on the basis of reigning formalist values. Not surprisingly, his main premise was "Afro-Americans have written artfully" (37). In an essay published in *College English* in 1970, he argued "it is both absurd and hypocritical to raise the question of academic respectability about the study of the literature of an ethnic group composed of people who have been publishing literary works in America for more than 200 years, who have created some of the best-known folktales, and who include among their number such distinguished writers as Jean Toomer, Countee Cullen, Richard Wright, Gwendolyn Brooks, Ralph Ellison, James Baldwin, Lorraine Hansberry, and LeRoi Jones."[50] The separatism common among black literary people of his generation was not part of Turner's makeup. As an Afro-Americanist, he sought assimilation of black culture into the mainstream of American life and learning. Accordingly, he became a leading, influential mediator between more radical black intellectual groups and white mainstream organizations, agencies, and power holders.

During the time that ethnic studies programs, departments, journals, anthologies, pedagogical guides, and organizations were being put together in American universities, similar efforts were being undertaken on behalf of women's studies, as we saw in chapter 11. Starting in the late seventies, some feminists worked to link women's studies and ethnic studies. Black feminists were increasingly active in this endeavor. A landmark event in this undertaking was the publication by Florence Howe's Feminist Press in 1982 of *But Some of Us are Brave: Black Women's Studies,* edited by Gloria T. Hull, Patricia Bell Scott, and Barbara Smith. This compendium offered materials on black women's studies by such active black literary intellectuals as Barbara Christian, Gloria T. Hull, Sonia Sanchez, Barbara Smith, Erlene Stetson, Alice Walker, and Mary Helen Washington, among many others. The collection included eight separate bibliographies, twenty sample syllabi (eight devoted to literature), eighteen articles, guidelines on racism for consciousness-raising groups, eighteen recommendations, and an introduction by Hull and Smith. Among the important reprinted pieces in the text were Barbara Smith's "Toward a Black Feminist Criticism" and the manifesto of the Combahee River Collective. All in all, this book provided a mine of valuable material on black women's studies, serving as a foundation for a new enterprise.

In "Three's a Crowd: The Dilemma of the Black Woman in Higher Education" (1973), Constance Carroll, a black university administrator, complained about the racism of women's studies and the sexism of black studies, urging black feminists to agitate for change from within both movements and to serve as bridges between them. She argued against the secession of black women from these two movements and against the creation of a separate third force. Unlike Constance Carroll, Gloria Hull and Barbara Smith, in their Introduction to *Black Women's Studies,* recommended the formation of a new autonomous discipline within academic institutions: "Ideally, Black women's studies will not be dependent on women's studies, Black studies, or 'straight' disciplinary departments for its existence, but will be an autonomous academic entity making coalitions with all three."[51] They advocated setting up journals, organizations, conferences, research centers, and programs devoted specifically to black women. They linked this enterprise with the earlier black liberation movement, the rise of feminism, and especially the renaissance of black female literature, which characterized Afro-American literary culture after the waning of the Black Aesthetic movement during the last days of the Vietnam War.

When Hull and Smith started to plan their book as members in the late seventies of the MLA Commission on the Status of Women in the Profession, they initially envisioned a text on "Third World Women's Studies," not "Black Women's Studies." They soon discovered that they lacked the required expertise, but they expressed the hope that their "volume on Black women helps to create a climate where succeeding works on American Indian, Asian American, and Latina women can more swiftly come into being" (xxxi). Significantly, their book appeared the same year as Houston Baker's collection for the MLA on *Three American Literatures: Essays in Chicano, Native American, and Asian-American Literature for Teachers of American Literature.* It was not uncommon for the generation of black literary intellectuals born after the start of World War II to associate black studies with ethnic studies of other minority groups. What these groups had in common was the indelible historical experience of internal colonialism, of racism, of economic exploitation, and of misrepresentation. The dominance of Anglo-Saxon values resulted in the denigration of their languages, literatures, and cultures. Because they constituted a long-standing third estate within America, they were historical allies sharing a similar fate. Common to these ethnic groups during the sixties and seventies were the phenomena of rising nationalism and radical activism, of modest sociopolitical gains and remarkable cultural flowering, and of increased access to higher education and emergent institutionalization of ethnic studies. During the conservative years of the seventies and eighties, progress on most fronts for minority ethnic groups slowed down when it did not halt or reverse itself. The main tasks of the eighties for minority group intellectuals seemed to be to preserve and solidify earlier gains, to forge coalitions and connect with the mainstream where possible, and to increase intellectual subtlety and sophistication. It was a time for regrouping, rethinking, and reconnoitering. Venturesome Third World women constituted something of an exception to this pattern: working against the grain was their métier. So they moved ahead with ambitious plans.

CHAPTER THIRTEEN

Leftist Criticism
from the 1960s to the 1980s

LEGACIES OF THE NEW LEFT
AND THE MOVEMENT

THE PERIOD from the late fifties to the early seventies in America witnessed the rise of numerous vociferous countercultural groups, ranging from the Beats, Freedom Riders, civil rights marchers, advocates of a new left, free speech student activists, and antiwar protestors to black nationalists, pacifists, feminists, hippies, homegrown Third World radicals, gay rights advocates, fellow-travelers of farm workers' unions, yippies, and commune organizers. Taken together, such groups formed the "Movement," which seemed singularly dedicated, despite its many fronts, to undermining the stability of settled social conventions and to fostering a multifaceted campaign for liberation. New modes of dress, speech, music, literature, criticism, political participation, sexual morality, and living proliferated, bearing witness to an emergent sensibility rooted in political irreverence and an antinomian spirit. In retrospect, these tumultuous and gaudy times, which were followed by an enduring conservative backlash, seemed nothing if not unstable, shifting, and ephemeral.

Perhaps no phenomenon of this period has been judged more heterogeneous and radical than the new left, which was a loose, protean set of temporary coalitions formed between 1960 and 1972 mainly by white university students. At the heart of the new left was the Students for a Democratic Society (SDS)—an organization named in 1960 and supported by the League for Industrial Democracy, a group of older leftist intellectuals and trade unionists originally founded by Upton Sinclair and Jack London in 1905. In 1960 Robert Alan Haber, a student at the

University of Michigan, became president of SDS. Soon he and a fellow student, Tom Hayden, were changing this modest campus association of liberals, socialists, and undesignated radicals into a more ambitious and left-leaning organization. The considerable importance of SDS was perhaps first signaled at the landmark annual convention in June 1962 at Port Huron, Michigan, the site of the United Auto Workers summer camp. Among the five dozen people at the meeting were representatives from the National Student Association, the Student Christian Movement, the Student Nonviolent Coordinating Committee, the Young Democrats, and the Young People's Socialist League. Drafted by Hayden and refined by diverse hands, the widely disseminated, lengthy *Port Huron Statement* soon became a founding document of the emerging new left. Showing the influence of early Karl Marx, Herbert Marcuse, Paul Goodman, C. Wright Mills, and William Appleman Williams, the SDS manifesto made clear the young radicals' loss of faith in American institutions and bureaucracies, their devotion to participatory democracy and nonviolence, their distrust of vanguard parties and left-authoritarianism, and their self-conscious disregard of the old left and the Cold War liberals. It criticized America's foreign policy, rabid anticommunism, two-party system, military-industrial complex, racism, poverty, and academic apathy. It called on activist students to form coalitions with allies in labor, civil rights, and other liberal causes. At the peak of its strength in 1968, SDS reportedly had 100,000 members in 500 chapters.[1]

When in 1965 SDS dropped its constitutional clause excluding communists, it lost the support of the League for Industrial Democracy. The next year it gained members from the Progressive Labor Party, which consisted of young Marxist-Leninist Maoists expelled from the Communist Party some years earlier. By 1969 this opening to the left and the growing radicalism of the times resulted in the fragmentation of SDS into numerous factions, including notably Progressive Labor (Maoists), Revolutionary Youth Movement I (terroristic Weathermen), Revolutionary Youth Movement II (old style Stalinists), feminists (namely WITCH and Redstockings), left-liberal community organizers (reminiscent of thirties Popular Fronters), and libertarian socialists (in the manner of certain European neo-Marxists). An analogous split had occurred several years earlier in the editorial collective of one of the leading new left journals, *Studies on the Left* (1960–67). Among other key factions of the new left were the Trotskyist Socialist Workers Party, the participants in the Free Speech Movement, the pacifists associated with *Liberation* magazine, and the yippies of the Youth International Party.[2]

Characteristic of the new left in its heyday were a distaste for party and electoral politics; a growing dismay about the weaknesses of "representative" democracy; an emphasis on cultural dissent and participatory process rather than on political revolution; a preference for economic and political decentralization; a preoccupation with personal as well as social liberation; an increasing focus on students and the intelligentsia rather than the proletariat as the central postindustrial alienated class; a rising discontent with the aridities, manipulations, and failings of American society; a broad sympathy for Third World liberation movements; a widening criticism of universities for conducting military officer training and warfare research, for supporting the status quo, and for making immoral investments with endowment funds; and a fragile, nonpartisan shifting set of coalitions of increasingly divergent sects and factions. From the outset there existed within the ranks of the new left continuous tensions between activists and intellectuals, between political and cultural radicals, and between socialists and anarchists. Significantly, missing from these struggles was a strong syndicalistic element linked with traditional labor and trade unions. Following the advice of C. Wright Mills in his "Letter to the New Left" (1960), the young leaders at the start of this radical decade abandoned the "labor metaphysic." Since the industrial class of blue-collar workers in the postwar period had become contented, it could not be expected to lead or support movements for revolutionary change. Later the various Marxist-Leninist factions within and outside SDS would forcibly reintroduce the labor metaphysic.

Not surprisingly, members of the "old left" were often extremely critical of the new left. This was particularly the case with many of the New York Intellectuals. In his autobiography, William Phillips, for example, explained the policy of the *Partisan Review* in the sixties as being at once sympathetic to the "innocence and idealism of youth" yet "critical of the counterculture and the new left for converting their ignorance, their petulance, their self-indulgence into an infantile left politics and pop culture that managed to be both alienated and modish."[3] Philip Rahv was more stern and pragmatic in his assessment of new leftists: "they have shown no understanding whatsoever of the first rule of revolutionary strategy, which is the education, build-up, and preservation of its leading cadres."[4] He deplored the new left's lack of organization and discipline, citing Lenin and Trotsky on the necessity of forming parties and gaining mass support. Irving Howe's reflections in his autobiography revealed sympathy for the early years and despair about the closing days of the new left. In particular, Howe faulted latter-day new leftists for glorifying authoritarian Third World radicals like Fidel Castro and Ho Chi Minh; for replacing the proletariat with the intelligentsia as the vanguard of revolution; for promoting impractical ideas of participatory rather than representative democracy; for succumbing frequently to intolerant moral righteousness (especially on the part of anarchists and pacifists); for renouncing completely the benefits of incremental reform and gradualism in favor of apocalyptic and violent alternatives; for disclaiming electoral politics, support from the masses, and careful political organization; for ignoring the lessons of American radical history as well as the experiences of the old left; and for degenerating into implacable sects and factions. During the late sixties, observed Howe, "the New Left kept moving away from its earlier spirit of fraternity toward a hard-voiced dogmatism, from the ethic of nonviolence toward a romantic-nihilist fascination with a 'politics of the deed.' In the years of the Vietnam war the New Left grew rapidly, mostly as a center of opposition, but by locking itself into a politics more and more like that of the old left-wing sects, it made certain that in the end it would do no more than reenact their collapse."5

While the old leftists of the thirties criticized with shrewdness the political and ideological weaknesses of the new left, they lacked insight into the cultural and moral preoccupations of the radical student movements of the sixties. Living in an era of affluence rather than in a time of depression, many new leftists disregarded economic issues as well as European radical theories rooted in economism, preferring instead to stress the values of expanded consciousness and moral rectitude. In these circumstances, political parties, disciplined cadres, and a proletarian ethic seemed irrelevant. The Movement had comparatively little use, consequently, for the classical Marxism of Marx and Engels, of Mehring and Plekhanov, or of Lenin and Trotsky. It found more suited to its special needs the Freudian Marxism of the Frankfurt School, particularly of Marcuse with his emphasis on false consciousness, alienation from love, and repressive tolerance. It was primarily after the demise of the new left that other European Marxists like Adorno, Althusser, Benjamin, Bakhtin, and Gramsci came into vogue among American university intellectuals. Ironically, the "Marxism" of older native radicals was spurned while the radicalism of Third World figures like Fanon, Guevara, and Mao gained a certain popularity in the late sixties.

The impact of the counterculture on literary studies manifested itself not only in the rise of feminist criticism and the Black Aesthetic, but also in the appearance of student-oriented reader-response criticism and the new hermeneutics. That the turn to European phenomenological and existential criticism occurred at the time of the emergence in the fifties of the early counterculture was not surprising: the emphasis on consciousness and freedom, on alienation and meaninglessness, and on loneliness and personal interaction preoccupied American scholars and students in numerous fields of postwar inquiry from sociology, psychology, and political science to philosophy, religion, and literature. Significantly, a surge of countercultural interest in leftist literary criticism among university intellectuals born between the late twenties and late thirties happened in the sixties, as we shall see in the next section when we discuss Bruce Franklin, Louis Kampf, Paul Lauter, and Richard Ohmann. Unlike these critics appearing in the sixties, some American literary leftists coming into prominence in the seventies turned to modern European Neo-Marxism for assistance, as did Fredric Jameson and Jeffrey L. Sammons, who are examined in the third section of this chapter. During the late seventies the rise of literary-critical theory as a powerful and growing subdiscipline prompted certain Leftist Critics, especially Gerald Graff and Frank Lentricchia, to mount wide-ranging political critiques of all the main critical schools and movements, as will be explained in section four. Some Marxist critics born after 1940 and emerging in the late 1970s and thereafter joined Marxism to deconstruction—a linkage effected by, among others, John Brenkman, Michael Ryan, and Gayatri Spivak, who are treated below in the section titled "Left-Deconstructionist Criticism." What characterized all these Leftist Critics of the Space Age was a dedication to cultural criticism in opposition to the pervasive practices of formalist criticism. Some adherents of cultural criticism, like Stephen Greenblatt and Edward Said, carried on their leftist projects without relying on Marxist traditions or dogmas, instead constituting a "post-Marxist" practice considered below under "Post-Marxist Cultural Criticism." These and other leftist literary critics extended the legacies of the new left and the Movement that rocked American society between 1960 and 1972. In the early eighties the various modes of leftist criticism converged in a project to develop "cultural studies," which is explored below under " 'Cultural Studies' in the Academy."

Here was how one observer in the early eighties depicted the rise of Marxism in the university between the sixties and the eighties:

American Marxism is now respectable. Its practitioners teach and sometimes get tenure at Ivy League schools as well as community colleges. Their scholarship appears under the imprint of university presses and mainstream quarterlies. And, in certain fields, American history for example, Marxism is the mainstream. . . . Just about every field, certainly every social science, has its own Marxist journal and its own radical caucus or subgroup that competes or meets with the main professional organization. Together these groups have more than 12,000 members, the largest and most important cohort of left-wing scholars in American history.[6]

Indeed, prominent literary leftists in the eighties taught at leading universities, edited and contributed to radical and mainstream journals, held leadership positions in major associations and institutes, and published with prestigious academic presses. Although the relations between the academy and leftist proponents of cultural criticism will be taken up later in this chapter, it is enough at the outset to observe that between the late sixties and mid-eighties a heterogenous and multifaceted movement of leftist literary critics rose to prominence. At the same time many of the older surviving left-wing New York Intellectuals—Howe, Kazin, Phillips, and Rahv, to name just four—came to occupy positions of eminence at leading universities. Needless to say, the interaction between these groups was minimal, though Richard Poirier, for example, sought to link the traditions of the old and new left through his journal, *Raritan* (established 1981). And Gerald Graff, as well as certain younger New York Intellectuals, sometimes joined together the insights of the new and the old left.

ASSAULTING THE INSTITUTION OF LITERARY STUDIES

The increasingly radical mood and ethos of the sixties was not limited to the student new left. Groups of former students, graduate students, professors, and young professionals started to organize in the closing years of the decade. In 1967, for instance, SDS set up the Movement for a Democratic Society to nurture radicalism among nonstudents. This same year Radicals in the Professions was formed; the following year the New University Conference (NUC) began operations. Attending the NUC organizing conference in March 1968 were several key SDS alumni, including Al Haber, Tom Hayden, Staughton Lynd, and Richard Flacks. According to its agenda, NUC aimed to organize campuses, encourage radical research, publicize the academy's complicity in fostering war and oppression, and develop radical perspectives in the professions. The latter goal was carried out by the formation of radical caucuses within the professions, which proliferated in mainstream disciplines between 1968 and 1972—the year

NUC folded. Among the members of the Steering Committee of NUC in 1968 was Louis Kampf, a thirty-nine-year-old associate professor and head of the Literature Section at the Massachusetts Institute of Technology. A few months earlier Kampf, an SDS member, had become Associate National Director of Resist, a group of activist clergymen, journalists, authors, intellectuals, and professors vehemently opposed to the Vietnam War and supportive of draft resistance, counting among its distinguished members Philip Berrigan, Noam Chomsky, William Sloan Coffin, Allen Ginsberg, Paul Goodman, Dwight MacDonald, Herbert Marcuse, Richard Ohmann, Linus Pauling, Susan Sontag, and Benjamin Spock.

On the first day of the 1968 convention of the Modern Language Association (MLA), held during December in New York with twelve thousand members in attendance, Louis Kampf and two graduate students were arrested in the lobby of the Americana Hotel following a scuffle with hotel guards over the right of these activists to put up NUC posters. This arrest outraged many MLA members and immediately became a *cause célèbre*. Hats were passed to raise bail money. Rumors spread, exaggerating the banal encounter with the law. Caught up in a growing celebrity, Louis Kampf was elected second vice-president of the MLA, succeeding to the presidency in 1971. At the same business meeting the six hundred literary scholars in attendance passed four political resolutions: one against the Vietnam War; one against the draft; one against repression of writers; and one against antiriot provisions in educational legislation. It was also at this meeting that the Commission on the Status of Women in the Profession was first proposed. This radical turn of the MLA constituted one instance, however modest, of the expansion of the Movement into the professions.

The person nominating Kampf at the business meeting was Richard Ohmann, the thirty-seven-year-old editor of *College English,* member of NUC, and convention roommate of Kampf. Both young professors were socialists increasingly critical of the institution of literary studies, including mainstream textbooks, pedagogical guides, journals, learned societies, foundations, presses, graduate programs, modes of financing, testing procedures, professional ethics, and reigning institutional ideologies. Written between 1965 and 1975, Ohmann's well-known *English in America: A Radical View of the Profession* (1976) avowed collaboration with Kampf: "After seventeen years of talking and working with him," wrote Ohmann in his Acknowledgments, "I am not sure which ideas are his and which mine, but I know that I would not have written this book without his comradeship."[7] Moreover, Ohmann noted, "I did much of my thinking and writing about the profession in collaboration with members of the Radical Caucus in English and the Modern Languages." Regarding the thirty-thousand member MLA, Ohmann deemed it, despite its momentary radical turn in 1968, an elitist "leviathan" that "pursued the politics of neutrality and guild interest, which means, basically, maintaining the status quo" (45). What he most deplored was the complicity of literary intellectuals with the professionalization of the discipline fostered by "bourgeois" society in its decaying phase of advanced industrial capitalism. Ultimately, he hoped for a socialist transformation of society and the profession.

According to Ohmann, literature possessed two forces: one was conservative and tradition-affirming; the other was critical and potentially revolutionary. The institution of English Studies denied the critical force at every turn, preserving a prophylactic view of literature and thereby ensuring the harmlessness of literary culture. All the schools of "bourgeois" criticism presented literature as a special and separate thing above circumstances, commercialization, politics, science, and technology: literature miraculously raised critics and students out of the present and made them one with timeless "tradition." In Ohmann's view, however, literature "comes out of specific times and social conditions, and it helps create the future. Like all art, it tends toward the rebellious and iconoclastic . . ." (58). But the dominant formalism of English departments domesticated such subversive force, engendering a politics of things-as-they-are and a delusive methodology of disinterestedness and value-free inquiry in harmony with the ivory tower model of the modern university and its ethic of professionalism. Professors of literature taught not only the skills of analysis, organization, and fluency, but the attitudes of detachment, caution, and cooperation, all of which were essential for the capitalist technostructure and for the smooth functioning of liberal society. Like all institutions, academic literary studies were part of the social order and survived by assisting in its maintenance. What society and its leaders wanted from literature and criticism was a culture supporting the social order and discouraging rebellion while sanctioning safe modes of nonconformity.

In constructing his views of literature and criticism, Richard Ohmann did not discuss writers, literary works, movements, and themes; rather he examined textbooks, professional associations, standardized tests, and departments. He was concerned not with an aesthetic realm of literary and human values, but with the current socioeconomic and political grounds of cultural institutions. From the sixties to the eighties, two methods of inquiry characteristic of leftist literary intellectuals were institutional and ideological analysis.

In a spate of essays published between 1967 and 1970 in such outlets as

Harper's Magazine, The Nation, and *Change,* Louis Kampf castigated reigning schools of criticism from formalism and myth criticism to existentialism and structuralism for refusing to relate literature to life and thought to action, and for making critical inquiry a passive, voyeuristic, schizoid technique practiced by alienated professionals. This debased mode of criticism served the corrupt interests of academic institutions in America. It was clear to Kampf that "the university is a servant of the economy, that its institutional function is to contribute to the technological triumphs of capitalism. In this process departments of literature are as deeply involved as departments of industrial management."[8] The main functions of academics were to support the status quo, to award credentials, to channel students into the social hierarchy, and to turn out industrial cadres. "The American university performs a variety of related functions. It produces war-related research, propagates ruling class ideologies, trains experts in counter-insurgency, helps develop strategies for riot control, and so forth."[9] What typified university departments of literature as well as other academic departments were careerism, bureaucratization, isolationism, aestheticism, and cooption by capitalist society, all leading to "quiet acceptance of intellectual and moral treason" ("SLS," 90).

Kampf held that literature played two contradictory roles: it engendered cultural oppression and it enabled emotional and intellectual liberation. In the dominant interests of the ruling class, the high culture of Western Europe (the "Great Books") took precedence over ethnic, women's, and working-class cultures. However, "force-feeding people on a rich diet of Western masterpieces will only make them more sick" ("TL," 30) by creating a sense of inferiority, immobilizing activity, and promoting acquiescence. Rather than an instrument or weapon of ruling-class oppression, literature was potentially liberating, provided it was set within a living context close to daily life and removed from its sacrosanct place in the great tradition. "In spite of our academic merchants, literature is not a commodity, but the sign of a creative act which expresses personal, social, and historical needs. As such it constantly undermines the status quo" ("SLS," 91). The task of the radical critic was to destroy received dogmas and procedures, letting literature be an instrument of agitation and resistance and a force for freedom and genuine liberation. "As members of the educated middle class, we must learn that our words should discredit our own culture. Those of us who are literary intellectuals and teachers ought to illustrate in our work that the arts are not alone available to those who are genteel . . ." ("TL," 32–33). The ultimate object of Kampf's anger was the division of capitalist society into classes and the complicity of the university in this pernicious social stratification—all of which the institution of literary studies both reflected and reinforced.

In a 1972 special issue of *TriQuarterly* on "Literature in Revolution," which contained contributions from such radicals as Noam Chomsky, Todd Gitlin, Carl Oglesby, and Raymond Williams, Frederick Crews presented a tough-minded critique of the new left and the Movement, singling out Louis Kampf for Stalinist tendencies, for confounding literature with propaganda, for confusing teaching with indoctrination, and for hating while loving bourgeois literature. As far as Crews was concerned, Kampf was like a preacher wedded to a whore whose wares he was obliged to sell. In a little-known essay of 1969 written for fellow radicals, Kampf substantiated Crews' wicked image: "When I last stood in the Piazza Navona, watching my fellow tourists more than Bernini's fountains, I hardly dared think of the crimes, the human suffering, which made both the scene and my being there possible. I stood surrounded by priceless objects—and I valued them. Yet I hate the economic system which has invested finely chiseled stone with a price."[10] In *A Margin of Hope* (1982), Irving Howe portrayed Kampf as a man "driven out of his wits by the *Zeitgeist*" (307). Kampf shrewdly confirmed as much in his article "The Humanities and Inhumanities" (1968) published in *The Nation*. Because industrial capitalism created severe divisions between people's values, their daily activities, and wider social reality, it sometimes forced them into irrational acts. Kampf's example was 300 students in Boston during 1967 turning in their draft cards and thereby rejecting their civilization. Like this mad and disfiguring act, the acts of critical resistance by radical intellectuals sometimes necessarily manifested themselves as witless or deranged. The social forces at play demanded that acts of resistance be deemed madness.

When the MLA put together its centennial issue of *PMLA* in May 1984, it commissioned Paul Lauter to write about the impact of society on the profession of literary criticism between 1958 and 1983. Lauter was a radical associated with the Movement in the sixties. Ohmann had benefited from his assistance, as noted in his Acknowledgments to *English in America*. Among Lauter's radical credentials were his teenage membership in the National Association for the Advancement of Colored People; his antiwar, antinuke, anti-ROTC, and pro-union activities in the sixties; his full-time work for the Quakers promoting peace; his teaching in the Mississippi Freedom Schools of 1964; his membership in SDS; his being jailed on several occasions for radical protests; his feminist activity, particularly the cofounding with Florence Howe (herself a radical) of the Feminist Press in 1969; and his coediting with Louis Kampf of *The Politics of Literature: Dissenting Essays on the Teaching of English* (1970), which contained a long introductory essay and eleven articles by such leftists as Bruce Franklin, Florence Howe, Richard Ohmann, and Lillian Robinson, several of whom originally contributed their articles to a special Marxist issue of *College English* published in March 1970. Like other radicals born in the thirties, Lauter started his academic career just when the "consensus" of the fifties was coming apart and the "crisis" of the sixties was beginning. And too, he came to professional maturity during the retrenchment of the seventies. Looking back over a quarter century from the vantage point of the early eighties, Lauter singled out three areas of special concern to him about literary studies in America: the state of the MLA; the status of the canon; and the situation of critical theory and practice.

According to Lauter, the MLA between the fifties and eighties had expanded and diversified immensely, yet "the hierarchy of the profession remains fundamentally unaltered, so—as yet—does the hierarchy of what we value."[11] Despite impressive gains in women's and ethnic scholarship, the canon of texts actually taught in university classrooms during the eighties showed "little significant improvement over a 1948 survey by the National Council of Teachers of English of ninety introductory courses" (425). This conclusion was based on two surveys of hundreds of syllabi collected from around the nation in the eighties. Just as the reigning critical ideology in the late 1950s was "formalism," so the dominant mode of criticism in the 1980s was "formalism," however expanded to include hermeneutics, semiotics, and poststructuralism, all of which criticism "accepts the formalist stance by analyzing texts, including its own discourse, primarily as autonomous objects isolated from their social origins or functions" (425). What most dismayed Lauter about such fashionable criticism were its alignment with linguistics and philosophy rather than history and sociology, its tendency to become obscurant self-referential metacriticism in a debauch of professionalism, its preference for a limited canon of elitist texts, its increasing abnegation of practical exegesis and humanistic values, and its deepening occupation of the core of the profession.

Kampf, Ohmann, and Lauter assaulted the institution of literary studies most memorably and dramatically in their focus upon the MLA, the leading national organization of academic literary professionals, which embodied and disseminated through its journals, newsletter, reports, books, conventions, and intricate networks of information and influence the reigning scholarly and pedagogical models and values shaping literary research and teaching in America. Although the activism in the MLA of the NUC, Radical Caucus, and various Movement people led to strong leftist resolutions, to the presidencies of Louis Kampf and Florence Howe, to the creation of the Commission on the Status of Women in the Profession, and to Marxist discussion groups and forums at the annual conventions, the impact on the MLA of such visible successes was minimal and short-lived, according to the retrospective judgments of Ohmann and Lauter. Following the radicalism of the late sixties and early seventies, "formalism" still held sway in scholarship and the canon remained largely unchanged in teaching. Ethnic, working-class, women's, and popular literature did not displace the "Great Books" of aristocratic and middle-class white males. Sociohistorical cultural criticism did not replace New Criticism, myth criticism, or existential criticism. Instead, hermeneutics, structuralism, and deconstruction arrived at the turn of the decade to strengthen the dominant practice of privatized antihistorical linguistic analysis, as did reader-response criticism in its own way. The leftist case against these new arrivals was most effectively made later by Frank Lentricchia in his widely read *After the New Criticism* (1980).

Yet, despite the rise of conservatism and the retrenchment characteristic of America in the 1970s, and despite the demise of the new left and the Movement, society seemed a long way from the Cold War consensus, the McCarthyism, and the purges carried out by the House Committee on Un-American Activities, all of which marked the 1950s. In a mid-seventies collection of eighteen essays by such Marxist critics as Lee Baxandall, Bruce Franklin, Fredric Jameson, Gaylord C. LeRoy, Lillian Robinson, and Paul Siegel, Norman Rudich argued that a modest Marxist Renaissance was underway, which *Weapons of Criticism: Marxism in America and the Literary Tradition* (1976) aimed to further. What was odd about the Marxist criticism of this Renaissance associated with the post-1950s new left and the Movement was its complete disregard of the old left. Mention was never made of V. F. Calverton, James T. Farrell, Granville Hicks, Bernard Smith, Edmund Wilson, or other Leftist Critics prominent in the thirties. The native tradition of radicalism stemming from the nineteenth century had been forgotten during the heyday of the literary new left. Portrayed in broad strokes as "sectarian," "communist," and "Stalinist," this stigmatized heritage interested only historians and some younger New York Intellectuals. Not only was the old belief in the proletariat as the sole vanguard of socialist revolution in serious question, but the aura and attractiveness of early

Soviet Marxism was dramatically diminished by latter-day Russian interventions in Hungary in 1956 and in Czechoslovakia in 1968 and by the Polish workers' strike in 1970. To the intellectuals in the Movement, Mao and Che Guevara were more interesting and available than Stalin and his discredited successors. Not until Frank Lentricchia published in 1983 an extended meditation on Kenneth Burke's early radical criticism did the new Marxism connect with the old in a productive way.

Appearances to the contrary, the status of Leftist Critics in universities during the early 1970s was precarious. Nothing illustrated this fact more for literary people than the firing in 1972 by Stanford University of Bruce Franklin, a tenured associate professor of English and American literature. (Parenthetically, the year 1972 witnessed the dissolution of the NUC, the end of Kampf's term as president of the MLA, and the resounding defeat in the national presidential election of the liberal George McGovern by the conservative Richard Nixon.) While Bruce Franklin's scholarly credentials were impeccable, his political views on the role of the university in war research were unacceptable to Stanford's administration because they led Franklin to advocate student protests against secret military research being carried out at the university. Two years after his dismissal, Franklin secured a one-year position at Wesleyan University where Ohmann and Rudich worked and then a permanent position at the Newark campus of Rutgers University, where he was named distinguished professor in 1980.

Bruce Franklin was a socialist in the early sixties who turned to Marxism-Leninism and Maoism in 1967, as he later explained in his autobiography, *Back Where You Came From: A Life in the Death of the Empire* (1975). Published in 1970 in *College English* and in Kampf's and Lauter's *The Politics of Literature*, Franklin's infamous personal essay on "The Teaching of Literature in the Highest Academies of the Empire" engaged in both angry criticism of the formalistic institution of literary studies and in Chinese-style self-criticism and autobiography. From the latter we learned Franklin came from the working class; he deplored aristocratic and bourgeois cultural values; his undergraduate education weaned him from his proletarian roots and preferences; he served as an intelligence officer during the mid-fifties in the Strategic Air Command, supporting spy planes which dropped agents to create provocations; he went to Stanford and earned his Ph.D. in 1961; and he was irate about his graduate education. Of the literature faculty, Franklin observed:

Not one was concerned with the major ideological questions of our century. Not one was familiar with the major ideas that attacked their own beliefs.

They were universally ignorant of Marx, Engels, Lenin, Mao, and Marxist criticism. (This was before they hired, for two years as it turned out, that noted professional anti-communist Irving Howe.)[12]

In Franklin's view, what was wrong with academic literary professionals was their thorough immersion in the bourgeois ideology of formalism, which itself was rooted in the counterrevolutionary antiproletarianism of the thirties. "In the present era, formalism is the use of aestheticism to blind us to social and moral reality" (113). The elite works championed by formalist doctrine despised the masses and their leaders. This regime relegated popular works like westerns and science fiction to "sub-literary" categories, as it did with the texts of women and ethnic authors. According to formalist dogma, human nature was corrupt whereas great literature was a transcendent human achievement separate from the constraints of social class and political struggle. For Franklin, however, "a thing is good only when it brings real benefit to the masses of the people," as his epigraph from Mao's talks at the Yenan Forum indicated.

The influence of the leading male Leftist Critics who had emerged at the height of the Movement, including Kampf, Ohmann, Lauter, Franklin, and others, diminished throughout the seventies not simply because of the conservative backlash, but mainly because they did not produce polemical pieces on the newest modes of criticism and theory that swept through the profession in the post-Vietnam era. This task was undertaken during the closing years of the decade most notably by the younger socialists Gerald Graff and Frank Lentricchia. What their immediate forerunners had accomplished was to create a highly public rebirth of socialist criticism, clearing a space for further developments within the institution of literary studies. As a result of the literary new left, certain major mainstream presses, journals, learned societies, research institutes, and graduate programs were comparatively more open to and interested in leftist research than they had ever been.

EUROPEAN NEO-MARXISM
AND DIALECTICAL THEORY

Starting in the 1970s, some American literary critics on the left sought to develop a sophisticated dialectical theory based on the works of leading European Neo-Marxists. The earliest and most important text in this endeavor was Fredric Jameson's *Marxism and Form: Twentieth-Century Dialectical Theories of Literature* (1971). Among other such books were Jeffrey L.

Sammons' *Literary Sociology and Practical Criticism: An Inquiry* (1977) and Fredric Jameson's later *The Political Unconscious: Narrative as a Socially Symbolic Act* (1981). What initially distinguished these and similar studies from the works of the Movement critics was a scholarly immersion in the Marxist projects of contemporary German and/or French theorists.

In *Marxism and Form*, Fredric Jameson offered a monograph-length final chapter titled "Towards Dialectical Criticism," preceded by detailed scrutinies of T. W. Adorno, Walter Benjamin, Herbert Marcuse, Ernest Bloch, Georg Lukács, and Jean-Paul Sartre. Jameson made it clear in his Preface that he was not interested in postrevolutionary Soviet Marxism, Third World peasant Marxism, or interwar American industrial Marxism. His preoccupation was with consumer capitalism and postindustrial society— the major concerns of contemporary Western European Neo-Marxism. The revealing opening words of his book were:

> When the American reader thinks of Marxist literary criticism, I imagine that it is still the atmosphere of the 1930s which comes to mind. The burning issues of those days—anti-Nazism, the Popular Front, the relationship between literature and the labor movement, the struggle between Stalin and Trotsky, between Marxism and anarchism—generated polemics which we may think back on with nostalgia but which no longer correspond to the conditions of the world today.[13]

Several pages later Jameson declared that "the reality with which Marxist criticism of the 1930s had to deal was that of a simpler Europe and America, which no longer exist. Such a world had more in common with the life forms of earlier centuries than it does with our own" (xvii). By arguing that different kinds of social reality required different forms of Marxism, Jameson was able to jettison the traditional burdens of orthodoxy, to justify various Neo-Marxisms, and to judge irrelevant the old left and the remaining leftists among the aged New York Intellectuals. On the role on the new left he was strangely silent, though he admired the works of Lukács, Marcuse, and Mills—tutelary figures for many Movement intellectuals. In his view, the successful importation and use of Continental dialectical Marxism faced serious challenges because of the entrenched position in America of empiricism, logical positivism, liberalism, antitheoreticism, and especially anticommunism.

Trained at Yale University in the fifties by Erich Auerbach and Henri Peyre, Jameson began his career in the sixties as a philological and phenomenological critic. Sometime early in the decade he evidently became a Marxist without, however, renouncing his previous critical commitments. In the work of Sartre he found a model of phenomenological Marxism which could be linked to Hegelianism and Marxist dialectics in the manner of Adorno. Essentially, Jameson wanted a rigorous stylistic and rhetorical literary criticism capable of expanding its scope to take into account political, socioeconomic, and historical reality. The job of dialectical criticism was to move from analysis of the private artwork of the individual consciousness to the public reality of collective history—from spirit to matter, literature to sociology, the cultural superstructure to the socioeconomic infrastructure, Hegel to Marx. This hermeneutic project entailed deliberate shifting of levels in dramatic leaps of transcoding. According to Jameson, the essential goal of dialectical analysis was "to reconcile the inner and the outer, the intrinsic and extrinsic, the existential and the historical . . . , transcending the sterile and static opposition between formalism and a sociological or historical use of literature between which we have so often been asked to choose" (330–31). Jameson characterized the crucial moment of linkage alternately as "incarnation" or as "totalization."

As a work of literature touched the ground of social history, it manifested its inevitable interrelations with class struggle, economic modes of production, and ideological orientations. Following various Neo-Marxists, Jameson avoided assigning a privileged role to purely economic determinants, personally preferring to ground literature in the human interactions embodied in social struggle. The trouble with vulgar or economistic Marxism was its idealistic or metaphysical view of class, which comported poorly with late American capitalism, whose lower classes were largely outside its borders in the Third World. What Jameson aimed to do was to free literary Marxism from its outdated mystique of the proletariat and from its commitment to mechanical economic determinism.

As a Germanist committed to sociological criticism, Jeffrey Sammons, like Frederic Jameson, was disturbed about the bifurcation of postwar European and American criticism. He wanted to import German literary sociology into the American academy in order to combat the "salvationist poetics" and "reactionary allegiances" fostered by formalism.[14] His basic premise in *Literary Sociology and Practical Criticism* was that "the relationship of literature and society, of imagination and reality, is reciprocal, or, as it is now common to say, dialectical" (xii). What motivated his project was the "extraordinary revival of Marxism in German scholarship" (6) and what frustrated it was the "failure of American criticism, increasingly fascinated by the current French fireworks, to come to terms with modern Marxist theory" (14). For Sammons, literature served important human ends, particularly truth, rationality, and liberation, and criticism needed to restore these humanistic ends to literary study by showing literature for what it was: "literature is a product of human beings in their relations with one another and speaks to human beings in their relations with one another" (177). Where Sammons most differed from Jameson was in his willingness to criticize the excesses and weaknesses of Marxist criticism and in his advocacy of critical pluralism.

In *The Political Unconscious*, Jameson developed a Marxist hermeneutic indebted not only to European Neo-Marxists, but a broad range of non-Marxist critics, as, for example, Jacques Derrida, Northrop Frye, A. J. Greimas, Jacques Lacan, and Paul Ricoeur. In other words, he sought to construct an interpretive model by selecting from and synthesizing the most powerful research in the areas of deconstruction, myth criticism, semiotics, psychoanalysis, and phenomenological hermeneutics. In addition, he made use of the work of contemporary Marxists, including, for instance, Louis Althusser, Mikhail Bakhtin, Claude Lévi-Strauss, and Pierre Macherey as well as certain British leftist intellectuals. *The Political Unconscious* was more broadly learned, scholarly, and eclectic than *Marxism and Form*, taking into account many schools and movements developed since the sixties and situating itself at the crossroads of contemporary theory. It was this book, if not his four earlier ones, that rendered Jameson the leading Marxist literary critic in America. Published in autumn 1982, a special issue of *Diacritics* on Jameson's book certified the significance of his project.

As we saw in the closing pages of chapter 7, Jameson constructed a twofold hermeneutic. The negative, destructive phase demystified illusions in an operation of ideological analysis. The positive, restorative phase provided access to utopian elements in cultural productions. Significantly, James adopted a "textualist" account of history and reality to ground his hermeneutic. Adapting poststructualist insights, he argued "that history is *not* a text, not a narrative, master or otherwise, but that, as an absent cause, it is inaccessible to us except in textual form, and that our approach to it and to the Real itself necessarily passes through its prior textualization, its narrativization in the political unconscious."[15] This textualization provided an escape from both empiricism and vulgar materialism, putting Marxist dialectics on an "equal footing" with contending Continental modes of analysis. Jameson had come some way from his criticism of structuralism in *The Prison-House of Language* (1972), which we examined at the conclusion of chapter 9. Whatever a Marxist hermeneutic of cultural works ultimately revealed, it could not, in Jameson's view, "be separated from a passionate and partisan assessment of everything that is oppressive in them and that knows complicity with privilege and class domination . . ." (299).

Perhaps the finest English-language history of the rise of European Neo-Marxism between the 1920s and the 1960s was Perry Anderson's *Considerations on Western Marxism* (1976). Born in the late thirties, Anderson was a British sociologist and editor of the influential *New Left Review*. In 1982 he delivered three lectures in the Wellek Library Lecture Series at the University of California at Irvine, where Frank Lentricchia was teaching at the time. Later published as *In the Tracks of Historical Materialism* (1984), Anderson's lectures reviewed the state of Western Marxism in the 1970s. In his judgment, Marxist theory thrived in the Space Age whereas Marxist political strategy withered badly. Not only did he lament the retreat from the classical Marxist goal of a realizable socialism, but he deplored the rise to prominence of structuralism and poststructuralism, both of which diluted further any interest in political action. Explicitly, Anderson criticized Marxist intellectuals for renouncing radical activity in favor of critical theory. Unlike the Movement critics, American Marxist literary theorists in the seventies labored under the charge of political inactivity and impotence— an accusation sometimes lodged against Fredric Jameson. Efforts like Lentricchia's to differentiate the political work of the specific intellectual from that of the radical intellectual did little to disarm such criticism, as we shall see momentarily.

THE POLITICS OF "THEORY"

Within the field of academic literary studies between the sixties and the eighties, the rebirth of leftist criticism and the expansion of the subdiscipline "theory" co-occurred. As discussed in chapter 6, a wave of Continental ideas started sweeping American criticism during the sixties, cresting throughout the seventies and eighties as hermeneutics, semiotics, deconstruction, Neo-Marxism, Lacanian psychoanalysis, German reception theory, and French feminism gained growing numbers of adherents in the universities. During this time the increasing expansion and institutionalization of the domain of literary-critical "theory" was signaled by the appearances of new specialized journals like *Diacritics, New Literary History, Critical Inquiry,* and numerous others; of new institutes like the School of Criticism and Theory and the International Summer Institute for Semiotic and Structural Studies; of new nationwide theory groups like the MLA's populous Division on Literary Criticism and the Society for Critical Exchange; of an onslaught of original and translated theoretical books from certain prestigious university presses like Chicago, Columbia, Cornell, Indiana, Johns Hopkins, Northwestern, and Yale (among others); of a growing number of special issues of journals and symposiums on theory; of an influx of new theoretical terms, issues, and questions; and of the spreading prominence of academic theorists as leading figures in the profession. Over the course of the period from the late sixties to the early eighties, the growing importance and centrality within aca- demic literary studies of theory resulted in its constituting the vanguard, if not the core, of the discipline. It became an ever more tumultuous site where new and old schools, movements, and factions pressed their contend- ing projects and points of view with such vigor as to make the earlier struggles of the thirties, forties, and fifties among Marxists, New Critics, Chicago Critics, New York Intellectuals, Myth Critics, and Existential Critics seem, in retrospect, to be modest skirmishes.

Actually, the growing importance of theory within the academy dates from the immediate postwar years, as marked by the appearance and broad success of Wellek's and Warren's *Theory of Literature* (1949) and later of Frye's *Anatomy of Criticism* (1957). By the time Hirsch's *Validity in Inter- pretation* (1967), Donato's and Macksey's *The Structuralist Controversy* (1970), de Man's *Blindness and Insight* (1971), and Bloom's *The Anxiety of Influence* (1973) registered their collective impact in the mid-seventies, the significance of theory was more or less firmly established. None of this was comforting to literary historians, period specialists, textual bibliographers, biographers, literary journalists, or creative writers. Long-standing tensions among scholars, nonacademic literary intellectuals, and university theorists broadened and deepened. After the mid-seventies, it was not unusual to read in scholarly articles or popular reviews sarcastic remarks about "the- ory," particularly deconstruction, which most captivated the antitheoretical imagination by its evident nihilism and sophistry. Within the ranks of theorists, meanwhile, interest in the politics of theory sharpened. As in the thirties and the sixties, so in the seventies and the eighties, it was the critics on the left who most often led the debates on politics, though it must be recalled that the New York Intellectuals had kept this tradition alive during the forties and fifties when other schools more or less repressed questions of politics.

In the immediate post-Vietnam era the two most celebrated Leftist Critics of the politics of vanguard theory were arguably Gerald Graff and Frank Lentricchia, the first born in 1937 and the second in 1940. Younger by several years than the Movement critics Kampf, Ohmann, Lauter, and

Franklin, Graff and Lentricchia exposed not only formalism, myth criticism, and existentialism—as did their new left predecessors—but also phenomenology, hermeneutics, reader-response criticism, structuralism, and deconstruction. Self-consciously, they assaulted the emergent ideologies of the discipline, criticizing especially any and all antihistorical and formalistic tendencies.

In the 50th anniversary issue of *Partisan Review* published in 1985, Gerald Graff offered a brief, revealing autobiographical account of his twenty years in the profession, recalling his turn to the left in the sixties: "in 1966, I had become a convert to the new Left. My new leftism was more theoretical than activist, though I took part in the usual teach-ins and demonstrations and signed the usual protest petitions. I read Marx, Lukács, and Noam Chomsky's articles in the *New York Review of Books,* and I started calling myself—when anybody asked—a democratic socialist."[16] Graff went on to characterize his special commitment to the rationalist old left and the New York Intellectuals as a conservative corrective to the chic irrationalism of the counterculture and radical new left and as a way to preserve for literary criticism the crucial linkage of traditional morality, politics, and cultural inquiry.

In *Poetic Statement and Critical Dogma* (1970), Graff had criticized New Critics and Myth Critics, arguing that poetic discourse was not only dramatic, experiential, and organically unified, but also propositional, assertive, and structurally semantic. Not denying that poems dramatized fictional attitudes and generated verbal tensions or that poems contained myths and archetypes, Graff insisted that such features did not exclude the expository and discursive elements of poetry, which offered statements on matters of fact, knowledge, belief, and morality. In essence, Graff sought to open literature to extrinsic as well as intrinsic criticism, to undermine exclusive belief in the sacred autonomy of the literary artifact, and to bring literature into contact with history, social reality, politics, and ethics. In an Appendix, he interrogated the decision of the Bollingen Prize Committee to make its award in 1949 to the anti-Semitic and fascist work of Ezra Pound, concluding that the poet's pernicious beliefs irretrievably marred his work and disqualified it from any prize. What the case of the Bollingen award illustrated, in Graff's account, was the inseparability of literature, politics, and morality.

It was in *Literature Against Itself: Literary Ideas in Modern Society* (1979) that Graff dramatically extended and deepened his assault on vanguard schools of criticism, including New Criticism, myth criticism, phenomenological criticism, existential criticism, various branches of Marxist criticism, hermeneutics, reader-response criticism, speech-act theory, structuralism, and deconstruction. Graff's main target was the set of modern or post-Romantic ideas constituting the core ideology of all the main schools and movements of contemporary criticism. As a defender of philosophical realism and traditional humanism, Graff located the critical turning point in Western culture during the early Romantic period when Kantian theories of truth as coherence displaced older notions of truth as correspondence. It was at this point that commitment to certain key ideas weakened, gradually undermining dedication to objectivity, reason, disinterested inquiry, and belief in facts and rational argumentation. As industrial capitalist society evolved in the modern era into postbourgeois consumer culture, the very ideas of social reality and literary realism, of linguistic reference and referentiality, and of objective interpretation and determinate meaning fell into disfavor, becoming the property of a conservative minority—a *cultural* right. The radicals on the *cultural* left championed antirepresentational and antimimetic philosophies of art. Eventually, two strands of decadent formalism emerged: one declared that literature was not about reality but about itself; the other asserted that "reality" itself was indistinguishable from literature. The one turned away from reality; the other absorbed reality by construing it as myth or fiction. In either case, literature was progressively denuded of its classical mimetic, expressive, and didactic functions, rendering it increasingly immune to political and social inquiry, historical and objective analysis, and ethical and moral judgment. What Graff contended was that this evolution in aesthetics paralleled the development of Western capitalism. As a result, vanguard literary intellectuals in our time unwittingly aided and abetted the "progress" of late consumer capitalism, abdicating their critical function in society. This renunciation was as characteristic of "progressive" Hegelian, Existential, new left, and Neo-Marxist Critics as it was of New Critics, Myth Critics, Phenomenological Critics, hermeneuticists, Reader-Response Critics, speech-act theorists, structuralists, and deconstructors. Even certain figures associated with the New York Intellectuals, including Leslie Fiedler, Richard Poirier, and Susan Sontag, promoted an antipolitical formalism. Paradoxically, all these cultural vanguardists and radicals encouraged political quietism.

From Graff's left-conservative perspective, "radical" modern and postmodern aesthetics constituted a natural cultural counterpart of late capitalism, which had no use for history, orthodoxy, or belief. Fully consonant with twentieth-century skepticism and relativism, this capitalism thrived on, by commercializing, narcissism, alienation, the pleasure and play principles, discontinuity, and indeterminacy. Thus, the antihistorical formalism propounded by literary intellectuals furthered the prospects of unrestrained personal consumption, renouncing the old critical tasks of opposition and resistance to capitalist society. Having effectively neutralized themselves, literary intellectuals were their own worst enemies. The more they severed literature from life, the less literature was able to serve as criticism of life. Significantly, Graff saw little hope of positive reconstruction within the academy short of drastically rearranging the way university departments of literature carried on their business.[17]

The year after Graff published *Literature Against Itself,* Frank Lentricchia brought out *After the New Criticism* (1980), which was a lengthy critical history of literary criticism and theory between 1957 and 1977. This text immediately became the standard history of contemporary criticism. Its accounts of myth criticism, existentialism, phenomenology, hermeneutics, reader-response criticism, structuralism, and poststructuralism were generally detailed, lucid, and informative. Whereas Graff engaged from start to finish in polemics in the mode of all-but-forgotten literary journalists, Lentricchia practiced scholarly exposition in the professorial manner of a textbook writer. Numerous other features distinguished the books of these Leftist Critics. Lentricchia devoted large stretches of his work to Continental theorists and philosophers while Graff alluded only on occasion to European influences. Lentricchia's leftist critiques, inspired primarily by the work of Michel Foucault, were discreetly embedded in his broad expository narrative, whereas Graff's leftist attacks, stemming from the old left, dominated his whole enterprise, rendering his expositions ironic when not argumentative. Unlike Graff, Lentricchia surprisingly had nothing much to say about psychoanalysis, the New York Intellectuals, or the Movement critics. Neither one mentioned the work of Feminist Critics or Black Aestheticians. Graff was concerned and Lentricchia was comparatively unconcerned about the academic institution of literary studies, that is, about departmentalization of knowledge, professional organizations, pedagogical practices, university journals and presses, conferences and symposiums, institutes and schools, literary canons and textooks, foundations and agencies, and specialized terminology and protocols of professionalism. In essence, Graff leaned toward institutional analysis and Lentricchia toward history of ideas which attended primarily to major figures and major works. Graff, unlike Lentricchia, situated literature and criticism amidst social history, taking into account at selected moments certain political events, economic reversals, and significant nonliterary cultural phenomena. Despite their differences, both critics regarded the main schools of contemporary literary criticism as formalistic, meaning given to antihistoricism, philosophical idealism, relativism, subjectivism, aestheticism, and apoliticism.

Not until the publication of *Criticism and Social Change* (1983) did Lentricchia abandon historical exposition and negative critique in order to offer a positive program for Marxist criticism. Here he was deeply concerned about the sociopolitical functions of the university, academic intellectuals, and literary pedagogues. He deplored the alienation, isolationism, and apoliticism of contemporary theory, which fostered ironic disengagement and quietism. He did not, however, want to abandon theory, but to publicize it or rather to focus on its inherent political dimensions. Meditating on the political paralysis promoted by de Manian deconstruction, Lentricchia sought resources in the early leftist work of Kenneth Burke. Along the way, he employed key insights from Michel Foucault, Antonio Gramsci, Herbert Marcuse, and Raymond Williams as well as other European leftists. He disregarded Soviet, Third World, old left, and most new left Marxists, seeking to avoid the pitfalls of earlier Marxisms and to forge an independent socialist criticism.

Building on the work of Gramsci and Foucault, Lentricchia depicted three kinds of intellectuals. The "radical intellectual" labored overtly and continuously with the working class. The "traditional intellectual" operated as a cosmopolitan figure in the world of letters, philosophy, and art, pursuing an idealistic vocation as connoisseur of ideas and curator of culture, standing outside power and politics, and prizing universal values and detached inquiry. Being concerned mainly about present-day academic critics, Lentricchia exhibited little interest in "radical intellectuals" and considerable despair over "traditional intellectuals" who populated the universities. He wanted Leftist Critics to work through and renounce their training as "traditional intellectuals" in order to become "specific intellectuals." The "specific intellectual" struggled against repression and sought social transformation at the precise institutional site where he or she was located and strictly within the domain of his or her expertise. The work of such a literary intellectual could not be, by definition, connected with, say, a teacher's union, a political party, or a public demonstration. However valuable such activities were, they did not relate to the academic intellectual's everyday, detailed functioning as a scholar-teacher of literature. In Lentricchia's view, "our potentially most powerful political work as university humanists must be carried out in what we do, what we are trained for."[18] In the case of literary people, this meant ideological analysis and struggle at the level of discourse. Following Gramsci and Williams, Lentricchia asserted that the production, distribution, and consumption of culture constituted a primary moving force in the creation, maintenance, and perpetuation of society and its ruling interests. In order to render such interests normative and inevitable, social institutions engaged in "educating" the people. The social dissemination of the dominant ideology engendered both cooperation and productivity within established political and social structures and without use of coercion or violence. By means of the family, church, school, job, media, courts, police, and other social institutions, the reigning ideas and values were so deeply and pervasively embedded in everyday existence as to form the unconscious bases of understanding, judgment, and feeling. Never a static or complete operation, the numerous processes insuring cultural domination or hegemony had continually to be modified and re-exerted to restrict resistances and changes. In this work, the traditional intellectual functioned, knowingly or not, as an agent of ideology whereas the specific intellectual labored as an oppositional critic who scrutinized suppressed ideas, inquired into the excluded and the marginal, and continuously reexamined the whole culture.

To further the counterhegemonic labor of specific intellectuals, Lentricchia sketched a project of "Marxist rhetoric." The main premise of this enterprise was that the substance of ideology was "revealed to us *textually* and therefore must be grasped (read) and attacked (re-read, rewritten) in that dimension" (24). The primary work of both counterhegemonic and hegemonic culture was done through language. In other words, the agent of change and action in society was rhetoric, which obviously could be used for good or ill. For the academic literary critic, rigorous textual and ideological analysis constituted the fundamentals of his or her Marxist rhetoric: these operations ideally opened the traditional text to a contemporary reception conscious of political effects, social values, and cultural continuities and changes. Self-consciously, the new Marxist rhetorician scrutinized the grounds of tradition-making and canon formation as well as the foundations of ideology, rendering viable the prospects for change and social transformation.

In constructing a theory of "literature," Lentricchia recalled that during the Renaissance "literature" designated the whole body of books and writings and that, significantly, during the Romantic period "literature" came to signify imaginative writing. Thus, "literature" in its modern sense had achieved identity and distinction "by attempting to empty itself of historical, scientific, and generally utilitarian values" (123). Ultimately, "literature" for moderns meant great works of aesthetic perfection. This progressive narrowing and purification of "literature" rendered it increasingly puerile. In his first book, *The Gaiety of Language: An Essay on the Radical Poetics of W. B. Yeats and Wallace Stevens* (1968), Lentricchia had reconstructed in a nonpartisan scholarly manner the reductive course of poetic theory through its Romantic, Naturalistic, Symbolist, and Modernist phases. In his later work, he tried to reverse the effect of the historical diminution of literature by enlarging its scope.

The literary is never only the elite canon of great books; it is also what we call "minor" literature and "popular" literature. But it is more even than what this expanded definition would allow. It is all writing considered as social practice. . . . The literary is all around us, and it is always doing its work upon us. (157)

By equating "literature" with social discourse embodying ideological and counterideological elements and forces, Lentricchia connected the literary with social reality and power, which had not only causes and effects but also links to history and present struggles. Moreover, literature as social writing, as text, and as rhetoric depended on willful and free activity, however limited by circumstances and preconditions. This much of traditional humanism Lentricchia retained—a belief in human will and freedom. While he sought to revive a Renaissance conception of "literature" by recourse to the broad postmodernist ideas of textuality and social discourse, he refused to adopt the postmodern doctrines of the "death of man" and the deconstructed subject. Like other leftists influenced by poststructuralism in the post-Vietnam era, Lentricchia opened "literature" not only to popular, working-class, and ethnic works, but to all discourse.

As the subdiscipline of theory expanded from the sixties through the eighties, critics on the left became concerned about its implicit and explicit political alignments and implications. What the work of Graff and Lentricchia illustrated was a growing preoccupation with the politics of theory. In this area the difference between early Movement critics and later leftists was most obviously the increased scope of theory. Graff, Lentricchia, and others in the post-Vietnam period took into account not only New Criticism, myth criticism, and existential criticism, but also phenomenological criticism, hermeneutics, reader-response criticism, structuralist criticism, and deconstruction. In the early eighties, feminist criticism would be added to this list. By the time that *Critical Inquiry* published a special issue in 1982 on "The Politics of Interpretation," the editor could declare as productive the proposition that "criticism and interpretation, the arts of explanation and understanding, have a deep and complex relation with politics, the structures of power and social value that organize human life."[19] The self-conscious linkages of literary theory with ideology and of literary criticism with cultural hegemony opened the work of all academic intellectuals to the domains of politics, sociology, ethics, economics, anthropology, and history. It was this crucial opening that constituted the grounds for an expanded, multidisciplinary project of critical analysis often nicknamed "cultural studies"—a theoretical practice conceived in opposition to that of traditional philosophical idealism, aestheticism, subjectivism, antihistoricism, and apoliticism.

What leftist "cultural studies" challenged was the reign of the traditional intellectual and the dominance of formalism. As far as Leftist Critics were concerned, literature needed to be redefined to encompass a much wider range of discourse than the old belletristic canon had allowed. And the tasks of teaching and criticism required reformulation to include ideological analysis and social inquiry as well as textual exegesis. Authority figures had to change. Not surprisingly, Marx took the place of Kant, and Foucault replaced Derrida. Lentricchia put Burke in place of Brooks. Graff preferred Lukács and the old American left to Frye and the New Critics. By the late seventies a significant shift from the "text" to the "social text" as object of inquiry had occurred. This change showed up in the non-Marxist work of Spanos, Fish, Scholes, Felman, and Baker, which meant that hermeneutics, reader-response theory, semiotics, deconstruction, and Black Aesthetics all registered the impact of the movement toward cultural studies. Notwithstanding Spacks, Jehlen, and certain others, feminist criticism from the outset formed a powerful parallel grouping. Millett, Robinson, and Howe, for example, all belonged to the new left in the sixties. The related projects of feminism, of Black Aesthetics, and of cultural studies were closely associated with the Movement, meaning they were born out of the sixties sociopolitical struggles rooted in resistance to oppressive economic and historical conditions. All of this is to say that *cultural studies* was a broad-based, heterogeneous movement, initiated in the late sixties and culminating in the eighties, involving some of the finest critics born between the late twenties and late forties, who vigorously contested the many facets of formalistic theory.

LEFT-DECONSTRUCTIONIST CRITICISM

Many leftist intellectuals were hostile to deconstruction, as, for example, Gerald Graff, Paul Lauter, and Frank Lentricchia in the United States and Perry Anderson, Terry Eagleton, and Raymond Williams in England. Other Leftist Critics, however, like the Americans Fredric Jameson and Edward Said and the Britons Rosalind Coward and John Ellis, used selected insights from deconstruction while remaining critical of its apolitical orientation. Significantly, as deconstruction gained ascendency in the late 1970s, some leftist literary critics, mostly born after 1940, began to construct a Marxist criticism in line with deconstructive theory. Among such left-deconstructionists were John Brenkman, Michael Ryan, and Gayatri Spivak.

As we saw in chapter 10, Gayatri Spivak linked Marxist feminism with deconstruction, stopping short of full support for the Yale School version of textuality, which she regarded as an idealistic construction that reduced socioeconomic, political, and historical forces to mere language. What was most useful in deconstruction for Spivak was its powerful critique of modern logocentric society in its patriarchal, capitalistic, racial, and class-bound forms.

Published in *Social Text*, John Brenkman's "Deconstruction and the Social Text" (1979) imbricated Marxism and deconstruction by reworking and expanding two central deconstructive formulations—textuality and intertextuality. To begin with, there were several problems with the deconstructive theory of textuality or rhetoricity. The referent or the Real was very narrowly conceived according to old notions of stable, fixed objects of perception; the concept of the unconscious was misconstrued, when not bypassed. Following Marx, Brenkman cast the referent or the Real as historically produced and socially organized, which accounted more adequately than Saussurean linguistics for the instability and discrepancy between signifiers and signifieds. Using Lacan, he added a psychoanalytic dimension to the theory of the sign to extend understanding of linguistic slippage: for all human subjects, utterances contained constitutive gaps, communicating something different from what was stated. In other words, the phenomenon of linguistic slippage had a psychological dimension rooted in fantasy life. The effect of thus resituating the theory of textuality on the grounds of Marxist and Freudian logics was to reconnect linguistic reference to social reality and the unconscious without giving up the crucial deconstructive notion of linguistic slippage. An added benefit was that the fictionality or rhetoricity of language, seen from a left-deconstructionist point of view, highlighted the power of literature both to criticize society by setting itself apart from the Real and to figure forth utopian possibilities by setting loose fantasy material.

Brenkman found the deconstructive theory of intertextuality extremely narrow and limited. He noted that literary texts referred not simply to other literary texts, but to a broad range of social writings, symbolic formations, and systems of representation. Intertextuality linked texts with religious, cultural, politicial, and economic discourses. Taken together, these heterogeneous textual fields constituted the general or "social text." By transforming the theory of intertextuality into the theory of the *social text*, left-deconstructionists joined poetic works not merely to literary tradition, but to cultural history. The result was a fundamental expansion of the enterprise of deconstructive dismantling and negation, extending it to the tasks of Marxist ideological critique and institutional analysis.

Perhaps the premier work of left-deconstructionism was Michael Ryan's *Marxism and Deconstruction: A Critical Articulation*, published in 1982 by the Johns Hopkins University Press. A student of Spivak's, Ryan had worked during the late seventies in France with Derrida and with the activist French Group for Research on Philosophic Teaching. Starting out as a new left Maoist in the late sixties, Ryan had come to favor a decentralized, democratic communism over Soviet-style bureaucratic Stalinism and Leninist disciplinarianism. He expressed sympathy for Third World socialism and feminist Marxism as well as French radical poststructuralism and contemporary British Marxist criticism. He was indebted to certain European Neo-Marxists and to the Italian theorist Antonio Negri, some of whose works he cotranslated. He had little use for American deconstructive criticism, which he thought fostered political conservatism, cultural traditionalism, epistemological nihilism, and de facto capitulation to the status quo.

Like Brenkman and Spivak, Ryan also linked the theories of textuality and intertextuality to the theory of the social text. He did this primarily by reconceptualizing Derrida's concept of radical otherness or *alterity*. "One cannot locate a proper ground of substance or subjectivity, ontology or theology, being or truth, that is not caught up in a web of other-relations or a chain of differentiation."[20] In effect, all concepts, objects, and phenomena were intermeshed in a network of heterogeneous relations, conventions, histories, and institutions. For literary criticism, this meant that text and social text were irrevocably interrelated. Accordingly, Ryan transformed deconstructive differential methodology into a form of dialectical criticism:

this way of thinking was both relational and differential. It differentiated all purified or essentialized concepts like primordial "speech" and "subjectivity" by subverting their self-enclosed substance and ideality and exposing them to constitutive otherness. Also, it doggedly related events and phenomena, as, for instance, literature and political economy. On the basis of this Marxist deconstructive process of differential and relational thinking, Ryan projected a radical pedagogy as well as a critical practice.

At the conclusion of his book, Ryan compared the philosophies and styles of the new left and of deconstruction. Deconstruction, like new left philosophy, exhibited certain crucial traits: "an emphasis on plurality over authoritarian unity, a disposition to criticize rather than obey, a rejection of the logic of power and domination in all their forms, an advocation of difference against identity, and a questioning of state universalism" (213). This decentralized and "anarchic" mode of operation functioned in strategic opposition to all centralized authority, whether in the form of party politics, state power, philosophical conceptuality, or canonized literary tradition. Adopting such new left and deconstructive values, Ryan argued the merits of enclave politics, particularly as developed by socialist feminists, Polish Solidarity, and the Italian "Autonomy" movement. In general, left-deconstructionists displayed sympathy for new left values, which was not particularly surprising since these radical critics came of age during the heyday of the new left and often took part in its activities.

Once again, many leftist intellectuals remained hostile to deconstruction, dismissing its usefulness for a Marxist politics and critical practice. For example, in 1985 one Marxist-Leninist published a vituperative critique of left-deconstructionism as well as Derridean and Yale School deconstruction. According to this condemnation, deconstruction—whether from the right, center, or left—dissolved the main Marxist concepts of class, of the proletariat, of party centralism, of the worker's revolution, and of the seizure of state power. Left-deconstructionism stood against communism, centralism, and revolution and for anarchism, coalition politics, and left pluralism. In this radical view, all deconstruction was an antiprogressive, formalistic idealism, which rendered the whole school politically bankrupt.[21] Left-deconstructionists were attacked from the conservative, moderate, and radical wings of the Marxist movement. Neither Graff, nor Lentricchia, nor many other leftists had sympathy for the merger of Marxism and deconstruction. Moreover, the works of left-deconstructionists were ignored by leading mainstream deconstructors, who did not relish playing the role of political reactionaries to the Marxists' radicalism.

POST-MARXIST CULTURAL CRITICISM

The emergence of leftist thinking in both Europe and America predated the appearance of Karl Marx and his followers. Socialism, syndicalism, and anarchism, for example, stretched back in time before the mid-nineteenth century. There was no reason to think that every future leftist philosophy and movement would necessarily be tied to Marxist thought and tradition. A post-Marxist left was not out of the question. In arguing that Marxism applied to nineteenth-century industrial capitalism and not to late twentieth-century consumer capitalism, certain Neo-Marxists had raised questions, sometimes inadvertently, about the continuing relevance of Marxism for contemporary Western societies. In particular, the potential for social revolution tied to the proletariat seemed increasingly remote. Progressive radical action had visibly shifted in the sixties from industrial workers to activists for peace, ecological balance, feminist rights, and racial empowerment. Such popular radicalism was very far from the factory. Historically speaking, class struggle in America appeared a relic compared with the authentic struggles against nuclear weapons, Asian wars, and racial segregation. The numerous different interests, goals, and ideologies of emergent popular movements increasingly undermined Marxist dominance on the left. Meanwhile, the credibility of Marxism had diminished in the Space Age with the Soviet interventions in Czechoslovakia and Afghanistan, with the workers' strikes against the Marxist government in Poland, and with the left-organized genocide in Cambodia. Coupled with the emergence of such prominent and credible non-Marxist radicals as Rudolf Bahro, Noam Chomsky, and Sheila Rowbotham, all these events made a post-Marxist movement and mode of analysis seem not only possible, but promising. Among a growing number of literary critics in the United States practicing a post-Marxist cultural criticism were the Renaissance scholar Stephen Greenblatt and the Palestinian-born, American-educated intellectual Edward Said. As we noted in earlier discussions, certain Leftist Critics like Paul Lauter and Kate Millett in the sixties, Florence Howe and Elaine Showalter in the seventies, and William Spanos and Robert Scholes in the eighties had advocated various projects of post- or non-Marxist cultural criticism.

In the seventies, Stephen Greenblatt developed a "poetics of culture" that culminated in his *Renaissance Self-Fashioning: From More to Shakespeare* (1980), which won the British Council Prize in the Humanities. As he worked on the book, Greenblatt discovered "that fashioning oneself and being fashioned by cultural institutions—family, religion, state—were inseparably intertwined" and that there existed "no moments of pure, unfettered subjectivity; indeed, the human subject itself began to seem remarkably unfree, the ideological product of the relations of power in a particular society."[22] Just as the autonomous self was an illusion, so too was the autotelic literary text; both had to be conceived dialectically in their complex interactions with social institutions. Whether he focused on the "self" of an author or of a literary character, Greenblatt positioned sixteenth-century subjectivity amidst a network of contending discursive forces, flanked on one side by hostile Others and on another by absolutist Authorities, both of which threatened to subvert identity. In the end, the constitution of an identifiable self entailed negotiating powerful cultural control mechanisms.

Although Greenblatt's poetics of culture relied on some local insights gleaned from Marxist scholarship, it was most indebted to contemporary anthropological work, especially Clifford Geertz's *Interpretation of Cultures* (1973). What Greenblatt most wanted to avoid were reductive literary biography, literary history, and literary sociology. The main problem with biography was that it limited itself to the behavior of authors and sacrificed attention to larger social networks. Conventional literary history relegated to the background the institutional and personal functions of literature, falsely rendering art either autonomous or timeless. And literary sociology depicted art too exclusively as a reflection of social rules and codes, isolating it in the ideological superstructure and diminishing the role of the author as creative-destructive improviser.[23]

As an historian of English Renaissance literature, Greenblatt found himself caught between the necessity to generalize about a century of cultural production and the desire to write a series of related but differentiated histories. "This book will not advance any comprehensive 'explanation' of English Renaissance self-fashioning; each of the chapters is intended to stand alone as an exploration whose contours are shaped by our grasp of the specific situation of the author or text. We may, however, conclude by noting a set of governing conditions common to most instances of self-fashioning . . ." (8–9). Of interest to Greenblatt were less the large-scale structural constraints underlying an enduring social formation than the particular conflicts and contradictions engendered by such constraints for specific authors. Significantly, a shift from holistic to differential analysis characterized the historiography of many post-Marxist intellectuals. The tutelary spirit here was the French poststructuralist historian Michel Foucault, whose works during the post-Vietnam era far outranked those of

Derrida or Lacan in terms of influence and applicability among certain American post-Marxist or non-Marxist cultural critics like Greenblatt, Said, Scholes, and Spanos.

Whereas Greenblatt concentrated exclusively on sixteenth-century scholarship and had little impact on general theoretical debates occurring in the late seventies and early eighties, Edward Said engaged in effective polemics against leading contending schools and movements, taking on "radical" critics and positioning himself in the midst of the struggles surrounding literary-critical theory. For over a decade he was the preeminent exponent of Foucault and of post-Marxist cultural criticism. It was in his polemical essays that Said first gained a wide audience. In addition, his theoretical stances were applied in examining and exposing distorted European and American views of Arab societies in a series of books, including *Orientalism* (1978), *The Question of Palestine* (1979), and *Covering Islam* (1981).

In "Reflections on American 'Left' Literary Criticism" (1979), published in Spanos' *Boundary 2,* Said registered a handful of complaints against ersatz "leftist" criticism, which he defined as criticism "adopting a position of opposition to what is considered to be established or conservative academic scholarship" and arguing "*as if* for the radicalization of thought, practice, and perhaps even society."24 One flaw in such criticism, whether it was Marxist or not, was its neutralization of historical research in the interests of rhetorical analysis and methodological systematization. Another weakness was the widespread inadvertent confirmation of prevailing values, definitions, and institutions as a consequence of refusing to scrutinize the complicity of scholarship with state authority. Significantly, Said singled out the work of Ohmann and Foucault as exceptions in this regard. A third failing was the literary "left's" willingness to accept the isolation of literary studies and to ignore larger social questions. This tendency appeared especially among Derrideans whose concept of textuality rendered the text homogeneous by restricting its reach to other texts similarly denuded of history and power. And this tendency also manifested itself in the easy governability'of leftist literary intellectuals whose passive devotion to masterpieces of culture posed no threat to reigning values or state agencies. A fourth weakness was the left's unconscious ethnocentric Occidentalism, which was related to contemporary Western racial hatred, colonial settlements, imperial wars, and economic manipulations of Third World countries. Citing the political engagement of the intellectual left in the 1930s and 1940s and recalling the exemplary earlier work of Edmund Wilson, F. O. Matthiessen, and Antonio Gramsci, Said lamented the avoidance of adversarial politics among Leftist Critics in the 1970s. He noted as a weakness the "absence of a continuous native Marxist theoretical tradition or culture" (166). And he urged intellectuals "to see culture as historical force possessing its own configurations, ones that intertwine with those in the socioeconomic sphere and that finally bear on the State as a State" (171).

However much Said aligned himself with genuine leftist politics and with Marxist traditions, he refused to regard himself as a Marxist. At the end of the introductory manifesto to his essay collection, *The World, the Text, and the Critic* (1983), he explained his views on Marxism. "Marxism is in need of systematic decoding, demystifying, rigorous clarification" (29). The work of Noam Chomsky was cited as exemplary in this connection. According to Said, the proper role of an oppositional intellectual was not to be a good member of a school, not to become immured in doctrine, and not to adhere to party discipline, but to remain forever skeptical of orthodoxy. Criticism had to be "secular," not clerical or "religious." Thus, for Said, "criticism modified in advance by labels like 'Marxism' or 'liberalism' is, in my view, an oxymoron. The history of thought, to say nothing of political movements, is extravagantly illustrative of how the dictum 'solidarity before criticism' means the end of criticism" (28). Even if Said were inclined to become a Marxist, there were other serious problems with present-day American Marxism, which was politically ineffectual.

Right now in American cultural history, "Marxism" is principally an academic, not a political commitment. It risks becoming an academic subspecialty. As corollaries of this unfortunate truth there are also such things to be mentioned as the absence of an important socialist party (along the lines of the various European parties), the marginalized discourse of "Left" writing, the seeming incapacity of professional groups (scholarly, academic, regional) to organize effective Left coalitions with political-action groups. The net effect of "doing" Marxist criticism or writing at the present time is of course to declare political preference, but it is also to put oneself outside a great deal of things going on in the world, so to speak, and in other kinds of criticism. (28–29)

Intellectually and strategically, to be a Marxist in America during the post-Vietnam period was to risk being cut off, marginal, and ineffective as well as doctrinaire, clerical, and noncritical.

Published in the seventies and eighties, Said's articles and books espoused and promoted activist cultural criticism in a post-Marxist vein. "My position is that texts are worldly, to some degree they are events, and, even when they appear to deny it, they are nevertheless a part of the social world, human life, and of course the historical moments in which they are located and interpreted" (*WTC*, 4). Not surprisingly, Said took inspiration from worldly criticism in its philosophical and philological forms as practiced by intellectuals from Vico to Auerbach, both of whom received special praise in Said's *Beginnings: Intention and Method* (1975). Said advocated rigorous textual analysis of affiliative networks, that is, of the many links materially connecting texts to authors, cultures, and societies. Any effacing of such affiliations or adjacencies in the name of humanism, formalism, structuralism, or anything else constituted capitulation of critical responsibility. Still, it was not enough merely to study the situational filiations and affiliations of discourse; in the event that a text promoted the dogmatic status quo or some form of domination, then resistance and opposition were necessary. Said admired oppositional critics and activists, from Swift to Chomsky, who advocated changes, alternatives, and interventions. At bottom, "criticism must think of itself as life-enhancing and constitutively opposed to every form of tyranny, domination, and abuse; its social goals are noncoercive knowledge produced in the interest of human freedom" (*WTC*, 29).

What most disturbed Said were all forms of orthodoxy, authority, dogma, systematization, and especially quietism. He advocated "secular" skepticism and irony against such "religious" forms and tendencies. To take one example, the deconstructive notions of undecidability and unreadability effectively counseled resignation from the world and encouraged private consumption of high culture. Any mode of criticism exclusively promoting refinement, reverence, and/or noninterference rendered itself irrelevant as well as impotent while enervating the enterprise of criticism by divorcing it from culture and society. Not only did the project of deconstructors anger Said, but so too did the late work of Foucault and his followers. "Foucault's eagerness not to fall into Marxist economism causes him to obliterate the role of classes, the role of economics, the role of insurgency and rebellion in the societies he discusses" (*WTC*, 244). The result of such effacements was unfortunately "to justify political quietism with sophisticated intellectualism" (245). This surprising criticism of Foucault led Paul Bové to observe that Said himself did not question the arrogant and self-interested role traditionally assigned to intellectuals—"the role of the [traditional] intellectual is to exercise critical consciousness *for* the oppressed to alleviate their oppression."[25] Taking another tack, Catherine Gallagher faulted Said because no specific politics attached to his worldly criticism. With Said, she argued, "politics becomes insubstantial, almost meaningless."[26] As a matter of fact, Said's politics, as was hinted in

Orientalism and later essays, championed libertarianism and veered toward anarchism, which explained his special aversions to dogmatism and authoritarianism as well as to orthodoxy and quietism.[27]

The intellectuals and critics admired by Said all exhibited "extraterritoriality." That is to say, they breached disciplinary and national boundaries in their practice of activist secular criticism. As far as Said was concerned, the "future of criticism or the critical function is, I believe, to be exercised in the traffic between cultures, discourses and disciplines, rather than in the appropriation, systematization, management, and professionalization of any one domain."[28] This statement explained the shifting boundaries of Said's project of worldly cultural criticism while reflecting his dedication to Comparative Literature and his exile from Palestine. For his part, Greenblatt less ambitiously advocated a sociological poetics of culture within the framework of English Studies. What these critics had in common were commitments to undertake interdisciplinary investigations, to study "discourse" (social text rather than literary texts), and to examine political and economic matters without being bound by the protocols of Marxism. In self-conscious opposition to circumscribed formalist and poststructuralist modes of inquiry, both critics recommended biographical, historical, ethical, and sociological analysis while accepting the demands of close reading.

"CULTURAL STUDIES" IN THE ACADEMY

What most readily distinguished leftist types of inquiry from various contending formalist kinds of criticism was a marked determination to situate aesthetic phenomena and artifacts in relation to both social foundations and other cultural works. This project required of literary critics not only textual analysis, but also investigations into the economic, political, social, institutional, and historical grounds of cultural production, distribution, and consumption. Accordingly, American academic Leftist Critics increasingly advocated totalizing modes of examination and wide-ranging programs of cultural studies. Given the different factions and approaches within the leftist movement in the Space Age, programs for cultural studies came in various forms.

Despite their temperamental, professional, and political differences, Leftist Critics broadly concurred on the inadequacies of and the need for changes in the institution of academic literary studies. From the sixties through the eighties a consensus among literary leftists existed that the scope of critical inquiry had to be dramatically expanded and that the concept of "literature" had to be significantly broadened. Assaults on the limitations of literary criticism and on the narrowness of the canon of great books were characteristic of leftist criticism. In the sixties, for instance, Florence Howe and Lillian Robinson argued for incorporating women's texts into the curriculum; Leslie Fiedler and Richard Poirier advanced the claims of popular culture; and Louis Kampf and Paul Lauter urged attention to working-class literature. All these critics insisted on the inescapable relevance of politics to literary criticism. In the seventies, to mention other examples, the dialectical criticism advanced by Fredric Jameson, the poetics of culture propounded by Stephen Greenblatt, and the secular criticism advocated by Edward Said all urged the linkage of politics and criticism and the redefinition of "literature" to encompass heretofore "nonliterary" materials. By the early eighties, the leftist project of redefining literature and reconceptualizing criticism took on the broadly accepted nickname "cultural studies."

In their Preface to *Criticism in the University* (1985), a collection of eighteen pieces by diverse hands, Gerald Graff and Reginald Gibbons observed, "If anything ties our contributors together and transcends their local differences, it is the feeling that a revived 'cultural criticism,' based on general ideas and the largest sense of literary culture, and taking in contemporary imaginative writing (and other media), is what is most sorely needed today to revitalize the humanistic study of literature" (10). They went on to assert that "the close, concrete reading of literary works, which remains one of the primary tasks of criticism, is not likely to recover the sense of mission that once informed it as long as it takes place in a vacuum—separated from historical, philosophical and social contexts" (10–11). Without wanting to denigrate or dismiss the important habit of close reading instilled by earlier formalists, Leftist Critics in growing numbers called for sociohistorical, philosophical, and political modes of critical analysis against the background of a growing loss of mission, an increasingly moribund humanities establishment, and an ever more hyperspecialized and disinterested academy. The projected renewal to be effected by cultural studies depended on an enlarged sense of literature to encompass contemporary as well as classic texts and to include other media. Here was how John Brenkman, in his "Theses on Cultural Marxism" (1983), explained the necessity to broaden the concept of "literature": "The humanities are no longer central to the cultural cohesion of capitalist society; they have been displaced by mass culture. . . ."[29] Given this historical shift, mass culture became an essential object for contemporary humanistic analysis and cultural study. Some literary leftists justified the project of cultural studies by calling for a return to earlier, richer modes of criticism, while others argued the necessity to respond to new and altered social realities. The former looked to previous times, as did Graff; the latter focused on the contemporary moment, as did Brenkman. One took inspiration from the New York Intellectuals; the other followed French poststructuralists. In both cases, the project of cultural studies construed "literature" and "criticism" very broadly, marking its difference from the numerous practices of contending critical schools and movements.

At the close of an interview given in 1982, Fredric Jameson declared that "Marxism is the *only* living philosophy today which has a conception of the unity of knowledge and the unification of the 'disciplinary' fields in a way that cuts across the older departmental and institutional structures and restores the notion of a universal object of study underpinning the seemingly distinct inquiries into the economical, the political, the cultural, the psychoanalytic, and so forth."[30] According to Jameson, the only effective cure for the fragmentation engendered by academic specialization and departmentalization of knowledge was the long-standing Marxist practice of cultural criticism, which was demonstrably superior to the ephemeral gimmickry fostered by contemporary interdisciplinary studies. In his own practice of cultural criticism, Jameson sought a grand synthesis not only of Neo-Marxism and (post)structuralism, but of myth criticism and hermeneutics. In constructing his ambitious Marxist hermeneutic in *The Political Unconscious,* he sought to offer the most capacious interpretative model for cultural studies available to literary critics in the United States.

Calls for the creation of effective contemporary cultural studies became increasingly common as the eighties wore on. For example, Robert Scholes in *Textual Power* (1985) urged:

[W]e must stop "teaching literature" and start "studying texts." Our rebuilt apparatus must be devoted to textual studies. . . . Our favorite works of literature need not be lost in this new enterprise, but the exclusivity of literature as a category must be discarded. All kinds of texts, visual as well as verbal, polemical as well as seductive, must be taken as the occasions for further textuality. And textual studies must be pushed beyond the discrete boundaries of the page and the book into institutional practices and social structures. . . .[31]

Replacing the traditional concept of "literature" with the poststructuralist notion of textuality, Scholes envisioned a project of "textual studies," which would examine all sorts of "texts" as well as social forms. Scholes was neither committed nor overtly hostile to Marxism. In a similar spirit, the editors of *Cultural Critique,* established in 1985 at the University of Minnesota, intended their journal to "occupy the broad terrain of cultural interpretation that is currently defined by the conjuncture of literary, philosophical, anthropological, and sociological studies, of Marxist, feminist, psychoanalytic, and poststructuralist methods."[32] Moreover, declared the editors, "the goal of *Cultural Critique* may be formulated most comprehensively as the examination of received values, institutions, practices, and discourses in terms of their economic, political, social, and aesthetic genealogies, constitutions, and effects" (5). This post-Marxist program for cultural studies self-consciously superseded the work of conventional literary criticism and theory. On the advisory board of the journal were numerous leading leftist intellectuals, including the Marxists Stanley Aronowitz, Fredric Jameson, Frank Lentricchia, and Hayden White; the nonsectarian leftists Paul Bové, Noam Chomsky, Edward Said, William Spanos, and Cornel West; the feminists Alice Jardine and Gayatri Spivak; and the British Marxists Terry Eagleton, Stephen Heath, Colin MacCabe, and Raymond Williams.

British leftists pioneered projects for cultural studies during the seventies and eighties. Among the most influential of these were the "cultural materialism" of Raymond Williams, the "cultural studies" of the Birmingham Centre for Contemporary Cultural Studies, and the Marxist "rhetoric and discourse theory" of Terry Eagleton, as outlined in his widely read *Literary Theory: An Introduction* (1983). Building on the work of Williams and others, Eagleton argued strenuously that "literature" was not an immutable ontological category or objective entity, but rather a variable functional term and sociohistorical formation: "it is most useful to see 'literature' as a name which people give from time to time for different reasons to certain kinds of writing within a whole field of what Michel Foucault has called 'discursive practices.' . . ."[33] The proper object for cultural study was not literature but discursive practices understood historically as rhetorical constructs linked with knowledge and power. Among discursive forms worthy of study, Eagleton named films, television shows, popular literary works, children's books, scientific texts, and, to be sure, classic "masterpieces." Regarding critical method, Eagleton promoted "pluralism" grounded in Marxist politics: "Any method or theory which will contribute to the goal of human emancipation, the production of 'better people' through the socialist transformation of society, is acceptable" (211).

In an examination of Raymond Williams and the Birmingham Centre,

Michael Ryan isolated three key moments in the progressive transformation of contemporary literary studies into cultural studies. To begin with, the combined effect of feminist, ethnic, and leftist criticism was to force recognition that literary texts were fundamentally documents and social events, having sociohistorical referents. Second, the projects of structuralism and semiotics demonstrated that texts were shaped by social codes, conventions, and representations, which rendered defunct the idea of literary autonomy. And, third, the rise in importance of the mass media and popular culture over the centrality of the literary classics compelled critics to admit the crucial formative and educational roles played by these new discourses.[34]

During the eighties, advocates of cultural studies influenced by poststructuralist thought advanced the argument that a pure pre-discursive, pre-cultural reality or socioeconomic infrastructure did not exist: cultural discourse constituted the ground of social existence as well as personal identity. Given this "poetic," the task of cultural studies was to study the conventions and representations fostered by the whole set of cultural discourses. The effect of this conceptualization was to collapse the classic Marxist doctrine of base/superstructure and thereby to scrap long-standing mimetic and reflectionist theories. Literary discourse did not reflect social reality; rather, discourse of all kinds constituted reality as a set of representations and narratives, which produced discernible affective and didactic effects in epistemological as well as sociopolitical registers.[35] It was this textualist poetics (or something like it) and the associated "discourse hermeneutic" that distinguished the later projects of cultural studies formulated by left-deconstructionists, post-Marxists, and certain Neo-Marxists from those developed earlier by new left and conservative Marxists. In one camp were such figures as Brenkman, Greenblatt, Jameson, Lentricchia, Pratt, Ryan, Said, Scholes, and Spivak and in the other camp were such people as Franklin, Graff, Florence Howe, Kampf, Lauter, Ohmann, Robinson, and Smith. To a considerable extent, the appeal and strength of leftist literary criticism in the late seventies and eighties resulted from its ability to incorporate and employ the insights of vanguard Continental philosophers without sacrificing its traditional political and ethical commitments.

In studying popular and working-class literature, mass media, and "subcultural" forms, the practitioners of cultural studies raised vexed questions, however inadvertently, concerning aesthetic value and evaluation. Isn't a Shakespearean play more valuable than the latest Harlequin romance? Invariably, the leftist reply was that "value" was not an intrinsic property; it derived from certain groups in specific situations in which particular criteria served given purposes. That is to say, value was historical and relative. Under certain conditions, a popular romance might have more value, aesthetic and otherwise, than a Shakespearean text.[36] One effect of such reasoning was to legitimize the serious academic study of diverse cultural discourses, as opposed to the study of only elite or canonical literature.

LEFTIST CRITICISM IN THE SPACE AGE

There were three stages in the emergence and development of academic leftist literary criticism in America during the Space Age. By the late sixties, a vital left was at work, which included members of the new left, black radicals, leftist feminists, New York Intellectuals, and independent radicals. A distinctive feature of this period was the popularity and influence of such Third World leftists as Castro, Fanon, Guevara, Ho, and Mao. During the seventies, the new left dissolved while the number of leftist feminists (white and black) rose. Certain New York leftists became increasingly conservative. Significantly, there emerged in the early seventies Neo-Marxists indebted primarily to the Frankfurt School and, in the late seventies, left deconstructionists and post-Marxists influenced by French poststructuralism. In this decade, unaffiliated leftists played a relatively minor role. During the early and mid-eighties, the scope and influence of various modes of leftist criticism, particularly feminist, Neo-Marxist, left-deconstructionist, and post-Marxist kinds, approached an evident high point, promising to continue with vitality throughout the decade. It was in the early eighties that key British and Italian Marxists had their maximum impact and that cultural studies became a broad-based movement, attracting nonleftists to its cause.

In the development of academic leftist literary criticism over the course of the sixties, seventies, and eighties, there was considerable diversity and a distinctive lack of continuity with thirties Marxism. So much of what deeply concerned the Depression-era radicals was of little or no interest to most Space-Age leftists, including membership in the Communist Party, the coming proletarian revolution, the stakes in the struggle between Stalin and Trotsky, the political functions of a successful Popular Front, the progress of Soviet society, and the state of international class conflict. Compared with the literary left of the thirties, the academic literary left between the sixties and eighties was fragmented, diversified, unorthodox, and indiscriminate. The success of leftist thinking in the university, however, depended to a considerable extent on its nonparty, non-Russian, and nonsubversive character, as Bertell Ollman and Edward Vernoft observed in the Introduction to their informative collection *The Left Academy: Marxist Scholarship on American Campuses* (1982).

The literary left during the Space Age was anything but homogenous. Among intellectuals associated in one way or another with the left were some New York Intellectuals, Existential Critics, hermeneuticists, Reader-Response Critics, semioticians, deconstructors, feminists, and Black Aestheticians as well as new left radicals, Marxist-Leninists, Neo-Marxists, and various mavericks and independents. In not a few instances, a Leftist Critic belonged to several of these schools, as, for example, in the cases of the new left Marxist feminist Lillian Robinson, the black Marxist feminist Barbara Smith, and the Third World Marxist feminist deconstructor Gayatri Spivak. Roughly speaking, the numerous American intellectuals more or less aligned at one moment or another between the 1960s and 1980s with leftist thinking included, among others, such different critics as Amiri Baraka, John Brenkman, Kenneth Burke, Harold Cruse, Judith Fetterley, Leslie Fiedler, Bruce Franklin, Gerald Graff, Stephen Greenblatt, Ihab Hassan, Florence Howe, Irving Howe, Fredric Jameson, Louis Kampf, Alfred Kazin, Paul Lauter, Frank Lentricchia, Kate Millett, Richard Ohmann, Mary Louise Pratt, Lillian Robinson, Michael Ryan, Edward Said, Jeffery Sammons, Robert Scholes, Elaine Showalter, Kaja Silverman, Barbara Smith, Susan Sontag, William Spanos, Gayatri Spivak, and Philip Rahv. Significantly, Leftist Critics drew on radical foreign sources as wide-ranging as the Britons Perry Anderson, Terry Eagleton, Juliet Mitchell, and Raymond Williams; the French Louis Althusser, Jacques Derrida, Michel Foucault, and Pierre Machery; the Germans T. W. Adorno, Jürgen Habermas, Karl Marx, and Herbert Marcuse; the Italians Antonio Gramsci and Antonio Negri; the Russians Mikhail Bakhtin, V. I. Lenin, and Leon Trotsky; the Third World thinkers Frantz Fanon and Mao Tse-Tung; and many, many others.

The leaders among American leftist literary intellectuals held positions in prestigious colleges and universities, published articles and books with major journals and presses, received grants and awards from prominent foundations and agencies, and served leadership roles in key professional organizations, societies, and institutes. Some leftists, like Baraka, Franklin, and Lauter, suffered dismissals and arrests for their political activism, while some others endured subtler forms of official discouragement. Although there was no particular leftist organization, society, press, or journal uniting the group, many members participated in the Modern Language Association; published books with university presses like California, Chicago,

Indiana, and Oxford; and contributed to such journals as *Boundary 2,* *College English, Critical Inquiry, Cultural Critique, Minnesota Review, New German Critique, New Literary History, Partisan Review, Praxis, Radical Teacher, Raritan, Representations, Social Text,* and *Telos.*

Politically, the diverse group of Leftist Critics exhibited a broad array of positions that ranged from the left-conservatism of Graff to the democratic socialism of Irving Howe to the nonsectarian leftism of Greenblatt and Lauter to the Neo-Marxisms of Jameson and Sammons to the Marxism-Leninism of Baraka to the Maoism of Franklin to the evident anarchist libertarianisms of Hassan, Ryan, and Said. Among the group were pacifists, socialists, communists, syndicalists, and anarchists as well as militant feminist, Third World, and race activists. Some advocated more or less radical reforms and others believed only revolution would do. Stylistically, their modes of address spanned a broad spectrum from outraged journalistic polemics to staid scholarship to philosophical speculation to utopian creative criticism. In the eighties, perhaps the most noteworthy feature of leftist criticism was its capaciousness in incorporating the diverse insights, findings, positions, and procedures of other schools and movements without renouncing its set of core beliefs, commitments, and practices.

Circumstances of History

HISTORY EVIDENTLY entails as much creation as discovery. Whenever historians engage in description, exposition, argumentation, evaluation, or narration, they inevitably include some things and exclude others. Unavoidably, certain subjects receive emphasis while others remain relatively unexplored. As achievable goals, totalization and disinterest are impossible. Competing historical texts exhibit numerous variations in what they include, exclude, stress, downplay, value, and criticize. Considered as writing, history makes up as much as it finds. Moreover, the effects of textual order and symmetry brought about by the unexceptional demands of syntax, style, and narration engender a fundamental literariness in historical discourse so that "creativity" can be deemed not only to characterize but to constitute history.

Quite obviously, however, the situation of the historian determines to a large extent the range of available materials, perspectives, and styles. Not all possibilities are always open. The epistemological matrix or configuration of an era—which operates something like a cultural unconscious—conditions the production of history. Also, contingencies of personal history, predispositions of temperament, and special commitments predetermine in crucial ways the shape and trajectory of historical discourse. What is beyond the grasp and control of the historian marks history perhaps as tellingly as what is within sight and reach.

To be plausible, history must seem not only clear and complete but directed. Here circumstance and chance may play as important a role as knowledge, planning, style, and intelligence. Direction results from complex combinations of fundamental forces which include, on one hand, the operations of grammar, discursive structure, intertextual alignments, and institutional conventions and, on the other hand, the workings of the will-to-knowledge, the desire for community, socioeconomic conditions, political allegiances, professional commitments, and ethical preferences. What is finally incalculable in this tangle of contending forces is just how much could be ascribed to conscious choice and how much to unconscious determination. Ultimately, the direction of historical discourse is determined but undecidably so. Accident and chance as well as choice and circumstance riddle the text of history.

Two contradictory circumstances marked the state of academic literary criticism in America between the early 1970s and the late 1980s—the period of my personal involvement. On one hand, the discipline of literary-critical theory experienced an epochal transformation, distinguished by an unprecedented proliferation of provocative, subtle, and important schools and movements within the university. On the other hand, the profession of academic literary studies entered a long period of decline, characterized variously by a gross overproduction of Ph.D.s, a precipitous drop in undergraduate literature and language majors, a gradual shift of pedagogical emphasis from literature to basic literacy, a progressive impoverishment of the professoriate, and an unprecedented crisis for thousands of unemployed and underemployed well-trained literary intellectuals. One consequence of this collective tragedy was a drastic exacerbation of the class system traditionally constituting the profession, consisting of a comparatively small cadre of decently paid literary scholars located primarily at elite graduate schools; a growing group of subsistence-level workers employed as part-time instructors of remedial literacy, temporary replacements, adjuncts, and "gypsy" scholars; and a vast number of literature professors little by little spending more time teaching literacy at four-year and community colleges for substandard wages. This institutional paradox was exacerbated by yet another contradiction.

Because the majority of critics contributing to the "revolution" in literary-critical theory wrote from within the ranks of the elite class, the token professionals and the rank-and-file intellectuals often perceived vanguard "theory" to be an instrument of elitist hegemony largely irrelevant to their more familiar labors. To counter this troubling perception, an emergent group of aspiring theorists came forth with growing numbers of guidebooks, anthologies, surveys, and introductions designed to elucidate the significance of the new theory for those seeking information and understanding. These brokers were sometimes condemned for domesticating and profiting from the so-called "boom" in theory. In part, *American Literary Criticism* and my previous book, *Deconstructive Criticism,* belong to this group of works. All such texts share the common fate of humanistic scholarship, which battens on the works of forerunners and renders them service-able, thriving on the take. Paradoxically, the dissemination and the "domes-tication" of elitist works assure their prominence, vitality, and pertinence as well as their demystification, mishandling, and profanation. This is how history is inscribed and lived. "Desecration," struggle, and flowering go hand in hand.

NOTES

CHAPTER ONE. MARXIST CRITICISM IN THE 1930S

1. George B. Tindall, *America: A Narrative History* (New York: Norton, 1984), p. 1052.

2. Hal Draper, "Pie in the Sky," *New York Review of Books*, 10 May 1984, pp. 25, 28–31; and Irving Howe and Lewis Coser, *The American Communist Party: A Critical History* (1957; New York: Praeger, 1962), pp. 225, 419.

3. Harvey Klehr, *The Heyday of American Communism: The Depression Decade* (New York: Basic Books, 1984), pp. 353–57.

4. Ellen Schrecker, "The Missing Generation: Academics and the Communist Party from the Depression to the Cold War," *Humanities in Society*, 6 (Spring & Summer 1983), 139–59.

5. For an attempt at a systematization of Marxist aesthetics and for a useful bibliography, see Lee Baxandall and Stefan Morawski, eds., *Marx & Engels on Literature and Art* (St. Louis: Telos Press, 1973).

6. Fredric Jameson, "Introduction," Henri Arvon, *Marxist Esthetics*, trans. Helen R. Lane (Ithaca: Cornell University Press, 1973), pp. xi–xiii.

In his "The Failure of Left Criticism," *The New Republic*, 9 September 1940, Granville Hicks observed there were two main schools of American Marxist criticism: one was concerned with "the importance of economic forces, the importance of the working class, the importance of the Marxist analysis of society"; the other "insisted on technical excellence, was concerned with problems of style and form" (346). The first group consisted mainly of historians; the second of aesthetic evaluators and literary reviewers.

7. Arnold L. Goldsmith, *American Literary Criticism: 1905–1965* (Boston: Twayne, 1979), p. 62. Goldsmith's book is the third of a three-volume survey of American literary criticism from 1800 to 1965.

8. V. F. Calverton, *The Liberation of American Literature* (New York: Scribner's, 1932), p. xi.

9. Daniel Aaron, *Writers on The Left: Episodes in American Literary Communism* (New York: Harcourt, Brace & World, 1961), p. 324.

10. Aaron, chap. 16; James T. Farrell, "The End of a Literary Decade," *American Mercury*, 48 (1939), 408–15.

11. Goldsmith, p. 68.

12. Granville Hicks, Review of Calverton's *The Liberation of American Literature*, in *The New Republic*, 7 September 1932, pp. 104–05. See also Hicks, "The Crisis in American Criticism," *New Masses*, 8 (February 1933), 4; and Terry L. Long, *Granville Hicks* (Boston: Twayne, 1981), pp. 51–59.

13. Granville Hicks, *The Great Tradition: An Interpretation of American Literature Since the Civil War*, rev. ed. (New York: Macmillan, 1935), p. ix.

14. Bernard Smith, *Forces in American Criticism: A Study in the History of American Literary Thought* (New York: Harcourt, Brace, 1939). For Smith's history of Marxist critics in the twenties and thirties, see pp. 368–80.

15. For brief historical accounts of the *Partisan Review*, see Aaron, pp. 297–303; Richard H. Pells, *Radical Visions and American Dreams: Culture and Social Thought in the Depression Years* (New York: Harper & Row, 1973), pp. 334–46; and Alan Wald, "Revolutionary Intellectuals: *Partisan Review* in the 1930s," *Literature at the Barricades*, ed. Ralph F. Bogardus and Fred Hobson (Univeristy: University of Alabama Press, 1982), pp. 187–203. We shall discuss the *Partisan Review* more fully in chapter 4.

16. See *AAUP Bulletin*, 21 (January 1936), 16–20.

17. Schrecker, pp. 150–52.

18. Malcolm Cowley,—*And I Worked at the Writer's Trade: Chapters of Literary History, 1918–1978* (New York: Viking, 1978), pp. 108–12.

19. Granville Hicks, *Where We Came Out* (New York: Viking, 1954), p. 178.

20. Granville Hicks, "Communism and the American Intellectuals," in *Whose Revolution? A Study of the Future Course of Liberalism in the United States*, ed. Irving DeWitt Talmadge (New York: Howell, Soskin, 1941), p. 86.

21. Martin Jay, *The Dialectical Imagination: A History of the Frankfurt School and the Institute of Social Research 1923–1950* (Boston: Little, Brown, 1973), p. 114.

22. Jay, p. 292.

23. Allen Tate, Preface to *Reactionary Essays on Poetry and Ideas* (1936), in *Essays of Four Decades* (Chicago: Swallow Press, 1968), p. 612.

24. For a recent leftist critique of American formalism, see John Fekete, *The Critical Twilight* (London: Routledge & Kegan Paul, 1977).

25. Cleanth Brooks, *Modern Poetry and the Tradition* (Chapel Hill: University of North Carolina Press, 1939), p. 47.

26. Granville Hicks, "Literary Criticism and the Marxian Method," *The Modern Quarterly*, 6 (Summer 1932), 47.

27. R. P. Blackmur, "A Critic's Job of Work" (1935), *Language as Gesture: Essays in Poetry* (New York: Harcourt, Brace, 1952), p. 384.

CHAPTER TWO. THE "NEW CRITICISM"

1. William E. Cain, *The Crisis in Criticism: Theory, Literature, and Reform in English Studies* (Baltimore: Johns Hopkins University Press, 1984), p. 105.

2. Cleanth Brooks, "New Criticism," *Princeton Encyclopedia of Poetry and Poetics*, enlarged ed., ed. Alex Preminger et al. (Princeton: Princeton University Press, 1974), pp. 567–68.

3. René Wellek, "The New Criticism: Pro and Contra," *Critical Inquiry*, 4 (Summer 1978), 618–19. In this retrospective assessment, Wellek found only one serious limitation of the New Critics: "They are extremely anglocentric, even provincial. They have rarely attempted to discuss foreign literature . . ." (623). This accounts, in part, for why New Criticism was more influential in departments of English than in other departments of literary study in America.

4. T. S. Eliot, *To Criticize the Critic* (New York: Farrar, Straus & Giroux, 1965), p. 25.

5. W. K. Wimsatt, *The Verbal Icon: Studies in the Meaning of Poetry* (Lexington: University of Kentucky Press, 1954), pp. 4–5.

6. Allen Tate, "Narcissus as Narcissus" (1938), *Essays of Four Decades* (Chicago: Swallow Press, 1968), p. 595. Hereafter *EFD*.

7. Cleanth Brooks, *The Well Wrought Urn: Studies in the Structure of Poetry* (New York: Harcourt, Brace, 1947), p. 177. Herafter *WWU*.

8. William K. Wimsatt and Cleanth Brooks, *Literary Criticism: A Short History* (1957; rpt. Chicago: University of Chicago Press, 1978), p. 749.

9. John Crowe Ransom, "Poetry: A Note in Ontology" (1934), *The World's Body* (1938; rpt. Baton Rouge: Louisiana State University Press, 1968), p. 139. Hereafter *WB*. Ransom likened the miraculous, mysterious element of literature to the latent dream content of Freudian theory—see "Poetry: The Formal Analysis," *Kenyon Review*, 9 (1947), 441.

10. Cleanth Brooks and Robert Penn Warren, *Understanding Poetry*, 3d. ed. (New York: Holt, Rinehart and Winston, 1960), p. 270. See also Brooks' "Metaphor and the Tradition," *Modern Poetry and the Tradition* (Chapel Hill: University of North Carolina Press, 1939), pp. 1–17.

11. Grant Webster, *The Republic of Letters: A History of Postwar American Literary Opinion* (Baltimore: Johns Hopkins University Press, 1979), pp. 100–2.

12. Cleanth Brooks, "The Formalist Critics," *Kenyon Review*, 13 (Winter 1951), 75.

13. Allen Tate, *Memoirs and Opinions 1926–1974* (Chicago: Swallow Press, 1975), p. 99.

14. Webster, pp. 95–97 and p. 310, n.7.

15. I. A. Richards, *Principles of Literary Criticism* (1924; New York: Harcourt, Brace, 1959), p. 248.

16. I. A. Richards, *Practical Criticism* (1929; New York: Harcourt, Brace & World, n.d.), p. 15.

17. René Wellek, "Literary Criticism," *Encyclopedia of World Literature in the 20th Century*, rev. ed., ed. Leonard S. Klein (New York: Frederick Ungar, 1983), 3: 122.

18. A. Walton Litz, "Literary Criticism," *Harvard Guide to Contemporary Writing*, ed. Daniel Hoffman (Cambridge: Harvard University Press, 1979), p. 57.

19. Kenneth Burke, "Formalist Criticism: Its Principles and Limits," *Language as Symbolic Action: Essays on Life, Literature, and Method* (Berkeley: University of California Press, 1966), p. 497.

20. Kenneth Burke, "Kinds of Criticism," *Poetry*, 68 (August 1946), 278–79. Hereafter "KC."

21. Kenneth Burke, "The Philosophy of Literary Form," *The Philosophy of Literary Form: Studies in Symbolic Action*, 3d ed. (1941; Berkeley: University of California Press, 1973), p. 1. Herafter *PLF*.

22. Kenneth Burke, *Counter-Statement*, 2d ed. (1931; Los Altos, Calif.: Hermes, 1953), p. 55.

23. William H. Rueckert, *Kenneth Burke and the Drama of Human Relations*, 2d ed. (Berkeley: University of California Press, 1982), pp. 83–84.

24. Murray Krieger, *The New Apologists for Poetry* (Minneapolis: University of Minnesota Press, 1956), p. 216, n.18.

25. Murray Krieger, *Poetic Presence and Illusion: Essays in Critical History and Theory* (Baltimore: Johns Hopkins University Press, 1979), p. 173. Hereafter *PPI*. (This volume collects seventeen essays published between 1968 and 1979.)

26. Murray Krieger, *Arts on the Level: The Fall of the Elite Object* (Knoxville: University of Tennessee Press, 1981), pp. 27–48. (This book consists of three lectures delivered in 1979.)

27. Victor Erlich, *Russian Formalism: History-Doctrine*, 3d ed. (New Haven: Yale University Press, 1981), pp. 272–76; and Ewa M. Thompson, *Russian Formalism and Anglo-American New Criticism: A Comparative Study* (The Hague: Mouton, 1971).

28. Leon Trotsky, *Literature and Revolution*, trans. not listed (New York: Russell & Russell, 1957), p. 179.

29. P. N. Medvedev/M. M. Bakhtin, *The Formal Method in Literary Scholarship: A Critical Introduction to Sociological Poetics*, trans. Albert J. Wehrle (Baltimore: Johns Hopkins University Press, 1978), p. 145.

30. Robert Penn Warren, "A Conversation with Cleanth Brooks," *The Possibilities of Order: Cleanth Brooks and His Work*, ed. Lewis P. Simpson (Baton Rouge: Louisiana State University Press, 1976), pp. 22, 25–26.

31. Yvor Winters, *In Defense of Reason* (Denver: Swallow Press, 1947), p. 11.

32. Geoffrey H. Hartman, *Criticism in the Wilderness: The Study of Literature Today* (New Haven: Yale University Press, 1980), pp. 285–86.

CHAPTER THREE. THE CHICAGO SCHOOL

1. Richard McKeon, "Criticism and the Liberal Arts: The Chicago School of Criticism," *Profession 82*, ed. Richard I. Brod and Phyllis P. Franklin (New York: Modern Language Association, 1982), p. 4. Hereafter "CLA."

2. R. S. Crane, ed., *Critics and Criticism: Ancient and Modern* (Chicago: University of Chicago Press, 1952), p. 5. Hereafter *CC*.

3. R. S. Crane, *The Idea of the Humanities and Other Essays Critical and Historical* (Chicago: University of Chicago Press, 1967), 2: 19. Hereafter *IH2*.

4. John Crowe Ransom, "Criticism, Inc." (1937), *The World's Body* (1938; rpt. Baton Rouge: Louisiana State University Press, 1968), p. 330.

5. R. S. Crane, *Critics and Criticism: Essays in Method*, abridged ed. (Chicago: University of Chicago Press, 1957), p. v. Hereafter *CC2*.

6. R. S. Crane, *The Languages of Criticism and the Structure of Poetry* (Toronto: University of Toronto Press, 1953), pp. 168–69. Hereafter *LCSP*.

7. R. S. Crane " 'The Chicago Critics,' " *Princeton Encyclopedia of Poetry and Poetics*, enlarged ed., ed. Alex Preminger et al. (Princeton: Princeton University Press, 1974), p. 117.

8. Wayne C. Booth, *Critical Understanding: The Powers and Limits of Pluralism* (Chicago: University of Chicago Press, 1979), p. 349.

In his *The Act of Interpretation: A Critique of Literary Reason* (Chicago: University of Chicago Press, 1978), Walter Davis—a third-generation Chicago Critic—sought to develop a sophisticated pluralism by relying on insights from phenomenological, existential, and hermeneutical criticism and philosophy.

9. Wayne C. Booth, "Between Two Generations: The Heritage of the Chicago School," *Profession 82*, ed. R. I. Brod and P. P. Franklin, pp. 20–22. For an account of the recent history of the Chicago School, see Remo Ceserani, *Breve viaggio nella critica americana* (Pisa: ETS, 1984), pp. 33–60.

10. W. K. Wimsatt, *The Verbal Icon: Studies in the Meaning of Poetry* (Lexington: University of Kentucky Press, 1954), p. 64.

11. Grant Webster, *The Republic of Letters: A History of Postwar American Literary Opinion* (Baltimore: Johns Hopkins University Press, 1979), p. 123.

12. Walter Sutton, *Modern American Criticism* (Englewood Cliffs: Prentice-Hall, 1963), pp. 173–74. Compare the assessment of Michael Sprinker, "What is Living and What is Dead in Chicago Criticism," *Boundary 2*, 13 (Winter/Spring 1985), 189–212.

13. The classroom texts by Walter Blair and Edward Rosenheim, both at the University of Chicago from the thirties through the sixties, have never been examined in relation to the Chicago School. This constitutes an area for future research and analysis.

CHAPTER FOUR. THE NEW YORK INTELLECTUALS

1. Irving Howe, "The New York Intellectuals" (1968), in *Decline of the New* (New York: Harcourt, Brace & World, 1970), pp. 211–65. This book collects seventeen essays. Hereafter *DN*. See also Howe, *World of Our Fathers* (New York: Harcourt, Brace, Jovanovich, 1976), pp. 598–607; and Howe, *A Margin of Hope: An Intellectual Autobiography* (New York: Harcourt, Brace, Jovanovich, 1982), chaps. 5 and 6.

2. "New York and the National Culture," *Partisan Review*, 44, 2 (1977), 177–78. This is a symposium of three critics (Howe included), convened by William Phillips in December 1976 at the City University of New York, followed by a question and answer session. See also *DN*, pp. 212–13; and Mark Krupnick, "Fathers, Sons, and New York Intellectuals," *Salmagundi*, no. 54 (Fall 1981), 106–20.

3. Alfred Kazin, *New York Jew* (New York: Knopf, 1978), p. 44.

4. Grant Webster, "New York Intellectuals: The Bourgeois Avant-Garde," *The Republic of Letters: A History of Postwar American Literary Opinion* (Baltimore: Johns Hopkins University Press, 1979), pp. 209–92.

5. Norman Podhoretz, *Making It* (New York: Random House, 1967), chap. 4.

6. On Rahv as the "representative" New York Intellectual, see William Barrett, *The Truants: Adventures Among the Intellectuals* (New York: Doubleday, 1982), esp.

chaps. 3 and 8. For a critique of Barrett's view, see William Phillips, *A Partisan View: Five Decades of the Literary Life* (New York: Stein and Day, 1983), pp. 290–93.

7. Edmund Wilson, *Letters on Literature and Politics 1912–1972,* ed. Elena Wilson (New York: Farrar, Straus and Giroux, 1977), p. 196. Hereafter *Letters.*

8. Edmund Wilson, *The Shores of Light: A Literary Chronicle of the Twenties and Thirties* (New York: Farrar, Straus and Young, 1952), pp. 518–33. This is a collection of eight dozen pieces. Hereafter *SL.*

9. Philip Rahv, *Essays on Literature and Politics 1932–1972,* ed. Arabel J. Porter and Andrew J. Dvosin (Boston: Houghton Mifflin, 1978), pp. 281–83. Hereafter *ELP.*

10. Lionel Trilling, *The Liberal Imagination: Essays on Literature and Society* (1950; rpt. New York: Doubleday, 1957), p. xii–xiii. Hereafter *LI.* See also Irving Howe, "Literature and Liberalism," *Celebrations and Attacks: Thirty Years of Literary and Cultural Commentary* (New York: Horizon Press, 1979), pp. 239–54. Hereafter *C&A.*

11. Lionel Trilling, ed., *Literary Criticism: An Introductory Reader* (New York: Holt, Rinehart and Winston, 1970), p. 19.

12. Irving Howe, ed., *Modern Literary Criticism: An Anthology* (Boston: Beacon, 1958), p. 32.

13. Alfred Kazin, *Contemporaries* (Boston: Little, Brown, 1962), p. 505. Hereafter *C.*

14. Richard Chase, "Art, Nature, Politics," *Kenyon Review,* 12 (1950), 591.

15. Edmund Wilson, *The Triple Thinkers: Twelve Essays on Literary Subjects,* rev. ed. (1948; London: John Lehmann, 1952), p. 243.

16. See Louis Fraiberg, *Psychoanalysis and American Literary Criticism* (Detroit: Wayne State University Press, 1960), which assesses six psychoanalytical critics: Burke, Van Wyck Brooks, Krutch, Lewishon, Trilling, and Wilson.

17. Irving Howe, "Literature on the Couch," *C&A,* pp. 150–54. See also William Phillips, ed., *Art and Psychoanalysis* (1957; Cleveland: Meridian, 1963), esp. "Introduction: Art and Neurosis," pp. xiii–xxiv.

18. Philip Rahv, "Freud and the Literary Mind," *Literature and the Sixth Sense* (Boston: Houghton Mifflin, 1969), p. 164.

19. Edmund Wilson, *The Wound and the Bow: Seven Studies in Literature* (New York: Oxford University Press, 1941), p. 289.

20. Lionel Trilling, "Some Notes for an Autobiographical Lecture" (1971), *The Last Decade: Essays and Reviews, 1965–75,* ed. Diana Trilling (New York: Harcourt, Brace, Jovanovich, 1979), p. 237.

21. Lionel Trilling, "Freud: Within and Beyond Culture," *Beyond Culture: Essays on Literature and Learning* (1965; New York: Viking, 1968), p. 108. Hereafter *BC.*

22. Leslie A. Fiedler, *Love and Death in the American Novel,* rev. ed. (1960; New York: Dell, 1966), p. 10.

23. Richard Chase, *The American Novel and Its Tradition* (New York: Anchor, 1957), p. 245.

24. Edmund Wilson, *Axel's Castle: A Study of the Imaginative Literature of 1870–1930* (1931; New York: Scribner's, 1943), p. 292.

25. Irving Howe, *Politics and the Novel* (New York: Horizon, 1957), p. 24.
   The dual mimetic-moral theory of realistic literature appeared in Erich Auerbach's

Mimesis at about the same time as the New York Intellectuals were developing it in the 1940s.

26. Philip Rahv, "Introduction: The Native Bias," *Literature in America: An Anthology of Literary Criticism* (Cleveland: Meridian, 1957), p. 15.

On the status and scope of theories of American literature in the pre-World War II era, see Howard Mumford Jones, *The Theory of American Literature* (1948; rpt. Ithaca: Cornell University Press, 1956) and Richard Ruland, *The Rediscovery of American Literature: Premises of Critical Taste, 1900–1940* (Cambridge: Harvard University Press, 1967).

27. Alfred Kazin, *On Native Grounds: An Interpretation of Modern American Prose Literature* (New York: Harcourt, Brace, 1942), p. vii.

28. Irving Howe, "This Age of Conformity," *Partisan Review*, 21 (1954), 13. This essay was part of the important symposium initiated by *PR* in 1952 on "Our Country and Our Culture."

29. Delmore Schwartz, "Our Country and Our Culture" (1952), *Selected Essays of Delmore Schwartz*, ed. Donald A. Pike and David H. Zucker (Chicago: University of Chicago Press, 1970), p. 401.

30. Alfred Kazin, *Contemporaries: From the 19th Century to the Present*, rev. ed. (New York: Horizon, 1982), p. 4.

31. Lionel Abel, *The Intellectual Follies: A Memoir of the Literary Venture in New York and Paris* (New York: Norton, 1984), p. 285.

CHAPTER FIVE. MYTH CRITICISM

1. Friedrich Nietzsche, *The Birth of Tragedy and The Genealogy of Morals*, trans. Francis Golffing (New York: Doubleday, 1956), p. 137.

2. Stanley Edgar Hyman, "The Ritual View of Myth and the Mythic" (1958), *Myth and Literature: Contemporary Theory and Practice*, ed. John B. Vickery (Lincoln: University of Nebraska Press, 1966), p. 54. Hereafter *ML*.

3. Richard Chase, "Notes on the Study of Myth" (1946), *ML*, pp. 70–71. See also Chase, *Quest for Myth* (Baton Rouge: Louisiana State University Press, 1949), pp. 69–74.

4. Ernst Cassirer, *Language and Myth*, trans. Susanne K. Langer (1925 in German; New York: Dover, 1946), pp. 7–15.

5. Bronislaw Malinowski, *Myth in Primitive Psychology* (New York: Norton, 1926), pp. 20–30, 91–92.

6. *ML*, p. ix. Sixteen years later Vickery repeated unchanged this same codification of myth criticism in his essay, "Literature and Myth," in *Interrelations of Literature*, ed. John-Pierre Barricelli and Joseph Gibaldi (New York: Modern Language Association, 1982), pp. 80–81. Hereafter *IL*.

7. C. G. Jung, "On the Relation of Analytical Psychology to Poetry" (1922), *The Spirit in Man, Art, and Literature*, trans. R. F. C. Hull (New York: Pantheon, 1966), p. 80. This book is vol. 15 in the *Collected Works of C. G. Jung*.

8. Maud Bodkin, *Archetypal Patterns in Poetry: Psychological Studies of Imagination* (1934; London: Oxford University Press, 1963), p. 315. Hereafter *APP*.

9. Leslie A. Fiedler, "Archetype and Signature" (1952), *The Collected Essays of Leslie Fiedler* (New York: Stein and Day, 1971), 1: 537.

10. Leslie Fiedler, "From Ethics and Aesthetics to Ecstatics," *What Was Literature? Class Culture and Mass Society* (New York: Simon and Schuster, 1982), p. 133. Hereafter *WWL*.

11. Northrop Frye, "The Archetypes of Literature" (1951), *Fables of Identity: Studies in Poetic Mythology* (New York: Harcourt, Brace & World, 1963), p. 18.

12. Philip Wheelwright, *The Burning Fountain: A Study in the Language of Symbolism* (Bloomington: Indiana University Press, 1954), chap. 4. Hereafter *BF*.

13. Giambattista Vico, *The New Science*, 3d ed. rev., trans. Thomas Goddard Bergin and Max Harold Fisch (Ithaca: Cornell University Press, 1968), p. 33.

14. The earliest self-conscious advocate among the American Myth Critics of integrated interdisciplinary study was Burke's younger colleague Stanley Edgar Hyman. See especially Hyman, *The Armed Vision: A Study in the Methods of Modern Literary Criticism*, rev. ed. (1948; New York: Vintage, 1955), esp. Preface, Introduction, and Conclusion. In his massive *The Tangled Bank: Darwin, Marx, Frazer and Freud as Imaginative Writers* (New York: Atheneum, 1962), Hyman concluded of the four figures under study, "In their integration lies our future" (p. 446).

15. Kenneth Burke, "The Philosophy of Literary Form" (1941), *The Philosophy of Literary Form: Studies in Symbolic Action*, 3d ed. (1941; Berkeley: University of California Press, 1973), p. 102n. According to William Troy, "If the impulse behind the symbolical or imaginative is above all integrative, that of the analytical is dissociative. Analysis is, therefore, by its very nature, hostile to the work of art as it has traditionally existed, that is, as a pattern of symbols."—"Thomas Mann: Myth and Reason" (1938; 1956), in *Selected Essays*, ed. Stanley Edgar Hyman (New Brunswick: Rutgers University Press, 1967), p. 243.

16. Joseph Campbell, *The Hero with a Thousand Faces*, 2d corrected ed. (1949; Princeton: Princeton University Press, 1968), p. 385.

17. Francis Fergusson, *The Idea of a Theater: A Study of Ten Plays—The Art of Drama in Changing Perspective* (1949; New York: Doubleday, 1953), p. 14.

18. Northrop Frye, *Anatomy of Criticism: Four Essays* (Princeton: Princeton University Press, 1957), p. 51.

19. Northrop Frye, *Spiritus Mundi: Essays on Literature, Myth, and Society* (Bloomington: Indiana University Press, 1976), p. ix.

20. Northrop Frye, "Literature and Myth," *Relations of Literary Study*, ed. James Thorpe (New York: Modern Language Association, 1967), p. 40.

21. Northrop Frye, *The Critical Path: An Essay on the Social Context of Literary Criticism* (Bloomington: Indiana University Press, 1971), p. 25.

22. Northrop Frye, "Criticism, Visible and Invisible" (1964), *The Stubborn Structure: Essays on Criticism and Society* (Ithaca: Cornell University Press, 1970), p. 82.

CHAPTER SIX. PHENOMENOLOGICAL AND EXISTENTIAL CRITICISM

1. J. Hillis Miller, "The Geneva School," *Critical Quarterly*, 8 (Winter 1966), 305–6. Pub. also in *Virginia Quarterly Review*, 43 (Summer 1967).

2. See J. Hillis Miller, "The Antithesis of Criticism . . . ," *Modern Language Notes,* 81 (December 1966), 564–65.

3. For critiques of this idealistic tendency, see the discussions by Frank Lentricchia, "Versions of Phenomenology," *After the New Criticism* (Chicago: University of Chicago Press, 1980), esp. pp. 62–81; and Terry Eagleton, "Phenomenology, Hermeneutics, and Reception Theory," *Literary Theory: An Introduction* (Minneapolis: University of Minnesota Press, 1983), esp. pp. 58–61.

4. *The Quest for Imagination,* ed. O. B. Hardison, Jr. (Cleveland: Case Western Reserve University Press, 1971), p. 196. See also Miller, "Hommage à Georges Poulet," *MLN,* 97 (December 1982), 1039–41.

5. Sarah Lawall, *Critics of Consciousness* (Cambridge: Harvard University Press, 1968), p. vii.

6. On the question of "intentionality" in phenomenological criticism, see Robert R. Magliola, *Phenomenology and Literature: An Introduction* (West Lafayette: Purdue University Press, 1977), pp. 29, 31, 97, 104, 110.

7. Paul Brodtkorb, Jr., *Ishmael's White World: A Phenomenological Reading of MOBY DICK* (New Haven: Yale University Press, 1965), p. 9.

8. Geoffrey H. Hartman, "Retrospect 1971," in *Wordsworth's Poetry: 1787–1814* (1964; Yale University Press, 1971), p. xii.

9. Geoffrey H. Hartman, *Wordsworth's Poetry: 1787–1814* (New Haven: Yale University Press, 1964), p. xi.

10. Geoffrey H. Hartman, *The Unmediated Vision: An Interpretation of Wordsworth, Hopkins, Rilke, and Valéry* (1954; New York: Harcourt, Brace & World, 1966), pp. xi, xii. In the 1950s knowledgeable critics regarded Hartman's *The Unmediated Vision* as a major phenomenological work—see the memoir by J. Hillis Miller, "Interview with J. Hillis Miller, Yale, Fall, 1979," *Criticism,* 24 (1982), 100–1; and the 1958 conference paper by Neal Oxenhandler, "Ontological Criticism in America and France," *Modern Language Review,* 55 (1960), 17.

11. Geoffrey H. Hartman, *Beyond Formalism: Literary Essays 1958–1970* (New Haven: Yale University Press, 1970), p. xi.

12. Geoffrey H. Hartman, *The Fate of Reading and Other Essays* (Chicago: University of Chicago Press, 1975), p. 260.

13. William V. Spanos, ed., *A Casebook on Existentialism* (New York: Crowell, 1966), p. v.

14. Susan Sontag, "The Aesthetics of Silence" (1967), *A Susan Sontag Reader* (New York: Farrar, Straus, Giroux, 1982), p. 189.

15. George Steiner, "Silence and the Poet" (1966), *Language and Silence: Essays on Language, Literature, and the Inhuman* (New York: Antheneum, 1967), p. 49.

16. Jean-Paul Sartre, *Existentialism,* trans. Bernard Frechtman (New York: Philosophical Library, 1947), p. 15.

17. William V. Spanos, *The Christian Tradition in Modern British Verse Drama: The Poetics of Sacramental Time* (New Brunswick: Rutgers University Press, 1967), p. 7.

18. Ihab Hassan, *Radical Innocence: Studies in the Contemporary American Novel* (Princeton: Princeton University Press, 1961), p. 97.

19. Ihab Hassan, *The Dismemberment of Orpheus: Toward a Postmodern Literature* (New York: Oxford University Press, 1971), p. x.

20. Ihab Hassan, *Paracriticisms: Seven Speculations of the Times* (Urbana: University of Illinois Press, 1975), p. xii.

21. Ihab Hassan, "Frontiers of Criticism: 1963, 1969, 1972," *Paracriticisms*, p. 28. The first part of this three-part critical manifesto was published in 1964, the second in 1970, and the third in 1972.

22. Ihab Hassan, "Postface 1982," *The Dismemberment of Orpheus: Toward a Postmodern Literature*, 2d ed. (Madison: University of Wisconsin Press, 1982), p. 271.

CHAPTER SEVEN. HERMENEUTICS

1. Paul Johnson, *Modern Times: The World from the Twenties to the Eighties* (New York: Harper & Row, 1983), pp. 544–67.

2. William Phillips, *A Partisan View: Five Decades of the Literary Life* (New York: Stein and Day, 1983), p. 294.

3. Richard E. Palmer, *Hermeneutics: Interpretation Theory in Schleiermacher, Dilthey, Heidegger, and Gadamer* (Evanston: Northwestern University Press, 1969), p. 7. Pub. in Northwestern's important series, "Studies in Phenomenology and Existential Philosophy."

4. Walter J. Ong, S. J., *The Presence of the Word: Some Prolegomena for Cultural and Religious History* (New Haven: Yale University Press, 1967), p. 228.

5. E. D. Hirsch, Jr., *Validity in Interpretation* (New Haven: Yale University Press, 1967), pp. 209–12. Hereafter *VI*.

6. E. D. Hirsch, Jr., *The Aims of Interpretation* (Chicago: University of Chicago Press, 1976), p. 7.

7. E. D. Hirsch, Jr., "Meaning and Significance Reinterpreted," *Critical Inquiry*, 11 (December 1984), 223.

8. Martin Heidegger, *Being and Time*, trans. John Macquarrie and Edward Robinson (1927 in German; New York: Harper & Row, 1962), p. 44. Hereafter *BT*.

9. William V. Spanos, "Breaking the Circle: Hermeneutics as Dis-closure," *Boundary 2*, 5 (Winter 1977), 427. Hereafter "BC."

10. William V. Spanos, "Repetition in *The Waste Land:* A Phenomenological Destruction," *Boundary 2*, 7 (Spring 1979), 229.

11. William V. Spanos, "Hermeneutics and Memory: Destroying T. S. Eliot's *Four Quartets*," *Genre*, 11 (Winter 1978), 563.

(As of 1986, Spanos was working on two related books tentatively titled *Repetitions: The Postmodern Occasion in Literature and Culture* and *T. S. Eliot's Poetry: A Destructive Reading*.)

12. William V. Spanos, "Heidegger, Kierkegaard, and the Hermeneutic Circle: Towards a Postmodern Theory of Interpretation as Dis-closure," *Boundary 2*, 4 (Winter 1976), 116. Hereafter "HK." This issue of *Boundary 2*, on the topic "Martin Heidegger and the Question of Literature," contained essays not only by Spanos, Heidegger, and Palmer, but by David Couzens Hoy and Joseph N. Riddel, who were both influential during the 1970s in furthering Heideggerian hermeneutics. We shall discuss Riddel in chapter 10 and Hoy later in this chapter. Significantly, this

issue of *Boundary 2* was published three years later as a book with a Preface and edited by Spanos, *Martin Heidegger and the Question of Literature: Toward a Postmodern Literary Hermeneutics* (Bloomington: Indiana University Press, 1979). The book bore the imprint of the series, "Studies in Phenomenology and Existential Philosophy," formerly published by Northwestern University Press, which had brought out Palmer's *Hermeneutics* ten years earlier. In a sense, the later book represented a certain culmination of the "new hermeneutics" in America.

13. As we saw in the case of Palmer, the "new hermeneutics" entailed a deep concern for "oral poetics." Spanos displayed such a concern: see, for example, "The Oral Impulse in Contemporary American Poetry," a special issue (edited by Spanos) of *Boundary 2*, 3 (Spring 1975).

14. Gerald L. Bruns, *Inventions: Writing, Textuality, and Understanding in Literary History* (New Haven: Yale University Press, 1982), p. 97. See also Bruns, "Structuralism, Deconstruction, and Hermeneutics," *Diacritics*, 14 (Spring 1984), 12–23.

In *Literary Meaning: From Phenomenology to Deconstruction* (New York: Basil Blackwell, 1984), William Ray structured the whole history of postwar literary criticism according to whether a critical theory promoted systems or individual instances. In this account, deconstruction self-consciously merged "instance" and "system," undermining the structuralist faith in systems. Ray and Bruns were in fundamental disagreement about Derrida and deconstruction.

15. Faced with the challenge of deconstruction, other theologically oriented critics opted for phenomenological hermeneutics. See, for example, the essays by Robert P. Scharlemann and Max A. Myers in *Deconstruction and Theology*, ed. Thomas J. J. Altizer et al. (New York: Crossroad, 1982).

With fourteen texts by such authors as Betti, Bruns, de Man, Gadamer, and Palmer, the collection *Hermeneutics: Questions and Prospects*, ed. Gary Shapiro and Alan Sica (Amherst: University of Massachusetts Press, 1984), commenced by admitting that Derridean deconstruction "hangs over this volume unacknowledged, the absent but necessary guest . . ." (p. 2). In other words, the confrontation of hermeneutics with deconstruction, however unwanted, was inescapable. The same point was made earlier in "A Symposium: Hermeneutics, Post-Structuralism, and 'Objective' Interpretation," *Papers on Language and Literature*, 17 (Winter 1981), 48–87, where the Hermeneutical Critics Robert Magliola, Vernon Gras, David Halliburton, Michael Murray, and James Swearingen examined the modern crisis in linguistic referentiality as recently exacerbated by deconstruction.

16. Richard Rorty, *Philosophy and the Mirror of Nature* (Princeton: Princeton University Press, 1979), p. 7. Hereafter *PMN*.

17. Richard Rorty, "A Reply to Dreyfus and Taylor," *Review of Metaphysics*, 34 (September 1980), 39.

18. Richard Rorty, "Nineteenth-Century Idealism and Twentieth-Century Textualism" (1980), *Consequences of Pragmatism: Essays 1972–1980* (Minneapolis: University of Minnesota Press, 1982), p. 150.

19. Richard E. Palmer, "Postmodernity and Hermeneutics," *Boundary 2*, 5 (Winter 1977), 386. This essay was originally presented at a symposium, hosted by Spanos and *Boundary 2*, in early 1976. Shortly before, a special issue on hermeneutics was published by *The Journal of Religion*, 55 (July 1975), which contained an

annotated bibliography on hermeneutics and contributions from Palmer and Hirsch, among others.

20. Fredric Jameson, *The Political Unconscious: Narrative as a Socially Symbolic Act* (Ithaca: Cornell University Press, 1981), p. 296.

CHAPTER EIGHT. READER-RESPONSE CRITICISM

1. Susan R. Suleiman, "Introduction: Varieties of Audience-Oriented Criticism," *The Reader in the Text: Essays on Audience and Interpretation,* eds. Susan R. Suleiman and Inge Crosman (Princeton: Princeton University Press, 1980), p. 6.

2. Jane P. Tompkins, "An Introduction to Reader-Response Criticism," *Reader-Response Criticism: From Formalism to Post-Structuralism* (Baltimore: Johns Hopkins University Press, 1980), p. ix.

3. Stanley Eugene Fish, *Surprised by Sin: The Reader in Paradise Lost* (1967; Berkeley: University of California Press, 1971), p. x.

4. Stanely E. Fish, "Literature in the Reader: Affective Stylistics," *New Literary History,* 2 (Autumn 1970); rpt. with omissions in *Self-Consuming Artifacts: The Experience of Seventeenth-Century Literature* (Berkeley: University of California Press, 1972); rpt. with omissions in Tompkins, pp. 70–100; and rpt. in Fish, *Is There a Text in This Class? The Authority of Interpretive Communities* (Cambridge: Harvard University Press, 1980), p. 49. *Is There a Text* contains sixteen articles— twelve of which were previously published between 1970 and 1980.

5. Paul de Man, "Literature and Language: A Commentary," *New Literary History,* 4 (Autumn 1972), 192.

6. Jonathan Culler, "Stanley Fish and the Righting of the Reader" (1975), in *The Pursuit of Signs: Semiotics, Literature, Deconstruction* (Ithaca: Cornell University Press, 1981), p. 131.

7. Stanley E. Fish, "Interpreting the *Variorum,*" *Critical Inquiry,* 2 (Spring 1976); rpt. in *Is There a Text,* p. 171.

8. Stanley Fish, *The Living Temple: George Herbert and Catechizing* (Berkeley: University of California Press, 1978), p. 172.

9. Stanley Fish, "Consequences," *Critical Inquiry,* 11 (March 1985), 438.

10. Edward W. Said, *The World, the Text, and the Critic* (Cambridge: Harvard University Press, 1983), p. 26.

11. Frank Lentricchia, *After the New Criticism* (Chicago: University of Chicago Press, 1980), p. 147.

12. Norman Holland, "UNITY IDENTITY TEXT SELF," *PMLA,* 90 (October 1975), 815.

13. Norman Holland, "The New Paradigm: Subjective or Transactive?," *New Literary History,* 7 (Winter 1976), 338.

14. According to Holland, "the same large principle seems to apply not only to interactions of people but to interactions by anything that can be said to have a style the way a person does: an institution, for example, or a culture or a nation"—*5 Readers Reading* (New Haven: Yale University Press, 1975), p. xiii. See also Holland, *The I* (New Haven: Yale University Press, 1985), pp. 145–55.

15. Frederick Crews, *Out of My System: Psychoanalysis, Ideology, and Critical Method* (New York: Oxford University Press, 1975), pp. 179–80.

16. David Bleich, *Subjective Criticism* (Baltimore: Johns Hopkins University Press, 1978), pp. 297, 9.

17. David Bleich, *Readings and Feelings: An Introduction to Subjective Criticism* (Urbana: National Council of Teachers of English, 1975), p. 81.

18. Bleich and Holland debated this difference in articles published in *College English* and *New Literary History* during 1975 and 1976.

19. Judith Fetterley, *The Resisting Reader: A Feminist Approach to American Fiction* (Bloomington: Indiana University Press, 1978), p. viii.

20. Mary Louise Pratt, "Interpretive Strategies/Strategic Interpretations: On Anglo-American Reader-Response Criticism," *Boundary 2*, 11 (Fall/Winter 1982–83), 209.

21. Wolfgang Iser, "Talk like Whales: A Reply to Stanley Fish," *Diacritics*, 11 (Fall 1981), 84.

22. Robert C. Holub, *Reception Theory: A Critical Introduction* (London: Methuen, 1984), p. xiii.

CHAPTER NINE. LITERARY STRUCTURALISM AND SEMIOTICS

1. Robert Scholes, *Structuralism in Literature: An Introduction* (New Haven: Yale University Press, 1974), p. 10.

2. Jonathan Culler, *Structuralist Poetics: Structuralism, Linguistics and the Study of Literature* (Ithaca: Cornell University Press, 1975), p. viii. Hereafter *SP*.

3. Claudio Guillén, "Literature as System" (1970), *Literature as System: Essays toward the Theory of Literary History* (Princeton: Princeton University Press, 1971), p. 376.

4. Roman Jakobson, "Linguistics and Poetics" (1958), in *The Structuralists: From Marx to Lévi-Strauss*, eds. Richard T. and Fernande M. De George (Garden City: Doubleday, 1972), p. 93.

5. Roman Jakobson and Claude Lévi-Strauss, "Charles Baudelaire's 'Les Chats'" (1962), in *The Structuralists*, p. 141.

6. Michael Riffaterre, "Describing Poetic Structures: Two Approaches to Baudelaire's 'Les Chats'" (1966), in *Structuralism*, ed. Jacques Ehrmann (Garden City: Doubleday, 1970), p. 197.

7. Jonathan Culler, "Riffaterre and the Semiotics of Poetry" (1981), in *The Pursuit of Signs: Semiotics, Literature, Deconstruction* (Ithaca: Cornell University Press, 1981), pp. 95–97; Guillén, pp. 9–10; and Robert Scholes, *Semiotics and Interpretation* (New Haven: Yale University Press, 1982), pp. 42–48.

8. Gerald Prince, *Narratology: The Form and Functioning of Narrative* (Berlin: Mouton, 1982), p. 101.

9. Hayden White, *Metahistory: The Historical Imagination in Nineteenth-Century Europe* (Baltimore: Johns Hopkins University Press, 1973), p. 30.

10. Seymour Chatman, *Story and Discourse: Narrative Structure in Fiction and Film* (Ithaca: Cornell University Press, 1978), p. 196.

11. Jonathan Culler, "Problems in the Theory of Fiction," *Diacritics,* 14 (Spring 1984), 2–11. See also the several issues devoted to narratology of *Poetics Today,* 1–2 (1980–81); and Harold F. Mosher, Jr., "Current Trends in Narratology," *Critical Texts,* 1 (Summer 1982), 1, 15–20. On the state of narrative theory just prior to the advent of structuralism in America, see the representative anthology of criticism edited by Philip Stevick, *The Theory of the Novel* (New York: Free Press, 1967), which observed on the opening page "the novel has had no poetics" (1). For an introduction to the developments in narratology between 1960 and 1985, see Wallace Martin, *Recent Theories of Narrative* (Ithaca: Cornell University Press, 1986), which has a detailed bibliography.

12. M. H. Abrams, *A Glossary of Literary Terms,* 4th ed. (New York: Holt, Rinehart and Winston, 1981), p. 189.

13. Michael Riffaterre, *Semiotics of Poetry* (Bloomington: Indiana University Press, 1978), p. 166.

14. Gerald Prince, "Introduction to the Study of the Narratee" (1973), trans. Francis Mariner in *Reader-Response Criticism: From Formalism to Post-Structuralism,* ed. Jane P. Tompkins (Baltimore: Johns Hopkins University Press, 1980), p. 7.

15. Michael Riffaterre, "Interview," *Diacritics,* 11 (Winter 1981), 13. See also *Semiotics of Poetry,* pp. 12, 150, 165.

16. Jonathan Culler, *On Deconstruction: Theory and Criticism after Structuralism* (Ithaca: Cornell University Press, 1982), p. 75.

17. Robert Scholes, *Textual Power: Literary Theory and the Teaching of English* (New Haven: Yale University Press, 1985), p. 24.

18. See also Jonathan Culler, "Phenomenology and Structuralism," *The Human Context,* 5 (Spring 1973), 35–42; and Donald G. Marshall, "The Ontology of the Literary Sign: Notes toward a Heideggerian Revision of Semiology," *Boundary 2,* 4 (Winter 1976)—rpt. in *Martin Heidegger and the Question of Literature: Toward a Postmodern Literary Hermeneutics,* ed. William V. Spanos (Bloomington: Indiana University Press, 1979), pp. 271–94.

19. See, for example, Eugenio Donato, "Structuralism: The Aftermath," *Sub-Stance,* no. 7 (Fall 1973), 9–26; and Josué V. Harari, ed., Introduction, *Textual Strategies: Perspectives in Post-Structuralist Criticism* (Ithaca: Cornell University Press, 1979), pp. 17–72.

20. Jonathan Culler, "Beyond Interpretation" (1976), *The Pursuit of Signs,* p. 9.

21. Kaja Silverman, *The Subject of Semiotics* (New York: Oxford University Press, 1983), p. viii. On the political uses of semiotics, see Marshall Blonsky, "Introduction—The Agony of Semiotics: Reassessing the Discipline," *On Signs,* ed. M. Blonsky (Baltimore: Johns Hopkins University Press, 1985), pp. xiii–li.

22. Thomas A. Sebeok, "Semiotics: A Survey of the State of the Art" (1974), *Current Trends in Linguistics,* ed. T. A. Sebeok (The Hague: Mouton, 1974), vol. 12, part 1, p. 231.

23. Donato, p. 25.

CHAPTER TEN. DECONSTRUCTIVE CRITICISM

1. Jacques Derrida, "Structure, Sign, and Play in the Discourse of the Human

Sciences" (pub. 1967), in *Writing and Difference*, trans. Alan Bass (Chicago: University of Chicago Press, 1978), p. 292. First published in English in *The Languages of Criticism and the Sciences of Man*, eds. Richard Macksey and Eugenio Donato (Baltimore: Johns Hopkins University Press, 1970)—which was republished in 1972 as *The Structuralist Controversy*, containing a new Preface, "The Space Between—1971," that opened, "Today we may question the very existence of structuralism as a meaningful concept . . ." (ix), signaling the move beyond structuralism enabled by deconstruction.

2. Paul de Man, *Blindness and Insight: Essays in the Rhetoric of Contemporary Criticism* (New York: Oxford University Press, 1971), p. viii. Hereafter *BI*.

3. Paul de Man, *Allegories of Reading: Figural Language in Rousseau, Nietzsche, Rilke, and Proust* (New Haven: Yale University Press, 1979), p. 300. Hereafter *AR*.

4. J. Hillis Miller, "Nature and the Linguistic Moment," *Nature and the Victorian Imagination*, eds. U. C. Knoepflmacher and G. B. Tennyson (Berkeley: University of California Press, 1977), p. 450. Hereafter "NLM."

5. J. Hillis Miller, "Tradition and Difference," review of M. H. Abrams' *Natural Supernaturalism*, in *Diacritics*, 2 (Winter 1972), 11.

6. Jeffrey Mehlman, "The 'floating signifier': from Lévi-Strauss to Lacan," *Yale French Studies*, no. 48 (1972), 11.

7. Jacques Derrida, *Speech and Phenomena: And Other Essays on Husserl's Theory of Signs*, trans. David B. Allison (Evanston: Northwestern University Press, 1973), pp. 80−81. Hereafter *SP*.

8. Paul de Man, *Blindness and Insight: Essays in the Rhetoric of Contemporary Criticism*, 2nd ed. rev. (Minneapolis: University of Minnesota Press, 1983), pp. 237, 240.

9. J. Hillis Miller, "George Poulet's 'Criticism of Identification,'" *The Quest for Imagination*, ed. O. B. Hardison, Jr. (Cleveland: Case Western Reserve University Press, 1971), p. 216.

10. J. Hillis Miller, "Deconstructing the Deconstructers," review of Joseph N. Riddel's *The Inverted Bell*, in *Diacritics*, 5 (Summer 1975), 29−30. Hereafter "DD."

11. Joseph N. Riddel, "A Miller's Tale," *Diacritics*, 5 (Fall 1975), 59.

12. Joseph N. Riddel, "From Heidegger to Derrida to Chance: Doubling and (Poetic) Language," *Boundary 2*, 4 (Winter 1976); rpt. in *Martin Heidegger and the Question of Literature: Toward a Postmodern Literary Hermeneutics*, ed. William V. Spanos (Bloomington: Indiana University Press, 1979), p. 248. Hereafter "HD."

13. Geoffrey H. Hartman, Preface, *Deconstruction and Criticism*, ed. Harold Bloom et al. (New York: Seabury, 1979), p. ix. Hereafter *D&C*.

14. Geoffrey H. Hartman, *Criticism in the Wilderness: The Study of Literature Today* (New Haven: Yale University Press, 1980), p. 261. Hereafter *CW*.

15. Geoffrey H. Hartman, *Easy Pieces* (New York: Columbia University Press, 1985), p. xii.

16. Jacques Derrida, *Of Grammatology*, trans. Gayatri Chakravorty Spivak (Baltimore: Johns Hopkins University Press, 1976), p. 5.

17. Paul de Man, "Literature and Language: A Commentary," *New Literary History*, 4 (Autumn 1972), 188, 184.

18. Paul de Man, "Nietzsche's Theory of Rhetoric," *Symposium*, 28 (Spring 1974),

51. When published in *Symposium*, this conference paper, later reprinted in *Allegories of Reading*, included de Man's responses to questions from the audience. This revealing material is available only in *Symposium* and not in *Allegories of Reading*.

19. J. Hillis Miller, "Fiction and Repetition: *Tess of the d'Urbevilles*," in *Forms of Modern British Fiction*, ed. Alan Warren Friedman (Austin: University of Texas Press, 1975), p. 68.

20. J. Hillis Miller, *The Linguistic Moment: From Wordsworth to Stevens* (Princeton: Princeton University Press, 1985), p. 422. Hereafter *LM*.

21. J. Hillis Miller, "Ariachne's Broken Woof," *Georgia Review*, 31 (Spring 1977), 59.

22. J. Hillis Miller, "Stevens' Rock and Criticism as Cure, II," *Georgia Review*, 30 (Summer 1976), 334. This essay promotes the Yale Critics.

23. Harold Bloom, *The Anxiety of Influence: A Theory of Poetry* (New York: Oxford University Press, 1973), pp. 94–95.

24. J. Hillis Miller, *Fiction and Repetition: Seven English Novels* (Cambridge: Harvard University Press, 1982), pp. 19–20.

25. Joseph N. Riddel, "Re-doubling the Commentary," review of Derrida's *Of Grammatology* and of Foucault's *Language, Counter-Memory, Practice*, in *Contemporary Literature*, 20 (Spring 1979), 242. Hereafter "RC."

26. Robert Young, ed., *Untying the Text: A Post-Structuralist Reader* (Boston: Routledge & Kegan Paul, 1981), p. 8. See also Philip Lewis, "The Post-Structuralist Condition," *Diacritics*, 12 (Spring 1982), 2–24, who prefers the term "critical structuralism" to "poststructuralism" and who positions deconstruction as part of "critical structuralism."

27. Jacques Derrida, "The Purveyor of Truth" (1975), partial trans. by Willis Domingo et al., in *Yale French Studies*, no. 52 (1975), 48.

28. Shoshana Felman, "Turning the Screw of Interpretation," *Literature and Psychoanalysis—The Question of Reading: Otherwise*, ed. S. Felman (Baltimore: Johns Hopkins University Press, 1982), p. 112. The volume was originally published as a double issue of *Yale French Studies* in 1977. Felman's monograph was reprinted in her *Writing and Madness: (Literature/Philosophy/Psychoanalysis)*, trans. Martha Noel Evans et al. (Ithaca: Cornell University Press, 1985), pp. 141–247.

29. Geoffrey H. Hartman, Preface, *Psychoanalysis and the Question of the Text*, Selected Papers from the English Institute, 1976–77, ed. G. H. Hartman (Baltimore: Johns Hopkins University Press, 1978), p. xvii.

30. Geoffrey H. Hartman, *Saving the Text: Literature/Derrida/Philosophy* (Baltimore: Johns Hopkins University Press, 1981), pp. 121, 138–39.

31. Harold Bloom, *A Map of Misreading* (New York: Oxford University Press, 1975), pp. 53–60, 115–19; and his *Poetry and Repression: Revisionism from Blake to Stevens* (New Haven: Yale University Press, 1976), p. 27. Hereafter *PR*.

32. Harold Bloom, "The Breaking of Form," *D&C*, p. 37.

33. Harold Bloom, *The Breaking of the Vessels* (Chicago: University of Chicago Press, 1982), p. 29.

34. Jacques Derrida, "Choreographies," interview with and translation by Christie V. McDonald, *Diacritics*, 12 (Summer 1982), 75. This special issue on feminist criticism was edited by Cynthia Chase, Nelly Furman, and Mary Jacobus. See also "Textual Politics: Feminist Criticism," *Diacritics*, 5 (Winter 1975).

35. James Creech, Peggy Kamuf, and Jane Todd, "Deconstruction in America: An Interview with Jacques Derrida," trans. J. Creech, *Critical Exchange*, no. 17 (Winter 1985), 30. Hereafter "DA." On the deconstruction of the male/female opposition, see Jonathan Culler, *On Deconstruction: Theory and Criticism after Structuralism* (Ithaca: Cornell University Press, 1982), pp. 165–75.

36. Barbara Johnson, "Gender Theory and the Yale School," *Rhetoric and Form: Deconstruction at Yale*, eds. Robert Con Davis and Ronald Schleifer (Norman: University of Oklahoma Press, 1985), p. 101.

37. Shoshana Felman, "Rereading Femininity," *Yale French Studies*, Special Issue on "Feminist Readings: French Texts/American Contexts," no. 62 (1981), 25.

38. Harold Bloom, *Kabbalah and Criticism* (New York: Seabury, 1975), p. 106.

39. Gayatri Chakravorty Spivak, "Displacement and the Discourse of Women," *Displacement: Derrida and After*, ed. Mark Krupnick (Bloomington: Indiana University Press, 1983), p. 185.

40. Gayatri Chakravorty Spivak, "French Feminism in an International Frame," *Yale French Studies*, no. 62 (1981), 171n.

41. Eugenio Donato, "Structuralism: The Aftermath," *SubStance*, no. 7 (Fall 1973), 23.

42. Gerald Graff, "Fear and Trembling at Yale," *American Scholar*, 46 (Autumn 1977), 470.

43. M. H. Abrams, "How to do Things with Texts," *Partisan Review*, 46, no. 4 (1979), 574–75.

44. W. Jackson Bate, "The Crisis in English Studies," *Harvard Magazine*, September-October 1982, p. 52. See Bate's retraction in "To the Editor," *Critical Inquiry*, 10 (December 1983): "My short paragraph on deconstructionism was admittedly testy and unfairly dismissive" (370).

CHAPTER ELEVEN. FEMINIST CRITICISM

1. K. K. Ruthven, *Feminist Literary Studies: An Introduction* (Cambridge: Cambridge University Press, 1984), pp. 20–21; Toril Moi, *Sexual/Textual Politics: Feminist Literary Theory* (London: Methuen, 1985), pp. 50–51, 70; Elaine Showalter, "Introduction: The Feminist Critical Revolution," *The New Feminist Criticism: Essays on Women, Literature, and Theory*, ed. E. Showalter (New York: Pantheon, 1985), pp. 5–10; and Gayle Greene and Coppélia Kahn, "Feminist Scholarship and the Social Construction of Woman," *Making a Difference: Feminist Literary Criticism*, eds. G. Greene and C. Kahn (New York: Methuen, 1985), pp. 1–5, 21–28.

2. Betty Friedan, *The Feminine Mystique* (New York: Norton, 1963), p. 34.

3. Kate Millett, *Sexual Politics* (Garden City, N.Y.: Doubleday, 1970), p. 363.

4. Ellen Moers, *Literary Women* (Garden City, N.Y.: Doubleday, 1976), pp. 62–63.

5. Elaine Showalter, *A Literature of Their Own: British Women Novelists from Brontë to Lessing* (Princeton: Princeton University Press, 1977), p. 7.

6. Sandra M. Gilbert and Susan Gubar, *The Madwoman in the Attic: The Woman Writer and the Nineteenth-Century Literary Imagination* (New Haven: Yale University Press, 1979), p. xii.

7. Elaine Showalter, "Women's Time, Women's Space: Writing the History of

Feminist Criticism," *Tulsa Studies in Women's Literature,* Special Number on "Feminist Issues in Literary Scholarship," 3 (Spring/Fall 1984), 35. Hereafter "WT."

8. Annette Kolodny, "Dancing Through the Minefield: Some Observations on the Theory, Practice, and Politics of a Feminist Literary Criticism," *Feminist Studies,* 6, no. 1 (1980); rpt. in Showalter, ed., *The New Feminist Criticism,* p. 161. Hereafter "DM." This important essay won the Florence Howe Award in 1980 from the Modern Language Association.

9. Elaine Showalter, "Toward a Feminist Poetics," *Women's Writing and Writing about Women,* ed. Mary Jacobus (London: Croom Helm, 1979) and her influential essay, "Feminist Criticism in the Wilderness," *Critical Inquiry,* Special Issue on "Writing and Sexual Difference," 8 (Winter 1981)—both rpt. in her *The New Feminist Criticism.*

10. Barbara Herrnstein Smith, "Contingencies of Value," *Critical Inquiry,* 10 (September 1983), 7. In addition to this special issue on "Canons," see Lillian S. Robinson, "Feminist Criticism: How Do We Know When We've Won?," *Tulsa Studies in Women's Literature,* 3 (Spring/Fall 1984), 143–51, which raises questions of race, class, and gender vis-à-vis aesthetic values and criteria of canonization.

11. Josephine Donovan, "Afterword: Critical Re-Vision," *Feminist Literary Criticism: Explorations in Theory,* ed. J. Donovan (Lexington: University Press of Kentucky, 1975), p. 80. Herafter *FLC.* See also Josephine Donovan, "Toward a Women's Poetics," *Tulsa Studies in Women's Literature,* 3 (Spring/Fall 1984), 99–110, which describes six social, economic, and psychological conditions determining women's world views and poetics.

12. Myra Jehlen, "Archimedes and The Paradox of Feminist Criticism," *Signs,* 6 (Summer 1981); rpt. in both *Feminist Theory: A Critique of Ideology,* eds. Nannerl O. Keohane, Michelle Z. Rosaldo, and Barbara C. Gelpi (Chicago: University of Chicago Press, 1982); and in *The SIGNS Reader: Women, Gender & Scholarship,* eds. Elizabeth Abel and Emily K. Abel (Chicago: University of Chicago Press, 1983), p. 73. For responses to Jehlen, see *Signs,* 8 (Autumn 1982), 160–76, and Moi, pp. 80–86.

13. Lillian S. Robinson, "Dwelling in Decencies: Radical Criticism and the Feminist Perspective" (1970), in her *Sex, Class, and Culture* (Bloomington: Indiana University Press, 1978), p. 17. This book collects a dozen Marxist feminist essays written between 1968 and 1977.

14. Catharine R. Stimpson, "On Feminist Criticism," *What is Criticism?,* ed. Paul Hernadi (Bloomington: Indiana University Press, 1981), p. 234.

15. Alice Jardine, "Gynesis," *Diacritics,* 12 (Summer 1982), 56–61. In her introduction to this 1981 conference paper, Jardine told her audience she had spent three years in Paris working with French feminists.

16. Elaine Marks and Isabelle de Courtivron, eds., *New French Feminisms: An Anthology* (New York: Shocken, 1981), p. xi.

17. For critical introductions to the works of Cixous, Irigaray, and Kristeva, see Ann Rosalind Jones, "Writing the Body: Toward an Understanding of *l'Écriture féminine,*" *Feminist Studies,* 7, no. 2 (1981), 247–63; and Moi, pp. 91–173.

18. Shirley Nelson Garner, Claire Kahane, and Madelon Sprengnether, eds., *The (M)other Tongue: Essays in Feminist Psychoanalytic Interpretation* (Ithaca: Cornell University Press, 1985), pp. 9–10.

19. Jane Gallop, *The Daughter's Seduction: Feminism and Psychoanalysis* (Ithaca: Cornell University Press, 1982), p. 125. See also Juliet Mitchell, *Women: The Longest Revolution* (New York: Pantheon, 1984), pp. 289–92.

20. Nancy Chodorow, *The Reproduction of Mothering: Psychoanalysis and the Sociology of Gender* (Berkeley: University of California Press, 1978), p. 199.

21. Editorial Collective, "Variations sur des thèmes communs" ("Variations on Common Themes"), *Questions féministes*, no. 1 (November 1977), trans. Yvonne Rochette-Ozzello, *New French Feminisms: An Anthology*, p. 214.

22. Carolyn G. Heilbrun, "A Response to *Writing and Sexual Difference*," *Critical Inquiry*, 8 (Summer 1982), 811.

23. Marilyn J. Boxer, "For and About Women: The Theory and Practice of Women's Studies in the United States," *Signs*, 7 (Spring 1982); rpt. in *Feminist Theory: A Critique of Ideology*, pp. 237–71.

24. Catharine R. Stimpson, "What Matter Mind: A Theory about the Practice of Women's Studies," *Women's Studies*, 1 (Fall 1973), 293–314. See also Stimpson, "The New Feminism and Women's Studies," *Change*, 5 (September 1973), 43–48.

25. Florence Howe and Paul Lauter, *The Impact of Women's Studies on the Campus and the Disciplines* (Washington, D.C.: National Institute of Education, 1980), p. 92. See also Howe, "Feminist Scholarship: The Extent of the Revolution" (1982), in *Myths of Coeducation: Selected Essays, 1964–1983* (Bloomington: Indiana University Press, 1984), p. 282—"teaching is a political act: some person is choosing, for whatever reasons, to teach a set of values, ideas, assumptions, and pieces of information, and in so doing, to omit other values, ideas, assumptions, and pieces of information. If all those choices form a pattern excluding half the human race, that is a political act. . . ." Hereafter *MC*.

26. For a conspectus on the special area of lesbian feminist criticism, see Bonnie Zimmerman, "What Has Never Been: An Overview of Lesbian Feminist Criticism," *Feminist Studies*, 7, no. 3 (1981), 451–75; rpt. both in Greene and Kahn, eds., *Making a Difference* and in Showalter, ed., *The New Feminist Criticism*.

27. Florence Howe, "Feminism and the Study of Literature" (1976), *MC*, pp. 190, 197–98.

28. Florence Howe, *Seven Years Later: Women's Studies Programs in 1976*, Report of the National Advisory Council on Women's Educational Programs (Washington, D.C.: Government Printing Office, 1977), p. 31.

29. Florence Howe, "The Past Ten Years: A Critical Retrospective" (1979), *MC*, pp. 236–37. For a retrospective assessment after fifteen years, see Ellen Carol DuBois et al., *Feminist Scholarship: Kindling in the Groves of Academe* (Urbana: University of Illinois Press, 1985).

30. Florence Howe, "Feminist Scholarship: The Extent of the Revolution," *MC*, p. 282.

31. Annette Kolodny, "The Feminist as Literary Critic," *Critical Inquiry*, 2 (Summer 1976), 830.

32. Alice Jardine, "Men in Feminism: Odor di Uomo or Compagnons de Route?," *Critical Exchange*, Special Issue on "Men in Feminism," no. 18 (Spring 1985), 29.

33. Zillah R. Eisenstein, "The Sexual Politics of the New Right: Understanding the 'Crisis of Liberalism' for the 1980s," *Signs*, 7 (Spring 1982); rpt. in *Feminist Theory: A Critique of Ideology*, pp. 77–98.

CHAPTER TWELVE. BLACK AESTHETICS

1. On the black arts movement, see Carolyn Fowler, *Black Arts and Black Aesthetics* (Atlanta: First World Foundation, 1981).

2. Malcolm X, "Statement of Basic Aims and Objectives of the Organization of Afro-American Unity" (June 1964), in *New Black Voices,* ed. Abraham Chapman (New York: New American Library, 1972), p. 563.

3. Hoyt W. Fuller, "Towards a Black Aesthetic," *The Critic,* 26 (April-May 1968); rpt. in *Afro-American Writing: An Anthology of Prose and Poetry,* 2d ed., eds. Richard A. Long and Eugenia W. Collier (University Park: Pennsylvania State University Press, 1985), p. 582. On Fuller's career as an editor, see Abby Arthur Johnson and Ronald Mayberry Johnson, *Propaganda and Aesthetics: The Literary Politics of Afro-American Magazines in the Twentieth Century* (Amherst: University of Massachusetts Press, 1979), pp. 187–96.

4. Larry Neal, "The Black Arts Movement," *tdr: The Drama Review,* 12 (Summer 1968), 39.

5. Stokely Carmichael, "Toward Black Liberation," *Massachusetts Review,* 7 (Autumn 1966); rpt. in *Black Fire: An Anthology of Afro-American Writing,* eds. LeRoi Jones and Larry Neal (New York: William Morrow, 1968), p. 128.

6. See Letitia Dace, "Amiri Baraka," in *Black American Writers: Bibliographical Essays,* eds. M. Thomas Inge, Maurice Duke, and Jackson R. Bryer (New York: St. Martin's, 1978), 2: 121–78.

7. Amiri Baraka, "Why I Changed My Ideology: Black Nationalism and Socialist Revolution," *Black World,* 24 (July 1975), 30–42; and Amiri Baraka, *The Autobiography of LeRoi Jones* (New York: Freundlich Books, 1984), pp. 202–313.

8. LeRoi Jones, "Hunting is Not Those Heads on the Wall" (1964), in *Home: Social Essays* (New York: William Morrow, 1966), p. 174.

9. Stephen E. Henderson, "'Survival Motion': A Study of the Black Writer and the Black Revolution in America," in *The Militant Black Writer in Africa and the United States* by Mercer Cook and S. E. Henderson (Madison: University of Wisconsin Press, 1969), pp. 65–129, esp. pp. 87, 93, 124.

10. Stephen Henderson, *Understanding the New Black Poetry: Black Speech and Black Music as Poetic References* (New York: William Morrow, 1973), p. 4.

11. Addison Gayle, Jr., ed., *The Black Aesthetic* (Garden City, N.Y.: Anchor, 1971), p. xvi.

12. Addison Gayle, Jr., *The Black Situation* (New York: Horizon, 1970), p. 221.

13. Addison Gayle, Jr., *The Way of the New World: The Black Novel in America* (Garden City, N.Y.: Doubleday, 1975), p. 313.

14. Harold Cruse, *Rebellion or Revolution?* (New York: William Morrow, 1968), p. 23.

15. "Harold Cruse: An Interview" (June 1969), in C. W. E. Bigsby, ed., *The Black American Writer* (Deland, Fla.: Everett/Edwards, 1969), 2: 237.

16. Harold Cruse, *The Crisis of the Negro Intellectual* (New York: William Morrow, 1967), pp. 530–43.

17. Darwin T. Turner, "Afro-American Critics: An Introduction," in *The Black Aesthetic,* p. 72.

18. Houston A. Baker, Jr., *Long Black Song: Essays in Black American Literature and Culture* (Charlottesville: University Press of Virginia, 1972), pp. 16–17.

19. Houston A. Baker, Jr., *The Journey Back: Issues in Black Literature and Criticism* (Chicago: University of Chicago Press, 1980), p. xii. Baker earlier relied on non-structuralist linguistic theory, as, for example, in his "On the Criticism of Black American Literature: One View of the Black Aesthetic," in *Reading Black: Essays in the Criticism of African, Caribbean, and Black American Literature,* ed. H. A. Baker, Jr., Monograph Series 4 (Ithaca: Cornell University Africana Studies and Research Center, 1976), pp. 48–58—a monograph containing essays by Addison Gayle, J. Saunders Redding, and three foreign critics.

20. Like Baker, the young black Christian theologian and leftist cultural critic Cornel West turned to "structuralist" thought in the eighties. See West's "The Dilemma of the Black Intellectual," *Cultural Critique,* no. 1 (Fall 1985), 109–24. See Houston A. Baker, Jr., "Generational Shifts and the Recent Criticism of Afro-American Literature," *Black American Literature Forum,* 15 (Winter 1981), 3–21, which was expanded in his *Blues, Ideology, and Afro-American Literature: A Vernacular Theory* (Chicago: University of Chicago Press, 1984), pp. 64–112; and his "Belief, Theory, and the Blues: Notes for a Post-Structuralist Criticism of Afro-American Literature," in *Belief vs. Theory in Black American Literary Criticism,* eds. Joe Weixlmann and Chester J. Fontenot (Greenwood, Fla.: Penkevill, 1986), pp. 5–30.

21. Henry Louis Gates, Jr., "Editor's Introduction: Writing 'Race' and the Difference It Makes," *Critical Inquiry,* Special Issue on " 'Race,' Writing, and Difference," 12 (Autumn 1985), 1–20.

22. Henry Louis Gates, Jr., ed., *Black Literature and Literary Theory* (New York: Methuen, 1984), p. 6. Eight of the thirteen essays collected in this volume were originally published in two special issues of *Black American Literature Forum,* 15, 4 (1981) and 16, 1 (1982), ed. H. L. Gates, Jr.

23. Henry Louis Gates, Jr., "The 'Blackness of Blackness': A Critique of the Sign and the Signifying Monkey," *Critical Inquiry,* 9 (June 1983); rpt. in *Black Literature and Literary Theory,* p. 313. In *Afro-American Literature in the Twentieth Century* (New Haven: Yale University Press, 1984), Michael G. Cooke altered Gates' intertextual theory of "signifyin(g)," casting it as a subconscious folk form and secret matrix (along with the blues) of modern Afro-American literature.

24. "Prison Interviews with Angela Y. Davis" (October 1970), in *If They Come in the Morning: Voices of Resistance,* eds. A. Y. Davis et al. (New York: New American Library, 1971), p. 198.

25. Diane K. Lewis, "A Response to Inequality: Black Women, Racism, and Sexism," *Signs,* 3 (Winter 1977); rpt. in *The SIGNS Reader: Women, Gender & Scholarship,* eds. Elizabeth Abel and Emily K. Abel (Chicago: University of Chicago Press, 1983), pp. 169–91.

26. "The Combahee River Collective Statement" (April 1977), in *Capitalist Patriarchy and the Case for Socialist Feminism,* ed. Zillah R. Eisenstein (New York: Monthly Review Press, 1979); rpt. in *Home Girls: A Black Feminist Anthology,* ed. Barbara Smith (New York: Kitchen Table—Women of Color Press, 1983), p. 272. Hereafter *HG.*

27. Hazel V. Carby, " 'On the Threshold of Woman's Era': Lynching, Empire, and Sexuality in Black Feminist Theory," *Critical Inquiry,* 12 (Autumn 1985), 262–77.

28. Michele Wallace, "A Black Feminist's Search for Sisterhood," *The Village Voice,* 28 July 1975, p. 7. See also Wallace's *Black Macho and the Myth of the Superwoman* (New York: Dial, 1979), which indicted black patriarchalism and scrutinized stereotypes of black women.

29. Barbara Smith, "Toward a Black Feminist Criticism," *Conditions: Two,* 1 (October 1977); rpt. as a pamphlet in Trumansburg, New York, by the Crossing Press; and rpt. in *The New Feminist Criticism: Essays on Women, Literature, and Theory,* ed. Elaine Showalter (New York: Pantheon, 1985), p. 170.

30. Erlene Stetson, ed., *Black Sister: Poetry by Black American Women, 1746–1980* (Bloomington: Indiana University Press, 1981), p. xxii.

31. See, for example, Gloria T. Hull, "Black Women Poets from Wheatley to Walker" (1975), in *Sturdy Black Bridges: Visions of Black Women in Literature,* eds. Roseann P. Bell, Bettye J. Parker, and Beverly Guy-Sheftall (Garden City, N.Y.: Anchor, 1979), pp. 69–86; her "Re-Writing Afro-American Literature: A Case for Black Women Writers," *The Radical Teacher,* 6 (December 1977), 10–13; and her " 'Under the Days': The Buried Life and Poetry of Angelina Weld Grimké," in *HG,* pp. 73–82.

32. Gloria T. Hull, "Afro-American Women Poets: A Bio-Critical Survey," in *Shakespeare's Sisters: Feminist Essays on Women Poets,* eds. Sandra M. Gilbert and Susan Gubar (Bloomington: Indiana University Press, 1979), p. 174.

33. Deborah E. McDowell, "New Directions for Black Feminist Criticism," *Black American Literature Forum,* 14 (1980); rpt. in *The New Feminist Criticism,* pp. 190, 192.

34. Barbara Christian, *Black Feminist Criticism: Perspectives on Black Women Writers* (New York: Pergamon, 1985), p. 149.

35. Toni Cade Bambara, Foreword, *This Bridge Called My Back: Writings by Radical Women of Color,* eds. Cherríe Moraga and Gloria Anzaldúa (Watertown, Mass.: Persephone, 1981), p. viii. This anthology offered materials by twenty-nine Third World women. See also *The Third Woman: Minority Women Writers of the United States,* ed. Dexter Fisher (Boston: Houghton Mifflin, 1980), which was the first major collection of literature by American Indian, Afro-American, Chicana, and Asian American women. In 1980, Fisher held an influential executive position with the Modern Language Association. See also Toni Cade, ed., *The Black Woman: An Anthology* (New York: New American Library, 1970), which collected poems, essays, and short stories by black women.

36. Audre Lorde, "The Master's Tools will Never Dismantle the Master's House" (1979), in *This Bridge,* p. 98. Lorde's articles and speeches from 1976 to 1984 were collected in her *Sister Outsider: Essays and Speeches* (Trumansburg, N.Y.: Crossing Press, 1984).

37. Alice Walker, *In Search of Our Mothers' Gardens: Womanist Prose* (San Diego: Harcourt, Brace, Jovanovich, 1983), pp. xi–xii.

38. Pat Parker, "Revolution: It's Not Neat or Pretty or Quick" (1980), in *This Bridge,* p. 241.

39. Mari Evans, ed., *Black Women Writers (1950–1980): A Critical Evaluation* (Garden City, N.Y.: Anchor, 1984), p. vii.

40. Werner Sollors, "Theory of American Ethnicity," *American Quarterly*, 33, no. 3 (1981), 257–83.

41. Alan Wald, "The Culture of 'Internal Colonialism': A Marxist Perspective," *MELUS*, 8 (Fall 1981), 18–27, which built on the work of Fanon and others.

42. Abdul Alkalimat and associates, *Introduction to Afro-American Studies: A Peoples College Primer*, 5th ed. (Urbana: University of Illinois Publication, 1984), pp. 1–27.

43. Dexter Fisher, Introduction, *Minority Language and Literature: Retrospective and Perspective*, ed. D. Fisher (New York: Modern Language Association, 1977), p. 7.

44. Wayne Charles Miller, "Cultural Consciousness in a Multi-Cultural Society: The Uses of Literature," *MELUS*, 8 (Fall 1981), 29–44.

45. The "Core Curriculum for Black Studies" was adopted at the Fourth Annual Conference of the National Council for Black Studies in March 1980. See Gerald McWorter and Ronald Bailey, "Black Studies Curriculum Development in the 1980s: Its Patterns and History," *Black Scholar*, 15 (March/April 1984), 18–31, and their "An Addendum to Black Studies Curriculum Development in the 1980s," *Black Scholar*, 15 (November/December 1984), 56–58.

46. Elias Blake, Jr., and Henry Cobb, *Black Studies: Issues in Their Institutional Survival*, Report for the U.S. Office of Education (Washington, D.C.: Government Printing Office, 1976), pp. 7, 9, 10, 14.

47. Carlos A. Brossard, "Classifying Black Studies Programs," *Journal of Negro Education*, 53 (Summer 1984), 280–87. This important special issue, titled "An Assessment of Black Studies Programs in American Higher Education," was edited by Carlene Young, Chairperson of the National Council for Black Studies; it contained fourteen essays on the state of black studies in the early 1980s.

48. Harold Cruse, "Contemporary Challenges to Black Studies," review of Maulana (Ron) Karenga's *Introduction to Black Studies*, in *Black Scholar*, 15 (May/June 1984), 47.

49. Darwin T. Turner and Barbara Dodds Stanford, *Theory and Practice in the Teaching of Literature by Afro-Americans* (Urbana: National Council of Teachers of English, 1971), pp. 11–12.

50. Darwin T. Turner, "The Teaching of Afro-American Literature," *College English*, 31 (April 1970); rpt. in *New Perspectives on Black Studies*, ed. John W. Blassingame (Urbana: University of Illinois Press, 1971), pp. 186–87. For similar formalist emphases, see George E. Kent, "Ethnic Impact in American Literature," in *Black Voices: An Anthology of Afro-American Literature*, ed. Abraham Chapman (New York: New American Library, 1968), pp. 691–97; and the programmatic Introduction to *Afro-American Literature: The Reconstruction of Instruction*, eds. Dexter Fisher and Robert B. Stepto (New York: Modern Language Association, 1979), pp. 1–6, which offered "formalist" essays by Stepto, Gates, and others. The practice of close textual analysis was recommended by Kent, Turner, Stepto, Baker, Gates, Christian, and McDowell, among others, creating a line of continuity from the sixties to the eighties.

51. Gloria T. Hull and Barbara Smith, "Introduction: The Politics of Black Women's Studies," *But Some of Us are Brave: Black Women's Studies*, eds. G. T. Hull, Patricia Bell Scott, and B. Smith (Old Westbury, N.Y.: The Feminist Press, 1982), p.

xxviii. On the situation of black women's studies in the seventies, see Marilyn J. Boxer, "For and About Women: The Theory and Practice of Women's Studies in the United States," *Signs*, 7 (Spring 1982); rpt. in *Feminist Theory: A Critique of Ideology*, eds. Nannerl O. Keohane, Michelle Z. Rosaldo, and Barbara C. Gelpi (Chicago: University of Chicago Press, 1982), pp. 253–56.

CHAPTER THIRTEEN. LEFTIST CRITICISM FROM THE 1960S TO THE 1980S

1. Irwin Unger, *The Movement: A History of the American New Left, 1959–1972* (New York: Dodd, Mead, 1974), p. 115. In his *The New Left in America: Reform to Revolution 1956–1970* (Stanford: Hoover Institution Press, 1974), Edward J. Bacciocco, Jr., gives the number of 1968 SDS chapters as 300 and members as 35,000, estimating that 6,000 members paid dues (p. 208).

2. Stanley Aronowitz, "When the New Left Was New," in *The 60s Without Apology*, eds. Sohnya Sayres et al. (Minneapolis: University of Minnesota Press, 1984), pp. 26–39.

3. William Phillips, *A Partisan View: Five Decades of the Literary Life* (New York: Stein and Day, 1983), p. 18.

4. Philip Rahv, "What and Where Is the New Left?" (1972), in his *Essays on Literature and Politics 1932–1972*, eds. Arabel J. Porter and Andrew J. Dvosin (Boston: Houghton Mifflin, 1978), p. 352.

5. Irving Howe, *A Margin of Hope: An Intellectual Autobiography* (New York: Harcourt, Brace, Jovanovich, 1982), p. 309. The young anarchist Richard Kostelanetz produced a stinging critique of Howe in his "The Perils and Paucities of 'Democratic Radicalism,'" *Salmagundi*, no. 2 (Spring 1967), 44–60. See also the Preface and Introduction to *Beyond Left & Right: Radical Thought for Our Times*, ed. Richard Kostelanetz (New York: Morrow, 1968), pp. xiii–xli.

6. Ellen Schrecker, "The Missing Generation: Academics and the Communist Party from the Depression to the Cold War," *Humanities in Society*, Special Issue on "Marxists and the University," 6 (Spring & Summer 1983), 139.

7. Richard Ohmann, *English in America: A Radical View of the Profession* (New York: Oxford University Press, 1976), p. v. See also Richard Ohmann, "*English in America*, Ten Years Later," *ADE Bulletin*, no. 82 (Winter 1985), 11–17.

8. Louis Kampf, "The Scandal of Literary Scholarship," *Harper's Magazine*, December 1967, p. 90. Hereafter "SLS."

On the theory and practice of institutional analysis, see the suggestive work of Peter Uwe Hohendahl, a German-born and -educated American Marxist critic, who collected and revised seven of his essays written in the seventies in the *Institution of Criticism* (Ithaca: Cornell University Press, 1982). Later, Hohendahl synthesized the important work on institutionalization of Talcott Parsons, Jürgen Habermas, Antonio Gramsci, Louis Althusser, and Peter Bürger in "Beyond Reception Aesthetics," trans. Philip Brewster, *New German Critique*, no. 28 (Winter 1983), 108–46.

9. Louis Kampf, "The Trouble with Literature . . . ," *Change*, 2 (May-June 1970), 28–29. Hereafter "TL."

10. Louis Kampf, "Notes Toward a Radical Culture," *The New Left: A Collection of Essays*, ed. Priscilla Long (Boston: Porter Sargent, 1969), p. 424.

11. Paul Lauter, "Society and the Profession, 1958−83," *PMLA*, 99 (May 1984), 417.

12. Bruce Franklin, "The Teaching of Literature in the Highest Academies of the Empire," *College English*, Special Issue titled "A Phalanx from the Left," 31 (March 1970); rpt. in *The Politics of Literature: Dissenting Essays on the Teaching of English*, eds. Louis Kampf and Paul Lauter (New York: Pantheon, 1970, 1972), pp. 110−11.

13. Fredric Jameson, *Marxism and Form: Twentieth-Century Dialectical Theories of Literature* (Princeton: Princeton University Press, 1971), p. ix.

14. Jeffrey L. Sammons, *Literary Sociology and Practical Criticism: An Inquiry* (Bloomington: Indiana University Press, 1977), p. 4.

15. Fredric Jameson, *The Political Unconscious: Narrative as a Socially Symbolic Act* (Ithaca: Cornell University Press, 1981), p. 35. See also Jameson, "Marxism and Historicism," *New Literary History*, 11 (Autumn 1979), 41−73.

16. Gerald Graff, "Teaching the Humanities," *Partisan Review*, 50th Anniversary Issue, 51, nos. 4 and 1 (1984 and 1985), 851.

17. See Gerald Graff, "The University and the Prevention of Culture," in *Criticism in the University*, eds. G. Graff and Reginald Gibbons, *TriQuarterly* Series on Criticism and Culture, no. 1 (Evanston: Northwestern University Press, 1985), pp. 62−82.

Typical of political criticism produced in the post-Vietnam era, Graff's work called into question the traditional differentiation of "right" and "left" in matters related to politics and culture. What was needed, no doubt, was a new terminology or a new way of conceptualizing political alignments.

18. Frank Lentricchia, *Criticism and Social Change* (Chicago: University of Chicago Press, 1983), p. 7.

19. W. J. T. Mitchell, "Editor's Introduction," *Critical Inquiry*, Special Issue on "The Politics of Interpretation," 9 (September 1982), iii. This issue contained essays by, among others, Booth, Fish, Hirsch, Kristeva, Said, Spivak, and White. See also Mitchell, ed., *Against Theory: Literary Studies and the New Pragmatism* (Chicago: University of Chicago Press, 1985), which is a collection of twelve essays published in *Critical Inquiry* between 1982 and 1985 on the controversial status and nature of "theory."

20. Michael Ryan, *Marxism and Deconstruction: A Critical Articulation* (Baltimore: Johns Hopkins University Press, 1982), p. 14.

21. Barbara Foley, "The Politics of Deconstruction," in *Rhetoric and Form: Deconstruction at Yale*, eds. Robert Con Davis and Ronald Schleifer (Norman: University of Oklahoma Press, 1985), pp. 113−34.

22. Stephen Greenblatt, *Renaissance Self-Fashioning: From More to Shakespeare* (Chicago: University of Chicago Press, 1980), p. 256.

23. Stephen J. Greenblatt, Preface, *Allegory and Representation*, Selected Papers from the English Institute, 1979−80, ed. S. J. Greenblatt (Baltimore: Johns Hopkins University Press, 1981), p. xiii; and *Renaissance Self-Fashioning*, pp. 227−28. Similar attempts at renewing sociohistorical criticism were sketched in *Historical*

Studies and Literary Criticism, ed. Jerome J. McGann (Madison: University of Wisconsin Press, 1985), which contained a dozen essays by diverse hands. During the mid-eighties, the work of Greenblatt, McGann, and various other critics was loosely labeled "the new historicism."

24. Edward W. Said, "Reflections on American 'Left' Literary Criticism" (1979), in *The World, the Text, and the Critic* (Cambridge: Harvard University Press, 1983), p. 159—which collects and slightly revises a dozen essays published between 1969 and 1982. Hereafter *WTC.*

25. Paul A. Bové, "Intellectuals at War: Michel Foucault and the Analytics of Power," *SubStance,* nos. 37/38 (1983), 46.

26. Catherine Gallagher, "Politics, the Profession, and the Critic," *Diacritics,* 15 (Summer 1985), 38.

27. Edward W. Said, *Orientalism* (New York: Pantheon, 1978), pp. 24, 327–28; and "Orientalism Reconsidered," *Cultural Critique,* no. 1 (Fall 1985), 91, 106.

28. Edward W. Said, "The Future of Criticism," *MLN,* 99 (September 1984), 956.

29. John Brenkman, "Theses on Cultural Marxism," *Social Text,* 3 (Spring and Summer 1983), 20.

30. Fredric Jameson, "Interview," *Diacritics,* 12 (Fall 1982), 89. See also Fredric Jameson, "Marxism and Teaching," *New Political Science,* nos. 2–3 (1979–80), 31–36.

31. Robert Scholes, *Textual Power: Literary Theory and the Teaching of English* (New Haven: Yale University Press, 1985), pp. 16–17.

32. Editors, "Prospectus," *Cultural Critique,* no. 1 (Fall 1985), 6. See also *Works and Days* (established in 1979), especially number 5, published in Spring 1985, which concentrated on "Cultural Criticism."

33. Terry Eagleton, *Literary Theory: An Introduction* (Minneapolis: University of Minnesota Press, 1983), p. 205.

34. Michael Ryan, "Cultural Studies—A Critique." I thank Professor Ryan for an advance copy of this article. For a critique of Raymond Williams and Terry Eagleton, see Catherine Gallagher, "The New Materialism in Marxist Aesthetics," *Theory and Society,* 9 (Spring 1980), 633–46. On the relationship of Eagleton to Williams, see Andrew Martin and Patrice Petro, "An Interview with Terry Eagleton," *Social Text,* nos. 13/14 (Winter/Spring 1986), 83–99.

35. For an introduction to five contending Marxist models of literature, see David Forgacs, "Marxist Literary Theories," *Modern Literary Theory: A Comparative Introduction,* eds. Ann Jefferson and David Robey (Totowa, N.J.: Barnes & Noble, 1982), pp. 139–67.

36. The work of the left-liberal literary theorist Barbara Herrnstein Smith most convincingly argued for the ultimate contingency of all literary value and evaluation. See her "Contingencies of Value," *Critical Inquiry,* Special Issue on "Canons," 10 (September 1983), 1–35.

INDEX